ILLINOIS REPORTS

VOL. 306 IRWIN 1923

VOL. 307 IRWIN 1923

VOL. 308 IRWIN 1923

VOL. 309 IRWIN 1924

Adjudicating Illinois:
Justices of the Illinois Supreme Court

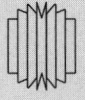

THE
DONNING COMPANY
PUBLISHERS

Adjudicating Illinois:
Justices of the Illinois Supreme Court

John A. Lupton, editor

Copyright © 2018 by Illinois Supreme Court Historic Preservation Commission

All rights reserved, including the right to reproduce this work in any form whatsoever without permission in writing from the publisher, except for brief passages in connection with a review. For information, please write:

The Donning Company Publishers
731 S. Brunswick St.
Brookfield, MO 64628

Lex Cavanah, General Manager
Nathan Stufflebean, Production Supervisor
Pamela Koch, Editor
Todd Erwin, Graphic Designer
Brooke Lauhoff, Project Research Coordinator
Katie Gardner, Marketing & Production Coordinator

George Nikolovski, Project Director

Library of Congress Cataloging-in-Publication Data

Names: Lupton, John A., 1966– editor.
Title: Adjudicating Illinois : justices of the Illinois Supreme Court / John A. Lupton, editor.
Description: Brookfield, MO : The Donning Company Publishers, 2018. | Includes bibliographical references.
Identifiers: LCCN 2018021704 | ISBN 9781681841892 (hard cover : alk. paper)
Subjects: LCSH: Judges—Illinois—Biography. | Illinois. Supreme Court—Biography.
Classification: LCC KF354.I53 A38 2018 | DDC 347.773/0350922—dc23
LC record available at https://lccn.loc.gov/2018021704

Printed in the United States of America at Walsworth

TABLE OF CONTENTS

Acknowledgments	8
Introduction	9
1. Joseph Philips, 1818–1822	12
2. John Reynolds, 1818–1825	15
3. Thomas C. Browne, 1818–1848	18
4. William P. Foster, 1818–1819	20
5. William Wilson, 1819–1848	21
6. Thomas Reynolds, 1822–1825	23
7. Theophilus W. Smith, 1825–1842	25
8. Samuel D. Lockwood, 1825–1848	27
9. Samuel H. Treat, 1841–1855	30
10. Thomas Ford, 1841–1842	32
11. Sidney Breese, 1841–1843, 1857–1878	34
12. Walter B. Scates, 1841–1847, 1853–1857	37
13. Stephen A. Douglas, 1841–1843	39
14. John D. Caton, 1842–1843, 1843–1864	42
15. John M. Robinson, 1843	45
16. James Semple, 1843	46
17. James Shields, 1843–1845	48
18. Jesse B. Thomas Jr., 1843–1845, 1847–1848	50
19. Richard M. Young, 1843–1847	53
20. Norman H. Purple, 1845–1848	56
21. Gustavus P. Koerner, 1845–1848	58
22. William A. Denning, 1847–1848	61
23. David M. Woodson, 1848	62
24. Lyman Trumbull, 1848–1853	64
25. Onias C. Skinner, 1855–1858	67
26. Pinkney H. Walker, 1858–1885	69
27. Corydon Beckwith, 1864	72
28. Charles B. Lawrence, 1864–1873	74
29. Anthony Thornton, 1870–1873	77
30. John M. Scott, 1870–1888	80
31. Benjamin R. Sheldon, 1870–1888	82
32. William K. McAllister, 1870–1875	85
33. John Scholfield, 1873–1893	87
34. Alfred M. Craig, 1873–1900	90
35. T. Lyle Dickey, 1875–1885	92
36. David J. Baker, 1878–1879, 1888–1897	95
37. John H. Mulkey, 1879–1888	98
38. Damon G. Tunnicliff, 1885	101
39. Simeon P. Shope, 1885–1894	103
40. Benjamin D. Magruder, 1885–1906	105
41. Joseph M. Bailey, 1888–1895	108

42. Jacob W. Wilkin, 1888–1907	111
43. Jesse J. Phillips, 1893–1901	113
44. Joseph N. Carter, 1894–1903	115
45. James H. Cartwright, 1895–1924	117
46. Carroll C. Boggs, 1897–1906	120
47. John P. Hand, 1900–1913	122
48. James B. Ricks, 1901–1906	125
49. Guy C. Scott, 1903–1909	127
50. William M. Farmer, 1906–1931	129
51. Orrin N. Carter, 1906–1924	132
52. Alonzo K. Vickers, 1906–1915	135
53. Frank K. Dunn, 1907–1933	137
54. George A. Cooke, 1909–1919	140
55. Charles C. Craig, 1913–1918	143
56. Albert Watson, 1915	146
57. Warren W. Duncan, 1915–1933	148
58. Clyde E. Stone, 1918–1948	150
59. Floyd E. Thompson, 1919–1928	152
60. Oscar E. Heard, 1924–1933	155
61. Frederic R. DeYoung, 1924–1934	157
62. Cyrus Dietz, 1928–1929	159
63. Paul Samuell, 1929–1930	162
64. Warren H. Orr, 1930–1939	164
65. Norman L. Jones, 1931–1940	167
66. Lott R. Herrick, 1933–1937	170
67. Elwyn R. Shaw, 1933–1942	173
68. Paul Farthing, 1933–1942	175
69. Francis S. Wilson, 1935–1951	177
70. Walter T. Gunn, 1938–1951	179
71. Loren E. Murphy, 1939–1948	181
72. June C. Smith, 1941–1947	183
73. William J. Fulton, 1942–1954	185
74. Charles H. Thompson, 1942–1951	187
75. Jesse L. Simpson, 1947–1951	190
76. Albert M. Crampton, 1948–1953	192
77. Joseph E. Daily, 1948–1965	195
78. Ralph L. Maxwell, 1951–1956	198
79. Walter V. Schaefer, 1951–1976	200
80. George W. Bristow, 1951–1961	203
81. Harry B. Hershey, 1951–1966	206
82. Ray I. Klingbiel, 1953–1969	208
83. Charles H. Davis, 1955–1960, 1970–1975	211
84. Byron O. House, 1957–1969	213
85. Roy J. Solfisburg Jr., 1960–1969	216
86. Robert C. Underwood, 1962–1984	219
87. Thomas E. Kluczynski, 1966–1976, 1978–1980	222

88. Daniel P. Ward, 1966–1990	224
89. Marvin F. Burt, 1969–1970	227
90. John T. Culbertson Jr., 1969–1970	230
91. Caswell J. Crebs, 1969–1970, 1975–1976	232
92. Howard C. Ryan, 1970–1990	234
93. Joseph H. Goldenhersh, 1970–1987	236
94. William G. Clark, 1976–1992	238
95. James A. Dooley, 1976–1978	240
96. Thomas J. Moran, 1976–1992	242
97. Seymour Simon, 1980–1988	244
98. Benjamin K. Miller, 1984–2001	247
99. Joseph F. Cunningham, 1987–1988, 1991–1992	250
100. Horace L. Calvo, 1988–1991	252
101. John J. Stamos, 1988–1990	254
102. Michael A. Bilandic, 1990–2000	257
103. James D. Heiple, 1990–2000	260
104. Charles E. Freeman, 1990–2018	263
105. John L. Nickels, 1992–1998	266
106. Moses W. Harrison II, 1992–2002	269
107. Mary Ann G. McMorrow, 1992–2006	272
108. S. Louis Rathje, 1999–2000	275
109. Robert R. Thomas, 2000–Present	277
110. Thomas R. Fitzgerald, 2000–2010	280
111. Thomas L. Kilbride, 2000–Present	283
112. Rita B. Garman, 2001–Present	286
113. Phillip J. Rarick, 2002–2004	289
114. Lloyd A. Karmeier, 2004–Present	291
115. Anne M. Burke, 2006–Present	294
116. Mary Jane Theis, 2010–Present	297
117. P. Scott Neville Jr., 2018–Present	300
Endnotes	304

ACKNOWLEDGMENTS

This book could not have been completed without the research and writing of Janice Petterchak and Theodore Hild. Janice and Ted performed the lion's share of the work in authoring first drafts of each of the justices. Interns Doris Weil and Kelsey Stybr also worked on several biographies and read over various parts of the full manuscript. My role as editor was to make the work of Janice, Ted, Doris, and Kelsey consistent. Much of the research was done at the Abraham Lincoln Presidential Library and Museum, the Illinois Supreme Court Library, the Illinois State Archives, the Illinois State Library, and the Supreme Court Historic Preservation Commission Archives, and my appreciation goes to them for their wonderful collections.

The Friends of the Supreme Court Historic Preservation Commission funded the publication of the book with donations from foundations, individuals, law firms, and bar associations. Major support came from the Jerome Mirza Foundation and the Illinois State Bar Association, and Joseph A. Power Jr.

The justices of the Supreme Court of Illinois have been very supportive of the Commission and its efforts, especially the publication of this book. Justice Rita B. Garman and Justice Anne M. Burke serve as liaisons to the Illinois Supreme Court Historic Preservation Commission. Chief Justice Lloyd A. Karmeier, Justice Robert R. Thomas, Justice Thomas L. Kilbride, Justice Mary Jane Theis, and Justice P. Scott Neville all have a deep appreciation for Illinois legal history.

Lastly, the Illinois Supreme Court Historic Preservation Commission provided necessary oversight and guidance. The Illinois General Assembly created the Commission in 2008, and over the course of its existence, the Commission has been managed by capable and involved Commissioners. All of the members of the Commission since 2008 are Jerold S. Solovy, chair; John B. Simon, chair; James R. Thompson, chair; Cynthia Y. Cobbs; Vincent F. Cornelius; Kirk W. Dillard; Kim B. Fox; Michael F. McClain; Marcia Meis; Pauline Montgomery; James M. Morphew; Joseph A. Power Jr.; William J. Quinlan; Jane Hayes Rader; J. William Roberts; and Michael J. Tardy. Members of the legal community have been very active in the programmatic activities of the Commission, particularly Appellate Justice Joy Cunningham, Appellate Justice Aurelia Pucinski, Cook County Circuit Court Judge Neil Cohen, Cook County Circuit Court Judge Margarita Hoffman, Scott Szala, Matthew Carter, Rachel Morse, and Penelope Campbell. Commission staff of Matt Burns and Virginia Geiger provided operational support on a daily basis.

This book would not exist if not for the 117 men and women who sat on the Illinois Supreme Court bench. Biographies were meant to be as inclusive as possible with personal information and career highlights. While biographies will mention other offices held, particularly those who served in the legislative or executive branches, they will focus on the person's career while in the judicial branch with special examination of several cases during that justice's tenure. Some justices certainly had more prolific and lengthy careers than others, either off or on the bench, but biographies are roughly equal in length. The biographies are also well documented with endnotes, allowing the reader to research further into a justice's life. Lastly, this work was a cumulative effort of several people over a seven-year period. While I have done my best to prevent errors, I have little doubt that some remain, and I accept responsibility for those errors.

INTRODUCTION

The Supreme Court of Illinois has gone through many changes during its two-hundred-year existence. With four Constitutions and several major structural changes, the Illinois Supreme Court has always had the important role as the supreme judicial body in Illinois with supervisory responsibility over all state courts and over the licensure and regulation of attorneys. Over time, the Court expanded and contracted in size. The Court moved from Illinois capital to Illinois capital; and even moved among three cities annually for a period of time in the nineteenth century. Most importantly, the Court consisted of individuals with varied backgrounds and life histories. This is the story of each of these justices within the context of their time and adjudicating cases that reflected the important issues of the day.

The 117 people who served as justices on the Court witnessed great change in the Illinois landscape: geographically, politically, socially, economically, and technologically. Legal cases mirrored the state's development as many early court cases examined whether a promissory note's consideration had failed. As the population grew, conflict became more prevalent, and when Illinois became a hub of manufacturing and transportation, legal cases soon followed to resolve disputes that had never been considered. The Court also recognized the evolution of the English Common Law system to a legal system unique to Illinois. More recent changes in Illinois law include modernization of contributory negligence and the elimination of the death penalty.

The Supreme Court of Illinois was established by the Illinois Constitution of 1818. It consisted of four justices who were appointed by the Illinois legislature. The legislature mandated that Supreme Court justices ride the circuit and hear trial-level cases in addition to appellate duty. Since there was no intermediate appellate court, the Supreme Court heard every case appealed. On several occasions, the legislature created circuit court judgeships, relieving the Supreme Court members of their duty to travel the circuit. The members of the Court also served on a Council of Revision, along with the governor, to review legislation. As a result, the Court did not hear many constitutional issues but dealt with a number of serious issues, such as slavery. After a politically charged Supreme Court case in 1839, the Democratic-controlled legislature expanded the Court from four to nine members to ensure a Democrat majority on the Court.

Legislative control of the Court was one reason Illinois met to create a new Constitution in the late 1840s. In 1848, the new Constitution took effect, reducing the Court from nine members to three members. Each justice would be popularly elected from a geographic district mirroring northern, central, and southern Illinois. The justices would meet in each of those districts annually with one term in Ottawa, in Mt. Vernon, and in Springfield. Justices served a nine-year term and stood for re-election in partisan races. The Court became a destination rather than a stepping-stone to higher political offices. As a result, the independence of the judiciary began to manifest itself during this period. Railroads became a revolutionary mode of transportation, and many lawsuits concerning right of way, damage to property, fencing, personal injury liability, and fellow servant rules found their way to the Illinois Supreme Court. The constitutionally mandated low salary of justices and increasing workload of only three members was one impetus for a new Constitution.

In 1870, Illinois adopted its third Constitution. The Court increased from three to seven members with each of the justices elected from one of seven geographic districts. The Court continued to hear cases in Ottawa, Springfield, and Mt. Vernon. The workload of the Court remained tedious and two justices resigned because of the workload. Relief finally came in 1876 when the legislature created the appellate court system. Travel for the justices remained an issue, but after a twenty-year effort, the legislature passed a law in 1897 to consolidate Court terms at one location in Springfield. The Court dealt with many different issues dealing with warehouse laws, taxation issues, licensing of women attorneys, and the separation of powers.

A movement to alter the make-up of the Court failed in the 1920s, but a sweeping reform occurred under the Civil Practice Act of 1933, which eliminated the old Common Law pleading requirements. An updated Civil Practice Act of 1956 further codified Illinois law. Other efforts to reform the judiciary were not successful because of the severe limitations on amending the 1870 Constitution. Once those restrictions were lifted, in 1962, Illinois voters approved an entirely new Judicial Article to the Constitution that completely restructured the Illinois courts.

Going into effect in 1964, the new Article kept the number of justices at seven, but reduced the number of geographic districts to five. Three justices would be elected from the First District, composed only of Cook County. The other four districts would elect one justice each from roughly northern (Second District), north-central (Third District), central (Fourth District), and southern Illinois (Fifth District). Justices were elected for ten-year terms in partisan races, but after serving ten years, the justices would run in retention elections. When the Fourth Illinois Constitution took effect in 1971, the Judicial Article of 1964 was adopted nearly in its entirety.

Illinois Supreme Court Building (Image courtesy of James Dobrovolny Collection, Illinois Supreme Court Historic Preservation Commission)

The Supreme Court began the Fourth Constitution after ending a crisis that saw two justices resign and one die, leaving only a four-member Court. The Court quickly dealt with new Constitutional issues as well as the death penalty and changes to issues such as contributory negligence, parental rights, and shackles in court. The Supreme Court continues to examine issues dealing with the technological revolution and social media. The Court takes it work seriously, deciding which cases to hear. While nearly 2,500 cases are filed each year, the justices choose to hear oral arguments in approximately 60–75 cases. In deciding whether to accept an appeal, the Court weighs the general importance of the question, the existence of a conflict between the decision sought to be reviewed and a previous decision of the Court or of the appellate court, the need to exercise the Court's supervisory authority, or the interpretation of the Illinois Constitution as well as the constitutionality of acts of the General Assembly.

In 2018, the Illinois judiciary commemorates its bicentennial, along with the State of Illinois. On August 26, 1818, the constitutional convention passed Illinois's first Constitution, which created the Supreme Court of Illinois. The date is memorialized on the State Seal and on the Supreme Court Seal. On October 9, 1818, the first General Assembly appointed the first four justices to the Court, marking the beginning of an uninterrupted chain of justices on the Supreme Court bench. On July 12, 1819, the Illinois Supreme Court met for its very first session in the capital city of Kaskaskia. Currently, it meets in the Supreme Court Building in Springfield, which has been the Court's home since 1908.

Illinois courts have adapted over time to meet the change from a frontier to a market economy, from horse-and-buggy transportation to major railroad and airport hubs, from subsistence farming to agribusiness, and from small general market stores to international corporations. Abraham Lincoln summed up this transformation perfectly when making an argument in a lawsuit that "adjudication and legislation must follow and conform to the progress of society." The history of law is the history of society.

JOSEPH PHILIPS, 1818–1822

Joseph Philips was born on October 6, 1784, in Kentucky, the fourth of nine children. His father, Philip Philips, speculated in land in Tennessee and co-owned nearly 7,000 acres, principally in what became Rutherford County, Tennessee. Joseph Philips had a classical and legal education and was licensed to practice law in Tennessee on July 3, 1809.[1] He practiced law in the county seat of Jefferson until 1812, handling debt collection cases.

When the War of 1812 broke out, Philips joined the war effort. In December 1812, he arrived at Fort Massac as captain of the new Twenty-fourth Regiment of Infantry, recruited from Tennessee and Kentucky. Soon in command of Fort Massac, Philips was unprepared for the large number of men to be trained for service in the War of 1812. He complained to the Secretary of War "of the insufficiency of the quarters" and that the troops lacked clothing, equipment, and supplies. In spring of 1813, after the Twenty-fourth Regiment received orders to move to Ohio, Philips remained at Fort Massac in command of a detachment of the Second Regiment of Artillery. A year later, the War Department ordered Fort Massac evacuated and the troops transferred to St. Louis.[2]

Moving to Kaskaskia, Captain Philips gained the reputation of "a dignified and pleasant gentleman," wrote author and attorney John M. Scott, "and as a man of the highest standing as a citizen." In 1816, Philips succeeded Nathaniel Pope as secretary of the Illinois Territory, holding the office for two years.[3] During this time, he issued a power of attorney to his brother-in-law, Robert Purdy, to handle his affairs relating to the estate of his father, Philip Philips.[4]

The 1819 court record book for the Illinois Supreme Court. (Image courtesy of Illinois State Archives)

During the October 1818 organizing session of the Illinois General Assembly, Joseph Philips received thirty-four of forty-one legislative ballots to become the state's first Chief Justice of the Illinois Supreme Court. He and the three associate justices assumed office on December 3, 1818, the date President Monroe signed the act admitting Illinois as the twenty-first state in the Union.[5]

Philips was also responsible for presiding at the trial level in the Third Judicial Circuit, initially comprised of Monroe, Randolph, Jackson, and Union Counties along the Mississippi River. In 1821, as the legislature created more counties, the third circuit enlarged with Jefferson, Fayette, Washington, and Bond Counties. At the first term of the Supreme Court in July 1819, the court heard no arguments in ten pending appeals to the General Court, the highest court of appeal in the Territory of Illinois. The justices presumably spent their time organizing the Court and creating a set of rules.

In the December 1819 term, the court handled twenty-six cases on the docket: ten cases carried over from the Territory of Illinois and sixteen cases new to the Supreme Court. Of the ten cases from the Territorial court, three were continued, three were dismissed, two were abated, and two were reversed and remanded to the lower court. Of the sixteen new cases, two were reversed and remanded, two were affirmed, three were dismissed, two were abated, and seven were continued to the next term. Only five of cases were reported in the *Illinois Reports*.[6]

The caseload at the Supreme Court continued to grow. The Court handled thirty-seven cases in the July 1820 term—the last at Kaskaskia—and at least forty-four cases in the December 1820 term—the first at the new capital of Vandalia.[7] John M. Palmer described Philips as "a lawyer of fine intellectual endowments."[8] There were only seventeen reported cases during his tenure as Chief Justice.[9] Since all opinions at that time were written by "The Court," published records indicated none of his individual opinions. Decades later, Scott noted that "a very large per cent of the opinions of the Court during the time of Chief Justice Phillips are still recognized as sound law and very few of them have ever been overruled. Most of them are models of terse and accurate statement. No doubt Chief Justice Phillips wrote his full share of the opinions of the Court delivered when he was chief justice and if so they are highly creditable to him as a lawyer and as a judge."[10]

The very first case on the Illinois Supreme Court docket was *Coleen and Claypool v. Figgins*. The case concerned the question of when the act creating the circuit court system in Illinois became valid. The Madison County Circuit Court issued a writ on March 31, 1819, but the act creating the circuit courts did not go into effect until April 1, 1819. In an opinion probably written by Chief Justice Philips, the Supreme Court reversed and remanded the case, declaring the writ to be void because the "clerk had no authority to issue the writ, and make it returnable to a court not in existence."[11]

Confident that he would be elected the state's second governor, the ambitious Philips resigned the office of Chief Justice in July 1822. A candidate of the state's pro-slavery faction, he supported a constitutional

The first Illinois statehouse at Kaskaskia held the first term of the Supreme Court. (Image courtesy of the Abraham Lincoln Presidential Library and Museum)

amendment permitting the "complete extension" of slavery into Illinois. The four-candidate race included another pro-slavery Supreme Court Justice, Thomas C. Browne. The two slavery proponents polled 59 percent of the vote, but Philips came in a close second to Edward Coles, leader of the state's anti-slavery movement. A former private secretary to U.S. President James Madison, Governor Coles effectively ended the state's pro-slavery activity. Had he and Philips been the only candidates, Philips probably would have won the election.[12]

Near the time he lost the election for governor, Philips also lost his wife, Elouise.[13] Hurt from the death of his wife and "[w]ith feelings of disgust at the ingratitude of the people," Philips decided to leave Illinois and return to his home state of Tennessee.[14] Philips settled in Davidson County, where he married recently widowed Dorothy Drake Sumner in 1825.[15] By 1830, the couple had moved to neighboring Rutherford County with their young children. The Philips family was intermarried with the prominent Childress family of Murfreesboro, Tennessee. John W. Childress married a daughter of Joseph and Dorothy Philips in 1851; Childress was the brother of Sarah Childress, who was the wife of President James K. Polk. A son of Joseph Philips married the daughter of Sarah Childress Polk's sister.[16]

Philips accumulated significant real estate south of Murfreesboro, built a home there in the 1830s, and purchased a number of slaves to work his farm. Philips never resumed the practice of law, instead concentrating on agrarian pursuits, but at various times, he served as an election judge, served on juries, acted as executor for his stepson's estate, and served as a court-appointed commissioner to set apart a widow's property.[17] By 1850, Philips decided to retire from agriculture and transferred much of his land and twenty-three of his fifty-five slaves to his son, but his son died a few years later at the age of twenty-eight. A neighbor remembered that Philips "used to go down the road every day, rain or shine, in his fancy, four wheel surrey."[18]

Joseph Philips died on July 26, 1857, and was buried in the City Cemetery in Murfreesboro, Tennessee. His estate was valued at $40,000, and his son-in-law, John W. Childress, was named as the administrator.[19] "Had Judge Phillips continued on the bench of the Supreme Court of the State and eschewed politics," observed Scott, "he would have built for himself a reputation equal to that of anyone that ever occupied a seat in that high tribunal."[20]

JOHN REYNOLDS, 1818-1825

A public officeholder for most of his adult life, John Reynolds served in all three branches of Illinois state government. His parents, Robert and Margaret Moore Reynolds, had emigrated from Ireland to Montgomery County, Pennsylvania, where Reynolds was born on February 26, 1788. A few months later, the family moved to Tennessee, joining relatives in the Knoxville area. "We left Tennessee in February, 1800, with eight horses and two wagons," Reynolds recalled, headed for Spanish territory along the Mississippi River. "Our company consisted of my parents, six children, I the oldest, three hired men, and a colored woman."[21] They settled in a colony near Kaskaskia, Illinois, and then seven years later, relocated to a farm in the Goshen Settlement southwest of Edwardsville.[22]

Reynolds learned arithmetic fundamentals from a neighbor, then in 1806 and 1807 attended a seminary north of Belleville, "a good school," he remembered, "taught by a competent teacher." He studied land surveying, navigation, reading, spelling, and writing.[23] At age twenty, Reynolds enrolled in a small private school near Knoxville, Tennessee, to study law, but health problems forced his return to Illinois. He served as a scout against western Native Americans during the War of 1812. "Soldiers from the adjacent States," Reynolds remembered, "saw the country and never rested in peace until they located themselves and families in it."[24]

Admitted to the bar at Kaskaskia, Reynolds opened a law office in the French village of Cahokia in 1814. Dealing primarily in land title litigation, he also speculated in land sales and operated two dry goods stores.[25] A contemporary described Reynolds as six feet tall, stout, and "always gentlemanly in appearance and apparel, with modest but ungraceful manners."[26]

Reynolds described the circumstances of his election as an associate justice of the first Illinois Supreme Court. "My friends urged me to visit, with them, the General Assembly in session at Kaskaskia, and I did so. When we reached the legislature, there was great excitement and turmoil in relation to the election of officers by the General Assembly. I had not been in Kaskaskia only a few days when it was urged on me to know if I would accept a judgeship, if I was elected. This broke in on me like a clap of thunder."[27]

Reynolds later recalled his first term as "a strange and novel business." His friends often failed to recognize the dignity of his office, reported historian Frederic B. Crossley, "and it is stated that the sheriff was in the habit of opening court by proclaiming without rising from the bench upon which he was sitting, 'Boys, the Court is now open. John is on the bench.'"[28]

During his six-year judicial tenure, Reynolds was present at nearly every session of the Supreme Court. Reynolds heard at least fifty cases on the bench. Ten opinions in

Illinois Reports listed him as the justice delivering the opinion of the Court, but justices were not named as writing the opinion until midway through his tenure. Reynolds also wrote dissenting opinions in at least two cases. In *Everett v. Morrison,* Reynolds dissented from the Court's reversal of judgment regarding David Everett's debt to William Morrison. While the majority of justices concluded that Everett was a collateral party to the actual debtor, Reynolds maintained Everett's liability: "I conclude that Everett was the person to whom the credit was given, and therefore liable."[29]

While performing his circuit duties, Justice Reynolds also presided at circuit court in St. Clair and neighboring counties. He ruled against anti-slavery Governor Edward Coles in a Madison County case involving the bonding of freed slaves. On appeal, however, the other Supreme Court justices reversed Reynolds's decision.[30] Reynolds also wrote an opinion in a case that he had decided at the trial level. U.S. Senator and former territorial governor Ninian Edwards had sued the sheriff of St. Clair County. The sheriff had levied a tax on Edwards's property, but Edwards refused to pay because he claimed to be a resident of a different county. Reynolds ruled for the sheriff, but Edwards appealed to the Supreme Court. In Reynolds's opinion, affirming his circuit court decision, he wrote that the legislature "on the subject of laying a tax on certain property, makes no distinction between residents and non-residents." The statute guiding taxes, Reynolds continued, "shows that the lien is created on the property to be taxed, and not on the owner of the property."[31]

In 1822, pro-slavery advocates called for a convention to consider a constitutional amendment allowing slaves in the state. "The convention question," Reynolds reported, "gave rise to two years of the most furious and boisterous excitement and contest that ever was visited on Illinois."[32] He joined Chief Justice Thomas Reynolds and fellow Justice Browne in publicly supporting the pro-slavery faction. By about a two thousand majority, however, voters defeated the call for a constitutional convention in 1824. "Thus, after one of the most bitter, prolonged, and memorable contests which ever convulsed the politics of this State," wrote Thomas Ford in his *History of Illinois,* the question of making Illinois a slave State was put to rest."[33]

With reorganization of the judiciary in 1824, Reynolds was not retained on the Supreme Court; "a sore disappointment," John M. Palmer reported.[34] Reynolds then served two terms in the Illinois House of Representatives, and in 1830, narrowly won election as the state's fourth governor, defeating Lieutenant Governor William Kinney. "A man of remarkably good sense and shrewdness," Ford wrote of Reynolds, who exhibited "mirthfulness and pleasantry when mingling with the people."[35]

In 1831, Governor Reynolds signed a treaty with Native Americans in Illinois that moved the Sauk west of the Mississippi. A year later he called for men to take up arms against contingents of Sauk and Fox who returned to northwest Illinois and frightened the white settlers. Reynolds commanded the state militia during the Black Hawk War, a conflict that was characterized, wrote historian Paul E. Stroble, "by lack of military discipline, serious misjudgments on both sides concerning each's intentions, white hatred of Indians, and the natives' sad defeat."[36] That defeat of Chief Black Hawk's tribes effectively ended Native American occupation in Illinois.[37]

Two years later, Black Hawk War participant John A. Wakefield of Vandalia published a documentary and contemporary account of the conflict to dispel what he considered unjust criticisms of Reynolds and the federal government. In the preface to his *History of the War Between the United States and the Sac and Fox Nations of Indians,* Wakefield hoped that "after the perusal of these letters and depositions, none will have the hardihood to say, that Governor Reynolds did wrong in the course he pursued to subdue those Indians."[38]

In 1834, two weeks before the expiration of his gubernatorial term, Reynolds resigned to accept election to the U.S. House of Representatives, filling the vacancy caused by the death of Charles Slade. Reynolds served until 1837. As political parties began to coalesce,

Reynolds joined the Democratic Party. His wife of seventeen years, Catherine Manegle, daughter of French-Canadian Indian trader Julien Dubuque, had died in 1834. Two years later, Reynolds married Sarah Wilson, a stately younger woman. He had no children by either spouse.[39]

Residing in a large home in Belleville, Reynolds and several associates built the first railroad in the Mississippi Valley, a six-mile track leading from his coal mine in the Mississippi bluff to the riverbank across from St. Louis. "The members of the company, and I one of them, lay out on the premises of the road day and night while the work was progressing; and I assert that it was the greatest work or enterprise ever performed in Illinois under the circumstances. But it well-nigh broke us all." The partners sold the railroad enterprise at a huge loss the following year.[40]

Reynolds again won election as U.S. Representative, serving from 1839 to 1843. Three years later, he was elected to the Illinois House of Representatives from St. Clair County, but was defeated in 1848 for the state Senate. Elected a state representative again in 1852, he served as Speaker of the House, then in 1858 ran an unsuccessful race for state superintendent of schools.[41]

Reynolds remained a Democrat but despised Stephen A. Douglas after Douglas broke with President James Buchanan over Kansas. In the 1858 U.S. Senate race, Reynolds supported Republican Abraham Lincoln and made a few speeches for him in southern Illinois. After Lincoln lost the election, Reynolds sent Lincoln a letter of consolation, writing that "I would much rather be defeated in principle and honesty; than succeed by fraud and corruption."[42]

For some years Reynolds edited a daily newspaper, *The Eagle,* published in Belleville. He strongly opposed Lincoln's policies as president. Reynolds died of pneumonia at his Belleville home on May 18, 1865, and was buried in the city's Walnut Hill Cemetery.[43]

THOMAS C. BROWNE, 1818-1848

A native of Kentucky, Thomas C. Browne was born about 1792. After studying law and gaining admittance to the bar in his home state, he settled in Shawneetown, Illinois Territory, and opened a practice in 1812. He soon became interested in politics, "chiefly in an effort to obtain office," according to historian Frederic B. Crossley.[44] Within two years of his arrival, Browne won election as Gallatin County representative in the second territorial legislature. In 1815, Governor Ninian Edwards appointed Browne as prosecuting attorney from his district, and in the third territorial legislature, he became a member of the council representing Gallatin County.[45]

Upon organization of Illinois state government in 1818, the first Illinois General Assembly elected Browne as one of three associate justices of the Supreme Court. "A good judge on account of his integrity of character and his valuable practical sense in all matters of business," wrote John M. Scott.[46] In the 1822 gubernatorial election, the question of slavery was the primary issue as Illinoisans contemplated a new constitution to legalize slavery. Both Browne and Chief Justice Joseph Philips became pro-slavery gubernatorial candidates. Together they garnered 59 percent of the vote but lost to the anti-slavery candidate Edward Coles.

The first General Assembly stipulated that the Illinois Supreme Court would be reorganized in 1824. When the Illinois Supreme Court was reorganized, the legislature again elected Browne as a Supreme Court justice. A contemporary had described Browne as "corpulent as Falstaff, vain, coarse, and effusive," but credited Browne as "a good lawyer and a capable judge."[47] Illinois attorney and later Chief Justice John Dean Caton recalled Browne to be an attentive listener who "would never express his opinion, especially in an important case, until he had heard all that could be said on either side by other members of the court."[48] In 1841, after the legislature divided Illinois into nine circuits, each justice on the expanded Supreme Court held court in one of the circuits. Browne became responsible for the Sixth Judicial Circuit in northwestern Illinois. As a result of this appointment, Browne moved more than 400 miles from Shawneetown to Galena.[49]

He was among the guests at the 1842 Springfield wedding of fellow attorney Abraham Lincoln to Mary Todd. When the groom promised, "With this ring I thee wed, and with all my worldly goods I thee endow," the unrefined Browne, who perhaps never before witnessed such an impressive ceremony, reportedly blurted loudly, "Lord A'mighty, Lincoln, the law fixes that!" Another guest recalled the incident as "one of the funiest things to have witnessed imaginable—No description on paper can possibly do it justice."[50]

In 1843, Browne became the subject of the state's second attempt to impeach a Supreme Court justice. Four members of the bar in Galena petitioned the House of Representatives charging Browne "for want of capacity to discharge the duties of his office," also described as "general incompetency."[51] But, according to Scott, "men of all political views rallied to his support. The newspapers attributed the attempt to a personal grudge between several members of the Galena bar and Joseph P. Hoge, Browne's son-in-law. Judge Browne was a pronounced Whig, but he found as many friends among the democratic members of the Legislature as among the members of his own political faith." Abraham Lincoln helped to defend Browne during the proceedings in the Illinois House. The impeachment attempt failed by a nearly unanimous vote and never went to the Senate for trial.[52]

While Browne did not author many opinions during his long tenure as a Supreme Court justice, he wrote several important ones on debt collection, a very important legal issue in a money-scarce society. In the December 1841 term, Browne delivered the Supreme Court opinion in *Nichols v. Ruckells*. After the Sangamon County Circuit Court upheld a justice of the peace decision in favor of the defendant, Samuel Ruckells, John Nichols retained Springfield attorney Abraham Lincoln for the Supreme Court appeal. Affirming the circuit court, Browne ruled that the justice of the peace acted within the legislative acts of 1827 and 1833, limiting his judgment to no more than $100. "We are of opinion," Browne wrote, "the justice of the peace may render a judgment for the defendant, for a sum less than one hundred dollars, though the account of the defendant may originally amount to more than that sum. His 'defense' covers only a sum within the jurisdiction of a justice of the peace, and we see nothing to prevent him from rendering a judgment accordingly. The law abhors a multiplicity of suits, and by this mode of proceeding it will unquestionably be avoided."[53]

In a circuit court case in Jo Daviess County, Daniel Harris, the losing party in the case, had purposefully consented to a nonsuit. Harris then wished to appeal the case to the Illinois Supreme Court. Browne refused to sign the bill of exceptions because of the voluntary nonsuit. Harris brought a mandamus suit in the Illinois Supreme Court against Justice Browne to force him to sign the bill of exceptions, but in a per curiam decision, the justices agreed with Browne, again represented by Abraham Lincoln, noting that the losing party "having voluntarily gone out of court, cannot call upon this court to reverse a judgment, which was entered at his own solicitation."[54]

Browne served continuously on the Supreme Court until 1848, when a new state constitution reduced the number of justices from nine to three. Browne served on the Supreme Court longer than any other justice in Illinois history. During that thirty-year tenure, "he maintained himself in office," according to Crossley, "through his political influence with members of the Legislature and was at no time popular with the people."[55] Judge Browne wrote at least forty-three opinions—"plain, common-sense statements," Scott reported. "Especially when questions of equal civil rights before the law were involved, Judge Browne always maintained the rights of all persons whether white or black to the enjoyment of these inalienable privileges."[56]

In the later years of his term, Browne resided in Galena, then in 1853 moved with his son-in-law Hoge, to San Francisco, California. Browne died there at the age of seventy in November 1862. He was originally interred at Laurel Hill Cemetery but moved to Cypress Lawn Cemetery in 1946.[57]

WILLIAM P. FOSTER, 1818-1819

One of the first three Associate Supreme Court justices, William P. Foster had been in the state for only a few weeks at the time of his election to the bench. "He was a man of pleasing address," wrote John M. Scott, "but artful and designing." In his history of the state, Thomas Ford described Foster as "a great rascal but no one knew it then."[58]

Foster's birth and death dates as well as information about his early life are unknown. He allegedly arrived in Illinois from Virginia without ever studying or practicing law. "The career of Foster affords a striking illustration of the possible success of a polished but unscrupulous adventurer, in a new country," explained historian John Moses. "An entire stranger in the territory, a lawyer by neither profession nor practice, in a few weeks, through his plausible address and skillful manipulation of credulous members, he succeeded in capturing one of the highest judicial offices in the gift of the legislature."[59]

Foster was one of nine candidates for an associate justice position. The legislature elected him and Thomas C. Browne on the first ballot with Foster winning twenty-six of the forty-one votes possible.[60] With no apparent legal training, Foster failed to perform his duties. Fearful of exposing his incompetence, Foster never met with the Supreme Court justices, nor did he ever preside over his assigned Second Judicial Circuit comprised of Crawford, Edwards, and White Counties in southeastern Illinois near or along the Wabash River. However, Foster did appoint Jesse Browne to be Circuit Clerk in Edwards County in April 1819.[61] In a letter from A. F. Hubbard to Elias Kent Kane, Hubbard noted that Foster had not held court in the upper counties of his circuit, and the citizens were quite angry. Hubbard later visited Foster in Vincennes, Indiana, and Foster explained that the Wabash River was too high for him to cross and that one of his children had been sick.[62]

Described by Ford as "a man of winning, polished manners . . . a very gentlemanly swindler," Foster resigned from the Supreme Court within a year on July 7, 1819, a week before the Court first met to organize. However, Foster "took care first to pocket his salary." He left Illinois, "moving from city to city and living by swindling strangers and prostituting his daughters, who were very beautiful."[63]

Scott blamed the "grave mistake" of Foster's Supreme Court position on the legislative election of judges. Partisan political and personal considerations, Scott argued, took precedence over a candidate's qualifications. Foster "never had any thing more than a mere nominal connection with the Court. His appointment is only mentioned as an historical fact to impress on the public mind the necessity for observing the utmost care and caution in choosing judges of the highest courts of the State—a lesson that should never be forgotten."[64] There is no known photograph or image of Foster, and the name of William P. Foster is not included on a tablet of justices displayed in the Illinois Supreme Court building.

WILLIAM WILSON, 1819-1848

William Wilson succeeded William P. Foster, one of the original Supreme Court justices, who never served in the position. Born in Loudoun County, Virginia, on April 27, 1794, Wilson studied law under John Cook, a distinguished attorney who became minister to France in the early 1800s. After military service in the War of 1812, Wilson moved to Kentucky and then in 1817 to southeastern Illinois Territory, where he was admitted to the bar. "He was very popular and greatly esteemed," wrote a biographer, "and before he had been in Illinois even one year he received fifteen votes in the legislature for an associate justiceship in the Supreme Court, which had just been organized."[65] He lost the election by six votes. Then in August 1819, at age twenty-five, he won the legislative election to fill the seat of Justice Foster, making him the youngest Supreme Court justice in Illinois history.[66]

The following year Wilson married Mary S. Davidson of Wheeling, Virginia, and they became the parents of ten children.[67] When the General Assembly reorganized the judiciary in 1825, legislators elected Wilson as the state's third Chief Justice, replacing Thomas Reynolds.[68] Wilson held the office for twenty-three years, the longest-serving Chief Justice in Illinois history. "As a writer," recalled Springfield attorney James C. Conkling, "his style was clear and distinct; as a lawyer, his judgment was sound and discriminating." Thomas Ford described Wilson as "a man of good education, sound judgment, and an elegant writer, as his published opinions will show."[69]

In one of his more important cases, *Coles v. The County of Madison,* Wilson ruled for Edward Coles, then governor of Illinois. In 1824, Madison County commissioners had penalized Coles $2,000 "for bringing into the county, and setting at liberty, ten Negro slaves, without giving a bond, as required by an act of the legislature of 1819." In early 1825, the legislature released all penalties incurred under that act, and Chief Justice Wilson reversed the Circuit Court decision and affirmed the legislative action releasing Coles from the penalty.[70]

Wilson's most well-known case, *Field v. the People ex rel. McClernand*, involved the removal of an appointed state official. In 1838, newly elected Governor Thomas Carlin chose fellow Democrat John A. McClernand to replace Whig Secretary of State Alexander P. Field. Field, a "pugnacious" appointee of Governor Ninian Edwards in 1829, refused to surrender the office, arguing that the state Constitution did not specify the duration of his term. The Whig Senate, along with a few Democrats, supported Field's "so-called rights." After the legislature adjourned, McClernand commenced legal proceedings for the office.[71]

Judge Sidney Breese of the Fayette County Circuit Court ruled in McClernand's favor, but the Supreme Court reversed the judgment in a 2–1 decision (Justice Browne recused himself because he was related to McClernand). Chief Justice Wilson wrote the majority opinion, ruling that a governor could appoint only when a vacancy existed. "A different rule would destroy all the stability and uniformity in the rule of law," Wilson wrote. "If every judge can decide according to his private sentiments, without regard to precedent and authority, there may be as many rules of decisions as there are circuits, and the decision of one day would furnish no rule for the decision of the next."[72]

The state capitol building in Vandalia housed the Illinois Supreme Court. (Image courtesy of Illinois Supreme Court Historic Preservation Commission)

In the next election, Governor Carlin and other Democrats campaigned on what they perceived to be an intensely partisan decision by the Court. After they gained control of the next legislature, Field subsequently resigned. Carlin then appointed Stephen A. Douglas to what became a brief tenure as Secretary of State. Three months later, Douglas won election to the Illinois Supreme Court. McClernand, during the Civil War, would become a leading general in the Union Army.[73]

In 1830, Wilson unsuccessfully sought the U.S. Senate nomination. In 1841, the Illinois General Assembly increased the number of Illinois Supreme Court justices to nine and reinstated the circuit court responsibilities. Wilson was assigned to the Fourth Judicial Circuit, in east central and southeastern Illinois. In 1845, in *Jarrot v. Jarrot,* Wilson upheld the opinion in the Supreme Court that residence in a free territory entitled a slave to his freedom. Justices Wilson and Samuel Treat expressed a similar opinion two years later in the Coles County Circuit Court, ruling that Kentucky resident Robert Matson could not force his Negro slaves to return with him from Illinois to his home state.[74]

With adoption of a new Constitution in 1848, Wilson retired from the bench. "During the long period of his occupancy," wrote historian Frederic B. Crossley, Wilson provided "the sort of solid, substantial service needed during the days of construction, perhaps more than the kind offered by more brilliant but less consistent minds."[75] Wilson returned to the practice of law in Carmi. In 1856, he and two other men chartered a town in eastern Sangamon County. Thomas Mathers of Springfield, who laid out the town, named it Wilson in honor of the retired judge.[76]

Justice Wilson and his wife entertained "in the old Virginia style," according to historian Joseph Wallace. "Seldom did a summer season pass at their pleasant country seat, about two miles from Carmi, on the banks of the Little Wabash, that troops of friends, relatives and distinguished official visitors did not sojourn with them. [Justice] Lockwood, Lincoln and Douglas were frequent visitors."[77] On April 29, 1857, at age sixty-three, Wilson died at his Carmi estate. His grave is in Carmi's "Old Cemetery."[78]

THOMAS REYNOLDS, 1822-1825

Succeeding Joseph Philips as Chief Justice of the Illinois Supreme Court in August 1822, Thomas Reynolds served in the position for three years. "Persons that knew him," wrote John M. Scott, "all bear the same testimony, he was a very able and learned lawyer and made a good judge."[79] Reynolds was born in Bracken County, Kentucky, on March 12, 1796, the son of Nathaniel and Catherine Vernon Reynolds. Completing his education while still in his teens and admitted to the bar as a young man, in 1817, he moved with his family to the Illinois Territory. Licensed to practice law in the Gallatin County Circuit Court, Reynolds entered politics as clerk of the Illinois House of Representatives from 1818 to 1822.[80]

Appointed Chief Justice of the Supreme Court, Reynolds also served as a Circuit Court judge. "This gentleman was a very talented lawyer of his day," wrote John M. Palmer, "the peer of Benton, Marshall and others."[81] On September 2, 1823, Reynolds married Eliza Ann Young in Bracken County, Kentucky, and in 1824 became parents of one child, Ambrose Dudley Reynolds.[82]

During Reynolds's short tenure on the bench, he heard at least thirty cases at the Illinois Supreme Court, writing opinions in at least eighteen of them. In *Gill v. Caldwell*, Reynolds overturned a case in which a witness raised his hand, but did not use a bible, to be sworn in. The question before the Court was whether the law recognized that kind of oath. Reynolds noted that "oaths are to be administered to all persons according to their own opinions, and as it most affects their consciences." By only uplifting his hand, the witness was correctly sworn in to testify.[83]

Thomas Reynolds emerged a leader in the movement to permit slavery in the state, helping to establish a pro-slavery newspaper in Kaskaskia. Both pro- and anti-slavery proponents distributed "fiery" handbills and pamphlets on the issue. "The State was almost covered with them," wrote Thomas Ford. "They flew everywhere, and everywhere they scorched and scathed as they flew. This was a long, excited, angry, bitter and indignant contest," with Reynolds joining three fellow justices in an unsuccessful call for a constitutional convention on the slavery issue.[84]

The legislature reorganized the judiciary in 1824, establishing circuit court judgeships to relieve the Supreme Court judges of that "onerous and even oppressive" responsibility of presiding in circuit court cases.[85] The legislature did not re-elect Reynolds as a justice on the Court, and he returned to the practice of law. In 1826, he won a seat in the Illinois House of Representatives. He became known as an outstanding orator, in both the courts and the legislature.

Moving to Missouri in 1829, the Reynolds family settled in Fayette, Howard County, where he practiced law. Elected as a Democrat to the Missouri House of Representatives in 1832, Reynolds was chosen as Speaker. Nominated by Governor Lilburn W. Boggs for the Second Judicial Circuit of Missouri in 1837, Reynolds served in that position for three years. At the 1840 state Democratic convention, "he was nominated for governor almost by acclamation." Reynolds won the general election to become the Missouri's seventh governor.[86]

During his gubernatorial tenure, Reynolds advocated states' rights, including the right of each state to decide the question of slavery, and he recommended life imprisonment for those who enticed slaves from service or aided in their escape. "In his warning against centralized government," Reynolds "seemed retrogressive in the midst of a changing economy."[87] He did have several significant accomplishments. With his support, the legislature formed fifteen new counties while improving voting requirements and abolishing the practice of debtor imprisonment.[88]

In the middle of his term, however, Reynolds began suffering from both physical and mental illnesses. Then, on February 9, 1844, "in a melancholic frame of mind, imagining his enemies were slandering him," he committed suicide with a rifle in his Executive Mansion office. At the time, he was the state's leading candidate for the United States Senate.[89] "Governor Reynolds's death was a tragedy," wrote a relative, Harriet Shoemaker. "He had no enemies, political or otherwise, for Thomas Reynolds was one of the most popular and beloved men in the state of Missouri." Two years after his death, officials erected a granite tombstone at his Woodlawn Cemetery grave in Jefferson City and named the county of Reynolds in his honor.[90]

THEOPHILUS W. SMITH, 1825-1842

Once described as "one of the striking characters in the history of the legal profession in Illinois," Theophilus Washington Smith holds the distinction of being the subject of Illinois's only judicial impeachment trial. Born in New York City on September 28, 1784, to Thomas and Mary Green Smith, Theophilus Smith served as a young man in the United States Navy.[91] A law student in the office of American political leader Aaron Burr and fellow student of Washington Irving, Smith was admitted to the New York bar in 1805. Three years later, he married Clarissa Harlow Rathbone of Stonington, Connecticut, and they would become parents of eight children.[92]

Moving to Illinois in 1816, the Smiths settled in Edwardsville, and he soon became one of the state's most powerful politicians. Losing to Samuel Lockwood for the position of Attorney General, Smith won election to the state Senate in 1822. He vigorously supported a new state constitution for the legalization of slavery and helped to edit the *Illinois Republican,* a newspaper published in Edwardsville for the pro-slavery faction in Illinois.[93] In 1823, he became a member of the first Board of Commissioners of the Illinois and Michigan Canal, then cashier of the Bank of Illinois branch at Edwardsville.[94]

Smith was the third associate justice elected at the 1825 session of the Illinois legislature. From 1828 to 1835, he also served as judge of the Fourth Judicial Circuit in southeastern Illinois. Attorneys and Illinois politicians Thomas Ford and John Reynolds both credited Justices Smith and Lockwood with revisions to more than thirty laws, including the criminal code, habeas corpus, and right of property.[95]

In the 1832 Black Hawk War, Justice Smith served as quartermaster-general on the governor's staff. Impeached that year on allegations of "oppressive conduct, corruption, and other high misdemeanors in his judicial office," the specific charges included selling a circuit clerk's office, swearing out fictitious writs returnable before himself, imprisoning a Quaker for not removing his hat in court, and suspending a lawyer for advising a client to apply for a change of venue.[96]

Three attorneys defended Smith: Ford, Sidney Breese, and Richard M. Young. Ford reported that during the Senate trial, Smith "procured some one to go into the Senate chamber regularly after every adjournment and gather up the scraps of paper on the desks of the senators upon which they had scribbled during the trial." That information allegedly enabled his defense counsel "to direct their evidence and arguments to better advantage."[97] The Senate voted a majority in favor of impeachment, 12 to 10, but the Constitution required a two-thirds vote for conviction. Afterwards, the House of Representatives passed a resolution for his removal, but that, too, failed in the Senate.[98]

As Illinoisans grew to favor the elimination of black servitude, so, too, did members of the Supreme Court, particularly noted in the opinions of formerly pro-slavery Justice Smith.[99] In the 1836 *Boon v. Juliet* case, he delivered the Court opinion that sharply reduced the legal basis for existing slavery in Illinois. He ruled that an 1807 territorial act regarding registration of servants did not affect the rights of the children, writing, "I am clearly of opinion that the children of registered negroes and mulattoes, under the laws of the Territories of Indiana and Illinois, are unquestionably free."[100] According to historian N. Dwight Harris, "The importance of this decision is at once apparent, when we remember that the larger proportion of the younger slaves were the offspring of Negroes who had been indentured under these Territorial laws. It is most difficult to determine at present [1904] just how many received their freedom through this act of the Supreme Court, but the number must have been considerable."[101]

In the highly political 1839 *Field v. People ex rel. McClernand* case, the lone Democrat Smith wrote the dissenting opinion. Democratic Illinois governor Thomas Carlin attempted to replace the Whig Secretary of State Field, but Field refused to leave the position because he could remain in office as long as he desired. The Illinois Supreme Court upheld Field's right to remain in office, but in his dissent, Smith held that since the Illinois Constitution was patterned after the U.S. Constitution—under which the President could dismiss the national Secretary of State, Democratic Governor Thomas Carlin could replace the incumbent Whig, Alexander P. Field.[102]

After the legislature in 1841 required justices to ride the circuit, Justice Smith was assigned to the Seventh Judicial Circuit, comprising six northeastern counties, including Cook, Will, and DuPage. In August 1842, the Springfield *Illinois State Register* published a lengthy attack on Smith, describing accusations that included drunkenness, nepotism, and harassment of politicians. "Under a cloud mostly of his own raising," wrote historian Theodore C. Pease, Smith resigned from the bench in December 1842.[103]

Throughout his legal career, according to Ford, Smith had been "an active, bustling, ambitious, and turbulent member of the democratic party. He had for a long time aimed to be elected to the United States Senate; his devices and intrigues to this end had been innumerable. In fact he never lacked a plot to advance himself or to blow up some other person." Smith was "a good lawyer and made an able judge," added John M. Scott, "but he was so much a partisan politician, it depreciated his usefulness as a lawyer and as a judge."[104]

Smith died in Chicago on May 6, 1845.[105] Most likely, he was interred in the City Cemetery. At some later point, his body was moved to Rosehill Cemetery in Chicago.

SAMUEL D. LOCKWOOD, 1825-1848

A young New York attorney who became prominent in Illinois politics, Samuel Drake Lockwood was born in Poundridge, New York, on August 2, 1789, the eldest of four children of Joseph and Mary Drake Lockwood.[106] Orphaned at the age of ten, Lockwood lived with an uncle who taught him law. In 1811, he obtained his law license and began practicing in Albany, also serving as justice of the peace and master in chancery.[107]

In 1818, the twenty-nine-year-old Lockwood traveled the Allegheny and Ohio Rivers to the new state of Illinois. He opened a law office in Carmi, then moved to Edwardsville in 1821 after the legislature elected him Attorney General.[108] In that position, he successfully prosecuted a defendant, William Bennett, accused of an 1820 murder by duel, which was illegal in Illinois. By that conviction and execution by hanging, wrote Thomas Ford in his history of Illinois, Lockwood prevented "the barbarous practice of dueling from being introduced" into Illinois.[109]

Less than two years after Lockwood became Attorney General, Governor Edward Coles appointed him as Secretary of State. Three months later, in April 1823, President James Monroe named Lockwood the receiver of public monies at the Edwardsville land office. "This carried a better salary, paid in gold, instead of the depreciated currency," wrote a Lockwood biographer, "so Mr. Lockwood resigned the secretaryship and accepted the federal office."[110]

In the ongoing issue of slavery in the state, he supported anti-slavery Governor Coles. Through columns in the anti-slavery *Edwardsville Spectator* newspaper, Lockwood argued against the call for a constitutional convention—helping to ensure that Illinois remained a free state. In other activities, as an appointed member of the state's first Board of Canal Commissioners in 1824, Lockwood contracted with engineers to survey the route of the Illinois and Michigan Canal.[111]

With the 1824 Supreme Court reorganization, the legislature elected Lockwood as an associate justice, and he served for twenty-four years. "He was a sound lawyer," wrote fellow attorney Usher F. Linder, "a scholar, a gentleman, and an honest man."[112] In one example of poor travel conditions, Lockwood and fellow Justice William Wilson were unable to cross the Kaskaskia River in the middle of winter. They chose to swim across and made the perilous journey, "but Lockwood nearly died of exposure."[113]

Among Lockwood's contributions were revisions of the Illinois statutes, a major undertaking to organize better Illinois laws. He also established a principle that voided unsigned indenture papers. "This was a small but an essential gain for the negroes," wrote historian N. Dwight Harris, "since this decision must have acted as an effectual check on all unscrupulous masters who, would, if it were possible, entice and browbeat free negroes

Illinois State Capitol Building in Vandalia (Image courtesy of James Dobrovolny Collection, Illinois Supreme Court Historic Preservation Commission)

into their service."[114]

Lockwood was involved in two politically charged cases in the 1820s and '30s. In *People ex rel. Ewing v. Forquer*, one of Lockwood's earliest cases in the Illinois Supreme Court, Acting Governor Adolphus F. Hubbard, who was sitting in the absence of Edward Coles, appointed Ewing to the position of paymaster-general. Secretary of State George Forquer refused to sign the commission. Ewing sued to force Forquer to sign the commission. In 1825, Lockwood wrote the opinion that Forquer did not have to sign the commission because Hubbard did not have the authority to make the appointment as an acting governor. In the 1839 highly politicized case of *Field v. People ex rel. McClernand,* Lockwood wrote a concurring opinion with Chief Justice William Wilson that the Illinois governor did not control the office of Secretary of State.[115]

In 1841, after the legislature divided Illinois into nine judicial circuits, Justice Lockwood became responsible for the First Judicial Circuit in western Illinois. In *Klein et al. v. Mather*, an 1845 case before the Morgan County Circuit Court, Lockwood rendered judgment for Thomas Mather to recover proportionate payments regarding the 1837 move of state government from Vandalia to Springfield. The Supreme Court affirmed that decision.[116]

In 1846, he delivered the Supreme Court decision in *Anderson v. Ryan*. Michael Ryan had sued Elias Anderson in the Coles County Circuit Court for the seduction of his daughter and the loss of her services while pregnant. The jury found for Ryan, and Anderson appealed to the Supreme Court. Justice Lockwood wrote the opinion affirming the circuit court judgment. He cited a New York opinion on seduction that "satisfactorily vindicates the modern doctrine, as more in accordance with the original design of the action for seduction. It has long been considered as a standing reproach to the common law, that it furnished no means to punish the seducer of female innocence and virtue, except through the fiction of supposing the daughter was a servant of her parent, and that in consequence of her seduction, the parent had lost some of her services as a menial. It is high time this reproach should be wiped out." He later added, "This action ought, then, no longer to be considered as a means of recovering damages for the loss of menial services, but as an instrument to punish the perpetrator of flagitious outrage upon the peace and happiness of the family circle."[117]

Lockwood represented Morgan County at the 1847 Illinois Constitutional Convention. In a speech on the judiciary, Lockwood commented that he believed "that long terms and competent salaries are the only sure basis of an independent, upright, and able judicial system—and I am yet to learn that the tenure of *good behavior* with a competent salary is not best calculated to secure these desirable results." Lockwood advocated gubernatorial appointment to the Court with fifteen-year terms, but the convention passed popular election and nine-year terms in addition to reducing the number of Supreme Court justices from nine to three.[118]

With implementation of the new Constitution, Lockwood retired from the bench. "The career of Judge Lockwood," wrote Frederic B. Crossley, "indicates he was one of the most popular and forceful men of his time, in that he was apparently never an office seeker, he held positions of trust and honor in the state for more than fifty years, to most of which he was elevated by administrations with whom he was not in political sympathy."[119] Former Justice John D. Caton noted, "If Judge Lockwood was not a great man, he was a good man and a good judge. His style of writing was easy and perspicuous."[120]

Lockwood married Mary Stith Nash in the 1820s, and they became parents of three daughters. In 1828, the family moved to Jacksonville, where he helped to establish Illinois College and served as a trustee for forty consecutive years (1828–1868). He also assisted in locating several state charitable institutions in Jacksonville.[121] In 1851, legislators elected Lockwood a trustee of the land department of the Illinois Central Railroad, a position he held for the remainder of his life. In 1853, he moved from Jacksonville to Batavia, where he died on April 23, 1874, at the age of eighty-five.[122] Lockwood was buried in the West Batavia Cemetery.

SAMUEL H. TREAT, 1841-1855

Born near Plainfield, Otsego County, New York, to Samuel and Elcy Tracy Treat on June 21, 1811, Samuel Hubbel Treat would become one of the longest-serving jurists in the early history of Illinois. Treat obtained his education in area schools, worked on his father's farm, and at age eighteen began the study of law at Richfield, New York, under Judge Holdridge, "a lawyer of eminence in that locality."[123]

After his admission to the New York bar, Treat came to Sangamon County, Illinois, in 1834 "traveling most of the way on foot." In Springfield, he formed a partnership with George Forquer, a former Illinois Secretary of State and Attorney General. In 1837, Treat married Ann Elizabeth Bennett, a native of Jefferson County, Virginia.[124] Treat's success at the Sangamon County bar was so rapid that in 1839 Governor Thomas Carlin appointed him to fill a judicial vacancy on the Eighth Judicial Circuit in east-central Illinois.

With the 1841 Supreme Court reorganization, Treat became one of the five new members of the Supreme Court, while retaining his circuit responsibility. The nine Supreme Court colleagues met twice each year in Springfield. The July term was frequently brief, perhaps the result of hot, humid central Illinois's summers, explained historian Robert W. Johannsen. The December term usually lasted until February, "thus affording the judges opportunity to participate in the political discussions of the state legislature."[125]

Presiding in an 1842 circuit court case, Treat showed an increasing judicial tendency toward granting blacks "full legal protection and justice." Historian N. Dwight Harris reported the case of an Arkansas resident who demanded the return of James Foster, a black man who had been living in Springfield for two or three years, as his slave. Judge Treat required that the "supposed master" provide disinterested witnesses to prove that the "the negro was his property." Harris considered the ruling "a step in the right direction . . . the practice of kidnapping Negroes had become so prevalent that the most stringent regulations were needed to protect the free blacks in Illinois."[126]

Springfield attorney Abraham Lincoln handled more than 900 circuit court cases and 167 Supreme Court arguments before Justice Treat.[127] In the 1852 *McAtee v. Enyert* case, Lincoln successfully represented William D. Enyert, who had sold ninety acres of land to Smith McAtee for $350, while the land was actually worth $1,000. In 1847, after twenty-two-year-old Enyert had been indicted for stealing a pair of shoes, neighbor McAtee pressured Enyert to sell him the land and then to flee the area to avoid imprisonment.[128] In the court case, Enyert contended that his former friend "used terror and intoxication to persuade him to take fraudulent advantage of him." The Sangamon County Circuit Court voided the sale and ordered the land returned to Enyert.[129]

"There is one feature of the case which demands especial notice," Justice Treat wrote in the Supreme Court opinion affirming the circuit court decree. Treat admonished McAtee for deliberately advising Enyert "to evade the demands of public justice," and as a result, "deserves no favor at the hands of a court of equity." Treat concluded that it "is the duty of every citizen to aid in the execution of the laws, and in no contingency is he at liberty to encourage their violation, or assist offenders to escape detection and punishment."[130]

Treat recalled a morning when Lincoln visited his office and joined the judge in a game of chess. "The two were enthusiastic chess-players," reported Lincoln biographer Jesse W. Weik:

> They were soon deeply absorbed, nor did they realize how near it was to the noon hour until one of Lincoln's boys came running with a message from his mother announcing dinner at the Lincoln home, a few steps away. Lincoln promised to come at once and the boy left; but the game was not entirely out; yet so near the end the players, confident that they would finish in a few moments, lingered a while. Meanwhile almost a half an hour had passed. Presently the boy returned with a second and more urgent call for dinner; but so deeply engrossed in the game were the two players they apparently failed to notice his arrival. This was more than the little fellow could stand; so that, angered at their inattention, he moved nearer, lifted his foot, and deliberately kicked board, chessmen, and all into the air. "It was one of the most abrupt, if not brazen, things I ever saw," said Treat, "but the surprising thing was its effect on Lincoln. Instead of the animated scene between an irate father and an impudent youth which I expected, Mr. Lincoln without a word of reproof calmly arose, took the boy by the hand, and started for dinner. Reaching the door he turned, smiled good-naturedly, and exclaimed, "Well, Judge, I reckon we'll have to finish this game some other time."[131]

Throughout Treat's fourteen years on the Illinois Supreme Court, he maintained a favorable reputation "for promptness in his decisions and was generally liked by the bar and the public," reported historian Frederic B. Crossley.[132] "He was a sterling Democrat, and as true as steel to that great and noble old party," added attorney Usher Linder, "but he never suffered his politics to mingle in the slightest degree with his judicial opinions or deliberations." Author John M. Palmer described Treat as an able jurist who wrote brief, clear opinions. "It was said of him that he could be depended upon to try issues of fact better than the most intelligent jury."[133]

Under the new Illinois Constitution of 1848, one justice would be elected from each of Illinois's Southern, Central, and Northern Divisions. Treat won the popular election in the Central Grand Division. The three justices needed to stagger their terms and drew lots for the nine-, six-, and three-year terms. Treat won the nine-year term and became the Chief Justice.[134] In 1855, President Franklin Pierce appointed Treat as judge of the newly created U.S. District Court for the Southern District of Illinois. With outbreak of the Civil War, Treat appointed a commission that determined membership in the secret antiwar Knights of the Golden Circle did not constitute treason to the United States.[135]

Treat held the federal position for thirty-two years. At age seventy-six, he died on March 27, 1887, at his Springfield residence. Following services at St. Paul's Episcopal Church, where he had been a founding member and longtime vestryman, Treat was interred beside his wife in Springfield's Oak Ridge Cemetery in an unmarked grave.[136] In 2008, the Illinois Bar Foundation and the Abraham Lincoln Association sponsored the installation of an obelisk monument at the Treat gravesite.

THOMAS FORD, 1841-1842

Thomas Ford served only a brief term on the Illinois Supreme Court before accepting the Democratic Party nomination for governor of the state. A Uniontown, Pennsylvania, native, Ford was born to Robert and Elizabeth Logue Ford on December 5, 1800. Four years later, he moved with his widowed mother and siblings to a rented farm in the area that became Monroe County, Illinois.[137]

With assistance from his elder half-brother George Forquer (who later served in the Illinois General Assembly, as secretary of state and as attorney general), Ford studied law for one term at Transylvania University in Lexington, Kentucky. He then returned to Illinois, where he farmed, taught school, and continued the study of law under Daniel Pope Cook, later a congressman from Illinois. Ford began his law practice in Waterloo before moving to Edwardsville. In 1828, Ford married Frances Hambaugh of Kentucky, and they would become the parents of five children.[138]

Moving to Galena in 1829, Ford edited the *Miners' Journal* and became a supporter of Andrew Jackson and active in the Democratic Party. The next year, he was named state's attorney for Illinois's Fifth Judicial Circuit in western and northern Illinois. In 1835, Ford became judge of the Sixth Judicial Circuit, covering the northern counties of Illinois. He served briefly as a municipal judge in Chicago, and later as judge of the Ninth Judicial Circuit, comprising the Rock River area. He was a defense counsel in the 1833 Senate impeachment trial of Supreme Court Justice Theophilus W. Smith.[139]

Ford described the administration of justice in Illinois during the early 1830s as "without much show, parade, or ceremony," in contrast with British courts. He considered most Illinois judges as men of "considerable learning and much good sense," who, whenever possible, avoided deciding questions of law. "They did not like the responsibility of offending one or the other of the parties," Ford explained, "and preferred to submit everything they could to be decided by the jury." Moreover, the justices rarely gave instructions to the jury, he complained, which he attributed to a lack of confidence in their own abilities and a fear of public censure for mistakes.[140]

With expansion of the State Supreme Court in 1841, the Democratic General Assembly elected Ford as one of the five new justices. Assigned to the Ninth Judicial Circuit, he moved with his family to Ogle County. Serving during the final reign of the Banditti of the Prairie, a gang of northern Illinois horse thieves and murderers, Ford denied that he unofficially recommended subjecting the criminals to bullwhip lashings.[141]

Ford had a brief career on the state's highest bench and only wrote a handful of opinions. In *Rogers v. Hall*, Ford commented on the importance of evidence as the appellant failed to file a proper bill of exceptions. Since the evidence was not certified to the Supreme Court and there was no error in the proceedings, "we have no means of judging upon the whole case. If it now fails to appear that injustice has been done, it is the fault of the plaintiff himself, in not stating, as he might have done, the whole of the testimony in his bill of exceptions. The party guilty of the omission must be the sufferer, and not the opposite party."[142]

Historian Robert P. Howard described Ford as "an able jurist, one of the best in Illinois. He reasoned clearly and might have had an eminent career on the Supreme Court . . . if he had not transferred to the executive branch."[143] With a reputation for "judicial probity and party loyalty," Ford resigned from the Court in 1842 to become the Democratic candidate for governor. Defeating Whig nominee Joseph Duncan, Ford assumed his first and only popularly elected office. Ford served as an effective governor, salvaging the state's credit after its enormous internal improvement debt, closing failed state-chartered banks, and expediting completion of the Illinois and Michigan Canal. He is also remembered, however, for the violent Hancock County conflicts with Mormon settlers and his failure to prevent the 1844 murders of Mormon leaders Joseph and Hyrum Smith.[144]

At the end of his term, Ford resumed the practice of law. Poor and in ill health, he moved his family to Peoria, where wealthy residents provided him with food, clothing, and bedding.[145] Hoping to leave a legacy for his children, Ford wrote *History of Illinois*, which was published posthumously. "Approaching the period of the state's history through which he had lived as an example of the futility of American politics," explained historian Theodore C. Pease, "he dissected with a merciless scalpel both politicians and political methods. . . . To him the period was one of little measures and little men."[146]

A few days following the death of his wife, Ford died of tuberculosis on November 3, 1850.[147] Anonymous acquaintances paid for his burial in the Peoria cemetery. The body was later removed to Springdale Cemetery in Peoria, where the state erected a monument in 1895. Ford County, organized in 1859, was named in his honor.[148]

SIDNEY BREESE, 1841-1843, 1857-1878

The son of wealthy aristocrats Arthur and Catharine Livingston Breese, Sidney Breese was born in Whitesboro, upstate New York, on July 15, 1800.[149] He attended Hamilton College and graduated at age eighteen from Union College in Schenectady, New York. A first cousin, Samuel Finley Breese Morse, invented the electric telegraph and devised the set of telegraph signals known as Morse code.[150]

Moving to Illinois in December 1818, Breese studied law in the Kaskaskia office of Secretary of State Elias Kent Kane, a New York schoolmate and later a United States Senator.[151] Admitted to the bar at age twenty, Breese, "from that time," wrote John M. Scott, "was prominent in both the legal and political history of the State. Writing his biography would be the history of the State during his active life."[152]

In 1820, Breese earned $25 for moving the state archives by wagon from Kaskaskia some one hundred miles to the new capital at Vandalia.[153] To supplement his law-practice income, the following year he became the Kaskaskia postmaster. His fortunes improved in 1822, when Governor Shadrach Bond appointed Breese as state's attorney for the Third Judicial Circuit, which included Kaskaskia.[154]

On September 4, 1823, Breese married Eliza Morrison, daughter of a wealthy pioneer Kaskaskia family, "a part of the aristocracy of commerce and land," wrote a Breese biographer, "which had already developed on the western frontier."[155] Through marriage, Breese shared in that social prominence, becoming acquainted with influential political friends of the Morrison family. Eliza and Sidney Breese would become parents of fourteen children.[156]

While not opposed to slavery where it existed in other states, Breese joined the Governor Edward Coles faction in opposing its extension into Illinois. Breese did not, however, take an active role against the call for a constitutional convention on the issue.[157] In 1827, President John Quincy Adams named Breese the U.S. District Attorney for Illinois. Breese published the *Illinois Reporter* newspaper at Kaskaskia from 1826 to 1828, editorially supporting the Adams administration. That public stance resulted in his dismissal as U.S. Attorney by President Andrew Jackson in 1829, cutting short his four-year term.[158]

In 1830 and again in 1832, Breese ran unsuccessfully for the U.S. Congress, on a platform of federal assistance for internal improvements and a high protective tariff. In addition to his Kaskaskia law practice, he made a contribution to the state's legal community—a compilation of Illinois Supreme Court decisions. He published *Breese's Reports, 1819–1831*, in 1831, even setting the type, while Kane assisted with proofreading.[159]

During the period covered in the *Reports*, Breese argued more than a dozen cases before the Supreme Court, primarily involving debts and land ownership—the two most common types of litigation in Illinois. Of his cases, Breese lost only two arguments. In an unusual case, Breese represented a black woman against a defendant who claimed her as an indentured servant under an 1807 law. The Supreme Court reversed a lower court decision, finding in favor of Breese's client.[160]

During the 1832 Black Hawk War, Breese enlisted as a private and rose in rank to become a lieutenant colonel of volunteers. After the war, he resumed the practice of law, by now recognized for clear and precise statements in addressing juries. Breese's legal defense in the 1833 impeachment trial of Supreme Court Justice Theophilus W. Smith brought him statewide attention. Both Smith and Breese had come to Illinois from New York, had become embroiled in factional politics, and evolved as supporters of Andrew Jackson and his policies. During the Senate proceedings, Breese prepared ten pleas in helping gain Smith's acquittal. Thereafter, Smith's friends and associates assisted Breese in beginning his own judicial career by supporting his candidacy for a circuit judgeship.

Appointed a judge of the Second Judicial Circuit in 1835, Breese traveled the circuit encompassing the state's most populous area. Realizing the necessity of moving from his "favorite" Kaskaskia, he settled with his family at Mound Farm, overlooking the village of Carlyle in Clinton County.[161] Breese "looked the judge while on the bench," recalled John M. Palmer. "He was industrious, prompt, energetic, and patient; he knew the law, and applied it to the cases before him."[162] In the 1839 case of *People ex rel. McClernand v. Field* brought in the Fayette County Circuit Court, Circuit Judge Breese ruled for McClernand, but the Supreme Court later reversed the decision.[163]

After an unsuccessful gubernatorial bid, Breese became a member of the Illinois Supreme Court after the legislature elected him in 1841 as one of the five additional justices.[164] He also continued as judge for the Second Judicial Circuit but resigned from the Court in December 1842, after legislators elected him to replace Richard M. Young in the U.S. Senate.[165] During his one senatorial term from 1843 to 1849, Breese advocated a transcontinental railroad as well as a north-south railroad through Illinois. He became the primary author of federal land grants to the Illinois Central Railroad, a project that,

Charles Lawrence, Sidney Breese, and Pinkney Walker constituted the Supreme Court in 1869. (Image courtesy of Abraham Lincoln Presidential Library and Museum)

according to Scott, "did more than any other one thing to develop the resources of the State."[166] Breese also introduced legislation that established a naval depot and dockyard at the confluence of the Ohio and Mississippi Rivers.[167]

Defeated for reelection by James Shields, a military hero of the Mexican War, Breese practiced law until his election to the state legislature in 1850, when he became Speaker of the House. In 1855, he was again elected a circuit court judge, and in 1857, won popular election to return to the Illinois Supreme Court. Breese "had a liking for some of Mr. Lincoln's—for whom he had an exalted opinion—stories," recalled Scott, "and would sometimes try to tell one of them, but he would quite as likely leave out the only point in it that would make it mirth-provoking."[168]

In the landmark *Munn v. Illinois* case, Justice Breese upheld the assertion that government could regulate a business in the public interest. In 1877, the U.S. Supreme Court, in the first of the "Granger" cases, affirmed every point in his ruling of the state's regulatory power over public service corporations.[169] Breese also maintained involvement in Democratic politics through his judicial tenure. In 1868, party leaders considered him as a presidential candidate, but, wrote historian Arthur Charles Cole, "it became evident that this was largely a compliment to a favorite son."[170]

Breese remained on the Supreme Court until his death in 1878, including terms as Chief Justice from 1867 to 1870 and 1873 to 1874. He served as a justice on the Court under three different Illinois Constitutions and wrote opinions on nearly every question affecting the welfare of the state. According to Scott, "as specimens of elegant judicial statements his opinions delivered in the Supreme Court will lose nothing in comparison with the best opinions of the most distinguished jurists of this country and England."[171]

Breese died of heart disease on June 27, 1878, in Pinckneyville, Illinois. Fellow Supreme Court justices served as pallbearers at his funeral. After services at the Clinton County Courthouse, Breese was buried in Carlyle Cemetery in Carlyle, Illinois.[172] The town of Breese in Clinton County is named in his honor.

WALTER B. SCATES, 1841-1847, 1853-1857

A native of South Boston, Halifax County, Virginia, Walter Bennett Scates was born on January 18, 1808, the fourth child of Joseph W. and Elizabeth Eggleston Bennett Scates.[173] In 1809, the family settled on a farm near Hopkinsville, Kentucky. Young Walter studied law in Louisville, Kentucky, before moving to Franklin County, Illinois, in 1831. Admitted to the Illinois bar, he served as county surveyor from 1831 to 1834, then as state's attorney pro tem. Two years later he won election to the office of Attorney General.[174]

Scates moved to the state capital of Vandalia in 1836 and married Mary Ellen Ridgeway, also a Virginia native. They became the parents of five sons and two daughters.[175] In December 1836, state legislators chose Scates as judge of the Third Judicial Circuit in southern Illinois. He served in that position until his election in 1841 as one of five new justices, "all nominal Democrats," of the Illinois Supreme Court.[176] Also in 1841, Scates moved to Mt. Vernon, Illinois.

Justice Scates heard more than 130 Supreme Court cases involving Springfield attorney Abraham Lincoln.[177] In the 1845 *Wren v. Moss et al.* case, Lincoln represented Clarissa Wren, whose husband, Aquilla Wren, had been granted a divorce based on her proven misconduct. He made a will leaving his property to people other than his former wife, and then died. An executor sold Wren's land to William S. Moss and Smith Frye, even though Clarissa had not released her right of dower. Moss's attorney argued that according to Illinois statute, a wife divorced for her own fault or misconduct lost her dower rights.

The Supreme Court, however, ruled in favor of Clarissa Wren, with Justice Scates writing the opinion. Clarissa Wren believed she had been injured by an erroneous divorce decree.[178] The Court granted a "writ of error," entitling her to a new trial. "We should frame such a writ of error," the justices decreed, "as will secure the interests of all who may be affected by it, while it affords a remedy to the plaintiff."[179]

In the 1846 Illinois gubernatorial contest, Scates was among six Democratic candidates, but lost the nomination to Augustus French, who became the state's ninth governor. Scates resigned from the Supreme Court in 1847. He served as a delegate to the 1847 Constitutional Convention and chaired the Committee on the Judiciary and was "one of the more active influences in the convention."[180] He supported statewide elections for Supreme Court justices, but the convention eventually adopted regional representatives from three grand divisions.

After his retirement from the Supreme Court, Scates returned to the practice of law and entered into several business ventures. His businesses failed, and when Lyman Trumbull resigned from the Illinois Supreme Court, Scates won the popular election to replace him in 1853. After two years on the Court, he became the Chief Justice.[181]

In 1855, Lincoln represented Oliver Browning in *Browning v. City of Springfield*. Browning alleged that while walking on a city sidewalk he fell and broke a leg. He charged that the city was negligent in its duty to maintain the streets and sidewalks. After the Sangamon County Circuit Court found in favor of the city, Lincoln and his partner William H. Herndon appealed to the Supreme Court. Reversing the lower court, Scates delivered the Supreme Court opinion that found the city liable, citing a legal obligation as well as the taxing authority to make such repairs. "We not only feel authorized," Scates concluded in the innovative decision, "but required to afford the protection sought."[182]

Scates's greatest contribution to Illinois may have been in 1857 as the principal compiler, along with Samuel H. Treat and Robert S. Blackwell, of *The Statutes of Illinois . . . and . . . Decisions of the Supreme Court Upon the Construction of Each Statute*.[183] Scates maintained a reputation "for ability and knowledge of the law," according to legal historian Frederic B. Crossley. "He was not a brilliant jurist, but his decisions are expressed with unusual clearness and are most noticeable for their conservatism and tendency to follow the existing authorities."[184]

Resigning from the Court in 1857, Scates and his family moved to Chicago, where he resumed the practice of law. With the outbreak of the Civil War, he joined the Union Army and in 1862 was commissioned a major on the staff of General John A. McClernand. Three years later, Scates became the assistant adjutant-general, with the rank of lieutenant colonel. He declined President Lincoln's offer of Chief Justice of the New Mexico Territory in March 1865. Mustered out of the service in 1866, he was brevetted brigadier general of volunteers. President Andrew Johnson appointed Scates as Collector of Customs in Chicago, where he remained until relieved by President Ulysses S. Grant in 1869.[185]

After retirement from judicial, military, and political offices, Scates practiced with Chicago attorney and Lincoln associate Henry Clay Whitney, who had served as paymaster of volunteers during the Civil War.[186] Scates died at his Evanston home on October 26, 1886, and was buried in Rosehill Cemetery in Chicago. "He was a grand old man, firm as a rock," recalled fellow attorney John M. Palmer. "He performed every duty firmly, ably and with an honest purpose. No power could drive him from what he thought was right. Had he been influenced by wealth and power he might have died worth millions instead of a few thousand dollars. The state should not forget the services of such a man."[187]

STEPHEN A. DOUGLAS, 1841-1843

One of Illinois's most prominent statesmen, Stephen Arnold Douglas was a native of Brandon, Vermont. Descended from Massachusetts and Connecticut ancestors, he was born on April 23, 1813, the second child of Sarah Fisk and Stephen Arnold Douglass. The father died when his son was just two months of age. "I have often been told," the younger Douglas later wrote, "that he was holding me in his arms when he departed this world."[188]

The widowed Sarah Douglass moved with her two children to her bachelor brother's adjacent farm, where young Stephen grew to adolescence. He attended a district school for three months each year, but most of his time was spent on farm chores for his uncle, "rather a hard master."[189] At age fifteen, Douglas apprenticed with a cabinetmaker, and then moved to Canandaigua, New York, where he resumed academic courses and began the study of law.[190]

Some five years later, he migrated westward, earning a position as schoolmaster in the village of Winchester, Illinois. Obtaining his law license in 1834, Douglas moved to the nearby larger town of Jacksonville, and in 1835, the legislature appointed him state's attorney for the First Judicial Circuit.[191] Dubbed the "Little Giant" for his diminutive physical stature, "his speed of action attracted friends, allies, and enemies equally," wrote historians David Kenney and Robert Hartley.[192]

An active Democrat, Douglas became chairman of the Democratic State Committee in 1836, helping the party carry Illinois for President Martin Van Buren along with an overwhelming majority in the state legislature. That same year, Douglas himself won election to the Illinois General Assembly and served with attorney Abraham Lincoln. Near the end of session, legislators voted to move the capital from Vandalia to Springfield. In the new capital city, Douglas accepted a commission as register of the land office. In 1838, he ran for Congress but narrowly lost against John T. Stuart, Lincoln's law partner.

Douglas also participated in several major politically charged lawsuits. He represented John McClernand in his legal attempt to gain the Secretary of State's position from Alexander P. Field. Douglas lost the case at the Illinois Supreme Court, but when Field later resigned, Governor Thomas Carlin appointed Douglas to the position in November 1840. Douglas also served as an attorney in a lawsuit concerning the right of aliens to vote in elections. Since many of the Irish immigrants tended to vote Democratic, Douglas worked to secure their voting rights.[193]

Anticipating the Whig-dominated Supreme Court to limit alien voting rights and after the adverse decision in *Field v. People ex rel. McClernand*, Douglas played a major role in expanding the Supreme Court from four to nine justices in order to gain a Democratic majority. While Douglas did not serve in the general assembly at the time, he shepherded the bill to expand the court through the legislature and secured its passage.[194]

As a reward for his services in managing the Supreme Court bill, also known as "Douglas's bill," the legislature elected him to one of the five new Supreme Court justice positions. At the age of twenty-seven, Douglas was one of the youngest justices in Illinois history. His election even caused some Democratic politicians to question whether Douglas had the necessary experience to be a judge. As part of his circuit duties, Douglas was assigned to the Fifth Judicial Circuit, a nine-county area in west-central Illinois, and he moved to Quincy and earned the reputation of a hard-working jurist.[195]

On the Supreme Court, Douglas heard twenty-four cases in which Lincoln represented clients. In *Grubb v. Crane,* Samuel Grubb had failed to pay the balance of a promissory note to William B. Crane. Lincoln and partner Stephen T. Logan represented Crane in suing Grubb in chancery. Crane won a judgment for the balance of the debt, then after Grubb failed to pay, purchased the land at public auction. The circuit court overruled Grubb's motion to set aside the judgment, and he appealed to the Supreme Court, with Lincoln and Logan again representing Crane. "We are of opinion," wrote Justice Douglas, "that substantial justice has been done according to the forms of law and the usages of chancery practice, and perceive no good reason for a reversal of the decree. The decree is affirmed."[196]

As judge in the circuit in which the Mormons resided, Douglas became involved in several issues regarding the religious group. In one opinion, Douglas decided that members of the Nauvoo Legion, the Mormon militia, were exempt from military duty. The decision emphasized the independence of the Mormons from the state of Illinois. In a second case, Douglas ruled that a Missouri indictment against Smith was not valid because a previous indictment had been returned unexecuted. Douglas's actions as judge endeared him to the Mormons, and Smith claimed that Douglas had "proved himself friendly to this people."[197]

On June 28, 1843, after serving on the Supreme Court for slightly more than two years, Douglas resigned to run for the U.S. House of Representatives. Defeating Whig Orville Hickman Browning by a margin of 461 votes, Douglas served as Congressman for two terms. A powerful and influential member of the national Democratic Party, in 1847 he won election to the U.S. Senate, succeeding James Semple.[198]

In Washington, Douglas had met Martha Martin, the daughter of a wealthy North Carolina plantation owner and a cousin of North Carolina Congressman David S. Reid. Senator Douglas married Martha Martin on April 7, 1847, and the couple moved from his Quincy home to the burgeoning city of Chicago, "a fitting base for Illinois' new Senator," wrote Douglas biographer Robert W. Johannsen.[199]

In early January 1853, as Douglas won reelection to the Senate, twenty-eight-year-old Martha gave birth to their third child and first daughter. Martha suffered complications from the delivery and died on January 19; she was interred in the family plot in North Carolina. A month later the couple's infant daughter died.

On Thanksgiving Day, November 20, 1856, Senator Douglas married Adele Cutts, the daughter of a government clerk and twenty-two years younger than her husband. She became a popular hostess in Washington and a loving stepmother to his two sons. In 1859, the couple became parents of a daughter, who, sickly from birth, died eight months later.[200]

Douglas, as chairman of the Senate Committee on Territories, led the Congress in its pursuit of continental expansion. He wrote the legislation that organized five territories and admitted five states to the Union. Douglas also supported legislation that provided a massive federal land grant for railroads in Illinois. His authorship of the Kansas-Nebraska Act of 1854, however, revoking the 1820 Missouri Compromise, placed Douglas at the center of the national controversy regarding slavery.

In the 1858 senatorial campaign, incumbent Douglas faced Republican candidate Abraham Lincoln. During one of their celebrated seven debates, Lincoln asked his opponent whether residents of a United States territory could lawfully exclude slavery prior to creating a state constitution. Douglas's response helped him in the Illinois contest but would doom his presidential aspirations two years later.[201] Illinois legislators reelected Douglas, but if the election had been a popular vote, Lincoln probably would have defeated Douglas.

In 1860, delegates to the Republican national convention in Chicago chose Lincoln as their Presidential nominee. At the Democratic national convention, Douglas failed to obtain the required two-thirds majority, and the convention ended without a candidate. The northern Democrats met separately from the southern Democrats and nominated Douglas, while the Southerners nominated John C. Breckinridge. The split in the Democratic Party allowed Lincoln to win the election.

With the fall of Fort Sumter in April 1861, Douglas pledged support to President Lincoln and rallied Illinoisans to the Union cause. Later in the month his "Preserve the Flag" address to a joint session of the state legislature encouraged thousands of young men to join the Union Army.[202] Shortly thereafter, Douglas contracted typhoid fever and died in Chicago on June 3, 1861. President Lincoln, recognizing Douglas's efforts on behalf of the country, called for thirty days of national mourning. The Little Giant was buried on the grounds of his Chicago home.

JOHN D. CATON, 1842-1843, 1843-1864

Born in Monroe, Orange County, New York, on March 19, 1812, John Dean Caton was the son of Robert and Hannah Dean Caton. Their ancestors immigrated to this country prior to the Revolutionary War, and Robert Caton served in the American army.[203] At age seventeen, John Dean Caton enrolled in a surveying course at a Utica academy. Then he taught school while also working as a farmhand and studying law, eventually gaining admission to the New York bar.[204]

In 1833, attracted by opportunities in the west, Caton moved to Chicago, Illinois, a town of fewer than three hundred residents.[205] "Young man, I shall give you a license," Justice Samuel Lockwood advised Caton after he passed the examination for admission to the Illinois bar, "but you have a great deal to learn to make you a good lawyer. If you work hard you will attain it." Nine years later, Caton would sit with Lockwood on the Illinois Supreme Court.[206]

Caton opened one of the first law offices in Chicago in a Lake Street back room with partner Giles Spring. "We had to live principally upon hope," Caton later related, "for the population was too scant and commerce too small to occupy much of the time or afford a decent support for two young lawyers just commencing professional life." According to John M. Palmer, Caton prosecuted the first criminal case in Cook County. Upon the defendant's conviction for stealing $46, Caton received $10 of the recovered money, which he described as his "greatest fee."[207]

Caton became active in Democratic politics and served as secretary of the first political convention held in 1834. That year, he won election as justice of the peace in Cook County. The following spring, he extended his practice to Putnam County in northeastern Illinois, traveling on horseback between the two locations. In July 1835, Caton married Laura Adelaide Sherrill of New Hartford, Oneida County, New York. They built the first house in the "school section" west of the Chicago River and became the parents of three children.[208]

In 1836, Caton formed a law partnership with Norman B. Judd and a year later became a Chicago alderman.[209] After the heavy workload began affecting his health, Caton accepted his physician's advice to relocate to a rural community, recuperating on a Will County farm, south of Chicago. By 1842, he had regained his health and moved to Ottawa, Illinois, but kept his Chicago home. He built a large residence on a bluff above Ottawa and continued to practice law.

Governor Thomas Carlin appointed Caton as an interim associate justice of the Illinois Supreme Court in August 1842, succeeding Thomas Ford, who resigned to run for governor. Seven months later, John M. Robinson defeated Caton for the position, but in May 1843 newly elected Governor Ford reappointed Caton to the Supreme Court, succeeding Robinson, who had just died.[210]

That year, while performing circuit duties in Bureau County, Caton became involved in a slavery case against abolitionist Owen Lovejoy. Convicted under an 1829 state law, which imposed penalties for harboring a black not possessing a certificate of freedom, Lovejoy appealed to the Bureau County Circuit Court. Caton, in his charge to the jury, stated, "By the Constitution of this State, slavery cannot exist here. If, therefore, a master voluntarily bring his slave within the State, he becomes from that moment free, and if he escape from his master while in this State, it is not an escape from slavery, but it is going where a free man has a right to go."[211] The jury acquitted Lovejoy, "the first instance," wrote historian N. Dwight Harris, "where the courts of Illinois declared that residence in a free territory entitled a slave to his freedom."[212]

With reorganization of the judiciary under the 1848 Constitution, Illinois voters in the northern third of Illinois elected Caton as one of the three Supreme Court justices, joining Samuel H. Treat and Lyman Trumbull. In one of the first cases under the new constitution, the court heard an appeal in which Caton was the circuit judge under the old constitution. In *Seeley v. Peters*, Caton issued one of his strongest dissents. Fencing laws were very important in antebellum Illinois as the English common law required property owners to fence in their livestock. Seeley's hogs entered Peters's property and destroyed a wheat crop. Peters sued Seeley and won the case at the circuit level, in which Justice Caton presided. Seeley appealed the case to the Illinois Supreme Court with former justice and former governor Thomas Ford representing him. The court reversed the decision claiming that the English common law requirement of fencing in livestock worked well in England where land was not plentiful, but that it did not apply to the open prairies of Illinois.[213]

Caton claimed to take great "care in examining the question, and thought I understood it thoroughly." He felt that his input during conference was disregarded. Perceiving that his colleagues ignored him because they did not want to upset him for overturning his decision, Caton wrote a twenty-page dissent. He later claimed the dissent was "unpardonably long, and that some of its expressions were more pungent than I wish they had been." Under the old constitution, Justice Caton had even overturned some of his own circuit-level decisions. He stood by his reasoning in the *Seeley* case, claiming that the court cannot overturn the common law because that was the legislature's responsibility.[214]

In the 1840s, Caton represented two New York friends in bringing one of the first telegraph lines into Illinois. He became a director and eventually the president and largest stockholder of the Illinois and Mississippi Telegraph Company. He expanded the operation into Iowa and Minnesota and contracted to install telegraph lines along railroad routes; soon those "lightning wires" provided news to nearly every town and village.[215] Caton, the "telegraph king of the West" eventually earned enormous income from leases to the Western Union system.[216]

When Justice Treat resigned to accept a federal judgeship in 1855, Caton became Chief Justice of the Illinois Supreme Court. Anti-slavery advocates attacked Caton for his commitment to the popular sovereignty stance of U.S. Senator Stephen A. Douglas. Despite the charges, Caton won re-election to the high court and served in the position until his retirement in 1864.[217]

In retirement, Caton replaced his Ottawa home with a brick mansion and became a major stockholder in a local glass factory, dividing time between Ottawa and Chicago. In 1865, Caton appeared before the Illinois Supreme Court to offer a formal resolution and eloquent personal recollections of assassinated President Abraham Lincoln, the former Illinois lawyer and legislator. "Who of this bar does not remember him as of yesterday," Caton recalled, "when he was among us relieving the hard labors of the profession by his enlivening presence? He will ever be remembered as one of our brightest ornaments, whose practice reflected honor upon the profession."[218]

An accomplished speaker and writer with an interest in natural history, he traveled extensively throughout the United States and Europe. A lifelong Quaker, on July 30, 1895, at age eighty-three, the wealthy and highly honored Caton died at his Chicago home. After services in Ottawa, he was buried in the Ottawa Avenue Cemetery.[219]

JOHN M. ROBINSON, 1843

John McCracken Robinson served on the Illinois Supreme Court for only a few months. The son of Jonathan and Jane (Jean) Black Robinson, John Robinson was born near Georgetown, Kentucky, on April 10, 1794.[220] After graduating with honors from Transylvania University in Lexington, he moved to Shawneetown, Illinois, and then to Carmi, Illinois, where in 1818, he was admitted to the Illinois bar. "Well known as a thorough lawyer," he won appointment as state's attorney for the area, a position he held until 1827. His brother James F. Robinson would later serve as governor of Kentucky.[221]

Active and interested in military affairs, John Robinson rose to the rank of major general in the Illinois militia "and was commonly known as General Robinson," reported biographer Daniel Berry. "Physically, he was a man six feet, four inches in height. . . . In personal appearance he could scarcely be excelled."[222]

In January 1829, Robinson married Mary B. D. Ratcliff, daughter of prominent Carmi resident James Ratcliff. The Robinsons became the parents of two children, James M. and Margaret Robinson, and resided in the town's oldest house, a building that had earlier served as the first White County courthouse.[223]

Upon the death of U.S. Senator John McLean, Illinois legislators in 1830 elected Robinson to the position, and he routinely supported the programs of Presidents Andrew Jackson and Martin Van Buren. Robinson chaired the Committee on Engrossed Bills and served on the Post Office and Post Roads committees.[224]

Completing McLean's unexpired term, Robinson won election to a full term in 1834. During that tenure, he followed a majority of state legislators' wishes in voting against President Jackson's proposal for an independent treasury, even though he personally favored the measure. "My political tenets lead me to believe," he explained, "that the representative is bound by the will of his constituents; and that so far as relates to a Senator in Congress, the Legislature is presumed to be the true exponent of that will."[225]

A few years after completing his term in the Senate, legislators elected Robinson on January 14, 1843, as an associate justice of the Illinois Supreme Court, succeeding John Dean Caton. While handling circuit duties in Ottawa, in the Ninth Judicial Circuit, Robinson died on April 27, 1843.[226] His remains were returned to Carmi for interment in the Old Graveyard Cemetery.

Since he died before being able to serve on the Supreme Court, he did not participate in any arguments nor write any opinions. Opening the January 1844 Illinois Supreme Court term, Chief Justice William Wilson expressed regret that Robinson "was not permitted to take his seat among us," then memorialized his "mature judgment, sterling integrity, and strong sense of the obligations of a public trust. . . . While steadfast in his principles, he was courteous and liberal to his opponents, and true to his personal friends."[227]

The Crawford County, Illinois, seat of Robinson is named in honor of John M. Robinson.[228]

JAMES SEMPLE, 1843

Born on January 5, 1798, the eldest of nine children of John Walker and Lucy Robertson Semple, James received a basic education in Greensburg, Kentucky, schools, supplemented by legal courses in Louisville. In 1814, at age sixteen, he joined the Kentucky militia and became active in Kentucky politics as early as 1817.[229] Semple moved to Edwardsville, Illinois, in 1818, but soon returned to Kentucky. In 1820, he married Ellen Duff Green, sister of journalist and Democratic politician Duff Green. The couple moved to Chariton, Missouri, where Semple served as assistant postmaster and then land office commissioner, while also commanding a regiment of the Missouri militia. After the death of his wife, Semple returned to his home state, resumed the study of law, and was admitted to the Kentucky bar.[230]

In 1828, he returned to Edwardsville, where he maintained a successful law practice. "He was diligent and careful," wrote John M. Palmer, "and, being a man of magnificent presence and fine manners, he rose rapidly to distinction."[231] During the 1831–1832 Black Hawk War in northwestern Illinois, Semple served on the staff of General Samuel Whiteside. In late summer 1832, he won election to the Illinois House of Representatives from Madison County, beginning a long record of public service. He briefly held the office of Illinois Attorney General before returning to the legislature.[232]

In 1833, Semple married Mary Stevenson Mizner, a widowed niece of Shadrach Bond, the state's first governor. The Semples became the parents of two daughters and a son. From 1834 to 1838, he served as Speaker of the Illinois House. A colonel of the Eighth Illinois Militia, Semple was commissioned brigadier general in 1835, "a title he enjoyed for the rest of his life," reported biographer William L. Burton.[233]

At the urging of senators and representatives from Illinois, President Martin Van Buren appointed Semple the Minister to Colombia, a position he held from 1837 to 1841. "On his return from Bogota," recalled fellow attorney Usher Linder, "I, being a member of the legislature, heard him deliver many interesting lectures in reference to that country."[234]

Semple returned to Edwardsville, and on January 14, 1843, the legislature elected him to the Illinois Supreme Court to succeed Sidney Breese. Three months later, however, Governor Thomas Ford appointed Semple to fill the unexpired term of deceased U.S. Senator Samuel McRoberts.[235] "It is difficult to predicate as to the judicial merits of Judge Semple," explained Palmer, "as he remained upon the bench but for a short time. He was bold, outspoken and frank; as a politician he was fearless, never hesitating to commit himself to any line of policy which his judgment approved. He was prompt in his decisions, assumed all the responsibilities of his place, and was popular with the bar and the public."[236]

In Semple's short few months on the Supreme Court bench, he authored the opinion in at least four cases and dissented in one. In *Bradley v. Case*, Case had sued Bradley in the circuit court and recovered payment from a promissory note. In his appeal to the Illinois Supreme Court, Bradley claimed that the consideration of the note had failed because of a conflict between federal and state laws on selling certain sections of land for school purposes. In his opinion affirming the judgment, Justice Semple compared at length federal and state legislation, concluding that these "considerations are, in my opinion, proper for investigation here. They form part of the history of the country. They throw light on the compact itself, and show conclusively, that the true construction to be given to the compact, is, that the lands were to be leased, or sold, as the state legislature, the sole manager of them, should think most beneficial to the people of the country."[237]

In Washington, D.C., Senator Semple enjoyed the friendship of fellow former Supreme Court justice Stephen A. Douglas, a newly elected Illinois congressman. "I am glad we will spend the winter in Washington together," Douglas wrote to Semple, "and propose that we make a mess of the entire delegation. They are all good fellows and would make pleasant companions."[238]

With the outbreak of the Mexican War in 1846, Semple sought a commission as brigadier general. President James K. Polk adamantly rejected the request, confiding in his diary that the solicitation was "disreputable" and stating that as a matter of policy he would not nominate members of Congress for military commissions. A month later, as Semple prepared to leave Washington to deal with a personal financial situation in Illinois, the Senate prepared to vote on a tariff bill supported by Polk. Without Semple's vote, the measure would be lost. At a White House meeting, the President appealed to Semple's patriotism and party loyalty; the Senator remained in Washington and helped pass the bill.[239]

In the fall of 1846, Semple announced that he would not be a candidate for the Senate seat. "I was never so sick in all my life as at present," he wrote shortly after Congress adjourned. "We have not yet heard a word of who is likely to take my place here, but suppose it will be Douglas." The Democratic caucus of the Illinois legislature unanimously nominated Douglas for the seat, which he won by a large margin over the Whig candidate.[240]

Semple retired to Edwardsville. There he created a model "prairie car," a steam-powered carriage that would operate on the open prairie "with no rails or elaborate right-of-way," explained biographer Burton. Lacking the necessary financial resources, Semple eventually abandoned the venture that came to be known in folklore as "Semple's Folly."[241]

Financially depleted, he settled with his family in Jersey County. In 1852, he became postmaster at Jersey Landing, on the banks of the Mississippi River, and joined a partnership to operate a ferry to St. Louis. A year later, Semple began developing a new town, named Elsah, at the Jersey Landing location. To encourage settlement, Semple offered free lots for home construction and built his own imposing residence. The town flourished, with grain-storage and shipping facilities, a distillery, and flour mill. In 1857, Semple erected a stone schoolhouse for the community.[242]

He died at Elsah on December 20, 1866, and was buried at historic Bellefontaine Cemetery in St. Louis. "Optimism and ambition informed Semple's public career," wrote Burton, "his experimentation with the prairie car, and his enthusiastic town building. He was representative of the class of men who moved in and out of public office and who capitalized on experience and personal contacts to promote business enterprise."[243]

JAMES SHIELDS, 1843-1845

A military hero and the only United States Senator to represent three different states, James Shields was a native of Altmore, Ireland. Born on May 6, 1806, to Charles and Anne McDonnell Shields, James immigrated to Canada in 1823, then in 1826 settled in Kaskaskia, Illinois, where he taught school while studying law. "His knowledge of the French language," wrote biographer William H. Condon, "his wit and genial disposition soon made him a general favorite."[244]

Admitted to the Illinois bar in 1832, Shields opened a law practice, for a time partnering with Belleville attorney Gustavus Koerner, and began participating in Democratic Party politics. "In conversation he spoke rapidly and vivaciously," recalled Koerner, "showing very little trace of the Irish brogue. He was not an orator, but a ready debater.... He really did not seek popularity, but yet had a sort of winning way about him that made him friends quite readily."[245]

Voters elected Shields to the Illinois General Assembly in 1836, and he served only one term. In 1841, Governor Thomas Carlin appointed Shields the state auditor, helping to restore the state's finances following the Panic of 1837.[246] Responding to anonymous newspaper accusations against his policies regarding the State Bank of Illinois, Shields assumed that Whig Representative Abraham Lincoln authored the criticisms and challenged him to a duel. Because dueling was illegal in Illinois, the men traveled to a Missouri location across from Alton.[247] "Did not wish to kill Shields," Lincoln later wrote, "the very thought was agony."[248] At the duel site, the two men settled their differences after their seconds intervened.

In 1843, Governor Ford appointed Shields to succeed James Semple on the Illinois Supreme Court. Shields also was responsible for the Second Judicial Circuit. In the St. Clair County Circuit Court, he ruled in *Jarrot v. Jarrot* that a slave could not sue his owner for wages.[249] He joined justices Samuel H. Treat and Jesse B. Thomas in dissent when the Supreme Court reversed the decision in 1844.[250]

During his two years on the Court, Shields "ranked high as a justice," wrote biographer Condon; "he was industrious, painstaking, impartial and strictly honest."[251] In delivering the Court opinion in *Eells v. People*, Shields upheld the 1843 circuit court decision against Quincy physician Richard Eells for aiding a fugitive slave. "If a State can use precautionary measures against the introduction of paupers, convicts, or negro slaves," Shields wrote, "it can undoubtedly punish those of its citizens who endeavor to introduce them."[252] Owing to "the notoriety gained in this case," wrote historian Theodore C. Pease, "Eells was elected president of the Illinois Antislavery Society in 1843 and nominated as the liberty party candidate for governor in 1846."[253]

In 1845, soon after legislative election to a full term on the Court, Shields resigned to accept President James K. Polk's appointment as Commissioner of the General Land Office in Washington, D.C. With the outbreak of the Mexican War, he resigned the Land Office position to become brigadier general of Illinois Volunteers. Sustaining serious wounds at Cerro Gordo and Chapultepec, he served throughout the war, leading New York and South Carolina troops at Churubusco.[254]

Brevetted major general and mustered out in 1848, Shields returned to Illinois a war hero. President Polk offered him the governorship of the new Oregon Territory, but Shields instead decided to challenge Sidney Breese for nomination to the U.S. Senate. The Democratic caucus chose Shields, and he easily defeated a weak Whig opponent. His election was voided, however, because he had not been a citizen for the required nine years. Shields waited a year for unquestioned eligibility, then again won the election.[255]

In the Senate, Shields joined fellow Democrat and close friend Stephen A. Douglas. An unenthusiastic supporter of the Kansas-Nebraska bill, extending slavery to the territories, Shields lost his 1854 reelection bid to anti-Nebraska candidate Lyman Trumbull. "The Anti Nebraska feeling is too deep," Shields wrote to Springfield friend Charles H. Lanphier, "more than I thought it was."[256]

Back in Illinois, ailing former Governor Thomas Ford asked Shields to arrange for publication of his *History of Illinois*. "Because of its caustic and outspoken criticism of public men," wrote historian Robert P. Howard, "Shields or the publisher reportedly excised more than half of the manuscript, which is regrettable in view of Ford's personal knowledge of the men and events he wrote about. . . . Even if he wrote with cynicism, his book has been recognized as a superior analysis of American politics and one of the most important volumes printed in Illinois before the Civil War."[257]

Disappointed at the Senate loss, Shields left Illinois in search of opportunity in the Minnesota Territory. After statehood in 1858, he was elected to a one-year term in the U.S. Senate. Relocating to California in 1859, Shields married Mary Ann Carr, a native of Longhall, Ireland. The couple settled in Mazatlan, Mexico, where he was part owner and manager of a mine. The couple became parents of five children, two of whom died in childhood.[258]

During the Civil War, Shields returned to Washington, D.C., to become a brigadier general, serving until March 1863. He then returned to San Francisco but three years later moved to Carrollton, Missouri, where he won election to the Missouri legislature, then appointment as railroad commissioner. In 1879, he was elected to complete an unexpired term in the U.S. Senate.[259]

Shields died suddenly on June 1, 1879, in Ottumwa, Iowa, while on a lecture tour. "He was a warm-hearted Irishman," wrote attorney Usher F. Linder, "and a brave and gallant soldier."[260] Following memorial services, he was buried at St. Mary's Cemetery in Carrollton, Missouri. A bronze figure of General Shields stands in the U.S. Capitol Statuary Hall.

JESSE B. THOMAS JR., 1843-1845, 1847-1848

The nephew of U.S. Senator from Illinois Jesse Burgess Thomas, Supreme Court Justice Jesse Burgess Thomas Jr. was born in Lebanon, Ohio, on July 31, 1806, the second son of Richard Symmes and Frances Pattie Thomas. Young Jesse graduated from Transylvania University in Kentucky in 1828. He moved to Edwardsville at his uncle's invitation and was admitted to the Illinois bar.[261]

On February 18, 1830, Thomas married Adeline Clarissa Smith, daughter of Illinois Supreme Court Justice Theophilus W. Smith. They became the parents of four sons and six daughters.[262] Later in 1830, legislators elected Thomas as Secretary of the Senate, and he served a second term in 1832. In 1834, as a Whig candidate, he won election as a Madison County representative to the General Assembly, "but was at no time considered a pernicious partisan," wrote historian John Francis Snyder; "his conservatism and moderation in politics being probably in deference to his illustrious father-in-law, who was one of the prominent leaders of the democratic party in Illinois."[263]

Thomas resigned from the legislature in 1835 to succeed Ninian W. Edwards as Illinois Attorney General, but a year later resigned that position to again become Secretary of the Senate. "In that era," explained Snyder, "the Attorney Generalship of Illinois was not the exalted and important position it is now considered to be, and almost every incumbent of it resigned just as soon as he could get into any other place, even one of as little consequence as Secretary of the Senate."[264] After legislators in 1837 elected Thomas judge of the First Judicial Circuit, he and his family moved to Springfield. Serving on the bench for nineteen months, "he became tired of the routine drudgery of the circuit" and resigned to resume his law practice.

In August 1843, Governor Thomas Ford appointed Thomas to the Illinois Supreme Court, succeeding newly elected U.S. Congressman Stephen A. Douglas. Thomas also presided over the nine-county western Illinois Fifth Judicial Circuit. In the 1843 *Sarah v. Borders* case, Thomas joined fellow Supreme Court justice Walter B. Scates in affirming a circuit court ruling that favored Randolph County resident Andrew Borders against one of his Negro indentured servants, Sarah. After her escape from Borders, "a man well known for his cruelty and rapacity," a justice of the peace declared her freedom, but Borders's lawyer immediately appealed the case.[265] Both Scates and Thomas cited Territorial acts as well as the state Constitution in upholding the lower court decision. "The Constitution of our State recognizes the indentures under consideration, as valid and binding contracts," Thomas wrote.[266]

"This decision excited much criticism throughout the State," reported historian N. Dwight Harris, "especially from the antislavery men. The Court was accused of corruption, and of subserviency to the slave power, and its opinion was a matter of great disappointment to many who had earnestly hoped that the Court would declare the holding of Negro indentured servants illegal."[267]

In 1844, Thomas heard a circuit court case involving Mormon prophet Joseph Smith. This case was the first in a series of events that led to Smith's murder. After several of Smith's followers destroyed the newly established anti-Mormon newspaper, the *Nauvoo Expositor*, a justice of the peace in the Hancock County seat of Carthage issued arrest warrants for Smith and his associates. Smith obtained a writ of habeas corpus to have the case brought before a Nauvoo, rather than the Carthage, justice of the peace. The Nauvoo court, according to Mormon historian Dallin H. Oaks, decided that Smith had acted under proper authority in destroying the *Expositor* and rendered his arrest "a malicious prosecution." The decision infuriated non-Mormons, and rumors of mobs organizing to destroy Nauvoo caused Smith to place the city under martial law.[268]

Non-Mormon Nauvoo authorities, doubting the legality of the court's action and reacting to the rising anti-Mormon hostility, asked the opinion of Justice Thomas, the presiding judge in that judicial circuit. Thomas advised that, "in order to satisfy the people," the defendants be retried before a non-Mormon magistrate. In the second trial, the non-Mormon justice of the peace heard numerous prosecution and defense witnesses and counsel before issuing a judgment of acquittal. That decision led to reports of anti-Mormon mobs forming around Nauvoo. Illinois Governor Thomas Ford intervened, declaring that only a trial before the Carthage justice of the peace who issued the original writ would "vindicate the dignity of violated law and allay the just excitement of the people."[269]

On June 25, Smith and his brother Hyrum voluntarily surrendered to the constable who had attempted to bring them to Carthage on the original riot warrant. Almost immediately, they were arrested on a charge of treason against the state for having declared martial law in Nauvoo. Two days later, an anti-Mormon mob overpowered the jail guards and murdered the brothers.[270]

Thomas resigned from the Supreme Court in August 1845 and moved to Chicago to open a law practice. In January 1847, the legislature again elected him to the Supreme Court, replacing Richard M. Young and presiding over the Seventh Judicial Circuit. Upon sitting on the Supreme Court, Thomas and his fellow justices heard *Garrett v. Stevenson et al.*, involving a labor contract. In 1839, Augustus Garrett had hired Andrew Stevenson and Orin

The state capitol building in Springfield housed the Supreme Court from 1840 to 1872. (Image courtesy of the Abraham Lincoln Presidential Library and Museum)

Wardwell to construct a house, but when Garrett failed to pay the amount due, the contractors sued to place a mechanic's lien on the property. Losing a circuit court decision on grounds that Garrett had not commenced the suit within the time frame required by an 1833 law, his attorney Abraham Lincoln appealed to the Supreme Court. In upholding the circuit court decision, Justice Thomas cited a later law that revoked the time limitation for initiating a suit.[271]

In 1848, when the new state Constitution provided for the election of only three justices, Thomas did not seek election. That same year, he formed a partnership with Patrick Ballingall, "a criminal lawyer of considerable local repute" in Chicago, reported historian John M. Palmer.[272] Thomas died in the city on February 21, 1850, at the age of forty-three, and was buried in Chicago's City Cemetery, but later his body was transferred to Rosehill Cemetery.[273]

RICHARD M. YOUNG, 1843–1847

A Jacksonian Democrat, Richard Montgomery Young served a term in the United States Senate before being chosen for the Illinois Supreme Court. Born on a Fayette County, Kentucky, farm on February 20, 1798, he was the son of Abner and Frances Bourne Young.[274] After attending country schools, Young enrolled in Forest Hill Academy, an exclusive school in Jessamine County. Completing the academy course at age sixteen, he studied law under a prominent area attorney, Colonel James Clark, and gained admission to the Kentucky bar in 1816.[275]

One year later, Young opened a law office in Jonesboro, Illinois. "His practice was not long confined to the meager litigation of Union county," wrote biographer John Francis Snyder, "but speedily extended to the courts of the several counties between Shawneetown to the east and Kaskaskia on the north, and to Missouri Territory beyond the Mississippi. He was a close and interested observer of the transition of Illinois in 1818, from a territorial form of government to that of a state, and actively participated in its embryo politics."[276]

In June 1820, a newly commissioned captain in the Illinois militia, Young married Matilda James, daughter of Judge William James of St. Genevieve County, Missouri. They became the parents of two daughters, Matilda James and Bernice Adelaide Young. At the general election just weeks after his military commissioning, voters elected Young to represent Union County in the second Illinois General Assembly.[277]

In his single term at Vandalia, Young championed controversial legislation that established a state bank. The bank system operated for four years before failing, a loss to the state of $300,000. "There is every reason to believe," wrote biographer Snyder, "that Mr. Young's constituents did not approve of, or forgive him for, his aid in establishing that State bank." He did not win endorsement for reelection, nor did he ever again win a popular-vote election to public office.[278]

In the 1824–1825 judicial reorganization, the Illinois General Assembly chose five judges for newly created circuit courts. On December 30, 1824, twenty-six-year-old Young won legislative election to the Third Judicial Circuit. He and his family moved from Jonesboro to Kaskaskia, center of the circuit. "He conducted his courts with dignity and conscientious rectitude," reported Snyder, "but neglected no opportunity to keep himself in the limelight of popular favor." In 1824, he participated in welcoming and entertaining the visiting French statesman Marquis de Lafayette.[279]

After legislators in the 1826–1827 session returned circuit court duties to the Supreme Court justices, Young resumed the practice of law, in partnership with U.S. Senator Elias Kent Kane. Then in 1829, the General Assembly formed the Fifth Judicial Circuit, comprising all of the state north and west of the Illinois River, and elected Young to serve that circuit. The Youngs moved from Kaskaskia to the populous and busy lead-mining town of Galena.

Two years later, "desiring a quieter place of residence for his family than Galena," he purchased a 120-acre farm east of Quincy and built a two-story frame farmhouse on the property. "He was a fine-looking, complaisant Kentuckian," wrote fellow attorney Charles Ballance, "who possessed not much legal learning, but a fine, high-blooded Kentucky horse, and knew well how to ride him." In May 1833, according to Ballance, Young "made his appearance in the Village of Peoria, and announced that he was on his way to Chicago to hold court. He had traveled about 130 miles, from Quincy, where he lived, and had to travel, as the trail then run, not less than 170 miles further, to hold the first court on his circuit. Just think of a horseback ride of at least 300 miles to hold a three days' court!"[280]

In addition to his circuit duties, Young traveled to Vandalia to attend Supreme Court and legislative sessions. "He was personally known to all the officials and politicians in the State," recalled Snyder, "and was himself one of the most popular and highly esteemed of the State's public men." When legislators in 1833 brought impeachment charges against Justice Theophilus Smith, Young won respect for his association with Sidney Breese and Thomas Ford in Smith's defense and acquittal.[281]

In 1835, Young sold his farm and the family moved to Quincy, to a newly built brick mansion on Hampshire Street (later the site of the Tremont House hotel).[282] Elected over five competitors to the United States Senate in 1836, Young resigned his judgeship on January 3, 1837, to begin the senatorial term. For two sessions, he chaired the Committee on Roads and Canals, supporting improvements within Illinois in the aftermath of a financial collapse.[283] "The march of Illinois is forward," he told fellow Senators, "and if her legislative guardians at home shall promptly discharge their duty in the preservation of her credit at home and abroad, who can not foretell that her destiny is no less than that of the Empire state?"[284]

In 1839, Illinois Governor Thomas Carlin, having exhausted money market possibilities in New York, sent Senator Young and former Governor John Reynolds to London, where they unsuccessfully sought loans of $4 million for completing the Illinois and Michigan Canal.[285] "It is doubtful if two other men so conspicuous in public life at that time," wrote Snyder, "could have been found, so little qualified—so destitute of financial skill, for such a difficult and important mission. . . . The people of Illinois never forgave Reynolds and Young for their bungling failure as special fiscal agents of the State. From that ill-judged junket of the two statesmen dated the decline of their popularity."[286]

Failing to win a second senatorial term, on January 14, 1843, Young assented to legislative selection as successor to Illinois Supreme Court associate justice Theophilus Smith. Young "accepted the Supreme Court Judgeship," Snyder explained, "because nothing better was then accessible, and found its laborious obscurity in too marked contrast with the dazzling eminence of the Senate."[287] In his new position, Young also had responsibility for the northern Illinois Seventh Judicial Circuit.

Snyder acknowledged that Young acquitted himself on the bench "with much credit . . . a superior lawyer and judge." In his first year, he delivered four court decisions and one dissenting opinion. In 1844, he wrote six decisions, one separate, and one dissenting opinion, and in 1845, delivered ten decisions, two separate, and two dissenting. "Well and concisely written," reported Snyder, "they are all clear and accurate judicial statements supported by ample references and sound reasoning."[288]

In the celebrated 1845 *Jarrot v. Jarrot* case, Young delivered a lengthy separate opinion upholding Justice Walter B. Scates's majority decision. The St. Clair County Circuit Court had ruled for slave-owner Julia Jarrot against slave Joseph "Pete" Jarrot, who brought legal action against her for services rendered.[289] According to Snyder, the Supreme Court decision "practically removed from the statutes the last vestige of authority for slavery in Illinois."[290]

In another 1845 case, *Eldridge v. Rowe,* Justice Young, writing for the majority, rejected the argument of Springfield attorney Abraham Lincoln regarding release of a contract. Barnabus E. Eldridge had hired Nelson Rowe as a farm worker for eight months, but Rowe worked for only four months before asking to be released from the contract. When Eldridge offered three options for completing the work, Rowe rejected the offers and hired Lincoln to sue for payment. Young wrote that Rowe had fairly entered the contract but failed to fulfill his obligations and rejected Eldridge's compromise options. Therefore, Young reasoned, Rowe should receive no compensation.[291]

Seeking a return to public prominence, Young in early 1846 made an unsuccessful attempt to become the Democratic nominee for governor. Senator Stephen A. Douglas then convinced President James K. Polk to appoint Young as Commissioner of the General Land Office, succeeding fellow Illinoisan James Shields.[292] On January 25, 1847, Young resigned from the Supreme Court to accept the federal appointment, and the Youngs moved from Quincy to Washington, D.C. From 1850 to 1851, he served as clerk of the U.S. House of Representatives, and then resumed the practice of law. Later in the decade he began suffering physical decline and mental illness, spending several months in 1860 in the Government Hospital for the Insane. Upon discharge, he remained secluded at his home, where he died on November 28, 1861, at age sixty-three. He was buried in the Congressional Cemetery in Washington, D.C.[293]

NORMAN H. PURPLE, 1845-1848

Successor to Justice Jesse B. Thomas Jr., Norman Higgins Purple was born on March 29, 1803, in Otsego County, New York.[294] The son of a carpenter and farmer, Purple received a common-school education, supplemented by academy courses. He began the study of law under Judge N. B. Eldred in Wayne County, Pennsylvania, and completed his legal education in Tioga County. After admittance to the bar in 1830, Purple opened a practice in Tioga County, and in January 1831, he married Ann Eliza Kilburn, daughter of Pennsylvania Judge Ira Kilburn.[295]

Six years later, the Purples moved to Peoria, Illinois, where he developed an extensive law practice. "As a practitioner at the bar," wrote John M. Palmer, "Purple was exact as well as exacting. He never presented a matter in court without due preparation. Keeping himself within the rules of the court, he expected the same of others."[296] From 1839 to 1842, Purple served as state's attorney for the ten-county Ninth Judicial Circuit, comprising most of northern Illinois. Strongly pro-slavery, Purple obtained a warrant against Bureau County abolitionist Owen Lovejoy for "keeping in his house, feeding, clothing, and comforting" two black women.

Purple argued that Lovejoy violated the Act of 1829, which imposed penalties for harboring any black not possessing a certificate of freedom. After a Bureau County inferior court apparently ruled for Purple, a circuit court jury heard the case in a nearly weeklong trial. In his charge to the jurors, Judge John Dean Caton "laid down the law distinctly, that 'if a man voluntarily brings his slave into a free-state, the slave becomes free.'" The jury acquitted Lovejoy, "a great triumph," reported historian N. Dwight Harris, "for the antislavery element."[297]

In addition to his lucrative law practice and judicial responsibilities, Purple ranked among the prominent citizens of Peoria. In 1843, he and several other residents obtained a state charter to establish a water supply from mineral springs on the west bluff two miles into the center of the city. The reservoir provided water for approximately fifteen years, until the rapidly increasing population required a larger source near the Illinois River.

In 1844, Purple served as a Democratic presidential elector for James K. Polk, and the following year, Democratic Illinois Governor Thomas Ford appointed Purple to the Illinois Supreme Court. With responsibility for the Fifth Judicial Circuit in western Illinois, the Purples moved from Peoria to Quincy.

During the December 1845 Supreme Court term, Justice Purple wrote the opinion in *Wright v. Bennett et al.,* regarding illegitimate children. Menard County Probate Justice of the Peace Asa D. Wright appealed a Menard County Circuit Court ruling that favored Richard E. Bennett against the mother of his illegitimate child. His attorneys had demanded possession of the child, basing their case on a state statute that if she did not relinquish custody, Bennett would not be responsible for court-ordered child support.

Although the courts intended that the law favor the child and its mother, fathers such as Bennett cited the statute in attempting to circumvent their child-support obligations. After "careful and attentive consideration of the law," Purple upheld the lower court ruling. "I am reluctantly compelled to admit that, if the reputed father of an illegitimate child, under the law as it existed at the time of the commencement of this suit, will have the inhumanity, in its helpless and dependent infancy, to demand its surrender by the mother, the law, upon her refusal, imposes upon him no further obligation to aid in its maintenance and support, at least so long as she persists in her refusal."[298]

In December 1846, the Illinois General Assembly elected Purple to the Supreme Court. In the slander case *Regnier v. Cabot et al.,* he affirmed the Morgan County Circuit Court judgment of insufficient evidence against Eliza Cabot. With Abraham Lincoln as her attorney, Cabot had sued Francis Regnier for publicly accusing her of fornication. "In my judgment," Purple wrote, "character is too valuable to permit it, in a Court of justice to be destroyed, or even sullied by a report derived from a majority of three persons only. It is general, and not partial, reputation in the neighborhood where the party resides which, in legal contemplation, establishes character for good or evil."[299]

With the 1848 Illinois Constitution that reduced the number of Supreme Court justices, Purple returned to the practice of law in Peoria. He edited and published a compilation of the state's real estate statutes in 1849, "a work of inestimable value to the profession in those days," reported fellow attorney John M. Palmer.[300] Purple also authored a compilation of general legislative acts, known as the "Purple Statutes," which contained references to Supreme Court decisions and statutes from 1818 to 1857. For nearly a decade he attended terms of the U.S. Circuit Court in Chicago, where "his clear legal mind, dignity of mien and unswerving integrity to his profession and clients, command the respect of all who saw him and heard him, and placed him upon the topmost round of his profession."[301]

Purple died at the Sherman House hotel in Chicago on August 9, 1863. He had been working on another compilation of statutes from 1857 to 1863. Survivors included his wife and five of their six children. After a funeral ceremony at the family home in Peoria, he was interred at Springdale Cemetery.[302]

GUSTAVUS P. KOERNER, 1845-1848

A native of Frankfurt am Main, Germany, Gustavus Koerner was born on November 20, 1809, the son of Bernhard and Marie Magdalene Kampfe Koerner. From age seven to nineteen, Gustavus attended Frankfurt schools, then the University of Jena, where he joined the student patriotic and revolutionary organization Burschenschaft. Completing law studies at the University of Heidelberg, he graduated with high honors.[303]

Remaining in Heidelberg, Koerner participated in Burschenschaft uprisings. On the evening of April 3, 1833, he was among sixty young men who assaulted a Frankfurt garrison. Wounded in the failed attack, he fled to France, then sailed with friends for the United States.[304] The ship *Logan* arrived in New York on June 17, and three days later he recorded in a New York City court his intention to become a U.S. citizen.[305]

Within a week of arrival, the immigrants traveled westward to St. Louis, then followed relatives and acquaintances to St. Clair County, Illinois. Koerner's friend Frederick Engelmann bought a farm in the same vicinity, and he and his family, along with Koerner, moved to the farm. Admitted to the Illinois bar in 1835, Koerner married Engelmann's daughter Sophie on June 17, 1836. They became parents of eight children, several of whom died in infancy.

"Life on the farm was of primeval simplicity," reported Koerner biographer R. E. Rombauer. "The produce of their land, and the game with which the country was then teeming, was sufficient to supply their simple table. The life of a farmer, however, was not congenial to Koerner's taste, and he decided to fit himself for his original profession, that of the law."[306]

Koerner enrolled in the one-year law course at Transylvania University in Lexington, Kentucky. Returning to Belleville, he passed the bar examination and formed a partnership with attorney Adam W. Snyder and later with James Shields. In other activities, Koerner established a German and English school in Belleville and served as its first teacher. He also joined with other area residents to found the Belleville Public Library. "This undertaking, very humble in its inception," wrote Rombauer, "grew rapidly under his fostering care." When the organizers transferred the library to the city of Belleville, Koerner continued as president of the board of directors until his death.[307]

Koerner wrote extensively for the German and English press and for several months in 1840 published *Der Freiheitsbote für Illinois*. A Democratic campaign organ, *Der Freiheitsbote* promoted the reelection of President Martin Van Buren and sharply rebuked the nativist movement.[308] "Since he spoke English, German and French with almost equal fluency," according to Rombauer, Koerner "soon became one of the most popular, and sought after political speakers. While small in stature his voice was sonorous and far-reaching . . . exercising a marked influence over his hearers." Strongly anti-slavery, Koerner as a young man witnessed the sale of a free Negro into temporary servitude under Illinois law. According to Rombauer, Koerner "paid with his slender means the fine of the Negro thus to be sold, and turned him free."[309]

In 1842, voters elected Koerner to the Illinois General Assembly. He served only one term and was a member of the Ways and Means and Judiciary Committees. After James Shields became a justice of the Illinois Supreme Court and Adam Snyder died, Koerner formed a law partnership with William Bissell, who in 1856 would become the state's first Republican governor.[310]

On April 2, 1845, Governor Thomas Ford selected Koerner to succeed Shields on the Illinois Supreme Court with trial level duties in the Second Judicial Circuit, "in deference," explained fellow attorney Usher F. Linder, to the "six to ten thousand" German Democrats in St. Clair County. "At that time there were more Germans in St. Clair County than in any other locality in the State."[311]

The following year, legislators elected Koerner to a full Supreme Court term. "To his profession," wrote historian Frederick B. Crossley, Koerner "brought a mind thoroughly trained and a conception of the law as one of the oldest and most fundamental professions, with something of a sacred character. His legal lore is said to have covered every department in the science of jurisprudence, and he won distinction at the bar among men of national reputation, including Lincoln [and] Douglas."[312]

In the December 1846 term, Justice Koerner delivered the opinion in *Munsell v. Temple*, in which Abraham Lincoln represented plaintiff Roswell Munsell against McLean County Treasurer William H. Temple. Munsell had purchased a Bloomington grocery store but failed to pay a $21.38 promissory note for the store's liquor license. Reversing the McLean County Circuit Court ruling that favored Temple, Justice Koerner wrote: "Licenses attach to the person, and cannot be used by others, even with the consent of the Court. . . . It is a plain violation of the express letter of the statute to issue a license on credit, and the undertaking of Munsell to pay was consequently founded on a contract against the express provisions and the general policy of the statute, and was therefore void in law, and cannot be enforced."[313]

Justice Koerner delivered a dissenting opinion in *Baxter v. People*. A Warren County Circuit Court jury had convicted John Baxter of murder and pronounced a death sentence. His attorney Onias C. Skinner appealed the decision, in part on grounds that the verdict was rendered on a Sunday, illegal by state statute. Justice John Dean Caton cited several judicial errors in delivering the majority opinion that voided the circuit court judgment. "Admitting that it were legal to receive a verdict on Sunday," Koerner argued in his nearly five-page dissenting opinion, "but illegal as the Court say, to pronounce judgment, what are the consequences of the reversal of the judgment? . . . As he was sentenced to the proper punishment, but on the wrong day, the verdict must stand. I cannot accede to this reasoning. . . . It seems to follow, that if Baxter had not taken the appeal, and had been executed, the sheriff would have been guilty of murder, as he then would have acted without any authority whatever."[314]

With reorganization of the judiciary in 1848, Koerner returned to his law practice. During nearly four years on the Court, Koerner's opinions, according to attorney Marshall W. Weir, had indicated "that he was an educated lawyer and an able and just judge. The state was then in its infancy; the courts had established but few precedents; the questions that arose were largely questions of first impression, and the labors of the justices were both difficult and responsible; and it may be said of Justice Koerner that he well performed the work of establishing precedents for his successors."[315]

From 1853 to 1857, Koerner served as lieutenant governor under Democratic Governor Joel Matteson. An outspoken opponent of the Kansas-Nebraska bill, which potentially allowed the expansion of slavery into U.S. territories, Koerner in 1856 served on a statewide committee to establish an "Anti-Nebraska" party.[316] Maintaining that the new Republican Party "meet all the important political issues clearly and distinctly," Koerner explained, "I could not cooperate with any party that did not, while asserting the principle that soil heretofore free shall remain free as long as it is territory, at the same time affirmatively maintain that the Constitutional rights of the Southern States should never be interfered with."[317]

The unsuccessful Republican candidate for Congress from the Belleville district, Koerner became a strong supporter of presidential candidate Abraham Lincoln. In April 1861, as the Civil War began, Koerner moved to Springfield and organized the Illinois volunteers, while also assuming responsibility for some of President Lincoln's law cases. For a time Koerner served as a colonel on the staffs of General John C. Fremont and his successor, General Henry W. Halleck.[318]

In 1862, Lincoln appointed Koerner the minister to Spain, where he endeavored to counteract British and French attempts for a joint recognition of the Confederacy and to cultivate the traditional friendly relations with Spain.[319] While there, he authored *Aus Spanien,* a book on Spanish art, natural beauties, and the ethnic characteristics of the diverse population.

Returning to the States in 1864, Koerner resumed his Belleville law practice with one son. In 1867, the elder Koerner became president of the board of trustees that organized the Soldiers' Orphans' Home in Bloomington.[320] In 1868, he served as president of the Illinois Electoral College and a Republican elector-at-large for Ulysses S. Grant. Three years later, intolerant of pervasive corruption in the Grant administration, Koerner joined the Liberal Republican movement. Nominated for governor by a coalition of Liberal Republicans and Democrats, he lost overwhelmingly to Republican Richard J. Oglesby.[321]

By 1876, Koerner retired from active political participation to focus on his law practice as well as literary works, including writing his autobiography. The oldest practicing attorney in Illinois, Koerner died in Belleville at age eighty-seven on April 9, 1896. His longtime friend and former Supreme Court Justice Lyman Trumbull delivered the funeral eulogy at Walnut Hill Cemetery in Belleville.[322]

WILLIAM A. DENNING, 1847-1848

Appointed as successor to Supreme Court Justice Walter B. Scates, William A. Denning served for nearly two years. Born in Kentucky about 1812 or 1817, Denning moved to Frankfort, Illinois, and began the practice of law. He resided for a brief time in Townmount before moving to the nearby Franklin County seat of Benton.[323] During the mid-1830s, Denning served as captain and then colonel in the state militia. In 1844, he won election as representative of the far southern Illinois counties of Franklin, Pulaski, and Alexander in the Illinois General Assembly. In 1845, legislators appointed Denning as state's attorney of the Third Judicial Circuit.

Two years later, he resigned his House seat to accept appointment to the vacated Supreme Court judgeship. "He was large in stature," wrote a county historian, "had a fine personal appearance, and was an able judge and powerful advocate."[324]

Denning heard many cases but wrote few of the Court's opinions. In serving part of the December 1846 term and all of the December 1847 term, he only authored two opinions. In *Woodford v. McClenahan,* he affirmed a Stark County Circuit Court decision on behalf of Elijah McClenahan. He had purchased a clock from W. H. Haywood, peddler for the seller, Bishop Higley & Co. When McClenahan complained that the clock was defective, company agent Samuel Woodford maintained that the signature on the warranty papers was not that of Haywood. "The evidence shows that Haywood sold clocks in the name of Bishop Higley & Co.," Denning wrote. "He did make the warranty in question; and Bishop Higley & Co., have ratified the act by accepting the note given for the clock warranted, and consequently are bound by it."[325]

Denning's term on the Illinois Supreme Court ended when the new Illinois Constitution took effect in 1848. Following his Supreme Court tenure, Denning won election as judge of the Third Judicial Circuit in southern Illinois. In an 1851 Hardin County trial, he ordered the discharge of a black man arrested under "slave laws of Illinois." Denning decreed those statutes null and void, having been "declared so by our Supreme Court." The Springfield *Illinois Journal* agreed with the decision: "We did suppose that every man in this state, who has paid any attention to the matter, understood the law of the case, as did Judge Denning."[326]

Denning resigned from the circuit court in 1854, then in 1855 unsuccessfully vied for the U.S. Senate nomination.[327] He died at his Benton residence on September 4, 1856, and was buried in the town's Old Cemetery.

DAVID M. WOODSON, 1848

Born on May 18, 1806, in Jessamine County, Kentucky, David Meade Woodson was the second son of prominent attorney Samuel H. and Anne R. Meade Woodson. The young Woodson attended Lexington schools and studied law with his father. He graduated from Transylvania University in Lexington. In 1831, Woodson won election as a Whig to the Kentucky House of Representatives. "His personal popularity," wrote a local historian, "and his ability led to his election and amid the shouts of the people he was borne in triumph on the shoulders of his friends through the streets of the town."[328]

Also in 1831, Woodson married Lucy McDowell, daughter of Major John McDowell of Fayette County, Kentucky. They became the parents of one son. Moving to Carrollton, Illinois, in the fall of 1833, Woodson began a fourteen-year law practice with another newly arrived resident, Charles D. Hodges. Woodson returned briefly to Transylvania University for additional courses and studied under George Robertson, chief justice of Kentucky.[329]

After the death of his wife in 1836, Woodson married Julia Kennett of Kentucky in 1838, daughter of Dixon H. Kennett. The couple became the parents of one daughter.[330] Also in 1838, Governor Joseph Duncan appointed Woodson as state's attorney in the First Judicial Circuit, comprised of eight counties in central Illinois.[331]

He served as lead prosecuting attorney in the murder trial of land office registrar Henry B. Truett, who had been accused of shooting Methodist preacher and physician Jacob M. Early during a heated political argument. Springfield attorney Abraham Lincoln, in one of his first murder trials, joined several other lawyers in defending Truett, while Stephen A. Douglas assisted Woodson in the prosecution. The prosecutors "described the expression of Truett's countenance before speaking to Early," wrote one observer, "the determined manner in which he spoke to Early, and the abuse, the repeated insults, and the provoking epithets—spoken by a cowardly man to one his superior in size, strength, and courage."

After five days of trial, the jurors deliberated for nearly three hours before rendering a verdict of not guilty. A decade later, Thomas Ford, who had served as Illinois governor and Illinois Supreme Court justice, explained such cases when he wrote, "There was now and then an indictment for murder or larceny, and other felonies, but in all cases of murder arising from heat of blood or in a fight, it was impossible to convict."[332]

In 1840, Woodson won election to the Illinois House of Representatives, serving for one term. In 1844, Woodson received the Whig nomination to challenge the incumbent Democratic Congressman Stephen Douglas. "Woodson was no match," according to Douglas biographer Robert W. Johannsen. "Both candidates traveled extensively about the district, but the Whig's efforts were at best half-hearted." Douglas won by more than 1,700 votes, with Woodson carrying only one county.[333]

In 1847, he served as a delegate to the Illinois Constitutional Convention, serving on the Committee of Law Reform.[334] When Justice Samuel D. Lockwood resigned from the Illinois Supreme Court, Woodson succeeded him on November 3, 1848. The new Illinois Constitution had already taken effect in April 1848, but the new Illinois Supreme Court of three members (Lyman Trumbull, Samuel H. Treat, and John D. Caton) had not yet been seated. When the new Supreme Court met in Mount Vernon in December 1848, Woodson's tenure of one month had expired. The Court held no sessions during that month, and Woodson neither heard any cases nor wrote any opinions.

In the 1848 judicial election, Woodson won the circuit court judgeship for the First Judicial Circuit, remaining in that position for eighteen years. "Judge Woodson was a gentleman of the old school," wrote fellow lawyer John M. Palmer, "and maintained the dignity of his court under all circumstances."[335]

Woodson became president of a western Illinois rail company, which eventually became the Chicago and Alton Railroad. In his honor, residents of a new Morgan County settlement along the rail line named their town Woodson.[336] He retired from the circuit court in 1867, succeeded by his former law partner Charles D. Hodges.[337] In 1868, "having in the meantime become an advocate of the Democratic party," Woodson again won election to the Illinois House of Representatives, serving one term.[338]

Woodson died at his Carrollton home on August 26, 1877. Following funeral services at the residence, he was buried in the City Cemetery.[339] "The favorable opinion which the world had passed upon him at the outset of his professional career," one county historian reported, "was in no degree set aside or modified throughout all the years of his practice or of his service upon the bench."[340]

LYMAN TRUMBULL, 1848-1853

Among the state's most eminent figures, Lyman Trumbull was a native of Connecticut, the grandson of a Congregational pastor who served as a military chaplain during the American Revolution. Born in Colchester on October 12, 1813, Lyman Trumbull was the seventh son of eleven children born to Benjamin and Elizabeth Mather Trumbull. Lyman attended Bacon Academy in Colchester, and then taught at a nearby school for four years. At age twenty, he moved to Greenville, Georgia, where he continued teaching while studying for the bar.[341]

In 1836, Trumbull traveled by horseback to Belleville, Illinois, the seat of St. Clair County. There he opened a law practice with former Governor John Reynolds, developing "not only a prospering law partnership," observed Trumbull biographer Mark Krug, "but an even more important political association that lasted for a number of years."[342] Trumbull possessed "rare intellectual endowments," according to historian N. Dwight Harris. "In politics he was an old-time Democrat, with no leanings toward abolitionism, but possessing an honest desire to see justice done the negro in Illinois. It was a thankless task in those days of prejudice and bitter partisan feeling to assume the role of defender of the indentured slaves."[343]

Trumbull won election to the state legislature in Springfield in 1840, but served only briefly, from November 23 to March 1, 1841. Governor Thomas Carlin appointed him to succeed Stephen A. Douglas as Secretary of State. While maintaining his Belleville residence and law practice, Trumbull took meals in a private home and slept in a statehouse committee room when in Springfield. Trumbull wrote letters to his family in Connecticut that the work of the Secretary of State was "very trifling." Among the duties, he provided handwritten copies of statutes, affixed documents with the state seal, and received election returns.[344] A popular bachelor, Trumbull enjoyed the Springfield social life.

After Thomas Ford succeeded Governor Carlin, Trumbull vocally opposed Ford's proposals to strengthen the state's precarious financial situation. In March 1843, Ford responded by removing Trumbull as Secretary of State. "From the nature of his office," Ford wrote, "he ought to have been my confidential helper and adviser." Ford described Trumbull as "a medium lawyer but no statesman . . . literally devoured by ambition" for political office.[345]

One of Trumbull's last duties as Secretary was to make an index for the House and Senate Journals, and the legislature appropriated $600 for the task. Trumbull did part of the work, received $400, and left the remainder to his successor Thompson Campbell. Campbell claimed that Trumbull took more than his fair share, sued Trumbull to obtain payment, and won a judgment for $200. Trumbull retained Abraham Lincoln and appealed to the Illinois Supreme Court. Justice Samuel Treat reversed the decision, arguing that Campbell could not sue Trumbull but had to sue the State.[346]

In June 1843 in Springfield, Trumbull married Julia Jayne, a close friend of Mary Lincoln, wife of Abraham Lincoln.[347] They became the parents of six sons, only three of whom survived to adulthood.[348]

Trumbull waged an unsuccessful campaign in 1846 for a congressional seat, then in 1848 won election as one of three Illinois Supreme Court justices. One justice was to serve three years, one six years, and the other nine years, the terms to be decided by lot. Thereafter, the term of each judge would be nine years.[349] Trumbull drew the lot for the three-year term, which pleased him. "If I should want to leave the bench," he wrote his wife, "it is fortunate that I have drawn the short term."[350]

Trumbull moved his family from Belleville to a house with acreage in Alton.[351] In 1852, he was elected to a full nine-year Supreme Court term. Among the cases in which he presented the Court opinion, *McKinley v. Watkins* involved Joseph Watkins and William R. McKinley, who had traded horses in 1845. After McKinley's horse soon died, they disputed the terms of the trade. McKinley maintained that he offered to pay Watkins $50 or give him a horse worth $50 in exchange for not filing a lawsuit. Justice Trumbull reversed the Logan County Circuit Court decision that had favored Watkins, finding no evidence that he had assented to McKinley's offer. "A mere offer, not assented to," wrote Trumbull, "constitutes no contract; for there must be not only a proposal, but an acceptance thereof."[352]

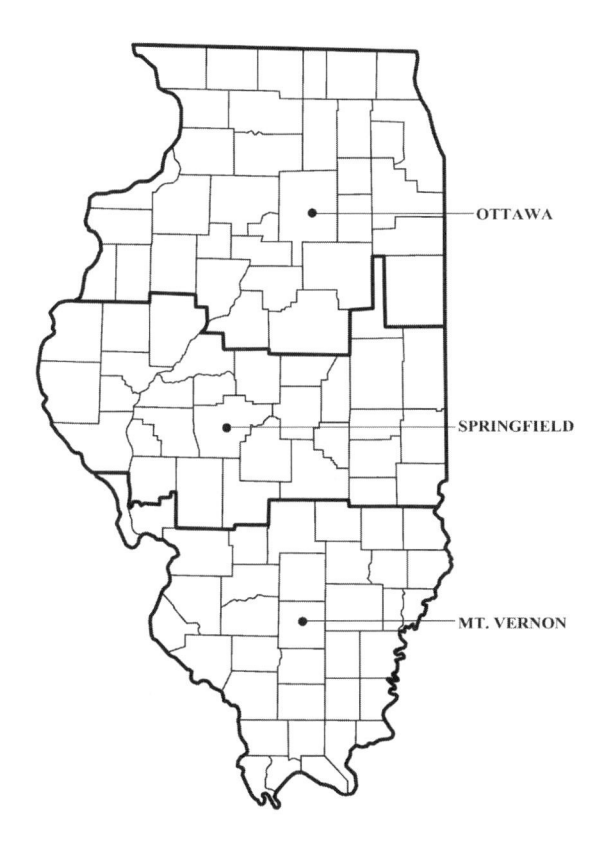

The three grand divisions of the Illinois Supreme Court (Map courtesy of Illinois Supreme Court Historic Preservation Commission)

In *Jones v. The People of the State of Illinois,* Trumbull affirmed a Morgan County Circuit Court decision against Samuel B. Jones, convicted of selling and serving liquor in his home. Jones contended that an 1851 statute prohibiting the retail sale of intoxicating drinks to be unconstitutional. "By virtue of its police power," Trumbull wrote, "every State must have the 'right to enact such laws as may be necessary for the restraint and punishment of crime, and for the preservation of the public peace, health, and morals of its citizens.' It is upon this principle that the sale of lottery tickets, and of cards, and other instruments for gaming is prohibited; and who ever questioned the constitutionality or validity of such laws? A government that did not possess the power to protect itself against such and similar evils would scarcely be worth preserving."[353]

Justice Trumbull "was not happy on the bench," observed biographer Mark M. Krug. He enjoyed participating in Illinois politics and "chafed under the customary restriction on political activities by judges," particularly as the slavery question became more prominent. Trumbull opposed the expansion of slavery into the territories. The Illinois Constitution fixed the salary of Supreme Court justices at $1,500 annually, which was not enough to support his family. Krug noted that after "considerable soul-searching he decided to resign from the bench and to resume the private practice of law in 1853."[354]

One year later, Trumbull left the Democratic Party in the aftermath of the 1854 Kansas-Nebraska Act.[355] He won election to Congress as an Anti-Nebraska opponent of Stephen A. Douglas's "popular sovereignty" stance on the slavery question. Before he could take his House seat, Illinois's Anti-Nebraska legislators failed to unite over the candidacy of Springfield attorney Abraham Lincoln to the U.S. Senate. Lincoln tossed his support to Trumbull, who won the election. "This produced some heart-burnings amongst some of Lincoln's friends," recalled fellow attorney Usher F. Linder.[356] Trumbull and Lincoln became the de facto leaders of the new Illinois Republican Party, and Trumbull campaigned for Lincoln when Lincoln vied to unseat incumbent U.S. Senator Stephen A. Douglas in 1858.

During the Civil War, Trumbull joined with Governor Richard Yates in allowing blacks as soldiers. Illinois authorized a regiment in 1863, but because of pay and benefit inequities, Illinois blacks in the war numbered fewer than three thousand.[357] Trumbull served as chairman of the powerful Judiciary Committee and was the principal author of the Thirteenth Amendment, which abolished slavery in the country.[358]

In 1868, Trumbull and six other Republican senators resisted pressure from party leadership and voted for the acquittal of impeached President Andrew Johnson. "I am a Senator and a judge," Trumbull explained to a friend. "The President is not guilty in manner and form as charged in any one of the articles of impeachment. I must so find and must so vote, without regard to consequences."[359]

In August 1868, following a lingering illness, Trumbull's wife, Julia, died at age forty-five. Eleven years later he married Mary Ingraham, of Saybrook Point, Connecticut. They became parents of two daughters, both of whom died in childhood.[360]

Trumbull broke with the Republicans in 1872 and contended for the presidential nomination of the short-lived Liberal Republican Party. Upon the expiration of his third senatorial term in March 1873, the sixty-year-old Trumbull and his family moved to Chicago, where he maintained a lucrative law practice. Returning to the Democratic Party, he became the 1880 gubernatorial candidate, "but the tide of Republicanism was too strong," reported the *Chicago Tribune,* and he lost to the incumbent, Shelby M. Cullom.[361] Trumbull then became a Populist, calling for "governmental ownership of monopolies affecting the public interest." He and fellow Chicago attorney Clarence Darrow petitioned the U.S. Supreme Court for a writ of habeas corpus on behalf of Eugene V. Debs, president of the American Railway Union. Debs had been convicted in circuit court of violating an injunction during the Pullman railway dispute. The Supreme Court, however, rejected the petition and affirmed the jurisdiction of the circuit court in issuing the injunction.[362]

Traveling to Belleville for the April 1896 funeral of his friend Gustavus Koerner, Trumbull became seriously ill and returned immediately to Chicago. He died there on June 25, at the age of eighty-two. "Judge Trumbull hated war and loved his country," wrote the *Chicago Tribune.* He was firm and true."[363] Orator William Jennings Bryan, who had resided with the Trumbulls while attending Union College of Law, delivered the funeral eulogy. The former senator's remains were interred in Oak Woods Cemetery in Chicago.[364]

"If he had remained true to his party," wrote Chicago newspaper publisher Joseph Medill, "Judge Trumbull, I believe, would have died with his name in the roll of Presidents of the United States. I have always thought that he could have been the successor of Grant. He stood so high in the estimation of his party and the nation that nothing was beyond his reach. . . . He could have been President instead of Hayes, or Garfield, or Harrison."[365]

ONIAS C. SKINNER, 1855-1858

A New York native, Onias Childs Skinner was born in Floyd, Oneida County, in 1817, the son of Onias and Tirza Bell Skinner. "A cabin boy on the Erie Canal, a sailor on the lakes," as a young man Skinner moved west, farming in Peoria County, Illinois, from 1836 to 1839.[366] Then he began the study of law in Greenville, Ohio, under future Congressman Hiram Bell and was admitted to the bar. Skinner returned to Illinois in 1840, practicing law in Carthage, the seat of Hancock County. Three years later, he married Adeline McCormas Dorsey, the daughter of Judge James M. Dorsey, in Greenville, Ohio.[367]

The couple moved to Quincy in 1844. "As a lawyer," wrote a local historian, "he was the most daring, speculative and successful litigant that ever practiced at the Adams County bar."[368] A member of a Hancock County anti-Mormon organization, he presented Governor Thomas Ford with the group's resolution calling for "extermination of the Mormons." Two weeks later, Skinner became special counsel to prosecute the Mormon founder Joseph Smith in a preliminary hearing on charges of treason.[369]

After the 1844 murder of Smith and his brother Hyrum, twenty-six-year-old Skinner served as a defense attorney in the trial of five men indicted for the crime. "Skinner was obviously an advocate of considerable skill," explained historians Dallin H. Oaks and Marvin S. Hill, "who concentrated his fire upon the prosecution's case, not upon the anti-Mormon or anti-Smith prejudices of the jury." Skinner ridiculed the testimony of Mormon witnesses, challenged the idea of a murder conspiracy, and in a three-hour summation asserted that the case against the defendants proved only that certain men thirsted for blood and desired "some victim offered up upon the gallows" to appease the name of Smith, "the idol of a powerful faction."[370] The jury deliberated for less than three hours before delivering not guilty verdicts for all five defendants. On the same day, after attorneys failed to appear in court to prosecute the indictment against the same defendants for the Hyrum Smith murder, that suit was dismissed.[371]

A Democratic member of the state legislature in the 1849 and 1850 sessions, Skinner "fulfilled all the duties devolving upon him with ability and energy, and by his bold advocacy of needed reforms through legislative enactment, took immediate rank with the representative men of the State." Serving for a short period as state's attorney, in 1851, he won election as judge of the western Illinois Fifteenth Judicial Circuit.[372]

Adeline Skinner died in 1849, and in 1853, he married Sarah Harris Wilton. They became parents of a daughter, Maud W. Skinner. Following the resignation of Supreme Court Justice Samuel H. Treat to become a United States District Judge, Skinner won the popular election on June 4, 1855, to fill the vacancy. He defeated Stephen T. Logan, a former law partner of Abraham Lincoln.[373]

In the 1855 case *Johnson v. Richardson et al.,* Justice Skinner affirmed a Sangamon County Circuit Court opinion regarding the responsibility of an innkeeper for the property of his guests. En route from Ottawa to Greene County, William B. Richardson and Henry L. Brush, one of Richardson's two business partners, lodged at Joel Johnson's Springfield City Hotel. During the night a thief stole Brush's money from their room. Richardson and the other partner sued Johnson and gained a $286 award, which was their two-thirds share of the stolen amount. "Every traveler must carry with him more or less money," Justice Skinner wrote in upholding the lower court decision. "To compel them to place their money in the custody of the innkeeper, his clerk, or servant, would create new perils in traveling, and place the guest at the mercy of the publican, honest or dishonest . . . . In this case, the sum was not unreasonably large to carry about the traveler's person and we cannot hold that he was at fault in not depositing it with the innkeeper."[374]

In the 1857 *Babcock v. Trice* case, Tandy H. Trice had sold and delivered a quantity of corn to a warehouseman. When the warehouse owner, Benjamin W. Babcock, noticed that some of the corn was "in a damaged condition and of less value than sound merchantable corn," he refused to complete the purchase. Trice successfully sued for payment in Warren County Circuit Court, after which Babcock appealed to the Supreme Court. "The duty of Trice," Justice Skinner wrote in reversing the lower court decision, "was to deliver a fair article, fit for use and market as a sound commodity; and his duty, under the contract, was not performed until he had done so."[375]

On April 19, 1858, just prior to the expiration of his term, Skinner resigned from the Supreme Court and resumed his Quincy law practice. He also pursued agricultural and railroad ventures, eventually serving as president of the Quincy & Carthage Railroad (later the Chicago, Burlington & Quincy Railroad). After the 1861 death of his wife, Sarah, in 1865 Skinner married Helen Reed Cooley, widow of Illinois Secretary of State Horace S. Cooley.[376]

Skinner represented Adams County in the 1870 Illinois Constitutional Convention and served as chairman of the Judiciary Committee.[377] "He was a sound, able lawyer," wrote fellow lawyer John M. Palmer, "gaining eminence by his excellent service on the supreme bench."[378]

Skinner died at his Quincy home on February 4, 1877, after having been thrown from his carriage by a team of frightened horses.[379] In the Supreme Court's memorial proceedings, Chief Justice John Scholfield remarked upon Skinner's contributions to the State of Illinois. "As judge, as legislator, and as a lawyer, he ably and honorably acted his part. His impress on our institutions and laws is strongly marked."[380]

PINKNEY H. WALKER, 1858-1885

The son of Kentucky attorney Joseph G. and Martha Scott Walker, Pinkney Houston Walker was born in Adair County, on June 18, 1815. He attended area schools and worked on his father's farm, and at age seventeen, he became a store clerk. Two years later, in 1834, Walker left Kentucky and settled in Rushville, Illinois, "at that time one of the most thriving and promising of the interior towns of the State."[381]

After clerking in a Rushville mercantile business for four years, Walker moved to Macomb, Illinois, where he studied law in the office of an uncle, Cyrus Walker. Examined for the bar by Supreme Court justices Samuel Lockwood and Thomas Browne, Walker opened an office in Macomb and in 1840, formed a partnership with his uncle.[382] On June 2 of that year, he married Susan McCroskey, an Adair County, Kentucky, native and daughter of Rushville merchant James McCroskey. They became the parents of five daughters and four sons.[383] In 1848, the family moved from Macomb to Rushville, and Walker partnered with the well-respected attorney Robert S. Blackwell in 1851.[384]

Future Supreme Court justice Damon G. Tunnicliff studied under Walker's tutelage. "Though his office was small," Tunnicliff recalled years later, "consisting of but a single room for himself, several students and a good law library, his uniform kindness and cheerfulness made all feel at home, and that they were never in the way, but always welcome there. His great fondness for the law, the delight he took in discussing it, and explaining its intricacies, as well as the kind, encouraging words he ever had for the beginner, rendered him not only a most valuable instructor, but caused him to be revered and loved by all who were so fortunate as to receive the benefit of his fostering care."[385]

In 1853, Walker won election as judge of the Fifth Judicial Circuit, comprising Schuyler, Pike, Brown, McDonough, Cass, and Mason Counties. He remained in that position until April 1858, when Governor William H. Bissell appointed him to fill a vacancy on the Illinois Supreme Court, replacing Onias C. Skinner, who had resigned his position. Popularly elected to the Supreme Court position in June 1858 for a nine-year term, Walker served as Chief Justice from January 1864 to June 1867. He was reelected for another nine-year term in 1867, and he was again Chief Justice from June 1874 to June 1875.[386]

Among his numerous opinions, Walker delivered the Supreme Court decision reversing an 1856 breach of warranty ruling. In the Edgar County Circuit Court, John Crabtree had won a judgment against William Kile and his partner, who sold Crabtree eighty-one warranted healthy cattle, many of which died of disease en route to the New York beef market. In *Crabtree v. Kile et al.,* Crabtree's attorneys argued that he had "sustained great damage by the said breach of the warranty of the plaintiffs, and incurred necessarily heavy expenses in doctoring and taking care of the cattle, and by the delays occasioned in consequence of the diseased condition of the cattle." Walker presented the Supreme Court opinion that Crabtree "had the undoubted right to rely upon the warranty, and to act in good faith upon the supposition that they were sound until the disease manifested itself; and then he had a right to sell them for the best price he could obtain for such cattle."[387]

Justice Walker delivered the Court opinion in an 1860 medical malpractice case. Dr. Powers Ritchey had treated Keziah West for a fractured and dislocated wrist, promising to examine her injury the following day. Ritchey failed to perform the reexamination, and West's wrist healed improperly. An Adams County Circuit Court jury found Ritchey guilty of malpractice and awarded West $700 in damages. Abraham Lincoln represented Ritchey in the appeal to the Illinois Supreme Court. "When a person assumes the profession of physician and surgeon," Justice Walker wrote in affirming the lower court judgment, "he must, in its exercise, be held to employ a reasonable amount of care and skill. For any thing short of that degree of skill in his practice, the law will hold him responsible for any injury which may result from its absence."[388]

Walker transitioned to the new 1870 Constitution, assuming his Supreme Court position from the Fourth Judicial District, which comprised twelve counties in western Illinois. Justice John Scholfield recollected that before the Appellate Court had been created in 1877, the work of the Supreme Court was very busy. In 1873, the court met in Ottawa to hear a great number of cases, working from eight in the morning to nine or ten at night. After the term ended, the justices were charged

The supreme court building in Ottawa hosted Supreme Court terms from 1859 to 1897. (Image courtesy of James Dobrovolny Collection, Illinois Supreme Court Historic Preservation Commission)

with writing opinions during the six-week vacation between the terms at Ottawa and Springfield. Scholfield reported that Walker wrote sixty-two opinions in those six weeks and read them in conference at Springfield.[389] Walker was elected without opposition for a third Supreme Court term in 1876, and again served as Chief Justice from 1879 to 1880.

In *Ruggles v. People,* on appeal from the Bureau County Circuit Court, Walker ruled in 1878 in what is considered among the Illinois Supreme Court's more important decisions of the nineteenth century. Morgan Lewis boarded a Chicago, Burlington and Quincy train at Buda, intending to ride six miles to Neponset. The ticket office was closed, so he offered the conductor, Neal Ruggles, the sum of eighteen cents (three cents per mile). Ruggles refused, demanding instead twenty cents, the regular fare charged by the CB&Q between the two towns, "which had been fixed by the board of directors and officers of said railroad company several years prior thereto." After Lewis refused to pay the additional amount, Ruggles stopped the train and unsuccessfully attempted to remove him. Lewis claimed that under the state law entitled "An act to establish a reasonable maximum rate of charges for the transportation of passengers on railroads in this State," approved April 15, 1871, he had the right to be carried from Buda to Neponset for eighteen cents.

Arriving in Neponset, Lewis had Ruggles arrested for assault and battery. A Bureau County justice of the peace found Ruggles guilty and fined him $10 and costs. Ruggles appealed to the circuit court, which affirmed the judgment. Ruggles then took an appeal to the Illinois Supreme Court, arguing that the legislative act "fixing the rate of fare to be paid by persons traveling on the road is unconstitutional and void." Walker affirmed the guilty verdict and $10 fine, relying on *Munn v. Illinois* and citing examples of legislative regulation, "as applicable to the police power of the State to the full extent that natural persons are subject to its control."[390]

Walker died at his Rushville home on February 7, 1885, having been on the Court two months short of twenty-seven years—one of the longest-serving justices in Illinois history.[391] He was buried in the Rushville City Cemetery. "Said to have written more opinions than any other Supreme Court judge in the United States," according to court historian Ralph M. Snyder, Walker's opinions appear in ninety-four volumes of *Illinois Reports*.[392]

CORYDON BECKWITH, 1864

Although serving only briefly on the Illinois Supreme Court, Corydon Beckwith earned the reputation of a skilled jurist. Born in Sutton, Caledonia County, Vermont, on July 24, 1823, Beckwith was the son of John and Matilda Shaw Beckwith.[393] Acquiring a rudimentary education in the vicinity of his home, young Beckwith pursued scientific and classical courses in Providence, Rhode Island, and Wrentham, Massachusetts. After studying law for three years, he was admitted to the Vermont bar in 1844 and formed a partnership with a distinguished area attorney, Frederick A. Schley.[394] Five years later, in 1849, Beckwith married Mary Ann Smith of St. Albans, Vermont.[395]

In the spring of 1853, the Beckwiths and their three children moved to Chicago, where he became associated with prominent attorneys Van H. Higgins and Bolton F. Strother, under the firm name Higgins, Beckwith & Strother.[396] The partners brought prominent cases in both state and federal courts. Beckwith "was remarkably successful," recalled one associate, "and was rarely beaten. If he found he was on the wrong side he would advise a settlement. He was never willing to go to a trial and expose his clients' interests where the chances were strongly against him."[397]

When John D. Caton decided to retire from the Illinois Supreme Court in early 1864, Governor Richard Yates accepted Caton's recommendation of fellow Chicagoan Beckwith to complete the term. As Caton's successor, Beckwith served from January to June 1864.[398] "Some of his decisions," reported the *Chicago Tribune,* "are models of brevity and are renowned for strength of statement."[399]

In *Miller v. Young's Administrator,* Beckwith delivered the Court opinion reversing a lower court decision. William H. Young had sued in the Logan County Circuit Court to rescind his purchase of what he contended was a fraudulent patent-right contract for the manufacture of cast iron cemetery tombs of a unique ornamental design. In payment for the contract, Young had conveyed 160 acres of land in Logan County to Reuben Miller, agent for the owner of the cemetery tomb patent. Young's attorney contended that the patent was void because not only was the design "of no utility" but also that it was not "novel," and that cast iron tombs made according to the design "were not as durable, saleable, and could not be manufactured as cheaply" as Miller represented. Circuit Court Judge David Davis ruled on behalf of Young and ordered Miller to return the 160 acres of land. In reversing the decree, Justice Beckwith cited an 1842 Congressional act in determining that a valid patent design "should be a new and an original one, but the law does not require that it should be useful." He further found that "the representations as to the durability and probable sale of the tombs" as "mere matters of opinion," not sustained by the evidence.[400]

Beckwith also delivered the opinion in *Happy et al. v. Morton et al.,* an unusual case involving a central Illinois church. Joseph Morton and several other members of the Jacksonville Church of Christ sued their preacher, Walter S. Russell, and his supporters, in the Morgan County Circuit Court. Morton charged that Russell did not hold to "the Bible doctrines as taught by the Christian church throughout the United States," and that he did not profess the theological views of the Jacksonville Church of Christ espoused by its founders in 1832. The circuit court found for Morton and the other complainants, transferring to them the church edifice and other property. Russell died in 1863, but some of his adherents, including William H. Happy, appealed the decision. In the January 1864 term of the Illinois Supreme Court, Justice Beckwith delivered the opinion reversing the lower court. "The original bill alleges that the property in question was purchased for the purpose and with the intention of erecting thereon a suitable building for the use of the Society called the Church of Christ, in which to worship Almighty God according to the teachings of the Christian or Reform Church," he wrote, "but it does not allege what the teachings of the Christian or Reform Church were, nor in what particulars these teachings had been departed from." Beckwith enumerated five "alleged doctrines" of the congregation, and then explained that he could find no substantial departure from those doctrines. "Before this court can declare the teachings of the Rev. Mr. Russell in this regard an abuse of the trust in question, the complainants must show a distinction between such teachings and their standard of faith, so that a difference can be perceived. . . . Mr. Russell considered his views essential, and undoubtedly he told his congregation that he so considered them, but they were not made a test of church membership or fellowship."[401]

Following his brief Supreme Court tenure, Beckwith partnered with Benjamin F. Ayer and F. H. Kales in Chicago. In 1873, he became general solicitor for the Chicago, Alton & St. Louis Railroad. "This appointment did not prevent him from engaging in a general practice," Ayer recalled. "He never confined his attention to any special branch of the law, but enjoyed a large general practice." Beckwith served as counsel for several large corporations, with a number of cases involving corporate rights and liabilities.[402] "Cases in which there are no precedents," wrote one biographer, "and in which he originates or discovers the necessary legal principles, are the cases in which he excels." Another writer described Beckwith as a remarkable attorney who "could originate lines of offense or defense better than any lawyer in Chicago at his time."[403]

Beckwith joined another former Supreme Court justice, Charles B. Lawrence, and prominent attorneys Robert G. Ingersoll and Orville Hickman Browning in representing three large railroads in an 1875 appeal to the U.S. Supreme Court. The U.S. Circuit Court had refused to uphold an Illinois Supreme Court decree that sustained an 1872 statute regarding the collection of corporate taxes. The federal circuit court ruling resulted in the suspension of corporate tax collections, seriously crippling the state's finances. In *State Railroad Tax Case*, the U.S. Supreme Court reversed the circuit court, a decision that established the right of the state to tax corporations under provisions of the 1872 law.[404]

Benjamin Ayer conjectured that Beckwith "earned more money in the practice of law" than any contemporary lawyer in Illinois. "He was always at work and gave himself no rest. I hardly ever knew him to take a vacation . . . . He has had a great deal to do with shaping the law of this State."[405] Beckwith died on August 18, 1890, at Highlands, his home near the Chicago suburb of Hinsdale. Following Episcopal services at the home, he was buried in the family lot at Rosehill Cemetery in Chicago.[406]

CHARLES B. LAWRENCE, 1864-1873

Born on December 17, 1820, in Vergennes, Vermont, Charles Brush Lawrence was the son of Viele and Betsy Woodbridge Lawrence.[407] Viele Lawrence was a merchant and a member of the Vermont State Senate. Charles Lawrence attended Middlebury College in Vermont and graduated in 1841 from Union College in eastern New York. A teacher in Lowndes County, Alabama, for two years, Lawrence then moved to Cincinnati, Ohio, and with college classmate David L. Hough studied law under Judge Alphonso Taft, who would become U.S. Attorney General in the administration of President Ulysses S. Grant.[408]

In the spring of 1844, Lawrence moved to St. Louis and continued his law studies in the office of Henry S. Geyer, later a U.S. senator from Missouri. Then Lawrence and Hough formed a partnership in Quincy, Illinois.[409] After Hough moved from the area, Lawrence partnered with Archibald Williams, specializing in litigation regarding titles to the large area of land known as the Military Tract.

When Charles Gilman, the Illinois Supreme Court Reporter, died in Quincy in July 1849, he had not yet completed the Reports of the Supreme Court. Lawrence undertook completing the task, which was about 80 percent finished. Lawrence commented that some of "the arguments of counsel are necessarily reported very briefly" because he could not locate them among Gilman's paperwork. Lawrence finished 5 Gilman, also known as 10 Illinois, in late 1849.[410]

In 1851 in Quincy, Lawrence married Margaret Marston, sister of Chicago attorney Thomas Marston. After spending two years in Europe "for the benefit of his health," the couple moved to a farm in Warren County, near Prairie City, where he intended to pursue agricultural interests. About a year later, they relocated to Galesburg, and he resumed the practice of law. They became the parents of five children, only one of whom survived to adulthood.[411]

A prominent Republican, Lawrence became a judge of the Tenth Judicial Circuit in 1861.[412] He held the position until his election to the Illinois Supreme Court on July 22, 1864, succeeding the appointed Corydon Beckwith. Lawrence became Chief Justice in 1870 when the new Illinois Constitution took effect.

The following year, he reversed an Edgar County Circuit Court decision in *Janney v. Birch.* Johnson J. C. Birch, administrator of the deceased Sarah E. Peake, sought payment of two notes by Eldridge S. Janney, totaling some $1,500. Janney denied signing the notes, and family relations complicated the issue: Peake had been Janney's sister and Birch's mother-in-law. The circuit court found for Birch, but, "In our judgment," wrote Chief Justice Lawrence, "the finding is against the decided preponderance of the evidence. It is true, three disinterested and credible witnesses, who knew the handwriting of the defendant, testify they believe the signatures on the notes to be his. On the other hand, there is an array of evidence going to show that if the notes were ever given they were settled with the payee in her life time, which, in our opinion, is irresistible."[413]

Lawrence also wrote the opinion in Myra Bradwell's case. Bradwell, the editor of *The Chicago Legal News*, applied for her license to practice law. The Supreme Court denied her application because she was a married woman and could not enter into contracts. Bradwell responded with an additional brief, citing laws giving her rights to enter into contracts. The Court again denied her application, with Lawrence writing an opinion "that when the legislature gave to this court the power of granting licenses to practice law, it was with not the slightest expectation that this privilege would be extended equally to men and women." Bradwell appealed her case to the U.S. Supreme Court, which upheld the Illinois Supreme Court's denial.[414]

In the early 1870s, farmers' organizations waged successful campaigns against railroad rates, and Illinois became the first state to enact railroad and warehouse regulations. Spurred by provisions in the 1870 Constitution, farmers' groups pressed for rigid enforcement of the Railroad and Warehouse Act that forbade rate discrimination by railroad carriers. An 1873 Supreme Court case, *The Chicago and Alton Railroad Company v. The People ex rel. Gustavus Koerner et al. Comrs.*, involved a suit brought against the Chicago and Alton Railroad for charging a greater rate for freight on lumber from Chicago to Lexington than from Chicago to Bloomington, both towns being in McLean County and the latter being the greater distance.[415]

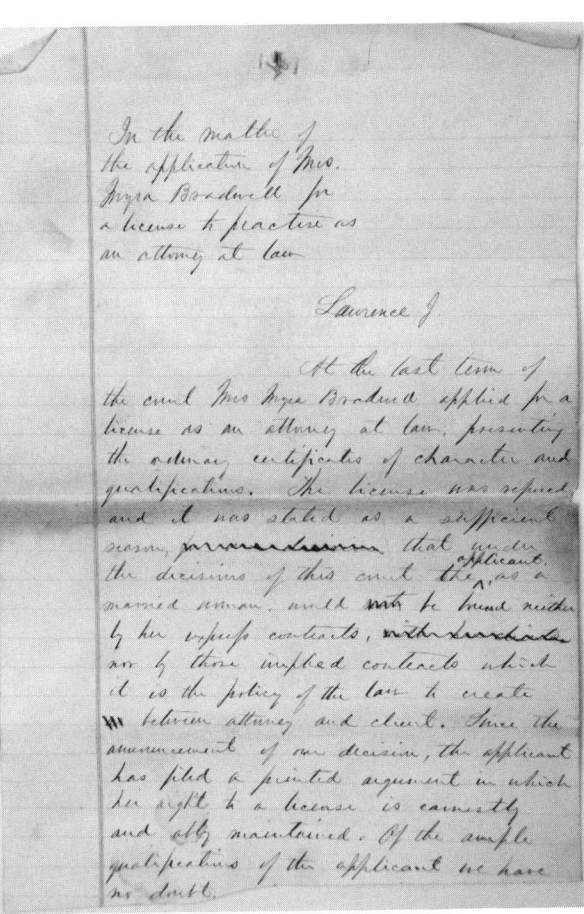

Lawrence wrote the opinion in the Myra Bradwell case. (Image courtesy of Illinois State Archives)

Chief Justice Lawrence expressed the Court majority in reversing the McLean County Circuit Court and declaring the law unconstitutional. "The existing act," he wrote, "does not prohibit unjust discrimination merely, but discrimination of any character, and because it does not allow the companies to explain the reason of the discrimination, but forfeits their franchise upon an arbitrary and conclusive presumption of guilt, to be drawn from the proof of an act that might be shown to be perfectly innocent. In these particulars the existing act violates the spirit of the constitution."[416] Because of Lawrence's decision in that case, farmers' groups led the opposition to his Supreme Court reelection bid several that case, farmers' groups led the opposition to his Supreme Court reelection bid several months later. In an overwhelmingly Republican district, Democratic Knox County attorney Alfred M. Craig defeated Lawrence by a large margin.[417]

He and his wife moved to Chicago that year, and Lawrence became a partner in the law firm Winston, Campbell & Lawrence. In 1877, he lost a fractious legislative election to the U.S. Senate. "If the fight had been kept up a day or two longer," recalled one contemporary, "the Democrats generally would have gone over to Lawrence and he would have been elected instead of David Davis."[418]

In 1882, Lawrence traveled to Springfield to deliver a eulogy for noted Quincy attorney Orville Hickman Browning, "a warm personal friend in the earlier years of his practice. The task was a veritable labor of love," reported the *Chicago Tribune,* "and the universal testimony of those who heard him was that no man could have performed it better."[419]

Traveling to Florida for a vacation with his wife and other relatives, Lawrence intended to revisit the Lowndes County, Alabama, area where he had taught as a young man. En route, however, the sixty-three-year-old Lawrence fell ill in a Decatur, Alabama, hotel and died there on April 9, 1883.[420] Following services at St. James Episcopal Church in Chicago, he was buried in Hope Cemetery, near Galesburg, alongside the graves of four of his children.[421]

"For personal integrity and uprightness of character," eulogized the Quincy *Daily Whig,* "Judge Lawrence was not less distinguished than for his legal and judicial ability." U.S. Supreme Court Chief Justice Melville W. Fuller wrote of Lawrence, "The qualities which made him eminent as a lawyer would have raised him to the highest rank in any walk of life. His works follow him and will perpetuate him, not as a ghost to haunt but as a guest to cheer."[422]

ANTHONY THORNTON, 1870-1873

One of seven Supreme Court justices elected under the new 1870 Illinois Constitution, Anthony Thornton was born on November 9, 1814, on a tobacco plantation near Paris, Bourbon County, Kentucky, to Anthony and Mary Towles Thornton. Both parents had descended from British immigrants to Carolina County, Virginia, and in 1807 nearly one hundred Thornton family members moved with their slaves from Virginia to Kentucky.[423]

Orphaned at the age of five, young Thornton resided with a grandfather and then an aunt. He attended county common schools, and at the age of sixteen, joined a sister in Gallatin, Tennessee, where he attended a preparatory school. He enrolled in Center College at Danville, Kentucky, then in the fall of 1834 graduated from Miami College in Oxford, Ohio. Returning to Kentucky, he studied law in the Paris office of an uncle, John R. Thornton, and obtained his law license before the age of twenty-two.[424]

In October 1836, Anthony Thornton traveled west by river and stagecoach, intending to settle in Missouri. Stopping at Shelbyville, Illinois, to visit an uncle, banker and merchant William F. Thornton, he decided instead to establish a law practice in that town. "When he arrived here," wrote a Shelbyville resident, "he found a town of only two hundred[,] the residences being nearly all made of logs, while the country surrounding was one vast expanse of timber and uncultivated prairie land."[425]

While in the state capital of Vandalia for his bar examination, Thornton met legislator Abraham Lincoln, and they and other attorneys rode the circuit together on horseback. "These twice a year trips about the circuit were not within a good deal of pleasure," noted a newspaper reporter. "There was more riding than court and there were hardships. In those days travelers were forced to ride through swamps and sloughs belly-deep in mud and swarming with venomous insects. But it was a brilliant and congenial company and it was an unmixed delight to drop into that charmed circle in the tavern where they happened to be spending the night."[426]

Thornton "was favored with success from the very start" of his Shelbyville practice, according to a county historian, "and during the first year had as much business as he cared to attend to in the courts of Shelby and adjoining counties."[427] Thornton garnered an excellent reputation and was "usually retained in all cases of importance." A Whig who strongly supported Henry Clay, Thornton became a delegate to the 1847 Constitutional Convention, which framed the state's second Constitution. Thornton served on the Committee for Law Reform and made a strong but unsuccessful effort for merit selection rather than popular election of judges.[428]

In 1850, he won election as a Whig to the Illinois General Assembly and served for one term. That same year, he married Mildred Thornton, the daughter of William F. Thornton of Shelbyville. They became parents of two sons before her death in 1856. After the passage of the Kansas-Nebraska Act in 1854, Anthony Thornton joined the Democratic Party. Thornton supported Stephen A. Douglas and the controversial Nebraska Act, granting citizens in newly organized territories the right to decide whether to permit slavery. During the presidential campaign of 1856, he participated in a debate against Abraham Lincoln on the slavery issue.

A few years later, during the Civil War, the Kentucky-born Thornton did not join in the conflict against Confederate relatives and friends. "My birthplace was in the South," he explained. "My sympathies were, therefore, with the Southern people. I never had a wish for their success in the mad attempt to disrupt the Union, and put out the light of liberty forever. But I could not engage in the deadly strife with brothers and near relatives. Still, at no time during the terrible struggle, did I falter in my devotion to the union of the States."[429] In 1862, Thornton again was a member of the state constitutional convention, but voters failed to ratify the proposed document.[430] The following year, he became the Shelby County agent for bounties to war draftees. "He handled over $100,000," reported a county historian, "without being called upon to give any security whatever."[431]

Then in the fall of 1864, he won election to the U.S. Congress and served on the Committee on Claims and Bankruptcy, handling vast numbers of war claims. In 1866, he married a Shelby County teacher, Katherine H. Smith, daughter of Addison Smith of Springfield, Ohio. The couple became parents of one son and one daughter.[432]

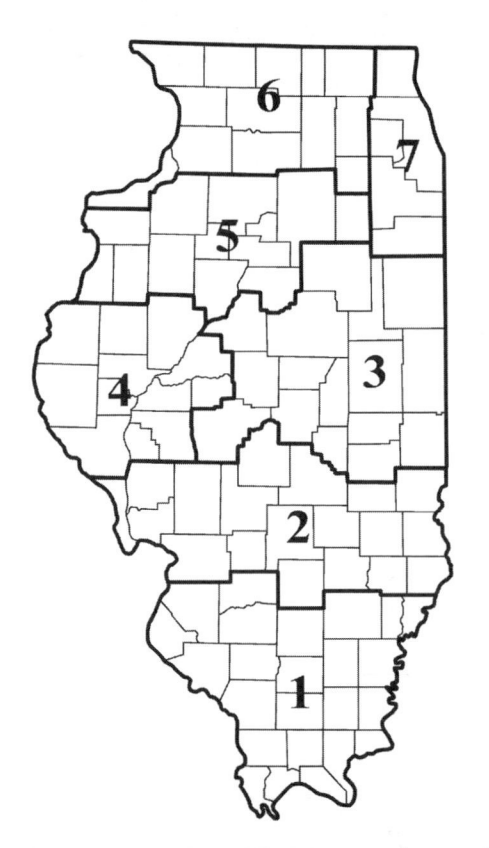

Declining re-nomination to the Congressional seat, Thornton returned to his law practice. The new 1870 Illinois Constitution increased the number of Supreme Court justices from three to seven, and other downstate Democrats insisted that candidates be selected by party convention. Thornton, however, restated his career-long belief that "a candidate for judge should be under no obligations to any party, and should not be chosen by a partisan convention."[433] In July 1870, he defeated Aaron B. Shaw by more than 8,000 votes to become a justice of the Illinois Supreme Court. "The judges were occupied during their entire time," he later observed. "Our practice was to read the abstracts and briefs, confer about the facts and law of the case, and then make a minute of our conclusions. All the judges were required to be present at these conferences. When the opinions were written, they were read in the presence of all the judges, and either approved or condemned."[434]

The 1870 Constitution divided Illinois into seven Supreme Court districts.
(Map courtesy of Illinois Supreme Court Historic Preservation Commission)

Biographer George D. Chafee further described Thornton's responsibilities: "While upon the bench he wrote one hundred and eighty-two decisions, reversed one hundred of these cases, and affirmed eighty-two. In addition to this he had to hear and join in considering an equal number of cases that each of the other judges wrote opinions upon."[435] Thornton heard approximately 2,000 cases during his short tenure.

In an 1870 case, *The People ex rel. Cutler v. Ford,* Thornton delivered the decision that removed George E. Ford from the roll of Illinois attorneys. Ford had made false representations regarding a land sale, "for the purpose of cheating the party out of his money," then refused to return the payment. "The defendant has neglected his duties, betrayed confidence, practiced deceit, and turned recreant to virtue," Thornton wrote. "He has not alone degraded himself—he has tarnished the fair fame of a profession always esteemed honorable."[436]

After three years on the Supreme Court, on May 31, 1873, Thornton resigned to return to private life. "The truth is," fellow attorney Usher Linder explained, "no man of his talents, who has a good practice as a lawyer as he had, can abandon it and forsake the pleasant walks of private and professional life for the insignificant compensation given to our Supreme Judges."[437]

Resuming his Shelbyville law practice, on January 4, 1877, Thornton and eighty-seven other lawyers met in Springfield and formed the Illinois State Bar Association. Elected its first president, Thornton served three successive terms.[438] In 1879, Thornton and his family moved from Shelbyville to nearby Decatur but returned to Shelbyville two years later. In 1895, Illinois Governor John P. Altgeld appointed Thornton to the State Board of Arbitration, his last public office. "Through his whole career as a lawyer," wrote Attorney General H. J. Hamlin, Thornton "always held to the view that the common law of this State was broad enough to reach most any question that could be presented for trial and decision."[439]

On September 10, 1904, eighty-nine-year-old Thornton died at his "Maple Hill" home in Shelbyville. Following an Episcopal service on the lawn of his home, he was interred in the family plot at Shelbyville's Glenwood Cemetery.[440]

JOHN M. SCOTT, 1870-1888

The first Illinois-born resident to become a member of the Illinois Supreme Court, John Milton Scott was born near Belleville, St. Clair County, on August 1, 1824, the son of Samuel and Nancy Briggs Scott. She was a Kaskaskia native, daughter of pioneer William B. Briggs, who arrived in Illinois with George Rogers Clark in 1778.[441] Young Scott attended public schools, supplemented by private instruction in English, Latin, and mathematics. He studied law in the Belleville office of William C. Kinney and future Illinois Governor William H. Bissell, then "among the most accomplished lawyers in the west," according to John M. Palmer.[442]

Scott was admitted to the Illinois bar in 1847 and moved to Bloomington, McLean County, the following year to establish his practice. "While an undeveloped section of the state," explained historian Frederic B. Crossley, members of its bar included Abraham Lincoln and Judge David Davis. "Scott soon became well known throughout the country and acquired a remunerative clientage."[443] Fellow attorney John Wickizer related one interaction between Scott and Lincoln in a court case in which the two lawyers were opposed to each other. The case lasted late in the evening before finally being submitted to the jury. Scott learned the next morning that he had lost the case. Lincoln saw him at the courthouse and asked what had become of it. Scott replied that "'it's gone to h—ll.' 'Oh, well,' said Mr. L., 'then you'll see it again.'"[444]

In 1849, Scott won election as county school commissioner in his first elective office. In 1852, he won election as judge of the McLean County Court, while also serving as Bloomington city attorney. In 1853, he married Charlotte A. Perry, daughter of Presbyterian minister David Perry, the first Bloomington city clerk. Both of their children died in infancy.[445] An ardent Whig, Scott became a member of the new Republican Party and, in 1856, won the party's nomination for state senator. "Although he made an active campaign," Crossley wrote, "and appeared as the first openly avowed anti-slavery man to deliver political speeches in his county, his district was overwhelmingly anti-republican," causing his defeat by a small majority to Joel S. Post of Decatur.[446]

Serving on the county court for ten years, Scott succeeded David Davis on the bench of the Eighth Judicial Circuit in 1862, after President Lincoln appointed Davis to the U.S. Supreme Court. Scott "held the circuit court," explained Palmer, "during the most troublous times of the civil war, and was called upon, in the discharge of his duties, to repress the violence of both sides, which he did with a fearlessness and courage worthy of the best age of the judiciary."[447]

With the 1870 Illinois Constitution increasing the number of Supreme Court justices from three to seven, Scott received the endorsement of the bar and in August 1870 won election for a nine-year term on the Supreme Court, representing the Third Judicial District.

"At the time Judge Scott became a member of the court," wrote Palmer, "he was in the prime and vigor of his life, and had acquired at the bar and on the bench a capacity for legal information which fitted him to deal intelligently and ably with all the questions which came before the court."[448]

In the 1874 *Lenfers et al. v. Henke et al.* case, Scott reversed the decree of the Jo Daviess Circuit Court. The case involved the dower interest of a widow in the mineral lands of her husband. That issue, according to Palmer, "had never been passed upon by any court, either in England or the United States." Judge Scott delivered the opinion "in a remarkably clear, original and well reasoned argument, showing his ability to deal with questions upon the broad ground of original thought, unaided by express authority."[449]

Scott won reelection to the Court in 1879 and served three terms as Chief Justice, in 1875, 1882, and 1886. He delivered the opinion in the 1884 *Ker v. People* case of Chicago bank cashier Frederick M. Ker, who had committed the crime of embezzlement and larceny, then fled to Peru. Since the Chilean military government possessed Peru at that time, American officials were unable to procure his return under any existing treaty. They arranged his forcible placement on a U.S. ship and return to Chicago. There, in the criminal court of Cook County, he unsuccessfully pleaded the illegality of his arrest and extradition.

Justice Scott rendered the opinion that sustained the criminal court decision. "Rejecting, as must be done," he wrote, "the erroneous assumption defendant had the right of asylum in Peru under the treaty between the two governments, and the argument for the defense is wholly without force. It is plain he had no right of asylum the law of either government would protect. The treaty as to the crime of larceny, with which defendant stood indicted, had provided no asylum that would secure him immunity from arrest for that crime in the country where he was domiciled."[450] The U.S. Supreme Court later upheld the opinion.[451]

Justice Scott's numerous decisions are included in volumes 54 through 125 of *Illinois Reports*, "a contribution to the body of judicial law," reported historian George W. Smith, "as important as the contribution of any member of the Supreme Court during the history of the state."[452] Scott's terms of service covered a formative period in the state "from which important litigation originated," including the park systems of Chicago, the railroad and warehouse commission, municipal taxation and real estate, and issues of corporation law. During that lengthy period, wrote Crossley, Scott "endeavored, as have too few judges, to interpret the law as a system of social and political philosophy and not as collection of arbitrary rules based on technical distinction."[453]

Retiring from the Court in 1888, Scott regularly attended annual meetings of the Illinois State Bar Association, participated in programs of the McLean County Historical Society, and wrote treatises on legal and local history.[454] In 1896, he wrote a history of the early days of the Illinois Supreme Court entitled *Supreme Court of Illinois, 1818, Its First Judges and Lawyers*. Scott died in his Bloomington home on January 21, 1898, and was buried in a granite mausoleum at Evergreen Cemetery.[455]

BENJAMIN R. SHELDON, 1870-1888

Benjamin Robbins Sheldon was born in Sandisfield, Berkshire County, Massachusetts, on April 15, 1811, to attorney Benjamin and Sarah Robbins Sheldon.[456] Young Benjamin attended college at Lenox and Stockbridge, and then at age nineteen, graduated from Williams College in Williamstown, Massachusetts. Completing legal studies at Yale University, he began his career in Pittsfield, Massachusetts. Sheldon soon relocated to northwestern Illinois, gaining admittance to the bar on January 12, 1835, and opening a practice in Hennepin in Putnam County. A few years later, he moved to the larger town of Galena, in Jo Daviess County.[457]

Under the 1848 Illinois Constitution, Sheldon won election as judge of the Sixth Judicial Circuit, known as the "Galena Circuit." During his term, the legislature created the Fourteenth Judicial Circuit, comprising Jo Daviess, Stephenson, and Winnebago Counties. Sheldon resigned his Sixth Circuit judgeship to become a candidate in the Fourteenth Circuit. "He made such a favorable impression upon the lawyers in the new counties in which he held court," reported an area newspaperman, "that the sentiment for returning him in the new district . . . was unanimous." His service on the Fourteenth Circuit began in 1851 and continued with terms in 1855, 1861, and 1867.[458]

In 1857, Sheldon presided over a notorious Winnebago County trial, in which Alfred Countryman, a married father of two infant children, stood accused of murdering Sheriff John F. Taylor. Arrested for cattle theft, Countryman had escaped from jail, and then shot and killed the pursuing Taylor. After capture by a group of local residents, a circuit court jury found Countryman guilty of murder and sentenced him to be hanged. "Your case is a sad instance of the mischief of the barbarous practice of carrying deadly weapons," Judge Sheldon admonished the defendant. "If you had not had that weapon of death concealed upon your person, you might have escaped a murderer's doom. In a well-ordered community like this, there is no need, under ordinary circumstances, to carry about such weapons of defence, and when carried they are much oftener used as the weapon of offence than of defence. The penalty of your high crime is the forfeit of your life—the terrible punishment the law inflicts not out of vengeance towards you, but for the protection of human life, to deter men from the commission of the crime of murder." According to a Winnebago County history, the hanging of twenty-seven-year-old Countryman was the area's first death penalty sentence.[459]

A staunch Republican, Sheldon won election to the expanded seven-member Illinois Supreme Court in 1870. The following year, he moved from Galena to reside with his sister in Rockford. "He did not care for popularity," wrote one biographer, "rather he did appear to shun it. He mingled but little with the people and yet those who knew him best say that he loved humanity. They say that he felt that in his career of jurisprudence it was his highest ambition to contribute to the public welfare and that he felt that the application of the law could not but benefit mankind."[460]

The *Petition of Alexander Ferrier* case, brought before the Supreme Court in 1882, provided one of Illinois's most significant cases regarding children's rights versus state responsibilities. Ferrier, a Chicago resident, filed a petition in the Cook County Court alleging that his neighbor's nine-year-old daughter, Winifred Breen, did not have proper parental care; she was truant from school and had "repeatedly been picked up by the police and others while wandering about the streets at night." The girl's father, a convicted felon, was presumed deceased, and her mother suffered periods of insanity, thus no longer a "fit person to have the custody of the child." By petitioning that she be committed to the Illinois Industrial School for Girls in South Evanston, Ferrier made the girl's home environment the subject of a public trial.

Industrial School president Helen Beveridge, wife of former Governor John L. Beveridge, testified in county court that the institution imposed "no more restraint upon their liberty than that imposed upon children in an ordinary family or institution of learning; that they are taught ordinary household duties, sewing, and the ordinary branches of English education." The young girl testified that "she was afraid of her mother; that she knew about this industrial school and wanted to go there."

Surprisingly, after the county court jury returned a verdict sending Breen to the Industrial School, her court-appointed attorney, Consider H. Willett, appealed the decision. Challenging the constitutionality of the state's reform school Industrial Schools Act, he played to fears of promoting dependency through state charity. In addition, he contended that not only was the state forcing Cook County to pay subsidies to private institutions but also that Chicago could become a center for child stealing. The possibility of a parent losing a child, he argued, undermined parental rights.[461]

In affirming the lower court's judgment, Justice Sheldon declared that the Industrial Schools Act procedures for hearing dependency cases contained such extensive due process protections that it did not violate the state Constitution. He defined the South Evanston Industrial School as truly a school, not a prison. "We perceive hardly any more restraint of liberty than is found in any well regulated school. Such a degree of restraint is essential in the proper education of a child, and it is in no just sense an infringement on the inherent and inalienable right to personal liberty so much dwelt upon in the argument."[462] With that decision, the Illinois Supreme Court began providing the framework for state care of dependent children.

In the 1874 *Peers v. Board of Education* case, Justice Sheldon delivered the judgment affirming a Madison County Circuit Court decision. Three years earlier, the Collinsville Board of Education had contracted with Wm. H. Phillips & Brother for the construction of a schoolhouse. The contractors ordered a quantity of lumber from J. W. Peers but did not pay him for it. Peers then sued the Board of Education. "We are of the opinion that the school directors had no authority to bind the school district by the acceptance of the order in question," Sheldon wrote. "In order to establish such a liability, the lumber should have been sold to the directors. But it was sold to Phillips & Bro. for the school house, and not to the directors. They never ordered or contracted with appellant for the lumber, and Phillips & Bro. alone are liable for it."[463]

In 1878, Sheldon affirmed a Cook County Circuit Court decision involving a Chicago man who died from injuries sustained when struck by a Chicago, Rock Island and Pacific Railroad Company yard engine. His widow, Johanna Austin, sued the railroad for negligence in preventing the accident. In *Austin, Admx. v. The Chicago, Rock Island and Pacific Railroad Company,* Sheldon ruled that by walking along the track the deceased "placed himself in the position of danger," then cited previous court decisions in similar cases. "To walk upon the track of a railroad, without looking in both directions to discover approaching engines or train, when the exercise of such precaution would discover either the one or the other, is such negligence as will preclude a recovery, unless the injury be willfully or wantonly inflicted by the defendant."[464]

During Sheldon's eighteen-year Supreme Court tenure, he served as Chief Justice in 1876, 1883, and 1887. Then in June 1888, at the close of his second term, Sheldon voluntarily retired from the bench.[465] The lifelong bachelor resumed the practice of law, traveled to Europe, wintered in California, and attended to various business enterprises. "Notwithstanding advancing years," wrote a contemporary attorney, "he was favored with mental vigor, so that he was able to keep abreast with the times and attend to the details of his business interests almost to the last."[466]

At the age of eighty-five, Sheldon died in Rockford on April 13, 1897. Following services at his North Court Street residence, he was buried in the now-named Greenwood Cemetery.[467] With an estate valued at $2 million, Sheldon provided generous bequests to Williams College, "expressive of lasting gratitude for the advantages which the college training had afforded him," and in Rockford to the Young Men's Christian Association and Rockford College.[468] "One of the ablest jurists who ever sat upon the supreme bench of Illinois," wrote John M. Palmer.[469]

WILLIAM K. MCALLISTER, 1870-1875

A New York native, William King McAllister was born in Salem, Washington County, on August 5, 1818. The son of well-to-do landowner William McAllister and his wife, Hannah Shoulder McAllister, young William remained on the family farm until entering college at the age of eighteen.[470] After discontinuing his formal education because of ill health, he prepared for the bar at the office of a Wayne County, New York, lawyer, and was licensed to practice law in 1844.

McAllister practiced law for ten years in Albion, New York, and during that period, wrote one biographer, "was brought in contact with the best legal minds in the State of New York, and this intercourse afforded him a discipline and an experience which must have been invaluable to him."[471] McAllister married Cordelia Andrews about 1840, and the couple would become parents of two sons and two daughters.[472] In 1854, the family moved to Chicago, where he soon secured a large clientele. As "an excellent lawyer and a citizen of high standing," wrote John M. Palmer, McAllister "possessed a logical, common-sense eloquence which, in his practice before juries, proved more successful than all the tricks of the insincere and more pretentious orator."[473]

John A. Jameson defeated him in his 1866 bid for the Cook County Superior Court, but in 1868, McAllister won election by an overwhelming vote as judge of the Recorder's Court of Chicago.[474] At that time, according to a biographer, "the city was overrun with garroters and criminals of all descriptions. Judge McAllister brought about a complete revolution. Toward the real criminal he was as inexorable as the law he administered, and they were sent to [the state prison at] Joliet in droves. But for the unfortunate victims of circumstances he had a compassion that at times encroached upon the law in the case. He knew the law, but he loved justice. Where his convictions were concerned he was a tower of strength."[475] In 1870, Independent candidate McAllister defeated Republican Charles Hitchcock for a seat on the Illinois Supreme Court—"a position of honor," according to historian Palmer, "more than of pecuniary reward."[476]

Among the cases during his five-year tenure, the 1872 *McElhanon et al. v. McElhanon, etc.* case involved whether a party to an action may appear in court as both plaintiff and defendant. In instituting a suit against James Hughes, John McElhanon was required to post a $500 bond, with James M. McElhanon as his security. John, averring that he was the assignee of Hughes in bankruptcy, brought debt upon that bond, against both himself and James as surety. "The case was brought to this court by writ of error," wrote McAllister in reversing the Washington County Circuit Court decision, "and the principal error assigned is the insufficiency of the declaration. Chitty says that 'it is an answer to an action that a party is legally interested in each side of the question. A party can not be both plaintiff and defendant in an action.' This rule will operate," McAllister concluded, "although the party appears on one side in his *personal* and on the other in his *official* character."[477]

In the 1874 case *Patten v. Patten*, Justice McAllister ruled on the validity of the 1861 Married Women's Property Act, which gave married women the right to possess the money that they brought into a marriage. Mary Patten had sued her husband Charles Patten to pay over the money that was due to her during the time they were married. The Cook County Circuit Court ruled in favor of Mary Patten, and Charles Patten took an appeal to the Illinois Supreme Court. Justice McAllister affirmed the lower court's judgment, writing that the 1861 Act abolished the common law practice of married women losing their estate to their husbands. Unless Mary Patten specifically gave her husband the agency to transact her business, then she had the right to recover.[478]

The 1870 Illinois Constitution had provided for the establishment of appellate courts after 1874, to relieve the four-year backlog of Supreme Court cases, "but delays and procrastination followed," reported Chicago Bar Association historian Herman Kogan.[479] The *Chicago Legal News* reported that "the dockets in the three grand divisions aggregate one thousand to twelve hundred cases per annum. Of these, not less than eight hundred require written opinions. Nearly one-half of the year is necessarily occupied in holding court and in consultation. The balance of the time must be devoted to writing opinions."[480] On the heels of Justice Anthony Thornton's resignation owing to the overworked and underpaid situation on the state's highest court, Justice McAllister followed suit. Herman Kogan added, the "intolerable situation confronting the overworked high court justices was dramatized in November 1875, when Justice William K. McAllister resigned his seat in protest against increasing burdens—the rise in cases stemming mainly from Chicago." Before his resignation, he had consented to run for, and subsequently won, election as Cook County Circuit Court Judge, with an annual salary of $7,000—a $2,000 increase from his Supreme Court pay.[481]

In June 1879, the Supreme Court justices appointed McAllister to the First District Appellate Court.[482] Reelected in 1885, he continued as both a circuit and an appellate judge for the remainder of his life. Praised by the *Chicago Times* as "a man of tender heart and the most generous sympathies," McAllister joined other Chicago judges and attorneys in unsuccessful clemency efforts for the eight men convicted of inciting violence at the 1886 riot in Haymarket Square.[483] On the circuit court, he heard the celebrated case against "the handsomest girl in Chicago," the wife of local gambling boss Michael C. McDonald. When Chicago police attempted to raid her family's living quarters in 1878, Mary McDonald responded with two pistol shots, one of which tore through an officer's coat sleeve. She was arrested and charged with the attempted murder of a police officer. After a studious examination of the case, McAllister found for the defendant, ruling that the police action, lacking sufficient warrant for entry into private quarters, constituted an unlawful invasion. That decision, reported historian Richard Lindberg, although immediately assailed by law-and-order advocates, "set an important precedent for years to come; one that would provide a modicum of protection to the gambling trust. The police had to be more circumspect in the proper execution of gambling raids."[484]

McAllister was "one of the greatest lawyers of Chicago," according to a city history. "His large number of printed opinions while upon the benches of the Supreme and Appellate Courts," reported legal historian James E. Babb in 1891, "have given him high rank for judicial ability."[485] His opinions were models of clarity and conciseness, and the "great controlling elements in his character were unflinching integrity, great love for suffering humanity and profound attachment to personal and constitutional liberty."[486]

On October 29, 1888, at age seventy, McAllister died suddenly at his Ravenswood home.[487] Funeral services were held at First Congregational Church of Ravenswood, followed by interment at Rosehill Cemetery in Chicago.[488]

JOHN SCHOLFIELD, 1873–1893

John Scholfield was born on his parents' farm near Martinsville, Clark County, Illinois, on August 1, 1834, the son of Pennsylvania Quaker Thomas Scholfield and his Ohio-born wife, Ruth Beauchamp Scholfield.[489] After his mother's death, sixteen-year-old Scholfield lived with an uncle, Jacob Anderson, in Martinsville, attending school and working in Anderson's stable and tavern on the National Road.

At age eighteen, Scholfield enrolled in a Congregational academy in nearby Marshall, intending to follow his mother's wish that he become a lawyer. He supported himself by performing chores for the county sheriff, Thomas Handy.[490] A biographer noted that Scholfield "never spent an idle hour in those days, joining the youngsters of his own age only in games of ball or other athletic sports, and returning immediately to his books. He had no time for loitering or gossip."[491]

In 1851, Scholfield accepted a teaching position while continuing his studies, and in 1854 sold a piece of land inherited from his uncle to finance the completion of his education. Two years later, at age twenty-two, he graduated from Louisville University Law School, returned to Marshall, and began the practice of law with James C. Robinson.[492]

Area resident Ralph H. Osborne, who studied law under Scholfield, recalled one of his cases. "A man came into the office and said, 'I wish to secure your service in a case I have.' From his statement it seemed through some technicality he would be able to secure forty acres of land belonging to two orphan children. Scholfield said, 'You old rascal! I never saw these children, but I am their attorney, and if you ever attempt to steal this land, I will do my best to send you to the "pen."' That was the last of that case."[493]

In 1856, Scholfield won election as State's Attorney for the ten-county Fourth Judicial Circuit. Spending three months each year riding the circuit by horseback or buggy, he gained the reputation of a fierce prosecutor, particularly in cases involving gambling, liquor sales to minors, and hog and horse theft.[494] He prosecuted a saloon keeper named Davis, who sold whiskey to a young girl for her "sad wreck" of a brother, after their father forbade Davis from selling liquor to the boy. Scholfield, recalled his former law student, portrayed Davis "as one of the worst criminals, a real scamp." Addressing the jury, Scholfield said, "Now men, you can only fine him, I plead with you to give him the full extent of the law. You cannot send him to the penitentiary. I do not want you to. He would corrupt the prisoners." According to Scholfield's student, the jurors, moved to tears, imposed "the full extent of the law, but was very inadequate then—a small fine."[495]

Illinois Supreme Court Justice Sidney Breese considered State's Attorney Scholfield "one of the most promising young lawyers in America. He has practiced regularly in our court in such cases as came up by appeal and writ of error from the

Wabash Courts, and I have had a good opportunity of estimating his ability, and know of no lawyer, old or young, that I can place above him."[496]

In December 1859, Scholfield married Emma J. Bartlett, daughter of John and Jane Archer Bartlett of Marshall. The Scholfields would become the parents of eight sons and two daughters. A Democrat, Scholfield had supported James Buchanan in the 1856 presidential contest, then Stephen A. Douglas in his 1858 Senate and 1860 presidential campaigns. Scholfield won election to the Illinois House of Representatives in 1860, and served one term. During that time, he also maintained a moderately large and constantly increasing law practice. In 1869, he was elected without opposition to represent Cumberland and Clark Counties in the Constitutional Convention.

In 1870, he became general solicitor for the Vandalia Railroad. Three years later, following the resignation of Supreme Court Justice Anthony Thornton, Scholfield defeated Judge A. N. Kingsbury of Hillsboro for the Court seat. "He is quite a young man to be elevated to so high a position," reported Usher Linder at the time, "but he is a bright and shining light in the legal world, and should he reach the age of fifty or sixty, will doubtless make himself a name that will deserve to fill a much larger place in our legal history than I can give to him at the present time."[497] Reelected without opposition in 1879 and 1888, Scholfield served as Chief Justice in 1877, 1884, and 1890.[498]

Among his most significant cases was the 1884 case, *Blake v. People for use of Caldwell,* involving the protection of agricultural lands against surplus water. In the Pike County Court, Judge Edward Doocy had rejected landowner M. M. Blake's challenge to his assessment for Sny Island Levee repairs, alleging as unconstitutional the state's 1879 Drainage Act. On appeal to the Supreme Court, Blake's attorneys contended that the Drainage Act embraced "more than one subject. Drains and ditches constitute a different subject from that of a levee." In upholding the Pike County Court, Scholfield confirmed the constitutionality of the 1879 law and approved the organization of sanitary districts within the state.[499]

The supreme court building in Mt. Vernon hosted terms from 1855 to 1897. (Image courtesy of James Dobrovolny Collection, Illinois Supreme Court Historic Preservation Commission)

In 1888, Scholfield declined recommendations by prominent jurists and legislators for nomination as Chief Justice of the United States Supreme Court. "The chief Justiceship of the United States is one of the most glittering prizes a man could be tempted with," he told a *Chicago Tribune* reporter at the time, "but I have not the courage to aspire to such a position, nor any confidence in my ability to meet its requirements. At any rate, my large family, their future and education, require that I should remain here."[500]

In failing health during the last few years of his life, Scholfield died on February 13, 1893, of peritonitis at his Marshall home.[501] He was buried in the Marshall City Cemetery. His "influence upon the jurisprudence of the State was very great," eulogized Supreme Court Justice Benjamin D. Magruder. "Many of his opinions are what are called among lawyers 'leading cases.' They illustrated and enforced principles which, at the time of his announcement of them, were new in the history of the court of which he was a member. Not a few of these cases have been since followed and used as the ground-work of numerous decisions, not only in Illinois, but in other States and in the Federal Supreme Court."[502]

ALFRED M. CRAIG, 1873-1900

An Illinois native of Scotch-Irish descent, Alfred M. Craig was born in Paris, Edgar County, on January 15, 1831. His father, David Craig of Philadelphia, Pennsylvania, had moved to Lexington, Kentucky, and married Minta Ramey, daughter of a friend of Daniel Boone and other frontiersmen. "Like thousands of the middle class in the southern States who were not slave holders and did not depend on the institution of slavery," wrote a family biographer, the Craigs moved from Kentucky, north to Illinois.[503]

Shortly after the birth of son Alfred, the Craigs relocated to a Fulton County farm near Canton, in the Military Tract. A millwright, David Craig built several mills along Spoon River, providing flour and feed for the early settlers. Alfred attended to farm chores while also attaining a common school education. He later enrolled in an academy in Canton and, in the fall of 1848, entered Knox College in Galesburg. Graduating with honors in 1853, he began the study of law in Lewistown under prominent attorney William C. Goudy.[504]

Admitted to the bar in 1854, Craig became a partner in the firm of Manning, Douglas & Craig, located in the Knox County seat of Knoxville. "By close application and determination he built up a large practice in a few years' time, riding the circuit as was customary in those days," wrote a Knox County historian. "It was not unusual for him to make the trip on horseback and on reaching Spoon river he would have to swim that stream astride his mount."[505]

In 1855, Craig succeeded Goudy as State's Attorney for the circuit comprising Knox, Henry, Mercer, Warren, Henderson, and Fulton Counties. Two years later in August 1857, Craig married Elizabeth Proctor Harvey, daughter of Curtis K. Harvey, a Galesburg attorney and delegate to the 1847 Illinois Constitutional Convention. The couple became parents of a daughter and three sons.[506]

In 1861, the Union Democrat Craig was elected Knox County judge, serving one four-year term. He unsuccessfully ran for state representative in 1868.[507] A year later, he served as a county delegate to the convention that framed the 1870 Constitution. "Judge Craig's familiarity with county affairs rendered him especially qualified to deal with township and county matters," explained his biographer. "He was on the committee of electoral and representative reform, along with Joseph Medill, O[rville]. H. Browning, Milton Hay and others; likewise a member of the committee on railroad corporations and on the committee on legislative apportionment."[508]

In the 1873 state Supreme Court election, Craig garnered support from Fifth Judicial District farmers to defeat decisively Chief Justice Charles B. Lawrence, who had delivered a Court decision that favored railroads against farmers.[509] Craig would be reelected in 1882 and 1891. During his twenty-seven-year tenure, he "never missed a single term of court nor failed to do his full share of the work of the court. During all that time he was recognized by his colleagues as an able coadjutor."[510]

The 1874 *Chase et al. v. Stephenson et al.* case involved whether school directors held the right to discriminate between white and black children by providing separate schools. The Supreme Court affirmed a McLean County Circuit Court ruling that, although a board of school directors had large and discretionary powers in the management and control of schools, the board had no power to make class distinctions, nor could it discriminate on the basis of color, race, or social position. "The conduct of the directors in this case," wrote Justice Craig, "in the attempt to keep and maintain a school solely to instruct three or four colored children of the district, when they can be accommodated at the school house with the other scholars of the district, can only be regarded as a fraud upon the tax-payers of the district, any one of whom has a right to interfere to prevent the public funds from being squandered in such a reckless, unauthorized manner."[511]

In the 1882 *People v. Wabash, St. Louis and Pacific Railway Company* case, Craig wrote the Court opinion that brought him national fame.[512] The case resulted from farmers' complaints that the Wabash railroad charged $65 for shipping a carload of grain from Gilman, Illinois, to New York; whereas, the charge on a carload from Peoria to New York, a longer distance, was only $39. In reversing the Ford County Circuit Court's decision favoring the railroad, Craig declared that "the State must be permitted to adopt such rules and regulations as may be necessary for the promotion of the general welfare of the people within its own jurisdiction."[513] The railroad appealed the case to the U.S. Supreme Court, which upheld Justice Craig's decision, firmly establishing that a state has power to regulate transportation within its borders.[514]

In 1898, he delivered the Court opinion in another railroad case, *Illinois Central Railroad v. The City of Chicago,* on appeal from the Cook County Superior Court. The Illinois Central, seeking to use submerged lands of Lake Michigan for railroad purposes, claimed its rights to the land under provisions of its charter.[515] Craig affirmed the superior court decision, declaring that the language of the charter "does not authorize the company to enter upon and take possession of any lands, waters and materials belonging to the State, as seems to be supposed, but the authority is to enter upon 'any lands, streams and materials.' The last clause of the section has an important bearing, showing that the authority conferred related to streams, and not to the lake." Craig's decision, according to one historian, "saved the lake for Chicago and kept it from being filled with roundhouses and other railroad structures and its announcement was hailed in Chicago with great pleasure."

In 1900, Craig ran for reelection but lost to Republican judge John P. Hand. Craig then became involved in area businesses. He owned several farms, became president and the largest stockholder of the Bank of Galesburg, and helped establish several private banks in neighboring communities. He served as a trustee of Ewing Female University in Knoxville, on the executive committee of the Knox College Board of Trustees, and reluctantly accepted appointment by Illinois Governor Charles S. Deneen to the State Tax Commission.[516]

Following the death of his wife, Elizabeth, in August 1904, Craig in July 1908 married Mary Davis of Galesburg. He died of pneumonia on September 6, 1911, and was buried in the family lot in the city's Hope Cemetery.[517] One of his sons, Charles Curtis Craig, won election to the Illinois Supreme Court in 1913.

T. LYLE DICKEY, 1875-1885

Theophilus Lyle Dickey, born on October 2, 1811, in Paris, Bourbon County, Kentucky, was the son of Presbyterian minister James Henry Dickey and his wife, Mary DePew Dickey. The family moved to Ross County, Ohio, where Mary died. Young Dickey then returned to Kentucky, residing on his grandmother's plantation. He attended schools in Ohio and Kentucky, studying Latin and mathematics at an academy, then graduated from Miami University in 1831.[518]

On December 6 of that year, at the age of twenty, Dickey married Juliet Evans, daughter of an area farmer.[519] The couple taught school for several years in Lebanon, Ohio, and Millersburg, Kentucky.[520] They became the parents of seven children. In the winter of 1834, the family moved to Macomb, Illinois, where he intended to farm. There he met Judge Cyrus H. Walker, uncle of future Illinois Supreme Court justice Pinkney H. Walker, who persuaded Dickey instead to study law.[521] Admitted to the bar in 1835, he practiced law in Macomb for nearly two years before the family moved to Rushville, where in addition to maintaining his law firm, he edited a Whig newspaper and speculated in real estate.[522]

"Overwhelmed with debt" from the Panic of 1837, the Dickeys moved to Ottawa in 1839, and he again practiced law and encouraged students in his office.[523] "You must know what the law is," as former pupil Judge Burton C. Cook later recalled Dickey's instruction, "and you must be able to render a reason."[524] In the first murder trial in Kendall County, Dickey defended Ansel Rider, a Georgetown carpenter who, in the process of arrest at his home for injuring a man during a tavern altercation, had shot to death another man, Charles McNeil. "McNeil was pretty full of whiskey when he arrived on the scene," recalled one witness, "making considerable noise and calling the posse a lot of cowards, and boasting that he could arrest Rider alone." Dickey, who intended to call the prisoner's seventeen-year-old son as a witness in his father's defense, took the boy to his Ottawa home, placed him in school there, and rehearsed his testimony and cross-examination. Aware that several jurors "had decided opinions of their own as to the extent of man's right to defend his own home and fireside against armed invasion by a howling mob," Dickey presented a strong defense. The "once awkward, diffident" son of the defendant "gave his testimony so promptly and so clearly that his testimony could not be shaken by the severe grilling on cross-examination." The adept Dickey secured Rider's acquittal, "and he went forth a free but ruined man, ostracized socially, bankrupt financially and morally depraved. On the 4th of December, 1843, Rider deeded his farm to Judge Dickey, and that was the price of his liberty."[525]

With the outbreak of the Mexican War in 1846, Dickey raised a company at Ottawa as part of the First Illinois Regiment, under Col. John J. Hardin. While serving in Texas,

Dickey became ill with dysentery and returned to Illinois. In 1848, he was elected judge of the Ninth Judicial Circuit, comprising LaSalle, Kendall, Kane, DeKalb, Ogle, Stark, Peoria, Marshall, and Putnam Counties, and for a time the county of Grundy. "For the next four years," Burton Cook remembered, "we rode the circuit, for the most part together, and shared in the experiences incident to a recently settled frontier country. In discharging the duties of a judge, he was noted for the clearness of his discrimination, and the facility with which he grasped the real points of a case, and the absolute integrity which guided his decisions."[526]

Resigning from the circuit court in 1852, Dickey opened a law office in Chicago while retaining his Ottawa residence, and eventually repaid his debts. Through his practice, he became friends with fellow attorney Abraham Lincoln. On Christmas Day 1855, Dickey's wife, Juliet, died. "My older brothers and sisters could get along very well," son Charles Dickey later recalled, "but my younger brothers and sisters and I were the problems. Lincoln and Judge [David] Davis knew this worried father. Lincoln offered to take me into his home in Springfield for the rest of the winter, and Judge Davis, then at Bloomington, offered to take my sister. I don't know what came up to prevent it, but my sister and I stayed that winter with Judge Davis. I always regretted the circumstances that deprived me of the great privilege of being a member of the Lincoln household even for such a short period of time."[527]

As the 1856 Whig nominee for Congress from the Third Congressional District, Dickey accepted advice from David Davis and withdrew from the race because Davis "feared defeat for his old-time friend." The candidate of the new Republican Party, Owen Lovejoy, an abolitionist Congregational minister, won by a 6,000-vote plurality over the Democratic candidate.[528] Two years later, Dickey became an ardent Democrat, campaigning for Stephen A. Douglas in the senatorial contest with Lincoln. In 1860, Dickey realized that Douglas could not win the presidential election and supported the candidacy of his friend Lincoln.

At the beginning of the Civil War, Dickey raised and became the colonel of the Fourth Illinois Cavalry. Joining General Ulysses S. Grant at Cairo in December 1861, Dickey participated in the capture of Fort Henry, led the advance at Fort Donelson, and took part in the battle of Shiloh, with two of his sons and a son-in-law, General William H. L. Wallace, who died in that conflict.[529] Later in 1862, Dickey became Chief of Cavalry under Grant, commanding four brigades of cavalry. "At one time," wrote a biographer, Dickey "selected six hundred men and engaged in an extensive and successful raid through a region of country swarming with confederate soldiers, and returned safely and without losing a man."[530]

Because of ill health, Dickey resigned his military command in 1863 and returned to Ottawa, where he established a law firm with John B. Rice. Dickey's son Sirus, with whom he had practiced prior to the war, was killed in the April 1864 battle at Red River.[531]

Dickey won the 1866 Democratic nomination for Congressman-at-Large, but lost to the Republican nominee, Civil War general John A. Logan. Dickey then accepted appointment as Assistant U.S. Attorney General, in charge of government suits in the Court of Claims and the U.S. Supreme Court. Again in ill health, he resigned the federal position and recuperated in Florida. Forming a partnership in Ottawa with Henry Boyle and Samuel Richolson, Dickey in 1871 married Beulah Risley Hirst of Maryland.[532] In 1874, the couple moved to Chicago, where he resumed his law practice and was appointed corporation counsel for the city.[533]

In 1875, Dickey won election to fill the Illinois Supreme Court vacancy created by the resignation of William K. McAllister. Dickey "gained a distinct popularity and uniform respect," wrote John M. Palmer. "Possessed of wonderful memory, and with a remarkable power of analysis, his judgments were always received with profound consideration, and his opinions on important cases have generally been sustained."[534]

Reelected in 1879, he succeeded Pinkney Walker as Chief Justice in 1880.[535] In one of the significant cases of the period, *Parker v. People,* Dickey dissented from Walker's 1884 opinion regarding the constitutionality of an 1879 law that provided "for the free passage of fish in the waters of this State." Michael C. Parker, who owned a dam across the Fox River in Kendall County, was prosecuted under the new law for "neglect or refusal to comply with" the requirement that he construct suitable fishways, "in order that the free passage of fish up or down or through such waters may not be obstructed." Parker's attorneys contended that his private dam had been built under a state charter some fifty years earlier and thus not subject to the new legislation.

After the Kendall County Circuit Court found Parker guilty, the Supreme Court heard the case and affirmed the lower court. In a fourteen-page dissent, Justice Dickey argued against "the police powers" of government. "The provision of our constitution protecting private property from being taken or damaged without just compensation is *unconditional.*"[536] Illinois court historian James E. Babb considered Dickey's dissent as "indicative of his industry, learning, logic, and skillful powers of discussion."[537]

In *Peck et al. v. Herrington,* Dickey again dissented from the other justices, on a property-rights appeal from the Kane County Circuit Court regarding surface-water drainage. Without explanation, he wrote, "I can not concur in this decision," disagreeing with the Court ruling reversing the circuit court that an owner could tile drain his land, even if it increased the flow of water on subservient land. That decision, according to court historian Ralph M. Snyder, enabled Illinois farmers to convert lowland prairie acreage into choice agricultural land.[538]

Dickey served on the Supreme Court until the summer of 1885, when he again became seriously ill. He and his wife traveled to Atlantic City, New Jersey, where he hoped to recuperate by rest and inhaling the sea breezes. His strength did not return, however, and he died there on July 22, 1885.

Dickey's remains were brought by train from Atlantic City to Ottawa, there conveyed to the Supreme Court Building. His swords from the Mexican and Civil Wars lay crossed on his coffin.[539] "His funeral was probably the most elaborate ever held in Ottawa," wrote one historian. "Special cars brought friends, soldiers, justices and others prominent in public life. His death preceded that of General Grant by one day. There was genuine mourning in Ottawa because of the deaths of these two great men who had served together."[540] Following Episcopal services Dickey was interred in the family cemetery, on a north bluff overlooking Ottawa.[541]

DAVID J. BAKER, 1878-1879, 1888-1897

A member of a prominent southern Illinois family, David Jewett Baker was born in Kaskaskia on November 20, 1834, the third son of Connecticut native David Jewett Baker and Sarah Fairchild Baker. The couple had moved to Kaskaskia in 1819, where the senior Baker served a long tenure as Probate Judge of Randolph County, "the equal of any contemporary lawyer at the Illinois Bar," according to court historian James E. Babb.[542]

Strongly opposed to the introduction of slavery into the state, the elder Baker engaged in a physical confrontation with the pro-slavery Supreme Court Chief Justice Thomas Reynolds on a Kaskaskia street in 1824.[543] According to a county historian, Baker sustained a bludgeon mark during the altercation that remained "to his dying day."[544] In late 1830, Governor Ninian Edwards named Baker to fill the unexpired term of deceased U.S. Senator John McLean. Returning to Illinois, Baker was United States District Attorney at the time of his son's birth.[545]

Acquiring an early education at area schools, the younger Baker graduated with honors in 1854 from Shurtleff College in Alton, and then studied law under his father's tutelage. In 1855, his brother Edward L. Baker, also an attorney and publisher of the *Alton Daily Telegraph*, purchased the *Illinois State Journal*, a Springfield newspaper strongly identified with the new Republican Party.[546]

David Baker, after admittance to the Illinois bar in 1856, began his practice in Alton. "From the beginning of his career," reported one historian, "he took an active part in politics, and with the example of his illustrious father before him was a vigorous opponent of slavery."[547] In 1856, Baker moved to Cairo, where he nurtured an extensive practice, in partnership with future Supreme Court justice John H. Mulkey, then with future circuit court judge William H. Green. Baker also served several terms as alderman and one term each as city attorney and mayor.[548] In July 1864, he married Sarah Elizabeth White, daughter of Captain John C. White of Cairo. The Bakers became the parents of two sons and three daughters.[549]

In March 1869, the Republican Baker won election as judge for the Nineteenth Judicial Circuit, comprising Alexander, Pulaski, Massac, and Pope Counties. In accordance with the 1870 Illinois Constitution, the General Assembly divided the state into twenty-six circuits, and Baker was elected without opposition as judge of the Twenty-sixth Judicial Circuit.[550] On July 9, 1878, his friend and Illinois Governor Shelby M. Cullom named Baker to fill the unexpired Supreme Court term of deceased justice Sidney Breese.

Among Baker's opinions during that yearlong tenure, *Norton et al. v. Richmond* concerned liability for grain purchases. Thomas Richmond, who bought and sold grain through Norton & Company, had refused to accept liability for purchases and sales made in his absence by his son Holland Richmond that resulted in heavy losses. After witnesses presented conflicting testimony as to whether the father had instructed his son to make those transactions, a Cook County Circuit Court jury found for Thomas Richmond. "The testimony of Holland Richmond tended to confirm that of his father," Baker wrote in affirming the Cook County decision. "Some of the circumstances in proof were corroborative of the statements of [Norton agent Charles E.] Hill, and some corroborative of those of Thomas Richmond. The jury were the judges of the fact, and it was their province to determine the degree of weight to be given the testimony of each witness. We see no sufficient reason for disturbing the verdict."[551]

Baker served in the Supreme Court until the election of John Mulkey in 1879. Later that year, the Supreme Court justices appointed Baker to the Fourth District Appellate Court, and to the Second Judicial District in 1882.[552] "He was thoroughly impartial and was extremely anxious to reach the correct conclusion," recalled fellow Appellate justice Oliver A. Harker. "I have seen judges who would feel terribly humiliated in changing, during trial, a ruling previously made, and so would prefer to let an error stand and escape the humiliation by subsequently setting aside a verdict on some other ground. Not so with Baker; I have seen him in a hotly contested trial, with the court room full of people[,] call a halt, reverse a previous ruling and give reasons for doing so. Is it any wonder then that he was with lawyers the most popular circuit judge of his day and was held in rare esteem by the people at large?"[553]

In 1885, Baker won the election to succeed Mulkey on the Supreme Court. "It is said," reported the *Chicago Legal News,* that when Baker "went upon the bench of the Supreme Court there was one important case held over in which the judges were three to three; that the chief justice said, 'Judge Baker, take the papers and write the opinion, for as you go, so goes the case, as we are three and three'; and that when he wrote the opinion it was so logical, clear and convincing that there was not a dissent, but all the judges concurred."[554]

Baker served as Chief Justice from June 1893 to June 1894. In January 1894, he delivered the majority opinion in *People ex rel. Bradley v. State Reformatory.* The case involved the imprisonment of two young men, one eighteen years of age and the other aged twenty, both convicted of burglary and larceny. Under provisions of the 1891 Illinois State Reformatory Act, the Peoria County Circuit Court jury had returned the guilty verdicts but did not determine the punishment or the term of imprisonment. A judge of the circuit court ordered the men confined in the Illinois State Reformatory at Pontiac "for and during a term of commitment to be terminated" by the Reformatory's board of managers. Lida Bradley, a relative of one of the convicted men, petitioned for a writ of habeas corpus and for the court to rule on the constitutionality of such indeterminate imprisonment.

"An adult convicted of burglary would be sentenced to the penitentiary," Baker wrote in dismissing the writ, "and to either solitary confinement or hard labor therein, and the statutes which consign him to such punishment must be regarded as highly penal":

> A minor, however, instead of being sentenced to solitary confinement or hard labor in a penitentiary, is committed to the State reformatory. The general scope and humane and benign purpose of the statute establishing the reformatory are clearly indicated by the following provisions found in section 6: "It shall be the duty of the managers to provide for the thorough training of each and every inmate in the common branches of an English education; also in such trade or handicraft as will enable him, upon his release, to earn his own support. For this purpose said managers shall establish and maintain common schools and trade schools in said reformatory."[555]

Baker concluded that there was no evidence that the boys were wrongfully imprisoned nor deprived of their liberty while at the reformatory.

Narrowly defeated for reelection in 1897 by Democratic candidate Carroll Boggs, Baker and his wife moved from Cairo to Chicago, where he engaged in general practice with his son John W. Baker.[556] His other son, Captain David J. Baker, was serving with the Twelth U.S. Infantry in the Philippines.[557]

On March 13, 1899, the sixty-three-year-old David Baker died suddenly of a heart attack at his Boyce Building office in downtown Chicago.[558] Following services at the Church of the Redeemer, Baker was buried in Mount Greenwood Cemetery in Chicago.[559] "He was considered one of the brightest lights of the Supreme Court, and his opinion was always respected by his colleagues," eulogized the *Chicago Tribune*. "His decisions, while on the Supreme Bench, had won for him the respect of scores of Chicago lawyers, and his office was daily visited by those wishing opinions on important cases, or interpretation of fine points in law."[560]

JOHN H. MULKEY, 1879-1888

Born in Monroe County, Kentucky, on May 24, 1824, of Scotch-Irish ancestry, John H. Mulkey was the second of nine children of Dr. Isaac and Abigail Ragen Mulkey. In his youth, John learned to become a tailor in Harrodsburg, Kentucky, and attended Bacon College in Hopkinsville. At the age of twenty-one, he moved to southern Illinois and accepted a teaching position in Benton. He also farmed, traded in stock, and operated a general store in Franklin County, then later in Blairsville, Williamson County.[561]

On March 23, 1846, in Benton, Mulkey married Margaret Cantrell, and they became the parents of eight children. During the Mexican War, he volunteered as a private in Company K, Second Illinois Regiment, and was later promoted to second lieutenant. He served from July 1847 to the end of the war the following July. Returning to Illinois, Mulkey resumed teaching, farmed 160 acres near Benton, and again became a merchant. "His career in this direction was brought to a sudden close, however, by an unfortunate adventure," reported a county historian. "He invested largely in lumber (hoop poles), loaded them on a flat-boat and started for the market, but danger was ahead of him. His craft struck a snag, and down into the waters of the Mississippi went boat, hoop poles, and all of the Judge's earthly effects, and left him in a seriously damaged condition; in fact, he was a 'busted merchant.'"[562]

About 1851, Mulkey began studying law, using books borrowed from a young Marion attorney and future judge, William J. Allen. The two men became lifelong friends and for many years partnered in practice. Admitted to the bar in 1853, Mulkey moved with his family to De Soto, Jackson County; he then practiced for about a year in Cairo before relocating to DuQuoin.[563]

During the Civil War, Mulkey was an outspoken critic of the Lincoln administration. Mulkey was one of thousands who were arbitrarily arrested and detained without charges. Mulkey was eventually released but not without the reputation of being involved in "disloyal activities."[564]

When Mulkey won election in 1864 as a judge in the Third Judicial Circuit, the family moved to Jonesboro, the central location in the circuit. After serving on that bench for less than a year, he and his family returned to Cairo, where he formed a partnership with future Supreme Court justice David J. Baker. Mulkey continued to practice in southern Illinois courts and served from 1861 to 1867 as Judge of the Court of Common Pleas in Cairo.

Following the death of his wife, Margaret, on June 2, 1871, Mulkey married Kate House of Metropolis on September 25, 1873. They became the parents of two daughters.[565] During that time, Mulkey served as senior member of the firm Mulkey, Linegar and Lansden.[566]

On June 2, 1879, the Democrat Mulkey won election to a nine-year term on the Illinois Supreme Court, succeeding David J. Baker. "The quality which enabled Justice Mulkey to succeed both at the bar and on the bench to a degree rarely ever attained by lawyers or judges," explained fellow justice Alonzo K. Vickers, "was his power to see further and deeper into abstract and close legal questions than others who may justly be called eminent jurists. He saw everything as it actually was. This quality might be properly called his mental reach or power of penetration, and was combined with a careful and painstaking mastery of every detail of fact connected with the case in hand; a power of analysis and a force of reasoning that was irresistible and convincing."[567]

Mulkey displayed his legal talent in the 1882 *County of McLean v. Humphreys* case, involving a seven-year-old dependent, Mary E. Stoner. The McLean County Circuit Court had awarded Laura B. Humphreys financial reimbursement from the county for payment to the Industrial School for Girls in South Evanston after the court sent Stoner to the school by decree. County officials appealed the decision, arguing as unconstitutional the 1879 act "to aid industrial schools for girls," for it not only compelled "counties to make donations" to private or sectarian organizations but also "deprived an unfortunate girl of her liberty."

In delivering the Supreme Court opinion, Mulkey forcefully affirmed the circuit court decision. "It is the unquestioned right and imperative duty of every enlightened government," he wrote, "in its character of *parens patriæ*, to protect and provide

The new state capitol building, completed in 1878, housed the Supreme Court until 1907. (Image courtesy of Abraham Lincoln Presidential Library and Museum)

for the comfort and well-being of such of its citizens as, by reason of infancy, defective understanding, or other misfortune or infirmity, are unable to take care of themselves."[568] That decision "cleared the way for the subsidy system to take root in Illinois," wrote legal historian David S. Tanenhaus. Mulkey's "powerful statement granted the state both the power as well as the responsibility to act as a parent" in order to safeguard dependent children in the state.[569]

Another of Mulkey's decisions, in the 1885 *Fort Dearborn Lodge v. Klein et al.* case was "one of the ablest legal opinions to be found in the history of our jurisprudence."[570] Fort Dearborn Lodge 214, an Independent Order of Odd Fellows, appealed a First District Appellate Court decision that a property owner could not enter that property "against the will of the occupant," Albert Klein. Chief Justice Mulkey delivered the opinion reversing the appellate court. "The paramount owner of a tract of land," Mulkey explained, "having a present right of immediate possession, may enter the same in a peaceable manner, though occupied by another, and he will not, by reason of such entry, become a trespasser."[571] Mulkey's opinion in "discussing the plea of *liberium tenementum* and incidentally the law of seisin and disseisin, has secured him many compliments."[572] Over the decades, attorneys have cited the decision in trespass cases throughout the nation.

Justice Benjamin D. Magruder described Mulkey's "vein of quiet humor" that often relieved tedium in the court. "In a proceeding where an attorney was charged with misappropriating property, and excused his doing by insisting that he was acting merely as trustee, and not as attorney, Judge Mulkey in a dissenting opinion said: 'This defense so forcibly reminds me of the old story of the profane bishop, who had the good fortune to be a duke also, I cannot refrain from telling it. An acquaintance, who happened to overhear him using profane language, asked him how it was that he, being a bishop, could be guilty of swearing. 'Ah, my friend,' replied his reverence, 'I swear as a duke, and not as a bishop.' 'But,' retorts the other, 'when the devil comes to get the duke, what will become of the bishop?'"[573]

Mulkey and the other justices unanimously ruled in the 1887 *Spies et al. v. People* murder-conviction appeal by the Haymarket Riot defendants. He added a statement, however, to Justice Magruder's formal opinion affirming the Cook County Criminal Court decision. "While I concur in the conclusion reached," Mulkey wrote, "I do not wish to be understood as holding that the record is free from error, for I do not think it is. I am nevertheless of opinion that none of the errors complained of are of so serious a character as to require a reversal of the judgment. In view of the number of defendants on trial, the great length of time it was in progress, the vast amount of testimony offered and passed upon by the court, and the almost numberless rulings the court was required to make, the wonder with me is, that the errors were not more numerous and more serious than they are."[574]

The Mulkeys had moved in 1884 from Cairo to Metropolis, on the Ohio River. Four years later, in June 1888, at the age of sixty-four, he retired from the Supreme Court. "Although upon the supreme bench but nine years," reported attorney Oliver A. Harker, Mulkey "left a wonderful record. No judge who ever sat in the bench could touch the very heart and soul of a lawsuit with more unerring certainty."[575]

A member of the Cambellite church in his youth, Mulkey professed to agnosticism as an adult. "But, strange to say," recalled a fellow judge, "after leaving this bench he took but little, if any, interest in the law, but devoted quite all his time to the subject of religion. He became a most ardent Roman Catholic and spent a great part of his time in religious devotion."[576]

In his final years, Mulkey lived as an invalid, the result of a fall while disembarking from a train in St. Louis. He died at his home on July 9, 1905. Following services at St. Rose Catholic Church, he was buried in the Metropolis Masonic Cemetery.[577]

DAMON G. TUNNICLIFF, 1885

A native of Herkimer County, New York, Damon George Tunnicliff was born on August 20, 1829, the son of George and Marinda Tilden Tunnicliff. Damon helped on the family farm until the age of fifteen, when he began working in an uncle's store in Ohio.[578] In 1849, Tunnicliff moved to Vermont in Fulton County, Illinois, where he operated his own general store. "His youth was almost devoid of opportunities for mental training," explained one biographer, "and the finished culture and broad, comprehensive grasp and power of minute analysis which made him a conspicuous and commanding figure in the forensic arena of Illinois, were the self-acquired attainments of his mature years."[579]

Eager for a professional career, Tunnicliff began legal studies in Rushville in 1853 under future Supreme Court Justice Pinkney H. Walker, and then in Chicago under Robert S. Blackwell. Admitted to the bar after only six months of study, Tunnicliff practiced with Blackwell and another leading Chicago attorney, Charles B. Beckwith.[580]

Moving to Macomb, McDonough County, in 1854, Tunnicliff partnered initially with Cyrus Walker, "one of the best criminal lawyers in the west," and Chauncey L. Higbee.[581] Retained in 1854 as counsel for the Northern Cross Railroad Company, he continued as legal adviser to the firm, which became the Chicago, Burlington & Quincy Railway Company, for the remainder of his life. After Higbee won an election as circuit judge, the firm dissolved in 1861, and Tunnicliff had a solo practice for nearly four years. In 1865, he began a ten-year partnership with Asa A. Matteson.[582]

"During these years of practice," observed a local historian, Tunnicliff "had been steadily developing in intellectual strength, broadening in scope and growing in legal knowledge and acumen, until he had attained an eminent position as the undisputed leader of the McDonough County Bar."[583] On January 11, 1855, he married Mary E. Bailey of Macomb, daughter of Colonel W. W. Bailey, an early McDonough County settler. The Tunnicliffs became the parents of six children before Mary's death in 1865.[584]

A "most intense" Republican and anti-slavery advocate, Tunnicliff served as an alternate delegate to the 1860 national convention that nominated Abraham Lincoln for the presidency. Tunnicliff was also an elector on the 1868 Ulysses S. Grant presidential ticket and a delegate to the 1876 convention that nominated Rutherford B. Hayes.

On November 4, 1868, Tunnicliff married Sarah A. Bacon, daughter of Larkin C. Bacon, and they became the parents of three daughters.[585] In 1874, he defended a notorious western Illinois outlaw, Ed Maxwell, on burglary and horse-stealing charges. In a victory for the defense, the court convicted Maxwell only of burglary and sentenced him to a year in the state penitentiary. "Most people of that era," explained historian John E. Hallwas, "wanted severe punishment for theft crimes, to instill fear in those socially marginal men, like Ed Maxwell, that the law was designed to control."[586]

When Tunnicliff's law partner, Matteson, moved to Galesburg in 1875, Tunnicliff practiced alone again until 1879, when he associated with James H. Baker, specializing in general law and collections. On February 16, 1885, Governor Richard Oglesby appointed Tunnicliff an associate justice of the Illinois Supreme Court, filling the unexpired term of his mentor, the deceased Pinkney Walker. *The New York Times* noted the appointment, describing Tunnicliff "as one of the ablest and most finished lawyers in the western part of the State."[587]

Tunnicliff served in the position for only five months and delivered few of the Court's opinions. He affirmed the Cook County Superior Court in *Gordon et al. v. Reynolds,* a case in which Charles Gordon conveyed real and personal property to his son William Gordon, in an attempt to "defeat, hinder and delay" the collection of a debt. Determining the transaction as "fraudulent," Tunnicliff wrote that appellee Frank P. Reynolds was "entitled to have the conveyance from Charles Gordon to William Gordon of the real and personal property set aside" in order for Reynolds to recover the debt.[588]

Tunnicliff ran for election for his own seat, but in a district that favored Democrats, the Republican Tunnicliff lost to Simeon P. Shope. After leaving the bench, he returned to his law practice, initially with son George, but his role was to act primarily as a consultant in cases. When his son George left the firm, Lawrence Y. Sherman became a partner and practiced with Tunnicliff. Sherman later had a significant political career as Illinois's lieutenant governor and a U.S. senator, helping to keep the United States out of the League of Nations after World War I.[589]

Tunnicliff and his family entertained at their spacious Macomb home, "Grove."[590] Following a brief illness, the seventy-two-year-old Damon Tunnicliff died at the residence on December 20, 1901. He was buried in the city's Oakwood Cemetery.[591]

SIMEON P. SHOPE, 1885-1894

Simeon Peter Shope was born in Akron, Ohio, on December 3, 1834, the son of Simeon P. and Linda Richmond Shope.[592] The family resided for two years in Michigan before moving to Illinois, settling first in Marseilles, then in Ottawa, and eventually on a farm near Metamora.

Young Simeon helped with chores, attended public schools, and enrolled briefly at Eureka College. At the age of fifteen, he began teaching school while also studying law in Peoria under former Illinois Supreme Court justice Norman H. Purple. In 1857, Shope married Sarah M. Jones, daughter of Wesley and Eliza Jones of Fulton County. They became the parents of four children, only two of whom would survive to adulthood.[593]

Admitted to the bar in 1858, Shope practiced briefly in Metamora before relocating to Lewistown, where he entered a partnership with Colonel Lewis W. Ross. Active in Democratic politics, Shope won election as a representative to the Illinois General Assembly in 1862. After serving one term, he returned to his practice while also attending state and local political conventions. He was a member of the national Democratic conventions that nominated Horace Greeley and Grover Cleveland for the presidency.[594]

"During the many political campaigns," recalled one observer, "he was in constant demand by his party, and there is not an old school house in the county whose walls has not rung with his impassioned and silver tongued oratory, and there are many living who tell of some of his remarkable pleadings as lawyer in the old court house."[595]

Shope also gained a reputation as an amusing storyteller, particularly tales concerning his friend and fellow attorney Abraham Lincoln. One of Shope's courtroom yarns involved Welcome Brown, a "shiftless, careless sort of lawyer. When Brown leaned over to speak to Shope, everybody in the room could see a big hole in the seat of his trousers. A young law student came up to Lincoln and asked him to subscribe for a new pair of pants for Brown. Lincoln looked, then wrote, 'I cheerfully contribute to the end in view, 25 cents.'"[596]

In 1871, Shope partnered with John A. Gray, and a few years later Harry M. Waggoner joined the partnership. "It was a strong firm," reported the local newspaper, "and enjoyed the patronage of a large clientele." Six years later, in 1877, Shope filled the unexpired term of Sixth Judicial Circuit Judge Joseph Sibley, then won election to the position. "His legal attainments," according to the newspaper, "his keen mind, his reputation as a judge, and his high character as a man and a citizen placed him at the head of his profession."[597] By 1879, according to one writer, Shope, "who had started in life with but little means," had accumulated "300 acres of fine farm land, 20 lots in Lewistown and a fine residence." His wife died on January 4, 1882.[598]

Shope continued as a circuit court judge until 1885, when he won election to the Illinois Supreme Court, defeating Damon G. Tunnicliff. Shope "possesses a clear, comprehensive, analytical mind, which, together with his thorough training and his retentive memory," wrote a biographer in 1890, "renders him peculiarly fitted for the honorable and useful office whose duties he is so ably discharging."[599]

Shope served as Chief Justice in 1889–1890, during which time he delivered the opinion in the slander case of *McLaughlin v. Fisher*. Daniel McLaughlin, president of the Illinois Miners' Protective Association, had brought the case in the Sangamon County Circuit Court, accusing Fisher of "contriving and wickedly and maliciously intending to injure the plaintiff in his good name and reputation," by "keeping up an agitation" among central and southern Illinois miners, "so that the mine owners of northern Illinois can get all the trade."

Shope affirmed the Third District Appellate Court decision on behalf of defendant Frank R. Fisher, ruling that "words not in themselves actionable can not be rendered so by an innuendo, without a prefatory averment of extrinsic facts which make them slanderous." He concluded, "It is not shown, in any way, that if the plaintiff had been guilty as charged in the language alleged to have been used by the defendant, it would have operated to the prejudice of the association or of the persons engaged in mining, or that the use of the language could have operated to the prejudice of the plaintiff."[600]

In the 1893 personal injury suit *Gartside Coal Company v. Turk,* Shope upheld the Fourth District Appellate Court decision on behalf of company employee William Turk, whose arm became so mangled in machine cog "that amputation became necessary." Gartside's attorneys maintained that a fellow employee, not the company, was responsible for the accident. "Appellee had been told by the superintendent," noted Shope, "that the workmen there would direct him what to do. . . . The injury to appellee arose, directly and proximately, from his obedience to the order and direction of the person in charge."[601]

Declining nomination for another term on the Supreme Court, Shope moved to Chicago to reside with his daughter. He established Shope, Mathis, Barrett & Rogers, with "commodious and pleasant" offices in the Title & Trust Company building. Shope served as general attorney for the Suburban Railway and several other major companies, and became a recognized authority on corporation law.[602] "Simeon P. Shope is to-day accounted one of the ablest members of the Cook county bar," attorney John M. Palmer wrote in 1899, "and was one of the best judges who ever occupied a seat upon the bench of Illinois."[603]

On January 23, 1920, Shope succumbed in Lake View Hospital from injuries he received several weeks earlier when struck by a passing automobile as he stepped onto a curb. "Up to that time," reported the Lewistown newspaper, "although 85 years of age he had been able to go down daily to his law offices in the city and was in his usual health."[604] Following services in Chicago and Lewistown, he was buried in the family lot at Lewistown's Oak Hill Cemetery.[605]

BENJAMIN D. MAGRUDER, 1885-1906

A Southerner who supported the Union during the Civil War, Benjamin Drake Magruder was born on a plantation near Natchez, Mississippi, on September 27, 1838. The family of his mother, Mary Bangs Magruder, resided in the vicinity of New Haven, Connecticut. His father, Professor W. H. N. Magruder, who graduated from Wesleyan University in Middletown, Connecticut, operated a private academy in Baton Rouge, Louisiana.[606]

At the age of fourteen, Magruder entered Yale University and graduated fourth in his class just before his eighteenth birthday.[607] His classmates included future United States Supreme Court justices David J. Brewer and Henry B. Brown.[608] Magruder taught at his father's academy for three years while studying law. He graduated as valedictorian of the 1859 University of Louisiana Law School, and opened a law office in Memphis, Tennessee. A year later, he began a two-year position as Master of Chancery.[609]

With the outbreak of the Civil War in 1861, Magruder moved to Chicago, forming a partnership with George F. Bailey under the firm name Bailey & Magruder. "While ever radically loyal" to the Union, wrote a Magruder biographer, "he refrained from enlisting or taking part in political discussions during the war, many members of his immediate family being in the Confederate service."[610] Later he partnered in Magruder & Norton, Magruder & Kerr, and Hervey, Galt & Magruder.[611]

On June 15, 1864, Magruder married Julia M. Latham of Springfield, and they became the parents of a son and a daughter. Four years later, he won appointment to succeed William Mather as Master in Chancery for the Superior Court of Cook County and held the position for fifteen years while also maintaining a large general practice. "Not only did he take advanced rank in his profession and secure a place among the foremost at the bar," remembered Chicago attorney Nathaniel M. Jones, "but he also gained an established place in what was known as the best of the city's social and intellectual life."[612] After the Magruder home at 7 Washington Place was destroyed in the Great Chicago Fire of 1871, he rebuilt on the site in 1873. A forty-year member of the nearby Fourth Presbyterian Church, he served for several years as a church elder.[613]

In October 1885, Magruder became the unexpected nominee for a vacancy on the Illinois Supreme Court. In a page one article titled "Chicago's Ring Beaten," the *New York Times* reported: "The Cook County Republican machine was given a very black eye to-day by the Seventh Judicial District Convention. The machine, after forcing its slate on the County Convention yesterday, blandly decided that it would to-day nominate George W. Stanford as the successor to the late Supreme Court Judge T. Lyle Dickey. There are, however, four counties outside of Cook in the judicial district, and they with the anti-machine men from Cook were enough to knock out Mr. Stanford. Mr. Benjamin D. Magruder, a reputable lawyer of this city, was nominated on the second ballot."[614]

With endorsement as well from the Democratic Party, Magruder won the Supreme Court seat without opposition, then was elected for nine-year terms in 1888 and 1897, and served as Chief Justice in 1891, 1896, and 1902. "He was ever and always a student," recalled fellow Justice Joseph N. Carter. "His days and nights were given to judicial labor. He never took a regular vacation, usually spending all of the summer between June and October working on his cases."[615]

In the 1889 case, *People ex rel. Peabody v. Chicago Gas Trust Company,* Magruder refused to enforce a restrictive covenant between the Chicago Gas Light and Coke Company and the Peoples Gas Light and Coke Company. In a "scathing" twenty-four-page opinion, he reversed a Cook County Circuit Court decision that allowed the Chicago Gas Trust Company to purchase stock in other gas companies. "The business of manufacturing and distributing illuminating gas by means of pipes laid in the streets of a city is a business of public character," Magruder wrote; "companies engaged in such business owe a duty to the public; any unreasonable restraint upon the performance of such duty is prejudicial to the public interest and in contravention of public policy. . . . Whatever tends to create a monopoly is unlawful as being contrary to public policy."[616]

Among other rulings in his twenty-one-year tenure, Magruder delivered opinions in two of the state's "most important" cases, according to historian Ralph M. Snyder. In the 1888 case, *Illinois Central Railroad Company v. The City of Decatur,* Magruder affirmed a Macon County Circuit Court decision regarding liability for special assessments. After the City of Decatur had assessed the Illinois Central for street paving along a portion of the right-of-way, the railroad argued in circuit court that its charter exempted "all taxation of every kind except as therein provided." A special assessment, Magruder wrote, "is not embraced within the meaning of the word taxation, because the owner of the property assessed gets back the amount of his assessment in the benefits received by his property, and, therefore, does not bear the burden of a tax." Snyder reported that Magruder's opinion, affirmed by the U.S. Supreme Court, became "the groundwork for cases holding that railroads with tax exempt charters may be liable for special assessments."[617]

Magruder delivered the opinion in one of the most well-known cases in Illinois court history, the 1887 *August Spies et al. v. People* case. August Spies and six other defendants in the 1886 Haymarket Riot bombing appealed their murder convictions that had been rendered by Judge Joseph E. Gary of the Cook County Criminal Court. Magruder, in a 167-page opinion, upheld Gary's decision, and, according to attorney Nathaniel Jones, "established in this State the doctrine that persons associating and conspiring together to aid and abet the killing of others are co-conspirators and are guilty of the crime of murder of the persons killed."[618]

Julia Magruder died in 1904, a few years after the death of the couple's daughter.[619] In 1906, Yale University conferred the LL.D. degree on Justice Magruder. That year a committee of prominent Chicagoans, including Democratic Mayor Edward Dunne and labor attorney Clarence Darrow supported his reelection to the Supreme Court. The *Chicago American* endorsed Magruder, editorializing that he "decided against the trusts and in favor of the people." The *Chicago Tribune* appeared to take a neutral stance, but according to the *Record-Herald,* which opposed his candidacy, Magruder had alienated many of his fellow justices with his antagonistic personality. Magruder had been the only dissenter in a 1903 decision affirming the state's Gas Consolidation Act. After the Democratic Party chose another candidate, Magruder ran as an independent but lost to Republican Orrin N. Carter.[620]

Magruder then resumed his Chicago law practice. He died of Bright's disease at his Chicago residence on April 21, 1910, at the age of seventy-two. Following Presbyterian services, he was buried in the family lot in Rosehill Cemetery.[621] "The opinions of this departed judge," eulogized the *Chicago Legal News,* "breathes the pure spirit of love for his fellow men of sympathy for the unfortunate."[622]

JOSEPH M. BAILEY, 1888-1895

A native of New York State, Joseph Mead Bailey was born in Middlebury Township in Wyoming County, on June 22, 1833, the third of eight children of Deacon Aaron and Maria Braman Bailey. She was a descendant of Richard Clarke, who immigrated on the *Mayflower.* Aaron's parents, Aaron and Mary Winchester Bailey, had moved from New England to settle in northern Illinois near Lena, Stephenson County.[623]

Joseph Bailey spent his youth on his father's New York farm and completed primary studies at Wyoming Academy. He "subsequently taught school or turned his hand to anything that would help him with funds to get into college," and entered the University of Rochester.[624] Upon graduation in 1854, he studied law under prominent Rochester attorney Ethan A. Hopkins. Bailey was admitted to practice in 1855, at the age of twenty-two.[625]

"Believing that in the West was to be found a wider and less encumbered field for the profitable exercise of skill and energy," wrote a biographer, Bailey followed his grandparents to Illinois and settled in Freeport, the Stephenson County seat in 1856. He formed a brief partnership with U. D. Meacham, state's attorney for the Fourteenth Judicial Circuit. Bailey "soon gained a reputation as a sound lawyer, safe counselor, careful pleader and persuasive advocate."[626]

In February 1859, Bailey returned to New York to marry Wyoming Academy classmate Anna Maria Olin, daughter of John and Maria Olin of Wyoming County. They became the parents of five children, one of whom died in infancy. Anna Bailey participated in Freeport charitable activities and founded the city's first kindergarten.[627]

Joseph Bailey began a partnership with F. W. S. Brawley, with offices in Freeport and Chicago. After the dissolution of that firm, Bailey partnered for ten years with Freeport attorney James I. Neff. In 1863, after Bailey convincingly argued his first case before the Illinois Supreme Court, Chief Justice Sidney Breese was heard to remark, "That young man will one day be a member of this court."[628]

In 1866, Bailey became known in statewide politics by winning a seat in the Illinois General Assembly as a Republican. He served as chairman of the committee on federal relations and as a member of the judiciary committee. Reelected in 1868, Bailey became chairman of the committee on railroads and a member of the penitentiary and municipal affairs and insurance committees.[629]

Among Bailey's prominent legal clients were the American Insurance Company of Chicago and the Illinois Central Railroad.[630] In 1869, he was an unsuccessful candidate for the Republican nomination to fill a Congressional vacancy in the Freeport district, and in 1876, he was a Republican elector on behalf of Rutherford B. Hayes.[631]

That same year, the legislature consolidated the twenty-six judicial circuits in Illinois into thirteen circuits and allowed an additional judge in each new circuit. Bailey won election to the Thirteenth Judicial Circuit, comprising Stephenson, Jo Daviess, Ogle, Carroll, Winnebago, Lee, and Whiteside Counties. In 1878, he was assigned to the First District Appellate Court in Chicago and reassigned in 1879, 1882, and 1885. "Six days a week find him hard at work in Chicago," the *Tribune* reported.[632]

"His opinions in the Appellate Court Reports have been quite widely cited," reported author James E. Babb. "While practicing at the bar and attorney for an Insurance Company, he wrote a book upon that subject, largely for the information of the local counsel for the Company. He was a trustee of the old University of Chicago, and is now a trustee of the new University of that name."[633]

In 1879, both the University of Rochester and University of Chicago bestowed Bailey the LL.D. degree for his merit as a jurist.[634] In 1887, he and fellow appellate court justice Thomas A. Moran founded the Chicago Evening Law Class, with Bailey tutoring law clerks for the new Illinois Bar Examination. By 1888, those evening sessions developed into formal classes of the Chicago College of Law, and Bailey became the College's first dean, followed by Moran.[635]

In 1888, Bailey won election to the Illinois Supreme Court, succeeding the deceased Benjamin R. Sheldon. "Judge Bailey came on the Supreme Court bench two years after I did," recalled Justice Simeon P. Shope, "but we were there together six years, and during that time I learned first to admire him, then to respect him, and finally to love him. He was a model Judge, combining as he did the widest learning with the most unwearied industry and the loftiest integrity. To that it must be added that he soon became noted for his powers of reach and his keen analysis. Well do I remember that away in the middle of the night, hours after the rest of the bench had cast off the cares of business and were devoting themselves to domestic pleasures and other recreations, I have passed Judge Bailey's room and discovered from the rapid click of his typewriter machine that he was still at work."[636]

In the 1889 case *Harris v. People,* Justice Bailey upheld the "common law right" to a jury trial in criminal cases. Nancy Harris had been convicted in the Cook County Criminal Court for larceny and concealing stolen property. Even though she had consented to trial without a jury, she appealed the verdict on grounds that the criminal court had no power or authority "to try her without a jury." The Supreme Court agreed. "We are of the opinion then, both upon principle and authority," wrote Justice Bailey, "that the Criminal court had no legal power to try the defendant without a jury, notwithstanding her consent and agreement in that behalf, and that the trial and conviction are therefore erroneous." He issued a verdict reversal and remanded the case to the criminal court.[637]

Bailey served as Chief Justice from 1892 to 1893. In the 1893 murder case of *Painter v. People,* Bailey delivered the Court opinion affirming a decision of the Cook County Criminal Court. George H. Painter had been sentenced to death for the 1891 strangulation death of Alice Painter in Chicago. His attorneys argued before the Supreme Court that "evidence of prior assaults on the deceased was calculated to inflame the minds of the jury." Before rendering the Supreme Court opinion, Bailey reiterated numerous details of the non-married couple's tumultuous relationship. He described the testimony of witnesses who heard loud noises from Alice's room, "as though some one was struggling, being bumped along the floor," and that several of the witnesses then saw George Painter leaving her room. He maintained that he had been at a saloon at the time of the murder, a statement corroborated by other saloon patrons, and that on his return to her room he found Alice dead. Bailey concluded that threats by the accused could be admissible to prove that he committed the crime.[638] "We have considered attentively the various propositions submitted by counsel for the defendant in their full and able argument," he wrote, "but we are unable to find any material error in the proceedings of the trial court, or any reason shown which makes it our duty to set aside the conviction and award a new trial. It follows that the judgment of the Criminal Court of Cook county must be affirmed."[639]

An assertive debater on the Court, he often argued with the equally formidable Justice Benjamin Magruder. "I have seen Judge Magruder jump on him and roast him unmercifully," recalled fellow Justice Shope, "but I could never see that it ruffled his temper any more than if a fly had lit on his shoulder. He was always a temperance man. The court was not composed of intemperate men by any means, but sometimes whisky would be given them and some of them would take a drink. But I never knew Judge Bailey either to drink with them or to rebuke them."[640]

On October 16, 1895, Bailey died at Freeport after a brief illness, at the age of sixty-two. His Supreme Court term would have expired in 1897.[641] At First Baptist Church, Dr. Galusha Anderson, a University of Chicago Divinity School theologian who had been Bailey's University of Rochester classmate, delivered the funeral sermon. "Farewell incorruptible Judge," Anderson concluded.[642] Bailey was buried in the family lot at the Freeport City Cemetery.

"Usually firm in his convictions," eulogized Justice Shope, Bailey "listened willingly to argument, impartially weighed it and yielded readily when convinced. No judge had greater respect for or yielded more readily to authority than he did. That great question, 'What is the truth?' seemed ever present before him, and he sought its solution with conscientious diligence."[643]

JACOB W. WILKIN, 1888-1907

A law student of future Illinois Supreme Court Justice John Scholfield, Jacob Wilson Wilkin was born near Newark, the seat of Licking County, Ohio, on June 7, 1837. He was the fifth of nine children of carpenter Isaac Wilkin and his wife, Sarah Burner Wilkin, both natives of Virginia. In 1844, the family moved to Crawford County, Illinois, where Isaac purchased 320 acres of land and became a successful livestock dealer. Jacob received an education in the country schools and enjoyed hunting in nearby forests.[644]

For two years, Jacob Wilkin pursued classical studies at McKendree College in Lebanon, Illinois. Following his father's advice, he began studying law in Scholfield's office in Marshall, Clark County, in 1861. During the Civil War in the spring of 1862, Wilkin interrupted his studies to enlist as a private in the Union Army. Promoted to captain of Company K of the 130th Illinois Infantry, he served with his regiment in the Army of the Cumberland, then in the Department of the Gulf, participating in campaigns at Vicksburg and the Red River. He fought at Sabine Cross Roads and assisted in the capture of Spanish Fort and Fort Blakely, near Mobile, Alabama, which were among the final battles of the war. Wilkin later served at the headquarters of General Ulysses S. Grant, before his discharge in August 1865 with the rank of major, "for gallant services in the field."[645]

Returning to Illinois, Wilkin married Alice E. Constable on September 21, 1865. She was the daughter of Judge Charles H. and Martha Constable of Marshall. The Wilkins became the parents of four children, one of whom died in infancy.[646] Wilkin resumed his law studies under Scholfield and in March 1866, at age twenty-eight, was admitted to the Illinois bar. The two men partnered under the firm name Scholfield & Wilkin until Scholfield's election to the Illinois Supreme Court in 1873. Wilkin then formed a partnership with a younger brother, maintaining, according to a court historian, "a general country practice, trying all kinds of law-suits, most of the trials being by jury, and full of excitement and interest to both clients and lawyers."[647]

Active in Republican politics, Wilkin was a presidential elector for Ulysses S. Grant in 1872 and became the unsuccessful candidate for the Fifteenth Congressional District two years later, losing to Democrat John R. Eden.[648] Wilkin also served on the board of trustees of the new Southern Illinois Normal University in Carbondale.[649] In 1879, he was elected judge of the Fourth Judicial Circuit, comprising the counties of Clark, Edgar, Coles, Vermilion, Douglas, Moultrie, Macon, Piatt, and Champaign.

Alice Wilkin died in March 1883, and in July 1885, he married Sarah E. Whitlock Archer, daughter of Judge William C. Whitlock of Marshall. Reelected circuit judge that year and assigned to the Fourth District Appellate Court, Wilkin moved with his family to the larger town of Danville. They became members of the Methodist Episcopal Church, and he served as a trustee.[650]

In 1888, he won election to the Supreme Court, succeeding the retired John M. Scott.[651] Wilkin "represented a large and populous district, which contains many able and ambitious lawyers," recalled an area attorney, "a district in which there is a sharp division between the two great political parties that represent the opposing political forces in this country; yet both of these parties practically united in supporting his election."[652] Wilkin enjoyed sharing the Supreme Court bench with his mentor John Scholfield. "The close intimacy of former years was renewed," added the attorney, "and remained unbroken until Scholfield's death, in 1893."[653]

Considered for the 1891 Republican senatorial nomination, Wilkin remained in the Illinois judiciary.[654] That year, he delivered the opinion in *Morgan v. People,* a case involving the inferred waiver of a trial by jury. After indictment in the Jefferson County Circuit Court for assault with intent to murder, defendant George Morgan entered a plea of not guilty. The judge, acting as "the court," found Morgan guilty and ordered him to serve six years of hard labor in the penitentiary. In reversing the decision, Wilkin wrote, "The record affirmatively shows, as we think, that plaintiff in error was tried for and convicted of a felony, upon his plea of not guilty, by the judge sitting as a jury. Consent of the defendant in an indictment for a felony can not confer jurisdiction upon the judge, or dispense with a finding of the fact of guilt by a jury." He remanded the case to the Jefferson County Circuit Court for a jury trial.[655]

In the 1893 *Friederich v. People* case, Wilkin reversed a St. Clair County Circuit Court attempted-murder judgment. During an argument, Edward Friederich had fractured the head of John Platt with a pine plank, causing his death some two months later. Friederich was found guilty of assault with intent to commit murder and appealed his conviction. In delivering the Supreme Court opinion, Wilkin enumerated the arguments of both Friederich and the state before ruling "that the blow was struck upon a sudden heat of passion, and without malice." He ordered the judgment reversed and the case remanded to the circuit court for further proceedings.[656]

Overwhelmingly reelected to the Supreme Court in 1897, Wilkin served as Chief Justice in 1894 and 1901. "His opinions are fine specimens of judicial thought," wrote one observer, "always clear, logical, and as brief as the character of the case will permit. He never enlarges beyond the necessities of the legal thought in order to indulge in the drapery of literature."[657]

On April 3, 1907, while working on court briefs, sixty-nine-year-old Wilkin died from acute Bright's disease. Following Methodist services in Danville, his remains were transported on a four-car train to Marshall. "This train bore the most distinguished funeral cortege in the history of eastern Illinois," reported the local newspaper. "There were the associate judges of the supreme bench, many men high in state positions, the entire bar of Vermillion county, as well as numerous close friends, beside the immediate family and other relatives, numbering more than 250, on the train."[658]

At Marshall Cemetery, Wilkin was laid to rest with military honors near the grave of his friend John Scholfield. "One loves to think of these two unknown and almost friendless young men," recalled Supreme Court reporter Isaac N. Phillips, "starting from the same law office in an obscure town of southern Illinois, without other aids than their own native ability and force of character, at length sitting together with credit on the highest court of their state, and, finally, in death, lamented and honored by the millions of a great commonwealth."[659]

JESSE J. PHILLIPS, 1893-1901

Born on a Montgomery County, Illinois, farm on May 22, 1837, Jesse J. Phillips was the seventh of eight children of Thomas and Jane Roberts Phillips. Jesse attended nearby Hillsboro Academy and at the age of nineteen was appointed a route agent on the Terre Haute & St. Louis Railroad. He resigned the position in 1857 and spent the next three years studying law under prominent Hillsboro attorney James M. Davis.[660]

Admitted to the bar in 1860, Phillips opened a law office in Hillsboro and "at once rose into prominence," recalled one resident. "He was a brilliant speaker, full of fire and magnetism which won him many friends." He had the "faculty of impressing his own convictions upon a jury so that he was soon known as the best jury lawyer in Central Illinois."[661]

Phillips practiced in Hillsboro until the outbreak of the Civil War. Upon hearing President Abraham Lincoln's first call for troops, Phillips "hung a flag from his office window and announced that he would raise a company to aid in preserving the Union." He was elected captain, then major, of his company, attached to the Ninth Regiment, Illinois Infantry. Soon ordered to the front, the company engaged in a number of battles, acquiring the name "Bloody Ninth."[662]

Their first engagement was in October 1861 near Eddyville, Kentucky, where Major Phillips, commanding three companies, attacked three hundred Confederates. Promoted to lieutenant colonel, he received a commendation from General Ulysses S. Grant for gallantry in the February 1862 battle of Fort Donelson. In the April battle of Shiloh, Phillips was twice shot through the thigh, and another bullet crippled his hand.[663]

In March 1863, the Ninth Regiment was mounted and served as a cavalry unit for the duration of the war. The following spring, the corps to which Phillips's regiment was attached advanced with the Army of the Tennessee. At the battle of Resaca, he was shot through the ankle. Resigning from the service in September, "having seen, perhaps, more hard fighting than any officer in the Union army," according to a county historian, Phillips was brevetted brigadier general "for gallant, meritorious and distinguished services."[664] "Few of the men whom Illinois gave to the armies of the union," declared the *Chicago Tribune*, "displayed greater personal bravery on the field of battle. Several times his horse was shot under him as he was leading a desperate charge, and he himself was so severely wounded at Shiloh that he never fully recovered his normal health."[665]

Before returning to his Hillsboro law practice, Phillips married Virginia Davis, daughter of planter Nicholas Davis, in Huntsville, Alabama. Active in Democratic politics, he was the unsuccessful candidate for State Treasurer in both 1866 and 1868. After the death of Virginia Phillips, on November 7, 1884, he married Mrs. Juliet Kendel Best of Hillsboro. Phillips had no children with either wife.[666]

Elected a judge of the Fifth Judicial Circuit in 1879, Phillips served on that bench for thirteen years. "He was a man of genial manners and striking appearance," reported the *Chicago Tribune,* with an erect and "soldierly" bearing, long black hair, and mustache. "Often the wounds which he received at Shiloh made it necessary for him to go about on crutches, but in the presence of congenial company he was always ready to forget his own suffering, relax for the moment his judicial dignity, and enter heartily into the spirit of jollity and good fellowship."[667]

Upon the death of Supreme Court Justice John M. Scholfield in 1893, Phillips won election by a wide majority to the vacancy and filled Scholfield's seat on the Court. "No man ever donned the ermine of the highest court in the state under more adverse and trying circumstances," reported the *Illinois State Journal.* "As the successor of Judge Scholfield, he knew that his opinions would be more closely criticized than had he been elected from any other district."[668]

Phillips soon became known as "fearless" for right and justice. "He readily left the established precedents and wandered into unexplored fields to find arguments in favor of his position," recalled fellow Supreme Court Justice Jacob W. Wilkin. "His discipline as a lawyer," added Simeon P. Shope, "and his broad training in the affairs of life, well fitted him for the work."[669]

In the 1893 case *Burke v. People,* Justice Phillips delivered the opinion affirming a decision of the Cook County Criminal Court. Thomas Burke and another man had been convicted of robbery. Burke appealed his conviction on grounds that not only had the prosecution failed to prove that he robbed the victim of anything specifically described in the indictment, but also that questions and remarks by the judge during examination of the victim's wife constituted error. Phillips affirmed the lower court's judgment. "Where, from the evidence, the force or intimidation, and taking from the person a thing of value, are shown," Phillips decreed, "a conviction may be had without a finding of value specifically." On the issue of judicial examination, Phillips found that "the error of the judge in that regard was not such that a new trial should be granted."[670]

In an 1894 case, *Erringdale et al. v. Riggs et al.,* Phillips delivered the opinion reversing a Mercer County Circuit Court decision and illustrating the insecurity of real estate titles during that era. After the death of his wife in 1892, Harrison W. Riggs, who had moved from Illinois to Texas nearly forty years earlier while his wife remained in Illinois, gave power of attorney to one of his sons to sell a parcel of his Illinois land. Although another son remained on the land on which he and his mother had resided, after her death, Riggs conveyed a half section to his former daughter-in-law, Eveline P. Erringdale. "The consideration was one dollar and past kindness in caring for him," according to court records, "and an agreement to support him the remainder of his life."

Eight of Riggses' sons filed suit, alleging that at the time of their mother's death, she, not their father, owned the parcel in dispute. The sons also alleged that Riggs "was not of sound mind" when he made the conveyance to Erringdale, "and that it was procured by undue influence." After the circuit court set aside the deed from Riggs to Erringdale, she appealed the decision. In delivering the Supreme Court opinion, Phillips determined that the wife could not own the property under the common law in effect at that time. Additionally, there was no documentary evidence to show that she indeed owned the land. Phillips reversed the circuit court decision and directed the lower court to dismiss the lawsuit.[671]

Reelected to the Supreme Court at the expiration of his first term, Phillips served as Chief Justice in 1897. Suffering poor health for more than a year, Phillips died on February 16, 1901. His body lay in state at the Montgomery County courthouse in Hillsboro, viewed by an estimated 10,000 people. Following funeral services, he was buried in Hillsboro's Oak Grove Cemetery.[672]

JOSEPH N. CARTER, 1894-1903

Joseph N. Carter was born on March 12, 1843, in Hardin County, Kentucky. He was the fourth of ten children of William P. Carter and Martha Mayes Carter, a family with modest means.[673] In 1857, the family moved to Charleston, Coles County, Illinois. One year later, they moved again to Tuscola, Illinois.[674] Young Carter received much of his primary education in the Douglas County public schools. Before entering college, Carter taught primary education for three years in Tuscola.[675]

In 1866, he graduated from Illinois College in Jacksonville with his bachelor's degree. He then chose to pursue a law profession, and in 1868, he graduated from the University of Michigan with his degree in law. He was admitted to the Illinois bar on November 3, 1869.[676] On December 3, 1879, Carter married Ellen Barrell of Springfield, Illinois. They had two sons and a daughter: Henry B. Carter, William Douglas Carter, and Josephine Carter Ferry.[677]

He settled in Quincy, Illinois, in 1869 and began his practice in law.[678] From 1869 to 1879, he was a partner in the Carter and Govert law firm with W. H. Govert. From 1879 to 1884, Judge Joseph Sibley also partnered in the law firm with Carter.[679] Then in 1888, Theodore B. Pape entered the firm and the name became Carter, Govert, and Pape. Carter remained with the law firm until his death in 1913.[680]

Carter won election to the Illinois General Assembly in 1878, serving two terms as a member of the Illinois House of Representatives in the 31st and 32nd General Assemblies. In 1882, he took part in the session that reapportioned the state into congressional and state legislative districts.[681] In 1882, the Republican Party nominated him for state senator, but he lost the general election.[682] He was also president of the Adams County Bar Association when he died in 1913.[683]

Carter was elected to the Illinois Supreme Court on June 4, 1894, as a Republican, taking over the seat held by Simeon P. Shope. He won the election in the Fourth Judicial District in a surprising vote from a democratic majority (12,000). He served from 1894 to 1903, and he served once as the Chief Justice from 1898 to 1899.[684] During his term on the court, Carter helped to expand the collection of the state's law library.[685] In his nine-year term, he authored 537 opinions contained in fifty-one volumes of the *Illinois Reports*.[686]

One case during his first year on the Court was *Fixmer v. People*. Benjamin Fixmer and John H. Lawrence attempted an abortion on Emma Stegmann, and she died due to complications from the procedure. The Sangamon County Circuit Court indicted Fixmer indicted as an accessory to the murder of Stegmann, but did not charge him as a principal. Illinois law stated that any person found to be an accessory must be tried as a principal. A jury found him guilty of manslaughter—as a principal—and sentenced him to ten years in prison.[687] Fixmer appealed the case, claiming that he was not the principal but rather an accessory in the case and that the indictment did not refer to him as a principal. The defense claimed that according to Illinois law, Fixmer was not properly charged and should have been acquitted. The defense also claimed and proved that John H. Lawrence, who had also been charged in the crime, was acquitted and one of the jurors had shown a biased opinion before the case began.[688] The Supreme Court reversed and remanded the case noting that Fixmer was not correctly charged with manslaughter.[689] Justice Carter gave the opinion of the Court, writing that "we cannot agree with counsel for the People that the indictment in the case at bar would have been sufficient […] to put defendant below on trial as an accessory before the fact to the crime of murder."[690]

Another case in which Carter wrote the opinion for the Court was *School Directors v. People*. In the case, a newly created school district in Ford County proposed a referendum to build a schoolhouse, but the voters rejected the referendum. The school directors therefore assumed that they no longer had an obligation to establish a location for the school despite Henry Heinreichs's offer to use his building. The People, on behalf of relator Heinreichs, petitioned the Ford County Circuit Court for a writ of mandamus to command the school directors to use Heinreichs's building. The Court granted the writ of mandamus and ordered that the school directors immediately designate a school site and hire a teacher.[691]

The Illinois Supreme Court affirmed the lower court's decision. Justice Carter wrote that after the school board was elected the district had the money and voter support for a new school. "The petition shows that sufficient children of proper school age reside in the district for such a school, and that by the neglect and omission of duty by the directors they [the children] are denied school privileges." Since Heinreichs had built a suitable building for the school "near the center of the district and easy of access from all parts of the district" and offered it to the district with or without rent, Carter said that it was "a clear case of neglect and disregard of official duty by these directors."[692]

Carter ran for reelection in 1903 but lost to Guy Scott. Carter resumed his law practice in Quincy, Illinois. He practiced law until February 6, 1908, when he suffered a stroke of apoplexy.[693] He never recovered from the stroke physically or mentally and was left paralyzed. He died in his home in Quincy on February 6, 1913, from prolonged complications of his apoplectic stroke.[694] After his death, Carter was remembered fondly in a memorial before the Illinois Supreme Court, and William Schlagenhauf said about Carter, "It is the life and character of such a man that makes life worth living and helps mankind to be happier, nobler and better."[695] Carter was buried in Woodland Cemetery in Quincy.

JAMES H. CARTWRIGHT, 1895-1924

Only two other justices served longer than James Henry Cartwright's twenty-nine years on the Supreme Court, and only a few others wrote more opinions than him. Born on the frontier in the first half of the nineteenth century and living well into the twentieth, his life and tenure on the court spanned periods of significant change in American society.

He was born in the Iowa Territory on December 1, 1842, one of six children of Barton Hall Cartwright, who was a descendant of an old New England family and second cousin to Reverend Peter Cartwright, the pioneer Illinois circuit-riding preacher. Barton Cartwright followed the same calling as his second cousin, which meant frequent relocation. The Cartwright family moved to Illinois in 1843 and resided in a number of communities in the western part of the state until settling in Mt. Morris in Ogle County in 1850.[696]

He took his schooling at the local Rock River Seminary, which was a regionally significant educational institution in the mid-nineteenth century. Although he did not receive a diploma, Cartwright was able to work as a teacher at a local school while still a teenager. In April 1862, he enlisted for Civil War service in the Sixty-ninth Illinois Infantry for ninety days. His father had joined General William T. Sherman's army as a chaplain, and the young Cartwright found it necessary to return home at the end of his ninety-day term to help manage family affairs. In June 1864, he enlisted again, this time for one hundred days in the 140th Illinois Infantry and at age twenty-two served as a captain. The 140th was mustered in for garrison duty at Memphis to free combat troops for concentrated action in the east. Cartwright took an active interest in the Grand Army of the Republic for his entire life. Locally, he was often referred to as "Cap," in deference to his Civil War rank.[697]

After his military service, he was a student at the University of Michigan and received a law degree in 1867. He was admitted to the Illinois bar that same year and joined the practice of Henry Mix, a prominent attorney in Oregon, Illinois, a few miles from the Ogle County seat of Mt. Morris. His law practice was always in Oregon even when serving, until 1876, as the general counsel for the short-lived Chicago and Iowa Railroad Company. During this period, he held two one-year terms as mayor of the city of Oregon in 1873 and 1875, and although active in civic affairs throughout his life and always voting Republican, he had no interest in politics after election to the bench.

In 1873, he married Hattie L. Holmes of Oregon and purchased his 365-acre Springdale Farm immediately north of the city boundary. The farm succeeded in producing more than two hundred trotting horses that were sold nationwide and established his reputation as one of the leading authorities in the United States on the pedigrees of trotting horses. He became president of the Illinois State Agricultural Society in the 1880s and undertook local conservation activities such as stocking the Rock River.[698] The marriage produced six children, five of whom survived. One son, James H. Cartwright Jr., also received a law degree from the University of Michigan, and his daughter Ada was among the few women admitted to the bar from the early part of the century.[699]

In 1876, he became Master in Chancery in Ogle County. As a resident of the Thirteenth Judicial Circuit, he was elected circuit judge in 1888. Reelected in 1891, he was soon assigned to the Appellate Court in what was then the second district sitting at Ottawa. In 1895, Cartwright ascended to the Illinois Supreme Court when he was elected to fill the unexpired term of Justice Joseph M. Bailey, who died in office. Cartwright was reelected in 1897, 1906, and 1915. He was nominated to run again, unopposed, in November 1924, but died before the election.[700]

During his time on the Supreme Court, he wrote more than 1,700 opinions. Of these, 150 addressed constitutional issues. Only Justice Pinkney H. Walker, whose service on the court ended in 1885, and Sidney Breese, who left the court in 1878, wrote more opinions than Cartwright with Walker writing 2,304 in his twenty-seven years as a Supreme Court justice, and Breese writing 1,962 in his twenty-three years.[701] Only Justice Thomas C. Browne, who served on the court from its beginning in 1818 until his retirement in 1848, and Justice Clyde E. Stone, who served from 1918 to 1948, sat on the Supreme Court longer than Cartwright.

One case was *Block v. City of Chicago*, for which Cartwright wrote the opinion as Chief Justice. In the spring of 1908, Jake Block, an exhibitor of motion pictures, was denied permission to show the films *The James Boys in Missouri* and *Night Riders* under the city's censorship ordinance that had been enacted the previous year. Block argued in the city's Superior Court and then the Illinois Supreme Court that motion picture exhibitors had been unconstitutionally singled out and suffered from burdensome regulation. Block argued further that depiction of historical events could not be determined obscene or immoral and pointed out that stage plays did not need approval from the censors before performances.

The Supreme Court upheld the city's ordinance and Superior Court's ruling in Cartwright's 1909 opinion, which held that motion pictures were indeed different from stage plays and could be regulated along with nickelodeons and similar forms of entertainment. He also found that censorship was a valid police power and that the City of Chicago did not abuse its power in the administration of the law.[702] Cartwright wrote, "there are people who differ upon the subject as to what is immoral and obscene," but it was important to have the local government apply the test in the case of motion pictures because the low price of admission allows for frequent attendance by children. Cartwright concluded that the audience must be protected from obscene and immoral depictions, and that the "welfare of society demands that every effort of municipal authorities to afford such protection shall be sustained."[703]

In another significant case, Cartwright issued the opinion in *Bliss v. Ward*. In a series of cases that reached the Illinois Supreme Court from 1897 to 1910, Montgomery Ward battled various entities that wanted to construct buildings on Chicago's Lake Park, citing the public dedication doctrine.[704] When Lake Park was dedicated in 1839, it was meant as public space to be "forever open clear and free" from buildings or obstructions. *Bliss* was the second of four cases and concerned whether the National Guard can build an armory and training ground on filled land east of the Illinois Central tracks. The first case determined that buildings could not be built west of the tracks.[705] Ward filed a bill for injunction when construction on the armory began, successfully winning the case in Cook County. Bliss and the Board of Commissioners appealed the case to the Illinois Supreme Court. Justice Cartwright wrote that "the extension grows upon the original park and becomes corporate with it and part of it,—in the one case by natural process, and in the other by artificial means, with the assent of the State."[706]

Off the bench, Cartwright had an active interest in the legal profession in addition to his other civic interests. He held membership in several bar associations, often speaking at meetings. In 1899, when the John Marshall Law School opened its doors for the first time, Cartwright served as one of the original faculty members.[707] Following the brand of the Supreme Court in Springfield in 1897, Cartwright served on the commission for the construction of the Supreme Court Building. Cartwright took his commission seriously, giving his attention to all the details of planning and the actual construction, which was completed on time and within its budget in 1908. His skill and knowledge as a jurist brought him some national attention when, in 1906, President Theodore Roosevelt considered appointing him to the United States Supreme Court. Ultimately Roosevelt chose his attorney general, William H. Moody, instead.[708]

In April 1924, at age eighty-two, Cartwright had to leave his duties in Springfield and return home to Oregon because of an undetermined illness. He died on May 18, 1924. His funeral was held at the Oregon Coliseum, the local civic center, in order to accommodate a large number of friends and neighbors and his colleagues from the Supreme Court. The Chicago Bar Association and the Illinois State Bar Association each sent a committee of more than thirty of their members, including three former governors. After his funeral, the *Chicago Legal News* reported that "he was recognized as the dean of the Supreme Court; his keen analytical mind, his lucid interpretation of the law, his application of common sense to the legal problems presented, with his long service and familiarity with the practices and decisions of the court made him in later life the outstanding figure in court."[709] He was buried in Riverside Cemetery in Oregon, on land that was once part of his Springdale Farm.

CARROLL C. BOGGS, 1897-1906

Carroll Curtis Boggs was born on October 19, 1843, in Fairfield, Wayne County, Illinois. His parents were Dr. Richard L. Boggs and Sarah A. (Wright) Boggs. He spent much of his early life with his mother's parents in Fairfield. He received his early education at the Fairfield public schools, and he earned a bachelor's degree from McKendree College in Lebanon, Illinois.[710] He spent one year studying literature at the University of Michigan but changed his studies to law in 1863. In 1864, he graduated from the University of Michigan with his degree in law.[711]

On February 25, 1866, Boggs was admitted to the Illinois bar. He first partnered with William H. Robinson in a law practice in Fairfield. Later, Colonel George W. Johns joined the practice. On October 31, 1870, he married Sarah A. Shaeffer of Fairfield. The couple had five children: Mary (Boggs) Elmore, Wreath, Edna, Richard L., and Joseph G. Boggs. Sarah (Shaeffer) Boggs died on July 6, 1914.[712]

Boggs had a successful political and legal career as a Democrat. He won his first election for State's Attorney of Wayne County and held that position for four years from 1873 to 1877. From 1878 to 1885, he held the office of county judge for Wayne County, and from 1885 to 1897, he was a judge in the Second Judicial Circuit. Boggs continued his judicial career to the appellate court when he was elected as a member of the Appellate Court for the Third District from 1891 to 1897.[713]

In 1897, Boggs narrowly defeated incumbent David J. Baker for the Illinois Supreme Court. He served until 1906 and was the Chief Justice from 1900 to 1901.[714] During Boggs's term as chief, the Illinois Supreme Court heard *Booth v. People*, and Boggs wrote the opinion. Alfred Booth had signed a contract that allowed him to buy corn for a fixed price for a period of ten days. The law, however, indicated that the buying or selling of grain under contract at a future time was considered gambling, and Booth was indicted and found guilty.[715] In the appeal, Booth's attorneys argued that under the 1870 Illinois Constitution the average citizen's right to contract was a right of both liberty and property. They added that there were many examples listed in the Criminal Code as gambling, but grain purchasing was not one of them. The Supreme Court affirmed the judgment, and Boggs agreed that Booth's contract was gambling or wagering on the market prices of grain.[716]

Another case heard before the Illinois Supreme Court in 1899 was the separate maintenance case of *Harding v. Harding*. Adelaide Harding did not divorce her husband, George F. Harding Sr., but left him because of her claims of cruelty and adultery. He never admitted to the adultery claim. She took the two youngest daughters of their seven children to her live with her and sued her husband for "separate maintenance and suit money, the custody of Susan and Madeline [the two minor daughters], an allowance for their support, maintenance, and education, and for general relief."[717]

George F. Harding Sr. was a wealthy man and owned a large portion of property in Chicago. Mrs. Harding claimed he was worth between $2 and $3 million, and when the entire family lived together, it took an average $15,000 per year to support the family's lifestyle. She also claimed that he had given her no money during their separation. Mr. Harding denied that he was worth $2 to $3 million, but he and his property was worth about $1 million. He also denied that it took $15,000 for annual support. His argument for not providing his wife with support money during their separation was that she already had her own small fortune, which she had acquired, according to Mr. Harding, from slowly stealing and hoarding money from him throughout their marriage. He also claimed that since she only wanted his money, he sought custody of the children.[718]

The lower court ordered Mr. Harding to pay $100 a month per daughter for child support and more than $26,000 for other fees and hardships, and they denied his claim of reductions to the alimony amounts.[719] The Illinois Supreme Court affirmed and remanded part of the decision. Boggs's opinion stipulated that that Mrs. Harding was to gain custody because the two daughters were "of tender age and require a mother's care." Boggs's opinion was based in part on an act in relation to married women, which stated that "a married woman who is living separate and apart from her husband without her fault may have her remedy in equity for reasonable support and maintenance, to be determined with reference to the condition of the parties life at the place of residence of the husband amid the circumstances of the respective cases."[720]

In 1906, Boggs ran for reelection to the Supreme Court but lost to Republican nominee Alonzo Vickers. Boggs returned to the practice of law in Fairfield but did not end his career in public service after his defeat. In 1907, he was nominated for the United States Senate by the Illinois House of Representatives. In 1908, he was a delegate to the Democratic National Convention. He was finally a delegate to the Fourth American Peace Congress in 1913.[721] Boggs died in Fairfield, Illinois, on December 16, 1923, and is buried in Maple Hill Cemetery in Fairfield. He was remembered fondly by the Illinois Supreme Court in a memorial service in 1924, stating, "He lived an exemplary life and by his death Illinois lost one of its noble sons."[722]

JOHN P. HAND, 1900-1913

John P. Hand was born on November 10, 1850, on a farm in Hanna Township, Henry County, Illinois. Hanna Township was named after Hand's grandfather and one of the pioneer settlers of the Illinois territory. His parents were Henry and Mary (Hanna) Hand.[723] Hand received some of his education in the public school in Hanna Township, and from 1866 to 1868, he was a student at Rock River Seminary in Mt. Morris, Illinois. Hand married Elizabeth Brayton of Mt. Morris on October 26, 1871. They had one son, Frederick Henry Hand, who also went into the law.[724] In 1875, John Hand graduated from Iowa State University with his degree in law.[725]

Hand was admitted to the Illinois bar in 1875. He was a partner in the Mock & Hand law firm with A. R. Mock from 1875 to 1885 in Cambridge, Illinois. From 1890 to 1895, he was a partner of the Hand, Milchrist & Smith law firm in Chicago. His final law firm, Hand & Hand, was formed in 1896 with his son. From 1885 to 1890, Hand served as a Henry County judge. In 1890, he became the Assistant United States District Attorney for the Northern District of Illinois.[726]

In 1900, Hand ran for the Fifth District seat on the Illinois Supreme Court. He defeated twenty-seven-year incumbent Alfred Craig. Hand served on the Supreme Court for thirteen years, winning reelection in 1909 against Charles Craig, Alfred's son. He served as Chief Justice from 1903 to 1904 and from 1907 to 1908. Hand was the Chief when he accepted the key to the new Illinois Supreme Court Building in February 1908. In his remarks at the dedicatory event, Chief Justice Hand noted the appropriateness that the Illinois Supreme Court "should be permanently located in a building which comports with the dignity and character of the court and the splendid history and commercial supremacy of the State." Hand also noted the importance of the court in a state with a large agrarian economy and rapid industrialization, "I venture the statement that . . . the opinions of no other State court are cited oftener or stand higher as an exposition of the principles of law than do the opinions of the judges of the Supreme Court of Illinois."[727]

One year later, Hand spoke on behalf of the Court to commemorate the centennial of the birth of Illinois's most famous lawyer, Abraham Lincoln. He commented that the fact that Lincoln "was a great lawyer when elected president has been largely overlooked" as well as "the training and development which enabled him to meet and solve the great questions which confronted him during [the Civil War] had been acquired while he was practicing law in the courts of Illinois."[728]

In one of his first cases heard on the Supreme Court, *Elmstedt v. Nicholson et al.*, Justice Hand wrote the opinion to affirm a Cook County Superior Court judgment that cancelled a land transfer from John Elmstedt to his wife Loenna Elmstedt. On her husband's deathbed, Loenna Elmstedt procured a transfer of four valuable Chicago lots to herself.

The other heirs of John Elmstedt's estate claimed that John Elmstedt had been mentally and physically weak, of unsound mind, and unable to comprehend the effect of his acts and was completely under the control of Loenna, his third wife. The Superior Court cancelled the transfer, and Loenna Elmstedt appealed the decision to the Illinois Supreme Court. In Hand's brief opinion, he stated in chancery cases, the master in chancery who took the evidence is best qualified to judge the weight of witness testimony, and the testimony fully sustains the decree.[729]

In 1909, the Woman's Ten-Hour Law restricted the number of hours women could work in a single day to ten hours. This applied only to women working in mechanical establishments, factories, and laundry facilities. The Illinois Manufacturers Association challenged the 1909 law limiting the hours per workday a female could be employed. The Association had won an earlier case in 1895 in the Illinois Supreme Court that an eight-hour workday for women was unconstitutional owing to the restrictions it placed on the right for employer and employee to negotiate a contract.[730]

In *Ritchie & Co. v. Wayman,* the W.C. Ritchie & Company, a manufacturer of paper boxes and paper box machinery, was accused of employing female employees for more than ten hours in a single day. The defense argued that the Woman's Ten-Hour Law of 1909 violated the Illinois 1870 Constitution because it took away the right to contract for property and labor rights. The case *Ritchie & Co. v. Wayman* came before the Illinois Supreme Court in 1910. Among the counsel for Wayman was Louis Brandeis, who submitted a longer version of the Brandeis Brief that he had prepared for *Muller v. Oregon.*[731] The Brandeis Brief, prepared with the assistance of former Illinois activist Florence Kelley and Josephine Goldmark, was innovative in that it relied on sociological and empirical data rather than legal arguments.

Young girls make paper boxes in a Cincinnati factory. (Image courtesy of Library of Congress)

Justice Hand delivered the opinion upholding the Woman's Ten-Hour Law. He reviewed the female workweek as well as the issues of manual labor and gender discrimination. Work environments in which machines dictated the pace of work, opposed to other manual labor jobs, created faster pace workdays and a greater chance to over-exert the employees. "The physical structure and maternal functions of women, and their consequent inability to perform, without effect upon their health and the vigor of their offspring, work which men may do without over-exertion, justify the discrimination between men and women made by the Woman's Ten-Hour Law of 1909."[732]

In December 1912, he suffered a stroke in his Illinois Supreme Court Building chambers. He had hoped that he would be able to return to the work of the court, but never fully recovered. Hand resigned from the Supreme Court in July 1913. Unable to return to the legal profession, he kept busy with several farming and business operations that he managed until his death. He also spent time in California for his health, although he developed heart problems. John Hand died at Long Beach, California, on May 22, 1923. He was buried at his family lot at Oak Wood Cemetery in Mt. Morris. At the Court's memorial service, Justice Hand was remembered as a generally positive person with strong convictions and a fine judicial temperament.[733]

JAMES B. RICKS, 1901-1906

James Benjamin Ricks was born on December 23, 1852, on a farm in Christian County, Illinois. His parents were John Bond Ricks and Dorcia B. (Haines) Ricks. He came from a long line of public servants. John B. Ricks was the sheriff and twice the circuit clerk of Christian County. He also served two non-consecutive terms in the Illinois legislature. James Ricks's grandfather, William Skinner Ricks, was an early Illinois pioneer and the first sheriff of Christian County. Ricks's great-grandfather was a soldier in the Revolutionary War and an early pioneer of Kentucky.[734]

James Ricks received his early education in the Christian County public schools. He continued that education at Wesleyan University in Bloomington, Illinois. On December 23, 1872, when Ricks was twenty years old, he married Pammie L. Geltmacher of Bloomington, Illinois. They had six children, and three survived into adulthood.[735] After graduating from Wesleyan University, Ricks studied law in the office of Judge Andrew Simpson and John B. Jones in Taylorville. During his apprenticeship, he helped to draft documents to change the village of Taylorville to a city.[736] He was admitted to the Illinois bar in 1874, and from 1874 to 1885, he was a solo practitioner. In 1885, he formed a partnership with J. C. Creighton, who was elected state's attorney. Creighton's health failed while still in office, and Ricks assumed his responsibilities and prosecuted the state's attorney's cases.[737]

Along with his law career, Ricks was also active in public service as a Democrat. From 1889 to 1891, he was the mayor of Taylorville. During his two-year term, he established a system of electric lights and doubled the capacity of the city's water works. In June 1892, Ricks was a delegate to the national Democratic convention in Chicago, and he campaigned in the presidential election for Grover Cleveland. After Cleveland's victory, Ricks was appointed as the supervising examiner of the pension bureau. He spent three years in Washington, D.C., with more than one hundred employees under him.[738] He returned to Taylorville in 1895, continued to practice law and to be active in the Democratic State Committee. Ricks also served as president of the Taylorville Township High School Board, the Benevolent Protective Order of Elks, and was a former grand chancellor of the Knights of Pythias.[739]

On April 12, 1901, a local Democratic convention in Litchfield nominated Ricks to the Illinois Supreme Court to fill the unexpired term of Jesse J. Phillips, who had died two months prior.[740] On May 21, 1901, Ricks was elected to the Court, defeating Republican George Cooper of Hillsboro. Ricks was described as "without experience on the bench, but he brought to the performance of his new duties a long and varied experience as a lawyer and legal abilities of high order."[741]

During his short tenure on the Court, Ricks wrote many opinions, but two opinions demonstrated support of large industrial companies. In 1904, the Illinois Supreme Court heard *Lloyd v. Catlin Coal Co.* Lloyd was a farmer who owned acres of surface land, and the Catlin Coal Company had claims to the minerals under his real property. Lloyd sued the mining company in the Vermilion County Circuit Court for damages to sixty acres of land and received a $6,000 judgment. Lloyd then sued again for an injunction to prevent the coal company from mining the coal in a certain way, demanding that veins be cut to leave half the coal in place for support and that the size of mining rooms be a certain size.[742] The Vermilion County Circuit Court dismissed Lloyd's bill because of the conflicting evidence "that it is impossible to tell whether the surface of [Lloyd's] land, or any part of it, will subside at all, or if so, when, to what extent, or whether [Lloyd] will be injured at all." Lloyd's case reached the Illinois Supreme Court, which affirmed the injunction's dismissal, stating that the court could not regulate the amount of coal the mining company had to leave behind to support the surface lands. Ricks wrote, "Each [party] has rights that must be recognized and conserved by the courts."[743]

The case *Mackey v. Northern Milling Company* was a case that also claimed negligence by a corporation. Thomas Mackey was an employee of the Northern Milling Company. A milling car was pushed onto him, and he died.[744] His widow, Lizzie Mackey, sued the milling company for negligence damages and won a judgment for $5,000, but the company successfully obtained a reversal at the appellate court due to the failure to state a good cause of action in the declaration. Mackie refiled a corrected declaration, but the Northern Milling Company argued that the statute of limitations had expired. The case reached the Illinois Supreme Court to answer the question whether the corrected declaration was a new case or a continuation of the previous case—the answer to which would determine if the statute of limitations expired. The Supreme Court agreed with the Northern Milling Company. Ricks wrote that this "identical question has been so clearly and repeatedly passed upon by this court that a new discussion of the proposition would seem to be useless."[745]

Ricks served on the Court for five years, with one year as Chief Justice (1904–1905), and announced his plan to run for reelection, but a diagnosis of cancer resulted in the retraction of his reelection bid. He retired from the Court on June 18, 1906, and died a month later on July 23 at his home in Taylorville. He was fifty-four years old and had suffered from the debilitating effects of cancer of the bowels for seven months. He was buried in Oak Hill Cemetery in Taylorville. Ricks was remembered as being "ambitious for office and power, but the glitter of gold tempted him not."[746]

GUY C. SCOTT, 1903-1909

Guy C. Scott was born in Henderson County, Illinois, on August 14, 1863.[747] He was the eldest child of eight to Samuel and Sarah Scott. His father was a native of Fountain County, Indiana, and moved to Illinois in 1858.[748] Guy Scott grew up on a farm near Keithsburg, Mercer County, Illinois. He received his primary education in Mercer County and one year at a preparatory school in Galesburg. He also attended Knox College for his higher education.[749]

Scott had a very diverse career in his early life. He taught school for many years in Mercer County. He spent two years working in Wyoming for a government surveying party, but he moved back to Illinois and settled in Aledo. He studied law beginning in 1882 with Aledo attorney Isaac N. Bassett.[750] In 1886, Scott was admitted to the Illinois bar. Also in 1886, he was appointed deputy county clerk, and later county clerk.[751] In 1886, he also spent a few short months in Trinidad, Colorado, with another lawyer James M. Brock. Scott returned to Aledo though, and called the town his home for the rest of his life.[752]

On September 1, 1887, he formed a partnership with John C. Pepper. The partnership lasted until 1896, when Pepper moved to Florida because of ill health.[753] In 1896, Scott formed a new partnership with George A. Cooke, which lasted until 1900. In 1900, Scott retired from practicing law for a couple of months because of his own ill health. Then he formed another partnership with James M. Brock, which lasted until Brock's death in 1902. Until Scott was elected a Supreme Court justice, he practiced law alone, and he represented many clients, including large companies such as the Chicago, Burlington and Quincy Railroad.[754]

Personally and socially, Scott was very active. Scott married Jessie Irvin, the daughter of Aledo doctor George Irvin on June 11, 1891. Guy and Jessie Scott had one daughter, Kathryn Scott, who was born on December 11, 1894.[755] In the winter of 1887 to 1888, Scott became a Mason and held several positions, including Secretary, Junior Warden, and eventually Sir Knight Templar.[756] Scott was not connected with any religious denomination.[757]

Scott was also active in Democratic politics, serving in various positions. In 1892, he was a delegate to the Democratic National Convention.[758] He was the mayor of Aledo from 1895 to 1899. In 1899, he declined reelection although, in 1901, he was reelected as mayor and served until 1905. In 1897, he was a candidate for the circuit bench, but he was defeated. He carried the vote in Mercer County, despite its Republican majority, by 2,300 votes. In 1901 and 1902, he was a member of the Illinois State Democratic Central Committee. Then in 1903, Scott defeated incumbent Joseph N. Carter as a justice for the Illinois Supreme Court in the Fourth Judicial District, "which his party seemed to be in a hopeless minority."[759] He served on the court from 1903 to 1909, and he was the Chief Justice from 1906 to 1907.

Among his cases, *Suchomel v. Maxwell* in 1909 dealt with Illinois labor conditions. The Cook County Circuit Court ruled that the Maxwell Brothers Company, owned by James Maxwell and Henry B. Maxwell, was negligent and owed $5,000 to one of their injured employees. Frank Suchomel injured his right eye while using a rotary saw and lost his vision. The court found Maxwell Brothers negligent for improperly maintaining the conditions of their equipment, especially the saw Suchomel used. The saw was not fixed with a hood or apron to block pieces of wood thrown from the saw from hitting the operator. The Maxwell brothers allegedly knew about the dangerous condition of the saw. The days before Suchomel's injury, he had complained twice about the working conditions and a foreman of the company said he would fix the saw within "reasonable time."[760]

An appellate court affirmed the circuit court's decision, and the Maxwell brothers appealed to the Illinois Supreme Court. Justice Scott wrote the opinion in the case affirming the Appellate Court's ruling. Scott wrote that while Suchomel's "statement of his conclusion that it was a piece of wood that hit him might properly have been stricken out, the court's refusal to sustain the motion to strike did not prejudice [the] appellants." Scott ruled that the injury was due to improper working conditions. The saw was not "defective or out of repair, while it is shown that the alleged difficulty was the result of lack of an additional appliance." The machine was not faulty, and it was the Maxwell brothers' responsibility as employers to provide safe working conditions for its employees.[761]

A railroad case, *Peabody Coal Co. v. Northwestern Elv. R.R. Co.*, brought before the Illinois Supreme Court in 1907, involved a dispute over clearance regulations and ownership of tracks. The Northwestern Elevated Railroad Company petitioned Cook County to gain access to twenty-five feet of land on the Peabody Coal Company's land to build an elevated track to continue its line of tracks granted by a previous ordinance from the City of Chicago. The petition showed that the track structure to be built would leave only fifteen feet of head clearance from the structures below. The Coal Company filed several cross-petitions to have the Northwestern Elevated Railroad Company's request denied. The cross-petitions claimed that the tracks to be built would not be the property of the Northwestern Elevated Railroad Company, but they would be the property of the land owners it crossed over, and that the construction plans of only fifteen feet of clearance would cause damage to the companies it crossed over.[762] The jury agreed with Railroad's right-of-way request and assessed compensation at $13,083 that the Railroad had to pay. Peabody Coal appealed to the Supreme Court.

The Supreme Court reversed and remanded the case. In Scott's opinion, he wrote that the court interpreted the original ordinance's purpose to create safety clearance rates and not to declare ownership.[763] Scott wrote that the purpose was "no doubt, to insure the safety of those traveling upon and operating trains on the steam railroads."[764] The clearance regulations were to ensure safety of citizens not the surrounding companies. Also, Scott wrote that the court determined that the dimensions of the tracks to be built were to be the decision of the railroad company because the Peabody Coal Company only used the tracts for commercial business.[765] Scott stated that "even though no boundaries for the right of way have ever been fixed, where the title to the track, and to the tract of land over which it passes, is in the same person."[766] It was the railroads responsibility to ensure safety of their tracks.

Scott suffered from appendicitis and underwent surgery to relive the condition. After two surgeries, Scott died from complications on May 24, 1909, at the age of forty-five.[767] Scott was remembered at a memorial by the Illinois Supreme Court and described by one speaker: "He was a just and fair minded man."[768] He died just shy of completing his full term as an Illinois Supreme Court justice. He was buried in the Aledo Cemetery.

WILLIAM M. FARMER, 1906-1931

William Maurice Farmer was born near Vandalia, Illinois, in Fayette County on June 5, 1853, and raised on the family farm. He was the son of Kentucky-born William Farmer and Vandalia-born Margaret Wright Farmer. He lived in Vandalia for all of his seventy-eight years, but conducted a life of public service in which his influence affected statewide public policy. As one of the longest serving justices of the Supreme Court he earned the sobriquet "Nestor of the Bench."[769]

He attended local public schools, and in 1871 headed fifty miles west to McKendree College at Lebanon to study for three years. He returned home to teach school, but soon began studying law in the office of Henry & Foulke in Vandalia. To receive a more formal legal education, he went to Chicago where he obtained a Bachelor of Laws degree from the Union College of Law, now Northwestern Law School, in June 1876, and immediately entered private practice. Between 1876 and 1897, when he assumed a circuit judgeship, he formed partnerships with Beverly Henry and George Chapin, and finally with John J. Brown, who was politically active and one-time candidate for governor.[770]

While he was enrolled in law school, he married Illinois Virginia Henniger of Vandalia on December 23, 1875. Together they had five children, but only two of them outlived their father.[771] His private practice soon gave way to public service when he was elected State's Attorney in 1880 for Fayette County. A half-century earlier, Vandalia was the capital of Illinois, and when state government moved to Springfield, the old capitol became the Fayette County courthouse. When Farmer was elected in 1888 to the House of Representatives, he had the unusual experience of moving his office from one capitol building into another. In 1890, he won election to the state senate.[772]

Farmer began his judicial career in 1897 with election to the circuit court in Fayette County. Under the state's 1870 constitution, circuit judges served as appellate judges when appointed to do so by the Supreme Court. Farmer was appointed to serve in the appellate court's second district in 1906, but he served only briefly because he was elected to fill a vacancy on the Supreme Court later that year. Farmer was a lifelong Democrat, and Fayette County was staunchly Democratic as well. Even though the Supreme Court district extended well beyond the county line, Farmer had become so popular in the region that the Republican Party ran no one against him. His only opposition was a Socialist Party candidate, whom Farmer beat by a margin of thirteen to one.[773] He was reelected in 1915 and again in 1924, on which occasion he again ran unopposed. The election of 1915, however, was much more troublesome for him.[774]

In his 1915 reelection bid, he ran a tight race against challenger William F. Bundy, and Farmer's victory was less than certain. There were issues raised about some of his opinions and beliefs. There had been much in politics concerning prohibition in the decades leading up to the eighteenth amendment to the United States Constitution. The "drys" in Farmer's district did not like his position against prohibiting alcohol. Second, he had opined that a schoolteacher had no right to read a Bible in class when the school superintendent had forbidden it. The issue was one of free speech and free practice of religion rather than separation of church and state. Third, Farmer had dissented in a case that would have extended a woman's right to vote.[775]

A suffrage bill enacted in Illinois gave women the right to vote for offices not established by the state constitution. In the 1914 case of *Scown v. Czarnecki*, the majority of the court found the law to be constitutional.[776] Justice Farmer and Justice George Cooke dissented, with Farmer writing in his dissent that when the constitution prescribed voting qualifications, it prescribed qualifications for voters in all elections for all offices, not just those created by the constitution itself. According to Farmer, whether the legislature or the state constitution created an elected office, the qualifications of electors for that office were to be determined by the constitution. Those supporting the right of women to vote disagreed with Farmer's dissent, but Farmer's opinion said nothing about the desirability of woman suffrage. He said that constitution needed to be changed in order for women to vote.[777]

In 1922, Illinoisans voted to accept or reject a proposed new state constitution. The 1870 constitution was more than fifty years old with a patchwork of amendatory provisions to help the state function in the modern world. Although the justices of the Supreme Court had no more authority over adopting the proposed constitution than any other individual voter, their opinions on the measure were eagerly sought. Farmer was one of three justices opposed to ratification because, he concluded, the new provisions for property taxes on farmland were not equitable. He also opposed returning to a system of decentralized Supreme Court hearings around the state. That system had been in place in a somewhat different form from 1848 until 1897, and no one found it efficient. As a farmer and a jurist, he was keenly interested in the issues and found the proposed provisions unacceptable.[778] The voters ultimately failed to ratify the measure, and Illinois would not get a new constitution until 1970.

The 1970 constitution would also undo a majority opinion written by Farmer in regard to constitutional amendments. In *People v. Stevenson*, a case to determine how many votes were necessary to pass an amendment, Farmer wrote, "amendments to the constitution shall receive a majority of all the vote cast for the general assembly."[779] The decision had a far-reaching effect in making amendments to the constitution nearly impossible because of the state's elector system that allowed up to three votes to be cast in each legislative district.[780]

Reelected in 1924 without opposition in a Republican landslide year, Farmer began his third and final term on the court. In 1926, he suffered from a relatively mild but partially paralyzing stroke that would eventually end his career. One year later, he celebrated thirty years on the bench, and at seventy-four years of age, he held the respected position of dean of the court.[781]

During his tenure on the Supreme Court, Farmer wrote 1,335 opinions for the majority and forty-one dissents. As cases arrived at the court they were distributed to the justices by rotation. Thus each justice was in charge of one in seven cases. In spite of his disability incurred by his stroke, Farmer never refused a case and never fell behind. He was soon unable to attend court but continued his work at home. His failing health raised concerns about compulsory retirement, but on June 5, 1931, his seventy-eighth birthday, he announced his resignation effective July 1, 1931, a full two years before his term expired.[782] After twenty-five years on the Supreme Court, as the court's grand old man, amid applause for his resolve in continuing his work on the bench, he returned home to Vandalia where just over one month later he died on August 8, 1931. Farmer was buried in South Hill

Cemetery in Vandalia. He had served thirty-four years as a judge on the circuit, appellate, and Supreme Court benches. He served as Chief Justice four times.[783]

ORRIN N. CARTER, 1906-1924

Orrin Nelson Carter was born in Jefferson County, New York, on January 22, 1854. His parents were Benajah Carter and Isabel (Cole) Carter. His father, a sailor on the Great Lakes, died in 1856 when Carter was two years old. His mother eventually remarried James W. Francisco, and the family moved to DuPage County, Illinois, in 1864.[784] He went to public schools in the county, and in 1877 he earned a Bachelor of Arts degree from Wheaton College in Wheaton, Illinois.[785] Carter worked his way through college as a janitor. The Doctor of Laws degree was also conferred to him twice by Wheaton College in 1889 and by Northwestern University in 1925.[786]

After receiving his college degree in 1877, Carter taught school at Dover Academy in Bureau County, Illinois, and then in Morris, Grundy County. He was the superintendent of the Grundy County school system from 1881 to 1883.[787] In his spare time he studied law, spending one year under the "tutorship" of Judge Murray F. Tuley and Gen. Israel N. Stiles. In 1880, he was admitted to the Illinois bar. Up until 1888 he practiced law with Judge Samuel C. Stough and Judge Russell C. Wing. In 1888, Carter moved with Wing to Chicago to practice law.[788]

Carter married Janet Steven in 1881. The couple had two children: a daughter named Ruth Carter and a son Allan J. Carter. Allan Carter followed in his father's footsteps and was also a lawyer.[789] They settled their family in Evanston, Illinois. The Carter home became the place of many community meetings and gatherings. He hosted the meetings of the Evanston Political Equality League and the Evanston War Board meetings during World War II. On November 3, 1898, Carter presented a well-received address about equal rights called "Loyalty" to the Ladies' Auxiliary of the Eighth Illinois Volunteer Infantry.[790]

Carter had a very successful legal career before he was elected to the Illinois Supreme Court. From 1883 to 1888 he served as State's Attorney for Grundy County.[791] From 1892 to 1894 Carter was the Chicago Sanitary District's general attorney. During that time, the great drainage canal project started in Chicago. Also, in 1894, he was nominated to the Republican ticket and elected to the office of County Judge for Cook County. He was reelected in 1898 and held that position until 1906.[792] In 1900, Carter was also the unsuccessful Republican nominee for governor.[793]

In June 1906, Carter was elected to the Illinois Supreme Court for the Seventh Judicial District, which had the largest population of all the districts in Illinois. It was quoted that "The seventh district may well be designated, 'The Colossus of the North.'"[794] He served on the court for eighteen years. During that time, he wrote more than 1,000 opinions, which appear in nearly one hundred volumes of the *Illinois Reports*. Carter was so highly regarded among his colleagues that during a meeting on December 30, 1911, he was unanimously endorsed by the Chicago Bar Association for the appointment to fill a vacancy on the

United States Supreme Court after the death of John Harlan. The Chicago Bar Association submitted their suggestion to President William Henry Taft on January 5, 1912.[795]

Carter was "liberal in his views as to the law, politics, and religion." He was also a supporter of black rights, claimed to be one of the first of the Illinois Supreme Court justices to declare openly for women's suffrage, and Carter and "his family were interested in the outlawing of the liquor traffic." The Women's Bar Association spoke at the Illinois Supreme Court Memorial after Carter's death because "[Carter] and Mrs. Carter were ardent workers in all movements aiming to give equal rights to men and women." Carter spoke at many banquets of the Women's Bar Association, and the Hon. Mary M. Bartelme, the first woman judge in Illinois, expressed that Carter's "friendliness to our organization gave women lawyers of Illinois recognition in the profession which few groups of women lawyers in other states ever received."[796]

One case in which Carter wrote the opinion was *People v. Pfanschmidt*. This case became known as the "blood-hound case." In September 1912, four citizens of Adams County, Illinois, were murdered on a farm just outside of Quincy. The victims were Charles and Matilda Pfanschmidt, their daughter Blanch, and a local schoolteacher Emma Kaempen. A jury found Ray Pfanschmidt, the son who worked and temporarily lived in Quincy, guilty for the murders.[797]

The Illinois Supreme Court eventually heard the appeal. The defense claimed that the Adams County Circuit Court made many errors, including improperly submitted testimony, unfair trial circumstances, and improperly submitted bloodhound evidence. The defense also claimed that it was impossible to create a jury for a fair trial. Several surveys of the citizens of Adams County found too many people felt that Pfanschmidt was overwhelmingly guilty, and the defense filed a motion to change the venue to another county, but the lower court denied the request.[798] The Illinois Supreme Court reversed and remanded the lower court's decision with specific directions. The venue of the new trial was to be moved to another county, and it was held that bloodhound evidence was deemed not admissible as evidence for any reason.[799]

After World War I, Americans still feared radical political groups and government break down. Illinois enacted a statute in 1919 to prohibit any person from distributing printed material of any kind or speaking badly of or overthrowing the government, no person could knowingly be a member of nor create societies to overthrow the government, and no flags, insignias, or banners could be displayed as a form of protest against the government. In 1922, the case *People v. Lloyd* came to the Illinois Supreme Court involving thirty-nine members of the Communist Labor Party. The grand jury in Cook County indicted them in March 1920 for conspiring against the government. After the trial, a jury found twenty of them guilty. Eighteen appealed their cases to the Illinois Supreme Court, and Bross Lloyd was one of them. Lloyd was recognized as a leader in the Communist Labor Party in the Chicago area.[800]

The defense claimed the statute of 1919 was unlawful because the "General Assembly of Illinois does not have the power and authority" to declare it unlawful for people to reform or overthrow any part of the government, and the only legislative body that had the authority and power to make it punishable was the United States Congress. The State's argument in support of the statute of 1919 was that the people of Illinois had a duty to the state and the United States government to secure and protect the safety and rights of all American citizens, therefore states could "require its citizens to refrain" from acting out against the government.[801]

The Illinois Supreme Court affirmed the case. All of the defendants were sufficiently advised of the charges against them, and despite much of the publications and public speeches submitted as evidence occurred before the 1919 statute, it was all properly submitted and accepted in the case. It was also ruled that the statute of 1919 was valid, and the states had a right to prohibit their citizens from speaking out or conspiring to overthrow the government.[802] Orrin Carter dissented. He wrote "the questions discussed in this case are so vital to our country's welfare that I feel compelled to express my views at some length in a separate opinion." He went on with strong language to say that "many of the views shown in this record to be held by them are most unwise and foolish and in my judgment are largely the result of ignorance or immature thought and the public expression of them may do harm to the country."[803] Carter felt the statute of 1919 was invalid and void because it was too vague and general and went against the American doctrine of freedom of speech. Carter urged, "Legislative enactments or decisions of courts cannot prevent people from believing that laws should be changed."[804] He welcomed civil democratic involvement.

A second case concerning submission of evidence in which Carter wrote the opinion was *People v Jennings*. This case was known as the "finger print case." The case "held for the first time by any court of last resort in this country that finger print evidence is admissible as a means of identification."[805] A jury found Thomas Jennings guilty for the murder of Clarence B. Hiller in Chicago. Jennings had attempted to rob the Hiller home, and upon entering the home, he held a railing on the porch that was covered in wet paint, leaving his fingerprints behind. The Chicago Police Identification Bureau and many other leading experts in the practice of fingerprinting testified at the trial for the identification process of fingerprints. Carter wrote "there is a scientific basis for the system of finger print identification and that the courts are justified in admitting this class of evidence."[806] The Illinois Supreme Court affirmed the death sentence of Jennings.[807]

During his service on the Illinois Supreme Court, Carter held many other positions. From 1905 to 1906, he was the chairman of the Chicago Charter Convention. He was a member of the Illinois State Bar Association and the Chicago Bar Association, and from 1913 to 1916, he was the chairman of the judicial section of the American Bar Association. He was the president of the American Institute of Criminal Law and Criminology from 1912 to 1913. In 1922, Carter was the chairman of the Citizen's Committee on the Constitutional Convention. It was thought that this position led to the breakdown of Carter's physical health. He also wrote several publications including the *Ethics of the Legal Profession* in 1915.[808]

Carter retired from the Court in 1924 and moved to Glendale, California, where he lived the last three years of his life. Shortly after retiring, he suffered a paralytic stroke and never fully recovered. Orrin Carter died on August 15, 1928, in Glendale, California.[809] He was seventy-four years old. His wife, two children, and his sister survived him. The memorial by the Illinois Supreme Court described Carter's life as the "American Dream." His humble poor beginnings as a farm boy made way for ambition and hard work, which led Orrin Carter to a distinguished position of the Illinois Supreme Court.[810]

ALONZO K. VICKERS, 1906-1915

Alonzo Knox Vickers was born in Massac County, Illinois, on September 25, 1853. Grandfather Thomas Vickers brought his family to Illinois from Warren County, Tennessee, and began farming. James, one of Thomas's nine children, married Celia Smith, born near Tuscumbia, Alabama, and the widow of his uncle Jacob Vickers. "Both she and her husband," wrote a local historian, "entered a small tract of Government land and then built a log house, of which the boards that covered the roof were rived by hand, and the rude chimney was made of earth and sticks."[811] James farmed in the area and operated a mercantile business in the county seat of Metropolis. Alonzo was the youngest of the couple's three sons.

Attending the district school in winter, Alonzo spent the rest of the year working on the family farm. His father died in 1861, and when the Civil War broke out that year, both of his brothers enlisted in the Union army. After high school in Metropolis, he earned a teaching certificate and taught for six years in area schools while also studying for the bar in the office of Judge R. W. McCartney. In 1877, he began practicing law in Metropolis and, two years later, purchased and became editor of the *Weekly Times* in Vienna, in adjacent Johnson County. After selling the newspaper in 1878, he returned to his law practice.

Vickers married Leora E. Armstrong in 1880, daughter of William and Anna Armstrong of Metropolis. They became the parents of two daughters and a son. The family moved to the Johnson County seat of Vienna, where Vickers associated in a law practice with William A. Spann, under the firm name of Spann & Vickers, and later with George B. Gillespie in Vickers & Gillespie.[812]

A Republican, he was elected to the Illinois legislature in 1886, serving one term, then won election in 1891 as judge of the First Judicial Circuit, a position he held for eleven years. "His rulings are sensible, practical & to the point;" wrote an acquaintance, "his decisions bear evidence of his familiarity with the last detail of the case under consideration."

In 1903, Vickers joined the Appellate Court of the Second District. In 1906, he sought the Republican nomination for the Supreme Court's First District. He lost to Charles Thomas of Belleville, but when Thomas died a few days after the nominating convention, the delegates selected Vickers. In the general election, he defeated the incumbent justice Carroll C. Boggs of Fairfield. At that time, the Vickers family moved from Vienna to a home he purchased in East St. Louis, "so as to be more convenient to Springfield where he was to spend so much of his time with his judicial duties."[813]

In 1907, he delivered the opinion affirming a Cook County Circuit Court decision regarding negligence, *Pauckner v. Wakem*. J. Wallace Wakem and his partners operated a general warehouse business in Chicago. Employees of the Chicago Tribune Company, including George Pauckner, went to the warehouse to retrieve stored machinery. After removing the items, Pauckner, "desiring to attend to a call of nature," received permission to use the toilet room. Walking through a dimly lighted passway, he fell into an unprotected elevator shaft and suffered severe injuries. After the Appellate Court of the First District affirmed a $5,000 judgment for Pauckner, the warehouse owners appealed to the Supreme Court. In affirming the verdict, Vickers wrote, "If appellee was on the premises at the time and place of the accident by the invitation, either express or implied, of appellants, they owed him the duty to exercise ordinary care for his safety while upon said premises."[814]

In *Dyrenforth v. Palmer Tire Company*, the issue involved a sales commission. Palmer Tire owners employed attorney Douglas Dyrenforth to seek a buyer for the firm, and he negotiated a sale to the B. F. Goodrich Company. After the sale, however, Dyrenforth and Palmer Tire disagreed as to Dyrenforth's compensation. He contended that they had agreed on 10 percent of the amount for which the property sold, while the Palmer Tire owners argued that the agreement was for 5 percent. Letters between the two parties further confused the issue, and upon the death of a Palmer owner, the successors refused to make further payments. Dyrenforth won a Cook County Circuit Court judgment, affirmed on appeal to the First District Appellate Court. On appeal to the Supreme Court, Justice Vickers upheld the verdict: "In view of the acquiescence of appellant for a period of seven years in this contract, during which time some thirty different payments were made to appellees under it, we think the decree of the circuit court below requiring appellant to complete the execution of this contract in good faith is equitable and just."[815]

Vickers owned a 300-acre farm northeast of Vienna and was involved in several business interests. He had organized Drovers' State Bank in Vienna and served as president of the St. Louis, Paducah & Southeastern Railroad Company.[816] Active in the Illinois State Bar Association, he also held memberships in several fraternal organizations, including the Masons, Knights of Pythias, Independent Order of Odd Fellows, and Benevolent and Protective Order of Elks.

By 1915, his eighth year on the Supreme Court, Vickers suffered from a combination of asthma and pneumonia. He died at age sixty-two at his East St. Louis home on January 21, 1915. Following Methodist services there, he was buried in the family lot at the Fraternal Cemetery, north of Vienna.[817] During his Supreme Court tenure, Vickers authored 514 written opinions and nineteen dissents. "His death was untimely," wrote Justice George A. Cooke, "but his work will remain as a perpetual monument to his ability and his unswerving devotion to duty."[818]

FRANK K. DUNN, 1907-1933

Frank Kershner Dunn was born November 13, 1854, in Mt. Gilead, Ohio. He was the son of Judge Andrew Dunn and Emily Armentrout Dunn. Andrew Dunn graduated from Kenyon College, where he was a classmate of Rutherford B. Hayes. When Hayes was governor of Ohio, he appointed Andrew Dunn to the bench of the Court of Common Pleas in 1876. Young Frank attended public schools there until his enrollment at Kenyon College in 1869. While there he was accepted into the Phi Beta Kappa scholastic fraternity. He graduated from Kenyon College with a Bachelor of Arts degree in 1873, and then went to Harvard Law School, from which he received a Bachelor of Laws degree in 1875.

He was admitted to the bar in Ohio that same year and practiced law with his father in Mt. Gilead. Although an established life was waiting for him in the community where his father enjoyed prominence, Frank decided to make his career in Illinois.[819] In 1878, he moved to Charleston, Illinois, to join his uncle James A. Connolly in the practice of law. He was admitted to the Illinois bar the same year. He did not cut his ties to his hometown in Ohio. He returned to Mt. Gilead for his June 1, 1882, wedding to Alice (Stroh) Trimble, who was from one of Mt. Gilead's oldest families. Their marriage produced three children.[820]

Dunn became involved in Republican politics in Illinois. After practicing privately for more than twenty years, he won election as judge of the Fifth Judicial Circuit in 1897. He served on the circuit bench until 1903, when he lost in a reelection bid, allegedly because of his ruling in a particular case that found disfavor with a dominant political faction. Although he failed in his reelection bid, his success as an impartial and rigorous jurist boosted the esteem of his supporters. In 1907, the death of Supreme Court Justice Jacob W. Wilkin created a vacancy in the district. Dunn won the nomination to run as the Republican candidate in the June special election.[821] He was elected and won reelection two more times. He retired from the court in 1933 and returned to private practice in Charleston. During his twenty-six years on the Supreme Court he served as Chief Justice for four separate terms.[822]

During his two and a half decades on the Supreme Court, Dunn was an active participant in the transition from one era to another. Dunn authored 1,700 opinions, including almost 250 dissents and more than 60 minority opinions. Particularly significant among them are *People v. Board of Education* and *Scown v. Czarnecki*. In the former he held that children in public schools cannot be compelled to join in any particular form of religious worship.[823] *Scown* came to the court holding that portions of the "Illinois Woman's Suffrage Act," which granted women the right to vote in certain elections, was unconstitutional. In February 1913, Dunn wrote the majority opinion reversing the lower court and upholding the validity of the law seven years before the women's suffrage amendment to the United

States Constitution.[824] His opinion in *Scown* was based entirely upon the logic of the law, not an affinity for a popular political movement. During the Great Depression, Dunn agreed in a per curiam Supreme Court decision to declare unconstitutional a state sales tax that Governor Henry Horner wanted to raise money for relief efforts.[825]

Dunn frequently pursued improvements in the laws of the state and the legal profession. He wrote articles and book reviews for law journals.

The *Illinois Reports* published opinions of the Illinois Supreme Court. (Image courtesy of the Illinois Supreme Court Historic Preservation Commission)

He was very active in the Illinois State Bar Association, even after his retirement from the bench.[826] Beginning in 1922, the Court instituted the practice of presenting successful candidates for bar admission to the Supreme Court and had a member of the Court address them. On one occasion in Springfield that December, Dunn told an audience of new lawyers that law is a science and explained that "the lawyer owes a great duty to the profession, but he should not forget that, in proportion to opportunities, he also owes a great deal to his country." He added, "Law is a profession where success is measured by service rather than money."[827]

Dunn's philosophy of law included the notion that the people make the laws. In a debate at the 1916 annual meeting of the Illinois State Bar Association, he argued that laws "are the expression of the public will, or public opinions, and the people have the right to criticize them or to amend or repeal them in the manner authorized by law and the constitution."[828] In 1919, at the end of the Progressive Era, a post–World War I surge of anti-radicalism questioned idea of initiative and referendum, which permitted a majority of voters to propose or repeal legislation when legislatures declined to act. Dunn felt that such measures would destroy constitutional limitations and would "empower the majority with autocratic control" that could damage the independence of the judiciary. There had actually been some public sentiment in support of judicial recall following some unpopular court decisions.[829]

In addition to his ideas about jurisprudence, he also involved himself in questions of practice. In an article that created something of a stir in the legal profession around the nation, Dunn claimed that the reasons for delays in proceedings and crowded dockets was not found in the laws or courts, but with lawyers who used technicalities to prolong cases.[830] He, along with other justices on the court, was also active in the effort to establish a new state constitution in 1922 and 1923. Although the justices could have only limited participation in the campaign for the constitution, they made their views public. Four of the seven justices including Dunn supported the proposed document. The electorate, however, voted to reject the proposal.[831]

After leaving the Supreme Court in 1933, he returned home to Charleston to resume the practice of law. His health declined rapidly after December 1939, but he was able to remain active. He died August 7, 1940, at his home not quite two months after the Illinois State Bar Association conferred the title of Senior Counselor in recognition of his service of more than sixty years as a member of the Illinois bar. His Presbyterian pastor officiated at his funeral service, which ended with his burial at Mound Cemetery in Charleston.[832]

GEORGE A. COOKE, 1909-1919

The descendant of Scotch-Irish immigrants, George Anderson Cooke was born on July 3, 1869, near New Athens, Ohio, in the hillside log cabin of his grandfather James Cooke. Family ancestors arrived in the United States in 1783 and initially settled in Washington County, Pennsylvania. Great-great-grandfather Robert Cooke moved to Harrison County, Ohio, in 1804, where he farmed with his son James Cooke.[833]

George Cooke was the second of three children of Dr. Thomas and Vanceline Downing Cooke. After his father died in 1872, Cooke and his family spent two years on the farm of his maternal grandfather, John Downing, in Mercer County, Illinois. They returned to Ohio, but after the death of their mother in 1880, a Mercer County aunt, Ellen Downing, reared the children.[834] According to a local attorney, Downing "gave to these children a motherly love and training which Judge Cooke never forgot and which he cherished as one of the most valued contributions in the building of his character. All his lifetime he gave credit to this motherly aunt, and lost no opportunity to repay her with his love and appreciation."[835]

Cooke attended public school during the winter terms until 1885, when he worked at odd jobs and "secured enough money to purchase an outfit of clothing and such school books as he would need" to attend Aledo High School. Graduating in 1888, Cooke entered Knox College, where he joined Beta Theta Pi fraternity and participated in debating and athletics. "During his college course both when in school and in vacation time, he engaged in every conceivable kind of work whereby he could earn money to meet his expenses. He sawed cord wood, mowed and raked lawns, acted as steward of a boarding club, was monitor of men in college, worked on the farm, sold books and other articles—in fact no work was too menial or humble for him."[836]

After receiving the Bachelor of Arts degree in 1892, Cooke studied law in the office of future Illinois Supreme Court Justice Guy C. Scott and was admitted to the Illinois bar at Mt. Vernon in July 1895.[837] Cooke briefly practiced in Galesburg, but then moved to Aledo to become the junior partner in the firm of Scott & Cooke until forming a partnership with John F. Main. Within a year, Main moved to Seattle, Washington, and eventually became a state Supreme Court justice. Cooke partnered with Alexander McArthur in 1900, and with John M. Wilson from 1905 to 1908, and then maintained a private practice.[838]

On October 20, 1896, Cooke married Sarah S. Blee, the only child of Robert and Martha Jane McHard Blee of Aledo and a fellow Knox College graduate. The Cookes became parents of two daughters and two sons.[839] Prominent in the Democratic Party, George Cooke represented the Thirty-third District in the Illinois House of Representatives from 1902 to 1906.[840] From 1903 to 1909, he also served on the Democratic State Central Committee.

On September 25, 1909, the forty-nine-year-old Cooke defeated Republican Milton McClure for a seat on the Illinois Supreme Court from the Fourth District, filling the unexpired term of his deceased mentor and former partner Guy Scott.[841] In 1912, with endorsements from several major Republican newspapers, Cooke won a full nine-year term, defeating circuit court judge Robert J. Grier.[842]

In a 1913 case, Chief Justice Cooke delivered the opinion in *Gillespie v. Ohio Oil Co.*, affirming a decision by the Lawrence County Circuit Court. Charles Gillespie and R. T. Gillespie, owners of ninety acres of Lawrence County land, leased the premises for $1 to James R. Poole, "for the purpose of developing, producing and marketing oil and gas therefrom." Terms of the lease required Poole to erect a well on the premises within one year or pay the lessors an annual rental of twenty-five cents per acre until completion of the well. As royalty, the Gillespies were to receive one-eighth of all oil produced, plus $100 per year for each well from which gas would be marketed.

Poole assigned the lease to the Ohio Oil Company, which did not begin drilling until five years later. From the time of the lease until completion of the well, the Gillespies received a total of $90 in rental fees. The well produced twelve barrels of oil per day for the first two days; then, even though the company pumped the well daily, the amount dwindled to ninety-six barrels in ten months. The Gillespies brought suit to nullify the lease, alleging that Ohio Oil should have further developed the land for oil and gas production. In affirming the circuit court judgment, Justice Cooke decreed, "Oil was produced continuously after the drilling of the well. It is true that the quantity produced was so small as to make the venture unprofitable, but the strict letter of the lease was complied with."[843]

Cooke also rendered the opinion in the 1916 *Crittenden v. Hindman* case. The Randolph County Circuit Court case involved Mary A. Hindman, widow of Alexander Hindman, whose children sued on the grounds that, since her previous marriage as Mary A. Head to Martin Hoover had not been dissolved by divorce, her marriage to Hindman was void. Hoover asserted that, prior to marrying Head, he had been married but not divorced, and a search of county court records found no divorce proceedings. Cooke affirmed the circuit court decision that Mary Hindman, as the lawful wife of Alexander Hindman, was "entitled to the interests which the statute gives the widow in his estate."[844]

In ten years on the court, including a term as Chief Justice from 1913 to 1914, Cooke wrote 531 opinions, "a monument to his industry and ability as a judge," wrote Justice Floyd E. Thompson. Cooke "was interested in all young lawyers and he was always ready to give them the benefit of his experience." Thompson added that as "a young lawyer I often availed myself of the privilege of visiting with him and he always made me feel that he was delighted to have me call. It was he who first suggested that I should be a candidate to succeed him on this court and who persuaded me that I should presume to a position of such importance and responsibility."[845]

Cooke decided to leave the court at the end of 1918 for a return to the practice of law. "He conferred with me about this matter," recalled an associate, "and remarked that while he owned a great obligation to the people who had so signally honored him, yet he could not escape the conviction that it would be unfair to his family to reject the offer of a private practice which would enable him better to provide for his family and give them advantages which they otherwise could not have."[846]

In his December 12, 1918, letter of resignation to Governor Frank O. Lowden, Cooke cited those financial considerations: "Notwithstanding the liberality of the state in the matter of salary, I am unable to make adequate provision for the future. This is largely due to the many demands made upon a public official of a nature which cannot be ignored, and the inability of one in a judicial position to become interested in any other line of endeavor."[847]

The Cookes moved to Chicago in early 1919, while also maintaining their Aledo residence.[848] He became senior partner in the Chicago firm Cooke, Sullivan & Ricks and chief counsel of Peoples Gas Light and Coke Company. "Cooke understood and liked people," recalled a fellow Chicago attorney, "and was able to make the most of the human elements that are present, although they may be latent, in every legal problem. He had a friendly and even fatherly manner that put persons at their ease when they came to him to tell him about their troubles. He showed the utmost interest, and it was not assumed but genuine. His hearing gave an impression of calm power, which inspired confidence. He was generous to opposing lawyers and refused to believe ill of them if there was any alternative. They also trusted him in return. These qualities made him an effective negotiator. He was skillful in relieving tension, softening asperities, and often brought fair settlements out of tangled and difficult controversies."[849]

"This has been one of the busiest decades in his long and useful career," wrote Edward F. Dunne of Cooke in 1933, "but to the majority of Illinois people the immediate suggestions arising from mention of his name are concerned with his service on the Illinois Supreme bench, a service lasting nearly a decade and in which he impressed his legal knowledge, his broad understanding and liberal spirit on many important decisions emanating from the courts."[850]

A thirty-year Illinois State Bar Association member, Cooke served a term as Association president. He was a congregant of the Presbyterian church, a Thirty-third degree Mason, Mystic Shriner, and a member of the Knights of Pythias, Elks, and Independent Order of Odd Fellows. Still in active practice, George Cooke died at age sixty-nine at his residence in Aledo on December 6, 1938. Following Presbyterian services, Cooke was buried in the family mausoleum in Aledo Cemetery.[851]

CHARLES C. CRAIG, 1913-1918

The son of Illinois Supreme Court Justice Alfred M. Craig (1873–1900) and Elizabeth Proctor Harvey Craig, Charles Curtis Craig was born in Knoxville, Illinois, on June 16, 1865. Descended from Scotch-Irish immigrants, his paternal grandparents were David Craig of Philadelphia, Pennsylvania, and Minta Ramey Craig of Lexington, Kentucky. Maternal grandfather Curtis Kendall Harvey, a native of Barnett, Vermont, became a lawyer in Galesburg, Illinois, served in the 1847 Illinois Constitutional Convention, and married Hanna Key Craig of Lebanon, Maine.[852] "From this parentage," recalled a fellow attorney, "the boy drew his interest and background in the law."[853]

After attending Knox County public schools and a private academy, Charles Craig studied at Knox College and Notre Dame University. In 1883, he gained an appointment to the United States Naval Academy but upon graduation, with "no liking for that life in time of peace," resigned his commission to study law at Columbia University in New York City.[854] There, in addition to educational curriculum, he learned the fundamentals of football.

Returning to Illinois because of an illness, Craig entered Illinois Wesleyan Law School in Bloomington, in February 1887. "I was passing the college building one day" that spring, he recalled years later, "when some of the boys were practicing with a new football. It rolled out my way and I picked it up and returned it with a long drop kick, which was apparently new to them." Students from Wesleyan and the neighboring Illinois State University asked him to help organize a team according to rules used by eastern colleges. "Prior to that time, football had been played in the western high schools and colleges with an inflated round rubber ball and the rules, if any, were different at different places. Generally speaking, any number could play on a side, and there was no regular distance between goals or bounds."

Craig helped fellow students mark off the bounds and erect goal posts, and he officiated as coach and referee. With the fall 1887 semester, the Wesleyan team practiced on vacant lots near the campus; "we were careful of our diet, not to leave anything on the table but empty plates." Craig played quarterback and captained the 1887–1888 team against Illinois State, winning two of their three games. "Wesleyan was not a large college then but the student body of co-eds made up in quality what they lacked in numbers; they were as fine a set of boys and girls as I ever knew, mostly from the farms and small towns of northern and central Illinois, honest, capable and high spirited. It takes some brains even to play football and they were the kind that would attempt anything and generally succeed."[855]

While a student, Craig studied law with Stevenson & Ewing in Bloomington, whose senior member was Adlai E. Stevenson. Admitted to the bar in 1888,[856] Craig began practicing law in Galesburg and, as a Democrat, lost the election for Knox County States

Attorney. On July 12, 1893, he married Louise Dary, daughter of Eugene and Sidonia Benedict Dary of New Orleans, Louisiana.

In 1897, Craig organized and became captain of the Illinois National Guard Battery B, First Artillery. Although volunteering for the Spanish-American War, his unit never engaged in combat service. He commanded troops at Pana and Virden during coal miner riots in autumn 1898, receiving "the thanks of the Governor for his successful control of the situation." Continuing in the National Guard for several more years, by 1912 Lieutenant Colonel Craig became Third Brigade ordnance officer and supervisor of rifle instruction for all state militia in the northern counties of Illinois.[857]

His career in public office began with service for two terms as a representative in the Illinois General Assembly from 1899 to 1902. He served on the Judiciary Committee during each legislative session and in 1904 chaired the Illinois Commission's Committee on Agriculture at the vast Louisiana Purchase Universal Exposition in St. Louis. "Visitors were advised to plan a stay of two weeks," reported one historian, "in order to see everything since in the agricultural building alone a spectator could walk past nine miles of different sights."[858]

Nominated in 1909 for the Illinois Supreme Court from the Fifth Judicial District, Craig lost the election to incumbent John P. Hand by a small margin. Four years later, in October 1913, he won election to the Court, succeeding Hand.[859] Craig served on the Supreme Court for five years, "a period in which an unusual number of vitally important questions arose and were decided," recalled Supreme Court Justice Clyde E. Stone. Craig "took a deep interest" in the significant cases, "and his opinions in those in which he wrote, show careful consideration and independent thought as do his dissents in some of them."[860]

Craig, along with Justices William Farmer and George Cooke, wrote strong dissents in the 1914 *Scown v. Czarnecki* constitutional issue. William J. Scown filed a bill in Cook County Superior Court to restrain the Chicago election commissioners, including Anthony Czarnecki, from expending funds for ballots and ballot boxes for women, as provided in the 1913 Woman's Suffrage act. His attorneys argued the act violated the Illinois Constitution by modifying or repealing existing statutes regarding voter qualifications. Justice Frank Dunn delivered the majority opinion that affirmed the rights of women to vote in "any election." In the dissent, Craig maintained that the Constitution specified voter qualifications. "No one except those designated in section 1 of the suffrage article of the constitution," he wrote, "is entitled to vote for any office specifically provided for by the constitution. That section limits the right of suffrage to male citizens above the age of twenty-one years."[861]

Craig served as Chief Justice from 1915 to 1916. In the 1916 case *Nice v. Nice,* he delivered the Court opinion in affirming a DeWitt County Circuit Court decision regarding legal rights of a stepchild's descendants. Erastus Nice made a will in 1888 that bequeathed his DeWitt and Macon county lands to his wife, Mary Elizabeth Nice, and at her death to be divided among his children as "equal heirs." His stepdaughter, Mary Emiline Bailey, daughter of his wife, died in 1903, and after Mary Nice died in 1915, Bailey's children sought their mother's portion of the estate. The circuit court agreed with a special master in chancery that although Erastus Nice intended that Bailey should have the status and all the rights of a child, "the devise was to her, only, and she having died before the testator, and not being a child or grandchild of the testator and not having the status of a child or grandchild under the language of the will, the devise to her necessarily lapsed" at her death.[862]

Retiring from the Court in 1918, Craig returned to his Galesburg law practice and, with his brother Dr. Harvey Craig engaged in extensive farming and business interests. A Knox College trustee, from 1918 to 1930 he served the Bank of Galesburg as director and then president. He held memberships in the Knox County Bar Association, Galesburg

Club, Elks, Masonic Lodge, Knights of Pythias, and Knights Templar. He was an honorary member and senior counselor of the Illinois State Bar Association.[863]

In failing health for several years, he withdrew from many of his former activities. On August 25, 1944, at age seventy-nine, Charles Craig died at his Galesburg home of an acute heart attack. His sole survivor was Louise Craig, his wife of fifty-one years. Following services, he was buried in Hope Cemetery in Galesburg.[864]

ALBERT WATSON, 1915

The youngest of three sons of Joel Franklin and Sarah Marena Taylor Watson, Albert Watson was born in Mount Vernon, "within a block of the Court House Square," on April 15, 1857. His grandfather Dr. John Wright Watson had moved from Virginia and then Kentucky to Illinois in 1821, where he farmed and became the first physician in Mount Vernon. Joel Watson attended Mount Vernon Academy, taught in area schools, and in 1842 won election as County Clerk, a position he held for sixteen years.[865]

His son Albert attended public school in Mount Vernon and graduated with honors from McKendree College in Lebanon in 1876. He taught in a country school for two years while studying law under Charles H. Patton. In 1880, he married Mary Eunice Way, an elementary school teacher and daughter of Newton E. and Lizzie H. Heaton Way of Mount Vernon. They would become the parents of five children.[866]

Admitted to the bar in 1880, Watson partnered with Patton for four years and served as Master in Chancery for Jefferson County. In the fall of 1892, the Democrat Watson became Mount Vernon's city attorney. He later served as Jefferson County state's attorney and became a director of King City Federal Savings and Loan Association and president of Ham National Bank, both in Mount Vernon, and an officer of First National Bank of Waltonville, Bank of Bonnie, First State Bank of Dix, and Ewing State Bank. In 1909, he served a one-year term as Grand Chancellor of the Knights of Pythias lodge and supervised construction of its Orphans Home in Decatur, Illinois.[867]

On February 17, 1915, Governor Edward F. Dunne appointed Watson to fill the unexpired term of Justice Alonzo Vickers, who had died the previous month.[868] Although he served only until June 7 of that year, Watson wrote a number of opinions, including *Dalbey v. Hayes*, the case of a feeble eighty-two-year-old widower, Aaron Dalbey, with no direct descendants. His "next friend" Fred Dalbey asserted that the widower was mentally incompetent when he conveyed his seventy-three-acre Vermilion County farm, home, and personal property to William S. Hayes, a nephew of Aaron Dalbey's wife, "for a purported consideration of one dollar." The transaction included a written agreement that Hayes would provide a home for Aaron Dalbey and would "do whatever should be necessary to properly care for him." Hayes assumed control of the farm and personal property, and Dalbey became "a member of the Hayes family." Eight witnesses testified to Dalbey's incompetence in business transactions, while twenty-nine considered him competent. "We are not convinced there is a preponderance of evidence showing mental incapacity in Dalbey to make the deed and contract in question," Watson wrote in affirming the Vermilion County Circuit Court ruling, "and such incapacity is not to be inferred from old age or feeble health, even when combined with a defective memory."[869]

Another 1915 case, *Burke v. The Toledo, Peoria and Western Railway Company*, involved the accidental death of freight brakeman Timothy Burke at the Gridley, Illinois, train station. Hanging onto the outside of a freight car, he fatally struck baggage trucks placed near the tracks. The Tazewell County Circuit Court awarded $7,500 in damages against the railroad for negligence in the death. In its appeal, the railroad contended that Burke violated company safety regulations. "Unless he saw the trucks and knew they were so near the car as to be a source of danger," Watson wrote in affirming the Circuit Court decision, "there is nothing in the position he occupied which could be charged as negligence. The fact that his attention was attracted toward the approaching passenger train, that smoke and cinders were blowing towards him from the freight train engine, and that he threw up his arms as if to shield his eyes from the dust and smoke, together with all the other circumstances, tended to prove that he did not see the trucks or their position in time to avoid the danger."[870]

Following his brief Supreme Court tenure, Watson served for many years as president of the State Board of Law Examiners. "Judge Watson reviewed the qualifications of would-be lawyers throughout two decades," reported the local newspaper, "giving personal attention to individual cases and influencing the careers of hundreds of successful attorneys."[871]

During World War I, he became chairman of the Jefferson County draft board and head of the district board. He served as attorney for several railroad companies and president of the Jefferson County Bar Association. Active in the First Methodist Church of Mount Vernon, Watson served as a trustee, taught Sunday school, and in 1928 was elected a lay delegate to the Methodist General Conference in Kansas City.

Watson maintained his law office on the north side of the downtown square until his mid-eighties, and in 1941 delivered the main address at the dedication of the new Jefferson County Courthouse. At the age of eighty-seven, Watson died at his Mount Vernon home on November 26, 1944. Burial in Oakwood Cemetery followed services at the First Methodist Church.[872]

WARREN W. DUNCAN, 1915-1933

Warren Webster Duncan was born January 21, 1857, in Lake Creek township in Williamson County, Illinois. The community, which was about six miles north of Marion, was named Shakerag, and later became part of the incorporated town of Johnston City.[873] When he was born, southern Illinois was barely one generation removed from the frontier era and must have still burned with the ardent patriotism of early nationhood since his parents, Andrew Jackson Duncan and Nancy Powell Duncan, named their son after Joseph Warren, a Revolutionary War hero killed at Bunker Hill, and Daniel Webster, one of the most popular statesmen of the nineteenth century.[874]

Young Duncan completed all of his courses at the local public schools and graduated from Ewing College with a Bachelor of Arts degree in 1879.[875] After a brief tenure as a public school teacher, he returned to his alma mater for a Master of Arts degree that he received in 1883. After obtaining his second college degree, he studied law briefly in the office of Judge W. H. Williams in Benton, the seat of neighboring Franklin County, then in the office of Judge George R. Young in Marion. A little more than a year later, in October 1884, he enrolled at St. Louis Law College and in less than a year obtained a law degree with honors in 1885. He received his law license on February 25, 1885, practicing in Mt. Vernon until August 1886, at which time he relocated to Marion, which remained his hometown the rest of his life.[876] That same year his election to a four-year term as county judge for Williamson County marked the beginning of his public service career.

He returned to the full-time practice of law in 1890 and except for his service as a presidential elector in 1896 as a Republican, he kept himself to the business of law. During this period, which ended in 1903, he earned a reputation as one of southern Illinois's most outstanding lawyers.[877] In 1903, he was elected as a circuit judge, serving for twelve years until his election to the Supreme Court in 1915. In 1909, the Supreme Court recognized his ability in the local circuit and appointed him to the Appellate Court for the Fourth District in Mt. Vernon. He remained on the appellate bench from 1911 until 1915 and had to serve in the First District in Chicago as a new state law precluded appellate judges from sitting on the bench in their home circuit.[878]

As a Republican, he ran successfully from the First Judicial District of the Supreme Court in 1915. In keeping with the court's practice of rotating the Chief Justice position, Duncan served as Chief Justice for the year commencing June 1919. His first term on the bench covered the entire period of the United States' involvement in World War I. As a member of the Court, he served on the executive committee of the State Council of Defense along with such prominent Illinoisans as Samuel Insull, Charles Deneen, Joseph Fifer, Edward Dunne, William Hale Thompson, and a score of others.[879]

In 1919, as Chief Justice he wrote the unanimous opinion in *Hagler et al. v. Larner et al.*, in which thirteen children sued the Granite City Board of Education for refusing their admittance to school because they had not been vaccinated for smallpox. Duncan wrote that a "child infected with small-pox may communicate the disease to hundreds of others, and the disastrous results therefrom are incalculable." He noted that some people chose not to vaccinate their children because of the risk of contracting the disease itself, but that a child's "right to enjoy school" should not "expose other people unnecessarily to dangerous diseases." Duncan concluded that the Board of Education did not have "an unreasonable requirement to prevent children from having the benefits of school unless vaccinated" affirming the Granite City Board of Education's and the lower court's decision.[880]

In another case, Governor Len Small may be remembered for a case in which Warren Duncan played a role. Small was elected governor in 1920 after serving a term as state treasurer. After he moved into the governor's mansion in Springfield, he and his lieutenant governor, Fred Sterling, and some of Small's associates from his hometown in Kankakee County were indicted for embezzling state funds during his time in the treasurer's office. The individuals were accused of investing the state's funds, rather than actually stealing the money, then keeping the proceeds for themselves. After several trials involving strained laws and uncertain facts, Small was acquitted in 1922. However, Edward Brundage, the Illinois Attorney General and Small's political enemy, brought a civil suit to force Small to pay more than $1 million to cover what he calculated as the state treasury's loss. The case ultimately went to the Supreme Court in early 1926. The court in effect agreed to a compromise in which Small would have to pay $650,000 into the treasury.[881] Warren Duncan and Oscar Heard dissented from the majority, with Duncan concluding that the Court was wrong because of "of a misconception of the facts in the record and a misconception in regard to the system of bookkeeping in the treasurer's office."[882]

He was reelected to the Supreme Court in 1924, but when he considered yet another term to begin in 1933, he decided to retire from the bench. After several serious operations within a few years, his health declined, and on the early morning of April 11, 1938, he died at his home in Marion at eighty-one years of age. His funeral and services were held at his home and a few blocks away at the Christian Church where he had been a member. He was buried in Rose Hill Cemetery in Marion.[883] His years of service on the Supreme Court coincided with the transition in the United States from the Progressive Era to the post–World War I world of the 1920s.

CLYDE E. STONE, 1918-1948

One of the longest-serving Illinois Supreme Court justices, Clyde Ernest Stone was born near Mason City, Illinois, on March 23, 1876. His grandfather William A. Stone, a native of Virginia, resided for a time in Kentucky before moving to Menard County, Illinois, in 1835 to farm. William's son Claudius L. Stone was the Mason City postmaster and a prosperous farmer. He and his wife, Mary Gertrude Marot Stone, became the parents of six children, including Clyde Ernest. Mary Stone died in 1884 from injuries when a cyclone destroyed the family home.[884]

Reared on the family farm, Clyde Stone attended rural schools and in 1894 graduated from Mason City High School. He taught in county schools for six years while also studying law at home. On November 14, 1900, he married Jessie Browning, daughter of Dr. Joseph and Lucy E. Harpham Browning of Havana, Illinois. The Stones would become parents of three daughters.

In 1901, Stone entered the University of Illinois pledging Phi Kappa Sigma, the Phi Delta Phi law fraternity, and earning a varsity letter in football.[885] After receiving his law degree in June 1903, Stone partnered in Peoria with Irwin I. Fuller and, in 1908, opened a law office with Joseph V. Graff, a veteran Peoria attorney and former member of the U.S. Congress.[886] "As a lawyer," wrote one Peoria historian, "Stone soon demonstrated his ability to handle intricate and involved problems of jurisprudence and to accurately apply the principles of the law to the points in litigation. His preparation of a case was ever thorough and comprehensive, his presentation clear and forceful and his deduction logical. He is seldom, if ever, at fault in the citation of principle or precedent and his success is due above all other things to his indefatigable industry."[887]

While maintaining his law practice, Stone also served for three years as assistant state's attorney. In 1910, he won election to the county court on the Republican ticket by a slight margin. "As a result of the energy of the new judge," recalled attorney Clarence W. Heyl, "his industry and intelligence, his firmness in requiring compliance with the adopted rules, it was but a short time until the trial dockets were up to date."[888]

Reelected by a large majority in 1914, Stone served on the county court until his election as judge of the Tenth Judicial Circuit in 1915. Then, in June 1918, a mere fifteen years after law school graduation, the forty-two-year-old won the election to succeed Fifth District Justice Charles C. Craig on the Illinois Supreme Court. "As a member of the bar of that circuit," Heyl continued, "I can testify that the movement to nominate [Stone] as a candidate for the Justice of this court came from the almost unanimous support of the lawyers of our circuit. . . . His ability as a circuit judge had been proven."[889]

Stone would be reelected in 1927, 1936, and 1945, and serve as Chief Justice in 1921, 1927, 1932, 1936, and 1942. Among his numerous opinions was *People of the State of*

Illinois v. Ernest J. Stevens, a famous case of alleged financial corruption. Chicagoan James W. Stevens, grandfather of future U.S. Supreme Court Justice John Paul Stevens, had made a fortune in insurance and in operating the LaSalle Hotel. In 1925, James and his sons Raymond and Ernest launched the Stevens Hotel Company, selling bonds to construct the world's largest hotel on Michigan Avenue and Seventh Street (now Balbo Drive). The new Stevens Hotel opened in May 1927 to great success. But during the Great Depression, after both the highly leveraged Stevens and the LaSalle lost millions of dollars, James and his sons authorized massive loans from the family-owned Illinois Life Insurance Company. They eventually filed for receivership, and when federal agents and a court-appointed administrator found a $13 million Illinois Life investment in the distressed hotels, a Cook County Grand jury indicted the three men for embezzlement.[890]

James suffered a massive stroke from the stress, and Raymond committed suicide; thus, Ernest Stevens stood trial alone. Even though the defense called prominent character witnesses, including former Illinois governors and business leaders, the jury found him guilty of embezzling $1.3 million. On appeal to the Illinois Supreme Court, Justice Stone delivered the opinion reversing the decision. "The transactions," he wrote, "were done in the regular course of business of the insurance company and approved by its board of directors. The officers of the insurance company had a right and power to loan money to the hotel company. In this whole record there is not a scintilla of evidence of any concealment or fraud attempted. . . . We are of the opinion that the record does not justify the verdict of guilty."[891]

Stone also wrote the opinion reversing the decision in the 1945 *Gabel Manufacturing Company v. Francis B. Murphy, Director of Labor,* regarding the state's Unemployment Compensation Act. The John Gabel Manufacturing Company of Chicago petitioned the Supreme Court after the Cook County Circuit Court ruled for the Illinois Department of Labor, seeking unemployment compensation assessments from the company. The issue involved several former employees who became independent contractors to lease, install, operate, and service Gabel-manufactured vending machines and automatic phonographs. "We see no difference in the arrangement" between the company and the contractors, Stone wrote, "from that of a farmer who owns a farm and machinery to operate it, and who also buys, sells and feeds livestock, and desiring to devote his entire time to his livestock business and to be free from the responsibility of cultivating the land, leases to a then hired employee, his farm and his farm equipment and the use of the farm land."[892]

A member of the First Presbyterian Church of Peoria, the local, state, and national bar associations, Stone also participated in local community affairs and several fraternal organizations. An avid outdoorsman, he supported wildlife conservation efforts of the Izaac Walton League.

On January 14, 1948, at age seventy-one, Stone died from a cerebral hemorrhage while caring for his ailing wife at their Tucson, Arizona, winter home. Following services in Tucson and at the Scottish Rite Cathedral in Peoria, he was buried in Peoria's Springdale Cemetery.[893] "For nearly thirty years," eulogized Illinois Governor Dwight H. Green, "he has been a distinguished member of the bench in this state. His exceptional ability and the high quality of his judicial service were widely recognized not only by the bar but [also] by all citizens. His place on the supreme bench will indeed be hard to fill."[894]

Only Thomas C. Browne's thirty-year tenure on the Illinois Supreme Court from 1818 to 1848 surpassed that of Stone. "It was Justice Stone's ambition," attorney Heyl recalled, "to continue his service in this court until he had at least served a period equal to that of Justice Browne. Had he lived until September 1948, he would have achieved that ambition."[895]

FLOYD E. THOMPSON, 1919-1928

Born on a farm two miles west of Roodhouse in Greene County, Illinois, on December 25, 1887, Floyd Thompson was the eldest of five children of Albert Alonzo and Sarah Edwards Thompson. More than a century earlier, Thompson ancestors had emigrated from the state of Virginia to the farmlands of the Mississippi Valley. Albert's great-grandfather John Thompson served in the Revolutionary War and, in 1815, settled with his family at the north edge of present-day Greene County.[896]

Floyd Thompson worked with his father on the family farm and attended district schools. Valedictorian of the Roodhouse High School Class of 1907, he taught school for two years. He became principal of the Manchester, Illinois, high school, studying law in the evenings and during summer vacations. "Through early training and by natural instinct," wrote *Roodhouse Record* editor Frank Merrill, "he was a gentleman, and an elemental trait which impressed his friends was his faithfulness and assiduity to the task at hand, qualities that have stuck to him."[897]

Never attending law school, Thompson passed the bar examination and was admitted to the Illinois and Tennessee bars in 1911. He opened a practice in East Moline, Illinois, while also publishing the *East Moline Herald*. "He had a good working knowledge of the law and some experience," reported the *Rock Island Argus,* "but that was all. He was among strangers, without funds or friends, and up against keen professional competition. Was he downhearted? Not a bit. He went out among people, picked up a little business on the strength, mainly, of his personality, and presently everybody in town knew who he was. In a year, he was so well advertised throughout the county that he was offered the Democratic nomination for state's attorney, a forlorn hope, it is true, for no Democrat ever had occupied that office."[898]

On a pledge to end rampant public corruption in Rock Island County, Thompson became the first Democrat elected State's Attorney in that area. He served as president of the Illinois State's Attorneys Association in 1916 and that year won reelection with a 2,300-vote plurality.[899] In 1918, Thompson married Irene Condit Worcester, a graduate of Roodhouse High School and Illinois Woman's College in Jacksonville. Irene and Floyd Thompson became the parents of one daughter, Mary Ellen Thompson.[900]

In addition to his prosecutorial duties, Thompson also served as president and director of the Rock Island County Fair. During World War I, he was a member of the District Appeal Board and the State Council of Defense. At Rock Island Arsenal, Thompson assumed responsibility for protecting the thousands of munitions workers while also keeping the federal property free from criminal influences.[901]

On April 1, 1919, Thompson won election to fill an Illinois Supreme Court vacancy from the Fourth District created by the resignation of Justice George A. Cooke. At age thirty-one, Thompson became the youngest popularly elected justice in Illinois Supreme Court history. That autumn the *Rock Island Argus* reported that Thompson had written opinions in thirty-eight cases, "almost a year's work in six months."[902]

In June 1921, with endorsements from the *Chicago Tribune* and other Chicago newspapers, he was elected to a full nine-year term. "The chief handicap that Justice Thompson had when he assumed office," editorialized the *Rock Island Argus,* "was his youth and inexperience, but this he has overcome through close application to his duties, his written opinions both as to volume and soundness having proved a pleasant surprise to his older colleagues of the bench."[903]

One year later, thirty-four-year-old Thompson was elevated as one of the youngest Chief Justices of the Illinois Supreme Court. During his tenure on the Court, according to a biographer, Thompson wrote opinions "in 643 cases in addition to all his other duties on the court, a record equaled by few and surpassed by none. The leaders of the Bar are free in their praise of the quality of his work."[904]

Justices sit for a portrait on the Supreme Court bench with Floyd Thompson as Chief. (Image courtesy of Illinois Supreme Court Historic Preservation Commission)

A number of prohibition-related cases came before the Illinois Supreme Court during the 1920s after the passage of the Eighteenth Amendment and the accompanying Volstead Act. Justice Thompson authored two opinions in cases regarding searches and seizures in 1926. In *People v. Wiedeman*, Florence Wiedeman was suspected of purchasing "white mule and homebrew," and a magistrate issued a search warrant for her house. The officer waited six days before searching, found the beer, and confiscated it. Wiedeman was found guilty and appealed, arguing that too much time had elapsed in executing the search warrant. Justice Thompson agreed with her argument in reversing the conviction, noting that the search warrant "is a powerful police weapon. The qualities which make it efficient as an aid to enforcing the law make it dangerous when abused." He added that promptness "in the service of the writ is not only necessary for the preservation of liberty of the citizen but also for the efficient administration of the law." In *People v. Daugherty*, Cornelius Daugherty believed that there was not enough evidence that he possessed liquor for a search warrant to be issued. Justice Thompson disagreed with his argument, and upheld the judgment of the lower court, noting that probable cause "for issuing a search warrant to seize contraband liquor does not exist unless the magistrate is convinced, by competent and material evidence, that there is reasonable ground for suspecting that the liquor is possessed for prohibited purposes."[905]

Chief Justice Thompson had the distinction of administering the oath of office to the first female state legislator, Lottie Holman O'Neill of DuPage County. She was among members of the Fifty-third Illinois General Assembly, sworn into office in January 1923. Representative Norman G. Flagg extended to O'Neill a "special welcome from every man in this house" and urged women in the audience "years hence when perhaps lady members occupy 152 seats in the house and one man is present, may you grant that man the same gracious consideration."[906]

Politically active, Thompson flirted with running for president of the United States in 1924.[907] In early 1928, with endorsements from the Democratic State Central Committee, the Cook County Democratic Committee, and other county committees, Justice Thompson became the unopposed Democratic candidate for governor of Illinois. His nomination, according to a campaign brochure, "was the result of a state-wide demand for a change in the administration of the public business. His simplicity, his honesty, his industry and his courage are traits which have endeared him to the people of Illinois."[908]

Thompson resigned from the Supreme Court on July 25, 1928, pledging statewide reforms to counter corruption during the administration of incumbent Republican Governor Len Small. Thompson's opponent, Secretary of State Louis Emmerson, had defeated Small in the primary election. In his campaign, Thompson promised legislation that would compel the publication of state payrolls and called for revisions of the criminal code and judicial system as well as worker-protection laws.[909]

Springfield's *Illinois State Register* described the candidate as "young, vigorous and personifying the finest idealism in public and private life." The *Chicago Tribune* praised his Court opinions and supported his call for reforming state politics.[910] Still, in the landslide election that brought Republican Herbert Hoover to the U.S. presidency, Thompson lost to Emmerson, 1,709,818 to 1,284,879.[911]

Following that defeat, Thompson became a partner in the Chicago law firm of Newman, Poppenhusen, Stern & Johnston. He specialized as a civil and criminal trial lawyer. In perhaps the most sensational criminal case of the Great Depression era, he served as lead defense counsel for Commonwealth Edison president Samuel Insull, charged with mail fraud as well as violations of antitrust and bankruptcy laws. In three federal and state trials during the 1930s, Thompson successfully defended Insull against the accusations.

By 1948, Poppenhusen, Johnston, Thompson & Raymond employed sixteen lawyers, the fifth-largest law firm in Chicago. Newly hired attorney Robert F. Fuchs recalled then-managing partner Thompson as "a gruff curmudgeon but a superb lawyer" and life in the firm as "strict and unrelenting." Partners and associates routinely worked on Saturdays and often into the evenings, Fuchs remembered, with vacations intended for bar association meetings or other law-related events. And, according to Fuchs, when associates petitioned Thompson to close the office at 1 p.m. on Saturdays, he crumpled and threw the request into a wastebasket.[912]

Throughout his Chicago law career, Thompson continued his involvement in professional legal organizations, serving terms as president of the Illinois State Bar Association and Chicago Bar Association. A board member of the American Bar Association, he chaired the ABA's criminal law section. When he became senior member of the law firm, the name was changed to Thompson, Raymond, Mayer, Jenner & Bloomstein (now Jenner & Block). He received an honorary doctorate in law from Knox College in Galesburg, Illinois.[913]

On the evening of October 18, 1960, after taking depositions in his office, the seventy-two-year-old Thompson died unexpectedly at his Evanston home.[914] Following services at First Presbyterian Church in Evanston, he was buried in Fernwood Cemetery in Roodhouse.[915]

OSCAR E. HEARD, 1924-1933

Oscar Edwin Heard was born June 26, 1856, in Harlem Township near Freeport in Stephenson County. He lived there his entire life of eighty-four years, more than sixty of which he spent in the profession of law and public service. He was the son of William and Sarah A. Swanzey Heard. His father was a farmer and merchant who died in 1871 when Oscar was fifteen years old. He received a diploma from Freeport High School then attended college at Northwestern University to study literature. He studied there for two years then returned to Freeport to read law in the office of J. S. Cochran. He was admitted to the bar at age twenty-three in 1879. Heard is one of the few people to ascend to the Supreme Court bench with neither an undergraduate degree nor a law degree. On Christmas Day 1879, he married Mary J. Peters in Freeport. Together they had one daughter, Emily, who would precede him in death, and one son, Oscar E. Heard Jr., who would, like his father, enjoy a lifelong career in the legal profession.[916]

His lack of a formal higher education did not prevent his earning the respect and trust of his fellow citizens. He served as a justice of the peace from 1881 to 1884, then was elected and reelected four times in sixteen years to the office of State's Attorney for Stephenson County. At the end of his final term as State's Attorney in 1900, he had won convictions in 2,241 criminal cases, including three murders.[917] In 1903, he was elected judge for the fifteenth judicial circuit on the Republican ticket.

In 1904, he presided over a sensational murder trial. Two men who had committed a robbery in the Carroll County town of Chadwick were pursued to the Mississippi River town of Thomson, about twenty miles away. While resisting arrest, one of the men shot and killed the town's mayor. Heard presided at the trial, and citizens all over the northwestern part of the state followed the trial.[918] Judge Heard sentenced the killer to life at hard labor in the Joliet penitentiary.

During the time that coincided with Heard's tenure on the circuit bench, it was the practice to have judges from circuits around the state send judges to preside in Cook County cases since the docket there was always too crowded to be handled efficiently by the number of judges in Cook County. Heard spent one part of each year for twenty years presiding in Chicago. Early in his career on the bench, he was selected under a special appointment from Governor Frank O. Lowden to preside over some of the cases arising from the East St. Louis race riot of 1917. As a trial judge, he earned a reputation for fairness, brevity, promptness, and maintaining dignity and order in his courtroom while treating everyone with respect.[919] Heard won reelection to the circuit bench in 1915 and 1921. After his last election to the circuit court, the Supreme Court appointed him to fill a vacancy in the second appellate district.[920]

He was elected to the Supreme Court in 1924, succeeding the deceased James Cartwright. His colleagues on the Supreme Court noted his seemingly unlimited energy and his willingness to devote himself to the work of the court during a period in which the docket was unusually heavy. One of his more notable opinions was that for *Fergus v. Marks*, in which the court refused to compel the General Assembly to assemble for the purpose of passing a legislative redistricting law despite the fact that twenty years had passed since the previous redistricting, which was a clear violation of an explicit constitutional requirement.[921] Based on the principle of separation of powers, the court would not compel the General Assembly to act because the Constitution left that obligation solely to the General Assembly.[922]

He served as Chief Justice twice, but he would serve only one term on the court itself. He failed in his attempt at reelection when Democrat Elwin R. Shaw edged him out in the vote count. The election was rather contentious for a judicial election. The issue of his age of seventy-seven years was raised against him, as were charges of nepotism. These issues combined with the disadvantage of being identified as a Republican in 1933 led to his loss in the election.[923]

Upon leaving the Supreme Court he returned to private practice with his son for the remainder of his life. During all his time in public service as a prosecutor and a judge, he always maintained a high level of interest and participation on his local and state bar associations. He served as president of the Stephenson County Bar Association and, from 1919 to 1924, sat on the board of governors of the Illinois State Bar Association. In June 1940, the state bar association conferred on him the title of Senior Counselor in recognition of service for more than fifty years as a member of the Illinois bar.[924]

He was also prominent in the civic affairs of his community. He was a member of the Freeport board of education for many years, and because of his interest in education, he wrote the Illinois teachers' pension law.[925] He was also active in the Odd Fellows and Freeport Country Club. As a Mason he was awarded the high honor of the thirty-third degree. He also served as the president of the Freeport library board and is generally credited with obtaining the grant from the Carnegie Foundation to construct the stately classical public library there.[926]

After an illness of only three days, Heard died at his Freeport home on July 15, 1940. His funeral was held in his home, and he was buried in Oakland Cemetery on the southwest edge of Freeport.[927]

FREDERIC R. DEYOUNG, 1924-1934

Frederic DeYoung was born on September 12, 1875. When he was a child, he exclaimed to his friends and family that he wanted to be a judge. His parents were both natives of the Netherlands, from which they emigrated as children, settling in Chicago. The family lived in the ethnically Dutch village of Roseland, which would be later annexed by Chicago. A few years later, the family moved to the town of South Holland, which was the center of Dutch settlement in the Chicago area. His father, Peter DeYoung, who had been born in Dordrecht Zuid in the Netherlands, obtained an appointment as postmaster for the town. Frederic attended the Christian School and later the Brennan School. He left school altogether at age twelve when the family moved back to the west side of Chicago in 1887. He never completed his primary and secondary education.[928]

Back in the heart of the city, he went to work for two dollars a week for a local jeweler who, in spite of DeYoung's young age, entrusted him with carrying jewels and money around the city for two dollars a week. In 1890 at the age of fifteen, he started working at the nearby Pullman train car factory as a timekeeper. He left there to enroll at the Bryant and Stratton Business College. He was unable to continue his courses there because of his health. In response, his father sent him to Europe during 1893. Upon his return to the United States, he enrolled at the Northern Indiana Normal School, now Valparaiso University. He graduated from there in 1895, then entered Northwestern University Law School from which he received his Bachelor of Laws degree in 1897 at the age of twenty-two.[929]

While attending college in Valparaiso, he met Miriam Cornell from nearby Boone Grove, Indiana. After graduation from law school and settling in his law career, he married her in 1901 on his twenty-sixth birthday. The young couple established their home in the southern Cook County village of Harvey, where they would live until his election to the Supreme Court almost twenty-five years later. The marriage produced a son, Herbert, and a daughter, Ruth. Herbert followed his father into the law profession. Years later, Herbert was admitted to the bar while his father served as Chief Justice of the Supreme Court.[930] Daughter Ruth also had a notable career. After her graduation from Smith College and marriage to Herbert Kohler, the manufacturer of plumbing products, she enjoyed more than ten years as a *Chicago Tribune* and WGN radio commentator on women's issues.[931]

As a law student and new attorney he was associated with the law office of I. T. Greenacre, a venerated and longstanding member of the local bar. In his private practice, he was also associated with a number of locally prominent attorneys, including former state representative Louis J. Pierson. Through these connections, DeYoung became involved in politics as a Republican. In 1907, he was elected city attorney for Harvey. He was reelected twice and served until 1919. In 1914, he was elected to the House of Representatives for the Forty-ninth and Fiftieth General Assemblies. He was reelected for a second two-year term in 1916 during which time he was the chairman of the committee on the judiciary.

At the end of his second term, he decided to run for judge of the Cook County probate court rather than continuing his legislative career. He lost this race to the incumbent Democratic judge Henry Horner, who would later become governor in the next decade. Rather than return to private practice, he secured appointment as the first assistant attorney for the Sanitary District of Chicago. He was yet able to realize his childhood ambition to become a judge in 1921 when Governor Frank O. Lowden appointed him to fill a vacancy in the Cook County Circuit Court. In 1923, he was elected judge of the Superior Court of Cook County, but held that position for less than a year due to his election to the Supreme Court in June 1924.

As a practicing attorney and judge, he was interested in solving problems in the state's outdated and cumbersome judicial system. DeYoung was instrumental in bringing about statutory changes through his service on regional and statewide council established to address those issues. The work of the bench and bar culminated in the Civil Practice Act of 1933. Before that he had served as a delegate to the unsuccessful constitutional convention in 1922 where he was the Chairman of the Committee on the Judicial Department. Following years of preliminary work and holding the convention itself, the state's voters declined to adopt a new constitution.[932]

As a lawyer and a jurist he had a reputation for prodigious amounts of work. During his ten years on the Supreme Court, he authored more than 440 opinions, which were known for their "uniformly high legal quality and their simple clearness of expression, but above all for their manifest respect for principles."[933] Two of his opinions had profound consequences for Illinois courts.

People v. Bruner in 1933 overturned a law that had been in effect since 1827, when the state's legislature and judiciary were less than ten years old.[934] The statute allowed juries in criminal cases to determine law as well as facts. In his majority opinion, DeYoung held that the hundred-year-old law was unconstitutional by infringing on the right of judges to interpret the law. The role of the jury, he argued, was simply to determine matters of guilt or innocence. The *Chicago Tribune* stated that DeYoung's opinion was "the biggest step forward in criminal procedure in the last fifty years."[935] A second opinion, also pertaining to criminal law, affected the rights of defendants. In *People v. Fisher*, DeYoung wrote that in a felony trial where the plea is not guilty the defendant can waive a jury trial and have the cause heard and determined by the judge.[936] A third opinion, involving land use, had nationwide consequences. In *City of Aurora v. Burns*, DeYoung wrote the first opinion supporting the constitutionality of zoning.[937] His opinion was quoted at some length by the United States Supreme Court in the landmark *Village of Euclid v. Ambler Realty Company*, which established the constitutionality of land-use zoning nationwide.[938]

He was reelected for a second term on the Supreme Court in 1933, but this term was cut short by his sudden death.[939] On November 16, 1934, shortly after serving ten full years on the Supreme Court, Frederic DeYoung died from a stroke while walking in downtown Chicago. His friends, colleagues, and all those looking forward to his continuing on the bench at least until the expiration of his term in 1942, were shocked to learn that DeYoung's brilliant career had come to an end at age fifty-seven. His funeral was held in his home in Chicago. His honorary pallbearers included the Justices of the Supreme Court, former Governors Dunne, Deneen, and Lowden. Governor Henry Horner, who had defeated DeYoung for a seat on the bench years before, was also in attendance. Burial followed at Chicago's Oak Lawn Cemetery (now Homewood Memorial Gardens).[940]

CYRUS E. DIETZ, 1928-1929

Cyrus Edgar Dietz was born on a farm near Onarga, Illinois, a town on the Illinois Central Railroad in Iroquois County, on March 17, 1875. His parents were Charles Christian Dietz and Elizabeth Orth Dietz. He was the youngest of eight children. His father was born in Philadelphia of Alsatian background. His mother came from a Moravian family that settled in Pennsylvania in the early eighteenth century. Elizabeth Orth Dietz's uncle was Godlove Orth, a friend of Abraham Lincoln's during the Civil War, a prominent lawyer in Indiana, serving in the state legislature, in the United States House of Representatives, and as minister to the court of Vienna.[941]

His education began at the Grand Prairie Seminary at Onarga. From there he went to Northwestern University and majored in speech and law, obtaining his Bachelor of Law degree in 1902. His brother Godlove Orth Dietz graduated with him.[942] While pursuing his double-major at Northwestern, he also played fullback for the university football team, an effort that earned him All-American status in 1901.[943]

After graduation he stayed near Northwestern to practice law in the Chicago office of William Dever, who would later become mayor of Chicago in the 1920s. After achieving some national fame as a college football player, he was not quite ready to give up sports. In 1902, he accepted the position of head coach for the football team at Kansas State Agricultural College, now Kansas State University. The following year, he took the head coaching position with the team at Willamette University in Salem, Oregon. In 1904, he moved to Moline and joined his well-liked and respected brother who had moved there to start a law practice. In that year, he became the Moline High School football coach and led the team to the Illinois state championship that season.[944]

He soon joined the office of Burton F. Peek, a former United States District Attorney and later the general counsel for John Deere & Company, which had its headquarters in Moline. He left Peek's office to join in practice with his brother from 1912 to 1918. After that time, he left his brother to form Kenworthy, Dietz, Shallberg, Harper, & Sinnett.[945] He took on important positions such as general counsel for the local Tri-City Manufacturers Association and the Chicago-based Associated Employers of Illinois in 1908 and 1925, respectively. His clients came from many states, and he represented them in state and federal courts and in front of legislative committees.[946]

Aside from his law practice he was also active in the Republican Party. In 1920, he was a delegate to the unsuccessful state constitutional convention. In 1924, he was a delegate to the Republican National Convention that nominated Calvin Coolidge; he attended again in 1928.[947] Probably because of his extensive practice and his political activity, he came to the attention of Republican Illinois Attorney General Oscar Carlstrom, who had also been a practicing attorney in the Rock Island-Moline community. Carlstrom appointed him Special Attorney General to represent Illinois in two high-profile cases.

Dietz represented the State of Illinois and the Chicago Sanitary District in a suit brought against them by the Great Lakes states of Wisconsin, Minnesota, Michigan, Ohio, Pennsylvania, and New York. Because the case was among states, the United States Supreme Court had original jurisdiction. In a suit known as the lake-levels litigation, the plaintiffs sought to prevent Illinois from diverting water from Lake Michigan down the Illinois Waterway into the Mississippi watershed. Suits between states over the waters of the Great Lakes were somewhat common. In this particular case, the plaintiffs claimed that the lowered levels of the lakes harmed shipping, commerce, and the public health. For three years, Dietz managed Illinois's defense in front of specially appointed Master in Chancery Charles Evans Hughes. Dietz argued that lower lake levels could not be altogether attributable to Illinois's usage. The resulting decision upheld the right of Illinois to divert water but limited the amount.[948] Hughes complimented Dietz on his work. The second important case was a suit against the Illinois Central Railroad in regard to fees and the company's charter. Dietz was able to effect a settlement in the case, which had been dragging on for twenty years, bringing $1.5 million into the state treasury.[949]

Early in 1928, Justice Floyd Thompson of the Fourth Judicial District announced that he would resign his seat on the Court to run as the Democratic candidate for governor. Since the western Illinois district generally returned Republicans to elected offices, five individuals from various parts of the area vied for the Republican nomination. After thirty-one votes in the party caucus, Dietz emerged the winner. In the November general election, he beat his Democratic opponent, Warren Orr, by more than 18,000 votes out of the 151,700 votes cast in the fourteen counties comprising the electoral district.[950]

Shortly after his election to the Supreme Court bench, his name surfaced in a payroll scandal in the Chicago Sanitary District, now named the Water Reclamation District. An investigation into the seemingly high number of employees in the sanitary district, some of whom made relatively large salaries, led to a sensational hearing. The former president of the district's board pointed out, with apparent vindictiveness, that the district had paid Cyrus Dietz $107,000 when he worked for the district in the lake-level litigation, with the obvious inference that Dietz had done something illicit. Dietz admitted that he had in fact been paid that amount but pointed out that his service was spread over three years and that his fee had been $100 per day, which was less than the average attorney fee of the day. He added that this amount included his travel expenses and fees paid to others.[951] The *Chicago Tribune* rushed to Dietz's defense, and in a prominent editorial averred vehemently that Dietz was never involved with any chicanery at the sanitary district and that "Justice Dietz is one of the ablest members of the Illinois bar."[952] The issue never surfaced again.

Serving on the Court for only ten months, Dietz authored twenty-four opinions of the Court. In *People v. Brown*, Justice Dietz reversed a Bureau County Circuit Court case in which S. G. Brown was found guilty of practicing medicine without a license. Dietz noted that the prosecution failed to be specific in its accusations, and therefore, Brown was unable to prepare a defense to the charge.[953] In *Bamberger v. Barbour*, Justice Dietz negated an unsigned will that had been admitted to probate in Cook County. Edwin Bamberger had written out his will and had two uninterested parties sign as witnesses, but Bamberger failed to sign it. Dietz acknowledged that prior cases on the subject "are in conflict," but he relied on a California case that concluded that "the document in question was not signed by the testator as required by" the statute relating to wills, "and that it is not entitled to probate."[954]

Justice Dietz was an avid horseman, a pastime he had enjoyed for many years. At eight o'clock in the morning of September 12, 1928, while he was enjoying his customary morning ride with nephew Carl Dietz, he was thrown from his horse when a truck bumped into him while negotiating morning rush hour traffic near the corner of Fourteenth Street and Third Avenue in Moline. He landed hitting his head and left knee on the pavement. He was awake and lucid, but as the pain was severe, he was taken to Lutheran Hospital where he soon lost consciousness and then died at 1:22 in the afternoon. The cause of death was given as "shock and internal injuries."[955] His horse Bravo was uninjured. When he landed on the ground, he broke his left leg, reproducing an identical injury that he suffered ten years earlier when he was thrown by another horse while riding at the nearby Rock Island Arsenal.[956] Ever since the earlier accident, he had been forced to walk with a cane.

His funeral was conducted in his home by his Congregational minister. Hundreds of friends and colleagues from the bench and bar attended the service followed by interment in the mausoleum at Riverside Cemetery in Moline. He left behind his widow, the former Roberta Louise Sleight of Moline. They were married in 1904 and had one adopted son, Hunter.[957] At the peak of a highly successful career as a prominent attorney, he won a seat on the Supreme Court only to die of injuries sustained in an equestrian accident barely nine months after his swearing-in, making his tenure one of the shortest in the Court's history.

PAUL SAMUELL, 1929-1930

Justice Paul Samuell represented the Fourth District on the Supreme Court for one year from his appointment in 1929 until he was replaced in the June 1930 election. Henry Paul Samuell was born near Havana in Mason County on October 2, 1886. He was one of four children born to the family of Hickman B. Samuell and Sarah Estep Samuell. He received his early schooling at Whipple Academy in Jacksonville, graduating from there in 1905. He stayed in Jacksonville to attend Illinois College but left there to complete his formal education at the School of Law at Illinois Wesleyan University in Bloomington where he earned a Bachelor of Laws degree in 1910. He was admitted to the Illinois bar the same year.[958]

He worked briefly for the *Bloomington Pantagraph*, and then moved to join his parents in Roundup, a small town on the plains of central Montana. He stayed there practicing law for three years before returning to Jacksonville. He was in private practice for only a few years when he was elected county judge in 1919 as a Republican. He was reelected in 1920. At the end of his second four-year term on the circuit bench, he formed the law firm of Bellatti, Samuell & Moriarty in 1924. He stayed with the firm, except when he was on the Supreme Court, until his death in 1938. Throughout the 1920s, he served on the Republican State Central Committee representing the Twentieth Congressional District.[959]

In addition to his legal career, Samuell was a member of Jacksonville's Elks Club and Masonic Lodge. With business partners Walter Bellatti and F. M. Morris, he owned the popular Dunlap Hotel in downtown Jacksonville.[960]

Justice Samuell's journey to the Supreme Court began when Fourth Judicial District Justice Floyd E. Thompson announced his resignation from the bench to run as the Democratic candidate for governor in 1928. Samuell immediately announced his candidacy for the seat in the special election called by Governor Lewis Emmerson for November 1928, the same day as the presidential election. Although Samuell had the backing of Governor Emmerson, the nomination went to Cyrus Dietz of Moline after thirty-one ballots taken at the district Republican convention. Dietz won the election easily and probably would have run again in the regular election for the Fourth District in 1930, but after serving on the Supreme Court bench for less than a year, he was killed in an equestrian accident.[961] When there is more than one year remaining in the term of a vacant Supreme Court seat, the governor is obliged to call a special election. When there is less than one year remaining in a term, the governor may appoint an individual to fill the vacancy. When Justice Dietz died, there was less than one year remaining in the term, and Governor Emmerson appointed Samuell to the seat.[962]

The regular Supreme Court election was scheduled for June 1930, barely nine months from Samuell's appointment. On this occasion, as the incumbent, his nomination by the Republican convention for the Fourth District was "smooth and harmonious," and although there were a few other candidates, Justice Samuell won the nomination "by a landslide" on the third ballot.[963] Samuell's opposition, the Democratic candidate, was Warren H. Orr, from Carthage. Orr had lost the special election in 1928 to Dietz. The district was largely Republican, but Samuell had earned editorial endorsements, including the *Chicago Tribune*, and local observers predicted that Samuell would beat Orr, perhaps by a larger margin than Dietz had in 1928. The ensuing Great Depression had eroded voters' confidence in the Republican Party since the 1928 election, and Orr beat the incumbent Samuell by 4,000 votes.[964]

During his time on the bench, Samuell wrote twenty-two opinions. In *Lundgren v. Industrial Commission*, Edward Iverson broke his leg while working for Carl Lundgren. He was unable to use his leg afterward and was unable to return to work but worked other jobs that did not require the use of his leg. Lundgren voluntarily paid him $17 per week until reaching the maximum benefit. Iverson applied to the Industrial Commission for further payment. The arbitrator ruled for Lundgren, but the Commission overruled the arbitrator. Lundgren took the case to the courts, but Iverson died before a judgment. The court ruled that Iverson deserved more workmen's compensation, and Lundgren appealed the decision to the Illinois Supreme Court. Justice Samuell reversed and remanded the judgment noting that Iverson "had been paid the maximum amount which he could have recovered" under the death benefit clause of the act and "was not entitled to any further award."[965]

In the criminal appeal of Carl Fiorita, Justice Samuell ruled on the importance of expert witnesses and eyewitness testimony. Fiorita was one of four defendants found guilty of killing a cashier at a bank in Madison, Illinois. Fiorita appealed to the Supreme Court. Two eyewitnesses to the crime said that they "thought Fiorita was one of the four men . . . or at least, it was somebody who looked like him." Another witness claimed to be an expert in ballistics but he had no experience in firearms other than owning a shooting gallery and brief work for the St. Louis Police Department. Justice Samuell reversed the judgment and remanded the case to the lower court. He wrote that the "jury might very properly have found plaintiff in error not guilty if the witnesses" had not been permitted to testify and the cross-examination of the ballistics expert had been properly limited.[966]

Although his tenure on the Supreme Court was brief, his colleagues agreed that he had "endeared himself to all his associates."[967] Even so, his public service was not over. He later served on the Illinois Commerce Commission in 1932–1933 and from time to time received appointments to conduct arbitration work for the state's executive branch. He was also given tasks such as the chairmanship of a commission to investigate evasion of the state's motor fuel tax.[968]

Following his electoral defeat, he decided he would no longer seek judicial office but would devote his time to his law practice.[969] His health, however, deteriorated after undergoing major surgery in 1932. He also developed a heart condition, and when fighting pleurisy, he died in his home in Jacksonville on March 21, 1938, at age fifty-two. He left behind his widow, Millicent Rowe Samuell, and his son, Rowe Samuell.[970]

To pay tribute to him, the Morgan County court and all the law offices in the Jacksonville were closed during the hours his funeral was occurring. The services were held in the Justice's home and conducted by Dr. M. L. Pontius of the Central Christian Church, and Dr. C. P. McClelland, the president of Jacksonville's MacMurray College. His friends and colleagues from the community, politics, and the Supreme Court were in attendance. His longtime associate Governor Lewis Emmerson could not attend because he was not well. Following the funeral services, Justice Samuell's remains were taken to the Valhalla Chapel of Memories in St. Louis for cremation.[971]

WARREN H. ORR, 1930-1939

Warren Henry Orr was born in Hannibal, Missouri, on November 5, 1886, to James H. and Louisa E. Watson Orr. He attended the local schools there. His high school commencement address was given by Samuel L. Clemens, who was also from Hannibal.[972] He received his higher education at the University of Missouri, and since his family was of modest means, he earned money for college by taking summer jobs on packet boats on the Mississippi River and reporting news of the state university to the *Kansas City Star*, the *St. Louis Post-Dispatch*, and the *Omaha Bee*. His plan was to become a journalist. He was so keen on the idea of creating a university-based journalism education program that he was instrumental in creating the nationally acclaimed school of journalism at the University of Missouri. Because of his part-time experience, Orr was one of the original instructors in the department, even though he was still a student.[973] He received his Bachelor of Arts degree in 1909, but at the request of his mother he stayed in school to receive a Bachelor of Laws degree in 1911.

He moved to Quincy, Illinois, where he was admitted to the bar in 1911. Shortly thereafter, he noted the construction of a new hydroelectric dam up the Mississippi River at Keokuk, Iowa. Anticipating a boom in the area, he moved to Hamilton across from Keokuk on the Illinois side of the river and opened a one-room law office with little more than a typewriter and a desk.[974] From 1913 to 1918, he served as the city attorney for Hamilton until he was elected Hancock County judge in 1918. He was reelected in 1922 and 1926. During his tenure on the local bench, he served as president of the Illinois County and Probate Judges Association in 1923. He earned a reputation for fairness; he never recommended one attorney over another. When he was called upon to place someone in a court-appointed position, he chose the individual from an alphabetical list of all the attorneys in the county.

During this period, judges were often assigned temporary circuit duties in Chicago to help alleviate the perennial burden of overloaded dockets. When Orr was sitting as a temporary municipal court judge in Chicago, he had the distinction of sentencing Frankie Lake, the notorious gangster from the Terry Duggan bootleg gang, to ninety days in jail for carrying a concealed weapon.[975]

Orr was the Democratic nominee in 1928 to succeed Floyd Thompson, who resigned his seat on the Supreme Court to run as the Democratic candidate for governor. In a district that usually voted Republican, he lost to Cyrus Dietz by 18,000 votes out of 151,000 cast in the election although he received more votes in his district than presidential candidate Al Smith, the head of the Democratic ticket. Dietz, however, died in an equestrian traffic accident after serving less than a year on the court. Because there was less than one year remaining in the regular nine-year term for the Fourth District, Governor Louis Emmerson was able to appoint Paul Samuell, an experienced jurist and Republican operative, to fill the seat until the judicial election in June 1930. Samuell was favored to win, but since the onset of the Depression that followed the 1928 election, voters had grown away from the Republican Party and gave the Democrat Orr a 4,000-vote majority.[976]

His entire career on the Supreme Court was played out against the backdrop of the Depression. In a special session in February 1932, the legislature passed an income tax law to raise money needed to help relief efforts. Legislators from Cook County worked to defeat the bill, but heavy support from rural areas downstate prevailed. Orr wrote the court's opinion denying the state's right to create an income tax. In *Bachrach v. Nelson,* the court said that the legislature exceeded its powers in adopting the measure and declared the law unconstitutional. Orr wrote that the Income Tax Act of 1932 was invalid as a tax on property, not being based on valuation as required by the constitution. There would be no state income tax for several more decades.[977]

He also wrote the opinion for the court's unanimous decision in *People v. Peoples Stock Yards State Bank*. In this case, the court determined that the employees and agents of the bank corporation named in the suit were in effect practicing law because of the status of the corporation. The court found that only lawyers, that is, licensed individuals admitted to the bar, could practice law. A corporate entity could not be a lawyer. If an employee of a corporation had to conduct law business such as appearing in court or filing suits, that employee must be a licensed lawyer. Orr's opinion was cited and quoted in law journals and briefs prepared for other jurisdictions.[978]

Orr was to serve only one term on the Supreme Court from 1930 to 1939 and served as Chief Justice from 1933 to 1934. These were tumultuous years that saw the Depression, the New Deal, and political upheavals that were to affect the nation for decades to come. Changes bring pressure on legal institutions either to legitimate or to reject those changes. Whereas Orr wrote opinions dealing with conventional cases such as the *Tribune Co. v. William Hale Thompson et al.*, which held in favor of the mayor against the newspaper's charges of malfeasance, he also had to write opinions that reflected the new temper of the time.[979] Thus, he wrote opinions upholding the right of Chicago's transit ordinances to create a unified transit system and make the construction of the subway system possible in *People v. City of Chicago*.[980] Similarly, he supported the consolidation of Chicago's parks from twenty-two separate systems into one.[981] At the same time, the Court directed much of its attention to writing a complete set of rules in accordance with the Civil Practice Act of 1933.

At the end of his term, he announced that he would not seek reelection to the Court even though

Warren Orr poses with his son Wallace Orr, who became an attorney while his father sat on the bench. (Image courtesy of Illinois Supreme Court Historic Preservation Commission)

he was guaranteed a unanimous nomination and probably an easy campaign. Having been a judge since he was thirty-two years old, he was concerned about the economic consequences for himself and his family. Even though he had some supporters who submitted his name to the President of the United States for appointment to the United States Supreme Court in the late 1930s, and others who would have liked him to run for governor in the mid-1940s, he chose to move to the Chicago area and engage in the practice of law.[982] He was briefly in former Supreme Court Justice George A. Cooke's firm of Cooke, Sullivan & Ricks. He subsequently formed the firm of Orr, Vail, Lewis & Orr—the last being his son—where he stayed until his retirement in 1958 due to failing eyesight.[983] In other business affairs, he was one of the organizers and the first president of the Belmont Bank on Chicago's north side. While he was in private practice, he kept up his active interest in the Democratic Party.[984]

In connection with his job as bank president, he was a member of the Lakeview Civic Association, and he was also a Thirty-second Degree Mason, a member of the Elks and Kiwanis Clubs. He also belonged to the Union League Club and the Illinois Athletic Club in Chicago. Other civic activities were the result of his love of the outdoors. He was an avid hunter of ducks and geese; during his earliest days in Hamilton, he was co-founder and longtime officer of a sportsman's club. His influence helped to have State Highway 96 placed directly alongside the Mississippi River between Hamilton and Nauvoo, which resulted in the road's later designation as a scenic byway. He was also instrumental in organizing the local park district in the Hancock County seat of Carthage.[985]

In the years following his judgeships, he lived in the North Shore suburb of Wilmette. It was there that he took sick and after a weeklong illness died at Evanston Hospital January 13, 1962. He left behind his wife Dorothy (Wallace) Orr, whom he had met and married after moving to Hamilton as a young man.[986]

NORMAN L. JONES, 1931-1940

Norman Lemuel Jones was born in Patterson, Illinois, in Greene County, on September 19, 1869, into a pioneer family of that area. His father was John Jones, a Civil War veteran and Greene County school superintendent. His mother, Minerva Patterson Jones, was from a Welsh family of early settlers dating to the time Illinois was a territory.[987] The Jones family had two sons and three daughters. After graduation from the local schools, Jones enrolled in Valparaiso University in Indiana in 1888. He was there for only one year when he was appointed to the United States Military Academy at West Point. He was compelled to drop out and return home when his father's health failed.[988]

Back in Carrollton, he became involved in politics and in 1890, at the age of twenty-one, was elected to the Illinois House of Representatives as the youngest member there. "Born, reared, and trained a Democrat," his distinguished career of public service was intertwined with the law. While serving in the state legislature, he read law in Carrollton in the office of H. C. Withers and was admitted to the bar in 1896 at age twenty-five. Subsequently, he was city attorney for Carrollton from 1902 to 1910, then State's Attorney for Greene County for a period of two years, beginning in 1912 and ending with his resignation in order to run for the circuit court in 1914. During this time, his law partner was Henry T. Rainey, Democratic congressman from Illinois who would become the powerful Speaker of the House during the early days of Franklin Roosevelt's New Deal legislative program. The partnership was dissolved when Rainey was elected to Congress and Jones was elected to the bench.[989]

With his career well under way, Jones married Almeda Pegram in 1906. They had one son, Norman Pegram Jones. When Jones sat on the Supreme Court years later he had the pleasure to administer the oath admitting his son to the bar.[990] After almost a decade and a half in state and local politics, Jones was elected judge to fill a vacancy on the Seventh Judicial Circuit. He was reelected for a full term in 1915, 1921, and 1926. In all these judicial elections, he ran unopposed. In 1921, he was appointed to the appellate court for the second district, which met in Ottawa. While on the appellate bench, he decided to run for governor in the 1924 general election.[991]

Jones was prominent in the Democratic Party. With connections from his own career in state and local politics and his relationship with Rainey, he won the Democratic nomination in the 1924 election. Illinois Republicans had been split and battered as a result of embezzlement charges against incumbent Governor Len Small. Many good-government Republicans defected to Jones, including lifelong Republicans such as Jane Addams; even the staunchly Republican *Chicago Tribune* endorsed Jones when their original candidate failed to unseat Small in the primary. Nevertheless, in the Coolidge Republican national landslide of 1924, Jones came out behind Small. Even so, Jones won over a half-million votes more than the rest of the Democratic ticket.[992]

If he could no longer claim statewide leadership of his political party, he at least retained the respect of it, as, for instance, when he was invited to be an honorary pallbearer at the funeral of assassinated Chicago Mayor Anton Cermak.[993] In 1931, Justice William Farmer of Vandalia resigned from the Supreme Court because of failing health, leaving a vacancy for which Jones sought election. He won the special election for the partial term handily and took his seat on the Supreme Court bench in September 1931. He was so well respected that the *Chicago Tribune* took the trouble to congratulate him on his ascension to the bench in an editorial. One of his friends would later remark in reference to his defeat in the gubernatorial election that "what the executive branch lost, the judicial branch gained."[994] He was reelected for a full term in the 1932 general election, this time a Democratic landslide with Franklin Roosevelt leading the ticket. The election gave the Democrats a five-to-two majority on the Supreme Court and thirty-six of the state's fifty-one circuit benches. Jones held the title of Chief Justice in 1934 and again in 1940.[995]

Shortly after assuming the Supreme Court bench in 1931, Jones wrote the opinion in *Graham v. City of Chicago*. Elise Graham had fallen on an icy sidewalk, injuring herself. The ice had formed when the city of Chicago purposefully flooded an area in a playground for children to ice skate, but the water had overflowed onto a sidewalk and froze. Graham sued the city and obtained a $16,000 judgment. On appeal at the Supreme Court, Justice Jones affirmed the judgment asserting that "a city is not liable for injuries resulting from the general slipperiness of its streets and sidewalks due to the presence of ice and snow which have accumulated as a result of natural causes." In this case, however, the ice did not accumulate naturally but by an act of the city. The city failed to remedy the problem for at least thirteen days and it "would have been no unreasonable undertaking . . . to have removed the ice . . . and the city should have used reasonable care to eliminate the danger."[996]

While Chief Justice, Jones affirmed the validity of a will in which a testator wrote the will and signed the name of the witnesses. The lower court had invalidated the will because it was not properly attested. The will had a codicil that was properly attested, and the question posed to the Court was whether the proper attestation of the codicil validated the improper attestation of the original will. Chief Justice Jones agreed that it did and that "there was no proof of fraud, compulsion, or other improper conduct in the execution of the instrument offered for probate."[997]

While serving on the high court, Jones was active in court reform serving on judicial advisory councils, which instituted changes to expedite the process of justice. Some of the changes included allowing jury waiver in criminal cases and strengthening the principle that juries could judge only the facts of a case and not the law.[998] During his tenure on the court, the state legislature passed the Civil Practice Act of 1933, which called for changes to all the rules of the Supreme Court. Jones played a significant role in developing the new rules because of his broad experience gained from being in private practice, serving as a public prosecutor, spending two decades on the bench, and working as a state legislator. Jones was more widely known than any other justice in the state as a result of his service in the legislature and as a candidate for governor. Senator J. Hamilton Lewis included Jones's name on a short list of candidates for a vacancy on the United States Supreme Court.[999]

On December 15, 1939, as a result of a recurring abdominal ailment for which he had been treated since the previous September, Justice Jones collapsed during a court session. He continued to decline, and on November 15, 1940, he died at Our Saviour's Hospital in Jacksonville two months after his seventy-first birthday. He was buried in the Carrollton Cemetery. Jones had spent fifty years, his entire adult life, in public service, including twenty-four years on the bench. His funeral was attended by Republicans and Democrats alike. Dignitaries came from all over the state, as befitting a person of his position, yet it appeared that genuine respect rather than protocol was the reason that hundreds of people turned out to say their goodbyes. As if to return the favor, a year after his death, Carrollton's Boyd Memorial Hospital was built on land that Jones had quietly donated for that purpose.[1000]

LOTT R. HERRICK, 1933-1937

Lott Russell Herrick was born December 8, 1871, in Farmer City in central Illinois to George W. and Dora O. Herrick. As a child, he attended the public schools in his hometown, ending his local education in 1888 when he graduated from Moore Township High School at age sixteen. The following semester, he enrolled at the University of Illinois, graduating there in 1892 with a Bachelor of Arts degree and memberships in the Sigma Chi fraternity and the Phi Beta Kappa honor society.[1001]

His father had a law degree from the University of Michigan, and Lott followed his father's footsteps north and received his own Bachelor of Law degree from that institution in 1894. Returning home, he was admitted to the Illinois bar and joined his father in the law firm of Herrick & Herrick. His career choice surprised no one. Since the age of eleven, he had been helping his father around the office during school vacations and Saturdays and continuing on to full partnership seemed natural. Having settled into his professional life, he married Harriet N. Swigart of Farmer City on April 2, 1896. Together they had two daughters, Helen and Mildred.[1002]

He became a county judge in DeWitt County in 1902. He resigned the position in 1904 after his father died to enable him to devote his full attention to the family law firm, which now included his brother.[1003] This move marked the beginning of a period of almost thirty years in which his partnership achieved eminence throughout the region, giving him wider experience in the practice of law than almost anyone who rose to the Supreme Court bench. His general practice, which included such clients as the Illinois Central Railroad, was successful enough that he and his brother opened another office in Clinton, the DeWitt County seat. His civic leadership was enhanced by his community participation in the Freemasons, the Knights of Pythias, and the local Elks club.[1004]

In 1908, he was involved in a sensational trial in Clinton that grabbed front pages around the state for more than five months. Thomas Snell, a wealthy landowner and successful businessman, died and in his will left a substantial amount of money in the form of an annuity to his youthful and attractive grandniece Maybelle McNamara. Snell's son Richard attempted to break the will claiming that McNamara had been a "baleful and evil influence" and that his aging father had been easily misled by various "temptresses." Lott Herrick served as the attorney for the estate to see that the terms of the will for the $2 million estate were carried out according to the wishes of the deceased, which meant that he argued in favor of allowing the annuity to go to the younger woman, whom some typified as a "vampire." In the end, Herrick lost the case when the court ruled not to break the will.[1005]

With a civil and criminal law practice that spanned decades and gave him a wide reputation for competence, he decided to run for the Supreme Court in the 1932 election as a Democrat. Although he had served only two years as a judge, he could claim with justification that as a trial lawyer he had "more cases in the Supreme and Appellate Courts than any other lawyer in his generation."[1006] He won the election after a bitter contest against Judge James Baldwin, who was a powerful Republican in neighboring Macon County. Herrick's victory could also be ascribed in part to the Franklin Roosevelt landslide of that year.[1007] Once on the bench, he earned a reputation for assertiveness and ceaseless work. The dramatic shift in politics occurring then reached into all aspects of government. Within a year of his ascent to the Supreme Court bench, Herrick was accused of playing politics with fellow Democrat Governor Henry Horner. A Republican state senator from Champaign County claimed that Herrick was using influence with Horner to affect appointments while Herrick himself had hired his own son-in-law as his law clerk. No one, however, suggested that "politics" played any role whatsoever in the cases before Justice Herrick.[1008]

Having served only four years on the court and having no great seniority, he did not write many opinions. In one case, he wrote the majority opinion involving the prosperous business of Albert Goodman. Goodman and his employees handled more than 8,200 workmen's claims for clients in front of the state's Industrial Commission. The Chicago Bar Association provided evidence to the state that Goodman represented clients without a law license. A Cook County court found him guilty of contempt and fined him $500. Herrick wrote the opinion affirming the contempt charge and the fine. In the course of telling Goodman that he was practicing law without a license, Herrick wrote that the power to define and regulate the practice of law is a prerogative of the Supreme Court. He also wrote that the right to practice law is in the nature of franchise but that such franchise cannot be assigned to a corporation or passed on to others. Much of this had been articulated and established by Justice James Cartwright in 1899 in *In Re Day*, but Herrick went further in asserting that only the court may determine what constitutes the practice of law and that only the court can decide what a law is in the first place even though the legislature is responsible for writing statutes.[1009]

Since 1848, justices have been popularly elected and campaign for their positions. (Image courtesy of Illinois Supreme Court Historic Preservation Commission)

In June 1936, Herrick became the Chief Justice of the Supreme Court and served for one year, but he would not be able to complete his first term on the Supreme Court. On August 27, 1937, he fell ill and returned from Springfield to his home in Farmer City for treatment by his family doctor. The doctor suspected blood clots on the brain and sent him to the Mayo Clinic in Rochester, Minnesota, for further diagnosis. He traveled there by private railcar with his wife and daughter in early September, but died there on September 18, 1937, from lesions on the brain. He was buried in Maple Grove Cemetery in Farmer City, close to where he was born.[1010]

ELWYN R. SHAW, 1933-1942

Elwyn Riley Shaw was born in Lyndon, Illinois, in Whiteside County on October 19, 1888, to William H. and Ella Moore Shaw. His father was a banker and owner of a grain elevator. He attended local rural elementary schools and, in 1903, enrolled in high school in nearby Sterling where he earned a reputation as one of the school's brightest students. After high school, he attended the University of Michigan, which granted him a Bachelor of Laws degree in 1910.[1011]

Rather than returning home after receiving his law degree, he moved to Freeport, Illinois, and lived with his brother Robert who practiced medicine there. After passing the bar in that same year, he worked in the law office of William N. Cronkite, one of the area's most prominent attorneys. In 1913, he opened his law office, marking the beginning of his notable career as a trial lawyer.[1012]

The year 1913 was also the year in which he married Edith Griffin. They met when both attended the University of Michigan and subsequently maintained their affection for each other after graduation. He traveled to Battle Creek, Michigan, Edith's hometown, for their wedding. They had two daughters, Mary Margaret and Joan. The marriage ended tragically when Edith, suffering from nervous disorders, shot herself to death in her home in 1942. In 1944, Shaw married Miss Mildred Voight of Freeport. The wedding ceremony took place in Washington, D.C., where his daughter Joan's husband was the recently appointed assistant choirmaster at the Washington National Cathedral. Elwin and Mildred Shaw had no children together.[1013]

Shaw's law office became a very busy place. It was so busy that he had to limit the number of his clients. He was interested in a more public life, serving, for example, as an alternate delegate to the 1932 Democratic National Convention, but as a Democrat in a heavily Republican region, he had little chance of gaining public office. However, he was such a popular person in the community that he successfully ran for the Freeport Board of Education in early 1933 as a test of whether that popularity could be turned into Democratic votes. As a result of that victory, he decided to run for the Illinois Supreme Court in the June 1933 election. He won, helped in part by Franklin Roosevelt's landslide election the year before.[1014]

As a jurist, Shaw held the modern belief that law is a science. Once when admitting new lawyers to the bar he reminded them metaphorically that while like any other science the law "constantly puts out new branches and twigs, the trunk and main branches always consist of the old and no longer questioned principles which know no change," and cautioned them with the admonition that "if you can learn to think along these scientifically correct lines you may safely allow yourself to feel your way out along the smaller branches, always remembering that when you find an idea which is foreign to the parent tree you are probably on the wrong track."[1015]

His opinion in *Sundquist v. Hardware Mutual Insurance Co.* was considered by some to be a masterpiece of learning and logic. He wrote that in civil cases involving arson, the arson must be established beyond a reasonable doubt, as in criminal cases, and persuaded the court to overrule prior law.[1016]

His reputation as a keen scholar did not help him politically. When Shaw ran for reelection to the court in 1942, the voters elected Republican William J. Fulton of Sycamore to the court by a margin of more than 22,000 votes. In the same election, Republicans gained a five-to-two majority on the Supreme Court and a majority in both houses of the state legislature as well as all statewide offices except for Secretary of State. Shaw had achieved the highest position in the state's judicial system, but even though he no longer sat on the bench, his legal career was far from over. As soon as his defeat became imminent, his supporters began a movement to have him appointed to fill a vacancy created by the death of Charles E. Woodward on the United States District Court for the Northern District of Illinois, which was located in Chicago.[1017]

The effort to have Shaw appointed to the federal bench was significant because it had been customary to have a jurist from Chicago fill the seat. Woodward, however, had been a resident of Ottawa, almost one hundred miles from Chicago. As a result, the downstate Democrats of northern Illinois had come to regard Woodward's seat on the court as a "downstate seat" and urged that the deceased judge's successor should also be from downstate. The President of the United States appoints federal judges, but in practice the president ordinarily acts upon the suggestion of a state's senior senator of the president's political party. In this case, the senator was Democrat Scott W. Lucas, who had several names in mind, including Shaw's. John P. Devine of Dixon, a former Speaker of the House in the state legislature, led Shaw's supporters. It would take almost two years before the appointment was made, but President Franklin Roosevelt appointed Shaw, who took his seat on the federal bench on May 9, 1944. He had taken the unusual step of moving from a court of last resort in a state legal system to a trial court in the federal legal system.[1018]

In the interim, Shaw served on the National Railway Mediation Board. These were the more difficult years of World War II when the problems of transition to a war economy unsettled normal procedures in business and industry. The ordinary tension between management and labor was exacerbated by the necessities accompanying the war effort. Shaw's specialties in practice had been insurance and contract law; his new position required him to become an expert on the laws dealing with capital and labor. He rose to the occasion, publishing many articles on the subject. As an added benefit, he developed a national outlook that would assist him as a federal judge.[1019]

Shaw was able to divide his time on the bench between the federal courthouse in Chicago and the courthouse in the District's western division in Freeport, allowing him to continue living on his farm near Cedarville, a few miles north of Freeport. He had developed a reputation as a legal scholar and enjoyed studying Abraham Lincoln, often using Lincoln quotes and references in his conversation and correspondence. He was welcomed in the highest offices in the land yet preferred to live in rural surroundings. He enjoyed hunting and fishing and professional sports. He came into contact with sports figures and enjoyed socializing with them. He considered the flamboyant baseball figure Connie Mack among his friends.[1020]

On the morning of July 18, 1950, he was at his farm preparing to catch the train to attend court in Chicago when he suffered a heart attack and died almost instantly. He was sixty-two years old and left behind a widow, two daughters, and two grandchildren. He is buried at Oakland Cemetery in Freeport.[1021]

PAUL FARTHING, 1933-1942

Paul Farthing was born in the small town of Odin in Marion County, a few miles west of Salem in south-central Illinois on April 12, 1887. He was one of two sons of William Dudley Farthing and Sarah Boyd (Phillips) Farthing. His complete name was William Dudley Paul Farthing, but he was called Paul even in official documents. He was blinded in a hunting accident when he was twelve years old, yet he never lost any time while pursuing his education and career.

He graduated from the Illinois school for the blind at Jacksonville in 1904 at the same age as any other high school student. He graduated with a bachelor's degree from McKendree College in Lebanon in southwestern Illinois five years later in 1909, and enrolled in the University of Illinois Law School from which he received his juris doctor degree in 1913. His academic career was successful because his brother Chester attended with him and read all of the material to him. Even so, he retained all the information because of his remarkable memory. His brother Chester received his law degree at the same time, and they would practice law together for many years.[1022]

He was a resident of Belleville for all his adult life. Initially, his law office was in East St. Louis, but later he moved his practice closer to home in Belleville. He began his public service as Master in Chancery of the city court of East St. Louis where he served in that capacity for six years. In 1924, he failed in his first attempt at election to the circuit court in St. Clair County, in which Belleville and East St. Louis are located. His disability may have been a factor in his defeat even though he insisted that he was "not running as a blind candidate, but as a Democrat on a Democratic ticket," and that as far as he was concerned, his blindness "cuts no ice" in his activities even as his wife, Harriet, drove him around during the campaign.[1023] A few years later, he did gain a seat on the St. Clair County bench and served as a county judge from 1930 to 1933. In 1933, he defeated Charles Miller for the First District seat on the Illinois Supreme Court. It was a bitter contest, and Farthing was helped by Franklin Roosevelt's Democratic landslide a year earlier.

He asked for no special consideration for his disability and set to work almost immediately, writing his first opinion in *People v. Scowley* in October 1933, just a few months after ascending to the Supreme Court.[1024] He was not a prodigious writer of opinions during the remainder of his single term of office. Much of the court's time in the first half of that decade was consumed by writing seventy-one new rules for the state's entire judicial system as a result of the passage of the Civil Practice Act of 1934. The sweeping new procedures were an attempt to satisfy current procedural needs that had not been addressed substantially since the enactment of the state's 1870 constitution.[1025]

Farthing was particularly proud of his dissenting opinion in the 1939 case of *Swing et al. v. American Federation of Labor* involving the right to strike in which the court's majority upheld a ruling that it was permissible to deny to a union to the ability to picket a workplace in which the pickets were not employed even if there was no threat of violence. When the case went before the United States Supreme Court, the Illinois Supreme Court was reversed in a majority opinion by Justice Felix Frankfurter using Paul Farthing's dissenting argument.[1026]

Remaining active in Democratic politics, he served as a delegate to the Democratic National Convention in 1936. In the election of 1942, however, the Republican Party swept forty-seven of the state's fifty-four circuits and gained a five-to-two majority on the Supreme Court. Paul Farthing was among the unseated Democrats.[1027]

After his reelection defeat after one term, he joined his brother Chester in their Belleville law practice in the firm of Farthing, Farthing and Feickert.[1028] In 1949, President Harry Truman had Farthing's name as one of six candidates for appointment to the United States Supreme Court. Truman eventually appointed his Attorney General Sherman Minton to fill the court position. His public service continued in two terms as a judge on the Court of Claims in Springfield from 1950 to 1954. He was appointed to his second term by Republican Governor William G. Stratton.[1029] In 1952, he and his brother donated to the DePaul University library their collection of imprints of the laws of Illinois going back to territorial times. It had taken them twenty-seven years to assemble a complete collection of 260 volumes valued in excess of $17,000.[1030] In July 1958, when his brother Chester retired, Farthing continued practicing by joining his son William in his law office in the middle of downtown Belleville. Paul Farthing retired from the practice of law altogether in 1966 at the age of seventy-nine.[1031]

Away from public office, he was a local civic leader. He was a founder of Belleville's Optimist Club and held leadership positions in the Presbytery in his Presbyterian Church. He was seen frequently on the streets of Belleville taking morning walks and commuting around town on the buses.

More than ten years after his retirement, Farthing died on December 2, 1976, at the age of eighty-nine at St. Elizabeth's Hospital in Belleville. Farthing could reflect on his life with satisfaction as expressed in his statement many years earlier that "if you can find work you can do which will be of some value to the world, I believe you will be that much happier." His sentiment had nothing at all do with his blindness.[1032] According to people who came into contact with him, he had "so completely conquered his disability that neither in personal contact nor in appearances in court is one conscious of his physical handicap."[1033]

FRANCIS S. WILSON, 1935-1951

Francis Servis Wilson was born in Youngstown, Ohio, on February 7, 1872, the only son of David M. and Griselda E. (Campbell) Wilson. His father maintained a successful law practice and at one time served in an Ohio constitutional convention. His mother studied voice and became a voice teacher after the death of her husband. Later, his mother moved to Chicago to live with her son, and she passed away in 1949 at the age of 103.[1034]

Wilson attended the public schools in Youngstown, then the Hudson Academy, a boarding school that is now the Western Reserve Academy, in Hudson, Ohio, about fifty miles west of Youngstown. He was a student and played football in Cleveland at Western Reserve University, now Case Western Reserve University, and received his Bachelor of Laws there in 1895. He was admitted to the Ohio bar in his hometown the same year.[1035]

Instead of entering a law office, he went to work for the *Youngstown Vindicator*, the local newspaper owned by John H. Clarke, who also was a lawyer and whom Woodrow Wilson would appoint to the United States Supreme Court in 1916. In 1896, Clarke sold his interest in the newspaper and moved to Cleveland. Apparently not wishing to remain on the newspaper staff without Clarke's leadership, or perhaps no longer needed at the newspaper without Clarke, Wilson moved to Chicago in 1897 and joined the law firm that with his arrival took the name Darrow, Masters and Wilson, whose two others partners, Clarence Darrow and Edgar Lee Masters, were already well known in the legal community. "His partners," according to a friend, "were both colorful and spectacular, while . . . Wilson was the quiet and scholarly, yet none the less famous, member of the firm." Wilson probably got the job with the famous partners because Darrow's then-wife was Wilson's cousin. In any case, this extraordinary first experience in a law firm undoubtedly helped him to develop "a temperament and understanding of both people and the law which eminently fitted him for the bench" in the future.[1036]

Wilson claimed that starting out as a young fellow he had "no idea of where he was going except that he didn't want to be a lawyer," yet upon moving to Chicago it was clear that the law would be his career. Having settled in Chicago, he married Caroline E. Siegfried in 1903. They had two children, David M., named after his father, and Francis Jr.[1037]

His public service began barely one year out of law school when he was elected probate judge in Mahoning County, Ohio, for which Youngstown is the seat. In Chicago, he went to work for the county attorney's office in 1911 and 1912, after which he returned to the private sector as the junior partner of Eli B. Felsenthal, who was fourteen years his senior, in the firm of Felsenthal and Wilson.[1038] As the nation prepared for entry into World

War I, Illinois Governor Frank O. Lowden made Wilson the legal advisor to the draft board in the Woodlawn community on the south side of Chicago. When the United States entered the war, Wilson enlisted and served as a captain in the army's Judge Advocate's Office at Camp Sherman in Ohio, leaving with the rank of major. After the war he was instrumental in establishing the Hyde Park American Legion Post in his Chicago neighborhood.[1039]

Wilson attempted to gain a seat on the bench of the Cook County Circuit Court when he ran as a Democrat with the backing of the William Randolph Hearst–sponsored Independence League and other civic reform organizations, including the Chicago Bar Association, to defeat Chicago Mayor William Hale Thompson's corrupting domination of the Cook County judiciary. From the 1890s to the 1920s, reformers in both political parties struggled to take politics out of judicial elections. The effort was a major movement in local politics, and it consumed much of the bar's time and energy in those decades. He failed to win initially but was elected to the circuit court to fill a vacancy in the important upset of the Thompson machine in 1920. He was reelected in 1921, 1927, and 1933 for six-year terms. The Supreme Court appointed him in 1927 to serve as a judge in the Appellate Court's First District.[1040] In 1935, he was elected to fill a vacancy on the Supreme Court left by the death of Justice Frederick R. DeYoung, whose term still had seven years remaining in it.[1041] At a testimonial dinner upon the occasion of Francis Wilson's election to the Illinois Supreme Court, a journalist pointed out that Wilson "was once a law partner of Clarence Darrow and Edgar Lee Masters, the poet, an alliance calculated to greatly instruct a man or to land him in nervous prostration."[1042]

During his tenure on the circuit and appellate benches, Wilson ruled in some interesting cases. One of these involved the signal of radio station WGES interfering with WGN's radio station signal. WGES beamed from the popular entertainment spot of the Guyon Hotel on Chicago's west side. WGN sued Louis Guyon, the Guyon Hotel owner, for the interference. Ultimately Wilson put Guyon in jail for ten days for contempt of court for continuing to broadcast against the court's order. An interesting aspect of the case was that Judge Wilson ruled, in the absence of yet-to-be-devised regulations and statutes concerning broadcasting, that a radio station could hold property rights to a wavelength.[1043] In another case that made headlines a few years later in the appellate court, Wilson took the opportunity to rule that boxing champion Jack Dempsey was liable for the Chicago Coliseum Club's $100,000 loss when Dempsey canceled a scheduled match with Harry Willis.[1044]

Wilson served as Chief Justice of the court for the year beginning June 1939, in accordance with the rotation of the title among the justices. He was reelected to the Supreme Court in 1942 after running unopposed. Although a Democrat at least as long as his association with John Clarke in Ohio, he had earned the support of both political parties for his Supreme Court election as well as his elections to the circuit court. In declining health after a fall in his home and a later bout with pneumonia requiring hospitalizations, he decided that he would not run for reelection to a second nine-year term in 1951.[1045]

On March 14, 1951, as he was preparing to attend a dinner in Springfield by Governor Adlai Stevenson at the Executive Mansion, he died in his apartment in the Supreme Court Building. Two days later his funeral was held at St. Paul's Episcopal Church in Hyde Park, close to his home on Forty-eighth Street. His widow, Caroline, and his two sons attended his funeral along with many government officials and civic dignitaries. Although he lived in the south side Hyde Park neighborhood most of his life, he was interred in Memorial Park Cemetery in the northern suburb of Evanston.[1046]

Perhaps the best remembrance of Francis Wilson was that offered by Edwin H. Cooke, who was the court's reporter of decisions for almost thirty-five years and knew every justice during his sixty-year period relationship to the court. Twenty-five years after Wilsons's death, Cooke could still say of him, "I think he was the most perfect gentleman I ever knew. He had a brilliant mind and a keen sense of humor."[1047]

WALTER T. GUNN, 1938-1951

Justice Walter T. Gunn was born in the Illinois River town of Seneca in LaSalle County on June 4, 1879. His parents, Luther V. and Alice E. Rogers Gunn, farmed there. The family relocated in 1890 to Hoopeston, just north of the Vermilion County seat of Danville. He attended local schools and later worked his way through Hoopeston's Greer College, from which he received a Bachelor of Science degree. Although his mother hoped that he would become a clergyman, his father wanted him to be an engineer. Consequently, he enrolled at the University of Illinois at Urbana to study engineering.[1048]

After the first year, however, he dropped out and enrolled in the law school at Illinois Wesleyan University in Bloomington. In preparation for his legal education, he claimed to have read William Blackstone's *Commentaries* four times before he entered law school. In this way, he was able to complete two years of schoolwork in one year. Even so, his money ran out before he could complete his courses. He taught school briefly for $15 a month. Before long he heard of a position in the Vermilion County State's Attorney's office that did not require a law license. He considered not taking the job, because it paid even less than teaching, until a friend advised him that experience in the county office would be invaluable. Because of that experience and four additional months of study, he passed the bar in 1902.[1049]

From 1903 to 1911, he partnered with John W. Keeslar in the firm Keeslar & Gunn. At the same time, he served as an Assistant State's Attorney for Vermilion County. In the latter capacity, he helped prosecute Iroquois Theater owner William J. Davis for manslaughter in the sensational trial in 1907 that followed the catastrophic 1903 fire in Chicago. The trial had been moved to Danville from Chicago after years of defense maneuvers. In the end, neither Davis nor any of the others charged with responsibility in the blaze that killed more than 600 people were found guilty. During this period he also served as Master in Chancery for the United States District Court from 1904 to 1911.[1050]

He decided to move to Los Angeles in 1911. He was admitted to the California bar and opened a law office with Jay Briggs of Hoopeston. Their plan was to specialize in oil and mining law. For unknown reasons, in about two years they closed their office and returned to Illinois. Back in Danville, Gunn began to build his law practice and to create a role for himself in the community.[1051] In 1904, he married Nina Dayton with whom he had two children, Horace E. Gunn and Margery Gunn Hickman. Later in his life, Gunn would practice law with his son, who would establish a lifelong practice in Danville.[1052]

After his return to Danville, he served as corporation counsel for the city from 1915 to 1919. He added the Masons (where he would be distinguished with the thirty-third degree), the Elks, Kiwanis, and the Knights of Pythias to his list of memberships, which also included his professional memberships in the Illinois State Bar Association and the

American Bar Association. He also found the time to serve as the president of the Danville Country Club, where he had been a founding member.[1053] He also tried his hand at business, becoming a founding partner, together with his former California law partner Jay Briggs, in a firm that was to manufacture railroad crossing gates, engines, and other machinery.[1054]

His practice covered all facets of the law. He became known as an aggressive, brilliant, and unrelenting lawyer, gaining the respect of his fellow attorneys. In the 1920s, he took over Walter C. Lindley's law practice when Lindley became a United States appellate justice. It became the firm Buchwalter, Gunn & Hickman, which included his son Horace and son-in-law Robert Hickman. He was with this firm his entire life, except for the period in which he served on the Supreme Court.[1055]

In September 1937, Supreme Court Justice Lott C. Herrick died in office, leaving the third district with a vacancy that had to be filled through a special election since there was more than one year remaining in Herrick's term. In May 1938, Gunn was nominated by a county convention to run for the bench as a Republican in the election that was scheduled for June 27. His opponent was Democrat Joseph L. McLaughlin of Sullivan. Although it was a judicial election, there was considerable and unpleasant campaigning. McLaughlin had the support of Governor Henry Horner, who was intent on having another Democrat on the Supreme Court. Republicans countered with the claim that the governor wanted to politicize the court.

After the short but bitter campaign, Gunn won the election by 15,000 votes out of the more than 147,000 cast. Gunn was sworn in on July 1, 1938, just a few days after the election.[1056] He was reelected to a full term without an opponent in the regular judicial election of 1942. He declined to run again in 1951 upon medical advice, after serving on the court for thirteen years that spanned the Depression, World War II, and postwar recovery. He was Chief Justice for the year beginning September 1940. During the war years, he made it known that he was a strong supporter of civil rights.[1057] He returned to his private office in Danville where for the remainder of his life he practiced with his son and son-in-law.[1058]

Gunn called himself "an ordinary country lawyer by profession and a liberal conservative philosophically." In his straightforward approach to the law, he said that he assumed "seventy-five percent of controversies are solved when you accurately know the facts."[1059] However modestly he may have portrayed himself, during his time on the bench, he was responsible for writing 481 opinions as well as numerous dissents. He had a remarkable memory and many times amazed attorneys and colleagues by quoting from memory the volume and page of the official reports of court decisions.[1060]

Gunn liked to read the works of Charles Dickens. In his opinion Dickens was "almost as universal as Shakespeare."[1061] Yet when it came to the laws of Illinois, Gunn liked to read the opinions of Justice John Scholfield, who served on the court from 1873 to 1893, the decades immediately following the adoption of the state's constitution of 1870. Scholfield's scholarship served as a guide for him to follow.[1062]

Walter Gunn died the day after he was admitted to Danville's Lake View Hospital on October 13, 1956. There was a small funeral service at the Berhalter Funeral Home followed by cremation.[1063] Following his death one of his colleagues on the court commented that "while he was always firm in his convictions and forthright in his expression of them, he was never harsh and never sought to force his will upon his colleagues. He was not moved by idea of self-aggrandizement and always gave the fullest consideration to the views of those who opposed him. His attitude was courteous and scholarly and could accept discussion and criticism of his position with [the] open judicial mind he possessed."[1064]

LOREN E. MURPHY, 1939-1948

Loren E. Murphy was born on July 23, 1882, to James W. and Ann Elizabeth (Deacon) Murphy in Cuba, Fulton County, Illinois. His great-grandfather had come to Fulton County from Ohio in 1832, and Murphy spent his childhood there living on the family farm and attended schools in Cuba.[1065] He graduated from the University of Michigan Law School in 1906, and he began practicing law in Monmouth, Warren County, Illinois, that same year. On November 26, 1910, he married Bessie Ditto, and they would have eight children.

Murphy held many professional positions during his career in Monmouth, and he was also quite civically engaged. In 1908, he formed a partnership with lawyer Clinton M. Huey until 1910 when Murphy won election as judge of Warren County. Reelected to this position in 1914, Murphy did not return to his private law practice until 1918, the year in which he was also elected to the Monmouth Hospital Board. His fellow lawyer John J. Kritzer, who was acquainted with Justice Murphy from 1917 to 1939, said of his law practice that, "his practice was made up of people from all stations of life—poor, rich, young, old, black and white. They came to his office. Why? Because he was kind, approachable, upright, understanding, honest, capable and attentive to business."[1066] Dedicated to public service, Murphy led the Monmouth park system free of charge and also served for a few years as the attorney for the park board.[1067]

He was elected the president of the Board of Education in 1923, and in 1924 he formed a partnership with John Kritzer after the death of Clinton M. Huey. He was elected circuit judge in 1932, a position that he was reelected to in 1933, the same year that he was appointed to the appellate court at Mt. Vernon. This election was significant because Murphy was the first Democrat elected to the Ninth Judicial Circuit since its creation in 1890, and his support by the Republican Party would last through his 1939 election to the Illinois Supreme Court.[1068] He served a nine-year term, succeeding Justice Warren H. Orr, who had just retired. Murphy served as Chief Justice of the court from 1942 to 1943 and 1947 to 1948.

In a memorial of Justice Murphy, Illinois Supreme Court Chief Justice Ray Klingbiel said, "His logical analysis of the law, the thoughts expressed, and the pleasing style with which they are presented all leave an enduring impression for depth in thought of kindliness in manner, and of conscientious devotion to duty. The products of his work are so well supported by sound reasoning that they are cited numerous times as precedent, and are frequently quoted because of their accuracy and conciseness."[1069] A reading of his recorded judicial opinions, which total approximately 334 and cover various subjects—including workmen's compensation, inheritance, murder, larceny, tax, collection, and insanity pleas—certainly reflects the depiction of Murphy as accurate and concise, and one may also add that he was quite thorough in his reasoning.

One case that exemplifies these descriptions is *People v. Maggi*, in which Murphy ruled in support of adhering to a minimum-wage law passed for women and minor workers. Jean Maggi, the defendant, was a beauty culturist who employed licensed workers in the field. She paid her employees a wage that did not meet the minimum standard set by the act because it did not apply to beauty professionals. Murphy analyzed the language of the act to conclude that it did apply to professional employees. To interpret the meaning of the act point by point, he employed and explained several official dictionary definitions: the *Webster*'s dictionary definition of industry, the *Anderson's Dictionary of Law* and *Encyclopedia Dictionary*'s definition of trade, and *Webster*'s definition of business.[1070] After identifying and defining the terms used in the act that were up for interpretation, Murphy wrote, "The words used to fix the meaning of the term occupation are almost as flexible in meaning and comprehensive in scope as the word which they are used to define. The primary purpose of statutory construction is to ascertain the intention of the legislature and in determining such intent it is proper for the courts to consider the language used, the evil to be remedied and the object to be obtained."[1071] He then concluded from his findings that the broad definitions of the key terms of the act made beauty culture professionals entitled to its benefits. He upheld the decision of the lower court, which ordered Maggi to meet the Illinois minimum wage standard.

Justice Murphy wrote the opinion for *People ex rel. Denny v. Traeger*, a case brought to the Illinois Supreme Court against jury commissioner John E. Traeger, who excluded a woman from participating on a jury. Murphy held that the language of the 1937 Jury Commissioner's Act did not support female exclusion from juries. He awarded a writ of mandamus, stating that Clara L. Denny "was excluded from jury service on the false theory of economic, sociological and legalistic inferiority and not by any positive statement found in any of the constitutional provisions guaranteeing the right of trial by jury."[1072] To support this claim, Murphy included various statements from the 1818, 1848, and 1870 Illinois Constitutions regarding the essential elements of a trial by jury.[1073] The decision was well received, and the *Chicago Tribune* reported on the significance of the ruling, stating, "More than 2,000 names will be in the hopper [device holding names of possible jurors] from which the list is chosen. Traeger estimated that at least half—and probably more—would be those of women. Based on the law of averages, this would mean that half of the September juries will be composed of women."[1074]

Murphy ran for reelection to the Supreme Court in June 1948 but was defeated by Republican Albert M. Crampton. Crampton, a former Moline city judge, yielded 28,461 votes to Murphy's 24,067 votes, and Murphy carried only two of fourteen counties in the fourth district: Schuyler County and Warren County.[1075] The *Chicago Tribune*, noting the strengthening of the Republican Party at the time of the election, attributed this loss to voter preference to elect a Republican as opposed to Murphy, who was a Democrat.[1076] Even though Republicans had supported Murphy in the past, his reelection campaign could not stand up against the local and national trend that favored Republicans. After Murphy's tenure on the Illinois Supreme Court, he served on the Monmouth Park Board and the Police and Fire Commission of Monmouth, and he also held the position of chief counsel of the Illinois Bankers Life Assurance Company until he retired in 1956.[1077]

Judge Murphy died on June 2, 1963, at his home in Monmouth, Illinois. He was survived by his wife, Bessie; his sister Marie; three daughters: Dorothy, Margaret, and Genevieve; and four sons: Loren Jr., Wayne, Darrell, and Lewis. His funeral services were held at First Methodist church in Monmouth, and he was buried at Warren County Memorial Park Cemetery.[1078]

JUNE C. SMITH, 1941-1947

June C. Smith was born at Irvington, Washington County, in the southern part of the state on March 24, 1876, son of farmer Isaac C. and Alma Maxey Smith. He was educated in local public schools, and attended Southern Illinois Normal School at Carbondale and Dixon College of Law in the northwestern part of the state. He received his LLB degree from Southern Normal University in Huntingdon, Tennessee, in 1899.[1079]

On September 30 the following year, he married Metta Bates, also of Irvington. They had two daughters: Ruth, who later married Robert J. Robler of LaGrange, Illinois, and Maureen, who married Bethuel Gross in Chicago, where she earned a reputation as an accomplished vocalist.[1080]

He was admitted to the Illinois bar in 1904 and the same year became State's Attorney for Marion County. Although Salem was the county seat, he set up his law practice about fifteen miles away in the larger city of Centralia, which would be his home for the remainder of his life. From 1908 to 1928, he was a partner with Frank Noleman in the firm of Smith & Noleman. Later he was in partnership with Hugh Murray as Smith & Murray from 1935 to 1941. During the same period, he served as an Assistant Attorney General from 1909 to 1913 under Illinois Attorney General William Stead.[1081] His practice in his Centralia office served an impressive client list including local banks; the Chicago, Burlington and Quincy Railroad; the Southern Railroad Company; the Marion County Coal Company; the Odin Coal Company; and local utility companies.[1082] He was also a thirty-second degree Mason, an Elk, a Moose, an Odd Fellow, and longstanding member of the American Legion.[1083]

He enlisted in the army in World War I and was commissioned as major of infantry, serving as Provost Marshal for Illinois. In this capacity he was in charge of administering the selective service law in Illinois from an office in Chicago.[1084] His public service in the military and government did not prevent his wholehearted participation in the legal profession. In the early 1920s, he had active roles in local and regional bar associations. In 1929, he was elected secretary for the Illinois State Bar Association. He became its vice president the next year and ultimately was elected president of the association for the year 1932–1933. His prominence in the state was boosted by his publication, along with Max Kidder, of the 890-page *Illinois Criminal Digest*, a series that included law, procedure, forms, and Supreme Court and Appellate Court decisions encompassing the preceding one hundred years.[1085] In addition to his law practice, he also invested in Centralia buildings and real estate.[1086]

In 1929, Governor Louis Emmerson appointed Smith to the newly created Illinois Judicial Study Commission. The commission's purpose was to examine the whole of the state's statutes with an eye to revision and to eliminate redundant and obsolete laws and laws that had been compromised by superseding legislation. Illinois was the twelfth state to create such a review body. One of the important results of the commission's work was the sweeping "Illinois Civil Practice Act" of 1933.[1087]

No stranger to politics, Smith was a contender for the Republican nomination in 1931 for the state Supreme Court seat in the Second District vacated by Justice William Farmer, who had to resign because of ill health.[1088] Smith did not get the nomination, and Democrat Norman Jones ultimately filled the vacancy. Before the end of his full term, Jones died in November 1940, bringing about a special election to fill the once-again empty seat on the Supreme Court. Republican county chairmen from the Second District assembled and quickly nominated June Smith to run in the special election to be held the following February.[1089] Smith defeated Democrat Franklin Dove, carrying twenty of the twenty-one counties in the district, which had been traditionally Democratic. Smith was the first Republican ever elected from that district. The staunchly Republican *Chicago Tribune* was so cheered by Smith's election that the newspaper marked the occasion with a page-one story and banner headline.[1090]

On March 1, 1941, four days after the special election and a few weeks before his sixty-fifth birthday, Smith was sworn in by Chief Justice Walter Gunn. Smith used his father's Bible opened to Psalm 19, which implored to "let the words of my mouth and the meditations of my heart be acceptable in thy sight, O, Lord."[1091] The term of office for his seat in the Second District expired in June the next year, which meant that he had to run in an election for his seat all over again. His reelection was easily accomplished, helped in part by a general swing to Republicans at the polls. Indeed, whereas his first election was precedent-setting, his second helped create a Republican majority on the Supreme Court.[1092]

While serving on the court, Smith wrote more than two hundred opinions. One of the most significant was *Zurn v. City of Chicago* in which the court upheld the constitutionality and implementation of the state's "Neighborhood Redevelopment Corporations Law" of 1943.[1093] The law enabled the public-private partnerships that were to have a critical effect in launching the era of post–World War II urban renewal in urban neighborhoods. Smith's opinion removed obstacles to the law's operation.[1094]

Toward the end of January 1947, he developed uremic poisoning. Although he was on his way to recovery, complications from pneumonia and a heart weakened by disease led to his death on February 8, 1947, in Centralia. The mayor of the city declared a half-day of mourning for the community's citizen, who was frequently in public where his friends and neighbors called him "Major" or "Judge." His funeral was held at the First Methodist Church, in which he was very active, and he was buried in Hillcrest Cemetery. After his passing it was said of him that "his ability as a judge and his appreciation of the purposes and relationships existing between the people and constitutional government have cut for him a niche in Illinois judicial history and constitute a substantial contribution to the government of his state and to the welfare of mankind."[1095]

WILLIAM J. FULTON, 1942–1954

A native of Lynedoch, Ontario, Canada, William John Fulton was born on January 14, 1875, the second of nine children of James and Jennie Gray Fulton. When William was about five years of age, the family came to the United States, settling near Waterman, Illinois, and then relocating to Hartford City, Indiana. Following his education in the Waterman and Hartford City public schools, the family moved to Sycamore, Illinois.

"Billy" Fulton enrolled in the University of Illinois and became the school's varsity second baseman and team captain on the baseball team. He led the team in hits during his senior year with a .400 batting average, and George Huff, the university's longtime director of athletics, would choose Fulton as a member of the "all time" Illini baseball team. "It was said by experts," reported the local newspaper, "that he could have been a major league player." He was a member of Phi Beta Kappa honorary scholastic fraternity as well as Phi Delta Theta social fraternity, and president of his senior class, graduating in 1898.[1096] Two years later, Fulton received his degree from the university's law school. Admitted to the Illinois bar in 1901, he married his college sweetheart, Laura Busey of Urbana, Illinois, on November 26 of that year. They became the parents of two sons and a daughter.[1097]

A lifelong staunch Republican, Fulton began his career in Sycamore as a law clerk and court reporter. From 1903 to 1909, he held the office of City Attorney and in 1913 won appointment as Master in Chancery of DeKalb County. During that period he was also a member of the firm of Faissler, Fulton & Roberts. In a 1923 special election, Fulton was chosen judge of the Sixteenth Judicial Circuit, winning reelection in 1927, 1933, and 1939.

In 1930, after the Supreme Court justices appointed Fulton a judge of the Fourth District Appellate Court, he served both the appellate and circuit courts. In 1932, he transferred to the Third District and was a member of that court for ten years.[1098] "Several years ago," the *Chicago Bar Record* reported in 1942, "he was the only Judge in his circuit for three years, during which time he alone kept up the dockets of the courts of that busy circuit."[1099]

Elected to the Illinois Supreme Court in 1942, the "small of stature, but possessed of boundless energy" Fulton carried eleven of the twelve counties in the Sixth District. He would serve for twelve years, including terms as Chief Justice in 1944–1945 and 1948–1949.[1100] In 1944, two years into his Supreme Court tenure, Fulton described the experience:

> It was something of a change for a man who had served on the Circuit bench for nearly twenty years. There I spent some of the happiest days of my lifetime. In the trial court one is surrounded by lawyers, witnesses, jurors, court fans and the

parties litigant. There is the daily friendly meeting and discussion in chambers and the open forum in the court room.

The Supreme Court is a new and vastly different character of service. There is no glamour or excitement about the duties of a Justice of this Court; there is plenty of hard work, interesting work, and I might say, fascinating work. The cases considered at each term involve nearly phase of human activity, constitutional, corporate and individual. The fact that most cases come to our court for final determination, and that our decisions must necessarily bring disappointment to some and happiness to others carries a sacred and grave responsibility to each member of the Court.[1101]

In the 1944 *Kinsley v. Kinsley* case, Chief Justice Fulton delivered the controversial decision that overruled the Cook County Superior Court in a divorce proceeding. That court had dismissed without prejudice a complaint for divorce filed by Frederick Roy Kinsley, who charged his wife, Verona Halla Kinsley, with adultery. According to his testimony, while he was overseas for eighteen months, his wife had given birth to a child by another man. The Superior Court cited a section of state law that prohibited a decree of divorce "without the appearance of the plaintiff in open court," even though Verona Kinsley admitted that her husband was not the father of the child.

"We are mindful of the public policy of the State," Fulton wrote, "in favor of preserving marriages and permitting divorces to be granted only upon strict compliance with the statute relating to divorce, but under the statute we have in Illinois, it appears to be clear that the chancellor should only be bound to exercise his discretion as to whether there is evidence which satisfies him the cause for divorce has been proved by reliable witnesses in open court. In determining that controlling factor, the court may take into consideration the presence or absence of the plaintiff in open court at the time of the hearing."[1102]

The decision attracted widespread legal and public interest. "The dangers of promoting so-called 'mail order' divorces," reported a Michigan bar journal, "must be weighed carefully against the many injustices which might well arise by reason of the absence in foreign lands of numerous individuals whose domestic difficulties have caused them to seek relief in the divorce courts, and who cannot appear in open court and testify in their own behalf."[1103]

In one of his final Supreme Court decisions, Fulton in 1954 delivered the opinion affirming the constitutionality of the Chicago Regional Port District. The Cook County Superior Court, in *People ex rel. Gutknecht v. Port District,* validated the 1951 legislation that established the Port District. In a twenty-page opinion, Fulton discussed and rejected Cook County State's Attorney John Gutknecht's constitutional objections to the Port District statute. "The action of the court in sustaining that legislation," wrote Chicago Bar Association President R. Newton Rooks in 1961, "has done much to foster the growth of Chicago as a world port, and the full benefit of the decision has not yet been realized."[1104]

After twelve years on the Supreme Court and continuous service on Illinois courts for thirty-one years, Fulton quietly resigned in 1954 because of his invalid wife's failing health. Remaining active in Sycamore civic affairs, he was a member of the town's Mason Lodge, Elks, and Chamber of Commerce, as well as the Illinois and DeKalb County Bar Associations. A longtime president of the Sycamore Board of Education, Fulton also helped organize and served as president of Sycamore Building & Loan Association.[1105]

On March 24, 1961, following months in the Sycamore Municipal Hospital, the eighty-six-year-old Fulton died. Services were held at Federated Church in Sycamore, with burial in Elmwood Cemetery beside his wife, who had died two months earlier.

CHARLES H. THOMPSON, 1942-1951

Charles H. Thompson was born on a farm near Harrisburg, Illinois, on December 11, 1886, to Lewis and Emma Monroe Thompson. In the years prior to the Civil War, Lewis and Emma Thompson moved to the farm from Mt. Vernon, Indiana. As a boy, Charles worked on the farm, sold newspapers, drove a delivery wagon, and later added coal mines and railroad yards to the list of places he worked.[1106]

He attended local schools and received his law degree from Chicago Kent College of Law in 1918. Having the barest means, he worked his way through law school as a stenographer and clerk in a law office for four years. He was admitted to the bar in 1919 at age thirty-one.[1107]

After law school he returned to Harrisburg with his wife, Ethel B. (Knight), of Harrisburg, whom he married in 1914. He was elected State's Attorney for Saline County in 1920 as a Republican. In that office he distinguished himself, and at one point, had twenty-one consecutive convictions. When his term ended in 1924, he returned to the private practice of law, yet his desire for public service led to his election to the Illinois State Senate in 1926.[1108]

By 1942, he would serve three nonconsecutive terms in the state senate. Owing to his background as a State's Attorney, he sat on the Senate's Judiciary Committee and served as the Republican floor leader as well. In 1927, he successfully sponsored a bill to change the method of execution in Illinois from hanging to electrocution.[1109] The last execution by hanging in the state took place in neighboring Franklin County not far from Harrisburg in 1928 just before the new law took effect.[1110]

While he was completing his third term in the Senate, he announced his candidacy for the Supreme Court for the June 1942 election. The Republican Party in Illinois had been regaining the offices it lost in Franklin Roosevelt's Democratic landslide in 1932. When Thompson succeeded in defeating his opponent for the Supreme Court seat, along with two other Republicans, the court had a Republican majority for the first time since 1933.[1111]

He earned a reputation as a dedicated and hardworking justice, often working well into the night with nighttime walks around the capital city on occasion. The opinions he wrote are contained in almost thirty volumes of the *Illinois Reports* and cover a range of subjects including *Klemme v. Drainage District No. 5* in regard to drainage laws in rural areas and *Continental Illinois National Bank and Trust Company v. Art Institute of Chicago*, which was a complex trust matter.[1112] In *Klemme*, the Will County Circuit Court dismissed William Klemme's appeal of classification of his lands under the newly passed Farm Drainage Act, which created amendments to a previous drainage act. The drainage district claimed that Klemme's appeal did not apply under the amended law. Justice Thompson reversed and remanded the case. Thompson noted that unchanged portions of amended statutes are still in force.[1113]

Supreme Court justices attend an Illinois State Bar Association event ca. 1945. (Image courtesy of Illinois Supreme Court Historic Preservation Commission)

He served as Chief Justice for two terms in 1945–1946 and 1949–1950.[1114] In January 1951, six months before the end of his nine-year term, he announced that he would not run for reelection to his seat. The announcement came as something of a surprise to the political establishment since it was generally conceded that he could be reelected easily had he chosen to run.[1115] Thompson's aim was to return to private practice, but he would find himself summoned to public service nonetheless.[1116]

After leaving the Supreme Court some months after his sixty-fourth birthday, he returned to his law office in Harrisburg and remained active in the profession through his practice and his affiliations with bar associations. In 1956, however, his former Supreme Court colleagues asked him to serve as a commissioner to examine questions surrounding some practices of labor union lawyers since the Supreme Court formulates the standards governing the practice of law. Over the preceding quarter-century, railroad unions had developed a function similar to a legal aid society. Years later the system had evolved to a point where the propriety of the union lawyers was uncertain. Thompson was the head of the special commission that would ultimately hold hearings involving twenty-seven railroad companies, the Chicago Bar Association, the Illinois State Bar Association, and the American Bar Association. In his report recommendations, which were implemented by statute a few years later, Thompson called for restricting practices of the union lawyers when it came to representing union members in court. The report, found in 13 *Illinois Reports* 2d 391, gained national attention.[1117]

Thompson continued to practice law in Harrisburg into his eighty-ninth year, for a long time in his old office in the Gregg Building, then later in the Harrisburg National Bank Building. He suffered a heart attack on October 27, 1972, but returned to his home. One month later he was hospitalized and died two days later on November 26, 1972. His wife had preceded him in death in 1967. They never had children. His only relatives at the time of this death were his cousins and several nieces.[1118] He is buried in Sunset Hill cemetery.

During his long life in public service, in which he became a "legendary figure in Illinois legislative, judicial, and Republican Parry circles," he also served on the Lincoln Memorial Commission in 1929–1932, the Illinois Century of Progress Commission in 1933–1934, and was the president of the Federation of Local Bar Associations for southern Illinois. He was a member of the Masons and the Knights Templar, and attended the Harrisburg United Methodist Church.[1119]

JESSE L. SIMPSON, 1947-1951

Jesse L. Simpson was born in the southwestern Illinois town of Troy in Madison County on January 13, 1884. Jesse and his father, George, were descendants of William Simpson, one of the state's earliest settlers, who moved into Johnson County in 1805, more than a decade before statehood. His family was poor, and after attending public schools, he worked his way through his higher education as a farm hand, a railroad telegrapher, and a section hand. He attended Illinois Wesleyan University Law School in Bloomington and was admitted to the bar in 1909. He set up a practice at the Madison County seat of Edwardsville and practiced law there for more than fifty years, beginning with the firm Simpson, Reed & Burroughs.[1120]

He soon began his career in public service as City Attorney for Edwardsville from 1914 to 1918, an Assistant State's Attorney for Madison County from 1919 to 1921, and Master in Chancery for all but one year between 1917 and 1923. In 1946, he was elected county judge for Madison County. He also served as the president of the Edwardsville Board of Education for eight terms, president of the Edwardsville National Bank and Trust Company, and president of the First Federal Savings and Loan Association of Edwardsville. He was also vice president of the Alton Memorial Hospital, led the Cahokia Mounds Council for the Boy Scouts of America, served as president of the Madison County chapter of the American Red Cross, and was chairman of the board of Emanuel Methodist Church for twenty years. He was elected president of the Madison County Bar Association in 1925.[1121]

He married Ella Kriege on July 25, 1914. They would have a daughter, Virginia, and a son, David, who like his father would establish a law practice in Edwardsville.[1122]

Early in 1947, the death of Justice June C. Smith left a vacancy on the state Supreme Court from the second district that included Madison County. Because there was more than one year remaining in Smith's term, there would be a special election to fill the seat. Republicans from the twenty-one counties in the second district met in May and nominated Simpson to run in the special election against Democrat Carl Preihs, a state representative from Pana. In the August 4 election, Simpson won with 59 percent of the vote. The results were surprising because no one expected a Republican do so well in a traditionally Democratic district. Even though Simpson was not the first Republican to be elected from there, his performance was especially surprising because of the unpopularity of the Republican-backed Taft-Hartley Act that many voters in the district's industrial and mining precincts construed as anti-labor and anti-union. Voters' reticence to elect a Republican was likely to have been offset somewhat by Representative Preihs's lack of judicial experience and his campaigning style, which many voters may have found objectionable for a judicial office.[1123]

The term to which Simpson was elected was due to expire in June 1951. When the time came for the March primary that year (party conventions were no longer utilized), Simpson ran unopposed for the nomination. This time he ran against Democrat Harry B. Hershey, a Springfield lawyer and losing gubernatorial candidate in the election of 1940. Simpson lost his bid for a full term by 184 votes.[1124] At age sixty-seven, Jesse Simpson retired from the Supreme Court after serving one month less than four years and having been Chief Justice for nine months.

While sitting on the bench, he earned a reputation among the other justices as an indefatigable worker and rightly suited to what some regarded a "lawyer's court" in which landmark cases were few. Instead, dockets were filled with felonies, local ordinances, taxing bodies, workmen's compensation, and wills and trusts. The substantive changes in the 1960s that brought, for example, new environmental laws, poverty- and race-related laws, and post-conviction remedies in criminal cases, were yet to come.[1125] Simpson's cases were very much products of their time. As such, he wrote, in 1949, the court's final opinion in *People v. Shafer*, which was a case involving a real estate broker accused and convicted of practicing law without a license. The case had lingered in the legal system for a number of years, and since it was important to the legal profession and the courts, Simpson's opinion upholding the conviction was greeted with satisfaction for conclusively delineating the boundaries of law practice.[1126]

Simpson returned to his law practice and myriad interests in Edwardsville with no intent to retire. He was soon to do even more: in December 1953, after appointment by Governor William G. Stratton, he assumed another public office as a member of the Illinois Commerce Commission. He served there until August 1963. He left the Commerce Commission and public office for good, and at age seventy-nine returned to his law practice with his longtime partner George Burroughs.[1127]

On May 6, 1973, after a brief illness, Jesse Simpson died at St. Joseph's Hospital in Highland, not far from his birthplace and the town where he practiced law for half a century. He left behind his wife, two children, and four grandchildren. His funeral was held at Edwardsville's United Methodist Church, and he was interred in Valley View Cemetery.[1128] More than twenty years had passed since he left the Supreme Court. He authored more than 130 opinions, but it could be argued that much of his legacy was the clear image he left behind that according to one colleague allowed that "you could see Justice Simpson, nodding from his big desk if you went by to borrow a book from their excellent library, or quietly strolling home and back at noontime. For lawyers, that could be a kind of serene and stabilizing image: Jess Simpson walking home . . . through the snow or under the green elms."[1129]

ALBERT M. CRAMPTON, 1948-1953

Albert M. Crampton was born in Moline, Rock Island County, Illinois, on January 7, 1900. His family was from a town in Henry County, Illinois, that was named Crampton after his grandfather, a pioneer settler. His father, George W. Crampton, was born and raised on the Crampton farm and moved to Moline as a young man to work for Deere & Mansure. He worked for John Deere for more than fifty years and became an executive of the company.[1130]

Albert Crampton attended high school in Moline and studied law at Cornell University, the University of Wisconsin, and Harvard. He was admitted to the bar of Illinois in 1923 and began practicing law that year in Moline. He married Josephine Von Maur, the daughter of a merchant from Davenport, Iowa, and they became the parents of four children: Gertrude, Kathryn, George, and Charles Albert.

Crampton was a very active citizen of Moline—socially, civically, and professionally—throughout his career. He chaired the executive committee of the Rock Island County Bar Association from 1927 to 1928, served as vice president in 1930, and president from 1945 to 1946.[1131] A colleague, Walter J. Klockau, explained that his participation in civic affairs was so extensive that he would only list a few to show the variety of his engagements, which included "service as past commander of the Moline Post, American Legion; judge advocate of the 14th district of the Legion; former treasurer Bethany Home orphanage of Rock Island; trustee of Moline high school students' aid fund; trustee of Moline Field House Association; and director, legal counsel and treasurer of the Moline Area Boy Scouts of America. From 1944 to 1947 Judge Crampton was a member of the Moline Board of Education, and during the last world war he directed the house-to-house canvas in his home city for the pledge of War Bond purchases. He was a member of the First Congregational Church of Moline, and was affiliated with many clubs and fraternal organizations such as the Elks, the Turners, the 40 and 8, and the After Dinner Club."[1132]

He also had an avid social life, and he was remembered as an "entertaining raconteur, with an inexhaustible fund of stories and anecdotes."[1133] In addition to his civic engagements and club memberships, Crampton enjoyed the outdoors and activities such as hunting, fishing, golf, and bowling.[1134]

He was elected to the Illinois Supreme Court in 1948, defeating incumbent Democrat Loren E. Murphy by a vote of 28,461 to 24,067 and carrying twelve of the fourteen counties.[1135] Murphy had beaten Crampton for the position nine years earlier in 1939, but the electorate swung to the Republican side to favor Crampton by 1948. Under the Illinois Supreme Court system of rotating chief justices annually, Crampton assumed that position in September 1953.[1136]

In regard to Crampton's work as a judge on the Illinois Supreme Court, Klockau said, "While no matter entrusted to him was too commonplace to receive his meticulous attention, he was unusually interested in cases involving broad and fundamental considerations of justice."[1137] Crampton's judicial opinions reflect this statement, and it seems that he may have been particularly concerned with assuring justice for those less-powerful members of American society at the time: women and children.

In a few of his written opinions, Crampton expressed concern for the rights of women and children. For instance, *Stalder v. Stone* was a 1952 case in which Adale Stauske contested the adoption of her child. Stauske had attempted to give the child up for adoption in the past, and her character was in question during the trial. Justice Ralph L. Maxwell delivered the opinion of the Court, ruling that Stauske was an unfit mother who could not provide her child with proper care. Crampton dissented to this opinion, arguing that she should retain custody because Stauske was then married and able to provide a stable home to her child. Crampton stated, "If her rehabilitation is not effected or complete, that question may be adjudicated in a different type of proceeding. On the other hand, to forever deprive this mother of her son, is, it seems to me, a grave injustice."[1138] Further upholding the importance of a mother's relationship with her child, Crampton rhetorically asked, "Are we to say this woman shall be denied the only highway of return to wholesomeness and send her, with all convenient speed, on down the road to perdition? And about the best interests of the child! Is he better off to be taken to his natural mother's breast at this still tender age and readily make his adjustment or wait until he later learns the inevitable truth untempered by any association with his mother."[1139] While the majority opinion for this case held that the mother in question was unfit, Crampton showed faith in the strength of a mother's nurturing qualities. Crampton's dissent, therefore, relied on what he felt was right or wrong, which is fitting with his characterization as concerned with justice.

Another significant case in which Crampton was involved, *People v. Levisen*, dealt with the application of the 1947 compulsory school attendance law. Crampton wrote the opinion of the court that upheld the rights of the Levisens to educate their child at home. The case was decided in 1950, when home schooling was not legal. The 1947 compulsory education law required parents to send their children to either a public or private school that met state education requirements. The defendants, the Levisens, were Seventh Day Adventists who had both religious and other reasons for educating their child from home.[1140] The court held that the compulsory education law was unconstitutional. Crampton noted that the home of the Levisens, two educated individuals whose child met state education standards, qualified as a private school.[1141] In supporting this construction of the law, Crampton said, "The law is not made to punish those who provide their children with instruction equal or superior to that obtainable in the public schools. It is made for the parent who fails or refuses to properly educate his child."[1142] In this way, Crampton provided for the rights of parents while also staying within the boundaries of Illinois law. Justice Jesse L. Simpson dissented to Crampton's decision, asking "If the compulsory attendance school law is not enforced, may not parents withdraw their children from school at any time desired, even in the middle of a term or semester so as to teach them at home?" and citing a Washington case that ruled against a parent's right to educate their child and "disrupt our common school system, and destroy its value to the state."[1143] The difference in opinion between Crampton and Simpson represent a debate that would continue in Illinois and other states for decades to come.

Some historians trace the "homeschooling renaissance" (termed as such because education in early America originated in the home) to the 1970s, but even in 1980 only three states—Utah, Nevada, and Ohio—had recognized home schooling rights by law.[1144] This case was concluded decades before home schooling became commonly accepted, but Crampton's opinion would ultimately prevail.

Crampton's judicial opinions, which total well over one hundred, show that he was actively engaged in promoting justice. Furthermore, in 1952, he gave a speech at the La Salle hotel to the Illinois Circuit and Superior Judges association, proposing an annual conference of judges and clerks of the court of records for the purpose of discussing judicial problems.[1145]

On the morning of March 12, 1953, Chief Justice Crampton opened the court's session at 9:30 a.m. After about an hour of hearing oral arguments on cases docketed for the March term, he fell ill and excused himself to a nearby conference room where he collapsed from a heart attack.[1146] Doctors were called to the scene, and he was rushed to the hospital and responded well to oxygen treatment, but the incident proved fatal. He died at Springfield's Memorial Hospital at 3:40 a.m. on March 13, 1953. Justice Walter V. Schaefer was named his successor as Chief Justice, and the business of the court was postponed for one week to honor Justice Crampton.[1147] His funeral services were held at the First Congregational Church in Moline, and he was buried at Riverside Cemetery in Moline.

JOSEPH E. DAILY, 1948-1965

Joseph Earl Daily was a precocious scholar even when measured against his extraordinary peers on the Illinois Supreme Court. He completed high school in three years, attended college, then graduated cum laude from Yale Law School and was admitted to the Illinois bar at the age of twenty-one, which was the earliest one could become a lawyer under the rules of admission.

Daily was born in Manito, Illinois, about twenty-five miles southwest of Peoria on January 22, 1888. His father was Joseph Sidney Daily, and his mother was Drusilla Robinson Daily. His grandfather arrived in the United States from County Tyrone, Ireland, in 1855. When he was still a child, his family moved to Chillicothe, Illinois, which also lay about twenty-five miles from Peoria, but to the northeast. After completing his education, he lived the whole of his adult life in Peoria.

His education began in the public schools in Chillicothe. It took him only three years to finish high school, and he was named class valedictorian at age fifteen in 1903. He worked briefly as a telegrapher for the Santa Fe Railroad in Chillicothe before attending the University of Illinois for two years. From there he went to the law school at Yale from which he graduated with honors in 1909. That same year he was admitted to the bar in Illinois, settling in Peoria to begin his professional career as an attorney.[1148]

His private practice was interrupted when he was elected to two terms as city attorney for the City of Peoria from 1911 to 1915. When he gained the office, he was only twenty-three and the youngest person ever to serve in that capacity. He married Audrey Woodward in 1914, and they had two sons. He resumed his practice after serving as Peoria's city attorney and served a public role as a clerk for Illinois Supreme Court Justice Clyde E. Stone. In June 1926, he was elected to fill a vacancy created by the death of the incumbent judge in the Tenth Judicial Circuit, consisting of Peoria, Tazewell, Stark, Marshall, and Putnam Counties. Although he announced himself publicly as a Republican, he obtained endorsements from both political parties for election and reelection to four six-year terms as a circuit judge. On the circuit bench, he earned a reputation for keeping trials moving and discouraging flamboyance.[1149] Indeed, during divorce conferences he would not let the participants be seated because in that way, he said, "agreements came more readily."[1150]

Because of the backlog of cases in Chicago, it was necessary and customary to have judges from the circuits surrounding Cook County to send judges to Chicago to help lessen the load on the dockets there. These "country judges" sometimes presided in as many as half of the trials in Cook County. Daily started coming to Chicago in 1927 to serve in circuit and superior court trials. Later on, when sitting on the Supreme Court, he was a significant actor in a concerted effort to petition the governor to call a special session of the General Assembly to create more circuit judgeships. He was considered an excellent trial judge as measured by the small number of his cases that were appealed; even fewer were re-tried.[1151]

Daily was president of the Peoria Bar Association and the president of the Federation of Bar Associations in the 1920s before becoming a circuit judge. He maintained a lifelong membership in the state and local bar associations and attended meetings regularly. In addition to his professional memberships, he also belonged to the Benevolent and Protective Order of Elks, the Knights of Pythias, the Shriners, and achieved the status of a thirty-third-degree Mason. He was a member of Peoria's Westminster Presbyterian Church. During his years on the Supreme Court, he was awarded honorary degrees from Bradley University in Peoria and John Marshall Law School in Chicago.[1152]

Daily joined the Supreme Court in 1948, when he was selected to fill the unexpired term of his deceased mentor, Justice Clyde Stone. Ernest H. Pool of Ottawa was also in the running for the seat on the bench at the Republican Party convention that March, ninety-one roll call votes were necessary before Daily got the nod to run in the June special election.[1153] For his reelections in 1954 and 1963, he enjoyed endorsements from both political parties as he had for his elections to the circuit bench. As a Supreme Court justice, he wrote more than two hundred opinions, which, according to his colleagues on the bench, were "models of clarity." Daily also served as Chief Justice from 1951 to 1952 and from 1958 to 1959. He was also noted for his prodigious memory that allowed him to call up cases, arguments, and precedents without consulting books.[1154]

His era was a tumultuous time to be on the Supreme Court. The state's judicial system, under the Constitution of 1870, had long operated with troublesome flaws. In the late 1950s and early 1960s, the bench and bar came together with the political structure and the citizens of Illinois to hammer out a new constitutional article to reorganize the state's judiciary. The court in that day also had to deal with some of the problems of modernization in the post–World War II world; for example, in 1964, Daily wrote the court's opinion approving municipal water fluoridation based on the principles of police power and public health.[1155]

The most controversial issue during his entire thirty-nine years on the bench was the application of George Anastaplo to the bar of Illinois. In November 1950, Anastaplo finished law school and passed his bar exam. When he went before the Supreme Court's Committee on Character and Fitness, he refused to answer a question about membership in the Communist Party. The committee refused to certify him, and the court did not admit him to the bar. The issue came before the Illinois Supreme Court, and Daily wrote the opinion for the court supporting the Committee on Character and Fitness's denial. Anastaplo maintained that any questions the Committee might have concerning his political philosophy were irrelevant to his bar admission and that he therefore did not have to answer inappropriate questions. Daily's opinion held that since the Communist Party intended to overthrow the United States government and the Constitution, and since an oath to support the Constitution was required for bar membership, the question was relevant. After a rehearing at the Illinois Supreme Court in 1960, the case was finally decided in 1961 at the United States Supreme Court. In a 5–4 vote, the U.S. Supreme Court refused to the review the matter, stating that Anastaplo's noncooperation was sufficient to deny bar admission. The case is still referred to by scholars and lawyers and is best known for Justice Hugo Black's dissent, in which he stated, "We must not be afraid to be free."[1156]

Anastaplo went on to a brilliant career producing scores of articles and books on the law, but he was never admitted to the bar. An interesting episode in the case occurred sometime after the court's denial when Justice Daily entered a taxi in Chicago and discovered that the driver was George Anastaplo, who was working as a cabdriver while he continued his education. Daily told Anastaplo that no one ever thought he was a communist and urged his driver to re-apply for the bar. On principle, he never did.[1157]

Years later, after a return to quieter cases, Daily took ill and was admitted to Columbus Hospital in Chicago on March 31, 1965. He never recovered and died four months later on July 1, 1965, without ever leaving the hospital. His wife, Audrey, having preceded him in death four years earlier, he was attended to by his sons who arrived from Florida and California. Governor Otto Kerner and Lt. Governor Sam Shapiro as well as the other members of the Supreme Court attended his funeral services at the Scottish Rite Cathedral in Peoria. He is buried in Park View Cemetery in Peoria.[1158]

RALPH L. MAXWELL, 1951–1956

Ralph L. Maxwell was born in Nashville, Illinois, on April 9, 1905. He was the second son of Ira and Laura Reidelberger Maxwell. His mother died when he was two weeks old. When he was thirteen, his father, who was a coal miner, was killed in a rock fall. He and his brother, Guy, were subsequently raised by their widowed grandmother.[1159]

He attended local schools, but when he entered high school, it became necessary for him to get a job to relieve the household's economic stress. He surmounted the problem of completing high school by doubling his course load and earning a diploma in two years instead of the customary four, while allowing him to earn money as a lineman for the regional Illinois Power Company. The demands of school and work left him little time for extracurricular activities, but he distinguished himself on the city's basketball and baseball teams.[1160]

He graduated from the University of Illinois with a Bachelor of Arts degree in 1931 at age twenty-six. He received his law degree from the College of Law at the University of Illinois the following year, essentially repeating his method of doubling his courses as he had done for his high school education. He completed seven years of college and law school in five years. He attended college and law school while married with a small child. He had married Beulah House of Nashville and together they had a daughter, Madalyn.[1161]

Immediately upon graduation and admission to the bar in 1932, he entered private practice in Nashville. Because of his skills and popularity, he was elected State's Attorney for Washington County in 1936. He was reelected in 1940 and again in 1944. He barely entered his third term as State's Attorney when he resigned the position in 1945 to run successfully for election to the circuit court. He completed his full six-year term on the circuit bench then in March 1951; he was nominated unanimously by a Republican convention to stand for election to the Supreme Court in the judicial election of June 1951. He succeeded Charles H. Thompson, who chose not to run for reelection.

As a circuit court judge, Maxwell was called upon to try cases from the state penitentiary at Menard in neighboring Randolph County. As a result he became an expert on penal law and other legal matters pertaining to convicts. He was therefore especially effective on the Supreme Court when a new post-conviction law swamped the courts with prisoners' claims of illegal detention. The law followed a decision by the United States Supreme Court in 1948 that overturned the Illinois practice of not allowing convicts to appeal their convictions. One of the results was a flood of hundreds of appeals by people in penitentiaries. Justice Maxwell "did more than his share of the work" in his careful reading and study of each petition.[1162]

One of the more interesting opinions he wrote for the court involved ending the ancient and rarely used common law practice of "purgation by oath," which was a rule in which a defendant could swear by oath that he was innocent of the crime of which he had been accused. If there were no proof of perjury, the case would be dismissed. In *People v. Gholson*, a Carroll County chiropractor had been accused of contempt of court for his alleged attempt to intimidate and influence the jury and the court by instigating public demonstrations in his defense in a separate case.[1163] Gholson used purgation by oath in seeking dismissal of the charge. As author of the majority opinion, Maxwell wrote, first, that Gholson had misapplied the practice and, second, ended the practice in Illinois forever. The practice had its roots in English common law and had been in use at least since the nineteenth century, but by the 1950s it had been eliminated in federal courts and many state courts. Claiming that purgation by oath actually bars the court from fulfilling its purpose, Maxwell said, it "will no longer be adhered to by this court and all previous decisions of this court upholding and applying [this anachronistic practice] are hereby expressly overruled."[1164]

Ralph Maxwell's accomplishments in the face of adversity were impressive. An orphan from adolescence on, attending high school, college, and law school under difficult, limited economic means tested his resolve and challenged his strength. In addition, in his ascent to the top of his profession, his seemingly unlimited energy allowed him to excel in sports as a young man. Later, and for his entire life, he fished and hunted whenever he could. Even as he organized camping trips with his friends, he earned a reputation as an excellent cook who would prepare complete meals for the whole group.[1165]

Early in 1956 he had not been feeling well. His family physician told him he had ulcers, but as he got worse, his colleagues on the Supreme Court and friends became concerned. He was prevailed upon to seek out more expert advice in Chicago. After examination at Presbyterian Hospital in June, he received a diagnosis of esophageal cancer. From there he went to the Mayo Clinic in Minnesota where the diagnosis was confirmed. Not one to give up, he traveled daily from his home in Nashville to Barnes Hospital in St. Louis for radiation therapy, then in its early days.[1166] His last public appearance was in June. He died early in the morning of August 29, 1956, at age fifty-one. His funeral was held at the First Presbyterian Church in Nashville, followed by his burial at Greenwood cemetery.[1167]

He was survived by his widow, Beulah. Beulah's brother Byron House was appointed to the seat on the court left vacant. His daughter, Madalyn, followed him onto the practice of law. It was not unusual for a justice to serve less than a full term on the Supreme Court, yet Ralph Maxwell's dramatic illness and death left those close to him stunned. His diagnosis came just three months before he was to have served his first term as Chief Justice. Although his commitment to the law and justice was intractable, his colleagues had heard him say that he would never remove the bandage from the eyes of justice, but that if it should slip, ever so little, he would wish it to show only the side of the weak and the oppressed.[1168]

WALTER V. SCHAEFER, 1951-1976

A highly regarded scholar who served on the Illinois Supreme Court for twenty-five years, Walter Vincent Schaefer was born in Grand Rapids, Michigan, on December 10, 1904. The son of Elmer Philip and Margaret O'Malley Schaefer, Walter's parents died when he was a boy; two aunts "reared, cared for, and inspired" the young Walter.[1169] He graduated from Hyde Park High School in Chicago. At the University of Chicago, he played on the baseball team and captained the tennis team that twice won the Big Ten championship. Graduating in 1926 with a philosophy degree, he intended to become an airplane pilot, but after a relative persuaded him to enter law school, he received his University of Chicago law degree in 1928. Admitted to the Illinois bar, he spent the next two years drafting statutes for the Legislative Reference Bureau of the Illinois General Assembly.[1170]

From 1929 to 1934, Schaefer associated with Tollman, Sexton & Chandler law firm in Chicago, spent a year in Washington, D.C., as litigation attorney for the Agricultural Adjustment Administration, then returned to Chicago for two years with the Reconstruction Finance Corporation. A principal author of the Illinois Civil Practice Act, adopted in 1933 to modernize the practice of Illinois law, Schaefer assisted Yale Law School dean Charles Clark in preparing the Federal Rules of Civil Procedure. Schaefer served from 1937 to 1940 as an assistant City of Chicago corporation counsel.[1171]

On June 3, 1940, Schaefer married Marguerite Moreland Goff, whom he had met while working at the Reconstruction Finance Corporation. They moved from Chicago to the suburb of Lake Bluff and had a daughter and three sons.[1172] A Northwestern University professor of law from 1940 to 1951, he taught, among others, John Paul Stevens, later a justice on the U.S. Supreme Court. Former pupils, whom he fondly called "the Kids," remembered Schaefer's "almost biblical pragmatism," and colleagues recalled his "wise and patient mentoring of junior faculty members." In addition to his teaching position, Schaefer served for a year as U.S. District Court bankruptcy referee and for two years as chair of the Illinois Commission to Study State Government, known as the Schaefer Commission. In 1949, he became chief legislative aide to newly elected Democratic Governor Adlai E. Stevenson.[1173]

In March 1951, Stevenson appointed Schaefer to the Supreme Court vacancy created by the death of Justice Francis S. Wilson. In June of that year, Schaefer won election to the position, was reelected in 1960 with support from both the Republican and Democratic parties, and was retained in 1970. Schaefer served as Chief Justice from May 1953 to September 1954 and again from September 1960 to September 1961.[1174]

Schaefer recalled the importance of one of his first cases on the high court: *People ex rel. Wallace v. Labrenz* in 1952. The parents of eight-day-old Cheryl Linn Labrenz refused on religious grounds to allow a blood transfusion to treat her steadily deteriorating blood condition. Two physicians testified in Cook County Circuit Court that without a transfusion the infant would die; a third stated that she might survive but would likely suffer permanent brain injury. The court appointed probation officer Alda Wallace as guardian of the child and directed him to consent to a blood transfusion. Following the procedure, the child's health greatly improved, and the parents regained custody. "The propriety of that action is challenged here upon a writ of error raising constitutional issues," Schaefer explained in delivering the opinion affirming the Circuit Court:

> We find that the present case falls within that highly sensitive area in which governmental action comes into contact with the religious beliefs of individual citizens. Both the construction of the statute under which the trial court acted and its validity are challenged. In situations like this one, public authorities must act promptly if their action is to be effective, and although the precise limits of authorized conduct cannot be fixed in advance, no greater uncertainty should exist than the nature of the problems makes inevitable. In addition, the very urgency which presses for prompt action by public officials makes it probable that any similar case arising in the future will likewise become moot by ordinary standards before it can be determined by this court. For these reasons the case should not be dismissed as moot.[1175]

"It was," Schaefer later recalled, "one of the most dramatic opinions, at least to me."[1176]

In what became a landmark death-penalty case in 1967, *People v. Witherspoon* concerned jurors "with scruples against capital punishment." William C. Witherspoon appealed his Cook County Circuit Court conviction and death sentence for the 1960 murder of a police officer. Witherspoon contended that he was denied the right to counsel prior to confessing to the crime, that his confession was coerced, and that eliminating prospective jurors with scruples against capital punishment violated his right to trial by a jury representing a cross-section of the community. Justice Schaefer wrote the opinion affirming the lower court, finding no evidence to support Witherspoon's contentions. Schaefer quoted *People v. Hobbs*, 35 Ill. 2d. 263 when he wrote, "Being not opposed to capital punishment is not synonymous with favoring it."[1177]

Witherspoon's attorneys appealed the decision to the U.S. Supreme Court. In *Witherspoon v. Illinois*, Justice Potter Stewart delivered the majority opinion in 1968 reversing the death sentence on constitutional grounds. When the Illinois courts, Stewart wrote, "swept from the jury all who expressed conscientious or religious scruples against capital punishment and all who opposed it in principle, the State crossed the line of neutrality. In its quest for a jury capable of imposing the death penalty, the State produced a jury uncommonly willing to condemn a man to die."[1178] Witherspoon was then sentenced to fifty to one hundred years in prison and obtained parole after serving twenty years.[1179]

Retiring from the Supreme Court in 1976, Schaefer returned to the private practice of law with the Chicago firm of Rothschild, Barry & Myers, and lectured at Northwestern University. He discussed his lengthy judicial career in a 1977 *Illinois Issues* interview. Regarding the most significant decisions of his tenure, he smilingly said, "The opinion a judge is working on at that precise moment is always, to him, the most important. By the time it becomes news generally, it's stale to him." In preparing an opinion, Schaefer recalled that he usually wrote several drafts. "I can write better if I work with something on paper in front of me," he explained. "Usually the essence of a case boils down to one or two sentences. You should write an opinion that is understandable. I usually try, if I have time enough, to write in words of one syllable. I think it's important, I think it helps." Sometimes, he recalled, he and his law clerks would thoughtfully argue the issues, noting one occasion involving law clerk Adlai E. Stevenson III, later a U.S. senator and son of the governor who appointed Schaefer to the Supreme Court. Stevenson, according to Schaefer, "insisted a particular case should be decided in a certain way. I felt otherwise; he came back, politely and insistently, and dammit he persuaded me, and the whole court was persuaded."[1180]

Schaefer held honorary degrees from John Marshall Law School, the University of Chicago, Northwestern University, University of Notre Dame, DePaul University, and Lake Forest College. He received numerous awards, including the American Bar Association's highest recognition, the Gold Medal, in 1969, only the thirty-fourth American lawyer bestowed that recognition. "Justice Schaefer has brought to the Illinois Supreme Court a comprehensive knowledge of the law, a broad vision, and a wide, humanitarian approach," read the award citation. "He is neither a liberal nor a conservative, neither a strict constructionist nor an activist. He is aware of both the obligations and the limitations of judicial office. He has helped to keep the law of Illinois abreast of the times without undue assertion of judicial prerogative."[1181]

Schaefer died of cancer at age eighty-one on June 15, 1986, in Lake Forest Hospital. His family held a memorial service at Northwestern University School of Law, followed by private burial. *Northwestern University Law Review* dedicated its December 1986 issue to Justice Schaefer, with remembrances from friends and associates. He "was completely devoted to freedom," wrote U.S. Supreme Court Justice William J. Brennan Jr., "and had supreme confidence in the principles that make our democratic society work. He was a man of principle, and a wholly compassionate, complete human being who never lost sight of the human dimensions of the great problems that confront society."[1182]

GEORGE W. BRISTOW, 1951-1961

George Washington Bristow was born on September 23, 1894, in the tiny Ohio River community of Grand Chain in Pulaski County. He would spend over half his life of sixty-seven years as a judge. His father, John David Bristow, was a judge. He lived with his parents and attended local public schools in Metropolis, then worked his way through college at the University of Illinois where he received a Bachelor of Arts degree in 1916.[1183]

He enrolled in Harvard Law School for the following autumn term, and all went well until near the end of the year when an eye disease from which he had been enduring worsened and nearly blinded him. He was unable to read, but since he refused to drop out, he had other people read aloud the course material necessary for completion of the term. He claimed later that he had to train himself to listen well and remember, skills that he said were very useful throughout his career. He completed his second year at Harvard shortly after the United States entered World War I. Anxious to serve, his efforts to enlist were rejected several times because of his bad eyesight. He managed to obtain a copy of the eye chart used by the army doctors to test recruits then memorized it so he could fool them into believing that his vision was not seriously impaired. He wound up spending twenty-three months in the army, fifteen of which were overseas. He was assigned to ordnance and spent his time "hauling ammunition to the front lines"[1184]

After the war he moved to Paris, Illinois, in 1920 to live with his uncle Frank Bristow while he completed his legal training in the law office of Frank Van Sellar. In that same year, he was admitted to the bar and was elected State's Attorney for Edgar County. Paris, the Edgar County seat, would be his home for the rest of his life. There, on June 24, 1921, he married Beryl Franklin Love of Danville, and together they had three children.[1185]

At the end of his term as State's Attorney in 1924, he was not reelected. He served a few years as Master in Chancery for Edgar County, and in 1927, at age thirty-three, he was elected judge of the circuit court as a Republican. He was reelected in 1933, when not many Republicans won elective office. He was reelected in 1939 to a third term and again in 1945 for a fourth term. During his years on the circuit bench, the governor appointed him to the Appellate Courts in Ottawa in 1938 and in Mt. Vernon in 1942. He was elected justice of the Supreme Court in the judicial election of June 4, 1951, to succeed Justice Walter T. Gunn, who had retired for health reasons. He was reelected for another nine-year term in June 1960, but he died sixteen months into his second term. He served as Chief Justice for the year beginning September 1954, and assumed the position again in September 1961, but filled that role barely two months before his death.[1186]

Bristow was on the Supreme Court during a tumultuous time in Illinois judicial history. The state was operating under a nineteenth-century constitution that was more than eighty years old. There were difficulties in applying the constitution to some of the legal problems of the post–World War II world, but the greatest problem was the years-long backlog of cases that put undue strain on the bench and bar and raised questions about the fair administration of justice for the state's citizens. Judges throughout the state called for an immediate solution by increasing the number of judges in the circuit courts. Supreme Court justices were at the apex of the judicial system. In that role Supreme Court justices also have responsibilities for the operation of the state's court system, so in June 1960, Justices Byron House and Joseph Daily joined George Bristow in petitioning Governor William Stratton to increase the number of judges by fifteen. Nothing, however, corrected the defects in the judiciary until the entire judicial article in the state's constitution was replaced in 1962. Bristow had been active in the constitutional crisis since the late 1950s when he was involved in statewide judicial conferences as part of the effort to ameliorate the constitutional problems.[1187]

Bristow wrote more than 300 opinions while on the Supreme Court, yet one of the opinions for which he was most noted was written while he sat on the Appellate Court. In the case of *Johnson v. Luhman* in 1947, he was responsible for the first higher court decision in Illinois holding that minor children might sue for damages against a woman for alienating the affections of their father and depriving them of his support and disrupting their home.[1188]

One of his more notable opinions while on the Supreme Court was his dissenting opinion in *In re Anastaplo*.[1189] The most controversial issue during his entire career on the bench was the issue of admitting George Anastaplo to the bar of Illinois. In November 1950, Anastaplo finished law school at the University of Chicago and passed his bar exam. When he went before the Supreme Court's Committee on Character and Fitness, he refused to answer a question about membership in the Communist Party. The committee refused to certify him, and the court did not admit him to the bar. The issue was to carry on for more than ten years until the United States Supreme Court, in a divided opinion, upheld Anastaplo's denied bar admission. The case is still discussed in literature on bar admissions. Anastaplo maintained that any questions the Committee might have concerning his political philosophy was irrelevant to his bar admission and that he therefore did not have to answer inappropriate questions.

Justice Joseph Daily's opinion for the four-to-three majority held that since the Communist Party intended to overthrow the United States government and the Constitution, and since an oath to support the Constitution was required for bar membership, the question was relevant. Bristow dissented on constitutional grounds in a scholarly opinion that impressed many who disagreed with him. In 1961 the United States Supreme Court refused to the review the matter, stating that Anastaplo's noncooperation was sufficient to deny bar admission. Anastaplo went to a brilliant career producing scores of articles and books on the law, but he was never admitted to the bar.[1190]

Early in October 1960, Bristow was diagnosed with pancreatic cancer. He was admitted to the hospital at the University of Illinois medical center in Chicago on October 25 and underwent surgery five days later. His recovery advanced and retreated for a short time but then he developed pneumonia and slipped into a coma. He died November 12, 1961, at age sixty-seven. His remains were returned to Paris where his funeral was held at the First Methodist Church, followed by interment at Edgar Cemetery. His funeral was attended by current Governor Otto Kerner, former Governor William Stratton, the other members of the Supreme Court, townspeople and members of the bench and bar from around the state.[1191]

Having served on the circuit bench in Paris for more than twenty years before joining the Supreme Court, he was a prominent and well-liked person in his community. He even had a reputation as a bridge master with national standing for that card game. To commemorate his contribution to the community and the Edgar County bench and bar, the local bar association created a foundation to establish and maintain the Justice George W. Bristow Memorial Library in the courthouse at Paris.[1192]

HARRY B. HERSHEY, 1951-1966

Harry Bryant Hershey was born in Mifflin, Ohio, on March 8, 1888, the son of F. B. and Anna Gongwer Hershey. The family moved to Taylorville, Illinois, about twenty miles southeast of the state capital. Hershey claimed that as a child helping out in his father's grocery store, he received early training in getting along with people. He graduated from the local high school and completed an undergraduate degree from the University of Illinois in 1909. He graduated from the University of Chicago school of law with honors in 1911.[1193]

After law school, Hershey was admitted to the bar and was elected City Attorney for his hometown all in the same year. His impressive record in municipal government led to his election in 1914 to State's Attorney for Christian County, a position in which he earned a reputation for talent and fearlessness in dealing with crime and criminals. He would be reelected and hold the office until 1922.[1194]

Hershey declined another reelection in order to devote time to building his private law practice with Charles Bliss in the law office of Hershey & Bliss. He continued his interest in politics and served two terms as mayor of Taylorville. He was also elected president of the Christian County Bar Association for the year 1924–1925. His law practice grew, and he found himself participating in a number of cases involving insurance. In addition to his law practice, he also accumulated holdings in local banking and widespread farmlands.[1195]

On May 27, 1912, he married Leah Stapleton of Assumption, a small farm town not far from Taylorville. Together they raised Auguste, born in 1913, and Richard, born in 1916. The younger son followed his father into the legal profession while the elder made a career in the field of chemical engineering. Hershey became a Mason, an Elk, and an Odd Fellow. He was also an active member in the congregation of Taylorville's First Presbyterian Church.[1196]

During the Depression he worked in Springfield as the head of the liquidation division of the state's Department of Insurance, a position created partly in response to the financial disasters of the Depression. A lifelong Democrat, he served as a State Central Committeeman and was an early supporter of Governor Henry Horner, becoming a close and trusted friend of the governor. He was elevated to the post of chairman of the Democratic State Central Committee for 1938–1939.[1197] His statewide significance to the Democratic Party was revealed when he became the party's candidate for the office of governor.

Henry Horner had ridden into the office of governor in the Democratic landslide of 1932. He served ably and with solid popularity until he suffered a crippling stroke in 1936 that took months of rest and recuperation before he could return to his office. As the general election of 1940 approached, it was clear that Horner could not run. There was also a threat of declining support for Democrats in the state and nation. Lieutenant Governor George Stelle wanted the nomination. However, Chicago politician Patrick J. Nash traveled to Springfield to meet in the Executive Mansion and agreed with Democratic downstate leaders to run Harry Hershey for governor. Hershey won the nomination, but in the general election, he lost to Republican Dwight Green, another University of Chicago law school graduate who had a substantial reputation as a federal prosecutor in the pursuit of Chicago's organized crime.[1198]

Having lost a major election at age sixty-two, Hershey returned to Taylorville uncomplaining about his defeat and grateful for all his friends.[1199] Nine years later, Adlai Stevenson, the state's newly elected Democratic governor who had beaten Dwight Green in Green's attempt at a third term, appointed Hershey to head the Illinois Department of Insurance, an agency in which Hershey had experience. His expertise in the legal aspects of the insurance industry aided in his work in the American Bar Association's Section on Insurance Law.[1200] He ran the department from 1949 to 1950, after which he was picked to run in the state Supreme Court election in 1951 as a Democrat for the twenty-one counties of the second district.[1201]

He ran against incumbent Justice Jesse L. Simpson from Edwardsville. It was a close race, but the campaign remained on a high level appropriate to a judicial election. The results from the June 1951 election showed that Hershey barely beat Simpson by fewer than 200 votes. Within weeks Republican committeemen from Simpson's county petitioned the circuit court of Madison County for a recount. There were no allegations of improprieties of any sort: Hershey and Simpson were both named as co-defendants in the suit, which claimed that there were errors in the vote-counting. The court ruled that Hershey won the seat on the Supreme Court by 184 votes out of a total exceeding 95,000 votes.[1202]

Hershey served on the court from 1951 until his resignation in November 1966. He had entered the law profession near the beginning of the century and had witnessed many changes by the time he reached the Supreme Court bench. Yet his decisions were never out of date. In judging Hershey's tenure on the court, his own colleagues held that "in many opinions he spoke for the court as it moved forward to improve legal procedure and to adopt rules of substantive law to changed conditions."[1203] During his long career, he adjusted and absorbed, for example, new tax laws, workmen's compensation, antitrust laws, and the enlargement of government. When he was serving as Chief Justice in 1961, he publically supported the proposal to replace the entire judicial article in the state's 1870 constitution with new wording that would adapt the state's judiciary to changed circumstances. Although neither Hershey nor the other justices could publicly support the new article, they privately expressed support for it.[1204]

That the times are clearly reflected in matters that come before the court is illustrated in some of his opinions. In 1954, Hershey wrote the opinion that permitted the City of Chicago to construct the enormous water filtration place in Lake Michigan near Navy Pier. Hershey held that construction of the plant would not infringe on the rights of nearby property owners and suggested that, since the United States Army Corps of Engineers had issued a permit allowing the construction, the authority of the federal government would supersede local authorities.[1205] Hershey also wrote the opinion banning the book *Tropic of Cancer* from Illinois bookstores. Since average readers would not be able to comprehend the unconventional plot and character development, he reasoned, only the "obscene" portions would be clear to them.[1206]

After fifteen years on the bench, Hershey decided to step down before his term expired. Although the new judicial article in the constitution was in effect, he pointed out that there were "more cases and harder cases." He said, "It is awfully hard work, and I am eighty years old." A few months after his remarks he retired, and less than a year after that, he died on August 30, 1967, at St. Vincent's Hospital in Taylorville, leaving behind his wife and two grown children. His funeral services were held at Taylorville's First Presbyterian Church, and he was buried at Taylorville's Oak Lawn Cemetery.[1207]

RAY I. KLINGBIEL, 1953-1969

Ray I. Klingbiel was born on March 2, 1901, in East Moline, Illinois. He attended local public schools and the University of Illinois, pledging the Phi Delta Phi legal fraternity. Attaining a law degree and admitted to the Illinois bar in 1924, Klingbiel returned to East Moline and rose in Republican Party political ranks, as a city attorney for twelve years and then as mayor for six years. He also served a term as president of the Illinois Municipal League. On October 5, 1928, he married Julia Stone, and they became the parents of two children.[1208]

In 1945, Klingbiel won election as circuit judge of the Fourteenth Judicial District, holding that position until 1953. Following the death of Illinois Supreme Court Justice Albert M. Crampton, the highly regarded Klingbiel was chosen for that vacancy, representing the third district. Later elected to the position, he would serve for sixteen years. "The Court does not blindly adhere to prior decisions," he explained in 1955 when discussing several cases in which the Supreme Court overturned lower court findings. "The law must, of course, have stability and continuity, and the importance of these values is not to be minimized. But our decisions also recognize that obsolete fictions and questionable holdings should not be perpetuated, and that the law must be adaptable to the progress of society, *to the end that justice will be dispensed and not dispensed with*."[1209]

Named "Citizen of the Year in East Moline" in 1957, Klingbiel received an honorary doctor of laws degree from Chicago-Kent College of Law. He served a term as president of the East Moline Rotary Club and was a thirty-third degree Mason. In 1965, more than six hundred guests attended a dinner in his honor, with actor Raymond Burr (television's attorney Perry Mason) as master of ceremonies and Democratic Illinois Governor Otto Kerner as speaker.[1210]

Among the significant cases in which Justice Klingbiel delivered the Court opinion, the 1959 *Molitor v. Kaneland Community Unit District* case involved tort liability of school districts. The father of Thomas Molitor, a minor, brought action against Kaneland Community Unit School District for injuries Thomas sustained when the school bus in which he was riding left the road, allegedly as a result of the driver's negligence, hit a culvert, and exploded. Molitor sustained severe burns and other permanent injuries. The Second District Appellate Court had affirmed the Kane County Circuit Court dismissal of the case on grounds that a school district is immune from tort liability.

"It is a basic concept underlying the whole law of torts today that liability follows negligence," Klingbiel wrote in a majority decision reversing the Appellate Court, "and that individuals and corporations are responsible for the negligence of their agents and employees acting in the course of their employment. The doctrine of governmental immunity runs directly counter to that basic concept. What reasons, then, are so impelling as to allow a school district, as a quasi-municipal corporation, to commit wrongdoing without any responsibility to its victims, while any individual or private corporation would be called to task in court for such tortuous conduct?"[1211]

Klingbiel served as Chief Justice in 1956–1957. In January 1963, following implementation of a new Judicial Article that provided for three-year terms on a seniority basis, Klingbiel again became Chief Justice. During that tenure he delivered the Court opinion in the 1966 case *People v. Hobbs*. A Sangamon County jury had convicted George Willie Hobbs of murdering Bertha Mae Scott in November 1964. Hobbs admitted firing the lethal shots but contended that he acted in self-defense. In addition, his attorneys questioned the meaning of "constitutional right of trial by jury," contending that prosecutors excluded "all persons expressing conscientious scruples against the death penalty." Hobbs claimed that after a drinking and sexual encounter, Scott stole $195 from his coat pocket and, on being confronted, attacked him with a knife; he responded by firing his pistol. A companion, however, testified that he did not see a knife in Scott's hand, that Hobbs took money from her purse, and then threw the purse, her rings, and watch, as well as shell casings into a river.

"The fact that defendant believed decedent had taken his money is not a circumstance in favor of his innocence," Justice Klingbiel wrote in affirming the verdict. He quoted a previous case, *People v. Mangano*, which stated when "a deliberate criminal act is proved the State is not required to prove a motive for it, as motive is not an essential element of the crime of murder."[1212] Klingbiel further ruled as proper the disqualification of jurors with conscientious scruples against capital punishment. "The constitutionally guaranteed right of trial by jury is in effect a right of trial by an impartial jury, consisting of persons favoring neither the prosecution nor the accused and being guided only by law and the evidence, and bias or prejudice, expressed or implied, constitutes ground for challenge for cause when directed toward the State or the accused."[1213]

In 1969, Klingbiel's judicial career ended in scandal. Chicago legal researcher Sherman Skolnick questioned the integrity of both Klingbiel and Chief Justice Roy Solfisburg regarding the 1967 case *People v. Isaacs*.[1214] Both justices had acquired stock in Civic Center Bank & Trust Company shortly before their ruling in the case, and Klingbiel wrote the Court's majority opinion dismissing corruption charges against the bank's general counsel Theodore J. Isaacs. A Special Commission of the Supreme Court investigated the "integrity of the judgment" in *People v. Isaacs*, co-chaired by the presidents of the Chicago Bar Association and Illinois State Bar Association. Anti-trust attorney and later U.S. Supreme Court Justice John Paul Stevens served as independent counsel to the Commission.[1215]

Despite Klingbiel's claim that he had accepted one hundred shares of CCB stock, worth approximately $2,500, not as a bribe but as a campaign contribution that he gave to his grandchildren, the Commission recommended the resignations of both Klingbiel and Solfisburg. They resigned from the bench on August 4, 1969. In a prepared statement, Klingbiel summarized his years of public service and said that, at age sixty-eight, he had intended to remain on the Court for only one or two more years. "However," he now concluded, "in view of the report of the special commission and the fact that four members of it decided to go beyond their authority and assume the prerogative of the constitutionally created Illinois court commission would place such pressure upon the health and happiness of my family, as well as myself, that in consultation within our own household, I have decided to retire from the Illinois Supreme Court. A letter to this effect will be directed to the governor on Monday. I wish to make it absolutely clear that in doing this I possess no sense of guilt." Klingbiel remained bitter over the "political push" that removed him from office, telling one friend that he was not a crook but a "damn fool," and refused to concede any wrongdoing.[1216]

Klingbiel's son described how the former Supreme Court justice spent much of his time after the 1969 resignation: "He baby-sat my children."[1217] On January 18, 1973, seventy-one-year-old Ray Klingbiel died unexpectedly in his Moline home.[1218] Following First Congregational Church services, he was buried in Rose Lawn Memorial Estates in Moline.

CHARLES H. DAVIS, 1955-1960, 1970-1975

Born in Fairfield, Wayne County, Illinois, on January 7, 1906, Charles Hubbard Davis was the son of Horace and Helen M. Decker Davis. Horace Davis owned a hotel on the courthouse square, and his son remembered that circuit lawyers lodged there during court sessions. Obtaining his elementary and high school education in Fairfield public schools, Charles Davis then attended the University of Illinois, intending to study medicine, but upon graduation in 1928 decided to enter the University of Chicago Law School. Graduating in 1931, Davis was admitted to the bar that year and moved to Rockford, where he opened a general law practice. On October 19, 1935, he married Ruth Peugh of Carroll County, and they would become the parents of five daughters and two sons.

From 1945 to 1955, Davis partnered with Charles S. Thomas in the firm of Thomas and Davis, specializing in education law. For nearly two decades, Davis represented the Harlem School District of Winnebago County and Rockford School District No. 205, while also guiding other northern Illinois districts through school consolidations and bond issues. A political activist, Davis served for fourteen years as chairman of the Winnebago County Republican Party. "I know more blacktop roads to more places in northern Illinois than anyone," he once joked, "between school business and campaigning I've been everywhere!"[1219]

In 1955, Davis won election to the Illinois Supreme Court from the Sixth District, succeeding William J. Fulton, and from 1957 to 1958 served as Chief Justice. During that tenure, the justices heard the appeal of Lloyd Eldon Miller Jr. A twenty-nine-year-old cab driver, Miller had been convicted in the Hancock County Circuit Court and sentenced to death for the 1955 murder of an eight-year-old girl. He appealed the verdict on grounds that he had involuntarily confessed to the crime after "an ordeal of endless questioning, accompanied by threats, promises, cajolery and violence, which led him to sign the document without knowing what it was."[1220]

Police and prosecutors convinced the jury that stains on clothing found at the scene was Miller's blood, even though state crime laboratory analysts reported that the stains were actually paint. The Supreme Court affirmed the conviction per curiam, and for ten years he waited on death row as the case moved through the federal appeals process. In February 1967, the U.S. Supreme Court reversed the Illinois decision. The state's contention was "totally belied by the record," wrote Justice Potter Stewart, citing the prosecutor's insistence that the clothing was encrusted with Miller's blood. After the federal decision, a U.S. District Judge in Chicago determined that the state had no basis for retaining Miller in custody. He was released from Stateville Prison in Joliet in March 1967, and the prosecution eventually dropped all charges against him.[1221]

Davis sought reelection to the Supreme Court in 1960, but lost the Republican nomination after his opponent, Roy J. Solfisburg Jr., appealed to convention delegates that Davis often voted with the Democratic judges. "The judicial process," Davis protested, "should take no cognizance whether the litigant is Republican or Democrat, rich or poor, influential or without influence, or of one race or creed or another."[1222]

Returning to private practice, Davis partnered in Thomas, Davis and Kostantacos from 1960 to 1965, and served another term as Winnebago County Republican chairman. In 1964, he was among the first full-time Appellate Justices elected under a new amendment to the Judicial Article of the 1870 Constitution, serving in the Second District Appellate Court in Elgin. In 1970, he won election to a ten-year term on the Supreme Court, succeeding Marvin F. Burt, who had succeeded Chief Justice Solfisburg after his resignation in 1969.

Among the cases during Davis's second tenure, *People v. Lindsay* concerned display of the American flag. Millikin University art department chairman Edward Lindsay and Decatur Art Institute president Marvin Klavens were convicted in the Macon County Circuit Court of violating the Illinois Flag Act by creating an exhibit sculpture that "was likely to provoke a breach of the peace." The art object, titled "Flag in Chains," consisted of two American flags sewn together, stuffed with foam rubber, and locked with a chain wrapped around the piece. The sculpture, Klavens explained, demonstrated their "patriotic concern for freedom for all." Hearing the case on appeal, Davis delivered the Supreme Court decision reversing the conviction. "The State did not prove beyond a reasonable doubt that there was a likelihood of a breach of the peace," he wrote. "It appears quite certain that a new trial will produce no additional proof that the exhibit 'Flag in Chains' would have caused public disorder."[1223]

In addition to his legal and judicial career, Davis served as chairman and director of Boone State Bank and Winnebago Farm School for Boys. He was a member of the Phi Delta Phi legal fraternity and Shriners, as well as the American Judicature Society, Fellow of the American College of Trial Lawyers, and the American, Illinois, and Winnebago County Bar associations.[1224] Active in the Rockford Second Congregational Church, he sang in the church choir for many years.

Davis retired from the Supreme Court in October 1975 because of ill health. On February 22, 1976, at the age of seventy, he died at his Rockford home. Following Congregational Church services, he was buried in Middle Creek Cemetery. "Judge Davis had one speed and that was 'full speed ahead,'" recalled Winnebago County Chief Circuit Judge John E. Sype. "He was an energetic man. He devoted himself to his work and I had great respect for him." Rockford attorney Peter C. Kostantacos, who began his career with Davis, described his admiration for the former justice. "He was a conscientious, dedicated hardworking man—one of the most thorough attorneys I knew. Anyone who retained him got 110 percent."[1225]

BYRON O. HOUSE, 1957-1969

Byron O. House was born on September 27, 1902, in St. Louis, Missouri, to Harold H. and Olive B. House. In 1904, the family moved to Oakdale, Illinois, about nine miles south of Nashville, then in 1906 moved to Ashley, about ten miles east of Nashville. Upon moving in 1908 to Nashville, House attended local public schools. He enrolled in the University of Illinois in 1921 and studied pre-law courses. He received a Bachelor of Laws degree from the law school there in 1926. That same year he was admitted to the bar and returned to Nashville where he was to live the rest of his life.[1226]

Before settling in Nashville, his father, familiarly called H.H., worked in railroad yards, and on streetcar lines while he attended Benton Law School in St. Louis. In Ashley, he worked as a schoolteacher and farm laborer. In Oakdale, he worked as a freight clerk for the Illinois Central railroad as he prepared for his bar examination. When he was admitted to the bar in 1908, he moved immediately to Nashville where he set up a law practice.[1227]

Byron House practiced law with his father until the latter died in 1944. His new partner became Wilbert J. Hohlt, although the firm retained the name House & House. Eventually his son, James B. House, joined the firm in 1955, and the firm eventually became Hohlt, House, DeMoss & Epplin.[1228]

House's family in Nashville included his parents, an older sister, Florence, and a younger sister, Beulah. His brother Lawrence was born in Nashville in 1912.[1229] Beulah later married Ralph L. Maxwell, who would precede House on the Supreme Court bench. House married Mildred Holston in 1925, a year before he completed law school. Their wedding date was planned around his semester final examinations. Their son, James, was born in 1927. Daughters Marilyn and Dorothy were born in 1929 and 1933, respectively.[1230]

His law practice was slow for the first several years, but the New Deal bank holiday of 1933 sent bankers looking for lawyers. Recognition of his good work brought in more and more clients. In addition, he found many new clients among the municipalities in his county that needed legal representation for the public works projects that were a large part of Franklin Roosevelt's New Deal programs.[1231] His practice grew, and after his father's death in 1944, he was working at his capacity. He was approached to serve as Washington County State's Attorney when his brother-in-law Ralph L. Maxwell left that post to sit on the circuit bench. House would have declined, but because World War II had depleted the county of manpower, including attorneys, he accepted the position for 1945 and 1946.[1232]

He returned to his law practice until 1956. In that year circuit judge William G. Juergens vacated his seat on the circuit bench to become judge of the United States District Court. Governor William G. Stratton appointed House to the circuit court in July 1956. He immediately gained a reputation as an outstanding judge. Therefore, it was not difficult for him to win the Republican nomination for the special election to fill the Supreme Court seat vacated by the death of his brother-in-law Ralph L. Maxwell.[1233]

House was first elected to the Supreme Court in a special election in 1957 following Maxwell's death. Maxwell's term was to have ended in 1960, so under the state's constitution, Governor William G. Stratton could either call for a special election or wait for the circuit court elections that were scheduled for the following June three months away. The Governor decided to call a special election over the objections of Democrats who hoped that an anticipated larger voter turnout in the June election would help them. Stratton, however, claimed that because of the court's heavy workload it was important to have all seven seats filled at the earliest opportunity. Observers close to the court also understood that the six sitting justices often had "bitter arguments" in the conference room that could be precluded by the presence of a seventh, tie-breaking justice.[1234] In the election on February 25, House handily beat the Democratic circuit judge from Benton, Frank P. Hanagan, by a margin of 56 percent to 44 percent.[1235] He took his seat on the bench after a swearing-in ceremony in Springfield on March 11, 1957.[1236] When he ran for reelection to a full nine-year term in 1960, House, a lifelong Republican, received support from Democrats because of his competence, efficiency, and experience.[1237]

His tenure on the Supreme Court began during the period of court reform that culminated in the entirely new article in the state constitution covering the judicial system. During the 1950s, congestion in the courts and outdated practices stimulated a growing demand for reform. By the end of the decade, which concluded with House's term as Chief Justice, the court could claim that it could keep its docket current, changed its rules to allow longer sessions and longer periods for issuing opinions, and urged the legislature to create more circuit judges.[1238] One of the reasons for the crowded docket was the flood of appeals from convicts in state penitentiaries who learned that they could exercise their right to appeal their convictions. Since House's former circuit was home to important state penal facilities, he had a familiarity with the corrections system that was useful in dealing with corrections laws.

Even though he carried the burden of the court's heavy workload, he made recreation an important part of his life. He had a lifelong passion for hunting, which his colleagues on the court supported by allowing him to take on more work at certain times of the year so that he could have time for hunting. Even though the family business, then in its third generation, was the practice of law, he also had a farm near Nashville where he spent time working as a farmer.[1239]

When the new judicial article in the constitution took effect in 1964, it created an administrative office responsible for the state's court system. House won the praise of his colleagues by voluntarily taking on the supervision of the court's budgetary and administrative matters. Thus, in addition to his duties as a jurist, he also worked with legislative committees on the budget and coordinated the development and even the invention of administrative policy.[1240]

One of House's last public appearances was for his testimony in July 1969 for the Supreme Court's Special Commission's investigation into allegations of judicial impropriety by two other justices of the court. House was the first justice to testify, and as far as anyone could remember, it was the first time a Supreme Court justice had ever been summoned as a witness to testify before attorneys. His testimony was for the most part concerned with court procedures and practices both formal and informal. The state's legal community always held House in the highest regard, and there was never the slightest suggestion that he had engaged in any impropriety.[1241]

On August 27, 1969, House suffered a stroke while attending the Hambletonian trotting race at the fairgrounds in DuQuoin. He was sent immediately to St. Mary's Hospital in Clayton, Missouri, fifty miles away, for emergency surgery to repair his carotid artery. Only his left arm and leg seemed impaired by the stroke, and complete recovery was anticipated. He had missed the opening of the September term for the Supreme Court, and since the resignation of two justices left the court with only five members, he was anxious to return to his duties in Springfield.[1242] He was recovering from the stroke and planned to be present at the court's January term, but while at home he developed abdominal trouble. Surgery on September 25 at St. Elizabeth's Hospital in nearby Belleville revealed advanced intestinal cancer. He died September 27, 1969, on his sixty-seventh birthday. He was survived by his widow, Mildred, his son and two daughters, and his brother, Lawrence. He was a member of the Presbyterian Church in Nashville. He was also a member of the Elks, Odd Fellows, Rotary, several bar associations, and the legal fraternity Pi Kappa Pi. He was buried in Greenwood Cemetery.[1243]

His death also precipitated a potential constitutional crisis for the Supreme Court. The constitution set a quorum at four of the seven members. Two had resigned, and House had died. The court could carry on provided that every decision by the remaining four members was unanimous. However, Daniel P. Ward, one of the four, had served as Cook County State's Attorney prior to his elevation to the court. Consequently, he had to excuse himself from any case in which his State's Attorney's office had been involved. Since no election could be held until the following year, the court had to take the unprecedented step of appointing temporary justices in order to avert crisis.

ROY J. SOLFISBURG JR., 1960-1969

A lifelong Aurora resident, Roy John Solfisburg Jr. was born in the city on September 9, 1916, the son of Roy J. and Helen Solfisburg and grandson of Christopher and Elizabeth Love Solfisburg.[1244] Roy Jr. attended local schools and graduated from East Aurora High School. After attaining his law degree from the University of Illinois in 1940, he joined his father's Aurora law firm and during World War II served as a lieutenant in the United States Navy.[1245] He and his wife, Edith Squires of Marietta, Ohio, would become the parents of three daughters and two sons.

Solfisburg served as Aurora corporation counsel from 1949 to 1953, a commissioner of the Illinois Court of Claims from 1953 to 1954, then as Master in Chancery of the Kane County Circuit Court.[1246] Politically active, he for a time was a Republican precinct committeeman and Kane County Republican Party chairman. Elected to a circuit court vacancy, Solfisburg won election to the position in 1956. "Lawyers say that Judge Solfisburg is methodical," wrote a local newsman, "knows constitutional law, and that he justified selection by others judges of the circuit as chief judge by excellent administration of the 16th Circuit's technical housekeeping." A year later the state Supreme Court justices appointed him a judge of the Second District Appellate Court.[1247]

In 1960, Solfisburg defeated incumbent Charles H. Davis for the Republican nomination for the Sixth District Supreme Court seat. Then, demonstrating what a local newspaper reporter termed "a master politician's knack," Solfisburg won a decisive victory over the Democratic candidate, Rockford trial lawyer B. Jay Knight.

Solfisburg began his Supreme Court tenure in June 1960 and was Chief Justice from 1962 to 1963. In a 1966 case, *People ex rel. Conn v. Randolph,* the Court considered the case of several attorneys seeking expenditure reimbursements from the State of Illinois, represented by Director of Public Safety Ross Randolph. They were appointed to defend four prisoners alleged to have murdered three guards during a riot at a state prison in Randolph County. Although all of the attorneys resided in the southern Illinois area in which the crime occurred, the Randolph County Circuit Court granted a change of venue to Sangamon County, approximately 150 miles distant. Those appointed attorneys, including David N. Conn, petitioned the Supreme Court for reimbursement above the statutory $500 compensation per defendant in a capital case. The attorneys contended that during the three-month trial, they lodged at their own expense and incurred significant costs in preparing the defense. The trial court had approved reimbursement of their itemized statements totaling approximately $31,000, but the treasurers of both Sangamon and Randolph Counties stated that "there were no funds" to cover the payments.

"Never before in the history of the State of Illinois has Court appointed counsel been asked to devote so much time, energy, incur so many expenses, and to expend so much of their own personal funds for the defense of any indigent persons in a trial of such lengthy duration and complexities," Solfisburg wrote in compelling the Department of Public Safety to cover the reimbursements from its fiscal appropriation. "We hold that upon the record presented here the petitioners are clearly entitled to payment of their costs and fees forthwith, as ordered by the trial court. A permanent solution of the problem presented is an appropriate subject for the legislature."[1248]

In 1967, fellow justices elected Solifsburg to a three-year term as Chief Justice. He delivered the Court opinion in a noted product liability case, *People ex rel. Gen. Motors Corp. v. Bua.* The plaintiff had claimed injuries resulting from a defective tie rod on a 1961 model Corvair, manufactured by General Motors. In a pretrial discovery order, Cook County Circuit Judge Nicholas J. Bua directed the company to produce voluminous records of model years 1960 through 1965, to determine whether the Corvair was negligently designed and manufactured. When General Motors had not produced the discovery documents several weeks later, Bua held the firm in contempt and entered a default judgment of liability as a sanction for failing to comply with his directive. General Motors appealed to the Illinois Supreme Court, which determined Bua's pretrial discovery order as too broad.

"We think that it was an abuse of discretion to order the production of complete records for Corvair model years through 1965 in the absence of a showing of relevancy or materiality," Solfisburg wrote. "Although we have determined that the production orders in this case were too broad we believe the trial judge has exercised extreme patience in this case, and it is to be hoped that counsel will adopt a spirit of co-operation with regard to further discovery so that all material matters will be expeditiously produced in order that the truth seeking purposes of the rules will be served."[1249]

In 1969, the *Chicago Tribune* reported that several Chicago attorneys and the National Conference of Metropolitan Courts recommended the highly regarded Solfisburg for the United States Supreme Court seat vacated by Justice Abe Fortas.[1250] A few months later, however, Chicagoan Sherman H. Skolnick, chairman of the Citizens Committee to Clean Up the Courts, requested that the Illinois Supreme Court investigate the integrity of its decision in the 1967 case *People v. Isaacs et al.* The Court had exonerated Civic Center Bank & Trust Company of Chicago's general counsel, Theodore J. Isaacs, on charges of conspiring to defraud the state while serving as Director of the Department of Revenue. Skolnick claimed that Solfisburg and Associate Supreme Court Justice Ray Klingbiel acted with impropriety, having purchased Civic Center Bank & Trust stock from Isaacs at a reduced price shortly before the Court decision.[1251]

Chicago Bar Association President Frank Greenberg chaired a five-member Special Commission of the Supreme Court to investigate the allegations, with Chicago antitrust attorney and later U.S. Supreme Court Justice John Paul Stevens as independent counsel. The Greenberg Commission interviewed twenty-one witnesses and examined more than one hundred exhibits before determining on July 31, 1969, that both Solfisburg and Klingbiel had engaged in "positive acts of impropriety" that tainted the Supreme Court decision regarding Isaacs. Commission members concluded that public confidence in the Court could "best be restored by the prompt resignation of the two Justices."[1252] Although Solfisburg denied any wrongdoing, he and Klingbiel resigned.[1253] "In all the previous history of the law courts in Illinois," reported legal historian George Fiedler, "no supreme court justice had ever been successfully impeached, nor removed by address, nor forced off the bench by demands of resignation."[1254] Marvin F. Burt completed Solfisburg's term to 1970.

Over the next few years, Solfisburg developed a private practice in Aurora, even arguing two cases before the Supreme Court, and in the early 1980s, taught constitutional law at

Aurora College.[1255] He held honorary degrees from Kent College and John Marshall law schools, and was a member of Trinity Episcopal Church, Aurora Union League, American Legion, Aurora Elks Club, the American, Illinois, and Kane County Bar Associations, and a past president of the Exchange Club. He retired shortly before his death, which occurred at age seventy-four on April 19, 1991, in Fort Myers, Florida. Interment followed graveside services at Spring Lake Cemetery in Aurora.

ROBERT C. UNDERWOOD, 1962-1984

Robert Charles Underwood was born in Gardner in Grundy County, Illinois, on October 27, 1915, the only child of Marion L. and Edith L. Frazee Underwood. His father worked in his grandfather's general merchandise and grocery store that served the surrounding farming community. His mother was a schoolteacher. The store provided a life without want, but when he was old enough to count, he was put to work counting eggs, and when he was old enough to drive a delivery wagon, he was put to work delivering groceries and soliciting orders from customers in the countryside.[1256] His father also owned a farm about fifteen miles east of Gardner where Rock Creek flowed into the Kankakee River. The property is now part of Kankakee River State Park. The farm played an important role in his life since his father and he spent time there hunting and fishing, in which he developed a lifelong interest.

He graduated from Gardner-South Wilmington High School in 1933, and then, partly because his family was active in the Methodist Church, he enrolled at Illinois Wesleyan University at Bloomington, about sixty miles to the southwest. While in college he worked in a food market and as a dishwasher in a restaurant to pay his two-dollars-a-week rent. He also took on odd jobs, including handyman work for an eccentric widow whom years later he committed to a mental hospital while serving on the circuit bench in Bloomington.[1257]

Following his graduation from Illinois Wesleyan in 1937, he enrolled in the law school of the University of Illinois from which he received his law degree in 1939. He was admitted to the state bar the same year. Also in that year he married Dorothy Roy of Chicago. He had planned to relocate and practice law in Minnesota because that state appeared better able to satisfy his love of the outdoors. He took the bar examination for Minnesota but did not receiving the results in a timely manner. In the meantime, he took the Illinois bar examination and passed. He decided, with his wife, to remain in Bloomington, where he entered private practice. Minnesota then notified him that he passed the bar examination, but he had already begun his career in Illinois that was to span fifty years.[1258]

From 1939 to 1946, he was in private practice in Bloomington and served as city attorney for adjacent Normal. During this period he was also assistant state's attorney for McLean County from 1942 to 1946. In 1946, he was elected judge. He was surprised at his nomination and election to the county bench because he felt he was too new to McLean County and to the legal profession. Voters, however, felt otherwise and demonstrated their support in reelecting him three times. His elevation to the Supreme Court was even more surprising to him.

Underwood attended the Republican convention in Champaign for the 1962 special judicial election to fill the Supreme Court seat vacated by the death of Justice George W.

Bristow. He attended the convention as a delegate with no inkling that he would become the nominee. Several people were keenly interested in the nomination, and the outcome was uncertain. To keep their options open, the McLean County delegation, which included Underwood, decided to run him as a favorite-son candidate. After sixteen hours and fifty-one contentious ballots, the convention deadlocked. Underwood's delegates decided to make their move, and after some quick electioneering, Underwood became the party's nominee on the fifty-second ballot. He modestly attributed his success to the notion that he "had not made any particular enemies." He was elected easily in the heavily Republican Third District in the April election, and Chief Justice Harry B. Hershey swore him in on May 2, 1962.[1259]

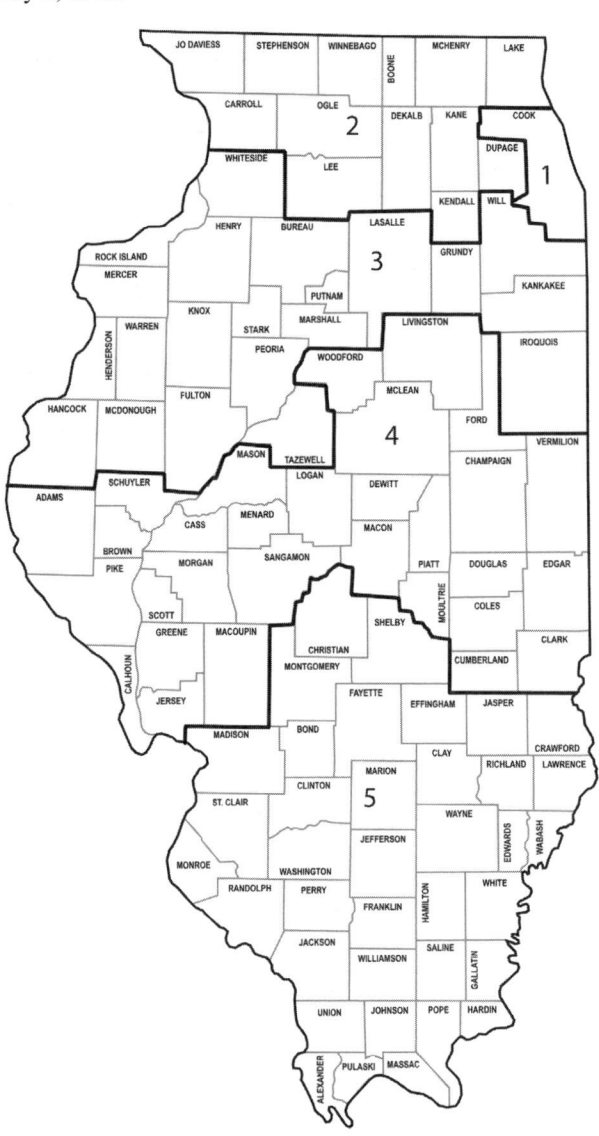

In the post–World War II decades, constitutional law, statutory law, and the common law in Illinois and the nation was in flux as social change presented new challenges to ideas such as criminal rights, the power of government, and family structures. In dealing with those issues, Underwood earned the respect of the bench and bar by showing his constant concern for the effect of his opinions upon people and not losing sight of the human element in pursuit of legal abstractions.[1260] Underwood admitted to conservative tendencies, as shown in his opinion in *Hewitt v. Hewitt*.[1261] In this case a woman was suing a man in what had become known as a palimony suit. The two had lived together for years and even raised children while she worked to put the man through medical school. The Supreme Court ruled against her because, as Underwood wrote, to rule in her favor would have the effect of legalizing common law marriages in Illinois when state statutes did not authorize them. The opinion was unpopular but matched his ideas concerning judicial restraint.

The Judicial Article of 1964 divided the state into five judicial districts. (Image courtesy of Illinois Supreme Court Historic Preservation Commission)

However, in *Hickey v. Illinois Central*, Underwood's opinion for the court came down on the side of local government in a property-ownership case of great consequence. The court held that the Illinois Central Railroad Company had no valid claim over lakefront property in Chicago that it had occupied for over a century. The land and landfill in question had become Grant Park, Lake Shore Drive, and some of the most densely developed and valuable property in the city.[1262]

During 1969, the worst scandal ever to involve the Supreme Court resulted in a serious crisis. Chief Justice Roy Solfisburg and Justice Ray Klingbiel resigned from the court after an investigating commission accused them of improprieties in accepting stock from a Chicago bank. At the same time, Justice Byron House suffered a stroke and was unable to execute his responsibilities. When the court convened for its September 1969 session, only four justices sat on the bench, which meant that all opinions would have to be unanimous since the state constitution required the agreement of four justices for a majority for the eight hundred cases pending before the court. Underwood was elected Chief Justice to serve through this extraordinary time.[1263] Underwood was the right person to represent the court to a doubting and uncertain public. His unimpeachable integrity restored confidence in the court as it faced new ethics rules and, in 1970, a brand new state constitution. Shorthanded on the bench, taking up the task of implementing new strict rules on judicial conduct, and assuming the responsibility for the administration of the state's entire judiciary as provided in the new constitution, Underwood's exemplary leadership earned him lifelong honor and respect.[1264]

The intelligence and love of the outdoors with which nature endowed him was not reflected in the weaknesses of his body. A congenital condition left him with noticeably enlarged hands and feet. In December 1963, he was stricken with an intestinal condition that left him hospitalized and near death for several weeks. His recovery required a transfusion of thirty pints of blood, many of which the legal community in Chicago provided.[1265] In 1977, he was afflicted with phlebitis, a condition that caused him to sit on the court bench with his leg raised, out of sight of those coming before him.[1266]

After twenty-two years on the Supreme Court bench, he announced his intent to retire on December 3, 1984, when his term came to an end. After more than twenty-two years as a Supreme Court justice, during which he frequently worked nights and weekends, he said that he had reached the point at which he preferred less demanding duties.[1267] His tenure of only six years as Chief Justice from 1969 to 1975 was among the longest in the history of the court. Although he left the bench, he did not retire from the law. He entered the Bloomington law firm of Dunn, Goebel, Ulbrich, Morel & Hundman.[1268]

During his long career, he held membership in more than a dozen professional groups and served on boards of directors for dozens of local and statewide organizations for legal and social issues. He achieved the rank of thirty-third degree Mason, was awarded four honorary degrees from colleges and universities in Illinois, the University of Illinois Outstanding Alumni Achievement Award, the Illinois State Bar Association's Award of Merit, and many others. A few days after his retirement, he was given special recognition in a legislative ceremony in the state capitol. Of all his awards and honors, among those he found most gratifying was the city of Normal's naming Underwood Park for him.[1269]

He collapsed and died in his kitchen at home on March 30, 1988, at age seventy-two. He was survived by his wife, Dorothy Roy Underwood, his daughter, Susan Louise Barcalow, and two grandchildren. His funeral was held at the First Methodist Church of Normal, followed by burial in the Funk's Grove Cemetery in nearby Funk's Grove.[1270]

THOMAS E. KLUCZYNSKI, 1966-1976, 1978-1980

Thomas E. Kluczynski was born in Chicago on September 29, 1903. He attended public and parochial schools. He received a Bachelor of Laws degree from the University of Chicago Law School in 1927, graduating cum laude and was admitted to the bar that same year. He was a general practitioner and specialized in trial work until 1948, when he was appointed to the Illinois Industrial Commission.[1271]

In 1950, Governor Adlai E. Stevenson appointed Kluczynski to a judgeship on the Cook County Circuit Court where he was assigned to the criminal division a few months later. In 1951, he was elected to a six-year term on the circuit court and reelected in 1957. He was the chief judge of the criminal court until 1952 after which he served as the presiding judge of the Family (Juvenile) Court until 1954 when he was assigned to common law civil trials. As chief judge of the criminal court, he earned a reputation as a stalwart supporter of the public defender system as a way to assure justice for indigent people.[1272] In 1958, he became the chief judge of the circuit court, and in 1962 was named chancellor of the circuit court, serving there until November 1963, when the Supreme Court assigned him to the First District Appellate Court until his election to the Illinois Supreme Court.[1273]

In 1959, while on the Cook County Circuit Court, he drew attention with his ruling to return four Russian children to their parents in the Soviet Union. The parents, George and Nadejda Kozmin, arrived in Chicago in 1950 as displaced persons but were unable to deal with their difficult situation and returned to Russia after institutionalization at Chicago State Hospital. Since the State of Illinois had taken custody of their four sons during their hospitalizations, the parents had to sue in the circuit court to have their children returned to them. With Cold War feelings running high, Kluczynski was under pressure to keep the children in the United States. After three years in court, Kluczynski ended the dispute by agreeing with the parents.[1274]

In 1961, Kluczynski had the support of United States Senator Paul H. Douglas for appointment to the federal district court in Chicago. He was unable to obtain the appointment and remained happily in the state court system. In 1964, a new judicial article in the state's constitution took effect and created three Supreme Court seats for Cook County. With the backing of the Cook County Democratic Party and approval from Chicago Mayor Richard J. Daley, Kluczynski was nominated and elected to the Supreme Court in 1966. Chief Justice Ray I. Klingbiel swore him in on December 13, 1966.[1275] Kluczynski's seat succeeded that of Harry Hershey's, the former downstate second district.

He served a ten-year term and left the court without running for reelection. Two years later, however, the court recalled him to his seat to fill the unexpired term of James A. Dooley, who died after serving just less than two years on the court. He served in this position from April 1978 until the judicial election of 1980, after which he returned to private practice.[1276]

After retirement in 1976, he formed the firm of Kluczynski, Dore, & O'Toole, located in downtown Chicago. The firm had some notable clients, including Joan Wrigley, who sued for divorce from William Wrigley, the chewing-gum heir, in a well-publicized case. The State of Illinois became another client when Illinois Attorney General William J. Scott hired the firm to handle the state's $260 million tax dispute against Illinois Bell Telephone Company.[1277]

One of Kluczynski's contributions was his service in the transition and interpretation of the new state constitution. He took his seat on the Supreme Court bench barely three years after voters chose to replace the entire judicial article of the state's constitution effective in 1964, and further changes were made when an entirely new constitution took effect on July 1, 1971. The new constitution made provisions for such concepts as the right to privacy and the right to a clean environment. Together with provisions for making constitutional amendments by petition and home rule for eligible sub-state units of government the Supreme Court during Kluczynski's tenure on the bench bore the responsibility for adjudicating and interpreting the constitutionality of issues where no precedent existed in Illinois.

One of Kluczynski's most important contributions was the opinion he filed November 30, 1972, in *Kanellos v. Cook County*, a case that sought to measure the limits of home-rule power. Prior to home rule, units of governments had to seek authority from state enabling statutes to carry out even the most mundane affairs of government; the new order of things obviated the necessity of local governments to ask permission from the state for many activities. In the case, Cook County had issued $10 million in bonds without first seeking a referendum to obtain public approval. Concerned citizens sued pleading that statutes in force before the new constitution took effect prohibited such behavior. Kluczynski upheld the right of Cook County to issue the bonds regardless of statute. In other words, he set a precedent granting substantial power to local government under home rule. He was also firm in ruling that should the legislature wish to require referenda for bond issues by local governments, it would have to do so with a two-thirds majority in both houses of the state General Assembly, as provided in the new constitution.[1278]

He was the brother of United States Congressman John C. Kluczynski, who served the Fifth Congressional District on Chicago's southwest side. The federal building in downtown Chicago is named for the congressman. After the death of John, Kluczynski's wife Melanie, a former fashion model, briefly sought the congressional seat.[1279]

He died at Northwestern Memorial Hospital on May 16, 1994, at age ninety. His funeral was held at Holy Name Cathedral on North State Street, within walking distance of his home on East Lake Shore Drive. He was buried at Resurrection Cemetery on Archer Avenue, close to the southwest side neighborhood of his birth.[1280]

DANIEL P. WARD, 1966-1990

Daniel Patrick (Patrick Daniel) Ward was born on August 30, 1918, the son of Chicago streetcar motorman Patrick Sarsfield Ward and his wife, Jane Convery Ward.[1281] Daniel attended Chicago and Oak Park parochial schools and graduated from Marmion Military Academy in Aurora. After attending St. Viator College, he graduated from DePaul University College of Law in 1941 and was admitted to the Illinois bar that year. He taught law at Southeastern University, Washington, D.C., before serving with the United States Army Forty-first Combat Engineers in World War II.

Opening a private law practice in 1945, Ward served as Assistant United States Attorney for the Northern District of Illinois from 1948 to 1954, including three years as chief of the criminal division. He married Marilyn Corleto on June 23, 1954, and they would become the parents of three daughters and a son. Named dean and professor of law at DePaul University College of Law in 1955, in 1960 the scholarly Ward was chosen by Democratic Mayor Richard J. Daley to challenge Republican Cook County State's Attorney Benjamin Adamowski. "Politicians were amazed to discover the zest with which he entered the political fray," remembered *Chicago Tribune* columnist Kenan Keise of Ward, "often being the last to leave a campaign rally."[1282] Ward won the election, and in 1964 the National District Attorneys Association named him the "nation's outstanding prosecutor." Reelected that year by the widest margin of any Cook County Democrat, Ward also served on the American Bar Association Committee on Fair Trial—Free Press, following the Warren Commission Report on the 1963 assassination of President John F. Kennedy.

In 1966, Ward resigned his position as State's Attorney to seek the First Judicial District vacancy on the Illinois Supreme Court, to succeed the deceased Justice Joseph E. Daily. Ward won the seat, and was reelected in 1974 and 1984, serving as Chief Justice from 1976 to 1979. "As judges we have to protect constitutionally insured rights," a position he maintained throughout his tenure. "I'm a firm believer that the law has a responsibility to keep abreast of society, that we certainly can't be held back by dead hands, if you will. Our society is evolutionary, it's changing, and the law is something that has to govern society. While courts are not legislatures, courts have to ensure that we do keep abreast."[1283]

In 1969, Ward wrote the opinion in *Continental National Bank v. Toll Highway Commission,* regarding the state's Toll Highway Authority Act. The legislation provided for dissolution of the Highway Commission and the transfer of toll highway management and operations to the newly established Highway Authority. Continental National Bank, on behalf of Commission bondholders, brought action in the Cook County Circuit Court seeking to have the Act declared unconstitutional, citing vague and conflicting language regarding transfer of the property and other assets: "that it leaves in doubt the status of the Commission and the relationship between the Commission and the Authority; and that it fails to bring into existence a fully functioning Authority to administer existing toll highways in this State." Ward upheld the circuit court judgment in affirming the Highway Authority Act. "It is not faultlessly drawn, as some of the numerous points raised by the appellant in behalf of the Commission's bondholders disclose, but, with respect to the objections presented for decision here, it does meet constitutional standards."[1284]

Other noted decisions authored by Ward included the 1985 *Chicago National League Ball Club, Inc. v. James R. Thompson, Governor, et al.* Ward's ruling upheld state legislation and a Chicago ordinance banning night baseball games at Wrigley Field, the only major league stadium with no night games. The Cook County Circuit Court had ruled against Chicago National League Ball Club, Inc., in its constitutional challenge to the state and city laws. "When the statute and ordinance are tested by the standards applicable to equal protection and special legislation challenges," Ward wrote in affirming the circuit court decision, "it appears that they are a reasonable attempt to protect the property and other rights of residents who live near the stadium." Three years later, a Chicago City Council ordinance allowed the Cubs a limited number of night games each season.[1285]

Ward delivered the opinion in a 1989 case that attracted national attention, *People v. Chicago Magnet Wire Corporation.* The Cook County prosecutor's officer had charged five officials of the Elk Grove Village company with aggravated battery, reckless conduct, and conspiracy to commit aggravated battery by knowingly permitting hazardous working conditions in their plant. The Cook County Circuit Court, determining federal preemption of state law, dismissed the indictments against the company. In the unanimous opinion reversing the circuit court decision, Ward wrote "There is nothing in the structure of OSHA [Federal Occupational Safety and Health Act] or its legislative history which indicates that Congress intended to preempt the enforcement of State criminal law prohibiting conduct of employers that is also governed by OSHA safety standards."[1286]

Ward delivered a nine-page dissenting opinion in the 1989 *In re Estate of Longeway*, in which a majority of the justices held that a guardian could refuse sustenance to a comatose, terminally ill patient. "Allowing a guardian to substitute his judgment for that of an incompetent ward," he wrote, "creates a grave risk that due to the guardian's own personal values, biases, or mistaken beliefs concerning the ward, there will be wards who will undergo the death described in frightening terms in the majority opinion, without ever having had such an intent to do so. It is fully understandable that the inherent risks of and the consequences of mistake which necessarily accompany the decision to terminate another person's life-sustaining treatment and take his life have led thoughtful commentators to reject the notion of substituted judgment."[1287]

In addition to his Court responsibilities, Ward served in administrative capacities, as liaison to the executive committee of the Illinois Judicial Conference, on the Committee on Character and Fitness, Attorney Registration and Disciplinary Commission, State Board of Law Examiners, and Committee on Professional Responsibility.

After twenty-four years as an Illinois Supreme Court Justice, Ward in 1989 announced his planned retirement the following year, stating that his only concern for a successor would be someone qualified to be a "fine judge"; "I have no preferences as to those superficial things of race, sex, what have you."[1288] Ward planned to remain in the legal profession, "but to a less intense degree," he explained. "This job has been a joy, the apex to a career in law, but it has been demanding. Now it is time for new challenges."[1289] He became of counsel to the Chicago firm of Bell, Boyd & Lloyd. His memberships included the Chicago and Illinois State Bar Associations, and the American Judicature Society.

In 1978, while Chief Justice, the popular Ward served as grand marshal of the Chicago St. Patrick's Day Parade, walking through the downtown Loop with Governor Jim Thompson and Mayor Michael Bilandic.[1290] Ward held honorary doctoral degrees from John Marshall Law School and DePaul University. "When one hears his name," remembered one colleague, "one immediately thinks of integrity. His large, robust body houses a giant intellect and a boundless magnanimity toward his fellow man."[1291]

Ward died on April 23, 1995, of complications from emphysema at Loyola University Medical Center, Maywood. Funeral services were held at Divine Providence Catholic Church, Westchester, followed by burial in Queen of Heaven Cemetery, Hillside. Justice Mary Ann G. McMorrow described her former Supreme Court colleague as "one of the most admired and respected jurists in Illinois history." Chief Justice Michael Bilandic, to whom Ward administered the oath of office as Chicago mayor in 1976 and who succeeded Ward on the Supreme Court in 1990, called him "one person that I believe everyone loved and respected."[1292]

MARVIN F. BURT, 1969-1970

A longtime public servant, Marvin F. Burt was born on November 20, 1905, in Freeport, Illinois, the son of Ralph and Isabel Marvin Burt. Educated in local schools, Marvin Burt graduated from Freeport High School in 1924. He continued his education at Harvard University, attaining a bachelor's degree. In 1931, he earned a law degree from Chicago-Kent College of Law. On June 17, 1930 he married Helen Woodruff, and they would become the parents of a son and a daughter.[1293]

Returning to Freeport to practice law, Burt also served as city attorney and as Master in Chancery of the Stephenson County Circuit Court. He also held terms as a director of the Lena State Bank, Rock City Bank, and Bankers Mutual Life Insurance Company, as well as a director and president of the Freeport YMCA.

Burt launched his political and governmental career in 1945 with election to the Illinois General Assembly as a representative. He held that position for four terms, then in 1952 won election to the state senate and reelection in 1956. There he headed the Illinois Commission on Care of Alcoholics and helped establish treatment programs for alcoholics, especially those confined to state mental institutions. He also helped draft a medical practice act to cover all health professionals and originated a banking act to prevent the infiltration of syndicate money into newly forming banks. During his second senate term, he led the Republican caucus.[1294]

In 1960, Burt made a bid for nomination to the United States Congress, but was defeated in the Republican primary by John B. Anderson of Rockford. Later that year, Burt won election to the Fifteenth Judicial Circuit and served as Chief Judge. On October 9, 1969, he was chosen for the Illinois Supreme Court, succeeding Chief Justice Roy J. Solfisburg, who resigned at the request of a special bar commission. Burt accepted the appointment with the understanding that he would not seek election to the seat at the expiration of the term.

Despite his brief tenure, Burt wrote the Court's opinion in several cases. *People v. O'Leary* involved the admissibility of a defendant's confession to a crime. In a 1968 Morgan County Circuit Court case, a jury found nineteen-year-old Kenneth O'Leary of Jacksonville guilty of burglary. According to police reports, during questioning he "began behaving like a child in a temper tantrum" and was administered tear gas and confined to a small cell. Half an hour later, calm but "still affected by the tear gas," he confessed to the burglary. In appealing the conviction, he contended that his constitutional rights had been violated, since he had not been adequately advised that he could remain silent or that he could have counsel present at his interrogation.

Burt wrote that the "defendant brought his troubles on himself, and the police reaction was understandable. However, we find it difficult to hold that the confession of this defendant, coming so soon after the gassing, was free and voluntary. The question in each case is whether a defendant's will was overborne at the time he confessed. If so, the confession cannot be deemed the product of a rational intellect and a free will. . . . This case must therefore be reversed and the cause remanded for a new trial."[1295]

In *People v. Howard,* T. G. Howard appealed his murder conviction by the Cook County Circuit Court, asserting that the arresting police officer failed to warn him of his constitutional rights to remain silent and have an attorney present. The conviction came approximately four months after the U.S. Supreme Court in *Miranda v. Arizona* affirmed "that statements stemming from custodial interrogation of a defendant may not be used unless procedural safeguards to effectively secure the privilege against self-incrimination have been followed." Since Howard voluntarily confessed to having shot the victim, the Illinois Supreme Court found the *Miranda* decision did not apply. "There is no showing at the time that the defendant was in custody," wrote Burt in affirming the conviction, "and, in fact, the *Miranda* decision indicates that volunteered statements of this type are admissible."[1296]

Burt served on the Supreme Court until December 1970, succeeded by Charles H. Davis, who had previously sat on the Supreme Court from 1955 to 1960. Burt then became counsel to the Freeport law firm of Kroeger, Burt & McClanathan and its successor firm, Schmelzle & Kroeger. In 1976, Illinois Attorney General William J. Scott named Burt as special assistant attorney general to investigate Illinois Secretary of State Michael J. Howlett, in the midst of a gubernatorial campaign against Republican James R. Thompson. Cook County Circuit Court Judge Raymond K. Berg had found no conflict of interest in the Democrat Howlett receiving an annual $15,000 salary from Sun Steel Company of Chicago while also serving as Illinois Auditor of Public Accounts and then Secretary of State, but Scott pursued the issue of whether to file a civil suit.

Howlett was first employed by Sun Steel as a vice president in 1952 and continued in the position after his election as state Auditor in 1962 and Secretary of State in 1972. After studying the case, Burt reported in July 1976 that he found no conflict of interest while Howlett was Auditor. A conflict of interest did arise, however, when he became Secretary of State. In that position, Howlett served as chairman of state programs for recycling wrecked and abandoned automobiles, which comprised a major portion of Sun Steel's business. Although no evidence surfaced that Howlett exerted influence on bills pertaining to the scrap metal business, Burt asserted that elected officials should not place themselves in positions that could involve personal interests. "Illinois case law," he wrote, "clearly established that a public official owes a fiduciary duty of undivided loyalty to the public and may not knowingly place himself in a position of temptation to act contrary to the best interests of the public."[1297]

A nature lover and twenty-five-year member of the Freeport Park Board, Burt helped establish and became the first president of the Jane Addamsland Park Foundation and the Pecatonica Prairie Path, an abandoned Rockford-to-Freeport railroad route. Also active in the Illinois Association of Park Districts, Burt served as its president in 1949, crusading for more parks throughout the state. In 1977, the Association of Park Districts bestowed Burt with its Presidential Award, citing his more than two decades of service for the betterment of parks and recreation in the state. "His activity consisted of much more than presiding or board-sitting," remembered a fellow Freeport attorney. "He participated in hiking, boating, swimming, ice skating and fishing and in other opportunities offered by the parks and natural resources of Illinois."[1298] Burt also held memberships in the Rotary Club, Freeport Consistory, and Elks and Germania clubs.

He died at age seventy-seven on October 15, 1983, at a Freeport nursing home. Following services at Grace Episcopal Church, he was buried beside his wife, who had died several years earlier, in Oakland Cemetery in Freeport.[1299] "I think he enjoyed his years in the Illinois State Senate the most," his son recalled. "He was in his natural element in the legislature. He was superlative at pulling people together in a quiet way. That was the height of his effectiveness. As a judge, he was fair and impartial, but it was not his natural element."[1300]

JOHN T. CULBERTSON JR., 1969-1970

Descended from a pioneer family that settled in Illinois prior to 1850, John T. Culbertson was born in Delavan on August 7, 1891, the son of John T. and Jennie McKinstry Culbertson. John Culbertson Jr. graduated in 1909 from Delavan High School and in 1913 from Illinois Wesleyan University Law School, Bloomington, where he pledged Phi Alpha Delta law fraternity. Admitted to the Illinois bar in 1913 and the Missouri bar in 1914, he taught at the Kansas City School of Law for two years. On November 25, 1915, he married Helen E. Read in Bloomington, and they became the parents of one daughter.[1301]

In 1916, Culbertson began practicing law in Delavan, joined several years later by his brother Robert M. Culbertson. Elected Tazewell County Judge in 1930, John Culbertson served a four-year term, and then won election as Circuit Judge of the Tenth Judicial Circuit, a position he held continuously until 1968. Appointed to the Fourth District Appellate Court in 1939, Culbertson served until 1964 when the new judicial article took effect and he moved to the Third District Appellate Court. On October 3, 1969, he was assigned to serve on the Illinois Supreme Court, filling the vacancy created by the resignation of Justice Ray I. Klingbiel. Culbertson accepted the stipulation that he would not be a candidate for the Court position in the November 1970 election.[1302]

A month after his Supreme Court assignment, Culbertson delivered the opinion in *People v. Sailor,* a case in which Marie Agnes Sailor appealed her Cook County Circuit Court conviction for petty theft and deceptive practices. In March 1967 she was a passenger in an automobile when a Chicago police officer stopped the driver for a traffic violation. The officer recognized items in the car as tools commonly used by burglars. Upon searching Sailor's purse, he found a credit card and papers bearing the surnames of two other individuals. Indicted for identity theft and deceptive practices for using the card to purchase a watch, Sailor contended at trial that she had found the items on the street but admitted possessing the credit card from the time of allegedly finding it.

The Supreme Court justices reversed the theft conviction, determining, wrote Justice Culbertson, "a total lack of proof" to support the decision. Regarding the charge of deceptive practices, however, Culbertson affirmed the conviction: "She freely admitted having sole possession of the credit card" on the date of the watch purchase, "and while she denied so using the card, the determination of her credibility was the function of the trial court."[1303]

In May 1970, Justice Culbertson affirmed the Cook County Circuit Court murder conviction of thirteen-year-old Michael Hammond. On appeal to the Supreme Court, his attorneys argued that the state had not proven the case beyond a reasonable doubt and that the circuit court violated Hammond's constitutional rights by failing to conduct a competency hearing prior to trial. They contended that he suffered from psychiatric and social disturbances at the time he shot twelve-year-old Robert Richardson. The Supreme Court justices determined that the trial court did not err in refusing to conduct a competency hearing "despite the brutal nature of the crime and the fact defendant had below average intelligence and a record of excessive absences from school and previous difficulties with authorities." They further found that evidence proved guilt beyond a reasonable doubt. "The testimony of an accomplice establishes that the defendant had participated in binding and shooting the decedent in his own bedroom before setting the room on fire . . . and there is no showing that the accomplice had received promises of leniency."[1304]

In addition to his lengthy judicial career and one-year Supreme Court tenure, Culbertson served as a director of the Tazewell National Bank of Delavan for forty years, twenty-five years as president, and as board chairman of Sheridan Village Bank of Peoria. A member of Delavan Presbyterian Church, he became a charter member of the local Rotary Club, also holding memberships in the Elks Lodge and Scottish Rite Masons. On July 26, 1982, a few days before his ninety-first birthday, Culbertson died at his Delavan home. He was buried in Prairie Rest Cemetery in Delavan.[1305]

"Throughout his career," recalled Peoria County Bar Association President Robert H. Miller, "Judge Culbertson displayed the finest judicial temperament. He was always cordial to and considerate of lawyers, litigants and court personnel. He tempered justice with kindness while conducting his court with decorum and impartiality. His warm personality was recognized and appreciated by all those who came in contact with him. It was a rewarding experience to appear in his court and it was also a delight to share his company at informal gatherings. His command of the language was unsurpassed and he could always be counted on for words of wit, wisdom and good fellowship. He was, above all, a gentle man."[1306]

CASWELL J. CREBS, 1969-1970, 1975-1976

Caswell Jones Crebs was born January 14, 1912, in Carmi in the southeastern part of the state. He was the son of Stewart L. and Dorothy Jones Crebs, both from locally prominent families. One of his grandfathers, William Caswell Jones, was a circuit court judge, and the other, John M. Crebs, was an officer in the Civil War and a United States congressman.[1307] When he was six years old, his family moved to California where he attended elementary and high school in Los Angeles. He completed his undergraduate degree in political science from the University of California at Los Angeles in 1932 and earned a Master of Arts degree the following year. He completed his first year in law school at the Law School of Southern California but transferred to the University of Illinois, graduating from the college of law in 1936. He was admitted to the bar the same year.[1308]

He entered the practice of law at Robinson, the seat of Crawford County, where he would reside the rest of this life. He formed a partnership with Hanby Jones in 1940. Here he would also begin his life of public service in 1941 when he served as an Assistant Attorney General until 1945. In 1941, he briefly served as supervising conciliation commissioner of the United States District Court for the Eastern District of Illinois. During World War II, Crebs served as chairman of the Crawford County Red Cross, war bond drives, and as a member of the Federal Rationing Board.[1309]

His career as a judge began in 1945 when he was elected circuit judge in the Second Judicial Circuit. At that time he was the youngest circuit judge in the state. He was reelected in 1951 and in 1957. In the last election he was so popular that no Democrat wanted to run against him, and no one in his own Republican Party wanted to challenge him for the nomination. As a result he was nominated by both political parties in that election.[1310] He earned a reputation as a lawyer's judge that preferred settlements to rancorous lawsuits. On several occasions lawyers arrived at settlements for court costs when he tossed his own money on the bench and offered to pay the costs himself. Each time the embarrassed attorneys settled quietly.[1311] He voluntarily resigned from the bench in 1964 after serving as chief judge in the circuit, returning to private practice.

In 1969, the Supreme Court appointed him to fill a vacancy created by the death of Justice Byron O. House. House's death precipitated a potential constitutional crisis for the Supreme Court. The constitution set a quorum at four of the seven members. Two had resigned and House had died. The court could carry on provided that every decision by the remaining four members were unanimous. However, Justice Daniel P. Ward, one of the four, had served as Cook County State's Attorney prior to his elevation to the court. Consequently, Ward had to excuse himself from any case in which his State's Attorney's office had been involved. Since no election could be held until the following year, the court had to take the unprecedented step of appointing temporary justices to avert a crisis. Crebs served on the court from October 1969 to December 1970 when the newly elected Joseph Goldenhersh took his seat. Crebs was appointed to the Supreme Court a second time to fill a vacancy created by the resignation of Justice Charles H. Davis. His second appointment lasted from October 1975 to December 1976. Between his appointments to the Supreme Court, the high court also appointed him to the Fifth District of the Illinois Appellate Court, serving from April 1971 to December 1974.[1312]

Among the opinions he wrote, *People v. Ward* is of special interest as it was a test of the state's obscenity statute. In this case appellant Ward, the operator of a Peoria bookstore, was convicted at a bench trial of selling obscene literature in 1971. He was sentenced to one day in jail and fined $200. Ward argued that Illinois's obscenity law was unconstitutionally vague and did not meet the guidelines for obscenity as expressed by the United States Supreme Court. Crebs wrote the court's opinion denying Ward's assertions and upholding the state law. Ward took the matter to federal court where the United States Supreme Court agreed with Crebs's opinion.[1313]

In addition to his career as a jurist and lawyer, he served as chairman of the board of directors of the First National Bank of Robinson, lieutenant governor of the Kiwanis Club, president of the Quail Creek Country Club, and Exalted Ruler of the Robinsons Elks Lodge. He was a founding member of the Robinson High School Academic Foundation and an ordained elder in the First Presbyterian Church of Robinson. In 1978, the Robinson Chamber of Commerce named him man of the year. He received the Masonic Thirty-third Degree and was named Illinois Mason of the Year in 1985.[1314]

His civic work extended beyond Crawford County. He had served as president of the Alumni Advisory Board of the University of Illinois Law School and established and funded in his name as scholarship program for minority students. He was member of the University's President's Council and co-chairman of his district for the University of Illinois Foundation.[1315]

Some years after his last and final retirement, Caswell Crebs died March 5, 1988, at age seventy-six in Pacifica Hospital in Huntington Beach, California, of a heart attack while visiting his daughter and son-in-law in adjacent Fountain Valley. He became ill the previous evening and died in the hospital the following morning. His funeral was held in Robinson on March 9 with interment in the Robinson New Cemetery.[1316]

HOWARD C. RYAN, 1970-1990

A native of Tonica, Illinois, Howard Christopher Ryan was born on June 17, 1916, the son of John F. and Sarah Egger Ryan. Reared on a farm and educated at Tonica public schools, he attended LaSalle-Peru-Oglesby Junior College and the University of Illinois. Graduating from the University of Illinois College of Law, he received his law license in April 1942. The following month he enlisted in the Army Air Corps, serving as a radio operator during World War II. After the Allies captured Paris in 1944, Ryan and his crew flew supplies into the city and returned wounded troops to the United States.[1317]

On October 16, 1943, he married Helen Cizek in Chicago, and they became the parents of three children, including a son who died in infancy. After the war, Ryan practiced law briefly in Decatur with the firm Evans, Kuhle and Leach. Returning to La Salle County, the Ryan family resided in Tonica, and he became a partner with Van Peursem, McNeilly and Ryan in nearby Peru. Appointed an assistant state's attorney in 1952, Ryan won election as county judge in 1954 as a Republican. Three years later he was elected a judge of the Thirteenth Judicial Circuit, serving as Chief Judge from 1963 to 1968, before being elected to the Third District Appellate Court. From that district, he won election to the Illinois Supreme Court in 1970, filling the seat of John Culbertson, who took office because of the resignation of Ray Klingbiel. Ryan was retained in 1976 and 1986, serving as Chief Justice from 1982 to 1985.

During the first decade of his Supreme Court tenure, Ryan expressed opposition to the Illinois death penalty law. He and two other justices strongly dissented from the majority opinion in the 1979 case of *Carey v. Cousins*, which upheld Cook County State's Attorney Bernard Carey regarding the constitutionality of the 1977 capital punishment statute. The dissenting justices agreed with Cook County Circuit Judge William Cousins Jr.'s refusal to convene a death-penalty hearing following a defendant's murder conviction. Writing the dissent, Ryan maintained that the statute "contains no directions or guidelines to minimize the risk of wholly arbitrary and capricious action by the prosecutor in either requesting a sentencing hearing or in not requesting a sentencing hearing. The vague belief of the majority that the State's Attorney will not request such a hearing unless he believes that there will be evidence which will persuade a jury that the requisite elements for a death sentence exist is meaningless." Without such guidelines, Ryan continued, the state's death penalty could be "wantonly and freakishly" imposed.[1318]

In the 1984 case *People v. Albanese*, however, he concurred in the Supreme Court's affirmation of the capital punishment statute. Charles Albanese, found guilty of the arsenic-poisoning murder of his mother-in-law, unsuccessfully appealed the verdict as well as his death sentence on several grounds. In a four-page opinion, Ryan explained his concurrence in the Court decision. "I must accept the fact that my opinion was wrong" in *Carey v. Cousins*, "because four members of this court said it was wrong. . . . The decision of the majority in *Cousins* is binding not because of the concept that it is right or correct as a proposition of law, but because it is the final statement on that issue made by the highest judicial tribunal that has considered it. . . . Simply because I dissent in a case does not mean that I must forever insist that I was right and the majority was wrong."[1319] In a 1991 *Chicago Tribune* interview, Ryan said that "he came to have fewer doubts about capital punishment and accepted it as the law of the land."[1320]

In the 1978 case *Kelsay v. Motorola, Inc.,* Ryan delivered a landmark opinion establishing that a worker may sue an employer for retaliatory discharge if terminated for asserting rights under the state's 1973 Workmen's Compensation Act. After the Livingston County Circuit Court awarded Marilyn Jo Kelsay compensatory and punitive damages against Motorola, the Fourth District Appellate Court reversed the judgment on grounds that an employee had no cause of action against an employer for retaliatory discharge. "An action for retaliatory discharge should be allowed," Ryan wrote in reversing the Appellate decision, "in order to prevent employers from putting employees in the position of choosing between their jobs and seeking their remedies under the Workmen's Compensation Act."[1321]

In a 1983 ruling, Chief Justice Ryan concurred with Rule 61 C (24) that banned media cameras in trial courts. "Having served as a trial judge for 14 years," Ryan wrote, "I am well aware of the fact that in conducting a trial, civil or criminal, of sufficient importance to attract the photographers and television crews into the courtroom, a trial judge has enough to do without having the additional responsibility of policing the conduct of a group of people who have no connection with the litigation." In 2012, the Supreme Court reversed the more than forty-year camera ban. "It gives the opportunity to bring the public's eye, through the media, into the courtroom," explained Chief Justice Thomas L. Kilbride. "Ultimately, we hope it's a good civics lesson."[1322]

In what he described as "his most challenging case" as an Illinois Supreme Court justice, Ryan delivered the majority opinion in *In re Estate of Longeway*. The guardian and daughter of Dorothy M. Longeway, an elderly comatose convalescent center patient who had not executed a "living will," appealed a DuPage County Circuit Court decision preventing the withdrawal of sustenance. The 1989 decision reversed the circuit court, recognizing the right of a guardian to refuse or to withdraw artificial nutrition and hydration from a terminally ill patient. "Because we believe the right to refuse artificial sustenance is premised on common law," Ryan wrote, "the legislature is free to streamline, tailor, or overrule the procedures outlined in this opinion to the extent that no constitutional doctrine is abrogated. The legislature is the appropriate forum for the ultimate resolution of the questions surrounding the right to die."[1323]

Conservative and independent, "I suppose that my decisions and my opinions probably reflect that I am not what they call an activist judge," Ryan mused in 1990. "I do believe that there is such a thing as separation of powers and that the Legislature should be performing legislative functions and the courts performing judicial functions. I do think that in the past a good many judges have not been happy with what the Legislature has [or has not] done and therefore have taken it upon themselves to do some of what probably rightfully can be called legislative work."[1324] Ryan strove to reduce delays in criminal case appeals and to develop alternate methods of resolving disputes, including a Supreme Court rule that established mandatory arbitration in civil suits seeking $15,000 or less in damages.[1325]

Retiring in 1990, six years before the expiration of his term, Ryan became of counsel to the Chicago firm Peterson and Ross. He held memberships in the LaSalle County, Illinois State, and American Bar associations, the American Judicature Society, Phi Alpha Delta law fraternity, American Legion, Odd Fellows, Elks, and was a Thirty-third Degree Mason. He died at age ninety-two on December 10, 2008, at the Manor Court nursing facility in Peru. After services at Tonica United Methodist Church, Ryan was buried beside his wife in Fairview Cemetery in Tonica.

JOSEPH H. GOLDENHERSH, 1970-1987

Joseph H. Goldenhersh was born in East St. Louis on November 2, 1914, one of five children born to Benjamin and Bertha Goldenhersh, who had immigrated to the United States in 1907. His parents owned a small store. He attended local elementary schools and East St. Louis High School. He graduated from Washington University Law School in St. Louis, Missouri, in the fall of 1935 and was admitted to the Illinois bar in the spring of 1936, having attended college and law school during the Great Depression.[1326]

He entered the practice of law in East St. Louis from 1936 until his election to the Illinois Appellate Court for the Fifth Judicial District in 1964. While in private practice, he served as city attorney of the City of Lebanon. He was special counsel to the City of East St. Louis and as attorney for the East Side Levy District Sanitary District. During World War II, he was an advisor to the local draft board. He was also president of the East St. Louis Bar Association.[1327] He was elected to the appellate bench to fill a seat created by the new judicial article in the state constitution.

After six years of service on the appellate court, he was elected to the Illinois Supreme Court in November 1970, on his fifty-sixth birthday, and was sworn in on December 7, 1970. He filled the seat vacated by the death of Justice Byron O. House. In the election he beat Harold Clark, the Republican candidate from Alton. His election victory gave the Supreme Court its first Democratic majority since 1942.[1328] He was reelected for a second ten-year term in 1980. During his time on the court, his colleagues chose him to be Chief Justice from 1979 to 1982.

As one of the more liberal justices, he wrote an above-average number of dissents and earned a reputation for his pithy, direct style of writing in which he was not afraid to include the occasional stinging comment aimed at his colleagues and attorneys appearing before the court. One of the most important decisions he wrote, however, was for the majority in *Jack Spring, Inc. v. Little*, a landlord-tenant dispute from Cook County. In his opinion, Goldenhersh overturned the common law rule absolving a landlord of any obligation to maintain or repair his property. Instead, the court recognized an implied warranty of habitability in all residential leases. This warranty imposed a duty on landlords to comply substantially with applicable municipal building code health and safety provisions. This decision gave tenants' rights advocates a useful tool for helping achieve fair treatment of tenants.[1329]

Goldenhersh also wrote the court's majority opinions upholding the conviction and death sentence of serial killer John Wayne Gacy. In 1980, a trial court found Gacy guilty of thirty-three murders and sentenced him to death, in compliance with the recently enacted death penalty law in Illinois. In the summer of 1984, the Supreme Court upheld Gacy's conviction and his execution by lethal injection. Goldenhersh wrote a ninety-two-page opinion affirming the convictions and the sentence of death coming at a time when constitutional issues surrounding death sentencing created controversy across the nation. Gacy began an appeal process in federal courts that ended with the United States Supreme Court's final denial of his petition in 1993. He was executed in May 1994.[1330]

Goldenhersh won reelection for a second ten-year term on the Supreme Court in 1980, while he was serving already as Chief Justice. Known for his diligence and extraordinary memory of case law and facts, he was also very busy with activities related to the judiciary. He served as the court's liaison to the Supreme Court Rules Committee, the executive committee of the Illinois Judicial Conference, and the administrative committee of the Illinois Appellate Court. He served as chairman of the Illinois Courts Commission from 1976 to 1979. The John Marshall Law School bestowed a Doctor of Laws on him to honor his contributions to the law profession.[1331]

His accomplishments were not all in the field of law. He also participated in many civic activities. He was a member of the Board of Trustees Executive Committee of the Christian Welfare Hospital in East St. Louis, a board member of the St. Clair County Heart Association, and president of the Jewish Federation of Southern Illinois. He was a member of the Missouri Athletic Club, the Masonic lodge in East St. Louis, and a member of Agudas Achim Synagogue in East St. Louis.[1332]

He would not be able, however, to complete his second term. He developed Parkinson's disease and became unable, in his own opinion, to fulfill his court duties satisfactorily. He worked at his home in Belleville as much as he could, but during 1987, he could not participate in three terms of the court because of frequent hospitalizations. With the best interests of the court in mind, he retired effective September 12, 1987, with more than three years remaining in his term.[1333] He had hoped to complete his second ten years, but his disease progressed faster than expected. He served on the court for seventeen years.[1334] After his retirement, his health continued to decline and became complicated with heart problems. He underwent a quintuple bypass surgery, but several weeks later, on March 12, 1992, at age seventy-seven, he died of a stroke in Barnes Hospital in St. Louis. He was buried the next day at Beth Hamadrosh Hagodol Cemetery in St. Louis following services at Berger Memorial Chapel.[1335]

He was survived by Maxine (Zelenka) Goldenhersh of Chicago, his wife of fifty-three years. She was an accomplished painter who studied at the University of Illinois and the Art Institute of Chicago. They had two children, Richard, who at the time of his father's death was an Illinois appellate court judge, and Jerry, a lawyer in private practice in Belleville.[1336] His approach to the law and his commitment to it were embodied in his own words when he said, "The Constitution is not the last word, it is the beginning."[1337]

WILLIAM G. CLARK, 1976–1992

William G. Clark was born July 16, 1924, in Chicago. His forebears were early settlers in the city and over the years became wealthy through real estate. His father, John S. Clark, was an alderman for Chicago and served a lengthy tenure as Cook County Assessor. His grandfather, also named John S. Clark, was a state legislator and alderman as well. He was born to John S. and Ita Kennedy Clark and had two brothers, John S. Clark and Don D. Clark.[1338] During his career of public service, which spanned nearly a half-century, he rose to positions of leadership in all three branches of state government.

He attended Resurrection Grammar School in his west side Austin neighborhood, and Campion High School in Prairie du Chien, Wisconsin. He attended Loyola University and the University of Michigan. Following service in the United States Army during World War II, he received a law degree from DePaul University Law School in Chicago and was admitted to the bar in 1947.[1339]

In 1952, after five years of private practice, Governor Adlai Stevenson appointed Clark attorney for the Public Administrator of Cook County. That same year, he was elected to the Illinois House of Representatives and held the seat occupied by his grandfather fifty years earlier. He was elected to the state senate in 1954, where he was chairman of a tax commission and played a leading role in passing legislation revising the state's tax laws.[1340] At the request of Mayor Richard J. Daley, he returned to the House in 1956 and was reelected in 1958. Clark had become close to the mayor when he was the head of "Citizens for Daley" in Daley's first mayoral campaign in 1955.[1341] In a tense contest facing powerful downstate Democrat Paul M. Powell, Clark was elected House Majority Leader for the Seventy-first General Assembly. He was thirty-four years old.[1342] In the House, he opposed personal property taxes on automobiles and household furnishings, reformed probate laws to lower costs, and co-sponsored the bill annexing O'Hare Field to the City of Chicago.[1343]

Early in 1960, he considered running against Cook County State's Attorney Benjamin Adamowski, a popular Republican. Instead, Democratic slatemakers put him up for Illinois Attorney General after briefly considering him for a gubernatorial candidacy.[1344] He was elected attorney general in November 1960 and reelected in 1964. He drafted legislation that became the state's first consumer fraud act and established the consumer fraud office to enforce the new law. He also accelerated water and air pollution control enforcement and supported legislation favorable to charities.[1345]

After two terms as attorney general, he decided that he would run for the United States Senate against incumbent Everett M. Dirksen after giving serious consideration to running for governor. The election of 1968 occurred during the peak years of the Vietnam era, and Chicago's Democratic National Convention was the center of the controversy. Clark made national headlines when he, a nominee for the Senate, spoke out against the president's

Vietnam policy and worked to have a "peace plank" included in the party's platform that year. Mayor Daley supported the president and saw Clark's position as disloyal. Clark lost the election. In the eighteen elections in which he ran during his lifetime, this was the only one he lost.[1346] He would never again have the support of Daley's political organization. Years later Clark remarked, typically, "I just have never been a rubber stamp."[1347]

After losing to Dirksen, he considered running to unseat Senator Ralph Smith, who had been appointed to the Senate following Dirksen's death in 1969. Clark withdrew from consideration when Adlai Stevenson III, son of the governor who first appointed Clark to public office, expressed his desire to run for the seat. Clark then turned his attention to the United States House of Representatives when a vacancy occurred in his old west side neighborhood after the death of Congressman Daniel Ronan. In the face of a crowded field and no certain support, he withdrew to private practice.[1348]

Out of public office for the first time in more than a decade, Clark returned to private practice in the prestigious and politically active Chicago firm of Arvey, Hodes, Costello, & Burman. He remained there until he ran for the Supreme Court bench in 1976 to occupy the seat vacated by the retirement of Thomas E. Kluczynski. Although he did not obtain Mayor Daley's support, he won the election to the astonishment of many observers.[1349]

He was the author of 524 majority opinions and 224 dissents while on the Supreme Court bench.[1350] Notable among them were *People v. Coslet* and *People v. Spreitzer*, both homicide cases dealing with attorney's conflict of interest involving representation of clients.[1351] In *Ostendorf v. International Harvester*, a product liability suit, he chastised the industrial giant for withholding evidence and obfuscating discovery procedures. "Discovery," he wrote, "is intended to be a mechanism for the ascertainment of truth, for the purpose of promoting either a fair settlement or a fair trial. It is not a tactical game to be used to obstruct or harass the opposing litigant."[1352]

Highlights of his work during his sixteen years on the Supreme Court included supporting merit selection of judges rather than the existing electoral system, inaugurating mandatory arbitration for smaller civil suits, starting a study of state funding for trial courts, establishing committees to evaluate judges' performance and the attorney disciplinary system, and working to improve the process for post-conviction review of death sentences. Most of these efforts were undertaken during his three years as Chief Justice from 1985 to 1988.[1353]

After retiring from the Supreme Court in 1992, he served of counsel to the Chicago law firm of his son, William G. Clark Jr.[1354] He was subsequently inducted as an Honorary Fellow in the Illinois Bar Foundation and received an honorary degree from The John Marshall Law School. For many years he held memberships in national, state, and local bar associations. He was also a Moose, an Elk, and belonged to the American Legion, Catholic War Veterans, Delta Theta Phi Law Fraternity, Ancient Order of Hibernians, the Chicago Athletic Association, the University Club of Loyola, and the Irish Fellowship Club of Chicago.[1355]

He said that his reason for leaving the court was that chronic neck and leg problems prevented him from giving his work the attention it required.[1356] In truth he suffered from diabetes. After nine years of the progressing illness, he succumbed to its complications on August 17, 2001, one month after his seventy-seventh birthday. A mass was held in Holy Name Cathedral with burial following at Calvary Cemetery in Evanston.[1357]

A few years before he died, Clark was the subject of a testimonial from Chicago newspaperman Steve Neal, who had a reputation for being hard on government officials. Clark had, he wrote, "set standards for leadership in three branches of Illinois government."[1358] The law library in the Illinois Attorney General's building in Springfield is named after him.

JAMES A. DOOLEY, 1976-1978

A Chicago native, James A. Dooley was born on August 7, 1914, to James and Agnes Dooley. Educated at Loyola University and Loyola University Law School, he received his law degree in 1937. An epileptic "in the days when modern drugs were not yet developed," Dooley "was quite a guy to overcome that," longtime friend and later Illinois Secretary of State Michael Howlett remembered. "He had great courage. He never took a backward step from anybody." The two met as youngsters at a neighborhood Knights of Columbus gymnasium.[1359]

Opening his practice in Chicago in 1941, Dooley soon began specializing in personal injury claims. "When Dooley became a trial lawyer," explained his friend Leonard Ring, "the courts were defense-oriented. They might award $10,000 to someone who lost a leg, but only if it was a child. Through relentless determination and work, Jim whittled away and turned the entire philosophy around."

Ring described one personal injury case of a severely burned fireman. "In those days you could not recover damages for injury to a firefighter. It was considered an assumed risk. Jim got $235,000 for the fireman, which in those days was considered tremendous, but more important he turned the law around so that a fireman can recover damages if the owner of the property is negligent and so contributes to bringing the fire on."[1360] Ring also recalled a case in which Dooley represented a woman blinded in her home by an exploding can of Drano drain cleaner. "Dooley won her a settlement of $900,000 and helped establish the idea of a company being held liable for its products."[1361]

Dooley married Virginia Rose Proesel on February 18, 1955, and they became the parents of one daughter. He served terms as president of the Illinois Trial Lawyers Association from 1951 to 1955, and the Association of Trial Lawyers of America from 1953 to 1954. He became a director of the International Academy of Trial Lawyers, serving as president in 1966. A delegate from the Illinois State Bar Association to the International Congress of Comparative Law in Paris, he served on the Chicago Board of Managers, 1957–1958.[1362] In addition, he lectured at the University of Chicago Law School, Northwestern University School of Law, Loyola University Law School, and DePaul University Law School.

In 1951, Clarke College conferred Dooley with the honorary degree of LLD for his leading work in the profession. He received awards from the Loyola Law School Alumni in 1967, the Law Science Academy of America in 1970, and Loyola University in 1975. A frequent contributor to various law reviews and legal publications, Dooley wrote *Modern Tort Law; Liability and Litigation,* published in 1977.[1363]

Regarded as one of Chicago's foremost courtroom lawyers, Dooley participated in more than 2,500 civil cases. Perhaps the most celebrated case of his practice was representing football linebacker Dick Butkus against the Chicago Bears and its team physician. Once the heart of the Bears' defensive unit, Butkus in 1974 filed a $1.6 million lawsuit against his former employers, charging that improper medical attention to his knee injuries significantly reduced the longevity of his career. He accused the physician of improper surgeries and the organization of causing him to be injected with high-powered drugs and painkillers during the 1972 and 1973 seasons, resulting in permanent knee damage. After a series of pretrial hearings, Dooley negotiated a $600,000 out-of-court settlement for Butkus.

Following the 1976 retirement of Illinois Supreme Court Justice Walter V. Schaefer, Dooley sought the support of Chicago Mayor Richard J. Daley and the Cook County Democratic organization for the position. When Circuit Court Judge and Daley law partner Joseph A. Power received the party backing, "A couple of judges," Dooley explained, "talked me into running as an independent. It was unprecedented but I decided to do it."[1364]

As an independent Democrat, Dooley pledged to make judicial appointments from the high court on a merit basis. "No one can do more damage or harm to the public and to the judiciary than an inexperienced or an ignorant judge."[1365] The Cook County Electoral Board ruled that some of his nominating petitions were defective and removed his name from the ballot, but Dooley, arguing his own case, won a reversal of the decision. "It was when they took my name off the ballot that any doubts I still had about running were resolved," he said. "And once I made the decision to run, I ran to win."[1366] With strong suburban support and a nearly $140,000 campaign funded primarily from his own considerable wealth, Dooley upset Power by a margin of 29,000 votes. In the general election campaign, Butkus campaigned for Dooley, and Daley pledged "100 per cent" support. Dooley defeated Republican Reginald G. Holzer by nearly 2 to 1 for the ten-year term.[1367]

Days before being sworn in as a Supreme Court justice, Dooley in late 1976 won a $1,250,000 personal injury settlement for a twenty-five-year-old Vietnam War veteran who became a quadriplegic as the result of an accidental shooting by a Chicago grocery store security guard.[1368] Taking his Supreme Court seat on December 12, 1976, Dooley soon, according to Ring, "came to love the bench and politics so much he called being a Supreme Court justice 'the best job in the state.'" Dooley's "written opinions were notable for their lack of complicated legal phrases," observed one Supreme Court reporter. "He stated the basic dispute in the first sentences of an opinion, and only then resorted to legal proofs."[1369]

Dooley drew upon his law-practice experience in delivering the 1977 Court opinion in *Sahara Coal Company, Inc. v. Illinois Industrial Commission*. Sahara employee Bob Bundren aggravated an existing back injury when the bulldozer he was operating struck a rock and swerved suddenly. Even though the sole medical expert described the disability as existing "a few weeks," both the Industrial Commission and the Saline County Circuit Court affirmed an arbitrator's award of temporary total disability for approximately one year. The physician testifying for the employer, Dooley noted, "did not examine the claimant during the year in question," even though the claimant had "constant medical treatment over that period." The Supreme Court affirmed the circuit court judgment.[1370]

The most celebrated and probably most controversial case during Dooley's tenure involved a peaceful demonstration by the swastika-bearing National Socialist Party of America (American Nazi party) in the predominantly Jewish Chicago suburb of Skokie. Only Justice William G. Clark dissented from the Court's January 1978 per curiam opinion upholding the organization's constitutional right to free expression.[1371]

Less than three months later, on March 5, 1978, after a tennis match, the physically active sixty-three-year-old Dooley died of a heart attack at his suburban Miami, Florida, winter home. He had been on the Illinois Supreme Court bench for only fifteen months of the ten-year term. "A grievous loss," said Chief Justice Daniel P. Ward. "He brought great scholarship and industry and vast experience to the court."[1372] Following a funeral Mass at Holy Name Cathedral, Dooley was buried at All Saints Cemetery in Des Plaines, Illinois.[1373]

THOMAS J. MORAN, 1976–1992

Thomas J. Moran was born in Waukegan on July 17, 1920. His forebears were among the earliest settlers in Lake County. His grandfather, Thomas Tyrell, helped raise him after his father left. His grandfather had been chief of police for Waukegan and later was in charge of the Lake County jail, where young Thomas brought cigarettes to the inmates. He claimed that his grandfather started him "on the straight and narrow."[1374]

Moran attended nearby Lake Forest College and worked in a local factory and in a theater where he earned twenty-five cents an hour as an usher. World War II interrupted his college work when he enlisted for service in the United States Coast Guard. He returned to the college after the war and received a bachelor's degree in 1947. Attending law school under the postwar GI Bill, he received a Bachelor of Laws degree from Chicago-Kent College of Law in 1950. He was admitted to the bar that same year and entered practice in Waukegan as a partner in the firm of Daly & Moran handling, he said, "whatever came through the door."[1375] He remained until he was elected Lake County State's Attorney in 1956.[1376] As State's Attorney he led an effort to rid Lake County of slot machines.[1377]

He began his judicial career when he was elected probate judge of Lake County. He was soon appointed to the circuit court to fill a vacancy. In 1961, he was elected circuit judge for the Nineteenth Judicial Circuit, which encompassed Lake and McHenry Counties. He was chief judge of the circuit court. In January 1964, the Supreme Court assigned him to the Appellate Court of Illinois for the Second Judicial District. He was elected an appellate judge in November 1964.[1378] As an appellate justice, he became active on the American Bar Association's Technology and the Courts Committee that was instrumental in producing the nation's first use of teleconferencing in a judicial proceeding. Counsels in the hearing for the plaintiff and the defendant presented their cases from New York City to a three-judge panel of the United States Court of Claims in Washington, D.C. He maintained his interest in technology, and while on the state Supreme Court, his knowledge of the appellate process and interest in technology led him to spearhead the court's computerized case-tracking system.[1379]

Moran was elected to the Supreme Court in the general election of November 1976. He defeated Democratic candidate Stanley Roszkowski of Rockford after winning the Republican primary election earlier that year by defeating three other candidates. He was elected to the Supreme Court to fill the vacancy created by the resignation of Justice Charles H. Davis. He was sworn in December 6, 1976, and upon his resignation effective December 7, 1992, served sixteen years on the court. Voters had retained him in 1986. He was Chief Justice for three years from January 1988 to January 1991. He would serve a total of thirty-four years as a judge.[1380]

Thomas Moran, better known to his friends as "T.J.," wrote almost five hundred opinions while on the Supreme Court, many dealing with crucial constitutional and public policy issues as well as questions involving legal practice and procedures.[1381] In criminal law, Moran wrote the opinion in the frequently cited *People v. King*, which is often referred to as the "King rule," which holds that a criminal defendant can be charged for only one criminal count when the criminal incident included closely related acts.[1382]

He was the author of the opinion in *Alvis v. Ribar*, which was one of the most important decisions in the history of Illinois Civil jurisprudence in changing the law of contributory negligence.[1383] As far back as territorial days, Illinois courts adhered to the common law doctrine of contributory negligence, which held that if a plaintiff contributed to his injury through his own negligence such as crossing an intersection against a traffic signal, he might not be awarded any damages, or often have little room for apportioning damages according to role of the parties involved. Moran's lengthy opinion, which traced the entire history of contributory negligence, abandoned the doctrine of contributory negligence and instead adopted the doctrine of comparative negligence, a rule under which damages could be apportioned between parties more easily. After Moran's opinion, Illinois joined thirty other states and the federal government in adopting comparative negligence.[1384]

During his term on the court, he did not hesitate to speak out on controversial subjects like his support for merit selection of judges because the current elective system was "fraud and a sham." He initiated and encouraged seminars for law clerks, served as chairman of the Illinois Courts Commission and on numerous judicial committees and committees for bar associations. He also was a faculty member of New York University Law School and Louisiana State University Law School seminars for judges. As Chief Justice he had the responsibility to oversee the implementation of new rules governing the Attorney Registration and Disciplinary Commission and ethics for lawyers in the Supreme Court's new Rules of Professional Conduct.[1385]

He developed a reputation for being tough on criminals, whether they were perpetrators of white crimes or street crimes. In civil law, where common law tenets drawn from England centuries ago were the basis for the state's legal traditions, he believed that interpretations evolved and consequently judges must take such change into account. He said, "If you live long enough, you can change things that strike you as wrong." In applying that concept, he authored some of the state's most important decisions.[1386]

He underwent surgery for prostate cancer in 1991 and retired from the court one year later. He did not publicly credit his cancer as a reason for retiring from the bench. After his resignation he became of counsel to the Waukegan law firm of Brydges, Riseborough, Morris, Franke & Miller. He remained at home as long as possible during his cancer treatment, but died at Lake Forest Hospital on September 14, 1995. He was survived by Mary Jane (Wasniewski) Moran, his wife of more than fifty years. After a funeral mass held at St. Mary's Catholic Church in Lake Forest, he was interred in the Ascension Cemetery Mausoleum in Libertyville.[1387]

SEYMOUR SIMON, 1980–1988

A fiercely independent voice on the Illinois Supreme Court, Seymour Simon was born in Chicago on August 10, 1915, the son of Russian immigrant Benjamin Simon and his wife, Gertrude Simon. Attending Roosevelt High School, Seymour graduated from Northwestern University, Phi Beta Kappa, in 1935 and the University Law School in 1938. He began working as an attorney in the Anti-trust Division of the U.S. Department of Justice. During World War II, he served in the U.S. Navy in the Pacific theater, receiving the Legion of Merit.

On his return to Chicago, Simon opened a law firm in 1946, handling primarily antitrust and corporate cases, and helped his Democratic precinct captain during the 1948 election campaign of President Harry S. Truman. In 1954, Simon married a widow, Roslyn Schultz Biel, and adopted two of her three children. The family resided in the Hollywood Park neighborhood.[1388]

By then the Fortieth Ward Democratic precinct captain, Simon built a power base among liberal independents, winning election as alderman in 1955. He served on the City Council until 1961, when he became the influential president of the Cook County Board of Commissioners, as well as president of the Cook County Forest Preserve District and a member of the Chicago Public Building Commission. In 1967, he won reelection to the City Council, and then resigned in 1974 for a successful bid to the First District Appellate Court.

In 1980, Simon challenged the Democratic machine candidate, Francis Lorenz, and four others in the primary election for the Illinois Supreme Court seat vacancy created by the death of Justice James A. Dooley.[1389] The Chicago Bar Association endorsed Simon, and the Council of Lawyers termed him "one of the most impressive judges" on the Appellate Court. "He has been willing to dissent where appropriate, and those dissents have helped sharpen the issues." Winning the primary by a large margin, Simon waged a successful, hard-fought campaign in the general election, defeating Republican Criminal Court Judge Robert Sklodowski by 435,000 votes.[1390]

In 1983, Simon broke ranks with fellow Democrats, joining the three Republican justices in denying a recount of the 1982 Illinois gubernatorial election results. He brushed aside charges that prior differences with the Democratic candidate, Adlai Stevenson III, influenced his key vote against the petition. "It certainly never crossed my mind in connection with the events of the past few months (recount controversy)," Simon said at the time, explaining that "he voted his conscience." Republican incumbent James R. Thompson officially won the office by roughly five thousand votes out of more than three million cast.[1391]

Simon wrote the 1984 Court opinion in *Michael Kalodimos v. Village of Morton Grove,* in which the Court upheld the Chicago suburb's ban on handgun possession and handgun sales. The U.S. Court of Appeals upheld the decision, and the U.S. Supreme Court refused to hear the case, leaving intact the ruling that the ban did not violate citizens' Second Amendment rights to keep and bear arms.[1392]

In a heavily publicized 1987 case, *In Re Edward A. Loss III,* Simon openly clashed with the other justices regarding their decision to deny a law license to a reformed petty thief and drug addict. Loss graduated near the top of his class at DePaul University Law School in 1984, and then employed former convicts at his moving company. Both the State Board of Law Examiners and the Supreme Court's Committee on Character and Fitness deemed Loss rehabilitated. After the other six justices voted to deny Loss's application for a law license, Simon wrote a stinging eight-page dissent. "The court's departure from any concept of fairness or regularity has been complete, and I would say, almost Kafkaesque," Simon fumed, adding that the Court violated its own rule for automatically admitting an applicant approved by the State Board of Law Examiners. "Edward Anthony Loss will not be permitted to practice law in this State," Simon wrote, "not because he has failed to follow the rules, but because we have."[1393]

When Simon joined the Supreme Court in 1980 he had hoped that the justices would rule the Illinois death penalty unconstitutional. Three had already voted against the law, but "they got timid when Simon's election gave them what should have been the decisive fourth vote," analyzed *Chicago Sun-Times* columnist Steve Neal. Simon "was appalled," according to Neal, "when two justices who had previously opposed capital punishment flip-flopped and voted to impose the death penalty" in the 1981 case *People v. Cornelius Lewis.* "It would be blatant folly," Simon wrote in dissent of the decision, "for this court to acquiesce in the execution of Cornelius Lewis without disclosing that four of the judges comprising the present court, either now or in the past two years, have viewed the death penalty statute as unconstitutional." He continued, "Because of the nature of the death penalty I do not believe that any judge should be expected to stifle his own viewpoint in the interest of uniformity. To follow the dictates of *stare decisis* in a case like this is to allow the conclusions of the past to be stamped indelibly upon the law without opportunity for correction. As the late Mr. Justice Douglas put it, 'It is, I think, a healthy practice (too infrequently followed), for a court to reexamine its own doctrine.'"[1394]

After *People v. Lewis,* Simon steadfastly dissented in every case, at least twenty-six times, in which the Supreme Court affirmed a death sentence, in part because the statute allowed each of the 102 state's attorneys arbitrarily to decide whether to pursue the death penalty. Consequently, Simon argued, "The death penalty is applied freakishly and unpredictably across the state, in violation of federal rulings."[1395]

Most executions took place in Stateville Prison in Joliet. (Image courtesy of James Dobrovolny Collection, Illinois Supreme Court Historic Preservation Commission)

Simon dissented in the 1985 *People v. Charles Walker,* who confessed in St. Clair County Circuit Court to the murders of a young engaged couple, but then appealed his death-penalty sentence. While the other Supreme Court justices affirmed the punishment, Simon maintained that the state's improper appeal "to the emotions of the jurors" flawed the penalty process, referring to the only two witnesses, both relatives of the murder victims, who testified during the sentencing hearing. "The obvious purpose for which the prosecution called these witnesses was to play upon the jurors' emotions in viewing the tragic deaths of the young victims." Simon also reiterated his firm belief "that the Illinois death penalty statute is unconstitutional and that therefore no sentence imposed under that statue can stand."[1396]

In January 1988, Simon delivered the opinion overturning the DuPage County Circuit Court conviction in *People v. Alejandro Hernandez.* That jury had found Hernandez guilty of the 1983 murder of ten-year-old Jeanine Nicarico and imposed the death penalty. Simon wrote that prosecutors had denied Hernandez a fair trial and that the physical evidence was not probative of his guilt. In addition, his statements to authorities contained widely varying accounts of the crime that were inconsistent with the known facts. Simon noted that Hernandez was "implicated by a witness whom he had no opportunity to confront and cross-examine, a violation of this court's precedents and an error of constitutional magnitude."[1397] Justice Howard C. Ryan wrote the opinion that overturned the conviction of Rolando Cruz for the same crime. Both defendants were convicted at second trials, but Cruz was exonerated in a third trial and the charges against Hernandez were eventually dropped.[1398]

When the "strong, intelligent, independent voice on the Illinois Supreme Court," retired at age seventy-two in February 1988, the *Chicago Tribune* editorialized that Simon "often was the lone angry man, a prod and a scold on a court that tended to be bland and lethargic."[1399] Having written some 200 majority opinions, 80 concurring opinions, and 175 dissents, "Simon's influence has been enormous," reported *Chicago Lawyer.* "Significantly, several of the minority positions he has taken on the court have been adopted later as the law of the land by the U.S. Supreme Court."[1400] His only major regret, he said at the time, was that the legal debate over the state's death penalty statute had not been resolved.[1401]

After retirement from the bench, Simon became a senior partner in Rudnick and Wolfe, one of Chicago's largest law firms, which later became DLA Piper.[1402] "I'm excited about the prospect of starting a whole new career," the seventy-two-year-old Simon told reporters at the time. "Heck no, I'm not ready to retire. My mother's birthday is today, and she is 97."[1403]

In addition to his law practice, Simon continued working for death-penalty reform. He advised Governor George H. Ryan that such penalties "could not be imposed fairly and uniformly because of the absence of sufficient standards to guide the 102 Illinois state's attorneys in deciding whether to request the death sentence." Simon described to Ryan the case of Girvies Davis, whose appeals had reached the Supreme Court five times. "If you were searching for individual Death Row occupants who were deserving of having their death sentences commuted," Simon wrote, "he would be a leading candidate were it not for the fact that he has already been executed [in 1995]." Ryan cited Simon's letter and the Davis case in his historic and controversial 2003 decision to commute the sentences of all Illinois's death-penalty inmates.[1404]

In a sixty-eight-year career as a lawyer and a public official, Simon was "both a loyal Democrat and a party maverick at the same time," assessed the *Chicago Law Bulletin.* On September 26, 2006, at the age of ninety-one, Simon died in Northwestern Memorial Hospital. Funeral services were held in the temple of Chicago Sinai Congregation, and he was buried in Chicago's Rosehill Cemetery. "This giant of the legal profession dedicated his life to public service," said Chicago Mayor Richard M. Daley, "and we will miss his many contributions and tremendous leadership."[1405]

BENJAMIN K. MILLER, 1984-2001

The first Illinois capital city native to serve on the Supreme Court, Benjamin K. Miller was born in Springfield on November 5, 1936, the son of optometrist Clifford C. and Mary Margaret Lutyens Miller.[1406] After graduation from Springfield High School in 1954 and Southern Illinois University Carbondale in 1958, Miller received his law degree in 1961 from Vanderbilt University. Graduating from the U.S. Army Intelligence School in Maryland in 1962, he served in the Army Reserves from 1961 to 1964, then in the Navy Reserves from 1964 to 1967.

Having established a law practice in Springfield that focused primarily on civil litigation, Miller also became active in community organizations. He served terms as president of the Greater Springfield Chamber of Commerce and the Springfield Mental Health Association and became a board member of Aid to Retarded Citizens and the Springfield-Sangamon County Youth Service Bureau.

In 1976, the Illinois Supreme Court appointed Miller to be a judge of the Seventh Judicial Circuit, and he won election to the position in 1978. He served as presiding judge in the Sangamon County Circuit Court Criminal Felony Division from 1976 to 1980. In 1979, he garnered notice for judicial efficiency and fairness when assigned to the largest civilian death penalty case in the nation's history: the Cook County prison-riot trials of seventeen Pontiac Correctional Center inmates. He presided over nearly two years of arduously slow pretrial hearings and jury selection for the case against ten of the defendants, who were accused of mob action and murder for causing the riot and slaying of three guards and critically injuring two others. After the defendants won acquittal in the eleven-week trial, prosecutors dropped charges against the remaining men.[1407] In 1981, Miller became Chief Judge of the Seventh Circuit and served in that capacity for a year, when he won election to the Fourth District Appellate Court.

In addition to judicial duties, Miller maintained an active membership in the Illinois State Bar Association, serving as treasurer from 1975 to 1976. Also a member of the Sangamon County Bar Association and American Bar Association, he became the first male member of the Central Illinois Women's Bar Association. He helped establish a Springfield center for battered women, providing legal advice to domestic-abuse victims. He developed the medical-legal curriculum at Southern Illinois University School of Medicine, where he served for several years as an adjunct professor in the Department of Medical Humanities.[1408]

In 1984, Republican Miller decided to seek the Illinois Supreme Court seat vacated by retired Justice Robert C. Underwood. Miller defeated fellow Appellate Court Justice Frederick Green of Urbana in the primary election, and then waged a hard-fought campaign against Springfield Democrat James C. Craven, an attorney and former appellate justice.

Miller defeated Craven to serve the remaining six years of Underwood's term, becoming the youngest member of the Court by more than a decade. In 1990, he would win retention with nearly 79 percent of the vote.[1409]

In the 1987 case of *People v. Wilson,* Miller delivered the opinion that reversed and remanded a murder conviction and death penalty sentence. After the Cook County trial judge denied Andrew Wilson's motion to suppress his confession as involuntary in the slaying of two Chicago police officers, the jury found him guilty of the crimes. In the appeal, Wilson maintained that he had been "punched, kicked, smothered with a plastic bag, electrically shocked, and forced against a hot radiator" by police interrogators. "The use of a defendant's coerced confession as substantive evidence of his guilt is never harmless error," Miller wrote in citing Chicago police brutality, "and the cause must therefore be remanded for a new trial."[1410] At the second trial, the jury convicted Wilson without the confession and imposed a life sentence.[1411]

In 1989, Miller wrote the majority opinion affirming the Rock Island County Circuit Court conviction of Leslie Foggy for aggravated criminal sexual assault and unlawful restraint. After an unsuccessful appeal to the Third District Appellate Court challenging the constitutionality of the state's "statutory privilege for communications made to rape crisis counselors," Foggy's attorneys presented his case to the Supreme Court. They cited other cases in which courts refused to recognize or enforce the "absolute" confidentiality privilege of counseling sessions. The Illinois Coalition Against Sexual Assault filed an *amicus curiae* brief in support of the statutory provision. "The defendant here has offered no reason to believe that the victim's counseling records would provide a source of impeaching material unavailable from other sources," Miller wrote. "We conclude that the defendant was not denied due process, nor was his confrontation right violated, by the trial judge's refusal in this case to conduct an *in camera* inspection of the victim's counseling records."[1412]

From 1988 to 1991, Miller chaired the Illinois Courts Commission, which is the constitutional body authorized to discipline or suspend members of the judiciary. In 1991, he received an Honorary Doctor of Law Degree from John Marshall Law School in Chicago.

In 1991, soon after assuming a three-year term as Chief Justice, Miller began working closely with former Supreme Court Justice Joseph Cunningham, newly appointed director of the Administrative Office of the Illinois Courts, to improve efficiency within the state's judicial system. "I'd like to see us look to the future rather than just react to problems as they arise," Miller explained. "Then we can try to make sure we're in a position to meet those needs as we work toward those goals."[1413]

Miller established the Special Commission on the Administration of Justice to examine the governance of Illinois courts, including the juvenile system. Also as Chief Justice, Miller convened the Illinois Family Violence Coordinating Council to improve court response regarding domestic abuse cases, and he began the practice of appearing personally before the Illinois General Assembly appropriations committees to present the judicial branch budget, a tradition that current chief justices maintain. "He has a real love of the Court, a love of the system, and a love of the institution," assessed fellow justice Charles E. Freeman. "The Court has always been something he has wanted to protect and keep in high esteem. That has always been very important to him, and it is a lesson and a goal that he has handed down to all of us."[1414]

In 1997, Miller moved briefly to the other side of the bench, serving jury duty in a Springfield personal injury civil trial. "It wasn't so much the case, but the process that was so interesting to me," he told reporters after the automobile-accident trial. "It reaffirmed my belief in the jury system—that 12 people would leave their jobs and resolve a dispute like that in a sincere and serious manner."[1415]

Chief Justice Miller delivered the majority opinion in the 2000 case *American National Bank & Trust Company v. The City of Chicago*. That decision allowed American National, administrator of the estate of Renee Kazmierowski, to bring an action alleging that municipal paramedics failed to properly respond to her emergency assistance call after an asthma attack. American National alleged that when the paramedics heard no response to a knock on her apartment door they did not attempt to enter the unlocked apartment, and the woman died. "Locating a person in need of emergency medical treatment is the first step in providing life support services. Not even that first step was taken here," Miller wrote in affirming the Cook County Circuit Court judgment.[1416]

In 2001, sixty-four-year-old Justice Miller decided to retire from the Supreme Court. "President Kennedy once remarked that change is the law of life, and those who look only to the past or present are certain to miss the future," Miller said in announcing his retirement. "Now it is time to move on to new adventures in the law and other areas that have long held an interest for me." During his seventeen-year tenure, Miller participated in more than 2,000 cases and wrote nearly 500 opinions.[1417]

In retirement, the bachelor Miller sailed his thirty-seven-foot boat *Adventure* on lengthy trips through the Caribbean and down to South America, and traveled in Europe and South Africa.[1418] "I thought at some point I would like to get involved again" in the law, he explained in 2003, deciding to become of counsel to Jenner & Block in Chicago. "Law has been my life and my big interest."[1419]

JOSEPH F. CUNNINGHAM, 1987-1988, 1991-1992

One of five justices to serve nonconsecutive terms on the Illinois Supreme Court, Joseph F. Cunningham was born in East St. Louis on February 25, 1924, the son of Joseph F. and Emily Hoffarth Cunningham. After graduating from the city's Central Catholic High School, he joined the Army Air Corps and performed research work during World War II. Receiving a chemical engineering degree from the University of Dayton in 1946, he earned a law degree from Washington University in St. Louis in 1952. That year he was admitted to the Missouri and Illinois bars and to practice before the U.S. Supreme Court and the Eighth Circuit Federal Court, and Eastern District, Missouri. On June 20, 1953, he married Mary Margaret Keeley, and they became the parents of a daughter and four sons, three of whom died in infancy.[1420]

In his early years of practice, Cunningham served as corporation counsel for two municipalities. In 1965, he became Magistrate for the Twentieth Judicial Circuit and Chief Magistrate four years later. The post was changed to Chief Associate Judge in 1970, and in 1972 he was appointed a circuit judge for the Twentieth Judicial Circuit, comprising of St. Clair, Monroe, Randolph, Washington, and Perry Counties. A Democrat, he won election to the position in 1974 and was retained in 1980 and 1986. He served as Chief Judge of the circuit from 1975 to 1984, and reelected in 1987.[1421]

As a trial judge, Cunningham garnered statewide attention for striking down Illinois's death penalty statute, which required the convening of a three-judge panel to determine whether a convicted death-eligible defendant should be executed. In a 1975 case involving two convicted murderers, Cunningham and two other judges refused to conduct a death-penalty hearing, contending that the 1970 Illinois Constitution limited the power to create courts to the judiciary, with no authority to the General Assembly. The prosecutor, St. Clair County State's Attorney Robert H. Rice, appealed to the Illinois Supreme Court for a writ of mandamus that would force the death-penalty hearing. In *People ex rel. Rice v. Cunningham,* the Supreme Court upheld Cunningham's ruling. Justice Thomas Kluczynski delivered the opinion that invalidated the statute.[1422]

In September 1987, the Supreme Court justices appointed Cunningham to fill the Fifth Judicial District vacancy created by the retirement of Justice Joseph M. Goldenhersh. The district comprises the state's thirty-seven southernmost counties, and Cunningham agreed not to seek election to the position that Goldenhersh had held for seventeen years. "I basically believe in fundamental fairness and following the law," Cunningham told reporters at the time of his appointment. "I've been on the bench for 22 years, and this will be the high point."[1423] Southern Illinois colleagues praised the choice of the soft-spoken, conscientious Cunningham. "He's fair to a fault," acknowledged Belleville lawyer Bruce Cook. "He goes overboard in letting each side offer anything they want before he rules. His patience sometimes gets people impatient."[1424]

As he assumed a seat on the state's highest court, Cunningham declined to offer insight into his judicial philosophy on potentially controversial issues. "I'll take them case by case as they are assigned to me and do the best job I can," he said. "When they come before me, that's when I'll make the decision."[1425]

During his tenure, Cunningham wrote the opinion in a 1987 disciplinary case, *In re Jiro Yamaguchi*. Chicago attorney Yamaguchi aided the unauthorized practice of law and engaged in fraudulent conduct by signing blank tax-appeal board complaint forms for a real estate broker as well as signing forms filled out by the broker without reviewing them. The Attorney Registration and Disciplinary Commission sought to disbar Yamaguchi, but Cunningham ordered only a six-month suspension, citing no proof that the lawyer had profited from the misconduct or that he had actually harmed or intended to harm anyone.[1426]

Completing the appointed term in December 1988, Cunningham was succeeded by fellow Democrat Horace L. Calvo. In 1990, Cunningham became Director of the Administrative Office of the Illinois Courts, assisting the Supreme Court justices in administering the state's court system. He served in that position until rejoining the Supreme Court in June 1991, to succeed Calvo, who died in office after serving less than two years.[1427]

Cunningham authored the Court opinion in a 1992 case, *In re Estate of Finley*, reversing the Fourth District Appellate Court regarding a wrongful death statute. In 1990, six-year-old Shawn Finley had been struck and killed by a semi-trailer. His parents received a settlement from the trucking firm and its insurance companies. His siblings, who were "expressly excluded from any recovery," sued for "loss of society" from their brother's death. Cunningham delivered the opinion establishing sibling rights in "proven loss of society" cases.[1428]

Moses W. Harrison II won the 1992 election to succeed the appointed Cunningham. During his two assignments on the Supreme Court, Cunningham participated in seventy-one majority opinions, one special concurrence, and one dissent.[1429] Following his second retirement, he maintained a law practice in Waterloo, Illinois.

Cunningham served as Chairman of the Conference of Chief Judges from 1979 through 1981 and was a member of the Executive Committee of the Illinois Judicial Conference. He also was president of the Illinois Magistrates Association, and president of the Illinois Judges Association. He received a Distinguished Alumni Award from Washington University and served as an adjunct professor at McKendree College, Lebanon. In 2002, the Illinois State Bar Association honored Cunningham as a Senior Counsellor.[1430] A member of the Knights of Columbus, he served as a Eucharistic minister at Our Lady of Assumption Catholic Church in Fairview Heights. On July 13, 2008, at the age of eighty-four, Cunningham died at St. Anthony's Medical Center, St. Louis. Following Mass of Christian Burial at St. Peter's Cathedral in Belleville, he was buried in the city's Mount Carmel Catholic Cemetery.

HORACE L. CALVO, 1988-1991

A four-term member of the Illinois General Assembly before serving on the Illinois Supreme Court, Horace L. Calvo was born in Chicago to working-class parents, Horace L. and Mary Drew Calvo, on January 4, 1927. The family moved to Mount Sterling, and young Horace graduated from St. Mary's Academy, Springfield Junior College, and the University of Illinois. He attended but did not graduate from Lincoln College of Law in Springfield and St. Louis University Law School. He served in the U.S. Army Air Corps from 1944 to 1947, and on June 28, 1947, he married Josephine Beth, daughter of William and Elizabeth Faust Beth.[1431] They became the parents of two sons and two daughters.

Calvo received his law license in 1956, at a time when a law degree was not a state requirement for legal practice.[1432] He practiced in Granite City until 1975 in the firm Calvo, Mateyke & Hill, specializing in worker compensation cases. From 1961 to 1968, he served as an Assistant Illinois Attorney General under William G. Clark, later an Illinois Supreme Court Justice. In 1968, Calvo won election to the Illinois House of Representatives, representing the Granite City area. He was a member of the House Committee investigating allegations of judicial impropriety against Supreme Court Justices Roy J. Solfisburg Jr. and Ray I. Klingbiel. "Observers considered the committee a high-powered group," reported the *Chicago Sun-Times,* "indicating the depth of concern in the General Assembly over the allegations against the two justices." As a result of the committee investigation, both Solfisburg and Klingbiel resigned from the Court.[1433]

In 1975, the Supreme Court appointed Calvo a judge of the Third Judicial Circuit, comprising Bond and Madison Counties, in the Criminal Felony and Civil Law divisions. He also served two terms as Chief Judge of the circuit. In 1987, he was assigned to the Fifth District Appellate Court in Mount Vernon, comprising thirty-seven counties across southern Illinois. Often called a "people's judge," Calvo earned praise for his common-sense approach on the bench. "Each case must be judged on its own merit," he commented, "and no two are alike."[1434]

In 1988, Democratic voters in southern Illinois followed the endorsement of local party leaders, nominating Calvo over three other candidates for the Supreme Court vacancy created by the retirement of Justice Joseph Goldenhersh and the temporary appointment of his successor, Joseph Cunningham. Calvo's lack of a law degree became an issue in the campaign. "You learn the law by your experience after you pass the bar exam, not before the exam," Calvo told reporters, adding that even though he did not complete the degree requirements, he had accumulated some 1,200 hours of law courses.[1435] Garnering labor support in the metropolitan areas of St. Clair and Madison Counties, he defeated fellow Fifth District Appellate Court Justice Thomas M. Welch of Collinsville in a hard-fought campaign for the ten-year Supreme Court term.[1436] At the swearing-in ceremony, Calvo remarked, "Did I ever think I would be ever here today? Not in my wildest dreams. It proves that the American dream does exist, can exist, and that if you work hard enough at your profession, it can happen for all of us."[1437]

In a *Chicago Daily Law Bulletin* interview after the election, Calvo said that the voters considered his "professional service and performance as a judge," not relying "on school background alone." He described his judicial temperament as moderate, but conservative on criminal law issues, and said that he would "try to make Justice Goldenhersh proud of his successor."[1438]

During what became a brief Supreme Court tenure, Calvo authored more than forty opinions, including six dissents, which often reflected his pragmatic and populist approach to the law. In *Business and Professional People for the Public Interest v. The Illinois Commerce Commission,* Calvo delivered the complex opinion that rejected the utility's request for a rehearing of the Court's December 1989 decision that disallowed a $480 million rate increase and ordered retroactive consumer refunds.[1439]

The 1989 *People v. R.G.* case involved a runaway minor child who did not want to return to his parents. The DuPage County Circuit Court ruled against the child, citing provisions of the Minors Requiring Authoritative Intervention (MRAI) statute as "violative of substantive and procedural due process, and equal protection provisions." Illinois Attorney General Neil Hartigan appealed the decision, and Calvo delivered the opinion reversing the circuit court and upholding the constitutionality of the MRAI statute. He wrote that the statute "permits the State to temporarily refuse parental demands for the return of a runaway who does not want to go home. . . . The statute survives strict scrutiny because of the State's compelling interest in providing shelter and care to runaways." Calvo's predecessor and eventual successor, Justice Cunningham, described the decision "as a fundamental component of juvenile laws."[1440]

In 1991, Calvo wrote a strongly worded dissent in *Wilder Binding Company v. Oak Park Trust and Savings Bank.* He disagreed with a majority of the Supreme Court justices who, reversing the Cook County Circuit Court, denied reimbursement to the bindery for the bank's payment of forged checks, each for less than $1,000 but totaling some $20,000. "Defendant did not manually verify signatures written for under $1,000, and had no system for verifying signatures on checks under that amount," Calvo argued. "Defendant's automatic payment of all checks drawn for less than $1,000, without manual verification of the signatures on those checks, conclusively established defendant's failure to exercise ordinary care" under the requirements of the Uniform Commercial Code.[1441]

During his judicial career, Calvo was an active member of the Illinois Judges Association, serving a term as president, and chaired the Illinois Courts Commission. A founding member of the Lawyers Assistance Program, Calvo served for many years on its Board of Directors. He also held memberships in the American, Illinois, Madison County, and Tri-City Bar associations.

Less than two years into his Supreme Court tenure, Calvo was diagnosed with cancer.[1442] Several months later, on June 3, 1991, at age sixty-four, he died at Jewish Hospital in St. Louis. Funeral Mass was held at St. Cecilia Catholic Church, Glen Carbon, with all of his fellow Supreme Court justices in attendance, followed by burial in Calvary Catholic Cemetery. "His strength was his down-to-earth approach to the resolution of legal problems," Illinois State Bar Association Past President Maurice Bone remembered of Calvo. "He was more of a people person than a legal technician. His presence and wisdom will be missed."[1443] On behalf of the Supreme Court, Chief Justice Benjamin K. Miller expressed deep regret at Calvo's death and remarked on his many contributions to justice in Illinois. "In addition," Miller stated, "his wry wit and judicial and legislative experience added to the collegiality of the court."[1444]

JOHN J. STAMOS, 1988-1990

A Chicago native, John James Stamos was born on January 30, 1924, the youngest of nine children of Greek immigrants James S. and Katherine Stamos.[1445] An amateur artist from the age of seven, John received an Art Institute of Chicago scholarship while attending elementary school. After graduating from Bowen High School, Stamos enrolled in pre-legal studies at DePaul University. With the outbreak of World War II, he interrupted his education to enlist in the U.S. Army, serving with the Army Medical Corps in the European theater. Discharged in late 1945, he returned to DePaul University under the GI Bill and received his law degree in 1948.[1446]

A Democratic precinct captain in Chicago's Tenth Ward, Stamos maintained a private law practice for several years while also serving as a trustee of SS. Constantine and Helen Greek Orthodox church. In 1951, he was appointed Assistant Corporation Counsel for the City of Chicago and a year later became Assistant Cook County State's Attorney. In 1955, Stamos wed Helen Voutiritras of Oak Park; they became the parents of four children. After Helen's death in 1981, Stamos married Mary Stamos, a widowed neighbor.

Following the 1960 election of DePaul University law professor Daniel P. Ward as Cook County State's Attorney, Ward named Stamos to head the criminal division. Six years later, Chicago Mayor Richard J. Daley and other Democratic leaders chose Stamos to succeed Ward, who won election to the Illinois Supreme Court.[1447] In the most infamous case of the era, Stamos continued Ward's prosecution of Richard Speck for the murders of eight young women. Ward had rejected Speck's offer of a guilty plea for a sentence of life imprisonment, and the jury convicted him of all charges, imposing the death penalty. In 1966, on appeal to the Illinois Supreme Court, Stamos and his staff successfully argued for affirmation of the verdict and sentence. "After Speck's conviction," Stamos later recalled, "the United States Supreme Court set aside all death cases which resulted in Speck receiving his life sentence after all."[1448]

Stamos recalled that after several trials, he and his staff interviewed jurors "and discovered it was an astonishing training experience which I believed improved our trial skills. We really developed insight into what juries perceived, etc."[1449] But in 1968, Mayor Daley refused to slate the quiet, sometimes seemingly "aloof" Stamos in the election for Cook County State's Attorney, suggesting that he instead seek the nomination for Illinois Attorney General. Spurning that offer, Stamos instead ran for and won election to the First District Appellate Court.[1450] He was retained in office in 1972 and 1982, with an unsuccessful primary bid for the Supreme Court in 1980. During his appellate tenure, Stamos co-chaired the Supreme Court Committee on Judicial Conduct and served for several years on the Illinois Courts Commission.

Viewed as a judicial moderate, Stamos dismissed charges against four juveniles in 1985 accused of beating a man because prosecutors failed to provide a speedy trial. He ruled that by waiting nearly 700 days after the beating occurred, the prosecution performed a "gross disservice" to both the juveniles and the victim with its "lackadaisical conduct that simply cannot be tolerated." Stamos wrote a 1986 opinion that struck down a Cook County ordinance regulating adult bookstores as a First Amendment violation of free speech. The Illinois Supreme Court later overruled the appellate decision.[1451]

In 1988, Justice Seymour Simon resigned from the Illinois Supreme Court, and in April 1988, the Supreme Court selected sixty-four-year-old Stamos from twenty-five applicants to complete Simon's term. In naming Stamos, they rebuffed efforts by Chicago Mayor Eugene Sawyer, Illinois Comptroller Roland Burris, and representatives of minority groups who urged naming the first black justice to the vacancy. "I wish to thank the court for appointing me and I hope to continue to merit their confidence," Stamos remarked after the selection announcement. "It is a bittersweet occasion leaving the appellate court after 19 years."[1452] Governor James R. Thompson praised the appointment, having worked for Stamos in the Cook County State's Attorney's office in the early 1960s. "He was chief of the criminal division when I was just a dog-eared assistant state's attorney," recalled the Governor, describing Stamos as "one of the finest judges in Illinois and one of the finest human beings I know."[1453]

Among the decisions during his Supreme Court tenure, Stamos delivered the 1988 opinion in the attorney discipline case of *In re Himmel*. Himmel had been hired by a client to recover money stolen from her by her previous attorney. Himmel obtained a favorable settlement for his client, but there was an agreement that they would not disclose the previous attorney's misconduct. Justice Stamos, writing for the Court, said that, "a lawyer should assist in maintaining the integrity and competence of the legal profession." Himmel had violated that rule by failing to disclose the attorney's misconduct to the Illinois Attorney Registration and Disciplinary Commission and called that conduct a "code of silence." Despite recommendations for a lenient sanction, the Court suspended attorney Himmel from the practice of law for one year.[1454]

In the 1990 *In re Estate of Greenspan* case, Stamos delivered the majority opinion that vacated the Cook County Circuit Court's refusal to allow the public guardian's termination of life-support systems for the elderly, unconscious, and unresponsive Sidney Greenspan. Stamos cited the 1989 case *In re Estate of Longeway* as precedent that "a patient's right to refuse medical treatment, including artificial nutrition and hydration, is supported by the common law."[1455]

Also in 1990, Stamos wrote the opinion that reversed the Bureau County Circuit Court case regarding the recently enacted Illinois and Mississippi Canal State Park Act. The circuit court had ruled that provisions of the Act violated the Illinois Constitution by imposing upon the County the obligation of maintaining bridges within the park. Governor James R. Thompson and the directors of the departments of Conservation and Transportation appealed the decision to the Supreme Court. "Where it was the United States government which originally acquired the land for the construction of the Illinois and Mississippi Canal and built the bridges connecting the county and township roads which cross it, there is no violation of the Illinois Constitution's provisions on special legislation and equal protection," Stamos explained, "in the fact that section 4 of the Canal Park Act provides that those local governments have an obligation to maintain those bridges once the land was reacquired by the State and converted into a State park."[1456]

For accomplishments during his legal and judicial career, Stamos received the Outstanding Prosecutor Award from the National District Attorneys Association, the Professional Achievement Award from the Illinois State's Attorneys Association, and the Liberty Bell Award from the Chicago Chapter of the Federal Bar Association. At the conclusion of his appointed term, Stamos decided to retire rather than seek election in 1990, then joined his son James Stamos's Chicago law firm.[1457] In addition, the former justice enjoyed painting at his Northbrook home and trips to the family homeland of Greece. Justice Stamos died at his home on January 28, 2017, and was buried at Memorial Park Cemetery in Skokie, Illinois.

MICHAEL A. BILANDIC, 1990-2000

A first-generation American who became mayor of Chicago, Michael Anthony Bilandic was born in the city on February 13, 1923. Both his father and mother, Mate and Lebedina "Minnie" Bilandzic (later changed to Bilandic) immigrated to the United States from Croatia. Michael's family, including three siblings, resided in the southwest Chicago neighborhood of Bridgeport. "We were both poor young boys who grew up looking to make it in a rough, tough world," said Michael's longtime friend Joseph N. Du Canto, "and we did it." Bilandic graduated from St. Jerome Grammar School and De LaSalle High School in Chicago, then St. Mary's College in Winona, Minnesota.[1458]

In World War II, Bilandic served as a U.S. Marine Corps first lieutenant in the Pacific theater. "We both served on Iwo Jima," Du Canto remembered, "and both of us lived our lives thereafter knowing every day was a gift." Attending DePaul University College of Law on the GI Bill, Bilandic graduated in 1949, and began his legal career as a $25-a-week clerk at the firm where he would later become a senior partner, Anixter, Delaney, Bilandic & Piggott.[1459] He served as a Master in Chancery from 1964 to 1967 and a special assistant Illinois Attorney General from 1965 to 1968. On the advice of his Bridgeport Eleventh Ward Alderman, Richard J. Daley, Bilandic became involved in Democratic Party politics and in 1955, campaigned for Daley in his first mayoral race. Fourteen years later, in 1969, Bilandic gave up his lucrative law practice to run for Daley's former aldermanic seat, overwhelmingly defeating the Republican candidate.

Quickly gaining the reputation of an effective Council alderman, Bilandic became chairman of the Environmental Committee, pushing legislation that banned phosphates from detergents and controlled asbestos in construction and demolition. In 1974, he became chairman of the powerful Finance Committee and Council floor leader for his mentor, Mayor Daley. After Daley's death in December 1976, Council leaders fought to determine a successor before agreeing on Bilandic, with support from the Daley family. "As a first-generation Croatian American," Bilandic later wrote, "this was an unexpected honor. I had worked with Daley for many years, and my life has been enriched for having known him."[1460]

The bachelor Bilandic, who resided with his elderly mother in Bridgeport, became a candidate in the special election to fill the remaining two years of Daley's sixth mayoral term. He won the April 1977 primary and the June general election. The next month at Holy Name Cathedral, Chicago Cardinal John Cody officiated at Bilandic's marriage to socialite Heather Morgan, director of the Chicago Council on Fine Arts. They would become the parents of one son.

As mayor, Bilandic ended a fifteen-year impasse on building a cross-town expressway, oversaw creation of the food and music ChicagoFest on Navy Pier, and helped organize and participated in the first Chicago Marathon. He also faced serious labor issues, however, including a gravediggers' strike and threatened strikes by butchers and the Lyric Opera orchestra.[1461] In January 1979, Chicago became virtually immobilized by a series of devastating snowstorms. Bilandic attempted to reassure concerned residents of improving conditions, even as buried cars blocked streets, garbage remained uncollected, and service on Chicago Transit Authority lines and at O'Hare International Airport came to a near-standstill. Bilandic lost the Democratic primary to his disgruntled former commissioner of consumer affairs, Jane M. Byrne. Winning the general election, Byrne became the first female mayor of Chicago.

Following his defeat, Bilandic joined the law firm of Bilandic, Neistein, Richman, Hauslinger & Young, specializing in corporate law. In 1984, he won election to the First District Illinois Appellate Court, and six years later, at age sixty-seven, became the Democratic candidate to succeed Daniel P. Ward on the Illinois Supreme Court. Declining campaign contributions, Bilandic spent $32,000 of his own funds. "This is my last hurrah," he explained. "I don't want to go there encumbered in any manner."[1462] He won election to a ten-year Supreme Court term, serving as Chief Justice from 1994 to 1997.

During his Court tenure, Bilandic would review thousands of cases and write more than two hundred opinions, including a high-profile death penalty case. In the 1995 *People v. Jimerson* case, Bilandic delivered the opinion ordering a new trial for death-row inmate Verneal Jimerson, who was convicted in the Cook County Circuit Court for the 1978 murder of two Chicago-area residents. Another defendant, the prosecution's key witness, stated that she had not been offered leniency for testifying against Jimerson, but after the trial, murder charges against her were dropped. The Supreme Court unanimously reversed Jimerson's conviction, achieved, as Bilandic wrote, with "knowing use of perjured testimony," and remanded the case for a new trial.[1463] Found guilty again, Jimerson spent nine years on death row before being exonerated of the crimes.[1464]

The 1997 *Johnson v. Edgar* case concerned action by the Illinois General Assembly. Donald Johnson, president of the Illinois State Federation of Labor and Congress of Industrial Organizations (Illinois AFL-CIO), filed suit in Cook County Circuit Court against Governor Jim Edgar and Attorney General Jim Ryan, challenging an article in the new Public Act 89-428 that permitted employers to monitor employee conversations. Introduced in 1995 as an eight-page bill regarding reimbursement to the state for prisoner incarceration expenses, Public Act 89-428 passed as a document that exceeded two hundred pages. The law included provisions for not only employer eavesdropping, but also such diverse subjects as environmental impact fees for the sale of fuel, child molestation, cannabis, and parole hearings.

The Supreme Court upheld the circuit court determination that Public Act 89-428 violated Article IV of the Illinois Constitution, prohibiting unrelated measures within a single bill. "One reason for the single subject rule is to prevent legislation from being passed which, standing alone, could not muster the necessary votes for passage," Bilandic wrote. "The single subject rule ensures that the legislature addresses the difficult decisions it faces directly and subject to public scrutiny, rather than passing unpopular measures on the backs of popular ones."[1465]

In 1999, Bilandic delivered the majority opinion in a landmark case regarding the liability of a health maintenance organization (HMO) for institutional negligence. In *Jones v. Chicago HMO Ltd.*, Sheila Jones sought medical malpractice action against Chicago HMO Ltd. of Illinois and one of its contract physicians. Jones charged in the Cook County Circuit Court that the HMO and the physician failed to adequately treat her three-month-old daughter, resulting in permanent disability. Bilandic wrote the opinion reversing a portion of the circuit court's summary judgment for Chicago HMO. "The law imposes a duty upon HMOs to conform to the legal standard of reasonable conduct in light of the apparent risk," he wrote. "It could be inferred that the doctor's failure to see the infant soon enough resulted from an inability to serve an overloaded patient population." The decision led to numerous HMO lawsuits in succeeding years.[1466]

As his Supreme Court term ended in 2000, Bilandic noted that his legal career had spanned half a century: three decades in practice and in government, then twenty years in the judiciary.[1467] Fellow justices praised his leadership as Chief Justice in the mid-1990s, which included rewriting rules of discovery, encouraging mandatory arbitration, and streamlining the Administrative Office of Illinois Courts. "Relocating and consolidating our administrative offices in Chicago and Springfield has provided a better working environment for our people and increased productivity," Bilandic said at the time. "Summary dispositions and page limitations on appellate opinions improved operations of our appellate courts and broke the logjam in the reporter's office."[1468]

After his Supreme Court tenure, Bilandic practiced law with the Chicago firm of Bilandic, Neistein, Richman, Hauslinger & Young and served on the Chicago Bar Association's Board of Managers. He maintained a longstanding exercise regimen as a runner and jogger, found enjoyment in art classes, photography, and visits to Croatia with his wife and son, exploring his family roots.[1469] On January 15, 2002, at age seventy-eight, Bilandic died unexpectedly from a heart rupture, a day before scheduled coronary bypass surgery at Northwestern Memorial Hospital in Evanston.[1470] Following a private funeral, he was interred beside his parents in St. Mary Catholic Cemetery in Evergreen Park. "He was a quiet and gracious and intelligent man," eulogized the *Chicago Tribune,* "who lost the best job in Chicago before he found the best job for him."[1471]

"If a person is ever granted immortality, it is perhaps the judiciary that comes closest to allowing that," said Supreme Court Justice Charles E. Freeman of Bilandic. "His words and opinions, his decisions will be quoted and followed by lawyers and judges for many years to come. He had a great impact on many important ground-breaking decisions."[1472] In March 2003, Illinois and Chicago officials renamed the twenty-one-story State of Illinois Building at 160 North LaSalle Street the Michael A. Bilandic Building.

The Bilandic Building in Chicago (Image courtesy of Wayne Lorentz, Artefaqs Corporation)

JAMES D. HEIPLE, 1990-2000

James D. Heiple was born in Peoria, Illinois, on September 13, 1933, the son of attorney and banker Rae Crane and Harriet Lucille Birkett Heiple. Attending grammar and high schools in Washington, Illinois, young Heiple graduated in 1955 from Bradley University and in 1957 from the University of Louisville Law School. On July 28, 1956, he married Virginia Duffield Kerswill at First Federated Church in Peoria, and they would become the parents of two sons and a daughter.[1473]

After passing the Kentucky and Illinois Bar examinations, Heiple joined the family law firm of Heiple & Heiple in Washington. In 1959, he opened an office in Pekin, developing an extensive practice in municipal law and as corporation counsel for several municipalities. He also served as an appellate law clerk, a public defender, and a Special Master in Chancery.

In 1970, the Republican Heiple won election to fill a Tazewell County Circuit Court vacancy and two years later was retained for a full-six-year term, and then retained again in 1978. In 1980, he won election to become a justice of the Third District Appellate Court. He was twice elected the Presiding Justice, and in 1988, received a Master of Laws degree from the University of Virginia. During his career, Heiple served as the Illinois Judges Association president, Tazewell County Bar Association president, held memberships in the Illinois, Kentucky, and federal bar associations, and chaired councils of the Illinois State Bar Association. In addition to his legal career, he partnered in an insurance agency and became a director of two banks.

In 1990, Heiple sought the Third Judicial District seat on the Illinois Supreme Court to succeed retired Justice Howard C. Ryan. Heiple campaigned as a "Common Sense Choice" in the twenty-one Third District counties of north-central Illinois. During the contest, observers called Heiple "feisty, his own man, and a writer of rather harsh dissents" during his appellate tenure. "One law professor predicted Heiple would shake up the court more than any other candidate then running."[1474] He defeated Democratic Illinois Appellate Justice Tobias Barry by less than one percentage point.

On the Supreme Court, Heiple proved a conservative "law and order" justice. In the 1991 *People v. Davis* case, he wrote the opinion affirming the death sentence of Girvies Davis, who had been convicted in the Madison County Circuit Court for shooting an eighty-nine-year-old man in the course of a robbery. After the Supreme Court in 1983 upheld the conviction but issued a divided ruling on the sentence, the state's attorney recommended life imprisonment. When the successor state's attorney again sought the death penalty, lawyers for Davis argued before the Supreme Court that double jeopardy precluded the state from a second death sentence for the same conviction. "No misrepresentations were made to the defendant regarding the maximum sentence he could receive," Heiple wrote in the brief opinion. "Further, the subsequent decision to seek the death penalty in this case was based on prosecutorial discretion of a new State's Attorney. Such scenario raises no *per se* presumption of arbitrariness or capriciousness under eighth amendment analysis" of cruel and unusual punishment.[1475]

In the 1994 *In re Doe* case, Heiple wrote the unanimous opinion that returned "Baby Richard," Daniel Kirchner, to his biological parents. The mother had relinquished her rights to the infant immediately after his March 1991 birth and refused to reveal the father's name to the adoptive parents. Several months later, she told the father of the child's existence, and he hired an attorney to challenge the adoption. Both the Cook County Circuit Court and First District Appellate Court agreed that the father had not shown interest in the boy within the first thirty days of his life, as required by law, thus abandoning his parental rights. The Supreme Court justices unanimously reversed the ruling, excoriating the adoptive parents for proceeding with the adoption "when they knew that a real father was out there who had been denied knowledge of his baby's existence." Illinois adoption laws, Heiple wrote, "are designed to protect natural parents in their preemptive rights to their own children wholly apart from any consideration of the so-called best interests of the child. If it were otherwise, few parents would be secure in the custody of their own children."[1476]

Illinois Governor Jim Edgar joined the adoptive parents in petitioning the Supreme Court for a rehearing of the highly unpopular decision. "The court has construed the Adoption Act in a manner, which if it remains unmodified creates a dangerous precedent for many adopted children," read the petition. "It allows a biological father to claim at any time that he did not know of the existence of his child and move to vacate an adoption." Edgar also supported and signed legislation that stressed a child's best interests in disputed adoption hearings.[1477] But in an emotionally charged majority opinion, Heiple refused to grant the adoptive parents' rehearing request.[1478] He criticized Governor Edgar's involvement as a "crass political move" and accused Appellate Justice Dom Rizzi of ignorance of basic legal adoption principles. In addition, Heiple charged *Chicago Tribune* columnist Bob Greene with "journalistic terrorism" for extensive "false and misleading" articles, "designed to discredit me as a judge and the Supreme Court as a dispenser of justice by stirring up disrespect and hatred among the general population."[1479]

A series of professional difficulties during Heiple's Supreme Court tenure emanated from four traffic violations in his hometown of Pekin. During the last incident, in January 1996, police accused him of speeding, then fleeing the traffic stop. Initially demanding a jury trial, Heiple eventually pleaded guilty to the speeding charge and to ignoring police orders. In exchange, prosecutors dropped the more serious offense of resisting a peace officer.[1480]

Neither the police incidents nor the disputes with Governor Edgar and columnist Greene deterred Heiple's election by his fellow justices to the rotating position of Chief Justice. "It is clear that Justice Heiple has a hard work ethic," evaluated editor Steven B. Levy in the *DuPage County Bar Association Journal*, "has self-reliant independence, is devoted to his family, has deeply felt religious convictions, has a desire for justice, and is an honorable and respected jurist. . . . His judicial independence, his libertarian (antiauthoritarian) bent, and his unswerving sense of moral rightness seem to emanate from this strong philosophical root."[1481]

Heiple assumed the three-year term as Chief Justice in January 1997, succeeding Michael A. Bilandic. Later that month, the state's Judicial Inquiry Board charged Heiple with misconduct for having repeatedly disobeyed police instructions during the Pekin traffic stops and for invoking his position to evade citations. In February, Justice Charles E. Freeman, a vocal Heiple critic, sought an Illinois Courts Commission investigation. "Considering the public's perception of the court and the entire judicial system, starting with the Baby Richard case and the further damage done by the several traffic incidents involving Chief Justice Heiple," Freeman asked his colleagues, "how can any member of this court even question the need for dialogue?"[1482]

The Courts Commission established a panel to investigate misconduct charges against Heiple. In a contentious move, he appointed Justice Moses Harrison II, arguably his closest colleague on the Supreme Court, to chair the five-member group. Heiple requested that the Commission make its determination based on already filed briefs. "We elect not to refute," his attorney stated.[1483]

Then in April 1997, for the first time in nearly 150 years, the Illinois House of Representatives unanimously authorized a bipartisan impeachment investigation of Heiple because of the Harrison appointment as well as Heiple's much-publicized traffic stops.[1484] In addition, the panel reviewed questionable lease arrangements for his Pekin law office and allegations regarding his choice of Appellate Justice William Holdridge, one of his former law clerks, to serve simultaneously as director of the Administrative Office of the Illinois Courts. Two days after the Courts Commission censured Heiple for damaging "the court system's integrity" and three days before the start of the House investigation, he reluctantly resigned his position as Chief Justice. "I refused to resign from the Supreme Court entirely; I had done nothing impeachable; and I was unwilling to allow my political and media enemies to prevail over my demise."[1485]

Former Illinois Governor James R. Thompson led the team of attorneys representing Heiple in the House proceedings, not only arguing the separation of powers within state government but also maintaining that none of the allegations merited removal from the Court.[1486] "It is our view that Chief Justice Heiple has a clear and undeniable property right in his office as a justice of the Supreme Court which neither this committee nor the House nor the Senate can deprive him of in violation of the constitution," Thompson stated. After the hearings, the members voted 8–2 against impeachment.[1487]

In December 2000, at the end of his ten-year term, Heiple did not seek retention on the Supreme Court. "It's difficult to always be on the firing line," explained his former publicist Thom Serafin. "But he fulfilled his term and feels he did it with a sense of dignity as a person who respected the law to the utmost."[1488]

In retirement, the widowed Heiple concentrated on operating two farms he owned near Peoria, while also vacationing at his Canadian cabin and rediscovering the enjoyment of reading. "While on the bench," he said, "I had to read so much—many hours every week—that I avoided reading for pleasure, but now I can enjoy a range of books by a variety of authors."[1489] He also continued championing the rights of biological parents in contested adoption cases. In 2003, he attended a reception honoring psychologist Karen Moriarty, author of *Baby Richard; A Four-Year-Old Comes Home.* Moriarty wrote that the boy had adjusted well to life with his birth parents and two younger sisters. "He's always so happy," she told reporters. "He just got straight A's on his last report card."[1490]

In 2011, Heiple responded to an Internet story that a Guatemalan court had returned a child from her U.S. adoptive parents to her native biological family. "If . . . the best interests of the child is to be the determining factor in child custody cases," he wrote in a colorfully worded agreement with the decision, "persons seeking babies to adopt might profitably frequent grocery stores and snatch babies from carts when the parent is looking the other way. Then, if custody proceedings can be delayed long enough, they can assert that they have a nicer home, a superior education, a better job or whatever, and that the best interests of the child are with the baby snatchers. Children of parents living in public housing or other conditions deemed less affluent and children of single parents might be considered particularly fair game."[1491]

CHARLES E. FREEMAN, 1990-2018

The first African American elected to the Illinois Supreme Court, Charles E. Freeman descended from slaves freed by Quakers before the American Civil War. Born in Richmond, Virginia, on December 12, 1933, Freeman attended high school and college with Douglas Wilder, who in 1989 in Virginia became the nation's first elected Black governor.[1492] Freeman completed undergraduate work at Virginia Union University in 1954 and in 1962 earned his JD degree from The John Marshall Law School in Chicago. He married Marylee Volker in 1960, and they became the parents of one son.

In private practice from 1962 to 1976, Freeman also served as an Illinois assistant attorney general, Cook County assistant state's attorney, and assistant attorney for the County Board of Election Commissioners. In 1965 Democratic Illinois Governor Otto Kerner appointed Freeman as an arbitrator with the Illinois Industrial Commission, where for nine years he heard thousands of work-related injury cases. Then, from 1973 to 1976, under Governor Dan Walker, Freeman served on the Illinois Commerce Commission, a regulatory agency for telephone, electric, and gas companies.

In 1976, Freeman won election to the Cook County Circuit Court and served for ten years. During that tenure he was the first African American to swear in a Chicago mayor when he administered the oath of office in 1983 to his longtime friend Harold Washington. For several years the two attorneys had shared an office in Chicago. "Harold was the hardest-working guy I've ever seen," Freeman recalled.[1493]

Elected to the First District Appellate Court in 1986, Freeman served that same year as Presiding Judge of the Third Division and member of the First District Executive Committee. In 1990, in a First Judicial District election to fill the Illinois Supreme Court vacancy of Seymour Simon, Democrat Freeman defeated Republican Robert Chapman Buckley 62 percent to 38 percent.

One of Freeman's most publicized cases was the 1994 decision involving DuPage County defendant Rolando Cruz, convicted of kidnapping, raping, and murdering ten-year-old Jeanine Nicarico, despite no physical evidence linking him to the crime. The Illinois Supreme Court in 1990 and 1992 upheld Cruz's conviction and death sentence, but heard the case again in 1994 after a sheriff's lieutenant admitted he had lied under oath about Cruz's statements regarding the murder. In delivering the *People v. Cruz* opinion reversing his conviction, Justice Freeman considered the "impact our decision will have upon Jeanine Nicarico's surviving family and friends." Yet, he reasoned, "we are duty bound to play a larger role in preserving that very basic guarantee of our democratic society, that every person, however culpable, is entitled to a fair and impartial trial. We cannot deviate from the obligation of that role."[1494] Another man eventually admitted to the murder, and in 2002 Cruz received a pardon from Governor George Ryan.

In 1997, the Supreme Court justices chose sixty-four-year-old Freeman to serve as Chief Justice, succeeding Justice James Heiple to become the first African American to lead a branch of Illinois government. Asked about the significance of being the first Black chief justice, Freeman responded, "I'm an African American who now has become chief judge; I'm not an African-American chief justice. I have no different perception on what course I would take because of my heritage."[1495] Freeman noted that "we're about to go into another century and I think the Court should start doing some things administratively that reflect the times."[1496] Freeman won retention to the Court in 2000 and 2010, both with nearly 80 percent of the vote.

Freeman has been praised for upholding defendants' rights and advocating prosecutorial reforms. R. Eugene Pincham, who served with Freeman on the Appellate Court, described him as tilting "slightly to the liberal side of the court" and that "probably more often than any justice dissents in criminal cases on the side of protecting" the rights of the accused.[1497] In *People v. McCauley*, the police refused an attorney's request to see his client when being interrogated. Freeman wrote in his majority opinion that the "day is long past in Illinois, however, where attorneys must shout legal advice to their clients, held in custody, through the jailhouse door. In this case, we determine that our State constitutional guarantees afforded defendant a greater degree of protection."[1498]

In the 2011 case *In re Jonathan C.B.*, Justice Freeman dissented in a case that juveniles charged with sex offenses were not entitled to a jury trial. Freeman's dissent focused on the shackling of juveniles, which not only creates prejudice against the accused, but also is an affront against the judicial process. He concluded, "A juvenile respondent has the right to appear in a courtroom free of unnecessary physical restraints unless justification is established."[1499] In 2016, the Supreme Court added Rule 943, which forbids the use of restraints on a minor during court proceedings except for specific reasons.

He also wrote the majority opinion in an adoptive parentage case that the equitable adoption doctrine does not apply to child custody proceedings. Maria and Jim engaged to be married. Maria was Slovakian and adopted Scarlett, also from Slovakia. Jim was not able to adopt Scarlett because he was non-Slovakian. Jim acted as a father and provided necessary support. Jim and Maria never married and broke up ten years later, and Jim asserted his parental rights, custody, and visitation. When the case reached the Supreme Court, Freeman noted that Jim lacked statutory standing to bring a custody petition because Illinois does not recognize functional parents. Only the adoptive mother has statutory parent-child relationship with child.[1500]

Freeman responded to a complaint that he appointed a friend to the bench, "I have done nothing different than any other judge who sits with me or any other judge before in the history of the Supreme Court," he told the *Chicago Sun-Times*. "We all receive calls. We all receive visits from politicians, from friends who made recommendations for appointments to the bench. We act on them sometimes. Sometimes we do not."[1501] He also expressed pride in having increased the number of African Americans and Jews on the bench, appointing eleven African Americans and nine Jews.[1502]

A resident of Hyde Park, Freeman enjoys boating, photography, and collecting cameo glass and soapstone. He is a member of many bar associations and has received numerous honors, including the Freedom Award from John Marshall Law School, Seymour Simon Justice Award from the Jewish Judges Association, the Earl Burrus Dickerson Award from the Chicago Bar Association, and the Ida Platt Award and the Presidential Award from the Cook County Bar Association. Freeman retired from the Supreme Court on June 14, 2018, after a long and distinguished career and the fifth-longest tenure on the Court. DePaul

University law professor Jeffrey Shaman complimented Freeman on "his reputation of being a solid judge, a very competent judge" and that his "opinions are well crafted."[1503] Prominent attorney James D. Montgomery also noted that Freeman's work on the Court leaves "a legacy that will endure for years to come."

JOHN L. NICKELS, 1992-1998

Born in Aurora, Illinois, on January 16, 1931, John L. Nickels was the son of Kane County dairy farmer Philip and wife Gertrude Rausch Nickels. John began his education at age four in a country school near Sugar Grove—one teacher for fifteen students in eight grades. When he was eleven years of age, the Aurora *Beacon-News* featured the Nickels family in an article on area farmers aiding the World War II war effort. The story included a photograph of John on a tractor. "Jackie can handle this tractor as easily as most youngsters pedal a bicycle," read the caption.[1504]

Graduating from Marmion Military Academy, a Catholic Benedictine high school in Aurora, Nickels worked on the family's 800-acre farm for five years, and then served for two years in the U.S. Army at Fort Knox, Kentucky, and in Louisiana, as an aircraft and engine mechanic. Discharged in 1956, he returned to the family farm and commuted to Northern Illinois University on the GI Bill.

On June 22, 1957, Nickels married artist Merita Smith at Holy Cross Catholic Church in Batavia, and they would become the parents of eight children. He graduated from NIU in 1958 at age twenty-seven, with a degree in business administration, and then received his law degree from DePaul University College of Law in 1961. The family lived briefly in Batavia before returning to the Sugar Grove area, building a home on a portion of the family farmland.[1505]

Nickels practiced law in DeKalb, Kane, and Kendall Counties for more than twenty years. Active in the business community and in public service, he won election to the first Waubonsee Community College Board of Trustees, and served on the Kane County Regional Planning Commission and Zoning Board of Appeals as well as the Board of Kane County Bank & Trust Company.

In 1982, Nickels was elected circuit court judge for the Sixteenth Judicial Circuit, serving DeKalb, Kane, and Kendall Counties. Eight years later, he won election to the Illinois Appellate Court, Second District. During his appellate tenure, he authored sixty-six majority opinions and three dissents.

Following the 1992 retirement of Second Judicial District Supreme Court Justice Thomas J. Moran, Nickels won an upset victory in the Republican primary for the seat. "I hope where I come from makes a difference," he told a reporter covering the campaign. "People have to make their decision based on a measure of the person. That's something you can't hand them on a resume or a campaign flyer. They want to look you in the eye. I hope when they look at me, they see something of themselves."[1506] He was unopposed in the general election.

In six years on the Illinois Supreme Court, Nickels participated in 820 cases, authoring 95 majority opinions, 45 dissents, and 10 special concurring opinions. He wrote a concurring opinion to the 1994 *People v. Cruz* majority ruling that overturned the conviction and death sentence of Rolando Cruz for the murder of Jeanine Nicarico of Naperville. Cruz was acquitted in his third trial, amid accusations of prosecutorial and police misconduct. Another man, Brian Dugan, was later found guilty of the crime.[1507]

In *City of Chicago v. Morales*, Nickels wrote the 1997 opinion that struck down the city's gang loitering ordinance as an unreasonable infringement on personal liberty. "Persons suspected of being in criminal street gangs are deprived of the personal liberty of being able to freely walk the streets and associate with friends," he wrote, "regardless of whether they are actually gang members or have committed any crime." He continued, "Many of the offensive activities the city claims the gang loitering ordinance will deter are already criminal acts. . . . However, the city cannot empower the police to sweep undesirable persons from the public streets through vague and arbitrary criminal ordinances."[1508] Two years later, the United States Supreme Court upheld Justice Nickels's decision, declaring the ordinance unconstitutional.

Although elected as a Republican, Nickels sided with the majority in the 1997 *Best v. Taylor Machine Works* that struck down a damages cap and other provisions of a tort reform law pushed by the Republican Party in the mid-1990s when it briefly controlled both legislative chambers and the governor's office.[1509]

In addition to hearing cases, Nickels was the Supreme Court liaison to the Lawyers Trust Fund of Illinois, credited with increasing legal aid programs for low-income residents. The Illinois State Bar Association recognized his success in securing the Lawyers Trust Fund rule that allowed their "pooled client accounts" to earn a higher rate of interest that substantially increased funding available for legal services. A staunch advocate of lawyers sharing their privilege, he championed free legal services not only to the poor, but also to the disadvantaged and vulnerable—"work of the Lord," he said.[1510] For those efforts, he received the Illinois State Bar Association's Access to Justice Award.

Nickels considered judicial independence as the cornerstone of democracy, "the sworn duty of judges to make the hard and unpopular decisions." In his keynote address at the 1998 annual Supreme Court dinner co-sponsored by the Illinois and Chicago bar associations, sixty-seven-year-old Nickels described as inappropriate recent attacks on "judicial independence," which he said "used to be confined to the fringe of society. Unfortunately, it has moved closer to the mainstream. Today's critics can be the President of the United States, state governors, state legislators, prominent members of Congress, and yes—even members of the bar—seemingly each with their own personal agendas." He criticized both President Bill Clinton and Republican Senate Leader Robert Dole for urging a judge's resignation or impeachment for suppressing evidence that had been seized in violation of the Fourth Amendment. "Regardless of the short-term political expediency of such comments," Nickels said, "they are outrageous."[1511] He urged judges to remain independent in the face of political pressure and for prosecutors to protect the rights of defendants. "In their exercise of prosecutorial discretion," he warned, "they must be keenly aware of what is fair and just."

Concluding the speech, Nickels announced his retirement from the bench. In a later *Chicago Tribune* interview, he said, "We can't lose sight of what we're all there for and that's to do justice. We have a larger responsibility to acquit the not-guilty person than we have to find guilty the guilty person. Some prosecutors lose sight of that aspect of it."[1512] Anticipating retirement, the farmer's son reflected on "going home. I am going back to the land that has always nourished my soul—back to the land that I never really got off of my hands or out of my heart."[1513]

Crediting his agrarian background for lifelong values of hard work, commitment, and loyalty, Nickels farmed throughout his legal and judicial career. At the Maple Park farm in DeKalb County he shared with his wife, he pursued no-till plowing to conserve topsoil, utilized computer programs for further resource conservation, and created a wildlife sanctuary. He was also an active member of St. Gall Catholic parish in Elburn.

After an extended illness, Justice Nickels died at age eighty-two on June 24, 2013, at his Maple Park home. Following services at St. Gall Church, he was buried in the parish cemetery. Nickels "was a gentle and most hospitable man," Illinois Supreme Court Chief Justice Thomas L. Kilbride said of his colleague. "He carried a wealth of compassion and internal resolve to bring out the best in all of us—to be respectful professionals. He was a real role model and epitomized that it was quite acceptable 'to agree to disagree.'"[1514]

MOSES W. HARRISON II, 1992-2002

Moses Wilkins Harrison II was born in Collinsville, Illinois, on March 30, 1932, the grandson of a physician and son of dentist Clarence Harrison and nurse Loretta O'Hara Harrison. After attending local public schools and working at a concrete-block plant, he earned money for college tuition as a Colorado ranch hand, truck driver, and organizer for the Teamsters union. Harrison graduated in 1954 with a degree in political science from Colorado College. "I saw a lot of hard times in my life," whose ancestors included coal miners; "My heart bleeds for the working man." He proudly carried his Teamsters card throughout his life.[1515]

Influenced by one college instructor who was also an attorney, Harrison returned to the Midwest to attend Washington University School of Law in St. Louis. Graduating in 1958, he was admitted to the Illinois and Missouri bars. For fifteen years he engaged in private practice, initially in an office next door to his father's dental practice, and eventually becoming senior partner of Harrison, Rarick, and Cadigan. On December 30, 1961, he married Sharon Phillips, whom he met in his father's dental office, and they became the parents of two sons.[1516]

"My shingle was out for everybody," Harrison explained. "I didn't do that much of any one thing, but I did a lot of everything," practicing corporate, domestic relations, and criminal law. "I sued a few banks, and I represented a few banks too." An East St. Louis case that he remembered years later involved an Appaloosa horse death at a sale barn. "The fellow that operated the sales put two stallions together in the same bin and, of course, they fight until one kills the other one." Harrison represented the horse's owner in suing the operator but was unable to obtain witnesses because many people were afraid to testify against the defendant because he was a prominent horse operator. Harrison "got a guy who owned thoroughbreds to testify, was a good witness. And we tried the case to completion and I got a verdict.... You think about it. Lawyers must have a big ego to go in there cold and try to convince twelve people that they're right about something."[1517]

While practicing law, Harrison was elected to the Board of Governors of the Illinois State Bar Association and as president of the Madison County Bar Association. He was also on the Collinsville City Council and served as the city's finance commissioner. Appointed by the Illinois Supreme Court in 1973 as a judge of the Third Judicial Circuit, the following year Harrison was elected as a Democrat to the position. He would serve two terms as chief judge of the circuit, comprising Bond and Madison Counties.

In 1979, the Supreme Court appointed Harrison to the thirty-seven-county Fifth District Appellate Court in Mount Vernon, and he was elected to that Court in 1980. Serving two terms as presiding judge of the Appellate Court, he won his retention election in 1990. In the 1992 contest to fill the vacancy of Illinois Supreme Court Justice Horace L. Calvo,

Harrison defeated "three worthy opponents," two in the primary and Republican Don W. Weber in the general election.[1518]

Five years later, Harrison figured in the judicial misconduct allegations against Supreme Court Chief Justice James Heiple for his behavior during four traffic stops, including a 1996 arrest. Harrison chaired the Illinois Courts Commission, handling cases of alleged judicial misconduct. Although critics characterized him as Heiple's closest ally on the court, Harrison refused to recuse himself from the case, stating that the Constitution offered no guidance on replacement. The Commission eventually censured Heiple, who resigned as Chief Justice, then retired in 2000.[1519]

In November 1998, Harrison gained national attention for his sole dissenting opinion in *People v. Bull,* a condemnation of the Court's opinion affirming the death sentence of Donald Bull for the murders of a mother and her three-year-old son. Citing the cases of nine men wrongly convicted of murder and sentenced to death, Harrison wrote, "Some would suggest that the freedom now enjoyed by these nine men demonstrates that our criminal justice system is working effectively with adequate safeguards. If there had been only one or two wrongful death penalty cases, I might be persuaded to accept that view. When there have been so many mistakes in such a short span of time, however, the only conclusion I can draw is that the system does not work as the Constitution requires it to. . . . When a system is as prone to error as ours is, we should not be making irrevocable decisions about any human life."[1520] Three months later, death row inmate Anthony Porter came within two days of execution before being exonerated in the slayings of two men.

In early 1999, shortly after *People v. Bull,* Harrison issued a stay of execution for Chicago gang member Andrew Kokoraleis, convicted of six murders, but a majority on the Supreme Court overturned the stay. "My colleagues seem to regard the existence of Kokoraleis' appeal [for the murder of Lorraine Borowski] as nothing more than a bureaucratic nuisance," Harrison lamented in his dissent. "They forget that under Supreme Court Rule 651(a), appeals from judgments of the circuit court in post-conviction proceedings involving judgments imposing death sentences are not optional or a matter for the court's discretion. Such appeals lie to the Supreme Court 'as a matter of right.'"[1521]

After Governor George Ryan denied clemency, Kokoraleis became the last person executed in Illinois. The following year, Ryan would order a moratorium on executions, and in 2011, Governor Pat Quinn signed legislation abolishing the death penalty. "If the system can't be guaranteed, 100-percent error-free," Quinn said, "then we shouldn't have the system."[1522]

In November 2000, Harrison became Chief Justice for a two-year term, succeeding Charles E. Freeman.[1523] Harrison guided the adoption of sweeping new rules governing the conduct and trial of death penalty cases. During his decade-long Supreme Court tenure, he authored 136 majority opinions, twenty-two special concurrences, and 195 dissents.

At age seventy and approaching the end of his ten-year term, Harrison announced his retirement from the Court in September 2002. Proud of his contribution to the death penalty debate, Harrison noted that when he made his landmark plea against the death penalty in *People v. Bull,* few shared his view.[1525] In 1999, the year before Illinois Governor George Ryan ordered a moratorium on executions pending a review of the system, Harrison had told a *St. Louis Post-Dispatch* reporter, "It is no answer to say we are doing the best we can do. If this is the best our state can do, we have no business sending people to their deaths."[1526]

During his lengthy career, Harrison held memberships in the Illinois State Bar Association, Metropolitan Bar Association of St. Louis, Tri-City Bar Association, Madison County Bar Association, American Bar Association, American Judicature Society, Justinian Society of Lawyers, and the Illinois Judges Association. Among many honors, in 2001, he received the Illinois State Bar Association's Access to Justice Award. The Justinian Society named an annual award in his honor for outstanding pro bono work.

A former senior warden of Christ Episcopal Church of Collinsville, in retirement he was a member of St. Michael's Episcopal Church, O'Fallon. After a lengthy illness, he died ate age eighty-one on April 25, 2013, at Missouri Baptist Hospital in St. Louis. "Moses Harrison was a great Supreme Court justice," said Illinois Governor Pat Quinn. "He served as a strong and passionate advocate against the death penalty and devoted his life to ensuring that justice was served fairly. He was a steadfast defender of everyday people. As he said best himself, his job as judge was to 'protect ordinary citizens against wrongdoing by the government, large corporations and powerful individuals.' He did this job well."[1527]

MARY ANN MCMORROW, 1992-2006

The first woman to serve on the Illinois Supreme Court, Mary Ann McMorrow attained a number of singular accomplishments in her legal career. A lifelong resident of Chicago's Northwest Side, she was born on January 16, 1930, one of three children of meat wholesaler Roman Grohwin and his wife, Emily. The Polish-American Catholic family lived in a small house near Addison Street and Central Park Avenue, where her parents, young McMorrow remembered, stressed the value of education. "They wanted us all to go to college," she said. "Dad would draw up long columns of math figures and have us compete to see who would solve it fastest. Mom was a great admirer of Eleanor Roosevelt and wanted her daughters to be like her and change the world."[1528]

An accomplished pianist, she attended Immaculata High School and graduated from Rosary College (now Dominican University) in 1950. On the advice of her admiring mother, she enrolled in the Loyola University Chicago School of Law. Although the only woman in the 1953 graduating class, Mary Ann's male peers elected her class president and associate editor of the *Loyola Law Review*.[1529]

After admission to the Illinois bar, she worked for the Riordan & Linklater general practice law firm before joining the Cook County state's attorney's office in 1955, where she became the first woman to prosecute major felony cases. "I especially loved the criminal cases and the jury work. Every kind of crime, from murder to embezzlement, I did them all," she said. "When you try a case in criminal court especially, you get totally absorbed in it. You get really pumped. But you can't let that impair your fairness."[1530]

While a prosecutor she met gregarious Chicago Police lieutenant Emmett McMorrow. They married in 1962 and had one daughter. For several years, she practiced civil law from their home in the Edgebrook neighborhood, near her parents' home.

In 1976, with virtually no political experience, McMorrow ran as a Democrat for Cook County circuit judge. A shy person, she disliked mingling among strangers. "At one event," she said, "my husband dropped me off at the door while he parked the car. By the time he got back, I simply wanted to go home. I didn't know a soul in there. But he said, 'Come on, go in, I'll help you.' I had to force myself to do it."[1531] She won the election and was retained in 1982. Three years later, she was appointed to the First District Appellate Court and was elected to the position in 1986.

In the 1992 election to succeed Justice William G. Clark on the Illinois Supreme Court, McMorrow defeated seven Democratic primary candidates and Republican Appellate Justice Robert C. Buckley, becoming the first woman elected to the Supreme Court. In the 1995 case, *Charles v. Seigfried*, Justice McMorrow dissented from the majority opinion against "social host liability" for serving alcoholic beverages to minors. The case involved the estate of Lynn Sue Charles, killed in a drunk-driving accident, against defendant Alan Seigfried. McMorrow termed the no-liability decision for injury and death resulting from minors being allowed to drink to intoxication "an injustice and an outrage. . . . Adult social hosts must realize that there are legal ramifications, but civil and criminal, to allowing teenage drunk driving. Unless that lesson is taught and learned, we all will suffer the ugly and tragic consequences, whether physical, emotional, social and economic, that are inflicted when minors are permitted to drink and drive."[1532]

McMorrow wrote the opinion in the 1997 *Best v. Taylor Machine Works* upholding the circuit court judgment. Laclede Steel employee Vernon Best suffered injuries when a Taylor Machine Works forklift assembly collapsed as he was moving slabs of hot steel, igniting hydraulic fluid that engulfed him. He filed a product liability action against Taylor, the forklift seller, and the hydraulic liquid manufacturer. In the lengthy decision, McMorrow affirmed the circuit court's ruling as unconstitutional the 1995 law, which benefited defendants regarding bodily injury death, negligent injury, and product liability. The justices ruled that the law's $500,000 cap on noneconomic damages invaded the power of the judiciary, in violation of the state's separation of powers clause, and that the legislation discriminated against seriously injured plaintiffs in favor of those who caused the injuries.[1533]

In the 2002 *Happel v. Wal-Mart Stores, Inc.*, McMorrow wrote the opinion that improved drug safety for customers. Heidi Happel sued Wal-Mart after a pharmacist dispensed prescription medicine without informing her that her allergies could cause a negative reaction to the drug. The Court decision required pharmacists to warn customers of known possible side effects from prescription medications.[1534]

Unanimously elected to a three-year term as Chief Justice in May 2002, McMorrow succeeded retired Justice Moses W. Harrison II to become the first woman to head any of the three branches of Illinois government.[1535] At her September installation ceremony, McMorrow outlined an agenda that included legal aid to the poor, speedier child custody cases, elder law initiatives, increased support for young lawyers, and improved public perception of the court system. In addition, "We must always be mindful," McMorrow said, "that death penalty cases must be subjected to the most severe scrutiny possible." She advocated legislative changes to limit the cases in which defendants could be subject to the ultimate punishment. In 2000, she had written the *People v. Blue* opinion reversing the conviction and death penalty sentence of Murray Blue for the murder of a police officer. The justices remanded the case for retrial based on errors and conduct that "deprived defendant of his due process right to a fair trial." On remand, Blue was again convicted but sentenced to life imprisonment.[1536]

In November 2002, McMorrow was retained for a second ten-year Supreme Court term. Named 2003 Person of the Year by *Chicago Lawyer*, McMorrow told an interviewer that "being the first [woman Chief Justice] was never a goal of mine. . . . But I knew that once I was in that position, I had to do my absolute best because it affects every single woman who comes down the line after you."[1537]

During her legal career, McMorrow received numerous accolades, including the American Bar Association's Margaret Brent Women Lawyers of Achievement Award, Loyola University School of Law Alumni Association's Medal of Excellence, the John Marshall School of Law's Freedom Award, the Illinois State Bar Association's Fellows Award for Distinguished Service to Law and Society, and the Women's Bar Association Myra Bradwell Woman of Achievement Award.[1538]

At the time of her 2006 retirement from the Supreme Court, seventy-six-year-old McMorrow had written 225 majority opinions and 85 separate concurring and dissenting opinions. Chief Justice Robert R. Thomas credited her with having "shattered gender barriers that for too long kept the law an artificially insular profession. She fought every step of the way, carving for herself a path that that none before had taken but that many since have had the privilege to follow."[1539]

In retirement, McMorrow remained involved in the legal community, serving on the Loyola law school faculty and mentoring women on legal career paths.[1540] On February 23, 2013, at age eighty-three, McMorrow died at Northwestern Memorial Hospital from complications of a brief illness. Funeral Mass was celebrated at her Chicago parish, St. Mary of the Woods. "Through her courage, perseverance, wisdom and character," wrote Chief Justice Thomas L. Kilbride, "she was a role model for all lawyers, regardless of gender. Her legacy looms large over the Illinois legal system."[1541]

S. LOUIS RATHJE, 1999-2000

S. Louis Rathje was born in Geneva, Illinois, on November 1, 1939. He would continue the Rathje family tradition of attorneys: in the 1920s, his grandfather Sylvanus Louis Rathje had been a circuit judge, and in the 1950s, father Bertram E. Rathje served as chief judge of the DuPage County Circuit Court. As a boy, the young Rathje later recalled, his mother, Margaret Peironnet Rathje, often told him and his siblings, "'Don't do anything that will embarrass your dad.' And that pretty much kept us on the straight and narrow."[1542]

Rathje attended Holmes Grammar School, Longfellow Junior High School, and Wheaton Central High School. He earned a bachelor's degree from Wheaton College in 1961 and law degree from Northwestern Law School in 1964. Admitted to the Illinois bar, he practiced at the Wheaton firm of Rathje, Woodward, Dyer & Burt, and partnered in the firm from 1970 to 1992, specializing in municipal and administrative law, land use litigation, environmental law, and civil appeals.[1543]

Rathje's judicial career began in 1992. After practicing law for twenty-eight years, he won election as a Republican for circuit judge from the Eighteenth Judicial Circuit, and two years later was elected to the Appellate Court, hearing cases from thirteen northern Illinois counties and writing fifty-six majority and twelve dissenting appellate decisions. Upon appeal, the Illinois Supreme Court adopted two of those dissents as majority opinions.[1544]

Following the 1998 retirement of Supreme Court Justice John L. Nickels, the other justices chose Rathje to fill the Second Judicial District vacancy. He began the fourteen-month appointment on January 1, 1999. Among cases heard during his brief tenure, Rathje wrote the opinion in *In re Estate of Sofia Gebis* vacating the trial court's judgment. Rathje cited the state's Probate Act of 1975 in determining that a trial court in a guardianship proceeding lacked the jurisdiction to adjudicate Gebis's son's statutory custodial claim against her estate. "Following the ward's death," Rathje wrote, "a custodian possessing a valid statutory claim could decimate the guardianship estate before the decedent's estate is opened, leaving the funeral home, the administrator, and every other creditor of the decedent's estate without recourse. This clearly is not the result that the legislature intended."[1545]

Another 1999 case, *First Springfield Bank & Trust v. Galman et al.*, involved the death of a French foreign exchange student in Springfield. May Phillippart sustained fatal injuries when struck by a car as she crossed Lawrence Avenue at mid-block. Her estate sued the driver, Angela S. Galman, as well as a truck driver and his employer for a tanker truck parked in a no-parking lane at that time of day—obstructing Phillippart's view in attempting to cross the street. Rathje wrote the opinion reversing the Appellate Court, agreeing with the defendants that the illegally parked truck "was not a proximate cause" of Phillippart's injuries and that "parking was specifically permitted at other times of the day."[1546]

Rathje delivered the majority opinion in the 2000 capital case *People v. Madej*. The Cook County Circuit Court convicted Gregory Madej of murder, armed robbery, rape, and deviate sexual assault. A native of Poland, Madej and the country's Consul General appealed the verdict under international law, alleging that the trial court violated Madej's rights under the Vienna Convention on Consular Relations to contact a consular official from Poland. "The trial court clearly had jurisdiction of the parties and of the subject matter," Rathje wrote, "and it had the inherent power to make or enter the orders involved."[1547]

In 2000, Rathje ran in the Supreme Court primary campaign against two Republican challengers, Appellate Court Justice Robert R. Thomas and DuPage County Circuit Judge Bonnie M. Wheaton. The Illinois State Bar Association gave all three candidates "well-qualified" ratings. "I have authored majority opinions addressing direct capital appeals, post-conviction capital appeals, the constitutionality of both state and local legislation, and questions of criminal and civil procedure," Rathje told the DuPage County Bar Association. "My opinions, concurrences, and dissents speak for themselves, and I stand by them as a testament to my qualifications for the office of Illinois Supreme Court Justice."[1548] Despite his lengthy legal and judicial career as well as support from Illinois Attorney General Jim Ryan and State Senate President James "Pate" Phillips, Rathje lost to Thomas, who then won the general election.

Following his Supreme Court tenure, Rathje served as chairman of the DuPage Water Commission and formed the law firm Rathje & Associates in Wheaton. He is a member of the DuPage County Bar Association, Illinois and Wisconsin state bar associations, and the Illinois Judges Association. He attends Trinity Episcopal Church in Wheaton and often accompanies his wife, prominent Chicago-area cardiologist Dr. Maria Rosa Costanzo, on her extensive lecture travels.

Asked in 2006 for advice on how to become a judge, he responded, "Know the law and keep up with the latest developments in the law. Cultivate a few trusted people who are seasoned lawyers and/or judges whose advice you can trust. Be able to listen to people and respect them. Keep an open mind and be able to articulate, both orally and in writing, the reasons for your decisions." Among the Illinois Supreme Court justices he admired from his time on the high court, "I could count on Justice John Nickels, Moses Harrison and Jim Heiple. All good judges amongst many good judges that helped me on the judicial path. You cannot look good in a black robe without some help."[1549]

ROBERT R. THOMAS, 2000-PRESENT

New York native Robert R. Thomas was born in Rochester, the son of a French-born father who had been a professional soccer player and coach. "When other kids were playing Little League baseball, soccer was my first love," Thomas recalled years later. "I played soccer starting when I was about eight."[1550] Attending McQuaid Jesuit High School in Rochester, Thomas lettered in both football and soccer, then after graduation enrolled at the University of Notre Dame. By his sophomore year, he became the starting football place kicker and, in the 1973 national championship Sugar Bowl, kicked the winning field goal against Alabama. As a senior, he was named an Academic All-American.

Following his graduation from Notre Dame in 1974, Thomas played twelve seasons in the National Football League, ten of them with the Chicago Bears. In the 1977 season, Thomas kicked a twenty-eight-yard overtime field goal that sent the Bears to the playoffs for the first time in fourteen years, and he remains the fourth-leading scorer in Chicago Bears history. While still playing for the Bears, Thomas attended Loyola University School of Law, where he was often seen studying after practice and between games. He graduated and was admitted to the Illinois bar in 1981.

Thomas worked in private practice with several law firms: Bochte & Kuzniar in Elburn; Bochte, Kuzniar & Thomas in St. Charles; John P. Callahan, P.C. and Kasey & Krippner in Geneva; and Guerard, Kalina, Mucial, Ulrich & Varchetto in Wheaton. In 1988, he was elected circuit judge in the Eighteenth Judicial Circuit, which is comprised of DuPage County. In the jury law division for six years, Thomas presided over more than one hundred jury trials, and from 1989 to 1994 served as the acting Chief Judge. In 1994, Thomas won election to the Second District Illinois Appellate Court, serving for five years.

In 2000, following the retirement of Illinois Supreme Court Justice John Nickels, Thomas declared his candidacy for the Second Judicial District seat. In the three-way Republican race that included Justice S. Louis Rathje, who had filled the term of retired Justice Nickels, Thomas won the Supreme Court primary contest and then the general election. Justice Thomas was elected by his colleagues on the Supreme Court to serve as Chief Justice from 2005 to 2008, making him the first Chief Justice from DuPage County in the Court's nearly 200-year history. "Ours is a position of service, not of power," Thomas said at the time. "The decisions we render are not personal achievements. They are the law, and they belong to the people of Illinois."[1551]

Upon his installation as Chief Justice, Thomas acknowledged the path that had brought him there: "Having served in both the trial court and the appellate court, I will never lose sight of the fact that the decisions rendered by the Supreme Court represent a mere sliver of the work that occupies the Illinois courts. Every day, in courtrooms from Lake County to Alexander County, decisions are rendered that will never be published, will never make headlines, and will never be reviewed by the Illinois Supreme Court. But these decisions are important, nonetheless. For they, as much as any decision rendered by the Illinois Supreme Court, affect the lives of real people." Thomas then committed himself to "serving the cause of justice, to walking humbly, and to never losing sight of the tremendous privilege that it is to wear the judicial robe, and to serve the people of this State."

One of the major accomplishments during Thomas's tenure as Chief was the establishment of the Supreme Court Commission on Professionalism, an outgrowth of the Special Supreme Court Committee on Civility, which was formed in 2001. The Commission promotes principles of integrity and civility among all Illinois lawyers and judges. "You hear a lot about how the practice of law is different now than in days past when a lawyer's handshake meant something and a lawyer's word was his bond," Justice Thomas said. "That may be an oversimplification, but in this day and age with competition in the profession for dollars and clients, activities sometimes degenerate into a Rambo-style, win-at-all cost attitude by attorneys."

Also during Justice Thomas's tenure as Chief Justice, the Court gave special attention to the implementation of information technologies that advance the services and functions of the Illinois courts. Among the most visible improvements was the streaming of the Court's oral arguments in video and audio format on the Court's website. The arguments are posted on the website shortly after they are formally heard by the Supreme Court. Justice Thomas's tenure as Chief Justice also saw the Illinois Supreme Court implement for the very first time a program of mandatory continuing legal education for all active Illinois lawyers and judges.

In his time on the Illinois Supreme Court, Justice Thomas has authored numerous notable opinions, including *People v. Lerma* (2016),[1552] which held that expert testimony concerning the reliability of eyewitness identifications is appropriate in certain cases; *DeHart v. DeHart* (2013), which for the first time recognized the theory of equitable adoption in Illinois; and *Ryan v. The Board of Trustees of the General Assembly Retirement System* (2010), which held that, as a result of his multiple federal felony convictions, former Governor George H. Ryan had forfeited the pensions he earned while serving in the General Assembly and as lieutenant governor.

In *People ex rel. Madigan v. Snyder* (2005), the case involved the 2003 decision by Governor George H. Ryan to grant "blanket clemency" for all 167 death-row inmates, commuting their sentences to a maximum of life imprisonment. Illinois Attorney General Lisa Madigan sought a writ of mandamus ordering Department of Corrections Director Donald N. Snyder Jr. and two correctional facility wardens to ignore the governor's commutation order. In a unanimous decision, Justice Thomas wrote that Ryan's blanket clemency grant did not violate the constitutional principle of separation of powers. "The 1970 Illinois Constitution does not provide that the Governor's power to grant clemency is subject to the legislature's regulation of the application process," Thomas wrote, and thus, the power of executive clemency is "essentially unreviewable."[1553]

In 2006, a Kane County jury awarded Justice Thomas $7 million in damages for a series of defamatory newspaper columns authored by *Kane County Chronicle* columnist Bill Page. The case later settled for a reduced amount after Page and the newspaper issued a statement apologizing to Justice Thomas for "publishing statements that the jury found to be false and in relying on sources who, based on the jury verdict, provided information that was not true" about Justice Thomas.[1554]

Thomas won his retention election in 2010 with 81 percent. He was named DuPage County Bar Association's Lawyer of the Year in 2001. In 2005, the Illinois Judges Association honored him with their "Professionalism Award." He received Loyola

University's Distinguished Jurist Award in 2006, and was named "Judge of the Year" in 2008 by the Illinois Chapter of the American Board of Trial Advocates.

In 1999, the NCAA Honors Committee selected Justice Thomas for the prestigious NCAA Silver Anniversary award, which recognizes former student-athletes who have distinguished themselves since completing their college athletics career twenty-five years ago. In September 2012, he was inducted into the Chicagoland Sports Hall of Fame. Justice Thomas and his wife, Maggie, reside in Glen Ellyn, Illinois. They have three children and five grandchildren.

THOMAS R. FITZGERALD, 2000-2010

The first Illinois Chief Justice to preside over the impeachment trial of a sitting governor, Thomas R. Fitzgerald was born in Chicago on July 10, 1941, the son of a circuit court judge. Graduating from the South Side's Leo Catholic High School, he attended Loyola University Chicago before enlisting in the United States Navy. Following his tour of duty, Fitzgerald entered John Marshall Law School, where he helped found and served as associate editor of the school's law review. Graduating with honors, he was admitted to the Illinois bar in 1968, and then began his law career as a prosecutor in the office of the Cook County State's Attorney. He married Gayle A. Aubry, and they would become the parents of five children.

In 1976, Fitzgerald won election as the county's youngest circuit judge. Eleven years later, he became Supervising Judge of the high-volume Traffic Court. In that position, he worked on Operation Greylord—a four-year federal bribery and case-fixing investigation that resulted in nearly one hundred convictions of judges, attorneys, and Cook County court personnel. "The amazing thing about it is that people who were involved in it lost everything," Fitzgerald said. "They lost their liberty, they lost their money, they lost their freedom, they lost their father's good name—which I always think of as being the most valuable thing of all."[1555]

Two years later, he returned to the Criminal Division as Presiding Judge of both Cook County Criminal Court and Illinois's first statewide grand jury. There he created an evening Narcotics Court to both help drug addicts receive treatment and relieve jail overcrowding and assigned floating judges to ensure full use of courtrooms.[1556]

From 1986 to 1996, Fitzgerald taught law at John Marshall Law School and the Einstein Institute for Science, Health and the Courts. At Chicago-Kent College of Law, he served as assistant coordinator of the trial advocacy program. Fitzgerald also worked to improve the quality of justice in the trial of capital cases, chairing a Supreme Court committee in 1999 that sought to improve capital punishment proceedings. The group drafted landmark rules, including a requirement that death penalty cases be tried only by well-experienced, court-trained attorneys.[1557]

In 2000, as a First District Democratic candidate for the Illinois Supreme Court to fill the seat vacated by Justice Michael A. Bilandic, Fitzgerald sought both a Republican and a Democrat to co-chair the announcement of his campaign. Former Governor James R. Thompson became his Republican supporter and former Illinois Comptroller and State Senator Dawn Clark Netsch as his Democratic backer. "The two of us presented him to the world," Thompson recalled. "When you've got a judge who is widely regarded as fair and hardworking, they stand out when they have that appreciation from not only the legal community, but also from the political community."[1558]

Defeating appellate judges William Cousins Jr. and Morton Zwick and attorney Christine Curran in the primary campaign, Fitzgerald then won the general election. In the 2002 case, *Donaldson v. CIPS Co.,* Fitzgerald authored the toxic tort opinion affirming the judgment favoring the plaintiff. The parents of Zachary Donaldson and those of three other children sued Central Illinois Public Service Company, alleging that actions of omission in the cleanup of a former manufactured gas plant in Taylorville, Illinois, caused their children to develop neuroblastoma, a rare peripheral nervous system cancer. After a four-month trial, the Christian County Circuit Court jury returned a $3.2 million verdict against CIPS, and the Appellate Court affirmed the judgment. "Plaintiffs' experts in the instant case relied upon the only available source of information to form the basis of their conclusions," Fitzgerald wrote, "similar, yet not identical, scientific studies and theories. From these studies, plaintiffs' experts concluded that coal tar caused these plaintiffs' neuroblastomas. CIPS offers no evidence to suggest that this method, extrapolation, is not utilized or generally accepted among the scientific community. . . . We find that extrapolation is sufficiently established to have gained general acceptance in these limited circumstances."[1559]

Early in his tenure on the bench, he worked with Justice Rita B. Garman to adopt rules for expediting child custody cases through the legal system. He also helped improve the delivery of free legal services to veterans and the rehabilitation of accused offenders with mental health issues.[1560] In 2008, his colleagues unanimously chose Fitzgerald to succeed Robert R. Thomas as Chief Justice. "It will be a unique honor to be first amongst equals at such a gathering of people," Fitzgerald said at the time. "There are no kings here, there are only people trying to do their job as best they can and they need a lot of help to do it. I will look to my colleagues for that help."[1561] That same year, he received the prestigious John Paul Stevens Award, a Chicago Bar Association and Chicago Bar Foundation honor to Illinois attorneys and judges who demonstrate extraordinary integrity and service to the community throughout their careers.

In January 2009, Fitzgerald presided over a first-of-its-kind Illinois Senate impeachment trial of Governor Rod Blagojevich for political corruption. "With scant precedent to work with—save for the impeachment proceedings of former President Bill Clinton and an Illinois Supreme Court judge back in 1833," reported the *Chicago Daily Law Bulletin,* "any move Fitzgerald made was magnified."[1562] Fitzgerald did not allow Senate members to break up a list of offenses that House members had approved for Senate consideration, equating the list to a "grand jury bill of indictment that should not be altered, but approved or rejected in full." Blagojevich was impeached and removed from office in 2009, and later convicted and sentenced to federal prison.

In 2010, Fitzgerald wrote a strongly worded opinion in *Lebron v. Gottlieb Memorial Hospital,* striking down a state law that limited noneconomic damages for medical malpractice. At issue was the case of Abigaile Lebron, born in 2005 with numerous permanent injuries, including cerebral palsy and cognitive mental impairment. Her mother, Frances Lebron, filed a malpractice action in Cook County Circuit Court against the hospital, her physician, and a registered nurse who assisted in the delivery. Lebron challenged the Illinois law that placed limits on noneconomic damages, alleging that her infant "sustained disability, disfigurement, pain and suffering to the extent that damages for those injuries will greatly exceed the applicable limitations on noneconomic damages under Public Act 94—677." Justice Fitzgerald wrote that such limitations in medical malpractice actions "violates the separation of powers clause of the Illinois Constitution . . . by permitting the General Assembly to supplant the judiciary's authority in determining whether a remittitur is appropriate under the facts of the case."[1563]

During his Chief Justice tenure, Fitzgerald spearheaded initiatives to enhance judiciary performance, including a requirement that each of the state's trial judges participate in a confidential performance evaluation program. He also advocated in the Illinois General Assembly for court funding of probation services as a viable tool for rehabilitation. Fitzgerald won retention to a second ten-year term in 2010, but in September he announced his retirement from the Court, citing a medical diagnosis of Parkinson's disease and adding that he feared making decisions that would harm the court. "Right now," he said in a written statement, "I'm fully capable of discharging its duties. I don't know how much longer that will be true."[1564]

To his Supreme Court colleagues, Fitzgerald became more than a respected judge—a storyteller, golf partner, and confidante—"a kind and gentle spirit who always looks for the best in both people and circumstance," Justice Robert R. Thomas said.[1565] An avid White Sox fan for more than a half century, Fitzgerald helped establish the Nellie Fox Society, which successfully advocated for the 1959 American League Most Valuable Player's admission to the Baseball Hall of Fame. In May 2012, Fitzgerald threw the ceremonial first pitch at the White Sox's "Justice Thomas Fitzgerald Appreciation Day," having practiced for the occasion, he said, by playing catch with a former law clerk and throwing against a backstop at a park near his home.[1566]

Fitzgerald served terms as president of the Illinois Judges' Association, chair of the Illinois Supreme Court Special Committee on Capital Cases, member of the Governor's Task Force on Crime and Corrections, chairman of several committees of the Illinois Judicial Conference. He served on the Chicago Bar Association's Board of Managers and as chairman of the Chicago Bar Association's committees on Constitutional Law and Long-Range Planning.

Fitzgerald died at his LaGrange home from Parkinson's complications on November 1, 2015, at the age of seventy-four. His life was celebrated at a Funeral Mass at his parish, St. Francis Xavier Catholic Church. "Having joined the court shortly after his election in 2000, I had the privilege of serving with Justice Fitzgerald for a decade," Chief Justice Garman reflected upon his death. "He was a warm and caring person, and even when on the bench, his demeanor revealed his genuine concern about the people who appeared before him. Tom Fitzgerald was dedicated to serving the people of Illinois and to making the judicial system as fair, efficient, and accessible as it could possibly be."[1567]

THOMAS L. KILBRIDE, 2000-PRESENT

A native of LaSalle, Illinois, Thomas L. Kilbride was born in 1953. Graduating from Bishop McNamara High School in Kankakee, he attended St. Mary's College in Winona, Minnesota, leaving school during his sophomore year to help Cesar Chavez and farm workers in California. "Having done that work, I saw how critical lawyers were to the process," Kilbride said years later in explaining his decision to return to college, attend law school, and work as a legal aid attorney.[1568] He received his BA degree magna cum laude from St. Mary's College in 1978 and law degree from Antioch School of Law in Washington, D.C., in 1981.

Kilbride and his wife, Mary, would become the parents of three daughters. He practiced law in Rock Island for twenty years, first as a legal services attorney for the poor, then in civil and criminal practice. He was admitted to the United States District Court of Central Illinois and the United States Seventh Circuit Court of Appeals.

In the 2000 election to succeed James D. Heiple for the Illinois Supreme Court's Third Judicial District seat, Democrat Kilbride, who had never served as a circuit or appellate judge, defeated Republican Carl E. Hawkinson, 52 percent to 48 percent, and began his tenure as a justice.

In 2007, Kilbride wrote the unanimous opinion in *People v. O'Connell,* a case involving the defendant's motion for DNA testing. John O'Connell had waived a jury trial and pled guilty to first-degree murder, robbery, and other charges in the stabbing death of a store employee. Sentenced to life terms, he subsequently filed unsuccessful motions for reconsideration of the sentences. He then filed for DNA testing of blood found at the time of the crime on his clothing and a knife, citing in his motions section 116-3 of 1998 legislation that permitted such testing when "not available at the time" of his 1990 plea. The Cook County Circuit Court denied O'Connell's motion, but the Appellate Court reversed that decision. "Defendants who plead guilty may not avail themselves of section 116-3," Kilbride wrote in reversing the Appellate opinion. "Those defendants are a separate group who have not contested identity at trial.... We reiterate, a defendant who pleads guilty may not use section 116-3 as a means to request DNA testing."[1569]

In *People v. Beaman*, Justice Kilbride authored the opinion reversing Alan Beaman's conviction for murder because prosecution violated his right to due process. Beaman had been found guilty of murdering Jennifer Lockmiller, an Illinois State University student. The prosecution successfully argued that Beaman, as a jealous former boyfriend, had the motive and opportunity to commit the murder. Beaman filed a post-conviction petition because the state failed to disclose important information about "John Doe," another former boyfriend and potential suspect who used steroids and had been previously charged with domestic battery. The circuit court denied the petition, and the Illinois Appellate Court upheld the denial. In a unanimous decision, the Supreme Court reversed the judgment, vacated the conviction, and remanded the case back to the circuit court. Kilbride noted, "There is a reasonable probability that the result of the trial would have been different if petitioner had presented the evidence establishing Doe as an alternative suspect."[1570]

In 2010 Kilbride voted with the Court's Democratic majority in striking down *Lebron v. Gottlieb*, a highly controversial decision written by Justice Thomas Fitzgerald that removed monetary limitations in medical liability cases.[1571] Then in October, he succeeded Fitzgerald as Chief Justice, while facing an expensive battle to retain his Third District seat. The pro-business Illinois Civil Justice Committee, funded by the U.S. Chamber of Commerce and the American Tort Reform Association, led efforts to unseat Kilbride, primarily because of his vote in the *Lebron v. Gottlieb* medical malpractice case. "I think there are going to be a lot of forces against him," said Illinois Civil Justice Committee President Ed Murname.

With a $2.8 million campaign fund, Kilbride successfully countered the effort, deriding his opponents' "bald-faced lies" and distortions regarding his medical-malpractice opinion as well as other decisions that his critics termed anti-business. "I didn't write the [Lebron] opinion," Kilbride said. "I am one of four votes." He retained his Supreme Court seat, with a 66 percent tally. Many observers consider that judicial race as exemplifying an increasingly corrosive monetary influence. "I frankly don't know what can be done, given the landscape that exists," he later remarked. "Constitutionally, the framework of what's permissible under free speech, given that lay of the land . . . the door is wide open. And who can be against free speech?"[1572]

As Chief Justice, Kilbride earned a reputation for his efforts to modernize the Illinois judicial system technologically. He supported implementing statewide standards for the electronic filing of civil case documents, expanding the legal process to low-income citizens, and increasing funds for probation services. He credited the members of the Access to Justice Commission, a group he formed in 2012, for helping in those endeavors. "Access to justice obviously means different things to different people," Kilbride said in a 2013 *Chicago Daily Law Bulletin* interview, noting that the idea is the same, "Our courts are to be equal justice under the law for everyone."[1573]

Also during his Chief Justice tenure, the Supreme Court changed the citation system for Illinois courts, allowing citations to online opinions, rather than pages in a printed book. Without the expense of costly bound volumes, the Court predicted more than $500,000 in savings over several years. "The greatest cost savings from the implementation of technological advances," he explained, "will come from e-filing and the use of the electronic record as the court's official record. Soon, the supreme court will issue standards and principles for e-business, enabling the court to manage documents without the necessity of paper."[1574]

Although Illinois has allowed limited use of cameras in the Supreme and Appellate courts since 1983, Kilbride in 2012 announced a pilot program for permitting news cameras and electronic news recording in trial courts. Since then, many counties and circuits allow photo and video coverage of specified case categories. "As a practical matter, I don't think the public or media has a desire to see everything in every single courtroom," Kilbride said. "But," he added, "I think it's sold itself already . . . the judges themselves who've participated have helped inculcate a sort of mindset that this isn't so terrible."[1575] In 2016 the Supreme Court made the camera program permanent, allowing television and radio coverage in courtrooms throughout the state.[1576]

Kilbride's three-year Chief Justice tenure concluded in 2013, when he was succeeded by Justice Rita B. Garman. Kilbride continues to represent the Third Judicial District; his current term extends to 2020. "I'm very pleased and impressed with the job that the chief justice has done," Kirk C. Jenkins, an appellate attorney, said of Kilbride in 2013. "I think he's been a superb representative for the Illinois judiciary."[1577]

Kilbride is a past president of the Illinois Township Attorneys Association, charter member of the Illinois Pro Bono Center, and member of the Illinois State and Rock Island County Bar associations. He received an honorary law degree from The John Marshall Law School in 2002. His other honors include the Harriet Beecher Stowe Voice of Freedom Award, and the Chicago Bar Association gave him the John Paul Stevens Award.

RITA B. GARMAN, 2001-PRESENT

Rita Bell Garman was born in Aurora, Illinois, on November 19, 1943, the youngest of three children of Dr. Sheldon Bell and Ellen Bell. She grew up in Oswego, where Dr. Bell had a dental practice and Mrs. Bell, a homemaker, also served as his business manager. She recalls that her parents encouraged all three children equally and that her father, in particular, "saw absolutely no reason why his daughters couldn't achieve as much as his son."[1578]

Rita Bell was valedictorian of her high school class and attended the University of Illinois. Although she was interested in a career in law, her undergraduate advisor steered her away from enrolling in a joint degree program in law and commerce, suggesting that as a young woman, she might not be admitted to the law school portion of the program. Thus, she majored in economics and graduated in 1965 with highest honors. While at the University of Illinois, she met Gill Garman of Urbana.[1579]

Both attended the University of Iowa College of Law, where she was one of only eight women in the entering class. She recalls some professors being overtly hostile to women law students, remarking that they were taking up spaces that belonged to men who would need to support their families, or accusing the women of attending law school only to meet a future husband. Rita, however, had already met her future husband. She and Gill married after their second year of law school.[1580]

They graduated in 1968 and passed the Illinois bar examination. When they were sworn in on the same day, their photograph appeared in the *Illinois Bar Journal* with the caption "Mr. and Mrs. Gill Garman."[1581] Dr. Bell was perhaps even more perturbed than his daughter that she was not identified as "Rita Bell Garman." The couple moved to Danville, Illinois, where Gill began the private practice of law, but jobs for a young woman lawyer were scarce in 1968. She was told by one firm that "no one wants to talk to a woman. No business person is going to come in here and share business issues with a woman. We don't know how we could possibly use you in this firm."[1582]

An opportunity did arise when the attorney who had been running the local legal aid office retired and she was offered a temporary position at the Vermilion County Legal Aid Society—just to "keep the doors open." "That's how I learned to practice law," she recalls. "The clients of Legal Aid didn't care that I was young, and they certainly didn't care that I was a woman. They were happy to see me."[1583] A year later, she was hired to handle family law cases in the State's Attorney's Office, and, in 1973, she joined the firm of Sebat, Swanson, Banks, Lessen & Garman.

When an associate judge position in Vermilion County became open in 1974, she was encouraged by several judges and colleagues to apply. When she was appointed associate judge, she became the first female judge in the Fifth Judicial Circuit—the first time, but not the last, that she would break new ground. After twelve years as an associate judge, she was elected Circuit Judge in 1986, again being the first woman to hold the position. She remained on the circuit court until 1995 and was Presiding Judge in Vermilion County for most of her tenure. Upon the retirement of Justice Carl Lund, Judge Rita Garman was assigned to the Fourth District Appellate Court and was then elected in 1996 to her own term. She was the Fourth District's first female justice.[1584]

When Justice Garman was appointed to the Illinois Supreme Court in 2001 to fill the vacancy created by the retirement of Justice Ben Miller, she was not the first woman in the room. Justice MaryAnn McMorrow had joined the court in 1992. Garman was elected to a ten-year term on the court in 2002 and retained for a second term in 2012. She served as Chief Justice from 2013 to 2016, becoming Illinois's second woman Chief Justice after Justice McMorrow. Following her installation ceremony, the new Chief Justice remarked: "The courts are where the people meet the promise of this nation. The four goals that I have set out—civility and professionalism, prompt decision-making, increased use of technology, and judicial education—all serve to make our courts more able to meet that promise."[1585]

Garman has served at every level of the Illinois judiciary and is the first chief justice to have done so: associate judge, circuit judge, presiding circuit judge, appellate justice, presiding appellate justice, supreme court justice, and chief justice. At present, she is the second longest serving judge in Illinois and the longest serving female judge.

Shortly after her arrival at the Supreme Court, she proposed the establishment of a Special Committee on Child Custody Issues to give priority to cases involving the custody, adoption, abuse and neglect of children, and the rights of parents. As a result of the committee's efforts, the Court has also adopted new procedural rules to expedite appellate review of such cases. While running for retention in 2012, she remarked that "Early in my tenure on the Supreme Court, I successfully urged the court to study and address the handling of juvenile cases in our court system. . . . We cannot afford to allow a child to grow up while the courts deliberate these issues."[1586]

During her tenure as Chief Justice, the Court established the Illinois Judicial College to elevate the professional education opportunities for Illinois judges and staff members of the court system; implemented mandatory electronic filing of court documents to reduce costs and increase efficiency of the court system; completed a pilot project on the use of media cameras

Opera baritone Nathan Gunn, great-grandson of Supreme Court Justice Walter Gunn, and his wife, Julie, visit the Supreme Court in 2014 at its rededication after a year-long restoration. (Image courtesy of Illinois Supreme Court Historic Preservation Commission)

in courtrooms and extended the program throughout the state; and created uniform standards and a certification process for problem-solving courts to bring uniformity, accountability, and administrative oversights to drug courts, mental health courts, and veterans courts throughout the state.

Also during her tenure as Chief Justice, Justice Garman and her colleagues twice invited the governor and the entire state legislature to attend special evening sessions of oral arguments. For the first time in over a century, the Supreme Court held proceedings in the evening to enable members of the other two branches of state government to, in her words, have "a window into the work that the Court performs for the people we all serve."

Of the many opinions she has authored, two milestone cases—one civil and one criminal—illustrate Justice Garman's scholarly, analytical, and disciplined approach to judicial decision making. The Illinois Supreme Court initially affirmed the conviction of Roy Caballes for cannabis trafficking, with Justice Garman and two other justices dissenting. During a routine traffic stop for speeding, a dog sniff of the vehicle had revealed the presence of marijuana. Although the sniff did not prolong the duration of the stop, the majority held that the canine sniff was not justified and that it impermissibly broadened the scope of the traffic stop, turning it into a drug investigation and violating the Fourth Amendment to the United States Constitution.[1587] The State of Illinois appealed to the United States Supreme Court, which held that the dog sniff was not a "search" and, thus, did not violate the Fourth Amendment.[1588]

When the case returned to the Illinois Supreme Court in 2006, Justice Garman wrote the opinion in *People v. Caballes*, which answered the additional question—even if the sniff was permitted by the U.S. Constitution, did it nevertheless violate the Illinois Constitution of 1970? The Court ruled that when a provision in the state constitution is virtually identical to the corresponding provision in the federal constitution, the two will be interpreted in "lockstep" unless the debates and the committee reports of the state constitutional convention indicate that the particular provision of our constitution was intended to be construed differently.

Thus, the dog sniff was not a prohibited search and the defendant's state constitutional rights were not violated. His conviction was, therefore, affirmed.[1589]

In 2009, Justice Garman authored the Illinois Supreme Court's unanimous opinion in *In re Estate of Feinberg*, a case that received national press coverage. Dr. Feinberg, a dentist, had created an estate plan that would have benefited his grandchildren if they married within the Jewish faith but would have excluded them if they married outside the faith. In litigation among the surviving family members, the circuit court found the restriction unenforceable on the basis that it violated public policy by discriminating on the basis of religion, and the appellate court affirmed. The Supreme Court reversed the judgment and found the so-called "Jewish clause" enforceable because an individual has the freedom to dispose of his property as he chooses.[1590]

Justice Garman is a member of the Vermilion County Bar Association, the Illinois State Bar Association, the Iowa State Bar Association, the Lincoln-Douglas Inn of Court, and the Illinois Judges Association. A champion of legal aid services and a strong advocate of pro bono service, she has received numerous awards including the Illinois Judges Association Lifetime Achievement Award in 2007, the Person of the Year Award from *Chicago Lawyer* magazine in 2013, and the Myra Bradwell Award from the Women's Bar Association of Illinois in 2016. Most notably, in March 2017, the Vermilion County Board voted unanimously to rename the county courthouse the "Rita B. Garman Vermilion County Courthouse" in her honor, and in April 2017, the Champaign County Bar Association named her a Pillar of the Profession.

Rita and Gill Garman had two children, Andrew and Sara, and four grandchildren. He passed away in 2014 after a long struggle with kidney disease.[1591]

PHILIP J. RARICK, 2002-2004

Philip J. Rarick was born in Troy, Illinois, on November 10, 1940. As a young boy and into adult life, he helped tend his family's farm and weeded crops on nearby farms. "Working outside and working with my hands came naturally to me," he told an interviewer. "I was fortunate that I escaped the coal mines," he added, "All of the men in my family were coal miners. I'm the first male to graduate from high school in my family."[1592]

Rarick attended Southern Illinois University Edwardsville, graduating in 1962, while working as a millwright helper at Granite City Steel to pay his tuition. "It was hot, dirty and dangerous work, and I loved every minute of it." He married Janet N. Arnovitz in 1963, and they became the parents of a son, also named Philip.

Earning a law degree from St. Louis University in 1966, he began his career with an East St. Louis law firm, primarily defending personal injury clients. Soon he opened a practice in Collinsville, became the city attorney, the Collinsville and Jarvis townships attorney, and then Madison County assistant state's attorney. In 1972, he became a partner in Harrison, Taylor & Rarick, which the next year became Harrison, Rarick & Cadigan.[1593]

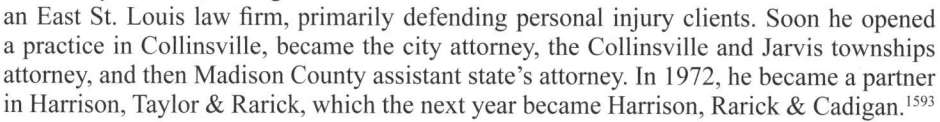

In 1975, Rarick was appointed Third Judicial Circuit associate judge and in 1982 was elected a Madison County circuit judge, serving through 1987. During his tenure, he presided over criminal cases that included the high-profile trial of James Lippert for the murder of his wife. Rarick sentenced the convicted man to a forty-year prison term. In the trial of Randy Brackett, prosecutors contended that his beating and raping of an elderly woman caused her death. After the guilty verdict, Rarick imposed a sixty-year sentence on Brackett. "You listen to each side. It's more than being an umpire," Rarick explained of the cases he heard. "It's based on law and evidence."[1594]

Rarick spent thirteen years with the Third Judicial Circuit in Madison County before winning election to the Fifth District Appellate Court in 1988. He was retained in office ten years later. For fourteen years, he traveled between the Mount Vernon Appellate courthouse and his home in Troy. In addition, from 1992 through 1999, he was a member of the Illinois Courts Commission and an alternate member from 1999 to 2000, hearing cases of judicial misconduct. He served on the executive committee of the Illinois Judicial Conference from 1987 to 2002 and as chairman of the Conference's Complex Litigation Study Committee from 1988 through 2001.

In September 2002, the Supreme Court appointed Rarick to replace retired Fifth District Justice Moses Harrison. The two men had been law partners from 1972 to 1975 and served together as judges in both trial and appeals courts.[1595] Rarick said that he was "greatly honored" to follow in Harrison's footsteps. "It's big shoes to fill, and I just don't mean size 11 or 12. He is a great man and a great jurist." Fifth District Appellate Judge

Terrence J. Hopkins called Justice Rarick "the most easy-going judge in the state," and added, "He's as common as can be. He has an intellectual capacity that sometimes could be underestimated."[1596]

Only a few months into his appointment, the sixty-two-year-old Rarick suffered a stroke. He quickly returned to work on court business while also undergoing extensive physical rehabilitation. Spending five months of the year in Springfield, Rarick usually prepared for cases at his Fairview Heights office. "I have to finish reading everything in these five boxes before I go to Springfield," he told a reporter in May 2004, a few days before the court started its two-week session. "He's so down to earth, and he's shown such courage dealing with the setback from the stroke," said attorney Mary Nalefsky, Rarick's administrative assistant.

Among the cases during his brief tenure, Rarick wrote the majority opinion in the 2002 *People v. Stehman.* Employee Michael Stehman had returned to Genoa Pizza in Sandwich, Illinois, after making deliveries in his own vehicle. As he walked toward the restaurant, a uniformed police officer approached him with an arrest warrant for failure to appear in court. The officer handcuffed Stehman and put him in the squad car. After searching and finding drugs in Stehman's vehicle, the officer arrested him on a criminal offense. Both the trial and appellate courts granted the defendant's motion to suppress evidence and quash the arrest. "The defendant had voluntarily exited his automobile and begun walking away before the officer initiated contact with him in order to arrest him on a warrant for an unrelated matter," Justice Rarick wrote in affirming the appellate judgment. "The more general criteria justifying a warrantless search incident to a lawful arrest . . . were not satisfied because the officer did not have any reason to fear for his safety and there was no possibility of destruction of evidence."[1597]

In the 2003 case *People v. Belk,* sixteen-year-old defendant John Belk had stolen a van and, in a high-speed police chase, crashed the van into a car, killing its two occupants. In the Cook County Circuit Court, Belk was convicted of felony murder and sentenced to life imprisonment. Justick Rarick affirmed the appellate court reversal of the circuit court conviction. "Aggravated possession of a stolen motor vehicle is not a forcible felony for purposes of the felony-murder statute," he wrote, "because the evidence does not support an inference that Belk contemplated that the use of force or violence against an individual might be involved in attempting to elude police."[1598]

Rarick's medical condition would cause him to not seek a full term at the expiration of his appointed term in December 2004. In the meantime, he continued to perform Court duties but explained that "it is not medically advisable to do both the court's business and be out on the road four or five nights a week campaigning in a 37-county area."[1599]

"Being able to serve on the Supreme Court was [the] greatest honor of my whole life," Rarick reflected on leaving the bench. "I am disappointed the appointment was cut short. If it weren't for my health, I would have run and I believe I would have won."[1600] In retirement, Rarick became an of counsel attorney in Granite City.

LLOYD A. KARMEIER, 2004-PRESENT

A southern Illinois native, Lloyd A. Karmeier was born January 12, 1940, in rural Washington County. He was raised on a small farm near Covington, the site of the first court session convened by a Justice of the Illinois Supreme Court following Illinois's admission into the Union in 1818.[1601] The third of five children, Karmeier attended a one-room grade school and went on to graduate as valedictorian of his class at Okawville Community High School in 1958. He received his BS degree in 1962 and his JD degree in 1964, both from the University of Illinois. While at the University of Illinois, Karmeier met his wife, Mary, who was also a student there, on a blind date. The couple married in 1965 and ultimately became the parents of two daughters.

Following admission to the bar, Karmeier became a judicial law clerk for Illinois Supreme Court Justice Byron O. House, who impressed on him the need for "clear and straightforward opinions" and "basically just to get it right." Karmeier served House from 1964 to 1968, and joined Hohlt, House, DeMoss & Johnson, the Nashville, Illinois, law firm founded by Justice House's father. In 1968, Karmeier was elected state's attorney of Washington County on the Republican ticket. When his term as state's attorney ended, he clerked for former U.S. District Court Judge James L. Foreman from 1972 to 1973. Karmeier then engaged in the private practice of law full-time with the Hohlt, House law firm until 1986, when a vacancy arose on the local circuit bench.

He was elected resident circuit judge of Washington County and took office in December of 1986. To avoid potential conflicts of interest involving his former law firm, Karmeier initially spent the majority of his time on the bench in St. Clair County, a much larger county in the same circuit. Voters retained Karmeier as circuit judge in 1992 and then again in 1998.

As Karmeier's third term as a circuit judge neared its conclusion, he decided to seek higher office and entered the race for Justice of the Supreme Court, Fifth District. The position had become vacant when the incumbent, then-Chief Justice Moses W. Harrison, decided to retire before the expiration of his term, and Philip J. Rarick, the former appellate court justice appointed to fill the vacancy, decided for health reasons not to seek a ten-year term.

Since adoption of the 1970 Constitution, the members of the Supreme Court elected from the Fifth District—geographically the largest of the five districts and one which encompasses both agricultural and industrial, rural and urban areas—had all run for the office as Democrats. Karmeier filed as a Republican. The resulting campaign, which pitted him against an appellate judge who was simultaneously seeking retention for his seat on the appellate court, proved to be a contentious one. Fueled by the debate over "tort reform" and concerns that Illinois's legal climate was causing doctors to leave the state, jeopardizing the availability of adequate health care for its residents, the election was considered to be the most expensive judicial race in Illinois history up until that time. Karmeier ultimately won by a sizeable margin, 55 percent to 45 percent, with the losing candidate also failing in his bid to be retained on the appellate court.[1602]

Wearing the same judicial robe used by his former boss and mentor Justice Byron House, Karmeier was sworn in as a member of the Supreme Court on December 6, 2004. Upon taking his seat on the bench, Karmeier noted that he would bring to the Court what his family taught him. "It taught us about responsibility to love and respect one another. Doing your job and doing it well without expecting any accolades."[1603]

Once on the Supreme Court, Karmeier assumed numerous administrative responsibilities in addition to his normal judicial duties. He continued his involvement with the Supreme Court Committee on Jury Instructions in Criminal Cases, but in a different capacity: Court liaison. He also took over as the Court's liaison to two of its most important administrative entities, the Attorney Registration and Disciplinary Commission (ARDC) and the Minimum Continuing Legal Education Board (MCLE), as well serving as liaison for the Court's New Judges Seminar. Effective October 26, 2013, the Court appointed Karmeier to the Courts Commission, an independent body established under the Illinois Constitution of 1970 to adjudicate complaints that a judge has engaged in misconduct or is no longer able to perform the duties of office. Shortly after joining the Commission, Karmeier was selected by its members to be its chairperson.

Since joining the Court, Karmeier has participated in the disposition of more than 1,000 cases on the merits following oral argument. In explaining his approach to deciding cases, Karmeier has written that when he first ran for the Supreme Court, he "made only one promise. It was a promise to the People of Illinois and the voters of the Fifth Judicial District that if elected, [he] would decide every case free of outside influence and based solely on the law and the facts."[1604]

Karmeier has thus far authored nearly 200 opinions, special concurrences, and dissents. The importance of judicial restraint and deference to the legislature are common themes in his writing. In a dissent that attracted national attention, Karmeier rejected the majority's decision invalidating a statute enacted by the General Assembly in response to the health care crisis in *Lebron v. Gottlieb Memorial Hospital*.[1605] The statute would have placed certain limits (caps) on the noneconomic damages that could be awarded in medical malpractice cases. In a similar vein is *People v. White,* where, this time writing for the majority, Karmeier wrote, "[W]e believe it appropriate to caution courts of review—particularly when constitutional issues are involved—that they are not free rangers riding about the legal landscape looking for law to make. Judicial restraint is a principle of review that the justices of the [United States] Supreme Court strive to observe."[1606]

When, however, the legislature has transgressed its constitutional bounds, Karmeier has spoken forcefully to invalidate its action. *In re Pension Reform Litigation* is perhaps the most notable example. Writing for a unanimous court, Karmeier held there that the General Assembly's attempt to reduce retirement annuity benefits for members of the state-funded pension systems violated the Pension Protection Clause of the Illinois Constitution. Rejecting the argument that the state's dire financial condition justified suspension of constitutional protections, Karmeier stated that the "financial challenges facing state and local governments in Illinois are well known and significant. In ruling as we have today, we do not mean to minimize the gravity of the State's problems or the magnitude of the difficulty facing our elected representatives. It is our obligation, however, just as it is theirs, to ensure that the law is followed."[1607]

Cases relating to the electoral process are also among Karmeier's more notable decisions. These include *Jackson-Hicks v. East St. Louis Bd. of Election Commissioners,* which declared that nominating petitions filed by an incumbent mayor should have been stricken because they did not contain the minimum number of valid signatures required by law. Karmeier rejected the theory that "substantial compliance" was sufficient to meet the law's numerical requirement.[1608] Also significant was his dissent in *Hooker v. Illinois State Board of Elections*; Karmeier argued that the voters of Illinois should have been permitted to consider a proposed ballot initiative to amend the system by which our state's legislative districts are drawn. The majority held that the proposed initiative failed to meet the requirements of the 1970 Constitution, which expressly authorizes the use of ballot initiatives to amend the current redistricting scheme set forth in Article IV of the Constitution.[1609]

Karmeier ran for retention in 2014, and the period leading up to the November election was largely uneventful. The ISBA screening committee recommended that Karmeier be retained. He received endorsements from such groups as the Illinois Education Association and the Illinois Fraternal Order of Police. Major regional and statewide newspapers urged voters to retain him.[1610] Just before the election, however, a handful of attorneys from Chicago, Missouri, California, Mississippi, and South Carolina expended more than $2 million on a last-minute media blitz opposing Karmeier's retention.[1611] With one exception, the lawyers or their law firms were counsel of record in past or pending cases before the Supreme Court. Their efforts proved unsuccessful. Karmeier received more than 60 percent of the votes cast, exceeding the threshold needed to continue in office.[1612]

In 2016, Karmeier succeeded Rita Garman as Chief Justice. On becoming Chief, he urged the legal community to be mindful of its members' shared responsibility to defend the integrity and independence of the courts. "Governments should be run by elected representatives," Karmeier recently observed. "Judges, even elected ones, represent no one. Their sole allegiance is to the law."[1613]

ANNE M. BURKE, 2006-PRESENT

Successor to the first woman to serve on the Illinois Supreme Court, Anne Marie McGlone was born on Chicago's South Side on February 3, 1944, the youngest of four children of George and Helen McGlone. As a student at St. Rita Grammar School, she struggled with dyslexia, a disorder that affects one's ability to learn. "I think the reason I always gravitated toward athletics and the arts was because of my dyslexia," she recalled. After a nun at the Catholic all-female Maria High School steered her toward pursuing a physical education degree, she enrolled in a physical education program at George Williams College in Hyde Park with a scholarship from the Chicago Park District. "It was 1962," Burke said, "and that college provided most of the physical education teachers and social workers for the YMCA throughout the country. I was a Park kid, so everyone knew me and my capabilities."[1614]

At the end of her freshman year, when the college relocated to a western suburb, she began working for the Chicago Park District, teaching physical education to mentally and physically disabled children and young adults. Witnessing the achievements of her students, she developed a proposal for a city-wide competition. With funding from the Kennedy Foundation, Burke organized the "Chicago Special Olympics." More than 1,000 special-needs children from the United States and Canada participated in the Chicago Special Olympics on July 20, 1968. The program eventually became the International Special Olympics, the world's largest sports organization benefiting children and adults with disabilities. "I never envisioned the impact that the first Chicago Special Olympics would have," she recalled. "My quest was simply to get as many children to the park as I could."[1615]

Marrying attorney Edward M. Burke in 1968, the couple are the parents of five children. Her husband became the Fourteenth Ward Alderman in 1969, an influential Democrat on the Chicago City Council. She resumed her education, graduating from DePaul University in 1976. Four years later, she enrolled in the Chicago-Kent College of Law. Graduating in 1983 at the age of forty, she obtained her law license and opened a neighborhood law practice focusing on cases of child neglect, abuse, delinquency, and custody. "There were other practitioners in the same building. We spent a great deal of time discussing the law and sharing ideas," she recalled. "Each of us had our own style, although we were each committed to the legal professions."[1616]

Burke was admitted to practice in the Northern District of Illinois federal court in 1983, and the United States Court of Appeals for the Seventh Circuit in 1985. In 1987, Governor James Thompson appointed Burke as the first woman to serve on the Illinois Court of Claims, and Governor Jim Edgar reappointed her in 1991. Three years later, she resigned to become special counsel for the state's Child Welfare Services. "She is very compassionate, and she's also very determined," Edgar said. "That's a pretty good combination for anyone in public service."[1617]

In 1995, Burke was appointed judge on the First District Appellate Court, and the following year won election to the seat as a Democrat, with no opposition.[1618] During her eleven-year tenure, she cited one case as particularly significant, a 2003 ruling in which the Court granted an evidentiary hearing to a Chicago man convicted of a double murder even though DNA tests had not proved his innocence.

In addition to her work on the Appellate Court, Burke led a national lay watchdog panel established by Roman Catholic bishops at the height of the clergy abuse crisis in 2002. At the end of her two-year tenure, she criticized the "mischievers at work" within the U.S. Conference of Catholic Bishops for attempting to squelch two years of "freedom and accountability." Burke "has shown a lot of growth and courage, especially speaking out recently about the backsliding of bishops across the country and their reneging on their reforms," said David Clohessy, national director of Survivors Network of those Abused by Priests, or SNAP.[1619]

When Justice Mary Ann McMorrow announced her retirement from the Supreme Court in 2006, the justices selected Burke to fill the vacancy. In November 2008, Burke won election to a ten-year term. In January 2009, she administered the oath of office to Illinois Governor Patrick Quinn, who replaced Governor Rod Blagojevich, and in 2012, administered the oath again after Quinn's election to a full term.

In the 2011 *People v. Almore* case, Burke wrote the opinion reversing the First District Appellate Court in a case of involuntary manslaughter of a "family or household" member, as defined in the state's Code of Criminal Procedure of 1963. Defendant James Almore had been convicted in the death of two-year-old Ethan Hampton, the son of Almore's girlfriend, Lovia Hampton. She and Ethan had been staying with the defendant at his temporary Chicago residence for the previous five days. The Circuit Court imposed an extended-term sentence of twelve years' imprisonment, based on its finding that the victim and defendant were "household or family members."

Almore appealed the extended sentence on grounds that the victim was not a family or household member. The Appellate Court vacated the sentence and remanded the case to trial court for resentencing. In delivering the unanimous Supreme Court judgment, Burke wrote, "The five days prior to Ethan's death was not the only time that Lovia, Ethan and defendant shared a common dwelling. . . . Lovia, Ethan, and defendant were members of each other's 'household' by virtue of the fact that they shared a common dwelling, even though the 'dwelling' was sometimes the Hampton family home and sometimes the residence defendant shared with his relatives." The justices concluded that the evidence supported the trial court's finding "within the meaning" of the Code of Criminal Procedure. "Accordingly, we reverse the appellate court judgment and reinstate defendant's 12-year extended sentence."[1620]

In 2013 case *Hope Clinic for Women, Ltd. v. Flores*, Burke wrote the opinion that the state's 1995 Parental Notice of Abortion Act requires physicians to notify an underage female's parents forty-eight hours before a planned abortion. The Hope Clinic had filed suit in Cook County Circuit Court seeking to enjoin enforcement of the Act. Defendants in the suit included Manuel Flores, Acting Secretary of the Illinois Department of Financial and Professional Regulation. In delivering the unanimous ruling, Burke cited several U.S. Supreme Court cases from across the country allowing for parent notification. "The [Illinois] Act is crafted narrowly to achieve its aim of promoting the minors' best interests through parental consultation. Accordingly, we find the Act is reasonable and, therefore, does not violate our state constitutional guarantee of privacy."[1621]

Burke was the lone dissenter in *People v. Martinez*. Esteban Martinez had been indicted in the Kane County Circuit Court for aggravated battery against Avery Binion and

Demarco Scott. At trial, Binion and Scott failed to appear as witnesses, and the circuit court judge empaneled the jury. Without the key witnesses, the prosecution refused to participate in the trial or present evidence. As a result, the court entered a not guilty judgment. The state appealed to the appellate court, which reversed the judgment and ordered a new trial. Martinez appealed to the Illinois Supreme Court that he was being subjected to double jeopardy after having been found not guilty. The Court affirmed the case with Burke dissenting, arguing that since "the jury was impaneled and sworn, and jeopardy attached, the State may not reprosecute defendant for the same offenses. Accordingly, the State was not permitted to appeal the trial court's judgment."[1622] Martinez appealed the case to the United States Supreme Court, which, in a per curiam decision, agreed with Burke's dissent.[1623]

In June 2014, Burke presided over two gay wedding ceremonies, the first member of the Supreme Court to marry same-sex couples since all Illinois counties began issuing such marriage licenses earlier in the month. "It's what the law permits," she explained. "Needless to say, I think there are people who would probably step back from this. I don't feel I should or would."[1624] Burke is a member of the American, Illinois State, Chicago, and Women's Bar associations, and the Illinois Judges' Association. In 2010 the Illinois Bar Foundation honored Burke with its annual Distinguished Award for Excellence.

MARY JANE THEIS, 2010-PRESENT

Illinois Supreme Court Justice Mary Jane Theis succeeded retired Justice Thomas R. Fitzgerald in 2010, becoming the fourth woman to serve on the high court. The only child of Cook County Circuit Court Judge Kenneth R. Wendt and his wife, Eleanore, Mary Jane was born in Chicago on February 27, 1949. "When I was in high school," she remembered, "I would go to his courtroom whenever I had an opportunity and watch the proceedings. It was a time when the law was changing very rapidly. He heard a lot of narcotics cases, and it was a time when issues about the Fourth Amendment were not only on the front pages of the newspapers, but also were important cases in the United States Supreme Court, and it seemed so compelling and exciting."[1625]

After graduation from Loyola University in 1971, Theis pursued a law degree from the University of San Francisco. She later said that an internship at the Marin County, California, public defender's office helped shaped her career. Returning to Chicago, she served as an assistant Cook County public defender until 1983, when she began her judicial career as a Cook County associate judge and in 1988 won election as a circuit judge. In 1993, she was assigned to the First District Appellate Court and was elected to the position in 1994, serving for seventeen years.[1626] Marrying criminal defense attorney John T. Theis, they became the parents of a son and a daughter.

In 2010, the Supreme Court appointed Mary Jane Theis to fill the Fitzgerald vacancy, effective October 26, 2010, through December 3, 2012. "I am humbled by the confidence the Illinois Supreme Court has placed in me," she told the Illinois State Bar Association at the time. "The fact is I love being a judge very much. I love the intellectual part of it. But most importantly, I have an opportunity to shape the law that affects the lives of the People of Illinois."[1627]

In February 2012, Theis wrote the opinion in *People v. Wrice*, regarding the 1983 conviction of Stanley Wrice for the abduction, rape, and deviate sexual assault of a Chicago woman.[1628] Wrice's attorneys claimed that after his arrest he had been severely beaten into a confession by two Chicago detectives, both of whom worked under Jon Burge, a police lieutenant who was promoted to commander before being suspended in 1991 and fired in 1993 for systematically torturing black suspects. At the trial, prosecutors introduced Wrice's alleged confession, and, although no physical evidence linked him to the crime, he was convicted by a jury and spent the next thirty-one years in prison.

In 2010, following special-prosecutor investigations of beatings by Chicago police, the Illinois Appellate Court ordered a hearing on Wrice's torture claim. Prosecutors appealed to the Supreme Court. Theis wrote the unanimous opinion, which held that "use of a defendant's physically coerced confession as substantive evidence of guilt is never harmless error. The defendant has satisfied the cause-and-prejudice test for successive postconviction petitions." The ensuing hearing culminated in Wrice's exoneration. At the time of his release from prison, the cases of twenty-five prisoners convicted in part from coerced confessions obtained by Burge and his subordinates were pending review by the Circuit Court, resulting from the Supreme Court decision.[1629]

In March 2012, Theis prevailed in a four-candidate Democratic primary race, aided by an endorsement from the Cook County Democratic Party. In the November election, she easily defeated Cook County circuit judge James G. Riley by about 50 percentage points, earning a full ten-year Supreme Court term. She remarked at the time that the seven justices share a healthy respect and ignore partisan divide. "There are those who like to pigeonhole people and say we're elected as Democrats and Republicans and, therefore, we must think a certain way," Theis said. "But if you really look at our cases, that's not what's

The Supreme Court Building, 2010 (Image courtesy of Illinois Supreme Court Historic Preservation Commission)

happening at all. I'm proud of that non-partisan sense in our court."[1630]

In 2014, Theis dissented from the Court's opinion in *People v. Patterson*, which addressed the constitutionality of the automatic transfer provision of the Juvenile Court Act.[1631] The majority upheld that statute, but Theis believed that it violated the Eighth Amendment of the United States Constitution and the proportionate penalties clause of the Illinois Constitution. At the end of her strong and lengthy argument, Theis concluded that "[o]ur state, home of the country's first juvenile court and once a leader in juvenile justice reform, should not be a place where we boast of locking up juveniles and throwing away the key. Illinois should be a place where youth matters, and we work to tailor punishment to fit the offense and the offender, as required by our federal and state constitutions. For juveniles, that starts with abolishing automatic transfers." Theis's words proved prescient. The following year, the General Assembly amended the statute, abolishing automatic transfers and restoring trial court discretion in all transfer rulings.

In 2016, Theis delivered the unanimous 5–0 ruling in *Mary J. Jones et al. v. Municipal Employees' Annuity and Benefit Fund of Chicago,* which struck down a 2014 state law intended to overhaul two of the city's financially struggling pension systems.[1632] The legislation, supported by Chicago Mayor Rahm Emanuel, scaled back retirement benefits, required city workers and laborers to increase their retirement contributions in phases over five years, and lowered annual cost-of-living increases for retired workers. In court filings, attorneys for the City contended that the pension systems, not the city, had responsibility for paying out benefits to retirees, and that the municipal fund had just 37 percent of the amount needed to pay future retirement benefits while the fund for laborers held slightly more than 50 percent of the needed money. "The Illinois Constitution mandates that members of the Funds have 'a legally enforceable right to receive the benefits they have been promised'—not merely to receive whatever happens to remain in the Funds," Theis wrote. "The General Assembly and the City have been on notice since the ratification of the 1970 Constitution that the benefits of membership must be paid in full."

In her seventeen years on the Appellate Court, Justice Theis served as a Presiding Judge. She was Committee Chair of both the Committee on Judicial Education and the Committee on Judicial Conduct of the Illinois Judicial Conference, and a member of the Supreme Court Rules Committee. She is currently the Supreme Court liaison to the Illinois Judicial College. Justice Theis was president of the Appellate Lawyers Association and the Illinois Judges Association, as well as president and founding member of the Illinois Judges Foundation. She has been a member of the Board of Governors of the Illinois State Bar Association and the Board of Managers of the Chicago Bar Association and is a member of the Women's Bar Association of Illinois.

Justice Theis has taught at numerous judicial education programs, as well as conferences and seminars for the ISBA and CBA, and at Loyola University School of Law, Northwestern University School of Law, and the John Marshall Law School. She has received various awards, including the Lifetime Achievement Award from the Illinois Judges Association, Catholic Lawyer of the Year from the Catholic Lawyers Guild, Celtic Lawyer of the Year from the Celtic Lawyers Society of Chicago, the Mary Heftel Hooten Award from the WBAI, and the Access to Justice Award from the ISBA. Justice Theis is the recipient of the American Constitution Society Legal Legend honor from the Chicago Lawyer Chapter.

P. SCOTT NEVILLE JR., 2018–PRESENT

Justice P. Scott Neville Jr. became the second African American to ascend to the Illinois Supreme Court, succeeding Justice Charles E. Freeman. He was born in Chicago and is the son of attorney P. Scott Neville Sr. and Alice Dempsey Neville. Neville was inspired to become a lawyer because his father and his father's brother were both attorneys. His grandmother, Eva Dempsey, was among those who instilled discipline and a strong work ethic in him, and he developed habits, like waking early in the morning to complete unfinished schoolwork, playing sports in the afternoon, and studying in the evening. Although Neville enjoyed playing baseball and basketball, he quit his college basketball team after playing only one game because his parents insisted that he excel in academics so he could become a lawyer. Neville's father insisted that he become a great orator, but his mother preferred that he become a great writer.

Neville received his bachelor's degree in history from Culver Stockton College in Canton, Missouri, in 1970, and he earned his law degree at Washington University School of Law in 1973. On May 21, 1974, he received his license to practice law and began his career as a law clerk for Appellate Court Justice Glenn T. Johnson, who was the second African American to sit on the appellate court in Illinois. Neville observed that Johnson was a mentor who "led by example, which is what great men do. He was a judge who was very influential as counselor and confidant, always willing to offer guidance."[1633]

In 1977, Neville began working for Howard, Mann & Slaughter, where he tried his first case with another mentor, George Howard. He began his own law firm in 1981, P. Scott Neville Jr & Associates, which merged in 1990 to become Howse, Howse, Neville & Gray. He argued cases in the United States Court of Appeals for the Seventh Circuit and in the Illinois Appellate Courts, and he practiced law and handled important cases with another mentor, Justice R. Eugene Pincham. One of those important cases, *Barrett v. Daley*, a class action, challenged the Chicago City Council's 1990 remap of Chicago's fifty wards and culminated with a change in the city's map. Former President Barack Obama was also a member of the legal team representing the plaintiffs.

Neville was elected to the Cook County Circuit Court in 2000 and served there until 2004, when he was appointed to the Illinois Appellate Court, First District. In 2012, he ran for election to retain his seat on the Illinois Appellate Court, defeating two other candidates in the Democratic primary. During his campaign, he explained that the moral arc of the universe bends toward justice, and he urged voters to support him because he would be fair, impartial, and a "strict constructionist, which means nothing more than applying the same rules in all cases."[1634] He was unopposed in the general election.

During Justice Neville's tenure on the appellate court, he wrote several significant and noteworthy opinions and more than twenty dissents. In *People v. Sanchez*, he authored an opinion overturning the murder conviction of Jesus Sanchez in the Cook County Circuit Court. Sanchez had been found guilty of murdering Rafael Orozco, in what appeared to be a gang-retaliation murder in 2013. At the time of the shooting, Sanchez was eighteen years old, and after being arrested illegally and after eleven hours of interrogation, he confessed and stated that he fired the gun accidentally. Despite strong evidence that Sanchez was not the perpetrator, the jury found him guilty, and Sanchez was sentenced to forty-five years in prison. He appealed the conviction. Justice Neville wrote that "the prosecution did not present sufficient evidence to sustain the conviction" since no one saw Sanchez with a gun and no one saw Sanchez near the spot from which the shot came.[1635]

Justice Neville also authored the opinion in *Ellis v. AAR Parts Trading, Inc.*, an appeal that resolved important questions arising from two lawsuits seeking recovery for wrongful death and survival act claims on behalf of 113 plaintiffs who were killed when Air Philippines Flight 541 crashed in the Philippines in April 2000. Deciding an issue of first impression in Illinois, the opinion held that defendants are not precluded from filing successive motions to dismiss based on the doctrine of *forum non conveniens*, where an amended complaint includes new factual allegations, theories of recovery, or parties that were not presented in the prior pleading or includes additional case law that had not been decided when the earlier motion was filed. The opinion further held that the circuit court of Cook County did not abuse its discretion in denying defendants' *forum non conveniens* motions because the balance of the private and public interest factors did not strongly favor transfer of the case to the Philippines.[1636]

Another significant case was *Frigo v. Silver Cross Hospital & Medical Center*, which reviewed the defendant hospital's challenge to a jury verdict in excess of $7 million in a medical malpractice action. The opinion held that the claim of negligent credentialing asserted in the amended complaint related back to the filing of the original complaint because it arose from the same transaction or occurrence as that asserted in the initial pleading. In addition, the opinion articulated for the first time in Illinois the elements of a negligent credentialing claim based on a hospital's independent, managerial duty to assume responsibility for the care of its patients. The opinion also rejected the hospital's arguments that the Medical Studies Act and the Hospital Licensing Act barred plaintiff's negligent credentialing claim and that the jury was not properly instructed regarding the hospital's liability for plaintiff's negligent medical treatment.[1637]

Finally, Justice Neville authored a noteworthy dissent in *People v. Aguilar*. He was the only appellate court justice (thirteen other justices reviewed the gun statute) on the Illinois Appellate Court, First District, to find that the statute criminalizing the carrying of operable firearms outside the home was unconstitutional because it violated the Second Amendment. Justice Neville opined that the gun statute defeated the core right protected by the second amendment—the right to use firearms for self-defense in public places. Justice Neville concluded that under *District of Columbia v. Heller* the statute sweeps with breadth disproportionate to its legitimate purpose of reducing gun violence and, therefore, was unconstitutional on its face. Justice Neville's 2011 dissent is significant because, in 2013, the Illinois Supreme Court ultimately reached the same conclusion and declared a section of the gun statute unconstitutional.[1638]

On May 17, 2018, the Illinois Supreme Court appointed Justice Neville to complete the unexpired term of Justice Charles E. Freeman, who retired from the Court.[1639] Justice Neville took the oath of office on June 15, 2018, and began his tenure on the bench during the September 2018 term. In addition to serving as an instructor and judge in the University of Chicago Law School's advance trial practice course for third-year students, he was also a guest lecturer at Loyola University Law School. Justice Neville cofounded the Alliance of Bar Associations, a diverse group of bar associations evaluating lawyers and judges for judicial vacancies, and is also a life member of the National Bar Association, a member of the Illinois State Bar Association, and a member of the Cook County Bar Association, serving as its president from 1997 to 1998. He also served as chairperson of the Illinois Judicial Council, and for more than twenty-five years has helped fund Cook County Bar Association and Illinois Judicial Council scholarships for law students.

Justice Neville is married to Sharon J. Neville, and they have two stepdaughters.

NOTES

1. "Joel Childress and Joseph Philips Families," *Rutherford County [Tennessee] Historical Society Publication No. 9* (Summer 1977), p. 23; Court Minutes Book C (1808–1810), 3 July 1809, p. 142, Rutherford County Archives, Murfreesboro, Tennessee.
2. Norman W. Caldwell, "Fort Massac: Since 1805," *Journal of the Illinois State Historical Society* 44 (1951), pp. 56–59.
3. John M. Scott, *Supreme Court of Illinois, 1818, Its First Judges and Lawyers* (Bloomington, IL: John M. Scott, 1896), p. 63; Alexander Davidson and Bernard Stuvé, *A Complete History of Illinois From 1673 to 1873* (Springfield: Illinois Journal Co., 1874), p. 300; Newton Bateman and Paul Selby, eds., *Historical Encyclopedia of Illinois* (Chicago: Munsell, 1900), p. 203.
4. Joseph Philips to Robert Purdy, 24 September 1817, Rutherford County Deed Record M, pp. 348–49, Rutherford County Office Building, Murfreesboro, Tennessee.
5. John M. Palmer, ed., *Bench and Bar of Illinois; Historical and Reminiscent*, 2 vols. (Chicago: Lewis Pub. Co., 1899), Vol. 1, p. 13; John Reynolds, *My Own Times, Embracing also the History of My Life* (Chicago: Fergus Printing Co.,1879), p. 158.
6. Issue Docket Book, December 1819 term, pp. 191–94, RS 901.002, Illinois State Archives, Springfield, Illinois. The five cases were *Coleen and Claypool v. Figgins*, 1 Ill. (1 Breese) 19 (1819); *Smith for use of Johnson v. Bridges*, 1 Ill. (1 Breese) 18 (1819); *Taylor v. Sprinkle*, 1 Ill. (1 Breese) 17 (1819); *Whiteside et al. v. People*, 1 Ill. (1 Breese) 21 (1819); and *Chipps v. Yancey*, 1 Ill. (1 Breese) 19 (1819).
7. Issue Docket Book, July 1820 term, pp. 197–204; December 1820 term, pp. 205–13.
8. Palmer, *Bench and Bar of Illinois,* Vol. 1, p. 13.
9. Those cases are reported in 1 Ill. (1 Breese) 17–36.
10. Scott, *Supreme Court of Illinois*, pp. 65–66.
11. *Coleen and Claypool v. Figgins*, 1 Ill. (1 Breese) 19 (1819).
12. N. Dwight Harris, *The History of Negro Servitude in Illinois and of the Slavery Agitation in that State, 1719–1864* (Chicago: A.C. McClurg and Co., 1904), p. 31; Theodore Calvin Pease, *The Story of Illinois* (Chicago: A.C. McClurg and Co., 1925), pp. 74–76.
13. "Joel Childress and Joseph Philips Families," p. 24; Carlton C. Sims, ed., *A History of Rutherford County* (Murfreesboro, TN: Carlton Sims, 1947), p. 75.
14. Davidson and Stuvé, *Complete History of Illinois*, p. 300; Bateman and Selby, *Historical Encyclopedia*, p. 423.
15. Tennessee State Marriages, Davidson County, TN, p. 301, Tennessee State Library and Archives, Nashville, Tennessee.
16. "Joel Childress and Joseph Philips Families," p. 35.
17. Rutherford County Minute Book X, p. 300; Rutherford County Minute Book Z, pp. 11, 115, 410; Rutherford County Minute Book AA, p. 234; all in Rutherford County Archives, Murfreesboro, Tennessee.
18. "Joel Childress and Joseph Philips Families," pp. 25–6.
19. Rutherford County Minute Book CC, p. 385; Rutherford County Record Book 19, pp. 78, 186; both in Rutherford County Archives, Murfreesboro, Tennessee.
20. Scott, *Supreme Court of Illinois*, p.74; Pease, *Story of Illinois,* p. 264.
21. *Illinois Biographical Dictionary* (New York: Somerset Pub., 1993), p. 296; Reynolds, *My Own Times*, pp. 13–14.
22. Reynolds, *My Own Times*, p. 64; Palmer, *Bench and Bar of Illinois,* Vol. 2, p. 1094.
23. Reynolds, *My Own Times*, p. 93; Jessie McHarry, "John Reynolds," *Journal of the Illinois State Historical Society,* 6 (1913), pp. 31–32.
24. James E. Davis, *Frontier Illinois* (Bloomington: Indiana University Press, 1998), pp. 155–56.
25. Scott, *Supreme Court of Illinois,* pp. 119–20.
26. McHarry, "John Reynolds," p. 29.
27. Reynolds, *My Own Times*, p. 135.
28. Frederic B. Crossley, *Courts and Lawyers of Illinois,* 3 vols. (Chicago: American Historical Society, 1916), Vol. 1, p. 163.
29. *Everett v. Morrison*, 1 Ill. (Breese) 79 (1823).
30. Robert P. Howard, *Mostly Good and Competent Men; Illinois Governors, 1818–1988* (Springfield: Illinois Issues, 1988), p. 50; *Coles v. County of Madison*, 1 Ill. (Breese) 154 (1826).
31. *Edwards v. Beaird*, 1 Ill. (Breese) 70 (1823).
32. Reynolds, *My Own Times,* p. 153.
33. Thomas Ford, *History of Illinois, From its Commencement as a State in 1818 to 1847* (Chicago: S.C. Griggs and Co., 1854), p. 33.

34. Palmer, *Bench and Bar of Illinois*, Vol. 1, p. 18.
35. Ford, *History of Illinois*, p. 69; David W. Lusk, *Eighty Years of Illinois: Politics and Politicians* (Springfield, IL: H. W. Rokker, 1889), p. 6; Bateman and Selby, *Historical Encyclopedia*, p. 449.
36. Paul E. Stroble Jr., *High on the Okaw's Western Bank: Vandalia, Illinois, 1819–39* (Urbana: University of Illinois Press, 1992), p. 98.
37. Theodore Calvin Pease, *The Frontier State, 1818–1848* (Chicago: A.C. McClurg, 1922), p. 172.
38. Stroble, *High on the Okaw's Western Bank*, p. 121.
39. Howard, *Mostly Good and Competent Men*, p. 52.
40. Reynolds, *My Own Times*, pp. 321–22.
41. *Illinois Biographical Dictionary*, p. 296.
42. John Reynolds to Abraham Lincoln, 28 December 1858, Robert Todd Lincoln Collection of Abraham Lincoln Papers, Library of Congress, Washington, DC.
43. Howard, *Mostly Good and Competent Men*, p. 53.
44. Crossley, *Courts and Lawyers of Illinois*, Vol. 1, p. 184; *San Francisco Cemetery Records, 1848–1863* (Daughters of the American Revolution, Tamalpais Chapter, 1938), found at www.sfgenealogy.com/sf/sfcem.htm; Daniel W. Stowell, et al., eds., *The Papers of Abraham Lincoln: Legal Documents and Cases*, 4 vols. (Charlottesville: University of Virginia Press, 2008) Vol. 4, p. 337.
45. Palmer, *Bench and Bar of Illinois*, Vol. 2, p. 855; Scott, *Supreme Court of Illinois*, pp. 77–78.
46. Scott, *Supreme Court of Illinois*, p. 80.
47. Jesse W. Weik, *The Real Lincoln, A Portrait* (Boston: Houghton Mifflin, 1922), p. 62. Browne is similarly described in Usher F. Linder, *Reminiscences of the Early Bench and Bar of Illinois* (Chicago: Chicago Legal News Co., 1879), p. 73.
48. John Dean Caton, *Early Bench and Bar of Illinois* (Chicago: Chicago Legal News Co., 1893), p. 174.
49. Douglas L. Wilson and Rodney O. Davis, eds., *Herndon's Informants; Letters, Interviews, and Statements about Abraham Lincoln* (Urbana: University of Illinois Press, 1998), 391; Martha L. Benner and Cullom Davis et al., eds., *The Law Practice of Abraham Lincoln: Complete Documentary Edition*, 2d edition (Springfield: Illinois Historic Preservation Agency, 2009), http://www.lawpracticeofabrahamlincoln.org, hereafter cited as *LPAL*.
50. Weik, *Real Lincoln*, p. 62; Wilson and Davis, *Herndon's Informants*, p. 665.
51. Bateman and Selby, *Historical Encyclopedia*, p. 63; Crossley, *Courts and Lawyers of Illinois*, Vol. 1, p. 185.
52. Bryon C. Andreasen, *Defending Judge Browne: A Case Study in the Legal, Legislative, and Political Workings on Abraham Lincoln's Illinois* (Springfield: Illinois Supreme Court Historic Preservation Commission, 2013); *Sangamo Journal* (Springfield, IL), 6 January 1843; *LPAL*; Scott, *Supreme Court of Illinois*, p. 81; Bateman and Selby, *Historical Encyclopedia*, p. 63.
53. *Nichols v. Ruckells*, 4 Ill. (3 Scam.) 298 (1841); Susan Krause and Daniel W. Stowell, *Judging Lincoln; The Bench in Lincoln's Illinois,* (2002, rev. ed., Springfield: Illinois Historic Preservation Agency, 2008), p. 10.
54. *People ex rel. Harris et al. v. Browne*, 8 Ill. (3 Gilm.) 87 (1846).
55. Crossley, *Courts and Lawyers of Illinois*, Vol. 1, p. 185.
56. Scott, *Supreme Court of Illinois*, pp. 87, 98, 99.
57. *San Francisco Cemetery Records*.
58. Scott, *Supreme Court of Illinois*, p. 14; Ford, *History of Illinois*, p. 14.
59. Palmer, *Bench and Bar of Illinois*, Vol. 1, p. 20.
60. *Illinois Senate Journal 1818*, pp. 18–19.
61. Edwards County Circuit Court Record A, p. 6, Albion, Illinois.
62. Solon J. Buck, *Illinois in 1818* (Springfield: Illinois Centennial Commission, 1917), p. 305.
63. Ford, *History of Illinois*, p. 14.
64. Scott, *Supreme Court of Illinois*, pp. 27–28, 33–34. The 1848 Illinois Constitution provided for an elected judiciary.
65. Sara John English, "William Wilson, Pioneer Judge in Illinois," *Journal of the Illinois State Historical Society*, 31 (1938), p. 222.
66. Palmer, *Bench and Bar of Illinois*, Vol. 1, p. 21.
67. English, "William Wilson," p. 223.
68. Pease, *The Frontier State,* p. 35.
69. Bateman and Selby, *Historical Encyclopedia*, p. 595; Ford, *History of Illinois*, p. 212.
70. *Coles v. County of Madison*, 1 Ill. (Breese) 154 (1826); B. D. Monroe, "Life and Services of William Wilson, Chief Justice of the Illinois Supreme Court," *Journal of the Illinois State Historical Society,* 11 (1918), p. 393.

71. *Field v. People ex rel. McClernand*, 3 Ill. (2 Scam.) 79 (1839); Scott, *Supreme Court of Illinois*, pp. 39–42; English, "William Wilson," pp. 221–24; Pease, *The Frontier State*, p. 278.
72. *Field v. People ex rel. McClernand*, 3 Ill. (2 Scam.) 79 (1839).
73. Howard, *Mostly Good and Competent Men*, pp. 74–75.
74. Harris, *History of Negro Servitude in Illinois*, pp. 112, 118; *Jarrot v. Jarrot*, 7 Ill. (2 Gilm.) 1 (1845); *In the Matter of Jane, A Woman of Color*, 5 *Western Law Journal* 202; Mark E. Steiner, *An Honest Calling: The Law Practice of Abraham Lincoln* (DeKalb: Northern Illinois University Press, 2006), pp. 103–36.
75. Crossley, *Courts and Lawyers of Illinois*, Vol. 1, p. 232.
76. The name was changed to Illiopolis in 1867. *Illiopolis, Historic Geographical Center, 1856–2006* (Illiopolis, IL: n.p., 2006), pp. 12–13.
77. Joseph Wallace, *Past and Present of the City of Springfield and Sangamon County, Illinois* (Chicago: S. J. Clarke, 1904), p. 1304.
78. Palmer, *Bench and Bar of Illinois*, Vol. 1, pp. 22, 126; English, "William Wilson," p. 222.
79. Scott, *Supreme Court of Illinois*, p. 134.
80. William G. Livingstone, "The Thomas Reynolds Confusion," *Journal of the Illinois State Historical Society*, 54 (1961), pp. 423–25. Some historians have confused this Thomas Reynolds with the brother of Illinois Governor and Supreme Court Justice John Reynolds.
81. Palmer, *Bench and Bar of Illinois*, Vol. 2, p. 1094.
82. Livingstone, "The Thomas Reynolds Confusion," p. 424.
83. *Gill v. Caldwell*, 1 Ill. (Breese) 53 (1822).
84. Ford, *A History of Illinois*, pp. 32–33.
85. Reynolds, *My Own Times*, p. 160.
86. Floyd Calvin Shoemaker, *Missouri and Missourians*, Vol. 1 (Chicago: Lewis Pub. Co., 1943), pp. 422–23.
87. Perry McCandless, *History of Missouri, Vol. II, 1820–1860* (Columbia: University of Missouri Press, 1972), p. 124.
88. Robert Sobel and John Raimo, eds., *Biographical Directory of the Governors of the United States, 1789–1978*, 4 vols. (Westport, CT: Meckler Books, 1978), Vol. 2, pp. 841–42.
89. Palmer, *Bench and Bar of Illinois*, Vol. 1, pp. 13–14.
90. Livingstone, "The Thomas Reynolds Confusion," pp. 424–25.
91. James E. Babb, "The Supreme Court of Illinois," *The Green Bag* 3 (1891), p. 226.
92. www.worldconnect.rootsweb.ancestry.com (database for Shinn, Healey, Berger, Willons and Allied families).
93. Franklin William Scott, *Newspapers and Periodicals of Illinois, 1814–1879*, Collections of the Illinois State Historical Library, VI, (Springfield: Illinois State Historical Library, 1910), p. 166; Bateman and Selby, *Historical Encyclopedia*, p. 489.
94. Howard, *Mostly Good and Competent Men*, p. 35.
95. Ford, *History of Illinois*, p. 37; Reynolds, *My Own Times*, p. 175.
96. Crossley, *Courts and Lawyers of Illinois*, Vol. 1, pp. 174–75.
97. Ford, *History of Illinois*, p. 113.
98. Krause and Stowell, *Judging Lincoln*, p. 54; Crossley, *Courts and Lawyers of Illinois*, Vol. 1, p. 175; Bateman and Selby, *Historical Encyclopedia*, p. 489.
99. Harris, *History of Negro Servitude in Illinois*, p. 121.
100. Pease, *The Frontier State*, p. 378; *Boon v. Juliet*, 2 Ill. (1 Scam.) 258 (1836).
101. Harris, *History of Negro Servitude in Illinois*, pp. 104–05.
102. *Field v. People ex rel. McClernand*, 3 Ill. (2 Scam.) 79 (1839).
103. Pease, *The Frontier State*, p. 282.
104. Ford, *History of Illinois*, p. 150; Scott, *Supreme Court of Illinois*, p. 288.
105. *Illinois State Register* (Springfield), 23 May 1845, p. 3.
106. William Coffin, *Life and Times of Hon. Samuel D. Lockwood* (Chicago: Knight & Leonard, 1889), p. 13.
107. Michael J. Howlett, *Keepers of the Seal: A History of the Secretaries of State of Illinois* (Springfield: State of Illinois, 1977), p. 29; Krause and Stowell, *Judging Lincoln*, pp. 22–23.
108. Palmer, *Bench and Bar of Illinois*, Vol. 1, pp. 22–23.
109. Crossley, *Courts and Lawyers of Illinois*, Vol. 1, p. 209; Ford, *History of Illinois*, pp. 28–29.
110. Quoted in *Jacksonville Journal-Courier*, Sept. 10, 2001.
111. Crossley, *Courts and Lawyers of Illinois*, Vol. 1, p. 209; Ford, *History of Illinois*, p. 33.
112. Linder, *Reminiscences of the Early Bench and Bar of Illinois*, p. 264.
113. Stroble, *High on the Okaw's Western Bank*, p. 101.
114. Harris, *History of Negro Servitude in Illinois*, p. 100.
115. *People ex rel. Ewing v. Forquer*, 1 Ill. (1 Breese) 104 (1825); *Field v. People ex rel. McClernand*, 3 Ill. (2 Scam.) 79 (1839).

116. *Klein et al. v. Mather*, 7 Ill. (2 Gilm.) 317 (1845).
117. *Anderson v. Ryan*, 8 Ill. (3 Gilm.) 583 (1846).
118. Arthur Charles Cole, ed., *The Constitutional Debates of 1847* (Springfield: Illinois State Historical Library, 1919), p. 763.
119. Crossley, *Courts and Lawyers of Illinois*, Vol. 1, p. 208.
120. Babb, "The Supreme Court of Illinois," p. 226.
121. Bateman and Selby, *Historical Encyclopedia of Illinois*, pp. 341–42.
122. Krause and Stowell, *Judging Lincoln*, p. 37.
123. *Portrait and Biographical Album of Sangamon County, Illinois* (Chicago: Chapman Bros., 1891), p. 633.
124. *United States Biographical Dictionary and Portrait Gallery of Eminent and Self-Made Men, Illinois Volume* (Chicago: American Biographical Pub. Co., 1883), p. 775; Bateman and Selby, *Historical Encyclopedia of Illinois*, p. 528; Daniel W. Stowell, *Samuel H. Treat; Prairie Justice* (Springfield: Illinois Historic Preservation Agency, 2005), p. 4.
125. Robert W. Johannsen, *Stephen A. Douglas* (New York: Oxford University Press, 1973), p. 100.
126. Harris, *History of Negro Servitude in Illinois*, pp. 109–10.
127. Stowell, *The Papers of Abraham Lincoln*, Vol. 4, p. 382; David Herbert Donald, *Lincoln* (New York: Simon & Schuster, 1995), p. 146.
128. *McAtee v. Enyart*, 13 Ill. 242 (1852); Stowell, *Samuel H. Treat*, pp. 20–21.
129. Stowell, *The Papers of Abraham Lincoln*, Vol. 2, pp. 106–130.
130. *McAtee v. Enyart*, 13 Ill. 242 (1852).
131. Wilson and Davis, *Herndon's Informants*, pp. 725–26.
132. Crossley, *Courts and Lawyers of Illinois*, p. 329.
133. Linder, *Reminiscences of the Early Bench and Bar of Illinois*, p. 388; Palmer, *Bench and Bar of Illinois*, Vol. 1, p. 35.
134. Stowell, *Samuel H. Treat*, p. 13.
135. Arthur Charles Cole, *The Era of the Civil War, 1848–1870* (Urbana: University of Illinois Press, 1987), pp. 308–09.
136. Palmer, *Bench and Bar of Illinois*, pp. 34–35; Krause and Stowell, *Judging Lincoln*, p. 66.
137. Bateman and Selby, *Historical Encyclopedia of Illinois*, p. 168; Robert P. Howard, *Illinois; A History of the Prairie State* (Grand Rapids, MI: Eerdmans, 1972), p. 227; *Illinois Biographical Dictionary*, p. 62; Howard, *Mostly Good and Competent Men*, p. 84.
138. *Illinois Biographical Dictionary*, 153.
139. Ford, *History of Illinois*, pp. xix, xxvi.
140. John W. McNulty, "Sidney Breese, the Illinois Circuit Judge, 1835–1841," *Journal of the Illinois State Historical Society*, 62 (1969), p. 177.
141. Howard, *Mostly Good and Competent Men*, p. 84.
142. *Rogers v. Hall*, 4 Ill. (3 Scam.) 5 (1841).
143. Ford, *History of Illinois*, p. xix; Howard, *Mostly Good and Competent Men*, p. 79.
144. Pease, *The Frontier State, 1818–1848*, p. 352.
145. Linder, *Reminiscences of the Early Bench and Bar of Illinois*, p. 106.
146. Pease, *The Story of Illinois*, p. 128.
147. *Illinois Daily Journal* (Springfield), 4 November 1850, p. 3.
148. Howard, *Mostly Good and Competent Men*, p. 87; Bateman and Selby, *Historical Encyclopedia of Illinois*, p. 168.
149. *Chicago Tribune*, 29 June 1878, p. 2; Linder, *Reminiscences of the Early Bench and Bar of Illinois*, p. 141.
150. *Illinois Biographical Dictionary*, p. 62; John W. McNulty, "Sidney Breese; His Early Career in Law and Politics," *Journal of the Illinois State Historical Society*, 61 (1968), p. 164.
151. Lusk, *Eighty Years of Illinois*, p. 269; Scott, *Supreme Court of Illinois*, p. 328.
152. Scott, *Supreme Court of Illinois*, p. 329.
153. Stroble, *High on the Okaw's Western Bank*, p. 18; Howard, *Illinois, A History of the Prairie State*, p. 120.
154. McNulty, "Sidney Breese; His Early Career in Law and Politics," p. 168.
155. Ibid., 168–69.
156. Ibid.
157. Scott, *Supreme Court of Illinois*, p. 165.
158. McNulty, "Sidney Breese; His Early Career in Law and Politics," p. 175.
159. The full title of the volume is *Reports of Cases at Common Law and in Chancery, Argued and Determined in the Supreme Court of the State of Illinois, from Its First Organization in 1819, to the End of the December Term 1830;* an appendix includes 1831 cases. 1 Ill. (1 Breese); McNulty, "Sidney Breese; His Early Career in Law and Politics," p. 177.

160. Under the Act of 1807, contracts of service could not pass to an heir but only to legatees or legal representatives. The defendant failed to meet that requirement. McNulty, "Sidney Breese; His Early Career in Law and Politics," pp. 178–79; *Phoebe, a woman of color v. Jay*, 1 Ill. (1 Breese) 268 (1828).
161. McNulty, "Sidney Breese, the Illinois Circuit Judge, p. 172.
162. Palmer, *Bench and Bar of Illinois*, Vol. 1, p. 34.
163. *Field v. People ex rel. McClernand*, 3 Ill. (2 Scam.) 79 (1839).
164. Pease, *The Frontier State*, p. 250.
165. Palmer, *Bench and Bar of Illinois*, Vol. 1, p. 34; Kenney and Hartley, *An Uncertain Tradition*, p. 27.
166. Scott, *Supreme Court of Illinois*, p. 340.
167. Lusk, *Eighty Years of Illinois*, pp. 266–68.
168. Scott, *Supreme Court of Illinois*, p. 334.
169. Howard, *History of Illinois*, p. 364; *Munn v. People of the State of Illinois*, 69 Ill. 80 (1873); *Munn v. People of the State of Illinois*, 94 U.S. 113 (1876).
170. Cole, *Era of the Civil War*, p. 410.
171. Scott, *Supreme Court of Illinois*, p. 342.
172. *Chicago Tribune*, 29 June 1878; *Carlyle Constitution and Union*, 4 July 1878, p. 2.
173. *Chicago Tribune*, 27 October 1886, p. 7.
174. Stowell, *Papers of Abraham Lincoln*, Vol. 4, p. 375.
175. *Chicago Tribune*, 27 October 1886, p. 7.
176. Palmer, *Bench and Bar of Illinois*, Vol. 1, p. 35; McNulty, "Sidney Breese the Illinois Circuit Judge," p. 185.
177. Krause and Stowell, *Judging Lincoln*, p. 47.
178. *Wren v. Moss et al.*, 7 Ill. (2 Gilm.) 72 (1845); Daniel W. Stowell, ed., *In Tender Consideration; Women, Families, and the Law in Abraham Lincoln's Illinois* (Urbana: University of Illinois Press, 2002), pp. 11, 216–20.
179. Stowell, *In Tender Consideration*, p. 217.
180. Cole, *The Constitutional Debates of 1847*, pp. xviii, 743.
181. *Chicago Tribune*, 27 October 1886, p. 7; Stowell, *Papers of Abraham Lincoln*, Vol. 4, pp. 375–76.
182. *Browning v. City of Springfield*, 17 Ill. 143 (1855); Krause and Stowell, *Judging Lincoln*, p. 46; *Lincoln Legal Briefs*, #75 (July–September 2005), p. 3.
183. Samuel H. Treat, Walter B. Scates, and Robert S. Blackwell, compilers, *The Statutes of Illinois* (Chicago: D.B. Cooke & Co., 1858); Palmer, *Bench and Bar of Illinois*, Vol. 1, p. 233.
184. Crossley, *Courts and Lawyers of Illinois*, Vol. 1, p. 318.
185. *New York Times*, 28 October 1886, p. 3.
186. Johannsen, *Stephen A. Douglas*, p. 776.
187. Palmer, *Bench and Bar of Illinois*, Vol. 1, p. 37.
188. Johannsen, *Stephen A. Douglas*, p. 6.
189. Ibid., p. 7.
190. Palmer, *Bench and Bar of Illinois*, Vol. 1, p. 37.
191. Stowell, *Papers of Abraham Lincoln*, Vol. 4, pp. 343–44.
192. Kenney and Hartley, *An Uncertain Tradition*, p. 32.
193. *Field v. People ex rel. McClernand*, 3 Ill. (2 Scam.) 79 (1839).
194. Johannsen, *Stephen A. Douglas*, p. 95.
195. Ibid., pp. 96–97.
196. *Grubb v. Crane*, 5 Ill. (4 Scam.) 153 (1842); Krause and Stowell, *Judging Lincoln*, p. 23.
197. Johannsen, *Stephen A. Douglas*, pp. 105–7.
198. Kenney and Hartley, *An Uncertain Tradition*, pp. 32–33.
199. Johannsen, *Stephen A. Douglas*, pp. 207–09.
200. Ibid., pp. 540–43, 713, 767.
201. Johannsen, *Stephen A. Douglas*, p. 670.
202. Howlett, *Keepers of the Seal*, p. 50.
203. 162 Ill. 15 (1896); Robert Fergus, *Biographical Sketch of John Dean Caton,* Fergus Historical Series, No. 21 (Chicago: Fergus Printing Co., 1882), pp. 3–4.
204. *Ottawa Free Trader*, 2 August 1895, p. 9.
205. Harry E. Pratt, ed., "John Dean Caton's Reminiscences of Chicago in 1833 and 1834," *Journal of the Illinois State Historical Society*, 28 (1935–1936), pp. 5, 8.
206. Crossley, *Courts and Lawyers of Illinois*, p. 267; Fergus, *Biographical Sketch of John Dean Caton*, p. 7.

207. Pratt, "John Dean Caton's Reminiscences of Chicago," p. 15; Palmer, *Bench and Bar of Illinois*, Vol. 1, p. 40; Vol. 2, p. 604.
208. 162 Ill. 15; Fergus, *Biographical Sketch of John Dean Caton*, p. 7; Palmer, *Bench and Bar of Illinois*, Vol. 1, p. 39.
209. Krause and Stowell, *Judging Lincoln*, p. 12.
210. Stowell, *In Tender Consideration*, p. 223; Fergus, *Biographical Sketch of John Dean Caton*, p. 7.
211. Crossley, *Courts and Lawyers of Illinois*, Vol. 1, p. 268; Harris, *History of Negro Servitude in Illinois*, pp. 110–12; Pease, *The Frontier State*, p. 379.
212. Harris, *History of Negro Servitude in Illinois*, p. 112.
213. *Seeley v. Peters*, 10 Ill. (5 Gilm.) 130 (1848).
214. John Dean Caton, *Early Bench and Bar of Illinois* (Chicago: Chicago Legal News, 1893), pp. 181–84.
215. Cole, *The Era of the Civil War*, p. 31.
216. Howard, *Illinois; A History of the Prairie State*, p. 241; *State Journal-Register* (Springfield, Illinois), 6 February 2005, p. 29.
217. Johannsen, *Stephen A. Douglas*, p. 479; Cole, *The Era of the Civil War*, p. 327.
218. Fergus, *Biographical Sketch of John Dean Caton*, p. 15.
219. *Chicago Tribune*, 31 July 1895, p. 3; *Ottawa Free Trader*, 2 August 1895, p. 9; Wayne C. Townley, *Two Judges of Ottawa* (Carbondale, IL: Egypt Book House, 1948), p. 29; Cole, *The Era of the Civil War*, p. 366; Palmer, *Bench and Bar of Illinois*, Vol. 1, p. 41.
220. Daniel Berry, "Forgotten Statesmen of Illinois; Hon. John M. Robinson," *Journal of the Illinois State Historical Society,* 7 (1914–1915), p. 77.
221. Palmer, *Bench and Bar of Illinois*, Vol 1, p. 43.
222. Berry, "Forgotten Statesmen of Illinois; Hon. John M. Robinson," p. 78.
223. Ibid.
224. Pease, *The Frontier State*, p. 138; Kenney and Hartley, *An Uncertain Tradition*, p. 21.
225. Berry, "Forgotten Statesmen of Illinois; Hon. John M. Robinson," p. 79.
226. 5 Ill. vi. Robinson's death date has been reported also as April 25, 1843; Berry, "Forgotten Statesmen of Illinois; Hon. John M. Robinson," p. 78.
227. 5 Ill. vi–vii.
228. Edward Callary, *Place Names of Illinois* (Urbana: University of Illinois Press, 2009), p. 298.
229. Palmer, *Bench and Bar of Illinois*, Vol. 1, p. 41; William L. Burton, "James Semple, Prairie Entrepreneur," *Illinois Historical Journal* 80 (1987), p. 67.
230. Burton, "James Semple, Prairie Entrepreneur," p. 67; Krause and Stowell, *Judging Lincoln*, p. 48.
231. Palmer, *Bench and Bar of Illinois*, Vol. 1, p. 42.
232. Burton, "James Semple, Prairie Entrepreneur," p. 68.
233. Ibid., pp. 68, 82–83.
234. Linder, *Reminiscences of the Early Bench and Bar of Illinois*, p. 219.
235. Crossley, *Courts and Lawyers of Illinois*, Vol. 1, p. 388.
236. Palmer, *Bench and Bar of Illinois*, Vol. 1, p. 42.
237. *Bradley v. Case*, 4 Ill. (3 Scam.) 585 (1842).
238. Johannsen, *Stephen A. Douglas*, p. 124.
239. Burton, "James Semple, Prairie Entrepreneur," pp. 72–73.
240. Johannsen, *Stephen A. Douglas*, pp. 187–89.
241. Burton, "James Semple, Prairie Entrepreneur," pp. 74–80.
242. Ibid., pp. 81–82.
243. Ibid., p. 83.
244. William H. Condon, *Life of Major-General James Shields* (Chicago: Blakely Printing Co., 1900), pp. 10, 26, 29. Shields's birth date has also been reported as May 9, May 10, and May 12, 1806, and as 1810. His mother's first name has been variantly reported as Catherine Shields. Francis O'Shaughnessy, "General James Shields of Illinois," *Transactions of the Illinois State Historical Society,* 1915, p. 114.
245. Kenney and Hartley, *An Uncertain Tradition*, p. 40.
246. O'Shaughnessy, "General James Shields of Illinois," p. 116–17.
247. Crossley, *Courts and Lawyers of Illinois*, Vol. 1, pp. 222–23; Stowell, *Papers of Abraham Lincoln*, Vol. 4, p. 376.
248. Wilson and Davis, *Herndon's Informants*, p. 31.
249. Harris, *History of Negro Servitude in Illinois*, p. 117.
250. *Jarrot v. Jarrot*, 7 Ill. (2 Gilm.) 1 (1845).
251. Condon, *Life of Major-General James Shields*, p. 51.

252. *Eells v. People*, 5 Ill. (4 Scam.) 498 (1843).
253. Pease, *The Frontier State*, p. 379.
254. Crossley, *Courts and Lawyers of Illinois*, Vol. 1, pp. 222–23; Palmer, *Bench and Bar of Illinois*, Vol. 1, p. 45.
255. Johannsen, *Stephen A. Douglas*, pp. 258–61; Howard, *Illinois; A History of the Prairie State*, p. 232.
256. Johannsen, *Stephen A. Douglas*, p. 461; Cole, *The Era of the Civil War*, pp. 126–27.
257. Howard, *Mostly Good and Competent Men*, pp. 87–88.
258. Condon, *Life of Major-General James Shields*, pp. 269–70; Kenney and Hartley, *An Uncertain Tradition*, p. 41.
259. O'Shaughnessy, "General James Shields of Illinois," p. 120.
260. Linder, *Reminiscences of the Early Bench and Bar of Illinois*, p. 66.
261. J. F. Snyder, "Forgotten Statesmen of Illinois: Jesse Burgess Thomas, Jr.," *Transactions of the Illinois State Historical Society,* 1904, p. 523.
262. Palmer, *Bench and Bar of Illinois*, Vol. 1, p. 177.
263. Snyder, "Forgotten Statesmen of Illinois: Jesse Burgess Thomas, Jr.," p. 523.
264. Snyder, "Forgotten Statesmen of Illinois: Jesse Burgess Thomas, Jr.," pp. 523–24; Palmer, *Bench and Bar of Illinois*, Vol. 1, p. 177.
265. Harris, *History of Negro Servitude in Illinois*, pp. 106–08.
266. *Sarah v. Borders*, 5 Ill. (4 Scam.) 341 (1843).
267. Harris, *History of Negro Servitude in Illinois*, p. 108–09.
268. Dallin H. Oaks, "The Suppression of the *Nauvoo Expositor,"Utah Law Review* (1964), pp. 862, 864–65.
269. Ibid., pp. 865, 866.
270. Ibid., pp. 866, 868; Pease, *The Frontier State*, p. 352.
271. *Garrett v. Stevenson et al.*, 8 Ill. (3 Gilm.) 261 (1846); Krause and Stowell, *Judging Lincoln*, p. 61.
272. Palmer, *Bench and Bar of Illinois*, Vol. 1, p. 44.
273. Chicago *Daily Democrat,* 22 February 1850, p. 2.
274. *Illinois Biographical Dictionary*, p. 347.
275. J. F. Snyder, "Forgotten Statesmen of Illinois: Richard M. Young," *Transactions of the Illinois State Historical Society* (1906), pp. 302–03.
276. Ibid., p. 303.
277. Ibid., pp. 303–04, 326; *Daily Herald* (Quincy, Illinois), 19 October 1905, p. 5.
278. Snyder, "Forgotten Statesmen of Illinois: Richard M. Young," p. 306; Ford, *History of Illinois*, p. 27.
279. Snyder, "Forgotten Statesmen of Illinois: Richard M. Young," p. 307.
280. Charles Ballance, *History of Peoria, Illinois* (Peoria: N. C. Nason, 1870), p. 63.
281. Snyder, "Forgotten Statesmen of Illinois: Richard M. Young," p. 314; Palmer, *Bench and Bar of Illinois*, Vol. 1, p. 43.
282. Snyder, "Forgotten Statesmen of Illinois: Richard M. Young," pp. 315–16; *Daily Herald,* 19 October 1905, p. 5.
283. Crossley, *Courts and Lawyers of Illinois*, Vol. 1, p. 233.
284. Palmer, *Bench and Bar of Illinois*, Vol. 1, p. 43.
285. Pease, *The Frontier State*, p. 225.
286. Kenney and Hartley, *An Uncertain Tradition*, p. 22; Snyder, "Forgotten Statesmen of Illinois: Richard M. Young," pp. 318–19.
287. Snyder, "Forgotten Statesmen of Illinois: Richard M. Young," p. 321.
288. Ibid., p. 320.
289. *Jarrot v. Jarrot*, 7 Ill. (2 Gilm.) 1 (1845).
290. Snyder, "Forgotten Statesmen of Illinois: Richard M. Young," p. 320.
291. *Eldridge v. Rowe*, 7 Ill. (2 Gilm.) 91 (1845); Krause and Stowell, *Judging Lincoln*, p. 75.
292. Johannsen, *Stephen A. Douglas*, p. 188.
293. Palmer, *Bench and Bar of Illinois*, p. 43; Snyder, "Forgotten Statesmen of Illinois: Richard M. Young," pp. 325–26; Kenney and Hartley, *An Uncertain Tradition*, p. 22.
294. Some sources report his birth year as 1806 or 1807 and his birthplace as Litchfield County, Connecticut.
295. Palmer, *Bench and Bar of Illinois*, Vol. 1, p. 45; David McCulloch, *History of Peoria County* (Chicago: Munsell, 1902), pp. 538–39; *United States Biographical Dictionary*), pp. 674–75.
296. Palmer, *Bench and Bar of Illinois*, Vol. 1, p. 300.

297. P. G. Rennick, "Courts and Lawyers in Northern and Western Illinois," *Journal of the Illinois State Historical Society,* 30 (1937–38), pp. 330–31; Harris, *History of Negro Servitude in Illinois,* pp. 110–11.
298. *Wright for use of Davidson v. Bennett and Bennett,* 7 Ill. (2 Gilm.) 587 (1845); Stowell, *In Tender Consideration,* p. 61; Stowell, *Papers of Abraham Lincoln,* Vol. 1, pp. 385–98.
299. *Regnier v. Cabot et al.,* 7 Ill. (2 Gilm.) 34 (1845).
300. Palmer, *Bench and Bar of Illinois,* Vol. 1, p. 46.
301. *Peoria Weekly Transcript,* 14 August 1863, p. 2.
302. Ibid.
303. R. E. Rombauer, "Life of Hon. Gustavus Koerner," *Transactions of the Illinois State Historical Society,* 9 (1904), pp. 286–87.
304. 162 Ill. 21.
305. Rombauer, "Life of Hon. Gustavus Koerner," p. 291.
306. Ibid.
307. Ibid. p. 292; 162 Ill. 29.
308. Ellen M. Whitney, comp., *Illinois History; An Annotated Bibliography* (Westport, CT: Greenwood Press, 1995), p. 487.
309. Rombauer, "Life of Hon. Gustavus Koerner," p. 306.
310. Ibid., p. 293.
311. Linder, *Reminiscences of the Early Bench and Bar of Illinois,* p. 190.
312. Crossley, *Courts and Lawyers of Illinois,* Vol. 1, p. 300.
313. *Munsell v. Temple,* 8 Ill. (3 Gilm.) 93 (1846); Krause and Stowell, *Judging Lincoln,* p. 31.
314. *Baxter v. People,* 8 Ill. (3 Gilm.) 368 (1846).
315. Palmer, *Bench and Bar of Illinois,* Vol. 1, p. 49.
316. Harris, *History of Negro Servitude in Illinois,* p. 198.
317. Koerner to the *Belleville Advocate,* quoted in Harris, *History of Negro Servitude in Illinois,* p. 200.
318. Rennick, "Courts and Lawyers in Northern and Western Illinois," p. 325.
319. Dumas Malone, ed., *Dictionary of American Biography,* Vol. X, pp. 496–97.
320. Crossley, *Courts and Lawyers of Illinois,* Vol. 1, p. 301.
321. Howard, *Mostly Good and Competent Men,* p. 139.
322. 162 Ill. 32; *Belleville Weekly Advocate,* 17 April 1896, p. 1. Trumbull became ill at the service and two months later died at his Chicago home.
323. *Franklin County, 1804–1818–1964,* (Sesser, IL: Print Shop, 1993), p. 18.
324. *History of Gallatin, Saline, Hamilton, Franklin, and Williamson Counties, Illinois* (Chicago: Goodspeed Pub. Co., 1887), p. 391.
325. *Woodford v. McClenahan,* 9 Ill (4 Gilm.) 85 (1847).
326. *Illinois State Journal* (Springfield, Illinois), 11 September 1851, p. 2.
327. *Illinois State Journal* (Springfield, Illinois), 24 September 1853, p. 3; Frank E. Stevens, "Life of Stephen Arnold Douglas," *Journal of the Illinois State Historical Society* 16 (1923–24), p. 489.
328. Edward Miner, *Past and Present of Greene County, Illinois* (Chicago: S.J. Clarke Publishing Co., 1905), pp. 338–41.
329. Ibid., p. 341.
330. Palmer, *Bench and Bar of Illinois,* Vol. 2, p. 1095.
331. Crossley, *Courts and Lawyers of Illinois,* Vol. 1, pp. 339–40; Palmer, *Bench and Bar of Illinois,* Vol. 2, p. 1095; *United States Biographical Dictionary,* p. 254.
332. Harry E. Pratt, "Abraham Lincoln's First Murder Trial," *Journal of the Illinois State Historical Society* 37 (1944), pp. 243–48.
333. Johannsen, *Stephen A. Douglas,* pp. 148–49.
334. Cole, *Constitutional Debates of 1847,* p. 66.
335. Palmer, *Bench and Bar of Illinois,* Vol. 1, p. 4.
336. *History of Morgan County, Ill., Its Past and Present* (Chicago: Donnelley, Loyd, & Co., 1878), p. 429.
337. Judge Cyrus Epler, "History of the Morgan County Bar," *Journal of the Illinois State Historical Society* 19 (1926–27), pp. 168–69.
338. Miner, *Past and Present of Greene County,* p. 341; *History of Greene and Jersey Counties, Ill.* (Springfield, IL: Continental Hist. Co., 1885), pp. 601–02.
339. *Daily Illinois State Journal* (Springfield), 28 August 1877, p. 2; *Carrollton Gazette,* 1 September 1877, p. 2.
340. Miner, *Past and Present of Greene County,* pp. 341–42.
341. Mark M. Krug, *Lyman Trumbull; Conservative Radical* (New York: A.S. Barnes & Co., 1965), p. 19–21.

342. Ibid., p. 24.
343. Harris, *History of Negro Servitude in Illinois*, pp. 122–23.
344. Howlett, *Keepers of the Seal*, p. 51.
345. Ford, *History of Illinois*, pp. 215, 272.
346. *Trumbull v. Campbell*, 8 Ill. (3 Gilm.) 502 (1846).
347. Ralph J. Roske, "Lincoln and Lyman Trumbull," in O. Fritiof Ander, ed., *Lincoln Images; Augustana College Centennial Essays* (Rock Island, IL: Augustana College Library, 1960), p. 65.
348. Horace White, *The Life of Lyman Trumbull* (Boston: Houghton Mifflin, 1913), pp. 326, 431.
349. White, *The Life of Lyman Trumbull*, p. 20.
350. Krug, *Lyman Trumbull; Conservative Radical*, p. 68.
351. White, *The Life of Lyman Trumbull*, p. 20–21.
352. *McKinley v. Watkins*, 13 Ill. 140 (1851).
353. *Jones v. People*, 14 Ill. 196 (1852).
354. Krug, *Lyman Trumbull; Conservative Radical*, p. 76–77.
355. Mario R. DiNunzio, "Lyman Trumbull, The States' Rights Issue, and the Liberal Republican Revolt," *Journal of the Illinois State Historical Society*, 66 (1973), p. 365.
356. Linder, *Reminiscences of the Early Bench and Bar of Illinois*, p. 167.
357. Kenney and Hartley, *An Uncertain Tradition*), p. 45.
358. White, *The Life of Lyman Trumbull*, p. 224; Krug, *Lyman Trumbull; Conservative Radical*, p. 11.
359. 165 Ill. 10; DiNunzio, "Lyman Trumbull, The States' Rights Issue, and the Liberal Republican Revolt," p. 366.
360. White, *The Life of Lyman Trumbull*, p. 412; Krug, *Lyman Trumbull; Conservative Radical*, p. 343–49.
361. *Chicago Tribune*, 26 June 1896, p. 9.
362. White, *The Life of Lyman Trumbull*, p. 414; DiNunzio, "Lyman Trumbull, The States' Rights Issue, and the Liberal Republican Revolt," pp. 347, 375.
363. Krug, *Lyman Trumbull; Conservative Radical*, p. 353.
364. White, *The Life of Lyman Trumbull*, p. 418.
365. *Chicago Times*, 26 June 1896, quoted in White, *The Life of Lyman Trumbull*, p. 425.
366. David F. Wilcox, *Quincy and Adams County, Vol. 1* (Chicago: Lewis Pub. Co., 1919), p. 149.
367. *Biographical Encyclopaedia of Illinois of the Nineteenth Century* (Philadelphia: Galaxy Pub. Co., 1875), p. 217
368. Wilcox, *Quincy and Adams County*, p. 149.
369. Dallin H. Oaks and Marvin S. Hill, *Carthage Conspiracy; The Trial of the Accused Assassins of Joseph Smith* (Urbana: University of Illinois Press, 1975), p. 94.
370. Ibid., pp. 66, 84, 94, 179–81.
371. Charles J. Scofield, ed., *History of Hancock County* (Chicago: Munsell Pub. Co., 1921), pp. 850–52.
372. "An act to establish the Fourteenth and Fifteenth Judicial Circuits, and for other purposes," 12 February 1851, *General Laws of the State of Illinois* (1851), p. 82.
373. Johannsen, *Stephen A. Douglas*, p. 479.
374. *Johnson v. Richardson*, 17 Ill. 302 (1855).
375. *Babcock v. Trice*, 18 Ill. 420 (1857).
376. *Biographical Encyclopaedia of Illinois*, pp. 216–17.
377. *Quincy Daily Herald*, 6 February 1877, p. 2.
378. Palmer, *Bench and Bar of Illinois*, Vol. 1, p. 54.
379. *History of Mercer and Henderson Counties* (Chicago: H.H. Hill and Co., 1882), p. 884.
380. 85 Ill. [725].
381. *Biographical Encyclopaedia of Illinois*, p. 440; Palmer, *Bench and Bar of Illinois*, Vol. 1, pp. 54–55.
382. *Rushville Times*, 12 February 1885, p. 4.
383. Emma Siggins White, *Genealogy of the Descendants of John Walker of Wigton, Scotland . . .* (Kansas City: Tiernan-Dart Print. Co., 1902), pp. 377, 381.
384. *History of McDonough County, Ill.,* (Springfield, IL: Continental Hist. Co., 1885), p. 335.
385. 113 Ill. 19.
386. *History of McDonough County*, p. 336.
387. *Crabtree v. Kile et al.*, 21 Ill. 180 (1859).
388. *Ritchey v. West*, 23 Ill. 385 (1860).
389. 113 Ill. 26.
390. *Ruggles v. People*, 91 Ill. 256 (1878); Ralph M. Snyder, "Ten Significant Decisions of the Illinois Supreme Court," *John Marshall Law Quarterly*, 5 (June 1940), p. 442.

391. *Rushville Times,* 12 February 1885, p. 4; Palmer, *Bench and Bar of Illinois,* Vol. 1, p. 54.
392. Snyder, "Ten Significant Decisions of the Illinois Supreme Court," p. 442.
393. *Chicago Tribune,* 19 August 1890, p. 3.
394. A. T. Andreas, *History of Chicago* . . . Vol. 2, (Chicago: A. T. Andreas Co., 1885), p. 465.
395. *Chicago Tribune,* 19 August 1890, p. 3.
396. Ibid.
397. Ibid.
398. Caton, *Early Bench and Bar of Illinois,* p. 194.
399. *Chicago Tribune,* 19 August 1890, p. 3.
400. *Miller v. Young's Administrator,* 33 Ill. 354 (1864).
401. *Happy v. Morton,* 33 Ill. 398 (1864).
402. Andreas, *History of Chicago,* p. 465.
403. *Biographical Encyclopaedia of Illinois,* p. 267; Crossley, *Courts and Lawyers of Illinois,* Vol. 1, p. 254.
404. Crossley, *Courts and Lawyers of Illinois,* Vol. 1, pp. 374–75; *Taylor v. Secor,* 92 U.S. 575 (1875).
405. *Chicago Tribune,* 19 August 1890.
406. *Chicago Daily News,* 20 August 1890, p. 2.
407. *National Cyclopaedia of American Biography,* (New York: James T. White & Co., 1907), Vol. 5, p. 437. The *Chicago Tribune* reported his middle name as Burral and spelled his father's first name as Ville. *Chicago Tribune,* 10 April 1883, p. 6.
408. Howard Louis Conard, "Hon. Charles B. Lawrence," *Magazine of Western History* 12 (May–Oct. 1890), p. 289.
409. Conard, "Hon. Charles B. Lawrence," p. 289; *Chicago Tribune,* 10 April 1883, p. 6.
410. 10 Ill. (5 Gilm.) iv.
411. *Chicago Inter Ocean,* 10 April 1883, p. 5.
412. Howard, *Illinois: A History of the Prairie State,* p. 363.
413. *Janney v. Birch,* 58 Ill. 87 (1871).
414. *In the matter of the application of Mrs. Myra Bradwell, for a license to practice law,* 55 Ill. 535 (1869); *Bradwell v. Illinois,* 83 U.S. 130 (1872).
415. John Moses, *Illinois, Historical and Statistical,* 2 Vols. (Chicago: Fergus Print. Co., 1895), Vol. 2, p. 1061.
416. *The Chicago and Alton Railroad Company v. The People ex rel. Gustavus Koerner et al. Comrs.,* 67 Ill. 11 (1873); John H. Keiser, *Building for the Centuries: Illinois, 1865–1898* (Urbana: University of Illinois Press, 1977), pp. 144, 163.
417. Edward F. Dunne, *Illinois: The Heart of the Nation,* 5 Vols. (Chicago: Lewis Pub. Co., 1933), Vol. 2, p. 130; Howard, *Mostly Good and Competent Men,* p. 167.
418. *Chicago Tribune,* 10 April 1883, p. 6; Ernest Ludlow Bogart and Charles Manfred Thompson, *The Industrial State, 1870–1893* (Springfield: Illinois Centennial Commission, 1920), p. 121.
419. *Chicago Tribune,* 10 April 1883, p. 6.
420. Chicago *Inter Ocean,* 10 April 1883, p. 5.
421. Chicago *Inter Ocean,* 13 April 1883, p. 3; Conard, "Hon. Charles B. Lawrence," p. 293.
422. *Quincy Daily Whig,* 10 April 1883, p. 4; *National Cyclopaedia of American Biography,* p. 437.
423. *Historic Sketch and Biographical Album of Shelby County, Illinois* (Shelbyville, IL: Wilder Pub. Co., 1900), p. 122; *Shelbyville Democrat,* 15 September 1904, p. 1.
424. Newton Bateman and Paul Selby, eds., *Historical Encyclopedia of Illinois and History of Shelby County,* 2 Vols. (Chicago: Munsell, 1910), Vol. 2, p. 729.
425. Palmer, *Bench and Bar of Illinois,* Vol. 1, p. 458.
426. Vandalia newspaper clipping, Abraham Lincoln Presidential Library vertical file.
427. *Combined History of Shelby and Moultrie Counties, Illinois* (Philadelphia: Brink, McDonough & Co., 1881), p. 161.
428. Charles C. Bingaman, "The Life and Times of Anthony Thornton, ISBA's First President," *Illinois Bar Journal* (January 1977), p. 314; Cole, *Constitutional Debates of 1847,* p. 66.
429. *Historic Sketch of Shelby County,* p. 134.
430. 216 Ill. 11.
431. *Historic Sketch of Shelby County,* p. 117.
432. 216 Ill. 16; Bateman and Selby, *Historical Encyclopedia of Illinois,* p. 73; Palmer, *Bench and Bar of Illinois,* Vol. 1, p. 459; *Shelbyville Democrat,* p. 1; *Historic Sketch of Shelby County,* p. 135.
433. *Historic Sketch of Shelby County,* p. 135.
434. 216 Ill. 11; *Historic Sketch of Shelby County,* p. 135.
435. *Historic Sketch of Shelby County,* p. 118.
436. *People ex rel. Cutler v. Ford,* 54 Ill. 520 (1870).

437. Linder, *Reminiscences of the Early Bench and Bar of Illinois*, p. 214.
438. Bingaman, "The Life and Times of Anthony Thornton," p. 315.
439. 216 Ill. 18.
440. *Shelbyville Democrat*, p. 1.
441. David Ward Wood, ed., *History of the Republican Party . . . Illinois Volume* (Chicago: Lincoln Engr. and Pub. Co., 1895), p. 217; *Portrait and Biographical Album of McLean County, Illinois* (Chicago: Chapman Brothers, 1887), pp. 969–70. In this publication, Nancy Scott's maiden name is recorded as Biggs.
442. Palmer, *Bench and Bar of Illinois*, Vol. 1, p. 55; Dunne, *Illinois: The Heart of the Nation*, Vol. 4, p. 32.
443. Crossley, *Courts and Lawyers of Illinois*, Vol. 1, p. 320.
444. Emanuel Hertz, ed., *The Hidden Lincoln from the Letters and Papers of William H. Herndon* (New York: Viking Press, 1938), p. 320.
445. *Bloomington Pantagraph*, 22 January 1898, p. 5; *Portrait and Biographical Album*, p. 970; Palmer, *Bench and Bar of Illinois*, p. 59.
446. Crossley, *Courts and Lawyers of Illinois*, Vol. 1, p. 320–21; *Portrait and Biographical Album*, p. 970.
447. Palmer, *Bench and Bar of Illinois*, Vol. 1, p. 56.
448. Ibid., p. 57.
449. *Lenfers et al. v. Henke et al.*, 73 Ill. 405 (1874); Palmer, *Bench and Bar of Illinois*, Vol. 1, p. 59.
450. *Ker v. People*, 110 Ill. 627 (1884).
451. Palmer, *Bench and Bar of Illinois*, p. 58; Crossley, *Courts and Lawyers of Illinois*, Vol. 1, p. 323.
452. 173 Ill. 18; George W. Smith, *History of Illinois and Her People,* 6 Vols. (Chicago: American Historical Society, 1927), Vol. 4, p. 366.
453. Palmer, *Bench and Bar of Illinois*, Vol. 1, p. 58; Crossley, *Courts and Lawyers of Illinois*, Vol. 1, p. 321.
454. 173 Ill. 18.
455. *Bloomington Pantagraph*, p. 5.
456. *Rockford Daily Republic,* 14 April 1897, p. 1, gives his birthplace as Marlborough, Middlesex County, Massachusetts, and the *National Cyclopaedia of American Biography* (New York: James T. White & Co., 1906), Vol. 13, p. 345, lists his birth year as 1812.
457. *Biographical Encyclopaedia of Illinois,* p. 476.
458. *Rockford Daily Republic*, p. 1.
459. *History of Winnebago County, Illinois, Its Past and Present* (Chicago: H. F. Kett & Co., 1877, rpt. Bowie, Md.: Heritage Books, 1990), pp. 306–10.
460. *Rockford Daily Republic*, p. 1.
461. David S. Tanenhaus, "Between Dependency and Liberty: The Conundrum of Children's Rights in the Gilded Age," *Law and History Review* 23 (Summer 2005), pp. 351–86.
462. *In re Ferrier*, 103 Ill. 367 (1882).
463. *Peers v. Board of Education of School District No. 3*, 72 Ill. 508 (1874).
464. *Austin v. Chicago, Rock Island, and Pacific Railroad Co.*, 91 Ill. 35 (1878).
465. 173 Ill. 12.
466. 173 Ill. 13.
467. *Rockford Daily Republic,* 16 April 1897, p. 1.
468. 173 Ill. 13; Newton Bateman and Paul Selby, eds., *Historical Encyclopedia of Illinois and History of Winnebago County* (Chicago: Munsell, 1916), p. 717.
469. Palmer, *Bench and Bar of Illinois*, Vol. 2, pp. 969–70.
470. *Chicago Times,* 29 October 1888, p. 1.
471. *Chicago Legal News*, 3 November 1888, p. 72; *Biographical Encyclopaedia of Illinois*, p. 267.
472. 1860 U.S. Census; 1880 U.S. Census.
473. Palmer, *Bench and Bar of Illinois*, Vol. 1, p. 60.
474. Crossley, *Courts and Lawyers of Illinois*, Vol. 1, p. 312; *Biographical Encyclopaedia*, p. 267.
475. *Chicago Tribune*, 30 October 1888, p. 3.
476. *New York Times,* 4 July 1870; Palmer, *Bench and Bar of Illinois*, Vol. 1, p. 60; *Industrial Chicago; Vol. 6, The Bench and Bar* (Chicago: Goodspeed Pub. Co., 1896), p. 74.
477. *McElhanon v. McElhanon for use of Le Compte*, 63 Ill. 457 (1872).
478. *Patten v. Patten*, 75 Ill. 446 (1874).
479. Herman Kogan, *The First Century: The Chicago Bar Association, 1874–1974* (Chicago: Rand McNally & Co., 1974), p. 46. With continued pressure from the Chicago Bar Association and other groups, the General Assembly in 1877 enacted legislation organizing the Appellate Court system within four districts: Cook County, and northern, central, and southern Illinois.

480. *Chicago Legal News*, 23 October 1875, p. 38.
481. Stephen Anderson, ed., "Wisdom and Deliberation," *Illinois State Bar Association News*, 1 June 2001; Richard C. Lindberg, *The Gambler King of Clark Street; Michael C. McDonald and the Rise of Chicago's Democratic Machine* (Carbondale: Southern Illinois University Press, 2009), p. 260.
482. Babb, "The Supreme Court of Illinois," p. 234; A. T. Andreas, *History of Cook County, Ill.* (Chicago: A. T. Andreas, 1884), p. 350.
483. *Chicago Times*, 30 October 1888, p. 1; Kogan, *The First Century: The Chicago Bar Association*, p. 75.
484. Lindberg, *The Gambler King of Clark Street*, p. 44–46.
485. *Industrial Chicago*, p. 74; Babb, "The Supreme Court of Illinois," p. 234.
486. *Chicago Legal News*, Nov. 3, 1888.
487. *Chicago Times*, Oct. 29, 1888; *Chicago Tribune*, 29 October 1888, p. 1.
488. *Chicago Tribune Supplemental Sheet*, 31 October 1888, p. 1.
489. *Biographical Encyclopaedia of Illinois*, p. 481; *Chicago Tribune*, 14 February 1893, p. 1.
490. *Chicago Tribune*, p. 1.
491. Ibid.
492. 145 Ill. 11.
493. Rev. R. H. Osborne, "Reminiscences of Judge John Scholfield" (Altamont, IL: pamphlet, n. d., n. p.). Copy in the Abraham Lincoln Presidential Library and Museum, Springfield, IL.
494. *Chicago Tribune*, p. 1.
495. Osborne, "Reminiscences."
496. Linder, *Reminiscences of the Early Bench and Bar of Illinois*, p. 231.
497. Ibid., p. 230.
498. Newton Bateman and Paul Selby, eds., *Historical Encyclopaedia of Illinois and History of Clark County* (Chicago: Middle West Pub. Co., 1907), p. 469.
499. *Blake v. People for use of Caldwell*, 109 Ill. 504 (1884); Snyder, "Ten Significant Decisions of the Illinois Supreme Court," p. 441; William T. Gard, *The Sny Story; The Sny Island Levee Drainage District and the Sny Basin* (North Richland Hills, TX: Smithfield Press, 2002), p. 31.
500. *Chicago Tribune*, p. 1.
501. *Chicago Times*, 14 February 1893, p. 2.
502. 145 Ill. 14.
503. 253 Ill. 9–10.
504. Newton Bateman and Paul Selby, eds., *Historical Encyclopedia of Illinois and History of Knox County* (Chicago: Munsell, 1899), p. 719.
505. *History of Knox County; Its Cities, Towns and People*, Vol. 2 (Chicago: S. J. Clarke, 1912), p. 258; Palmer, *Bench and Bar of Illinois*, Vol. 1, p. 61.
506. Bateman and Selby, *Historical Encyclopedia of Illinois and History of Knox County*, p. 719; 253 Ill. 11.
507. Chas. C. Chapman & Co., *History of Knox County, Ill* (Chicago: Blakely, Brown & Marsh, 1878), pp. 418–19.
508. 253 Ill. 11.
509. Dunne, *Illinois: The Heart of the Nation*, Vol. 2, p. 130.
510. 253 Ill. 12.
511. *Chase v. Stephenson*, 71 Ill. 383 (1874); *History of Knox County*, pp. 259–60.
512. *People v. Wabash, St. Louis, and Pacific Railway Co.*, 104 Ill. 476 (1882); *History of Knox County*, pp. 258–59.
513. 104 Ill. 476.
514. *History of Knox County*, p. 259.
515. *Illinois Central Railroad v. City of Chicago*, 173 Ill. 471 (1898).
516. 253 Ill. 12, 15; Chapman, *History of Knox County, Ill.*, pp. 598–601/
517. 253 Ill. 13, 16; *Galesburg Evening Mail*, 7 September 1911, pp. 2, 9 September 1911, pp. 1–2.
518. *Biographical Encyclopaedia of Illinois*, p. 125.
519. *Chicago Times*, 23 July 1885, p. 3.
520. James S. Ewing, "Memorial Address; Life and Services of T. Lyle Dickey," *Proceedings of the Illinois State Bar Association . . . 1885* (Springfield, IL: 1885), p. 63.
521. Wayne C. Townley, *Two Judges of Ottawa* (Carbondale, IL: Egypt Book House, 1948), pp. 11–12.
522. 121 Ill. 10; Townley, *Two Judges of Ottawa*, p. 13.
523. *Ottawa Free Trader*, 25 July 1885, p. 4.
524. 121 Ill. 13.

525. Avery N. Beebe, "Judge Theophilus L. Dickey and the First Murder Trial in Kendall County," *Journal of the Illinois State Historical Society,* 3 (January 1911), pp. 49–50.
526. 121 Ill. 13.
527. Quoted in C. C. Tisler, *Lincoln's In Town* (Ottawa: 1940), p. 27.
528. Beebe, "Judge Theophilus L. Dickey," pp. 52–58.
529. 121 Ill. 10–11.
530. *Chicago Times,* p. 3.
531. *Biographical Encyclopaedia,* p. 125; Townley, *Two Judges of Ottawa,* p. 14; *Ottawa Free Trader,* p. 4.
532. *Daily Republican Times* (Ottawa), 26 March 1923, p. 4.
533. 121 Ill. 11.
534 Palmer, *Bench and Bar of Illinois,* Vol. 1, p. 63.
535. *National Cyclopaedia of American Biography,* Vol. 12 (New York: James T. White & Co., 1904), p. 223.
536. *Parker v. People,* 111 Ill. 581 (1884).
537. Babb, "The Supreme Court of Illinois," p. 235.
538. *Peck v. Harrington,* 109 Ill. 611 (1884); Snyder, "Ten Significant Decisions of the Illinois Supreme Court," pp. 441–42.
539. *Ottawa Free Trader,* 1 August 1885, p. 4.
540. Townley, *Two Judges of Ottawa,* p. 15.
541. *Ottawa Free Trader,* p. 4.
542. Babb, "The Supreme Court of Illinois," p. 236.
543. *Daily State Register* (Springfield, Illinois), 15 March 1885, p. 2.
544. *Combined History of Randolph, Monroe and Perry Counties, Illinois* (Philadelphia: J. L. McDonough & Co., 1883), p. 182.
545. 53 Ill. i; 183 Ill. 9; Kenney and Hartley, *An Uncertain Tradition,* p. 19.
546. Wilson and Davis, *Herndon's Informants,* pp. 251, 738; Dunne, *Illinois: The Heart of the Nation,* Vol. 3, p. 25. Edward Baker later served for twenty-three years as U.S. Consul at Buenos Aires, Argentina. *Daily State Register,* p. 2; Bateman and Selby, *Historical Encyclopedia of Illinois,* p. 32.
547. W. T. Norton, ed., *Centennial History of Madison County, Illinois and Its People, 1812–1912* (Chicago: Lewis Pub. Co., 1912), Vol. 1, p. 968.
548. *The United States Biographical Dictionary and Portrait Gallery of Eminent and Self-Made Men, Illinois Volume* (Chicago: American Biographical Pub. Co., 1876), p. 647; John M. Lansden, *History of the City of Cairo* (Chicago: R. R. Donnelley & Sons Co., 1910), p. 180.
549. *The Citizen* (Cairo), 16 March 1899, p. 1.
550. *United States Biographical Dictionary,* p. 648.
551. *Norton v. Richmond,* 93 Ill. 367 (1879).
552. *Chicago Times-Herald,* 14 March 1899, p. 12.
553. Oliver A. Harker, "Fifty Years With Bench and Bar of Southern Illinois," *Transactions of the Illinois State Historical Society,* 27 (1920), p. 50.
554. *Chicago Legal News,* 18 March 1899, p. 253.
555. *People ex rel. Bradley v. Superintendent Illinois State Reformatory,* 148 Ill. 413 (1894).
556. *Chicago Daily Tribune,* 15 June 1897, p. 2; 183 Ill. 10.
557. 183 Ill. 11.
558. *Chicago Tribune,* 14 March 1899, p. 5.
559. *The Citizen* (Cairo), 23 March 1899, p. 1.
560. *Chicago Tribune,* p. 5.
561. "Commemorative of the Hon. John H. Mulkey, Deceased," *Transactions of the Illinois State Historical Society,* 11 (1906), p. 341; Palmer, *Bench and Bar of Illinois,* Vol. 1, pp. 63–65.
562. William Henry Perrin, ed., *History of Jefferson County, Illinois* (Chicago: Globe Pub. Co., 1883), p. 163.
563. "Commemorative," p. 342; Palmer, *Bench and Bar of Illinois,* Vol. 1, p. 64.
564. Cole, *The Era of the Civil War,* pp. 302–03.
565. "Commemorative," p. 345.
566. *Cairo Bulletin,* 11 July 1905, p. 6.
567. Palmer, *Bench and Bar of Illinois,* Vol. 1, p. 65.
568. *County of McLean v. Humphreys,* 104 Ill. 378 (1882).
569. David S. Tanenhaus, "Between Dependency and Liberty: The Conundrum of Children's Rights in the Gilded Age," *Law and History Review* 23 (Summer 2005), pp. 351–86.
570. Palmer, *Bench and Bar of Illinois,* Vol. 1, p. 65.
571. *Fort Dearborn Lodge v. Klein et al.,* 115 Ill. 177 (1885).

572. Babb, "The Supreme Court of Illinois," pp. 235–36.
573. 217 Ill. 13–14.
574. *Spies et al. v. People*, 122 Ill. 1 (1887), Mulkey's statement is found at 266–67; Francis X. Busch, "The Haymarket Riot and the Trial of the Anarchists," *Journal of the Illinois State Historical Society,* 48 (1955), p. 265.
575. Harker, "Fifty Years With Bench and Bar of Southern Illinois," p. 48.
576. Palmer, *Bench and Bar of Illinois*, Vol. 1, p. 65; 217 Ill. 11–12.
577. "Report of Necrologist," *Illinois State Bar Association* (1909), p. 398.
578. 196 Ill. 9.
579. Newton Bateman and Paul Selby, eds., *Historical Encyclopedia of Illinois and History of McDonough County* (Chicago: Munsell, 1907), p. 1029.
580. 196 Ill. 10.
581. *Macomb Daily Journal,* 21 December 1901, p. 5.
582. Bateman and Selby, *Historical Encyclopedia of Illinois and History of McDonough County*, p. 1030.
583. Ibid.
584. Ibid.
585. *Macomb Daily Journal,* p. 5; *History of McDonough County, Illinois* (Springfield: Continental Historical Co., 1885), pp. 392–93.
586. John E. Hallwas, *Dime Novel Desperadoes; The Notorious Maxwell Brothers* (Urbana: University of Illinois Press, 2008), pp. 60–61.
587. *New York Times,* 17 February 1885, p. 2.
588. *Gordon et al. v. Reynolds,* 114 Ill. 118 (1885).
589. Kenney and Hartley, *An Uncertain Tradition*, pp. 105–09.
590. Gordana Rezab, *Place Names of McDonough County, Illinois: Past and Present* (Macomb: Western Illinois University, 2008), p. 112.
591. *Macomb Daily Journal,* p. 5.
592. *History of Fulton County, Illinois* (Peoria: Chas. C. Chapman & Co., 1879), p. 813, reports Shope's birth year as 1835. Newton Bateman and Paul Selby, eds., *Historical Encyclopedia of Illinois and History of Fulton County* (Chicago: Munsell, 1908), p. 1104, report the year as 1836. Palmer, *Bench and Bar of Illinois*, Vol. 2, p. 1181, George W. Warvelle, *Compendium of Freemasonry in Illinois, Vol. 2* (Chicago: Lewis Pub. Co., 1897), p. 329, and E. R. Pritchard, ed., *Illinois of To-Day and its Progressive Cities* (Chicago: Illinois of To-Day, [1897], p. 21, list the year as 1837.
593. 294 Ill. 15, 19; *Portrait and Biographical Album of Fulton County, Illinois* (Chicago: Biographical Pub. Co., 1890), p. 891.
594. Palmer, *Bench and Bar of Illinois*, Vol. 2, p. 1182; Bateman and Selby, *Historical Encyclopedia of Illinois and History of Fulton County*, p. 1104; Pritchard, *Illinois of To-Day*, p. 21.
595. *Fulton Democrat* (Lewistown, Illinois), 28 January 1920, p. 1.
596. "Simeon P. Shope," *Journal of the Illinois State Historical Society,* 12 (1919–1920), p. 647. There is a variant of this story; Ward Hill Lamon refers to himself as the one with the torn trousers and that Lincoln "contributes nothing to the end in view." Ward Hill Lamon, *Recollections of Abraham Lincoln, 1847–1865* (Chicago: McClurg and Co., 1895), pp. 16–17.
597. *Fulton Democrat*, p. 1.
598. *History of Fulton County*, p. 813; *Fulton Democrat*, p. 1.
599. *Portrait and Biographical Album of Fulton County,* p. 891.
600. *McLaughlin v. Fisher*, 136 Ill. 111 (1890).
601. *Gartside Coal Company v. Turk*, 147 Ill. 120 (1893).
602. Warvelle, *Compendium of Freemasonry in Illinois*, p. 330; Palmer, *Bench and Bar of Illinois*, Vol. 2, p. 1182.
603. Palmer, *Bench and Bar of Illinois*, Vol. 2, p. 1182.
604. *Fulton Democrat*, p. 1.
605. *Chicago Daily Tribune,* 24 January 1920, p. 15; *Chicago Legal News*, 29 January 1920, p. 213; *Fulton Democrat*, p. 1.
606. *Industrial Chicago, Vol. 6, The Bench and Bar* (Chicago: Goodspeed Pub. Co., 1896), p. 327; 247 Ill. 17.
607. *Chicago Legal News,* 22 October 1910, p. 85.
608. 247 Ill. 18; Babb, "The Supreme Court of Illinois," p. 237.
609. *Industrial Chicago*, p. 327.
610. Bateman and Selby, *Historical Encyclopedia of Illinois*, p. 349.
611. *Industrial Chicago*, p. 327.
612. 247 Ill. 17; *Chicago Legal News,* 23 April 1910, p. 297.

613. 247 Ill. 10; *Chicago Legal News,* 22 October 1910, p. 85.
614. *New York Times,* 23 October 1885, p. 1.
615. 247 Ill. 26.
616. *People ex rel. Peabody v. Chicago Gas Trust Company,* 130 Ill. 268 (1889); Werner Troesken, *Why Regulate Utilities; The New Institutional Economics and the Chicago Gas Industry, 1849–1924* (Ann Arbor: University of Michigan Press, 1996), pp. 49–50.
617. *Illinois Central Railroad Company v. City of Decatur,* 126 Ill. 92 (1888); Snyder, "Ten Significant Decisions of the Illinois Supreme Court," p. 442; *Illinois Central Railroad Company v. City of Decatur,* 147 U.S. 190 (1893).
618. *Spies et al. v. People,* 122 Ill. 1 (1887); 247 Ill. 21; Snyder, "Ten Significant Decisions of the Illinois Supreme Court," p. 440; Michael J. Schaack, *Anarchy and Anarchists; A History of the Red Terror and the Social Revolution in America and Europe* (Chicago: F. J. Schulte & Co., 1889), pp. 608–11.
619. 247 Ill. 11.
620. Troesken, *Why Regulate Utilities,* pp. 50–51.
621. *Chicago Daily Tribune,* 22 April 1910, p. 7; *Chicago Legal News,* 23 April 1910, p. 297.
622. *Chicago Legal News,* 22 October 1910, p. 85.
623. *Chicago Tribune,* 30 March 1888, p. 7. Maria Bailey's maiden name is also reported as Brannan.
624. *Freeport Daily Bulletin,* 17 October 1895, p. 4; *Chicago Tribune,* 30 March 1888, p. 7.
625. *Portrait and Biographical Album of Stephenson County, Illinois* (Chicago: Chapman Bros., 1888), p. 752; *Daily Inter Ocean* (Chicago), 17 October 1895, p. 1; *Freeport Daily Bulletin,* 19 October 1895, p. 4.
626. *In the Foot-Prints of the Pioneers of Stephenson County, Illinois* (Freeport: Pioneer Pub. Co., 1900), p. 347.
627. *Chicago Tribune,* 17 October 1895, p. 5; Stephenson County Genealogical Society, "City Cemetery Inscriptions (Freeport)," Vol. 5, p. 247.
628. *Freeport Daily Bulletin,* 17 October 1897, p. 5.
629. *Freeport Daily Bulletin,* 17 October 1897, p. 4; Bateman and Selby, *Historical Encyclopedia of Illinois,* p. 31.
630. *Biographical Encyclopaedia of Illinois,* p.134.
631. *Freeport Daily Bulletin,* 17 October 1895, p. 4.
632. *Chicago Tribune,* 30 March 1888, p. 7.
633. Babb, "The Supreme Court of Illinois," p. 237.
634. Bateman and Selby, *Historical Encyclopedia of Illinois,* p. 31; *Daily Inter Ocean,* 17 October 1895, p. 1.
635. *Chicago Tribune,* 17 October 1895, p. 5; Babb, "The Supreme Court of Illinois," p. 237; "Judge Bailey," *The Commentator* 13 (April 2007), p. 5.
636. *Chicago Tribune,* 17 October 1895, p. 5.
637. *Harris v. People,* 128 Ill. 585 (1889).
638. Michael H. Graham, *Handbook of Illinois Evidence, 9 Edition* (New York: Aspen Publishers, 2008), p. 779.
639. *Painter v. People,* 147 Ill. 444 (1893).
640. *Chicago Tribune,* 17 October 1895, p. 5.
641. Ibid.
642. "Judge Bailey," *The Commentator,* p. 5.
643. 162 Ill. 12.
644. Isaac N. Phillips, "Judge Jacob W. Wilkin—An Appreciation," *Illinois Law Review* 2 (June 1907), pp. 68–69.
645. 229 Ill. 14–15; *Past and Present of Vermilion County, Illinois* (Chicago: S. J. Clarke Pub. Co., 1903), pp. 1087–88; *Portrait and Biographical Album of Vermilion County, Illinois* (Chicago: Chapman Bros., 1889), pp. 608–09; *Robinson Argus,* 10 April 1907, p. 4.
646. *Clark County Herald* (Marshall, Illinois), 10 April 1907, p. 8; William Henry Perrin, ed., *History of Crawford and Clark Counties, Illinois* (Chicago: O. L. Baskin & Co., 1883), p. 56; *Portrait and Biographical Album,* p. 608.
647. Palmer, *Bench and Bar of Illinois,* Vol. 1, p. 68.
648. *New York Times,* 31 October 1874, p. 3.
649. William Eaton, "Scholarship, Virtue, and Religion; Robert Allyn and McKendree College, 1863–1874," *Illinois Historical Journal* 78 (1985), p. 140.
650. *Past and Present of Vermilion County,* p. 1088.
651. *Portrait and Biographical Album,* p. 608.
652. 229 Ill. 18.

653. Phillips, "Judge Jacob W. Wilkin," pp. 71–72; 229 Ill. 15; Palmer, *Bench and Bar of Illinois*, Vol. 1, p. 69.
654. Babb, "The Supreme Court of Illinois," p. 237.
655. *Morgan v. People*, 136 Ill. 161 (1891).
656. *Friederich v. People*, 147 Ill. 310 (1893).
657. *Past and Present of Vermilion County*, p. 1089.
658. *Clark County Herald*, p. 8; *Robinson Argus*, p. 4; 229 Ill. 16.
659. Phillips, "Judge Jacob W. Wilkin," p. 72.
660. *Portrait and Biographical Record of Montgomery and Bond Counties, Illinois* (Chicago: Chapman Bros., 1892), pp. 501–02; William Henry Perrin, ed., *History of Bond and Montgomery Counties, Illinois* (Chicago: O. L. Baskin, 1882), p. 329.
661. *Hillsboro Journal,* 22 February 1901, p. 1.
662. Jacob L. Traylor, *Past and Present of Montgomery County, Illinois* (Chicago: S. J. Clarke Pub. Co., 1904), p. 100.
663. Bateman and Selby, *Historical Encyclopedia of Illinois*, p. 423; Traylor, *Past and Present of Montgomery County*, p. 103.
664. *Biographical Encyclopaedia of Illinois*, p. 327; Traylor, *Past and Present of Montgomery County*, p. 103.
665. *Chicago Tribune,* 17 February 1901, p. 38.
666. Illinois Statewide Marriage Index, 1763–1900, Montgomery County; *Biographical Encyclopaedia of Illinois,* p. 327; Cole, *The Era of the Civil War*, p. 398.
667. *Chicago Tribune*, p. 38.
668. *Illinois State Journal* (Springfield)*,* 16 February 1901, p. 1.
669. *Hillsboro Journal*, p. 1; 191 Ill. 43.
670. *Burke v. People*, 148 Ill. 70 (1893).
671. *Erringdale et al. v. Riggs et al*., 148 Ill. 403 (1894); Isaac Newton Bassett, *Past and Present of Mercer County, Illinois,* Vol. 1, (Chicago: S. J. Clarke Pub. Co., 1914), pp. 319–20.
672. *Hillsboro Journal*, pp. 1–2.
673. 260 Ill. 16; *Portrait and Biographical Record of Adams County Illinois* (Chicago: Chapman Bros, 1892), p. 233; David F. Wilcox, *Quincy and Adams County History and Representative Men* (Chicago: Lewis Publishing Company, 1919), p. 165.
674. 260 Ill. 16; William H. Collins and Cicero F. Perry, *Past and Present of the City of Quincy and Adams County, Illinois* (Chicago: The S.J. Clarke Publishing Co., 1905), pp. 366–369; *Portrait and Biographical Record of Adams County*, p. 233.
675. 260 Ill. 12.
676. 260 Ill. 12, 16; Wilcox, *Quincy and Adams County History*, p. 165; *Portrait and Biographical Record of Adams County*, p. 233.
677. *Chicago Tribune,* 7 February 1913, p. 17; 260 Ill. 17; *Portrait and Biographical Record of Adams County*, p. 369.
678. *Portrait and Biographical Record of Adams County*, p. 233.
679. Collins, *Past and Present of the City of Quincy*, p. 366.
680. 260 Ill. 16.
681. *Portrait and Biographical Record of Adams County*, p. 234.
682. 260 Ill. 17; Wilcox, *Quincy and Adams County History*, p. 165.
683. 260 Ill. 16.
684. *Portrait and Biographical Record of Adams County*, 234; Wilcox, *Quincy and Adams County History*, p. 166.
685. 260 Ill. 12.
686. 260 Ill. 23.
687. *Fixmer v. People*, 153 Ill. 123 (1894).
688. 153 Ill. 123.
689. 153 Ill. 123.
690. 153 Ill. 123.
691. *School Directors v. People*, 186 Ill. 331 (1900).
692. 186 Ill. 331.
693. 186 Ill. 331; *Portrait and Biographical Record of Adams County*, p. 233; Wilcox, *Quincy and Adams County History*, p. 165.
694. *Chicago Daily Tribune*, 7 February 1913, p. 17.
695. 260 Ill. 20.
696. 314 Ill. 12 (1925). Much of this memorial of Cartwright in a Supreme Court ceremony was delivered by his Oregon neighbor and friend Frank O. Lowden.
697. 314 Ill. 13; *History of Ogle County, Illinois* (Chicago: H.F. Kett and Co., 1878), p. 491.

698. Newton Bateman and Paul Selby, *Historical Encyclopedia of Illinois and Ogle County, Illinois* (Chicago: Munsell Publishing Co., 1909), p. 868; 314 Ill. 22–23.
699. "Memorials," *Chicago Bar Record* 37 (1955–1956), p. 465.
700. 314 Ill. 14.
701. Orrin N. Carter, "Constitutional Decisions of Justice Cartwright," *Illinois Law Review* 15 (November 1920), p. 237.
702. *Block v. City of Chicago*, 239 Ill. 251 (1909).
703. Comments on *Block v. Chicago* have been in the literature on film for more than thirty years. See for example Peter Sklar, *Movie-made America, A Cultural History of American Movies* (New York: Random House, 1975); Ray Broadus Borone et al., *Laws of Our Fathers: Popular Culture and the U.S. Constitution* (Bowling Green: Bowling Green State University Press, 1986); Charlie Keil et al., *America's Cinema Transitional Era: Audiences, Institutions, Practices* (Berkeley: University of California Press, 2004); and Lee Grieveson, *Policing Cinema: Movies and Censorship in Early Twentieth Century America* (Berkeley: University of California Press, 2004).
704. Joseph D. Kearney and Thomas W. Merrill, "Private Rights In Public Lands: The Chicago Lakefront, Montgomery Ward, And The Public Dedication Doctrine," *Northwestern University Law Review* 105 (2011): p. 1439.
705. *City of Chicago v. Ward*, 169 Ill. 392 (1897).
706. *Bliss et al. v. Ward et al.*, 198 Ill. 104 (1902).
707. William Wleklinski, *A Centennial History of John Marshall Law School* (Chicago: John Marshall Law School, 1998), p. 10.
708. Gov. Charles Deneen speaking at the dedication ceremony for the opening of the Supreme Court Building in February 1908. 232 Ill.10 (1908); 314 Ill. 20.
709. *Chicago Legal News*, 22 May 1924, p. 349.
710. 315 Ill. 12 (1924).
711. Walter A. Townsend, *Illinois Democracy: A History of the Party and Its Representative Members- Past and Present* (Springfield, Il: Democratic Historical Association, Inc., 1935), Vol. 2, p. 22.
712. 315 Ill. 12.
713. Crossley, *Courts and Lawyers of Illinois*, Vol. 3, p. 1224.
714. 315 Ill. 314.
715. *Booth v. People*, 186 Ill. 44–46 (1900).
716. 186 Ill. 51–53.
717. *Harding v. Harding*, 180 Ill. 483–484 (1899).
718. 180 Ill. 483.
719. 180 Ill. 496.
720. 180 Ill. 512–513.
721. Crossley, *Courts and Lawyers of Illinois*, Vol. 3, p. 1224.
722. 315 Ill. 14.
723. 310 Ill. 18 (1923).
724. *The History of Henry County Illinois, Its Tax-Payers and Voters* (Chicago: H.F. Kett & Co., 1877), p. 292.
725. Crossley, *Courts and Lawyers of Illinois*, Vol. 3, p. 1192.
726. 310 Ill. 19.
727. 232 Ill. 26 (1909).
728. 238 Ill. 12 (1909).
729. *Elmstedt v. Nicholson et al.*, 186 Ill. 580 (1900).
730. *Ritchie v. People*, 155 Ill. 98 (1895).
731. *Muller v. Oregon*, 208 U.S. 412 (1908).
732. *Ritchie & Co. v. Wayman*, 244 Ill. 509 (1910).
733. 310 Ill. 20 (1923).
734. *The Daily Breeze* (Taylorville, Illinois), 23 July 1906, p. 1.
735. Ibid.
736. 223 Ill. 10 (1906); *Illinois State Register* (Springfield, IL), 27 July 1906, p. 1.
737. *The Daily Breeze*, 23 July 1906, p. 1.
738. Ibid.
739. *Illinois State Register* (Springfield, IL), 22 May 1901, p. 1.
740. *The Daily Breeze*, 23 July 1906, p. 1.
741. 223 Ill. 10–12 (1906).
742. *Lloyd v. Catlin Coal Co.*, 210 Ill. 460 (1904).
743. 210 Ill. 460.
744. *Mackey v. Northern Milling Company*, 210 Ill. 115 (1904).
745. 210 Ill. 115.

746. 223 Ill. 9 (1906); *The Daily Breeze*, 23 July, 1906, p. 1.
747. 242 Ill. 9; Warvelle, *A Compendium of Freemasonry*, p. 508; W.A. Lorimer, Newton Bateman, and Paul Selby, eds., *Historical Encyclopedia of Illinois and Mercer County* (Chicago: Munsell Publishing Company, Publishers, 1903), p. 724.
748. Warvelle, *Compendium of Freemasonry*, p. 508.
749. Lorimer, *Historical Encyclopedia of Illinois*, p. 724; Warvelle, *Compendium of Freemasonry*, p. 508.
750. 242 Ill. 9.
751. 242 Ill. 9.
752. 242 Ill. 10.
753. Lorimer, *Historical Encyclopedia of Illinois*, p. 725.
754. 242 Ill. 10.
755. Lorimer, *Historical Encyclopedia of Illinois*, p. 725.
756. Warvelle, *Compendium of Freemasonry*, p. 508.
757. 242 Ill. 11.
758. Lorimer, *Historical Encyclopedia of Illinois*, p. 725; Warvelle, *Compendium of Freemasonry*, p. 508.
759. 242 Ill. 10.
760. *Suchomel v. Maxwell,* 240 Ill. 231 (1909).
761. 240 Ill. 231.
762. *Peabody Coal Co v. Northwestern Elevated Railroad Co.*, 230 Ill. 214 (1907).
763. 230 Ill. 214.
764. 230 Ill. 214.
765. 230 Ill. 214.
766. 230 Ill. 214.
767. 242 Ill. 11.
768. 242 Ill. 11.
769. *Chicago Daily Tribune*, 4 May 1931, 346 Ill. 11 (1932).
770. 346 Ill. 12; *Vandalia Leader*, 3 September 1931, p. 1.
771. Ibid.
772. 346 Ill. 14.
773. *Chicago Daily Tribune*, 6 June 1906, p. 2.
774. 346 Ill. 13.
775. *Chicago Daily Tribune*, 15 May 1915, p. 6.
776. *Scown v. Czarnecki,* 264 Ill. 305 (1914).
777. *Chicago Daily Tribune*, 14 June 1914; *Chicago Daily News Almanac and Year Book, 1915* (Chicago: Chicago Daily News, 1915), p. 554.
778. *Chicago Daily Tribune*, 1 December 1922, p. 7.
779. *People v. Stevenson*, 281 Ill. 1 (1917).
780. Snyder, "Ten Significant Decisions of the Illinois Supreme Court," p. 442.
781. *Chicago Daily Tribune*, 11 June 1927, p. 13.
782. *Chicago Daily Tribune*, 20 May 1931, p. 3.
783. 346 Ill. 11–26; *Illinois Bar Journal* 20 (October 1931) p. 6; *Vandalia Leader*, 3 September 1931, p. 1.
784. Frederick B. Crossley, "Editorial Notes: Orrin Nelson Carter 1854–1928," *Illinois Law Review* 23 (1928), pp. 371–372.
785. 333 Ill. 13–14 (1929).
786. 333 Ill. 15.
787. Crossley, "Orrin Nelson Carter," p. 372.
788. 333 Ill. 14.
789. *Chicago Daily Tribune*. 17 August 1928, p. 1.
790. 333 Ill. 23.
791. *Chicago Daily Tribune*, p. 1.
792. 333 Ill. 15.
793. *Chicago Daily Tribune*, p. 1.
794. 333 Ill. 19.
795. 333 Ill. 24.
796. 333 Ill. 21–23.
797. *People v. Pfanschmidt,* 262 Ill. 411 (1914).
798. Motion for New Trial and Grounds in Support of Same, 6 May 1918, case file 2055, Adams County Circuit Clerk, Quincy, Illinois.
799. 262 Ill. 411.

800. *People v. Lloyd et al.*, 304 Ill. 23 (1922).
801. 304 Ill. 23.
802. 304 Ill. 23.
803. 04 Ill. 23.
804. 304 Ill. 23.
805. Crossley, "Orrin Nelson Carter," p. 373.
806. *People v. Jennings*, 252 Ill. 534 (1911).
807. 252 Ill. 534.
808. 333 Ill. 461–462.
809. Crossley, "Orrin Nelson Carter," p. 371.
810. 333 Ill. 15.
811. *Biographical Review of Johnson, Massac, Pope and Hardin Counties* (Chicago: Biographical Pub. Co., 1893), pp. 578–79.
812. 269 Ill. 15.
813. *Vienna Times,* 28 January 1915, p. 4; Crossley, *Courts and Lawyers of Illinois*, Vol. 3, p. 447.
814. *Pauckner v. Wakem*, 231 Ill. 276 (1907).
815. *Dyrenforth v. Palmer Pneumatic Tire Company*, 240 Ill. 25 (1909).
816. O. J. Page, *History of Massac County, Illinois,* 1900; rpt. (Salem, Mass.: Higginson Book Co., [ca. 1998]), pp. 355–56.
817. *Daily Journal* (East St. Louis), 22 January1915, p. 1; *Chicago Legal News,* 15 January 1915, p. 197.
818. 269 Ill. 25.
819. Abraham Baughman and Robert F. Bartlett, *History of Morrow County, Ohio*, v. 2 (Chicago and New York: Lewis Publishing Company, 1911), pp. 413–16.
820. 375 Ill. 11–19; Baughman and Bartlett, *History of Morrow County, Ohio*, pp. 413–16; E. Duane Elbert, "Smile, Work, and Serve, the Legacy of an Illinois Officer in World War I," *Illinois History Journal*, 79 (Spring 1986), p. 36.
821. *Chicago Tribune*, 1 May 1907, p. 6.
822. *Charleston Daily Courier*, 8 August 1940, p. 1; 375 Ill. 11–19.
823. *People ex rel. Ring v. Board of Education*, 245 Ill. 334 (1910).
824. *Scown v. Czarnecki*, 264 Ill. 305 (1914); 375 Ill. 16; *The Public* 17 (16 January 1914), p. 586.
825. *Chicago Tribune*, 11 May 1933, p. 1; *Winter v. Barrett*, 352 Ill. 441 (1933).
826. *Charleston Daily Courier*, 8 August 1940, p. 1; 375 Ill. 11–19.
827. Frank K. Dunn, "The Lawyer's Duty and Function," *Illinois Law Review* 18 (February 1923), p. 414.
828. "Fortieth Annual Meeting, Illinois State Bar Association," *Illinois Law Review* 11 (November 1916), pp. 194–195.
829. *Chicago Tribune*, 30 November 1919, p. 4; *Chicago Tribune*, 20 May 1913, p. 4.
830. Frank K. Dunn, "Delays in Courts of Review in Criminal Cases," *Journal of Criminal Law and Criminology* 2 (May–March 1912), pp. 843–48.
831. *Chicago Tribune*, 23 November 1922, p. 6.
832. 375 Ill. 12; *Charleston Daily Courier*, 8 August 1940, p. 1.
833. George W. Smith, *History of Illinois,* 4 Vols. (Chicago: American Historical Society, 1927), Vol. 4, p. 339.
834. 373 Ill. 11; Newton Bateman and Paul Selby, *History of Illinois and History of Mercer County* (Chicago: Munsell, 1903), p. 725; Dunne, *Illinois: The Heart of the Nation*, Vol. 3, p. 148.
835. 373 Ill. 14.
836. *Aledo Democrat,* 23 April 1912, p. 1.
837. Crossley, *Courts and Lawyers of Illinois*, Vol. 2, p. 687.
838. Crossley, *Courts and Lawyers of Illinois,* Vol. 2, p. 687.
839. *Aledo Times Record,* 7 December 1938, pp. 1, 7; Crossley, *Courts and Lawyers of Illinois,* Vol. 2, p. 688.
840. Crossley, *Courts and Lawyers of Illinois,* Vol. 2, p. 687.
841. Daniel T. Johnson, *History of Mercer County, Illinois, 1882–1976* (Aledo: Mercer Co. Bicentennial Committee, 1977), p. 705; Walter A. Townsend, *Illinois Democracy* (Springfield: Democratic Historical Association, 1935), Vol. 2, p. 58.
842. *Aledo Democrat,* 26 March 1912, p. 1; 30 April 1912, p. 1; 21 May 1912, p. 1.
843. *Gillespie et al. v. Ohio Oil Company*, 260 Ill. 169 (1913).
844. *Crittenden et al. v. Hindman*, 271 Ill. 577 (1916).
845. 373 Ill. 16.
846. 373 Ill. 14.
847. *Aledo Democrat,* 17 December 1919, p. 1.

848. *Aledo Times Record*, 27 April 1932, p. 3.
849. 373 Ill. 18–19.
850. Dunne, *Illinois: The Heart of the Nation*, Vol. 3, p. 148.
851. *Chicago Daily Tribune,* 6 December 1938, p. 9; *Aledo Times Record,* 7 December 1938, p. 1; 14 December 1938, pp. 1, 3.
852. Newton Bateman and Paul Selby, *Historical Encyclopedia of Illinois and Knox County* (Chicago: Munsell, 1899), pp. 770–71.
853. 389 Ill. 11–18.
854. *Chicago Tribune,* Oct. 21, 1913, p. 2.
855. Craig to Fred Young, *Daily Pantagraph* (Bloomington, Illinois), 29 November 1940 (Craig, 1888, Charles Curtis, "First Football Team" (1940). *History*. Paper 2). http://digitalcommons.iwu.edu/athletics/athletics_hist/2.
856. Bateman and Selby, *Historical Encyclopedia of Illinois and Knox County*, p. 771.
857. *History of Knox County, Ill.* (Chicago: S. J. Clarke, 1912), Vol. 2, p. 591; *Daily Register-Mail* (Galesburg, Illinois), 25 August 1944, p. 2.
858. Paul C. Nagel, *Missouri; A Bicentennial History* (Nashville, TN: American Association for State and Local History, 1977), p. 29.
859. *Chicago Tribune,* 21 October 1913, p. 1.
860. 389 Ill. 17.
861. *Scown v. Czarnecki*, 264 Ill. 305 (1914).
862. *Nice v. Nice*, 275 Ill. 397 (1916).
863. 389 Ill. 14.
864. *Daily Register-Mail* (Galesburg, Illinois), 25 August 1944, p. 2.
865. *Portrait and Biographical Record of Clinton . . . and Jefferson Counties, Illinois* (Chicago: Chapman Pub. Co., 1894), pp. 382–84; *History of Jefferson County, Ill., 1810–1962* (Mt. Vernon, IL: Continental Historical Bureau, 1962), pp. H-16, W-29–32.
866. William Henry Perrin, ed., *History of Jefferson County, Illinois* (Chicago: Globe Pub. Co., 1883), Pt. 4, p. 42.
867. John A. Wall, *Wall's History of Jefferson County, Ill.* (Indianapolis: B. F. Bowen, 1909), p. 254; Perrin, *History of Jefferson County, Illinois*, p. W-30; *Illinois State Journal-Register* (Springfield), 26 November 1944, p. 17.
868. *Chicago Legal News*, 20 February 1915, p. 343; 10 April 1915, p. 427.
869. *Dalbey v. Hayes*, 267 Ill. 521 (1915).
870. *Burke v. The Toledo, Peoria and Western Railway Company*, 268 Ill. 615 (1915).
871. *Mount Vernon Register-News,* 27 November 1944, p. 1.
872. Ibid., pp. 1, 2.
873. *Marion Daily Republican*, 11 April 1938, p. 1.
874. Remarks by Hosea V. Ferrell of Marion in a memorial service, 369 Ill.12 (1938).
875. Remarks by Charles Rundall of the Illinois State Bar Association in a memorial service, 369 Ill. 11–12 (1938); *Marion Daily Republican*, 11 April 1938, 1. Ewing College was in operation from 1867 to 1925.
876. Ibid.; 369 Ill. 12.
877. Ibid., 14.
878. Ibid., 15; 15 *Law Notes* 113 (September 1911); *Marion Daily Republican*, 11 April 1938, p. 1.
879. *Chicago Tribune*, 14 April 1919, p. 2.
880. *Hagler et al. v. Larner et al.*, 284 Ill. 547 (1918).
881. Howard, *Illinois: A History of the Prairie State*, pp. 465–67. Small was able to pay the money in large part by forcing state employees to contribute to his campaign fund.
882. *Chicago Tribune*, 18 February 1926, p. 10; *People v. Small*, 319 Ill. 437 (1926).
883. 369 Ill. 16; *Marion Daily Republican*, 11 April 1938, p. 1; *Carbondale Free Press*, 12 April 1938, p. 1.
884. George W. Smith, *History of Illinois and Her People* (Chicago: American Historical Society, 1927), Vol. 4, p. 34.
885. *History of Peoria County* (Chicago: S. J. Clarke, 1912), Vol. 2, p. 152; *Peoria Journal Star*, 22 December 1997, p. B3.
886. Smith, *History of Illinois and Her People*, p. 34.
887. *History of Peoria County*, p. 153.
888. 400 Ill. 14; *Peoria Journal Star,* 22 December 1997, p. B3.
889. 400 Ill. 14.
890. "Heartbreak Hotel," *Chicago (*August 2006).
891. *People v. Stevens*, 358 Ill. 391 (1934).
892. *Gabel Manufacturing Company v. Francis B. Murphy, Director of Labor*, 390 Ill. 455 (1945).

893. *Illinois State Journal,* 15 January 1948, p. 1; *Peoria Journal,* 16 January 1948, p. 21; *Mason City Banner Times,* 22 January 1948, p. 1.
894. *Peoria Journal and Transcript,* 15 January 1948, p. 27.
895. 400 Ill. 14.
896. *Life Story of Floyd E. Thompson, Democratic Nominee for Governor of Illinois,* [1928], p. 2, pamphlet in the Abraham Lincoln Presidential Library, Springfield, Illinois.
897. R. B. Pearce, *Greene County, Illinois, and the War of the Revolution; Dedication of Government Markers . . . by Chief Justice Floyd E. Thompson* (White Hall: Greene County Board of Supervisors, 1923), p. 5, pamphlet in the Abraham Lincoln Presidential Library.
898. *Rock Island Argus,* 19 February 1919.
899. *Life Story,* p. 9.
900. *Who's Who in the Midwest* (Chicago: A. N. Marquis, 1949).
901. *Rock Island Argus,* 19 October 1960, p. 1; *Life Story,* pp. 3–4.
902. *Life Story,* p. 10.
903. *Rock Island Argus,* 19 March 1921.
904. *Life Story,* p. 4.
905. *People v. Wiedeman,* 324 Ill. 66 (1926); *People v. Daugherty,* 324 Ill. 160 (1927).
906. "Editorial," *Journal of the Illinois State Historical Society,* 15 (April–July 1922), pp. 719, 721.
907. *Chicago Tribune,* 25 November 1923, p. 4.
908. *Life Story,* p. 2.
909. Donald F. Tingley, *The Structuring of a State: The History of Illinois, 1899 to 1928* (Urbana: University of Illinois Press, 1980), pp. 386–87.
910. Tingley, *The Structuring of a State,* p. 387.
911. Ibid., p. 389.
912. *Illinois Bar Association News,* 29 (15 June 1999).
913. *Chicago Tribune,* 19 October 1960, p. 1.
914. *Chicago Sun-Times,* 19 October 1960, p. 52.
915. *Chicago Tribune,* 20 October 1960, Pt. 5, p. 10.
916. *History of Stephenson County* (Chicago: S.J. Clarke Publishing Company, 1910), p. 691; 375 Ill. 20–27; *Freeport Journal-Standard,* 16 July 1940, p. 1.
917. *Chicago Tribune,* 5 December 1920, p. 12.
918. E. George Thiem, ed., *A Goodly Heritage: A History of Carroll County, Illinois* (Mt. Morris, IL: Kable Printing Company, 1968), p. 8.
919. *History of Stephenson County,* p. 691; *Freeport Journal-Standard,* 16 July 1940, p. 1.
920. *Freeport Journal-Standard,* 16 July 1940, p. 1; *Illinois Blue Book,* (Springfield, IL: Illinois Secretary of State, 1921), pp. 555, 563; *Law Notes,* v. 23, no. 10 (January 1920), p. 174.
921. *Fergus v. Marks,* 321 Ill. 510 (1926).
922. *History of Stephenson County,* p. 691.
923. *Chicago Tribune,* 21 May 1933, p. 18; *Chicago Tribune,* 30 May 1933, p. 6; *Chicago Tribune,* 6 June 1933, p. 1.
924. Ibid.; *Law Notes,* v. 23 (August 1919), p. 93.
925. *Freeport Journal-Standard,* 16 July 1940, p. 1.
926. *History of Stephenson County,* p. 691; *Freeport Journal-Standard,* 16 July 1940, p. 1.
927. Ibid.
928. 359 Ill. 11–26; *Chicago Bar Record,* v. 16, no. 5 (1934–1935), pp. 212–213.
929. Ibid.
930. 359 Ill. 11–26.
931. *Chicago Tribune,* 6 June 1940, p. 26.
932. Ibid.
933. Charles P. Megan, representing the Chicago Bar Association at memorial services held for DeYoung, December 12, 1934, 359 Ill. 14.
934. *People v. Bruner,* 343 Ill. 146 (1933).
935. *Chicago Tribune,* 19 February 1933, p. 4.
936. *People v. Fisher,* 340 Ill. 250 (1930). Both opinions are noted in *Chicago Bar Record,* v. 16, no. 5 (1934–1935), pp. 212–213.
937. *City of Aurora v. Burns,* 319 Ill. 84 (1925).
938. *Village of Euclid v. Ambler Realty Company,* 272 U.S. 365 (1926).
939. 359 Ill. 11–26; *Chicago Bar Record,* v. 16, no. 5 (1934–1935), pp. 212–213.
940. *Chicago Tribune,* 18 November 1934, p. 18.
941. 337 Ill. 12.
942. *Chicago Legal News,* 18 January 1902, p. 348.
943. *Chicago Daily Tribune,* 14 September 1929, p. 23; 337 Ill. 12; *Moline Daily Dispatch,* 7 November 1928, p. 14; *Moline Daily Dispatch,* 13 September 1929, p. 23.

944. *Rock Island Argus*, 13 September 1929, p. 14.
945. *Moline Daily Dispatch*, 13 September 1929, p. 23.
946. Ibid.
947. Ibid.
948. *American Bar Association Journal* 15 (1929), pp. 146–148; *Chicago Daily Tribune*, 27 February 1927, p. 14; 337 Ill. 13; *Wisconsin et al. v. Illinois*, 279 U.S. 821 (1929).
949. *Rock Island Argus*, 13 September 1929, p. 14.
950. *Moline Daily Dispatch*, 7 November 1928, p. 14.
951. *Chicago Daily Tribune*, 24 January 1929, p. 1.
952. *Chicago Daily Tribune*, 26 November 1926, p. 12; *Chicago Daily Tribune*, 28 November 1929, p. 12.
953. *People v. Brown*, 336 Ill. 257 (1929).
954. *Bamberger v. Barbour*, 335 Ill. 458 (1929). The California case was *In re Manchester's Estate*, 174 Cal. 417 (1917).
955. *Chicago Daily Tribune*, 14 September 1929, p. 1.
956. *Moline Daily Dispatch*, 13 September 1929, p. 1.
957. *Moline Daily Dispatch*, 16 September 1929, p. 1; *Moline Daily Dispatch*, 13 September 1929, p. 23.
958. 369 Ill. 1; *Jacksonville Courier*, 21 March 1938, p. 12.
959. Ibid.
960. Ibid.
961. *Moline Daily Dispatch*, 7 November 1928, p. 14.
962. *Chicago Daily Tribune*, 1 October 1929, p. 7.
963. *Chicago Daily Tribune*, 11 April 1930, p. 5.
964. *Chicago Daily Tribune*, 1 June 1930, p. 7; *Chicago Daily Tribune*, 2 June 1930, p. 12.
965. *Lundgren v. Industrial Commission, Iverson, et al.* 337 Ill. 246 (1929).
966. *People v. Fiorita*, 339 Ill. 78 (1930).
967. 369 Ill. 1
968. *Chicago Daily Tribune*, 10 September 1931, p. 4; *Chicago Daily Tribune*, 21 October 1931, p. 16; *Chicago Daily Tribune*, 30 June 1933, p. 12.
969. 369 Ill. 1.
970. *Jacksonville Courier*, 21 March 1938, p. 12; *Chicago Daily Tribune*, 22 March 1938, p. 12; *Chicago Daily Tribune*, 4 August 1932, p. 1.
971. *Jacksonville Courier*, 22 March 1938, p. 8; *Jacksonville Courier*, 23 March 1938, p. 12.
972. 31 Ill. 2d. 11.
973. 31 Ill. 2d. 11.
974. 31 Ill. 2d. 11.
975. *Chicago Daily Tribune*, 13 September 1928, p. 6.
976. *Chicago Daily Tribune*, 4 June 1930, p. 7.
977. *Bachrach et al. v. Nelson et al.*, 349 Ill. 579 (1932); *Chicago Daily Tribune*, 23 October 1932, p. 3; Jo Desk Lucas, "No Property Taxes under the Illinois Constitution," *University of Chicago Law Review* 25 (Autumn 1957), pp. 63–108.
978. *People ex rel. Illinois State Bar Association v. Peoples Stock Yards State Bank*, 344 Ill. 462 (1931); *State Bar Journal* 9 (March 1934), pp. 53–54.
979. *Tribune Company v. Thompson et al.*, 342 Ill. 503 (1930).
980. *People v. City of Chicago et al; Bass et al v. City of Chicago et al.*, 349 Ill. 304 (1932).
981. *Chicago Daily Tribune*, 24 October 1931, p. 2; *Chicago Daily Tribune*, 27 July 1932, p. 2; *Chicago Daily Tribune*, 24 August 1934, p. 3.
982. *Chicago Daily Tribune*, 11 May 1939, p. 11
983. 31 Ill. 2d. 11.
984. 31 Ill. 2d. 11; *Chicago Daily Tribune*, 5 May 1937, p. 4; *Chicago Daily Tribune*, 11 January 1938, p. 3; *Chicago Daily Tribune*, 24 December 1943, p. 5; *Chicago Daily Tribune*, 18 January 1944, p. 2; *Chicago Daily Tribune*, 4 December 1947, p. 29.
985. *Chicago Bar Record* 43 (1961–1962), p. 513; 31 Ill. 2d. 11.
986. Ibid.
987. *Carrollton Gazette*, 22 November 1940, p. 1.
988. 376 Ill. 11.
989. 376 Ill. 11.
990. 376 Ill. 11.
991. 376 Ill. 11; *Chicago Daily Tribune,* 23 August 1931, p. 9.
992. *Chicago Daily Tribune*, 20 October 1924, p. 8; *Chicago Daily Tribune*, 24 October 1924, p. 4.
993. *Chicago Daily Tribune*, 9 March 1933, p. 1.

994. Memorial of Gilbert H. Hutchins of Carrollton, 376 Ill. 11.
995. *Chicago Daily Tribune*, 10 September 1931, p. 18; *Chicago Daily Tribune*, 16 November 1940, p. 12; *Chicago Daily Tribune*, 7 June 1933, p. 7.
996. *Graham v. City of Chicago*, 346 Ill. 638 (1931).
997. *Eschmann v. Cawi*, 357 Ill. 379 (1934).
998. *Chicago Daily Tribune*, 10 September 1931, p. 18; *Chicago Daily Tribune*, 16 November 1940, p. 12; *Chicago Daily Tribune*, 7 June 1933, p. 7.
999. *Chicago Bar Record*, v. 18 (1936–1937), p. 231.
1000. 376 Ill. 11; *Carrollton Gazette*, 22 November 1940, p. 1; *Carrollton, Illinois 1818–1968* (Carrollton: Carrollton Business and Professional Women's Club, 1968), p. 3.
1001. 367 Ill. 11.
1002. 367 Ill. 11; *Michigan Alumnus*, v. 44 (October 16, 1937), p. 39.
1003. "Justice Herrick," *Chicago Bar Record*, v. 19 (1937–1938), p. 4.
1004. *Chicago Daily Tribune*, 28 September 1937, p. 2.
1005. The *Chicago Daily Tribune* carried the story periodically from beginning to end. See the *Tribune's* beginning and ending articles on January 1, 1908, p. 1, and May 29, 1908, p. 1.
1006. 367 Ill. 11.
1007. *Chicago Daily Tribune*, 19 September 1937, p. 18.
1008. *Chicago Daily Tribune*, 26 April 1934, p. 7.
1009. *In re Day*, 181 Ill. 73 (1899); *People v. Goodman*, 366 Ill. 346 (1937); "Notes on Latest Supreme Court Picture," *Chicago Bar Record*, v. 18 (1936–1937), p. 231.
1010. *Chicago Daily Tribune*, 19 September 1937, p. 18; 367 Ill. 11.
1011. *Chicago Bar Record*, 32 (1950–1951), p. 140; *Freeport Journal-Standard*, 18 July 1950, p. 1; 407 Ill. 11.
1012. Ibid.
1013. *Chicago Daily Tribune*, 7 June 1938, p. 2; *Chicago Bar Record*, p. 140; *Freeport Journal-Standard*, 18 July 1950, p. 1; 407 Ill. 11.
1014. Ibid.; *Freeport Journal-Standard*, 18 July 1950; *Chicago Daily Tribune*, 7 June 1938, p. 2.
1015. Excerpts from Response on Behalf of the Court to motion from admission of sixty-five new lawyers in the Supreme Court of Illinois, 14 December 1933, *Kansas City Law Review* 2 (1933–1934), p. 88.
1016. *Sundquist v. Hardware Mutual Insurance Co.*, 371 Ill. 360 (1939); 407 Ill. 22.
1017. *Chicago Daily Tribune*, 3 June 1942, p. 4.
1018. Ibid.; 407 Ill. 15–16.
1019. Ibid.; *Chicago Bar Record*, p. 140; "Elwyn R. Shaw," *Journal of the National Association of Referees in Bankruptcy*, 24 (1950), p. 136.
1020. 407 Ill. 11–22.
1021. Ibid.; *Chicago Bar Record*, p. 140; *Freeport Journal-Standard*, 18 July 1950, p. 1.
1022. *Chicago Tribune*, 12 December 1976, p. B15; *Twenty-eighth Annual report of the Trustees, Superintendent and Treasurer of the Illinois Institution for the Education of the Blind* (July 1, 1904), p. 3; *Twenty-seventh Report of the Board of Trustees of the University of Illinois* (Urbana, 1914), p. 14; Memorial to Justice Farthing, 78 Ill. 2d xv–xxi (1980).
1023. *Chicago Tribune*, 16 March 1924, p. 13.
1024. *People v. Scowley*, 353 Ill. 330 (1933).
1025. Albert E. Jenner and Walter V. Schaefer, "The New Rules of the Illinois Supreme Court under the Illinois Civil Practice Act," *University of Chicago Law Review*, 1 (1933–1934): p. 752.
1026. *Swing et al. v. American Federation of Labor et al.*, 372 Ill. 91 (1939); *American Federation of Labor et al. v. Swing et al.*, 312 U.S. 321 (1941).
1027. *Chicago Tribune*, 2 June 1942, p. 13.
1028. *Chicago Bar Record* 33 (1951–1952), p. 451.
1029. *Chicago Tribune*, 17 July 1953, p. 11. He resigned before completing two full terms on the Court of Claims. According to the *Tribune* article, Stratton's office said that Farthing wanted to increase his state pension and, having done that, resigned.
1030. *Chicago Tribune*, 18 May 1952; "Membership News," *Law Library Journal* 48 (1955), p. 251.
1031. *Chicago Tribune*, 4 December 1976, p. B15; "Law Office Notes," *Illinois Bar Journal* 46 (1957–1958), p. 924.
1032. "Blind Illinois Judge to be Chief Justice," *St. Petersburg (FL) Times*, 30 April 1937, p. 16.
1033. "Chief Justice Farthing," *Chicago Bar Record* 18 (1936–1937), p. 188.
1034. Memorial by Joseph Hinshaw of the Illinois State Bar Association, 409 Ill. 11–17 (1951).
1035. Ibid.

1036. On Wilson's relationship to his partners, see Ibid; on his relationship by marriage to Darrow, see "Mother of Illinois Justice is 100," *Chicago Tribune*, 22 March 1946; on his relationship to Clarke and his newspaper career, see "Two Illinois Justices Former Newspapermen," United Press wire service article in *Binghamton (NY) Press*, 20 February 1936, p. 18.

1037. 409 Ill. 12.

1038. Thomas William Herringshaw, ed. and comp., *Herringshaw's American Blue Book of Biography* (Chicago: American Blue Book Publishers, 1919), p. 179.

1039. 409 Ill. 12; *Chicago Tribune*, 15 March 1951, p. 1.

1040. Much has been written about the bench and bar during Thompson's administration. See, for example, Herman Kogan, *The First Century: The Chicago Bar Association 1874–1974* (Chicago: Rand McNally & Company, 1974), pp. 99–121; for Hearst's Independence League and the other organizations' roles in elections, see especially pp. 113–115.

1041. *Chicago Tribune*, 4 June 1939, p. 20.

1042. "Francis S. Wilson, Justice of the Supreme Court of Illinois for the Seventh District," *Chicago Bar Record* 17 (1935–1936), p. 15

1043. *Chicago Tribune*, 25 November 1926, p. 32; *Chicago Tribune*, 8 December 1926, p. 32.

1044. *Chicago Tribune*, 17 March 1932.

1045. *Chicago Tribune*, 11 March 1949, p. 3; *Chicago Tribune*, 1 October 1949, p. 3; *Chicago Tribune*, 12 April 1942, p. 5; 409 Ill. 13.

1046. Ibid.; "Justice Wilson Dies," *Chicago Tribune*, 15 March 1951; "Officials Pay Tribute to Judge Wilson," *Chicago Tribune*, 17 March 1951, p. B4.

1047. Edwin H. Cooke, "Sixty Years with the Supreme Court," unpublished typescript, Box 5, Illinois State Bar Association Collection, Abraham Lincoln Presidential Library and Museum, Springfield, Illinois.

1048. 12 Ill. 2d. 14; *Chicago Tribune*, 1 July 1938, p. 9; *Danville Commercial-News*, 13 October 1956, p. 1.

1049. *Chicago Bar Record*, vol. 39 (1957–1958), p. 475; *Chicago Tribune,* 1 July 1938, p. 9; Sylvester Quindry, *Practicing Law, When Where and How* (Washington, D.C.: Washington Law Book Company, 1938), p. 127.

1050. *Chicago Bar Record*, vol. 39 (1957–1958), p. 475; *Chicago Tribune,* 1 July 1938, p. 9.

1051. *Proceedings of the Illinois State Bar Association 43 Meeting*, 1919 (Danville: Interstate Publishing Printing, 1919), p. 96; Joseph Clement Bates, *History of the Bench and Bar of California* (San Francisco: Bench and Bar Publishing Company, 1912), pp. 335–336.

1052. Ibid.; James Fifield Clarke, *American Bar 1962* (Minneapolis: J.F. Clarke, 1962), p. 19; *Chicago Bar Record*, vol. 39 (1957–1958), p. 475.

1053. Ibid.; *Danville Commercial-News*, 13 October 1956, p. 1.

1054. *Iron Age*, vol. 54, no. 4 (January–June 1915), p. 276.

1055. *Danville Commercial-News*, 13 October 1956, p. 1.

1056. 12 Ill. 2d 14 (1957); *Chicago Tribune*, 7 May 1938, p. 8; *Chicago Tribune*, 29 June 1938, p. 2.

1057. *Chicago Bar Record*, vol. 23 (1941–1942), p. 353.

1058. 12 Ill. 2d 14; *Chicago Tribune,* 12 April 1942, p. 5; *Chicago Tribune,* 9 September 1941, p. 8.

1059. *Chicago Tribune*, 1 July 1938, p. 9.

1060. Donald S. Baldwin in a memorial delivered May 13, 1957, 12 Ill. 2d 14.

1061. *Chicago Tribune*, 1 July 1938, p. 97.

1062. Justice Joseph Daily in a memorial delivered May 13, 1957, 12 Ill. 2d 19.

1063. *Danville Commercial-News*, 13 October 1956, p. 1.

1064. Justice Joseph Daily in a memorial delivered May 13, 1957, 12 Ill. 2d 19.

1065. *Chicago Tribune*, 24 May 1939, p. 7.

1066. 31 Ill. 2d 25.

1067. *Chicago Tribune*, 24 May 1939, p. 7.

1068. *Chicago Tribune*, 24 May 1939, p. 7.

1069. 31 Ill. 2d 29.

1070. *People v. Maggi*, 378 Ill. 595 (1942).

1071. 378 Ill. 595.

1072. *People ex rel v. Traeger*, 372 Ill. 11 (1940).

1073. 372 Ill. 11.

1074. *Chicago Tribune*, 9 August 1939, p. 1.

1075. *Chicago Tribune*, 8 June 1948, p. 1.

1076. *Chicago Tribune*, 9 June 1948, p. 6.

1077. "Judge Murphy Dead," *Monmouth Review Atlas*, 3 June 1963, p. 1.

1078. *Monmouth Review Atlas*, 3 June 1963, p. 1.
1079. *Chicago Tribune*, 4 January 1941, p. 8; 397 Ill. 11; *Chicago Bar Record*, Vol. 28, No. 9 (1946–1947), p. 390.
1080. Ibid.; *Centralia Sentinel*, 7 February 1947, p. 1.
1081. Ibid.; *Chicago Bar Record*, Vol. 28, No 9 (1946–1947), p. 390.
1082. *Chicago Bar Record*, Vol. 22, No. 4 (1940–1941), p. 233; James Clark Fifield, *The American Bar* (Minneapolis: JC Fifield Company, 1918), pp. 128–129.
1083. *Chicago Bar Record*, Vol. 28, No. 9 (1946–1947), p. 390, 17, 18
1084. *Chicago Bar Record*, Vol. 28, No. 9 (1946–1947), p. 390; 397 Ill. 11; *Chicago Tribune*, 25 December 1917, p.8.
1085. *Illinois Criminal Digest* (Chicago: BJ Smith & Co., 1920), and following years.
1086. *Chicago Bar Record*, Vol. 28, No. 9 (1946–1947), p. 390.
1087. *Chicago Tribune*, 18 July 1929, p. 14; *Illinois Law Review*, Vol. 24 (1929–1930), pp. 564–565.
1088. *Chicago Tribune*, 2 July 1931, p. 18.
1089. *Chicago Tribune*, 10 December 1940, p. 15.
1090. *Chicago Tribune*, 26 February 1941, p. 1.
1091. *Chicago Tribune*, 2 March 1941, p. C15; *Chicago Tribune*, 2 April 1941, p. 20.
1092. *Chicago Tribune*, 2 June 1942, p. 1.
1093. *Zurn v. City of Chicago*, 389 Ill. 114 (1945).
1094. *Chicago Tribune*, 18 January 1945, p. 2.
1095. 397 Ill. 11.
1096. *Chicago Bar Record*, Vol. 23 (1941–1942), p. 419.
1097. *True Republican* (Sycamore), 28 March 1961, p. 1.
1098. *Chicago Bar Record*, Vol. 42 (1960–1961), p. 478.
1099. *Chicago Bar Record*, Vol. 23 (1941–1942), p. 419.
1100. *Chicago Bar Record*, Vol. 23 (1941–1942), p. 420.
1101. *Illinois Bar Journal*, Vol. 33 (1944), 70–71.
1102. *Kinsley v. Kinsley*, 388 Ill. 194 (1944).
1103. *Michigan State Bar Journal*, Vol. 23 (1944), p. 587; *Chicago Bar Record*, Vol. 26 (1944–45), p. 23.
1104. 21 Ill. 2d. 5.
1105. *Chicago Bar Record*, Vol. 42 (1960–1961), p. 478.
1106. "New Justices of the Illinois Supreme Court," *Chicago Bar Record*, Vol. 23, no. 10 (July 1942), p. 419; *Harrisburg Daily Register*, 27 November 1972, p. 2.
1107. Ibid.; *Illinois Blue Book 1949–1950* (Springfield, IL: Secretary of State, 1950), p. 90.
1108. "New Justices of the Illinois Supreme Court," p. 419.
1109. Ibid.; 53 Ill. 2d. xxii; *Chicago Tribune*, 7 July 1927, p. 14; John Clayton, *The Illinois Fact Book and Almanac 1673–1968* (Carbondale: Southern Illinois University Press, 1970), pp. 419–420.
1110. Howard, *Illinois A History of the Prairie State*, p. 465.
1111. *Chicago Tribune*, 29 January 1942, p. 10; *Chicago Tribune*, 2 June 1942, p. 1.
1112. *Klemme v. Drainage District No. 5*, 380 Ill. 221 (1942); *Continental Illinois National Bank and Trust Company v. Art Institute of Chicago*, 409 Ill. 481 (1951).
1113. *Klemme v. Drainage District No. 5 of the Township of Crete*, 380 Ill. 215 (1942).
1114. *Illinois Blue Book 1949–1950* (Springfield, IL: Secretary of State, 1950), p. 90.
1115. 53 Ill. 2d. xxiv.
1116. *Chicago Tribune*, 11 January 1951, p. 6.
1117. *Journal of the American Judicial Society*, Vol. 40, no. 2 (August 1956), p. 57; Illinois State Bar Association, *Unauthorized Practice of Law News*, v. 22, no. 4 (December 1956), p. 76; 53 Ill. 2d. xvi.
1118. 53 Ill. 2d. xiv; *Harrisburg Daily Register*, 27 November 1972, p. 2.
1119. Ibid.
1120. H.L. Motsinger, "Simpson Family First to Settle in Johnson County in 1805," *Daily Register* (Harrisburg, Illinois) 24 January 1952, p. 24; James Clark Fifield, *The American Bar 1928* (Minneapolis: James C. Fifield Co., 1928), p. 255; 53 Ill. 2d. xvii.
1121. Ibid., *Illinois Blue Book* (Springfield, IL: Secretary of State, 1919), p. 217.
1122. *Edwardsville Intelligencer*, 7 May 1973, p. 1.
1123. *Chicago Tribune*, 23 July 1947, p. 16; *Chicago Tribune*, 5 August 1947, p. 1; *Chicago Tribune*, 6 August 1947, p. 18.
1124. *Chicago Tribune*, 7 June 1951, p. B10; *Chicago Tribune*, 19 June 1951, p. 22.
1125. Remarks by James O. Monroe at Simpson's memorial service held in the Supreme Court room in Springfield, May 29, 1973, 53 Ill. 2d. xvii.

1126. *People ex rel. Illinois State Bar Association, et al. v. Frank Shafer*, 404 Ill. 45 (1949).
1127. 53 Ill. 2d. xvii.
1128. *Edwardsville Intelligencer*, 7 May 1973, p. 1.
1129. 53 Ill. 2d. xvii.
1130. *Chicago Daily Tribune*, 22 May 1939, p. 9.
1131. 1 Ill. 2d. 12.
1132. 1 Ill. 2d. 12.
1133. 1 Ill. 2d. 14.
1134. 1 Ill. 2d. 14.
1135. *Chicago Daily Tribune*, 8 June 1948, p. 1.
1136. *Illinois State Register*, 13 March 1953, p. 1.
1137. 1 Ill. 2d. 14.
1138. *Stalder v. Stone*, 412 Ill. 488 (1952), 500.
1139. Ibid., 500.
1140. *People v. Levisen*, 404 Ill. 574 (1950), 575.
1141. Ibid., 576.
1142. Ibid., 577.
1143. Ibid., 580.
1144. James C. Carper and Thomas C. Hunt, *The Dissenting Tradition in American Education* (New York: Peter Lang Publishing, 2007), pp. 243–45.
1145. *Chicago Daily Tribune*, 14 December 1952, p. 15.
1146. *Illinois State Register*, 13 March 1953, p. 1.
1147. *Chicago Daily Tribune*, 14 March 1953, p. A7.
1148. James Montgomery Rice, *Peoria City and County*, v.2 (Chicago: S.J. Clarke Publishing Company, 1912), p. 570; "Joseph E. Daily, 1888–1965," *Illinois Bar Journal* 54 (November 1965), pp. 230–31.
1149. 35 Ill. 2d. 11.
1150. "Joseph E. Daily," *Illinois Bar Journal*, p. 230–31.
1151. *Chicago Bar Record*, Vol. 42, No. 9 (1960–1961), p. 213; 35 Ill. 2d. 15; "Judge Daily Viewed as a Candidate for State Supreme Court," *Chicago Daily Tribune*, 17 January 1948, p. 10.
1152. Rice, *Peoria City and County*, p. 570; 35 Ill. 2d. 11–17.
1153. *Chicago Daily Tribune*, 16 February 1948, p. A1; *Chicago Daily Tribune*, 26 March 1948, p. B7.
1154. Eulogy by Justice Ray I. Klingbiel, *Chicago Tribune*, 2 April 1965, p. 1.
1155. Ibid.
1156. *In re Anastaplo*, 3 Ill. 2d. 471 (1954); *In re Anastaplo*, 348 U.S. 946 (1955); *In re Anastaplo*, 349 U.S. 903 (1955), 349 U.S. 908 (1955); *In re Anastaplo*, 18 Ill. 2d. 182 (1960); *In re Anastaplo*, 366 U.S. 82 (1961).
1157. Andrew Patner, "The Quest of George Anastaplo," *Chicago Magazine* ((December 1982), p. 184ff.
1158. Ibid.
1159. *Nashville Journal*, 30 August 1956, p. 1.
1160. Ibid.
1161. Ibid.; 11 Ill. 2d. 15.
1162. Ibid., p. 15; *Chicago Tribune*, 17 January 1960, p. A13.
1163. *People v. Gholson et al.*, 412 Ill. 294 (1952).
1164. 412 Ill. 294, p. 303.
1165. 11 Ill. 2d. 17.
1166. Ibid.
1167. *Journal of the Illinois State Bar Association*, v. 4, no. 3 (November 1956), p. 3; *Nashville Journal*, 30 August 1956, p. 1.
1168. 11 Ill. 2d. 13.
1169. *Northwestern University Law Review* (December 1979), p. 694.
1170. *Northwestern University Law Review* (December 1986), p. 1148.
1171. *Northwestern University Law Review* (December 1979), pp. 680, 707; *Illinois Bar Journal* (September 1969), p. 66; John R. Vile, ed., *Great American Judges; An Encyclopedia* (Santa Barbara, CA: ABC-CLIO, 2003), p. 678.
1172. *Northwestern University Law Review* (December 1979), pp. 679–80, 699.
1173. Vile, *Great American Judges*, p. 679; Bill Barnhart and Gene Schlickman, *John Paul Stevens; An Independent Life* (DeKalb: Northern Illinois University Press, 2010), p. 80.
1174. *Chicago Tribune*, 17 June 1986, p. 10.
1175. *People ex rel. Wallace v. Labrenz*, 411 Ill. 618 (1952).

1176. Ed Nash, "Retiring justice of Illinois Supreme Court: Walter V. Schaefer," *Illinois Issues* (January 1977), p. 9. http://www.lib.niu.edu/1977/ii770108.html.
1177. *People v. Witherspoon*, 36 Ill. 2d. 467 (1967).
1178. *Witherspoon v. Illinois*, 391 U.S. 510; Evan J. Mandery, *Capital Punishment: A Balanced Examination* (Sudbury, MA: Jones and Bartlett, 2005), pp. 464–68.
1179. *Chicago Tribune*, 6 March 1990, Sec. 2, p. 8.
1180. Nash, "Retiring justice of Illinois Supreme Court: Walter V. Schaefer," p. 9.
1181. *Illinois Bar Journal* (September 1969), p. 66.
1182. *Northwestern University Law Review* (December 1986), p. 1146.
1183. *Paris Beacon-News*, 13 November 1961, p. 1.
1184. 26 Ill. 2d. 11.
1185. *Paris Beacon-News*, 13 November 1961, p. 1.
1186. 26 Ill. 2d. 11; *Chicago Tribune*, 13 November 1961, p. 1.
1187. "Judicial Conference of Illinois," *Journal of the American Bar Association*, Vol. 44 (September 1958), p. 837; "The Need for Judges Now," *Chicago Bar Record*, Vol. 42, No. 5 (1960–1961), p. 213.
1188. *Johnson v. Luhman*, 330 Ill. App. 598 (1947); 26 Ill. 2d. 11.
1189. *In re Anastaplo*, 18 Ill. 2d. 182 (1957).
1190. *In re Anastaplo*, 366 U.S. 82 (1961).
1191. 26 Ill. 2d. 11; *Paris Beacon-News*, 11 November 1961, p. 9; *Paris Beacon-News*, 13 November 1961, p. 1.
1192. 26 Ill. 2d. 11.
1193. 39 Ill. 2d. xi (1968); Newton Bateman and Paul Selby, *Historical Encyclopedia of Illinois and History of Christian County*, 2 Vols. (Chicago: Munsell Publishing Co., 1918), Vol. 2, pp. 901–02.
1194. Ibid.
1195. Ibid.; *Law Notes*, Vol. 28 (1924–1925), p. 114; *Chicago Tribune*, 1 September 1967, p. 12.
1196. Ibid; 39 Ill. 2d. xi (1968); Bateman and Selby, *Historical Encyclopedia*, pp. 901–02.
1197. 39 Ill. 2d. xi (1968); *Chicago Tribune*, 1 September 1967, p. 12.
1198. Charles Van Devander, *Politics and People* (New York: Arno Press, 1974), p. 284; "Illinois: the Horner Pie," *Time*, 22 April 1940, n.p.
1199. 39 Ill. 2d. xi.
1200. ABA Section of Insurance, Negligence and Compensation Law Proceedings, Vol. 1 (1940), pp. x–xii.
1201. *Chicago Tribune*, 1 September 1967, p. 12.
1202. *Chicago Tribune*, 3 June 1951, p. 1; *Chicago Tribune*, 11 July 1951, p. A7; *Chicago Tribune*, 14 July 1951, p. 5.
1203. Justice Walter V. Schaefer in the Court's memorial to Hershey, 19 September 1968, 39 Ill. 2d. xviii.
1204. *Chicago Bar Record*, Vol. 43, No. 5 (February 1962), pp. 247–250; *Chicago Bar Record*, Vol. 43, no. 2 (December 1961), p. 113.
1205. *Chicago Tribune*, 25 May 1954, p. 5.
1206. Quoted in Rosa Eberly, *Citizen Critics* (Urbana: University of Illinois Press, 2010), pp. 98–99.
1207. 39 Ill. 2d. xi; *Chicago Tribune*, September 1, 1967, p. 12.
1208. *Moline Daily Dispatch*, 19 January 1973, pp. 1, 3.
1209. *Illinois Bar Journal*, November 1955, p. 213.
1210. *Moline Daily Dispatch*, 19 January 1973, p. 3.
1211. 18 Ill. 2d. 11–29, quotation on p. 20.
1212. *People v. Mangano*, 375 Ill. 72 (1940).
1213. *People v. Hobbs*, 35 Ill. 2d. 263 (1966).
1214. *People v. Isaacs et al.*, 37 Ill. 2d. 205 (1967).
1215. Kenneth A. Manaster, *Illinois Justice; The Scandal of 1969 and the Rise of John Paul Stevens* (Chicago: University of Chicago Press, 2001), pp. 208–09, 225.
1216. George Fiedler, *The Illinois Law Courts in Three Centuries, 1673–1973* (Berwyn, Ill.: Physicians' Record Co., 1973), pp. 333–34; Manaster, *Illinois Justice*, pp. 240–41; Barnhart and Schlickman, *John Paul Stevens*, p. 144.
1217. Manaster, *Illinois Justice*, p. 275.
1218. *Moline Daily Dispatch*, 19 January 1973, p. 1. Since he died during the night of January 18, some sources list the date of death as January 19.
1219. 64 Ill. 2d. xvi.
1220. *People v. Miller*, 13 Ill. 2d. 84 (1958).

1221. www.law.northwestern.edu/cwc/exonerations/ilMlllerLSummary.html; *Time,* 31 March 1967, www.time.com/time/printout.
1222. 64 Ill. 2d. xvi.
1223. *People v. Lindsay,* 51 Ill. 2d. 399 (1972).
1224. Clyde C. Walton, *Illinois Lives* (Hopkinsville, Ky.: Historical Record Assn., 1969), pp. 202–03.
1225. *Morning Star* (Rockford), 23 February 1976, p. 1, 24 February 1976, p. A4.
1226. *Nashville Daily Register,* 29 September 1969, p. 1; *Chicago Tribun*e, 28 September 1969, p. 3; "This Is Your Life," typed transcript in Byron House file, Illinois Supreme Court Library, Springfield, Illinois, April 1960, pp. 1, 4. At a testimonial dinner given for House during his reelection campaign by close friends and family, the transcript preserved the evening's entertainment that included a presentation of the justice's life in a format copied from a popular television program of the period and preserved in the transcript.
1227. Ibid.
1228. *Nashville Daily Register,* 29 September 1969, p. 1.
1229. "This Is Your Life," p. 1.
1230. Ibid., p. 5.
1231. Ibid.
1232. Ibid., p. 8.
1233. Ibid., p. 10.
1234. *Chicago Tribune,* 24 February 1957, p. 16; *Chicago Tribune,* 12 March 1957, p. A7.
1235. *Illinois State-Journal Register* (Springfield), 26 February 1957, n.p.
1236. *Chicago Tribune,* 3 January 1960, p. 5; *Chicago Tribune,* 17 January 1960, p. A13.
1237. *Chicago Tribune,* 22 May 1960, p. 19.
1238. *Chicago Tribune,* 17 January 1960, p. A13; *Chicago Tribune,* 12 September 1960, p. B14.
1239. *Chicago Tribun*e, 28 September 1969, p. 3.
1240. 44 Ill. 2d., xviii.
1241. Manaster, *Illinois Justice,* pp. 88–95; *Chicago Tribune,* 4 September 1969, p. 12.
1242. *Chicago Tribun*e, 4 September 1969, p. 12; *Nashville Daily Register*, 15 September 1969, p. 8; *Illinois State-Journal Register* (Springfield), 4 September 1969, p. 1.
1243. *Nashville Daily Register,* 29 September 1969, p. 1.
1244. ancestry.com (Roy John Solfisburg). Some sources list his birth year as 1912.
1245. *Aurora Beacon-News,* 7 June 1960, clipping in Solfisburg file, Illinois Supreme Court Library.
1246. *Aurora Beacon-News,* 22 April 1991, Sec. C, p. 3.
1247. *Aurora Beacon-News,* 7 June 1960.
1248. *People ex rel. Conn v. Randolph,* 35 Ill. 2d. 24 (1966).
1249. *People ex rel. General Motors Corporation v. Bua,* 37 Ill. 2d. 180 (1967).
1250. Manaster, *Illinois Justice,* pp. 57–58.
1251. *Time,* 29 August 1969, www.time.com.
1252. Barnhart and Schlickman, *John Paul Stevens,* p. 144.
1253. *Chicago Tribune,* 25 April 1991, Sec. 2, p. 8.
1254. Fiedler, *The Illinois Law Courts in Three Centuries,* p. 334.
1255. 49 Ill. 2d. 441; 101 Ill. 2d. 428; Manaster, *Illinois Justice,* p. 301.
1256. *Pantagraph* (Bloomington, IL), 31 March 1988, p. B7.
1257. Ibid.
1258. *Kankakee Daily Journal,* 3 October 1983, p. 5.
1259. *Illinois State Journal* (Springfield), 27 January 1962, n.p.; *Illinois State Journal-Register,* 2 May 1962, n.p. Quotation on his lack of enemies is a lengthy feature article by Bernie Schoenberg, "Justice Robert Underwood's Life of Law and Justice," *Bloomington Pantagraph,* 25 November 1984, pp. A4–A5.
1260. Walter V. Schaefer, "Tribute to Justice Underwood," *University of Illinois Law Review* (1984), p. 861.
1261. Nina Burleigh, "The Views of Bob Underwood, Retired But Not Reticent," *Illinois Issues* (March 1985), pp. 13–18; *Victoria L. Hewitt v. Robert M. Hewitt,* 77 Ill. 2d. 49 (1979).
1262. *Lawrence P. Hickey et al. v. Illinois Central Rail Road Company,* 35 Ill. 2d. 427 (1966); 364 U.S. 918.
1263. *Illinois State Journal,* 9 September 1969, p. 1. Every media outlet in the state covered the scandal through the spring and summer of the year.
1264. See for example his obituary in the *Chicago Tribune,* 31 March 1988, p. 14.
1265. Note to Chief Justice Ray Klingbiel, 20 January 1964, in Robert C. Underwood file, Illinois Supreme Court Library.

1266. Unsigned note, 21 June 21, 1977, in Robert C. Underwood file, Illinois Supreme Court Library.
1267. News release from Supreme Court Administrative Office, 3 October 1983, in Robert C. Underwood file, Illinois Supreme Court Library. He made the announcement more than a year in advance to allow ample time for potential candidates prepare their nominating petitions.
1268. *Bloomington Pantagraph,* 31 March 1988, p. B7.
1269. *Kankakee Daily Journal,* 13 December 1984, p. 24; *Bloomington Pantagraph,* 12 September 1982, p. A4.
1270. Ibid.
1271. Illinois State Bar Association, *Judicial Administration Newsletter,* vol. 7, no. 5 (November 1976), pp. 2–3; *Chicago Sun-Times,* 18 May 1994, p. 80.
1272. *Chicago Sun-Times,* 2 February 1960; Samuel Rubin, "Justice for the Indigent," *American Bar Association Journal* 39 (October 1953), p. 931.
1273. Illinois State Bar Association, *Judicial Administration Newsletter,* vol. 7, no. 5 (November 1976), pp. 2–3.
1274. *Chicago Sun-Times,* 18 May 1994, p. 80.
1275. *Chicago Sun-Times,* 14 July 1966, p. 18; *Chicago Bar News* (January 1967).
1276. *State Journal-Register* (Springfield, Illinois), 28 March 1978.
1277. *Chicago Tribune,* 31 October 1977; *Chicago Sun-Times,* 1 November 1977; *Chicago Tribune,* 29 March 1978; *Chicago Tribune,* 2 October 1978.
1278. *Kanellos v. Cook County,* 53 Ill. 2d. 161 (1972); *State Journal-Register* (Springfield, Illinois), 13 September 1995, p. 9.
1279. *Chicago Sun-Times,* 22 August 1972, p. 7.
1280. *Chicago Sun-Times,* 18 May 1994, p. 80.
1281. Familysearch.org/pal:/MM9.1.1/N73M-RHV.
1282. *Chicago Tribune,* 25 April 1995, Sec. 2, p. 8.
1283. Illinois State Bar Assn., *Bench & Bar* (October 1990), p. 2.
1284. *Continental Illinois National Bank and Trust Company of Chicago v. Illinois State Toll Highway Commission,* 42 Ill. 2d. 385 (1969).
1285. *Chicago National League Ball Club v. Thompson,* 108 Ill. 2d. 357 (1985).
1286. *People v. Chicago Magnet Wire Corporation,* 126 Ill. 2d. 356 (1989).
1287. *In re Estate of Longeway,* 133 Ill. 2d. 33 (1989).
1288. *Chicago Tribune,* 14 November 1989, Sec. 2, p. 3.
1289. Illinois Supreme Court news release, 11 November 1989, Ward file, Illinois Supreme Court Library.
1290. *Chicago Tribune,* 17 March 1978, Sec. 2, p. 1.
1291. Illinois State Bar Assn., *Bench & Bar* (October 1990), p. 1.
1292. *Chicago Daily Law Bulletin,* 24 April 1995, Ward file, Illinois Supreme Court Library; *State Journal-Register,* 13 September 1995, p. 9.
1293. 127 Ill. 2d. xix..
1294. 127 Ill. 2d. xxi.
1295. *People v. O'Leary,* 45 Ill. 2d. 122 (1970).
1296. *People v. Howell,* 44 Ill. 2d. 264 (1970).
1297. *Illinois Issues,* 6 November 1976; www.lib.niu.edu/1976/ii761106.html.
1298. 127 Ill. 2d. xxii.
1299. *Freeport Journal-Standard,* 17 October 1983, p. 3.
1300. *Chicago Tribune,* 22 October 1983, Sec. 2, p. 12.
1301. *Peoria Journal-Star,* 26 July 1982, p. B-6.
1302. "Presentation of Jon W. DeMoss, President, Illinois State Bar Association," 27 November 1984, typescript in Illinois Supreme Court Library.
1303. *People v. Sailor,* 43 Ill. 2d. 256 (1969).
1304. *People v. Hammond,* 45 Ill. 2d. 269 (1970).
1305. *Peoria Journal-Star,* 26 July 1982, p. B-6.
1306. "Resolution of the Peoria County Bar Association in Memory of John T. Culbertson, Jr.," 27 November 1984, typescript in Illinois Supreme Court Library.
1307. *Robinson Argus,* 10 March 1988, p. 1; 129 Ill. 2d. xxvii–xxxiii.
1308. Ibid.
1309. Ibid.; *Robinson Daily News,* 7 March 1988, p. 1; *Robinson Argus,* 10 March 1988, p. 1
1310. 129 Ill. 2d. xxvii–xxxiii.
1311. Ibid.
1312. Ibid.; *Illinois Issues* (January 1976), p. 29.
1313. *People v. Ward,* 63 Ill. 2d. 437 (1976); *Ward v. Illinois,* 431 U.S. 767 (1977).

1314. Ibid.
1315. Ibid.
1316. *Robinson Daily News,* 7 March 1988, p. 9.
1317. mywebtimes.com/archives/Ottawa/print_display.
1318. *People ex rel. Carey v. Cousins,* 77 Ill. 2d. 531 (1979).
1319. *People v. Albanese,* 104 Ill. 2d. 504 (1984).
1320. *Chicago Tribune,* 17 December 2008, Sec. 1, p. 45.
1321. *Kelsay v. Motorola, Inc.,* 74 Ill. 2d. 172 (1979).
1322. www.qconline.com/archives/qco/print_display.
1323. *In re Estate of Longeway,* 133 Ill. 2d. 33 (1990); *Chicago Tribune,* 17 December 2008, Sec. 1, p. 45.
1324. Illinois State Bar Assn., *Bench & Bar,* Special Issue (October 1990), p. 4.
1325. Springfield *State Journal-Register,* 11 October 1989, p. 8.
1326. *St. Louis Globe-Democrat,* 25–26 September 1971, p. 6F.
1327. 143 Ill. 2d. xxv–xxix.
1328. *St. Louis Globe-Democrat,* 25–26 September 1971, p. 6F; *Chicago Tribune,* 12 March 1992, p. 11.
1329. *Jack Spring, Inc. v. Little,* 50 Ill. 2d. 351 (1972); Anthony J. Fusco, et al., "Damages for Breach of the Implied Warranty of Habitability in Illinois—A Realistic Approach," *Chicago-Kent Law Review* 55 (1979), pp. 337–360.
1330. *People v. Gacy* 103 Ill. 2d. 1 (1984). The federal appeal process begins with *John Wayne Gacy, Petitioner-appellant, v. Thomas Page, Warden, Respondent-appellee* 24 F.3d 887.
1331. *Bench and Bar* 18 (No. 5, 1987), pp. 1–3.
1332. Ibid.; "Biographical Information," typescript, Joseph H. Goldenhersh file, Illinois Supreme Court Library.
1333. *Springfield State Journal-Register,* 9 September 1987, p. 12.
1334. Ibid.; Illinois State Bar Association, *Bench and Bar* 18 (No. 5, 1987), pp. 1–3.
1335. *Chicago Tribune,* 12 March 1992, p. 11.
1336. Ibid.; *St. Louis Globe-Democrat,* 25–26 September 1971, p. 6F; 143 Ill. 2d. xxv–xxix.
1337. *Bench and Bar* 18 (No. 5, 1987), pp. 1–3.
1338. *Chicago Tribune,* 7 January 1960, p. 1; *Illinois Blue Book 1963–1964* (Springfield, IL: Illinois Secretary of State), p. 86.
1339. *Chicago Sun-Times,* 19 August 2001, p. 66A.
1340. "Biography of Chief Justice Clark," *Sullivan's Review* 1 (Spring 1986), p. 5.
1341. *Chicago Tribune,* 7 January 1960, p. 1.
1342. *Chicago Tribune,* 13 January 1959, p. 1.
1343. *Illinois Blue Book 1963–1964,* p. 86.
1344. *Chicago Tribune,* 5 January 1960, p. 3; *Chicago Tribune,* 16 January 1960, p. 3.
1345. "Biography of Chief Justice Clark," p. 5; *Chicago Tribune,* 21 November 1981, p. 7.
1346. Illinois State Bar Association, *Bar News,* 4 September 2001, n.p.
1347. *Chicago Sun-Times,* 19 August 2001, p. 66A; *Chicago Tribune,* 22 August 1968, p. 1; "Biography of Chief Justice Clark," p. 5.
1348. *Chicago Tribune,* 20 September 1969, p. N7.
1349. *Chicago Tribune,* 3 November 1976, p. 10; *Chicago Tribune,* 4 November 1976, p. B6.
1350. *Memorial Service Held in the Supreme Court on the Life, Character, and Public Service of the Late Justice William G. Clark and Justice Michael A. Bilandic,* May 22, 2002 (Springfield: State of Illinois, 2017).
1351. *People v. Coslet,* 67 Ill. 2d. 127 (1977); *People v. Spreitzer,* 123 Ill. 2d. 1 (1988).
1352. *Ostendorf v. International Harvester,* 89 Ill. 2d. 273 (1982).
1353. "Biography of Chief Justice Clark," p. 5; *Chicago Sun-Times,* 21 April 1999, p. 3.
1354. Illinois State Bar Association, *Bar News,* 4 September 2001, n.p.
1355. *Illinois Blue Book 1963–1964,* p. 86; Illinois State Bar Association, *Bar News,* 4 September 2001, n.p.
1356. *State Journal-Register* (Springfield, Illinois), 5 December 1991, p. 2.
1357. *Chicago Tribune,* 18 August 2001, p. 77.
1358. *Chicago Sun-Times,* 21 April 1999, p. 3.
1359. *Chicago Tribune,* 10 March 1978, Dooley file, Illinois Supreme Court Library.
1360. *Chicago Tribune,* 10 March 1978.
1361. Ibid.
1362. "Introducing James A. Dooley" 1976 campaign literature, Dooley file, Illinois Supreme Court Library.
1363. *Chicago Daily Law Bulletin,* 6 March 1978, pp. 1, 3.

1364. *Chicago Tribune,* 22 August 1976, Sec. 1, p. 6.
1365. *Pantagraph* (Bloomington), 6 March 1978, p. A-3.
1366. *Chicago Tribune,* 22 August 1976, Sec. 1, p. 6.
1367. Ibid.
1368. *Chicago Tribune,* 1 December 1976, Dooley file, Illinois Supreme Court Library.
1369. *Chicago Tribune,* 10 March 1978; *Daily Journal* (Kankakee), 6 March 1978, Dooley file, Illinois Supreme Court Library.
1370. *Sahara Coal Company v. Industrial Commission,* 66 Ill. 2d. 353 (1977).
1371. *Village of Skokie v. National Socialist Party of America,* 69 Ill. 2d. 605 (1978).
1372. *Daily Journal* (Kankakee), 6 March 1978, Dooley file, Illinois Supreme Court Library.
1373. *Chicago Sun-Times,* 7 March 1978, p. 58.
1374. Ibid.
1375. *Chicago Sun-Times,* 7 December 1987.
1376. Ibid.; "Alumni News and Biographical Footnotes," *Brief* (Phi Delta Phi) 60 (1964–1965), p. 173.
1377. *Chicago Tribune,* 16 September 1995, Sec. 1, p. 15.
1378. *Chicago Sun-Times,* 7 December 1987; "Tribute to Retiring Supreme Court Justices Clark, Moran and Cunningham," *Bench and Bar* 23 (Special Issue October 1992), p. 6.
1379. "US Claims Court Uses Long-Distance TV System to Hear Contract Case," *Judges' Journal* 14 (No. 4, 1975), p. 4; Illinois State Bar Association, *Bar News,* 2 October 1995.
1380. *Chicago Tribune,* 6 November 1975; *Chicago Tribune,* 2 November 1976.
1381. "Tribute to Retiring Supreme Court Justices Clark, Moran and Cunningham," p. 6.
1382. *People v. King,* 66 Ill. 2d. 551 (1977).
1383. Carol Isackson, "Pure Comparative Negligence in Illinois," Chicago-Kent Law Review 58 (April 1982), pp. 599–629.
1384. *Alvis v. Ribar,* 85 Ill. 2d. 1 (1981).
1385. "Tribute to Retiring Supreme Court Justices Clark, Moran and Cunningham," p. 6.
1386. Ibid.
1387. 143 Ill. 2d. xxv–xxix; *Chicago Tribune,* 16 September1995, Section 1, p. 15.
1388. *State Journal-Register* (Springfield), 20 December 1987, p. 6; *Chicago Tribune,* 27 September 2006, p. 27.
1389. *State Journal-Register,* 13 January 1983, p. 10.
1390. *Chicago Lawyer* (November 1980), Simon file, Illinois Supreme Court Library; *Chicago Sun-Times,* 6 November 1980, p. 28; *Illinois Issues* (January 1983), p. 11.
1391. *Chicago Daily Law Bulletin,* 13 May 1983, pp. 1, 8; *State Journal-Register,* 16 January 1983, p. 14.
1392. *Kalodimos et al. v. Village of Morton Grove,* 103 Ill. 2d. 483 (1984).
1393. *In re Edward A. Loss III,* 119 Ill. 2d. 186 (1987).
1394. *People v. Lewis,* 88 Ill. 2d. 129 (1981).
1395. *State Journal-Register,* 13 April 1988, p. 3.
1396. *People v. Walker,* 109 Ill. 2d. 484 (1986).
1397. *People v. Hernandez,* 121 Ill. 2d. 293 (1988).
1398. *People v. Cruz,* 121 Ill. 2d. 321 (1988); *Chicago Sun-Times,* 5 November 2003, p. 55.
1399. *Chicago Tribune,* 18 January 1988, Sec. 1, p. 18.
1400. *Chicago Lawyer (*February 1988), Simon file, Illinois Supreme Court Library.
1401. *Sunday Journal* (Kankakee), 31 January 1988, p. 12.
1402. *State Journal-Register,* 7 January 1988, p. 1.
1403. *St. Louis Post-Dispatch,* 7 January 1988, p. 6A.
1404. *Chicago Sun-Times,* 5 November 2003, p. 55. In 2011, Governor Pat Quinn signed legislation abolishing the death penalty in Illinois.
1405. *Chicago Tribune,* 27 September 2006, pp. 1, 27.
1406. *State Journal-Register* (Springfield), 3 February 1984, p. 4, 27 June 2012, p. 23.
1407. *State Journal-Register,* 16 November 1980, pp. 1, 2; *New York Times,* 2 June 1981, www.nytimes.com/1981/06/02/us/around-the-nation; *Pantagraph* (Bloomington), 22 July 2008, pp. A1, 10.
1408. "Supreme Court of Illinois" news release, 16 January 2001, Miller file, Illinois Supreme Court Library.
1409. *Chicago Sun-Times,* 16 January 2001, p. 27.
1410. *People v. Wilson,* 116 Ill. 2d. 29 (1987).
1411. In a 1996 civil trial, Wilson prevailed in abuse charges against the City of Chicago, www.chicagoreader.com/chicago/the-persistence-of-andrew-wilson.
1412. *People v. Foggy,* 121 Ill. 2d. 337 (1988).

1413. *State Journal-Register*, 2 January 1991, p. 7.
1414. "Supreme Court of Illinois" news release, 16 January 2001.
1415. *Peoria Journal-Star,* 22 February 1997, p. A11.
1416. *American National Bank & Trust Company v. City of Chicago*, 192 Ill. 2d. 274 (2000).
1417. "Supreme Court of Illinois" news release, 16 January 2001.
1418. *Chicago Daily Law Bulletin,* 6 August 2003, pp. 1, 24; "Supreme Court of Illinois" news release, 16 January 2001.
1419. *Chicago Daily Law Bulletin,* 6 August 2003, p. 1.
1420. *Belleville News-Democrat*, 15 July 2008, p. B2.
1421. *Illinois Issues* (August–September 1990), Cunningham file, Illinois Supreme Court Library.
1422. *People ex rel. Rice v. Cunningham*, 61 Ill. 2d. 353 (1975); *Chicago Lawyer* (January 1988), Cunningham file, Illinois Supreme Court Library.
1423. *State Journal-Register* (Springfield), 16 September 1987, p. 1.
1424. *Chicago Lawyer* (January 1988).
1425. *Chicago Tribune*, 16 September 1987, Sec. 1, p. 3.
1426. *In re Yamaguchi*, 118 Ill. 2d. 417 (1987); *Chicago Lawyer* (January 1988). Two years later, the Supreme Court disbarred Yamaguchi, following Attorney Registration and Disciplinary Commission findings that he had converted to personal use more than $225,000 in client funds. *Chicago Tribune,* 31 March 1989, Sec. 2, p. 1.
1427. *Chicago Law Bulletin,* 11 June 1991, Cunningham file, Illinois Supreme Court Library.
1428. *In re Estate of Finley*, 151 Ill. 2d. 95 (1992).
1429. Clerk of the Supreme Court of Illinois to Chief Justice Thomas Fitzgerald, 20 April 2009, Cunningham file, Illinois Supreme Court Library.
1430. Illinois State Bar Association, *Bar News* (August 2008), Cunningham file, Illinois Supreme Court Library.
1431. *Cemeteries of Brown County, 1825–1972* (Astoria, IL: Brown County Board of the Schuyler Brown Historical and Genealogical Society, 1975), p. 162; "Illinois County Marriages," https://famillysearch.org/pal:/MM9.1.1/X253-6J4.
1432. Since 1967, a lawyer must have obtained a law-school degree prior to taking the bar examination.
1433. Manaster, *Illinois Justice*, pp. 19, 289; *Chicago Sun-Times*, 13 June 1969, p. 3.
1434. *Granite City Journal*, 30 November 1988, p. 1.
1435. *St. Louis Post-Dispatch*, 11 March 1988; *Chicago Tribune*, 17 March 1988, Sec. 2, p. 4; 4 June 1991, Sec. 2, p. 9.
1436. *Chicago Daily Law Bulletin,* 9 November 1988, Calvo file, Illinois Supreme Court Library.
1437. *Pantagraph* (Bloomington), 6 December 1988, Sec. B, p. 4.
1438. *Chicago Law Bulletin,* 9 November 1988.
1439. *Business and Professional People for the Public Interest v. Illinois Commerce Commission*, 136 Ill. 2d. 192 (1990); *Chicago Tribune,* 4 June 1991, Sec. 2, p. 9.
1440. *People v. R.G., a minor*, 131 Ill. 2d. 328 (1989); 142 Ill. 2d. xxix.
1441. *Wilder Binding Company v. Oak Park Trust and Savings Bank*, 135 Ill. 2d. 121 (1990).
1442. *Belleville News-Democrat*, 6 June 1991, Sec. B, p. 3.
1443. *State Journal-Register* (Springfield), 4 June 1991, p. 15.
1444. *Chicago Tribune,* 4 June 1991, Sec. 2, p. 9.
1445. *Chicago Tribune,* 1 December 1966, p. 2.
1446. "Oral History Transcript, John J. Stamos," August 2010, Stamos file, Illinois Supreme Court Historic Preservation Commission, Springfield, Illinois.
1447. *Chicago Tribune,* 1 December 1966, p. 1.
1448. *People v. Speck*, 41 Ill. 2d. 177 (1968); *Chicago Daily Law Bulletin,* 14 July 2011, www.chicagolawbulletin.com/News-Extra/martin; John J. Stamos, "Criminal Court and Other War Stories," undated typescript, pp. 45–46, copy in Stamos file, Illinois Supreme Court Historic Preservation Commission, Springfield. Speck died in prison in 1991.
1449. Stamos, "Criminal Court and Other War Stories," p. 37.
1450. *Chicago Tribune,* 21 April 1988, pp. 1, 6; *Chicago Sun-Times,* 22 April 1988, pp. 20, 32.
1451. *Chicago Tribune,* 21 April 1988, p. 6.
1452. "Supreme Court Clerk" news release [19 April 1988], Stamos file, Illinois Supreme Court Library.
1453. *State Journal-Register* (Springfield), 21 April 1988, p. 1.
1454. *In re Himmel*, 125 Ill. 2d. 531 (1988).
1455. *In re Estate of Greenspan*, 137 Ill. 2d. 1 (1990).

1456. *County of Bureau v. Thompson*, 139 Ill. 2d. 323 (1990).
1457. *State Journal-Register*, 22 September 1989, p. 15.
1458. www.stjeromecroatian/org./eng/biladic.html; *Chicago Daily Law Bulletin*, 16 January 2002, Bilandic file, Illinois Supreme Court Library.
1459. *Chicago Daily Law Bulletin*, 16 January 2002.
1460. Michael Bilandic, "The Marathon Mayor," Adrienne Drell, ed., *20 Century Chicago; 100 Years, 100 Voices* (Chicago: Chicago Sun-Times, Bannon Multimedia Group, 2000), p. 166.
1461. Drell, *20 Century Chicago*, pp. 166–67.
1462. *Chicago Tribune*, 17 January 2002, p. 1.
1463. *People v. Jimerson*, 166 Ill. 2d. 211 (1995).
1464. *Chicago Sun-Times*, 9 February 1999, p. 8.
1465. *Johnson v. Edgar*, 176 Ill. 2d. 499 (1997).
1466. *Jones v. Chicago HMO Ltd. of Illinois*, 191 Ill. 2d. 278 (2000); *Chicago Tribune*, 17 January 2002, p. 1.
1467. *Chicago Daily Law Bulletin*, 17 August 2000, p. 25.
1468. *Chicago Daily Law Bulletin*, 1 November 1996, Bilandic file, Illinois Supreme Court Library.
1469. *Chicago Daily Law Bulletin*, 16 January 2002.
1470. *Chicago Sun-Times*, 16 January 2002, p. 2.
1471. *Chicago Tribune*, 17 January 2002, Sec. 1, p. 22.
1472. Illinois Supreme Court news release, 17 January 2002, *Chicago Daily Law Bulletin*, 16 January 2002, both in Bilandic file, Illinois Supreme Court Library.
1473. *Illinois Bar Journal* (January 1997), p. 6; "Justice James D. Heiple, Supreme Court of Illinois," Heiple file, Illinois Supreme Court Library.
1474. *State Journal-Register* (Springfield), 25 September 1994, pp. 1, 7.
1475. *People v. Davis*, 144 Ill. 2d. 349 (1991). In 1986 and again in 1987, the Supreme Court had denied a Davis appeal (112 Ill. 2d. 78, 119 Ill. 2d. 61), and in 1994 the U.S. District Court and the Seventh Circuit Court of Appeals denied his petition for federal *writ of habeas corpus*. He was executed in 1995.
1476. *In re Petition of John Doe and Jane Doe*, 159 Ill. 2d. 347 (1994).
1477. *Chicago Tribune*, 6 July 1994, Sec. 1, p. 7.
1478. *Chicago Tribune*, 8 July 1994, pp. 1, 7.
1479. *In re Petition of John Doe and Jane Doe*, 159 Ill. 2d. 347 (1994); *State Journal-Register*, 13 July 1994, pp. 1, 3.
1480. *State Journal-Register*, 27 September 1996, p. 1.
1481. *Daily Herald* (Arlington Heights), 2 October 1996, Heiple file, Illinois Supreme Court Library.
1482. *Chicago Sun-Times*, 12 February 1997, p. 16.
1483. *Chicago Tribune*, 25 March 1997, Sec. 5, p. 1.
1484. The previous Illinois House effort to remove a judge took place in 1842–1843, when legislators targeted Supreme Court Justice Thomas Browne. His attorney, Abraham Lincoln, successfully argued against impeachment; the attempt failed by a nearly unanimous vote. Bryon C. Andreasen, *Defending Judge Browne: A Case Study in the Legal, Legislative, and Political Workings of Abraham Lincoln's Illinois* (Springfield: Supreme Court Historic Preservation Commission, 2013).
1485. Heiple to Supreme Court "Colleagues," 2 May 1997, Heiple file, Illinois Supreme Court Library; Karen Moriarty, *Baby Richard; A Four-Year-Old Comes Home* (Palm Coast, FL: Open Door Publishing, 2003), p. 407; *Chicago Tribune*, 3 May 1997, pp. 1, 14.
1486. *Chicago Tribune*, 29 April 1997, Sec. 2, p. 6.
1487. "Justice James D. Heiple: Impeachment and the Assault on Judicial Independence," *Loyola University Chicago Law Journal* 29 (1998), pp. 741–840; "Heiple Impeachment Report," *Chicago Daily Law Bulletin*, 16 May 1997, p. 3; *Chicago Tribune*, 30 April 1997, Sec. 1, pp. 1, 8; 1 November 1998, Sec. 1, p. 2.
1488. *Chicago Sun-Times*, 7 December 1999, p. 19.
1489. Moriarty, *Baby Richard*, p. 399.
1490. *Chicago Sun-Times*, 18 November 2003, Heiple file, Illinois Supreme Court Library.
1491. familypreservation.blogspot.com/2011/08.
1492. *N'Digo*, 10–16 July 1997, p. 6.
1493. Ibid.
1494. *People v. Cruz*, 162 Ill. 2d. 314 (1994).
1495. *Chicago Sun-Times*, 13 May 1997, p. 1.
1496. *N'Digo*, 10–16 July 1997, p. 6.

1497. *Chicago Tribune,* 13 May 1997, p. 1.
1498. *People v. McCauley,* 163 Ill. 2d. 414 (1994).
1499. *In re Jonathan C.B.,* 2011 IL 107750.
1500. *In re Scarlett Z.-D.,* 2015 IL 117904; https://www.isba.org/cases/illinois/supreme/2015/03/19/reparentagescarlettz-d.
1501. *Chicago Sun-Times,* 24 October 2000, p. 6.
1502. *Chicago Sun-Times,* 24 October 2000, p. 7.
1503. *Chicago Tribune,* 13 May 1997, p. 1.
1504. Supreme Court of Illinois news release, 24 June 2013.
1505. *ISBA Bar News,* 4 January 1999, pp. 1, 5; "Oral History Transcript, John L. Nickels," 15 July 2010, Nickels file, Illinois Supreme Court Historic Preservation Commission, Springfield, Illinois.
1506. Supreme Court of Illinois news release, 24 June 2013.
1507. *People v. Cruz,* 162 Ill. 2d. 314 (1994); *Chicago Tribune,* 12 December 1998, Sec. 1, p. 7.
1508. *City of Chicago v. Morales,* 177 Ill. 2d. 440 (1997).
1509. *Best v. Taylor Machine Works et al.,* 179 Ill. 2d. 367 (1997); *Chicago Daily Law Bulletin,* 25 June 2013, p. 1.
1510. Supreme Court of Illinois news release, 24 June 2013.
1511. *DCBA Brief* (December 1998).
1512. *Chicago Tribune,* 21 February 1999, Sec. 2, p. 3.
1513. *State Journal-Register* (Springfield), 12 December 1998, p. 32.
1514. Supreme Court of Illinois news release, 24 June 2013.
1515. "Oral History Transcript, Moses Harrison," 30 June 2010, Harrison file, Illinois Supreme Court Historic Preservation Commission, Springfield, Illinois.
1516. Ibid.
1517. Ibid.
1518. Ibid.
1519. *State Journal-Register* (Springfield, Illinois), 14 May 2002, p. 9.
1520. *People v. Bull,* 185 Ill. 2d. 179 (1999).
1521. *People v. Kokoraleis,* 189 Ill. 2d. 721 (1999).
1522. *Chicago Daily Law Bulletin,* 24 April 1999, p. 22; washingtonpost.com, 9 March 2011.
1523. *Chicago Daily Law Bulletin,* 12 January 2000, p. 1.
1525. *Chicago Sun-Times,* 14 May 2002, p. 16.
1526. *St. Louis Post-Dispatch,* 14 May 2002, p. B4.
1527. *Illinois Issues* (June 2013), p. 34.
1528. *Chicago Lawyer* (December 2003).
1529. *Chicago Tribune,* 25 February 2013.
1530. *Chicago Lawyer* (December 2003), p. 10.
1531. Ibid., p. 66.
1532. *Charles v. Seigfried,* 165 Ill. 2d. 482 (1995).
1533. *Best v. Taylor Machine Works et al.,* 179 Ill. 2d. 367 (1997).
1534. *Happel et al. v. Wal-Mart Stores, Inc.,* 199 Ill. 2d. 179 (2002).
1535. *Illinois Issues* (November 2002), p. 21.
1536. *Chicago Daily Law Bulletin,* 10 September 2002; *Illinois Issues* (November 2002), p. 21.
1537. *Chicago Daily Law Bulletin,* 5 April 2006.
1538. *Chicago Daily Law Bulletin,* 7 March 2005.
1539. *St. Louis Post-Dispatch,* 6 April 2006.
1540. "Oral History Transcript, Mary Ann McMorrow," 29 October 2009, McMorrow file, Illinois Supreme Court Historic Preservation Commission, Springfield, Illinois.
1541. Supreme Court of Illinois news release, 25 February 2013.
1542. *Chicago Tribune,* 13 March 2000.
1543. *Chicago Daily Law Bulletin,* 24 April 1999, p. 27.
1544. chicagotribune.com, 17 December 1998; *Chicago Sun-Times,* 17 December 1998, p. 31.
1545. *In re Estate of Gebis,* 186 Ill. 2d. 188 (1999).
1546. *First Springfield Bank & Trust v. Galman,* 188 Ill. 2d. 252 (1999).
1547. *People v. Madej,* 193 Ill. 2d. 395 (2000).
1548. *DCBA Brief* (March 2000), p. 22.
1549. *Journal of the DuPage County Bar Association* 19 (2006–07).
1550. articles.chicagotribune.com/1995-10-22/sports/9510220426.
1551. *Chicago Daily Law Bulletin,* 8 September 2005.
1552. *People v. Lerma,* 2016 IL 118496; cwcblog.law.northwestern.edu/2016/01/22/Illinois-embraces-eyewitness-expert-testimony.

1553. *People ex rel. Madigan v. Snyder*, 208 Ill. 2d. 457 (2004); dcba.org/mpage/vol160404art5.
1554. articles.chicagotribune.com/2007-10-12/news/0710111023; ballotpedia.org/Robert_Thomas.
1555. *Chicago* (December 2010/January 2011), p. 20.
1556. *Illinois Bar Journal* (September 2008), p. 449.
1557. *Chicago Daily Law Bulletin,* 3 November 2015, p. 6; Supreme Court of Illinois news release, 3 November 2015.
1558. *Chicago* (December 2010/January 2011), p. 21; *Chicago Daily Law Bulletin,* 3 November 2015, p. 6.
1559. *Donaldson et al. v. Central Illinois Public Service Company*, 199 Ill. 2d. 63 (2002).
1560. *Chicago* (December 2010/January 2011), p. 22.
1561. *Chicago Daily Law Bulletin,* 19 May 2008, p. 20.
1562. *Chicago Daily Law Bulletin,* 3 November 2015, p. 6.
1563. *Lebron v. Gottlieb Memorial Hospital*, 237 Ill. 2d. 217 (2010); *Chicago Daily Law Bulletin,* 3 November 2015, pp. 1, 6.
1564. *State Journal-Register* (Springfield, Illinois), 4 November 2015, p. 19.
1565. *Chicago Daily Law Bulletin,* 3 November 2015, p. 1.
1566. *Chicago Daily Law Bulletin,* 25 May 2012, pp. 1, 22.
1567. Supreme Court of Illinois news release, 3 November 2015.
1568. *Chicago Daily Law Bulletin,* 14 April 2011, p. 1.
1569. *People v. O'Connell*, 227 Ill. 2d. 31 (2007).
1570. *People v. Beaman*, 229 Ill. 2d. 56 (2008).
1571. *Lebron v. Gottlieb Memorial Hospital*, 237 Ill. 2d. 217 (2010).
1572. *Chicago Daily Law Bulletin,* 16 July 2010; *Quad-Cities Online*, 2 November 2010, qconline.com/archives/qco/print.
1573. *Chicago Daily Law Bulletin,* 25 October 2013, p. l.
1574. *Illinois Bar Journal* (November 2012), isba.org/ibj/2012/11/thehighpriceoflowfunding.
1575. *Chicago Daily Law Bulletin,* 25 October 2013, p. 22.
1576. *Illinois Times,* 25 February 2016, p. 7.
1577. *Chicago Daily Law Bulletin,* 25 October 2013, p. 22.
1578. *State Journal-Register* (Springfield, Illinois), 21 October 2013, p. 4.
1579. chicagolawyermagazine.com/Elements/pages/print.aspx?printpath.
1580. Ibid.
1581. *Illinois Bar Journal* 57 (January 1969), p. 378.
1582. *State Journal-Register* (Springfield, Illinois), 21 October 2013, p. 4.
1583. Ibid.
1584. *Chicago Daily Law Bulletin*, 28 October 2013, p. 1.
1585. Supreme Court of Illinois news release, 12 December 2013.
1586. "Responses by Justice Rita B. Garman to Illinois Civil Justice League 2012 Judicial Retention Questionnaire," Garman file, Illinois Supreme Court Historic Preservation Commission, Springfield, Illinois.
1587. *People v. Cabelles*, 207 Ill. 2d. 504 (2003).
1588. *Illinois v. Caballes*, 543 U.S. 405 (2005).
1589. *People v. Caballes*, 221 Ill. 2d. 282 (2006).
1590. *In re Estate of Feinberg*, 235 Ill. 2d. 256 (2009).
1591. *Chicago Daily Law Bulletin*, 3 June 2014, pp. 1, 23.
1592. *Chicago Daily Law Bulletin,* 13 May 2002, p. l.
1593. Ibid., p. 22.
1594. *Belleville News-Democrat Magazine,* 6 June 2004, p. 11.
1595. *Chicago Daily Law Bulletin,* 5 September 2003, p. 24.
1596. *Chicago Daily Law Bulletin,* 13 May 2002, p. 22.
1597. *People v. Stehman*, 203 Ill. 2d. 26 (2002).
1598. *People v. Belk*, 203 Ill. 2d. 187 (2003).
1599. *Chicago Daily Law Bulletin,* 5 September 2003, p. l.
1600. mywebtimes.com, 11 September 2003.
1601. D. Vock, "Illinois Supreme Court: Humble Beginnings and a Rich History," *Chicago Daily Law Bulletin,* 23 April 2005, p. 1.
1602. Kevin McDermott, "All Eyes on the Fifth," *Illinois Issues* (September 2004); Editorial, "Gordon Maag's Revenge," *Chicago Tribune*, 24 December 2004; https://ballotpedia.org/Lloyd_Karmeier.
1603. M. Adrian, *The Southern Illinoisan*, 7 December 2004.

1604. *Philip Morris USA Inc. v. Appellate Court, Fifth District*, No. 117689, Order by Justice Karmeier, 24 September 2014), www.illinoiscourts.gov/supremecourt/specialmatters/2014/102114_117689_Order.pdf.
1605. *Lebron v. Gottlieb Memorial Hospital*, 237 Ill. 2d. 217 (2010).
1606. *People v. White*, 2011 IL 109689.
1607. *In re Pension Reform Litigation*, 2015 IL 118585.
1608. *Jackson-Hicks v. East St. Louis Board of Election Commissioners*, 2015 IL 118929.
1609. *Hooker v. Illinois State Board of Elections*, 2016 IL 121077.
1610. "A Voice of Confidence for Supreme Court Justice Lloyd Karmeier," *Chicago Tribune*, 27 October 2014; "Vote to Retain Karmeier," *Belleville News Democrat*, 25 October 2014; "Retain Karmeier," *The Southern Illinoisan*, 31 October 2014.
1611. Illinois State Board of Elections, D-1 and A-1 Reports for Campaign for 2016
1612. A. Maher, "Ill. SC Justice Fends Off Class Action Attorneys' Campaign, Wins Second Term*," Legal NewsLine*, 7 November 2014.
1613. Lloyd A. Karmeier, "2017: Reflections on the Past—Hopes for the Future," Appellate Lawyers Association, Union League Club, Chicago, IL, 23 February 2017.
1614. Yale Center for Dyslexia & Creativity, undated report, Burke file, Illinois Supreme Court Historic Preservation Commission, Springfield, Illinois.
1615. *State Journal-Register*, 2 August 2006, Burke file, Illinois Supreme Court Historic Preservation Commission; *Chicago Daily Law Bulletin*, 3 March 2015, pp. 3, 24.
1616. professionalism.jmis.edu/justice-burke-conversation/.
1617. *State Journal-Register*, 7 July 2006, p. 9.
1618. *Chicago Daily Law Bulletin*, 6 July 2006, p. 1.
1619. bishop-accountability.org/news2006/03_04/2006_04_05_Chase_PriestAbuse.
1620. *People v. Almore*, 241 Ill. 2d. 387 (2011).
1621. *Hope Clinic for Women, Ltd. v. Flores*, 2013 IL 112673.
1622. *People v. Martinez*, 2013 IL 113475.
1623. *Martinez v. Illinois*, 134 S. Ct. 2070 (2014).
1624. *Chicago Tribune*, 7 June 2014.
1625. ISBA *Bench and Bar* 42 (August 2011).
1626. *Chicago Daily Law Bulletin*, 15 July 2011, pp. 1, 22.
1627. ISBA *Bench and Bar* 42 (August 2011).
1628. *People v. Wrice*, 2012 IL 111860.
1629. law.umich.edu/special/exoneration/pages/casedetail.aspx?caseid=4323.
1630. *Chicago Daily Law Bulletin*, 7 November 2012, pp. 1, 24.
1631. *People v. Patterson*, 2014 IL 115102.
1632. *Jones v. Municipal Employees' Annuity & Benefit Fund*, 2016 IL 119618; chicagotribune.com/news/local/politics/ct-chicago-pension-law-ruling.
1633. *Chicago Tribune*, 30 November 2010.
1634. P.Scott Neville PSA. https://www.youtube.com/watch?v=DCviT81dT5w.
1635. 2018 IL App (1st) 143899.
1636. 357 Ill. App. 3d 723 (2005).
1637. 377 Ill. App. 3d 43 (2007).
1638. 408 Ill. App. 3d 136 (2011).
1639. Supreme Court of Illinois news release, 17 May 2018.

ILLINOIS REPORTS. 302 VOL. 302 IRWIN. 1922

ILLINOIS REPORTS. 303 VOL. 303 IRWIN. 1922

ILLINOIS REPORTS. 304 VOL. 304 IRWIN.

ILLINOIS REPORTS. 305 VOL. IRWIN. 1923